Family Therapy

Family Therapy

THEORY AND PRACTICE

Edited by

Philip J. Guerin, Jr., M.D.

Center For Family Learning

For American Orthopsychiatric Association

GARDNER PRESS, INC.

Distributed by Halsted Press

Division of John Wiley & Sons, Inc.

New York · Toronto · Sydney · London

GARDNER PRESS, INC.
32 Washington Square West
New York, New York 10011

Distributed solely by the Halsted Press Division of
John Wiley & Sons, Inc., New York

Library of Congress Cataloging in Publication Data
Main entry under title:

Family therapy: theory and practice.

Includes index.
1. Family psychotherapy. I. Guerin, Philip J.
II. American Orthopsychiatric Association.
RC488.5.F35   616.8'915   76-8409
ISBN 0–470–15089–0

Designed by Raymond Solomon

CONTENTS

Preface

The field of family therapy has celebrated its first quarter century of existence. The celebration marks the proliferation of family systems ideas and clinical practice throughout the mental health field. This volume brings together a series of original contributions from the most distinguished leaders in the field. Its purpose is twofold—to provide a reference text for teachers and students, and an organized presentation of theory and technique for the clinical practitioner. It is indeed fitting that the American Orthopsychiatric Association, the national organization most responsible for fostering the growth of family therapy, be the sponsor for this book.

I wish to thank personally each of the contributors for taking time out from already oppressive schedules to put together their chapters. Special thanks to Marie Maffucci and Julie Lanza of the CFL administrative secretarial staff for their typing: David Berenson, M.D.; Elizabeth Carter, M.S.W.; Edward Gordon, Ph.D.; Katherine Guerin, M.A.; Monica Orfanidis, M.S.W.; and Eileen Pendagast, M.A., M.Ed., all of the CFL Staff and faculty, for their assistance in reviewing the chapters. A special note of appreciation to Barbara Fried for her major editorial contribution, and to Ernest Herman of the American Orthopsychiatric Association for his advice and counsel.

P.J.G., Jr.

Contributors

IAN ALGER, M.D.
Visiting Associate Professor of
Psychiatry, Albert Einstein College of
Medicine; Training Psychoanalyst, New York Medical College

HARRY J. APONTE, A.C.S.W.
Director, Philadelphia Child
Guidance Clinic

CAROLYN L. ATTNEAVE, PH.D.
Professor of Psychology and
Director of American Indian Studies,
University of Washington, Seattle

LESTER BAKER, M.D.
Associate Professor of Pediatrics,
University of Pennsylvania
School of Medicine

MARIANO BARRAGAN, M.D.
President of Family Institute
of Mexico; Professor of Psychiatry,
University of La Salle

C. CHRISTIAN BEELS, M.D.
Assistant Clinical Professor of
Psychiatry at the College of
Physicians and Surgeons of Columbia
University; Attending Psychiatrist,
Washington Heights Community Service

JOHN ELDERKIN BELL, M.D.
Psychologist, Palo Alto Veteran's
Administration Hospital; Associate
Professor, Stanford University School
of Medicine; Associate Professor,
Department of Psychiatry and Behavioral
Science; Lecturer, University of California at
San Francisco, Department of Psychology

DAVID BERENSON, M.D.
Director of Research,
Center for Family Learning

DONALD BLOCH, M.D.
Director, Nathan Ackerman
Family Institute

MURRAY BOWEN, M.D.
Professor of Psychiatry
and Director of the Family
Center, Georgetown University
School of Medicine

ELIZABETH A. CARTER, M.S.W.
Associate Director and Director
of Education, Center for Family Learning

THOMAS FOGARTY, M.D.
Senior Faculty, Center for Family
Learning
Assistant Clinical Professor of
Psychiatry, Albert Einstein College of
Medicine, Bronx Psychiatric Center

JAMES L. FRAMO, PH.D.
Professor of Psychology,
Temple University

DORIS GREINER, R.N. M.S.
Associate Professor, University of
Alabama, Birmingham

KATHERINE B. GUERIN, M.A.
Staff and Faculty, Center For
Family Learning

PHILIP J. GUERIN, JR., M.D.
Director, Center for Family Learning;
Assistant Clinical Professor of
Psychiatry, Albert Einstein College
of Medicine, Bronx Psychiatric Center;
Adjunct Associate Professor Psychology
(Psychiatry), Fordham University

LYNN HOFFMAN, M.S.W., C.S.W.
Assistant Professor, Downstate Medical Center;
Director of Family Therapy for the
Division of Child and Adolescent
Psychiatry

MICHAEL HOLT, PH.D.
Clinical Psychologist,
Jefferson County Department of
Public Health

LAWRENCE S. JACKMAN, M.D.
Director of the Division of
Human Sexuality, Department of
Obstetrics and Gynecology, Albert
Einstein College of Medicine

H. PETER LAQUEUR, M.D.
Associate Professor of Clinical
Psychiatry, University of Vermont;
Director of Family Therapy, Vermont
State Hospital

RONALD LIEBMAN, M.D.
Psychiatrist-in-Chief,
Children's Hospital of Philadelphia;
Assistant Professor of Child
Psychiatry and Pediatrics, University
of Pennsylvania School of Medicine

SALVADOR MINUCHIN, M.D.
Director, Family Therapy
Training Center, Philadelphia
Child Guidance Clinic; Professor
of Child Psychiatry and Pediatrics,
University of Pennsylvania School
of Medicine

MONICA McGOLDRICK ORFANIDIS, M.S.W.
Clinical Assistant Professor,
Rutgers Medical School;
Coordinator of Family Therapy Training,
Rutgers Mental Health Center;
Faculty, The Center for Family Learning

PEGGY PAPP, M.S.W.
Senior Supervisor, Nathan Ackerman
Family Institute;
Consultant to Community Programs; Senior Facul-
ty, Center for Family Learning

EILEEN G. PENDAGAST, M.A., M.ED.
Staff and Faculty of Center for
Family Learning; Editor, *The Family*

NORMAN L. PAUL, M.D.
Lecturer in Neurology,
Boston University School of
Medicine

BERNICE ROSMAN, PH.D
    Director of Research,
    Philadelphia Child Guidance
    Clinic

JOHN WEAKLAND
    Mental Research Institute,
    Palo Alto, California

CARL WHITAKER, M.D.
    Professor of Psychiatry,
    University of Wisconsin
    School of Medicine

Part I

OVERVIEW

CHAPTER 1

FAMILY THERAPY: The First Twenty-Five Years

Philip J. Guerin, Jr., M.D.

This chapter is written in the spirit of the freedom of information. Most of the information is one or another person's particular version of factual events, and as such should not be construed to represent the absolute truth, but rather many different people's version of the truth. The reports of historical happenings included here, in addition to being personal versions, also represent the way human relationship systems operate, and are not a function of malice and/or paranoia on the part of any one individual or group of individuals.

HISTORICAL DEVELOPMENT

The years from 1950 to 1975 may be said to constitute the first quarter century of the field of family therapy, and it is within this chronological framework that I propose to explore the history of the movement. My main purpose is to clarify the developmental history of the field so as to enable future students of family therapy to organize and distinguish between old and new ideas. I will focus on three major areas: the context determinants that went into the formation of the family movement; the professional network of people and their interconnections with one another throughout the United States; and a theoretical classification of the family field.

The family movement had its beginnings in the late 40s and early 50s in different, somewhat isolated areas throughout the country. At that time the nation was going through the aftermaths of World War II, the Korean conflict, and the bomb; one of the noticeable reactions was an increased amount of family togetherness, a backlash to the separations of World War II. Psychiatry had become an attractive specialty; and psychoanalysis, having become firmly established as an ideology, was moving from the sanctuary of its institutes back into the medical schools.

As soon as any ideology becomes established, professional outsiders—"change merchants"—in the field become impatient with its limitations and set out to establish new frontiers and new ways of thinking. The major thrust for the development of the family perspective was due to frustration on two counts, namely, from the attempts being made to apply conventional psychiatric principles to work with schizophrenic families, and from the attempts to deal with behavior difficulties and delinquency in children. All of the important work in the family movement was being done under the rubric of research. Murray Bowen emphasized this in an article about developments in the field for *The American Handbook of Psychiatry.*

A psychoanalytic principle may have accounted for the family movement remaining underground for some years. There were rules to safeguard the personal privacy of the patient/therapist relationship and to prevent contamination of the transference by contact with the patient's relatives. Some hospitals had a therapist to deal with the carefully protected intrapsychic process, another psychiatrist to handle the reality matters and administrative procedures, and a social worker to talk to relatives. In those years this principle was a cornerstone of good psychotherapy. Finally, it became acceptable to see families together in the context of research.

Family research with schizophrenia was the primary focus of a majority of the pioneers in the family movement: Bateson, Jackson, Weakland, and Haley in California; Bowen in Topeka and Washington; Lidz in Baltimore and then in New Haven; Whitaker and Malone in Atlanta; Scheflen and Birdwhistle in Philadelphia.

Nathan Ackerman, perhaps the most widely known pioneer in the family field, came to the family movement by a different route. A card-carrying psychoanalyst, he was also a child psychiatrist; and as early as 1937, at the age of 28, he published a paper on "The Family as a Social and Emotional Unit." Donald Bloch, now director of the Ackerman Family Institute in New York, has described Ackerman's paper thus:

The 1937 paper appeared in the *Bulletin* of the Kansas Mental Hygiene Society; indeed it was the lead article. Its title was "The Family as a Social and Emotional Unit." It was written while Ackerman was a staff member at the Southard School, the children's division of the Menninger Clinic. The paper is short, barely five pages long; to read it now illuminates the spirit of the man, his awareness of human interrelatedness, his compassion, and, above all, his intuitive feeling for the ambiguous quality of intimate networks. The first paragraph has a grand architectural quality:

"None of us live our lives utterly alone. Those who try are doomed to a miserable existence. It can fairly be said that some aspects of life experience are more individual than social, and others more social than individual. Nevertheless, principally we live with others, and in early years almost exclusively with members of our own family."

Ackerman saw his work and the work of his colleagues in the Child Guidance movement as the "real" beginning of the family movement. In a 1967 paper, "The Emergence of Family Diagnosis and Treatment, A Personal View," he said:

The family approach arose in the study of nonpsychotic disorders in children as related to the family environment. The relative prominence of recent reports on schizophrenia and family has somewhat obscured this fact.

The necessity of remaining under the protective umbrella of research also affected the child wing of the family movement, as demonstrated by the Wiltwyck Project. In the early 1960s, Minuchin, working at Wiltwyck School, began with others a research project to study the families of delin- quent boys. This project was designed to study those families who had two delinquent boys, both of whom had been in trouble with the law. Richard Rabkin, a New York psychiatrist and author of such controversial papers as "Is the Unconscious Necessary?" says that the Wiltwyck project was possible because of the "hopeless nature" of the patient population—that is, since there was no effective way to work with these boys, research along the family lines was possible.

Between 1950 and 1975 the family movement went through a series of fascinating developments. From 1950 to 1954, it was more or less under- ground. By that I mean that research was being done that was based on a view of the family as the unit of emotional dysfunction, but the work was isolated and disconnected. No one mentioned this research in the profes- sional literature or at national meetings. During these years, however, Bateson was forming his communications project in California, and Bowen was well into his work on mother/child "symbiosis," schizophrenia, and the family at the Menninger Clinic.

In 1950 William Menninger prodded GAP to form a committee on family, and John Speigel was assigned the task of surveying those who were working on family. He focused on finding out what it was like to work with a family rather than with an individual. He immediately saw it was neces- sary to define the matter in terms of family process rather than intrapsychic experience; he therefore proceded to define a *family,* and to note the contextual forces operating on it. His report, therefore, does not list those who were working with families, or where and how they were doing it. In fact, he failed to pick up the research in California and Topeka, and he discovered only sociologists working with families. Actually, Speigel, aided by Florence Kluckhorn, tried to make the concept of working with family process comprehensible to traditional psychiatry.

Meanwhile, the work of John Rosen, a psychiatrist, with schizophrenic patients in Bucks County, Pennsylvania, had begun to influence several of the family therapy pioneers. Rosen originated direct confrontational analysis of schizophrenics, and in 1948 had visited the Menninger Clinic for a period of about a month to demonstrate his method using selected case material and a one-way screen room. As Bowen puts it, "By the time Rosen left, all one hundred psychiatric residents were into trying some version of Rosen's direct analysis." Bowen himself tried it for a couple of years, but by 1950 had moved into formulating and refining his ideas about mother/child symbiosis and its role in schizophrenia. Bateson's group, organized in 1952 in California, was also interested in Rosen's work and came to Philadelphia to observe it. Also, Whitaker, Warkenton, and Malone, working on a somewhat similar model in Atlanta, were also tuned into Rosen's work, as was Al Scheflen in Philadelphia.

Chestnut Lodge in Rockville, Maryland—the home of Frieda Fromm-Reichman, Otto Will, and Harold Searles—was outside the family movement, although its philosophy, strongly influenced by Sullivan, permitted the focus of therapy to shift away from purely intrapsychic toward interpersonal examination. Don Jackson and Don Bloch were both residents at Chestnut Lodge from 1950 to 1953. Jackson left to return to California, where he soon joined the Bateson project. Jackson and Bowen were later introduced by Tetzlaff, who had been a medical school classmate of Jackson's.

In 1957 and 1958, the family movement surfaced nationally. In 1956, Speigel had first heard of Bowen's work, by then already well underway at NIMH, as well as Lidz's work, begun in Baltimore and then moved to Yale-New Haven. Speigel organized a panel on Family Research for the March, 1957, Ortho program. This was the first national meeting at which these family schizophrenia research ideas were presented. In addition to Speigel, that panel included Bowen, Lidz, and David Mendel of Houston —then working on family groups with Seymour Fischer, and later to become widely known for Multiple Impact Family Therapy. Fifty people attended, Bowen recalls.

Three months later at the APA Meeting, also in Chicago, Spurgeon English, then chairman of Psychiatry at Temple, organized a panel on Family. Nat Ackerman was secretary to that panel; Jackson participated in addition to Bowen and Lidz. This meeting led to Jackson's book *The*

Etiology of Schizophrenia. The 1957 APA Meeting provided another network connection. Bob Dysinger, a coworker of Bowen's in the NIMH project, invited a classmate of his from the University of Illinois to the panel on Family: Charles Kramer, since then the founder and Director of the Chicago Family Institute.

Jackson published *The Etiology of Schizophrenia* in 1959. In that same year Bowen published "Intensive Family Therapy," a paper on the NIMH project, in which he talked about the concept of triangulation, which at that time he was calling the interdependent triad. By 1960 Nat Ackerman founded the Family Institute in New York City to provide himself a place for organizing and teaching his work. In 1962 he joined Jackson to produce the field's first journal, *Family Process.*

From 1964 to 1968, large numbers of central publications and the first audiovisual productions appeared. Birdwhistle and Scheflen produced the Hillcrest Series, four 16-mm. sound color movies showing Ackerman, Bowen, Jackson, and Whitaker, each interviewing the same family. The Philadelphia Family Institute was formed in 1964 by a group of approximately twelve family clinicians and researchers. Nagy and Framo together edited *Intensive Family Therapy,* bringing together in one volume much of the work being done around the country with schizophrenic families. In 1966, Bowen published the first major theoretical paper on family systems, "The Use of Family Theory in Clinical Practice." Watzlawick and Jackson published "Pragmatics of Human Communication," and Virginia Satir published *Conjoint Family Therapy.*

Toward the end of this period, a number of geographical moves took place. Whitaker left Atlanta to become a full professor at the University of Wisconsin; Satir left MRI and went to Esalen; Haley left MRI, and went to Philadelphia to join Minuchin, who had left New York and brought Montalvo and Rossman with him to Philadelphia. Al Scheflen left EPPI and Temple to come to New York to begin his human communications research project under the administrative umbrella of Israel Zwerling at Bronx State, Einstein. A few years earlier Zwerling had set up the Family Studies Section at Bronx State. In mid-1968 I left Georgetown, and with my friend and colleague Tom Fogarty joined the Family Studies Section at Bronx State. In January of 1969, the family of family therapists experienced the loss of one of its most significant pioneers with Don Jackson's death.

In the late 60s and early 70s Minuchin's work with anorexia was published. Haley's writing and reputation began to grow. The Georgetown University Symposium on Family expanded from a reunion for alumni of the residency program to a meeting attended by over a thousand people each year. The Family Studies Section at Bronx State became known as a teaching and training center throughout the country. In 1970, using the liaison between Einstein and Fordham that I had established in 1969, I produced the first of the three annual Fordham/Einstein Symposiums on Family Therapy. These served to stimulate an ever-increasing number of family therapy meetings throughout the country. In 1972 the publication of *The Book of Family Therapy* further established Bronx State Family Studies Section at home and throughout the country.

Also during the late 1960s and early 1970s, an antitheory trend was developing, along with an intensified ideological war between analysis and systems people. The battles centered around issues like the sanctity of the transference, and the necessity of the concept of the unconscious. This warfare cut across the field and reached deeply into the center of the family movement. However, with the death of Nat Ackerman in 1971, the family movement lost its most creative and zealous psychoanalytic proponent, and after it, the center of the field moved swiftly toward systems.

CALIFORNIA

In 1952, Gregory Bateson received a grant to study human communication. The study was housed at a VA hospital where Bateson was the Ethnologist, and it was not a clinical project. The first two people Bateson hired to work with him on this grant were Jay Haley and John Weakland. In 1954, Don Jackson, a supervising psychiatrist in residency programs at the same VA hospital, came into the project as a psychiatric consultant and clinical supervisor. Out of their work came the most important paper on the double bind, "Toward a Theory of Schizophrenia." In his book, *Steps to an Ecology of the Mind,* Bateson divides the credit for the concept of the double bind as follows:

> To Jay Haley is due credit for recognizing that the symptoms of schizophrenia are suggestive of an inability to discriminate the Logical Types, and this was amplified by Bateson, who added the notice that the symptoms and etiology could be formally described in terms of a double bind hypothesis. The hypothesis was communicated to D.D. Jackson and found to fit closely with his ideas of family homeostasis. Since then Dr. Jackson has worked closely with the project. The study of the formal analogies between hypnosis and schizophrenia has been the work of John H. Weakland and Jay Haley.

Bateson's work is central to the development of systems thinking in relation to human behavior. Perhaps the best single demonstration of this is his paper, "The Cybernetics of Self," a theory of alcoholism. Thus Bateson, the anthropologist, and Jackson, the clinician, moved to develop systems concepts, with the assistance and collaboration of Haley and Weakland.

In 1959, as some of the energy was waning from the Bateson Project, and as family therapy was becoming nationally known, Jackson formed the Mental Research Institute. The Bateson Project didn't officially end until 1962, but during these three years of coexistence there was no formal link between the project and MRI. Ideas and staff were interchanged, but there was no formal connection. At the end of the Bateson Project, Haley joined Jackson at MRI.

Also in 1959, Virginia Satir moved from Chicago to California. While in Chicago, Satir had worked and taught at the Chicago Psychiatric Institute. In 1958, her interest in family brought her to visit the Bowen Project at NIMH. The next spring, having moved to California, she met Bowen at the Ortho meeting and he in turn suggested she seek out Jackson. Satir joined Jackson at MRI, and quickly found herself at the center of the family therapy movement. She brought the ideas at MRI and elsewhere around the country together in her 1967 publication, *Conjoint Therapy*. Satir's ability to synthesize ideas, combined with her creative development of teaching techniques and general personal charisma, gave her a central position in the field. Satir and Haley left MRI around the same time, in the mid-1960s; Virginia went into the fast-developing growth movement, and became the first director of Esalen.

Haley, on the other hand, went to Philadelphia to further develop his ideas about the family as a system. He has become known for being especially antigrowth, emphasizing all its negative connotations. Early in his years at Philadelphia, he collaborated with Minuchin on the development of structural family treatment; more recently, he has turned his energies to strategic therapy, and to furthering the work begun by Milton Erickson.

The loss of Jackson, Haley, and Satir in a short period of time was a severe blow to MRI. It faded from national view in the years immediately following Jackson's death, and only recently, under the leadership of Watzlawick, Weakland, and Fisch, has it again surfaced. This threesome has successfully taken some of the ideas of Bateson, Jackson, and Haley, added them to the mathematical productions of Paul Watzlawick, and produced an excellent monograph called *Change*. *Change* is a treatise on the concept of clinical change and its relationship to human systems and brief strategic family therapy.

TOPEKA—WASHINGTON, D.C.

The history of Washington, D.C. and the family movement is the history of Murray Bowen, NIMH and Georgetown University School of Medicine, Department of Psychiatry. Bowen's work with families had actually begun in Topeka. In 1951 he requested the use of a cottage on the grounds of Menninger for use in study of schizophrenics and their families. He began asking the mothers of his schizophrenic patients to come to Topeka and stay for one to two months at a time, to move into the cottage and take over at least partial care of their schizophrenic offspring. In 1952 and 1953 he began to include some fathers in the research, but the main focus was around mother/child symbiosis.

In 1954 Bowen left Menninger to come to NIMH. There he set up the landmark project of hospitalizing whole families of schizophrenics for observation and research. This project was seen by Bowen and others, particularly Jackson, as the Camelot of family research, out of which would come a revolutionary way of conceptualizing about human emotional dysfunction that would turn psychiatry toward a totally new direction.

Well underway by 1956, this project aroused considerable national and international interest. By mid-1956, however, the project was already experiencing an administrative squeeze. Bowen attributes the fall of this Camelot to the fact that much of what his project was producing was heretical to prevalent ideologies. The presentations and publications of the project work were censored by delay and restrictions on space. Administrators asked questions like, "Are you sure you mean that?" and "Don't you think you ought to have harder scientific evidence before presenting that data?" Pressure to change direction was applied through administrative edicts that restricted operating space, budgets, and procedures.

Bowen began to search for a place to relocate his project. He decided to go to Georgetown University because of the vision and support offered by George Raines, then chairman of the Department of Psychiatry at Georgetown Medical School. Shortly after Bowen left NIMH for Georgetown and before his project staff could relocate, George Raines died of cancer. Bowen's project staff never made it to Georgetown.

Lyman Wynne took over the family section from Bowen. He continued there through the 60s and early 70s, when he left to assume the chairmanship at University of Rochester. During this time Wynne's project produced a number of significant papers, as well as talented researcher clinicians like Shapiro, Beels, and Reiss. Its ideology was more traditional than Bowen's, and perhaps most closely resembles the work of Ted Lidz at Yale-New Haven.

Still at Georgetown Bowen received a grant in 1973 to train third, fourth, and fifth year residents full time in family systems theory and intervention. Bowen, also working at the Medical College of Virginia, established probably the most extensive video project of ongoing therapy in existence. This project has produced a number of excellent video teaching tapes, the most noteworthy of which is *Steps Toward a Differentiation of Self.*

ATLANTA-MADISON

From approximately 1943 to 1945, Carl Whitaker was working with John Warkenton in Oak Ridge, Tennessee. They began doing co-therapy, seeing the identified patient and then adding another family member and finally even bringing the children to the sessions. They were doing work with children around the issues of behavior problems and delinquency. Later, in 1945 and 46, they became interested in schizophrenia.

In 1946 Whitaker went to Emory University in Atlanta and became Chairman of the Department of Psychiatry, and Workenton went with him. They were joined by Thomas Malone, who provided an analytic background. Their studies centered on schizophrenics and their families. In 1948 the trio began to have meetings every six months that would last about four days. During these meetings, they made use of one-way screening rooms with the individual patients on one side and the three of them on the other. They took turns going in and working with the patient; in addition to observing individual patients, they observed groups of patients and families, and each other's work. In 1953, at the tenth meeting of this group, they moved the site to Sea Island, Georgia, and invited Rosen, Scheflen, Bateson, and Jackson to join them. Thus a large number of therapists worked alternately on the same family or individual, and each learned something from the others.

In 1955 Whitaker left Emory University, and his whole group, including Warkenton and Malone, went into private practice in Atlanta. Then, in 1965, Whitaker was appointed full professor at the University of Wisconsin doing only family therapy. Workenton and Malone are still in Atlanta in group private practice. Whitaker's work had shifted to a study of normal families, which in turn led him to his present concentration on the role of the extended family in the therapeutic process. He began by inviting maternal and paternal grandparents to the sessions, and now he includes many other family members; sometime as many as 35 or 40 people meet for a weekend therapy session.

At such marathons, Carl serves mainly as a reacter who allows things to happen among family members while he refrains from orchestrating it and gears his comments to what he observes. He taunts the family about their failures and weaknesses, and attempts to open up the left sides of their brains—that is, he encourages them to expose the unresolved, crazy things that are usually covered over with the organized structures of the dominant cerebral hemisphere activity. He exposes his own left-sided craziness to the family to make them feel it's safe to delve into theirs. Some see him as having a one-sided brain, but others who watch more closely see the artistic control with which he orchestrates his "craziness."

After Whitaker had left Atlanta for Wisconsin, Frank Pittman came from Colorado to Emory to be Director of the Crisis Clinic. While in Colorado, he had been a central investigator of a project that successfully prevented psychiatric hospitalization by using crisis intervention with families. Within a year after its completion, everyone central to the project had left Colorado. The entrenched system had triumphed again. Pittman also ran into trouble with his crisis work at Emory, and in a short time he too found himself in private practice in Atlanta, where he has remained to the present.

PHILADELPHIA

Philadelphia has been central to the development of family since the mid-50s. At that time Spurgeon English as Chairman of Psychiatry at Temple was encouraging the work of Rosen, Scheflen, and Birdwhistle. With the advent of EPPI more things began to happen. Scheflen, in political trouble at Temple because of his research purism, moved to EPPI in 1960 and joined Birdwhistle to study the structure and process of psychotherapy. Ivan Nagy came to EPPI in 1958 to set up research on family and schizophrenia. Nagy's staff included Jim Framo, Dave Rubenstein, and Geraldine Lincoln Spark. In the early 1960s, Ross Speck was a psychiatric resident at EPPI; he and John Sonne and Al Freidman from the Philadelphia Psychiatric Center began a project to study the treatment of families in the home. The Philadelphia Family Institute was formed in 1964, with most of the people in the area as founders. From 1965 to 68 the direction of the family movement changed as Ross Speck, together with Carolyn Attneave, got into network intervention as a method of ministering to the accumulated ills of the family. Carolyn Attneave's Indian tribal heritage especially prepared her for this type of work. Also during this period, Jay Haley and Salvador Minuchin came to Philadelphia, and Al Scheflen left to go to New York.

In the late 1960s, Philadelphia Child Guidance formed its boundaries. Jim Framo made an attempt under the auspices of Jefferson Medical School to form a family treatment unit in a community mental health center. He too ran into massive systems reactivity to his work, and in the end he and his Bowen-trained associate, Rick Crocco, left in despair to pursue other ventures. Nagy has continued his work, and recently with Geraldine Spark published *Invisible Loyalties,* a view of reciprocity in intergenerational family therapy. Ross Speck has moved from networks to studying the alternative life styles of our present culture. The Philadelphia Child Guidance Clinic has successfully introduced family therapy into work with lower socioeconomic families. Minuchin, true to the tradition of the Wiltwyck Project, took on a clinical project with the urban poor in Philadelphia. The Philadelphia Child Guidance Clinic team under Minuchin's and Haley's leadership was able to take some of the basic family system concepts of Bateson, Bowen, Erickson, and Jackson, add to them Haley's strategic brilliance and Minuchin's considerable clinical artistry, simplify them, concretize them, and demonstrate their effectiveness in a clinical setting with families, and in teaching other family therapists. A number of excellent videotapes of the work of this group have been produced.

In the University of Pennsylvania Pediatric and Child Psychiatry Departments the beginnings of success with psychosomatic families and structural family interventions have already been published. Minuchin, using his clinical operation, was able to bring together a highly motivated creative staff. Those who have evolved a special place in the structure of Philadelphia Child Guidance Clinic are Braulio Montalvo as a conceptualizer and commentator on Minuchin's clinical artistry; Harry Aponte, a New York born Puerto Rican social worker just named to succeed Minuchin as Director of Philadelphia Child Guidance Clinic, who has become an expert on intervening with lower socio-economic families; and Ron Leibman, a child psychiatrist who skillfully advances the Minuchin methods in the psychosomatic arena.

Of added import for work in Philadelphia was the move of Israel Zwerling from Bronx State, Einstein, to Chairman of Psychiatry at Hanneman.

NEW YORK

In New York, Nathan Ackerman was the dominant figure in family psychiatry. Since the depression years of the 1930s, when he had become interested in the effect of chronic economic hardship on families, Ackerman had been interested in families. He was perhaps most moved by his experience in visiting an impoverished mining community in western Pennsylvania. A 1937 paper documents his observations of the unemployed miners.

I went to see, first hand, the mental health effects on the families of unemployed miners. This experience was a shocker; I was startlingly awakened to the limitless, unexplored territory in the relations of family life and health. I studied twenty-five families in which the father, the sole breadwinner in the mining community, had been without work for between two and five years. The miners, long habituated to unemployment, idled away their empty hours on the street corner, or in the neighborhood saloon. They felt defeated and degraded. They clung to one another to give and take comfort and to pass away the endless days of inactivity. Humiliated by their failure as providers, they stayed away from home; they felt shamed before their wives. The wives and mothers, harassed by insecurity and want from day to day, irritably rejected their husbands; they punished them by refusing sexual relations. The man who could no longer bring home his pay envelope was no longer the head of the family. He lost his position of respect and authority in the family; the woman drove him into the streets. Often, she turned for comfort to her first son. Mother and son then usurped the leadership position within the family. Among these unemployed miners, there were guilty depressions, hypochondriacal fears, psychosomatic crises, sexual disorders, and crippled self-esteem. Not infrequently, these men were publicly condemned as deserters. The configuration for family life was radically altered by the miner's inability to fulfill his habitual role as provider.

By the late 40s and early 50s Ackerman had begun to send his staff on home visits to study the family. During this time his public clinical work centered on individual child therapy and the psychoanalysis of adults. In his private practice he experimented with his own particular brand of family therapy.

One of Ackerman's most prominent analysands was Israel Zwerling, who together with Marilyn Mendelsohn, an analysand of Don Jackson's, put together the Family Studies Section at Albert Einstein College of Medicine. Andy Ferber was named Director in 1964.

Ackerman was a consultant to the Family Studies Section on a one day a week basis from 1964 to 67. In 1967 the Section began bringing in people with different ideologies. To Zwerling and Ferber's lasting credit, they managed to assemble the most diverse group of family therapists ever to work under the same roof—not only that, for over five years they maintained an environment that fostered this diversification.

By 1965, Nat Ackerman had founded the Family Institute, moved it to New York, and hired Judy Leib as Executive Director. One of Ackerman's proudest accomplishments at the Family Institute was the establishment of a low to moderate cost clinic for the practice of family therapy, thereby not restricting it to middle and upper class families. He introduced a sliding scale there because he still remembered the psychic pain he'd seen in the miners' families during the Depression.

Nat Ackerman lived and died a staunch psychoanalyst; nonetheless this orthodoxy did not save his heretical ideas about families from the establishment system's automatic response. Two events emphasize this point. While he was on the Faculty of Columbia Presbyterian Psychiatric Institute, his Family Therapy Conferences were scheduled to conflict with other conferences that were mandatory for residents. And in the fall of 1971, at the GAP meeting following his death, and even though he was instrumental in the founding of GAP, his name was left out of the traditional opening memorial service.

After Ackerman's death, the Family Institute was renamed the Ackerman Family Institute. The Directorship was assumed by Don Bloch, who had previously been working with Otto Will as Director of Research at Austen Riggs in Stockbridge, Massachusetts.

In 1970 I assumed the position and responsibility of Director of Training at Family Studies Section, Bronx State, Einstein. I did so predicated on Ferber and Beels, together with Al Scheflen, taking on the project of developing a new systems residency program at Bronx State. The demand for training from outside the Einstein Medical School network was increasing. In order to meet this need and provide funds for videotape projects, I set up an extramural training program in Family Therapy at Bronx State. Soon there were 150 inhouse and extramural trainees, professionals and paraprofessionals, a year. Betty Carter and Monica Orfanidis joined the extramural program; Peggy Papp also became interested in Tom Fogarty's and my work, and she joined the section as a part-time faculty member.

In 1972, with the residency project underway, Andy Ferber was reluctantly ready to move back into the Family Studies Section. For a number of political and administrative reasons, it was decided that I would take the extramural training program up to Westchester, and set up a center which would both house the extramural training program and offer a program of continuing education for families in the community about how family systems operate. Hopefully, this program would be effective in prevention of emotional dysfunction, and also aid in developing a clinical service to provide a different kind of elective experience for Bronx State residents. Then Israel Zwerling left Bronx State and Einstein to assume the Department of Psychiatry chairmanship at Hanneman. As part of the turmoil to be expected in any system after the loss of a leader as powerful as Zwerling, Ferber, certainly one of Zwerling's favorite sons, left Bronx State and moved to Westchester and Harlem Valley Psychiatric Center, where he is Director of Training. In 1973, along with Betty Carter, Tom Fogarty, and Peggy Papp, I founded the Center for Family Learning in New Rochelle, New York.

In addition to these major centers, several other places have been important to the development of family therapy.

In Chicago—where the 1957 American Orthopsychiatric Association Meeting launched family therapy nationally, and where Virginia Satir began her work—there are two foci of family therapy. One is the Chicago Family Institute, formed by Chuck and Jan Kramer; it has ongoing training and clinical programs, and has just recently affiliated with Northwestern University School of Medicine. Across town is the Institute for Juvenile Research, where Irv Borstein, with frequent visits from Carl Whitaker, has put together a clinical training program. Len Unterberger, a psychologist, was one of the central people in Borstein's program, but has since moved on to other things.

In Boston, several family therapy centers have developed independently of each other. Since the early days of family therapy, Norman Paul has been held in high esteem. He has appeared on national television to promote the cause of family therapy throughout the country; his work on operational mourning is widely recognized. He has, however, also experienced pressure from the academic system to change his views on family therapy. A few years ago, he resigned from academic psychiatry to join the neurology faculty at Boston University.

Fred Duhl bypassed some of this system difficulty by setting up the Boston Family Institute. In addition to his wife Bunny, his mainstays early on were David Kantor and Sandy Watanabe. BFI has its own clinical and training programs in family, and has recently added an elaborate video production division to its organization.

Sandy Watanabe left Boston to go to the Chicago Family Institute. Kantor, author of *Inside the Family* and one of the orginators of family sculpting, recently formed the Cambridge Family Institute with Carter Umbarger, a Minuchin-trained family therapist. John Pearce left the Ackerman Family Institute in the late 60s to go to Boston, where he was active with Marvin Schneider, a psychologist, in forming and nurturing the Boston Society for Family Research and Therapy. That organization, still active in the Boston area, is presently under the leadership of Bob Alymer, Eve Welts, and Jim Krainen.

And finally, this overview must mention Houston, and the multiple impact family work there.

THEORETICAL CLASSIFICATION

As any new field of study develops, a certain degree of chaos and disorganization is unavoidable. It is difficult to define the similarities and differences in pioneering work, and any attempts to arrive at an overview fall prey to predictable responses. Some therapists perceive all ideas and techniques as basically the same; others define their own work as totally different from everyone else's.

Still others attempt to organize the chaos by classifying it. There are to date three attempts at classification: the GAP report, *The Treatment of Families in Conflict;* the Beels and Ferber classification published in *Family Process* as "Family Therapy, a View"; and my own classification, presented in a paper at the Georgetown University Symposium on Family Therapy in 1970. The Beels and Ferber classification and mine were later combined into a video training tape called *The Field of Family Therapy.*

In 1970 the Family Committee of GAP published a monograph on family therapy titled *Treatment of Families in Conflict.* At the time of publication the committee's chairman was Norman Paul, and the membership included, among others, Nagy, Bowen, Mendell, Speigel, Wynne, and Zwerling. One chapter, "Premises About Family Therapy," classified family therapists from A to Z.

> Position A will locate those one-to-one therapists who occasionally see families but retain a primary focus upon the individual system, and Position Z those who use exclusively a family system orientation. One should keep in mind that both positions involve the practice of treating whole families and that, between these two positions, most therapists combine these interests in differing proportions. No attempt is made to put specific people at points on the scale.

Al Scheflen had a significant influence on the Beels and Ferber classification; he shared with them a decade of interest in studying the structure and process of psychotherapy by direct observation. Adopting direct observation as their basic method, Beels and Ferber also assumed that a therapist's theory was just a rationalization for his or her clinical behavior. One negative aspect of this assumption was that it fostered an antitheory position, and overemphasized the therapist's personal style. A positive aspect was that in the long run it taught theory zealots like myself to understand that theory is an abstraction of a natural process, and as such each theory represents merely one among many possible abstractions.

Beels and Ferber did direct on-site viewing of therapy sessions, and studied films and videotapes of therapists at work. They then organized their observations around the concept that therapists could be classified according to their therapy session behavior as either conductors or reactors.

Conductors are therapists with aggressive, public, charismatic personalities; they have a strong value system, and they carry their beliefs into their work with families. Nat Ackerman, who broke all family rules with

warmth and humor; Virginia Satir, who teaches people how to live; Sal
Minuchin, who moves in fast to break established patterns of family dysfunction; and Murray Bowen, who orchestrates the family's progress by his
never-ending quest for research—all are conductors.

Reactors are described as less public personalities who get into families
playing different roles at different times. Reactors are divided into two
further groups; analysts and systems purists. Among the analyst reactors
are Whitaker, who invades the family and takes over roles with a cotherapist functioning as his life line; Nagy and Framo, who identify and
relabel phasic interactive patterns of the family; and Wynne and Searles,
who openly register their own feelings of anger, confusion, and futility to
the family. Haley and Jackson are classified as systems purists reactors—
critical observers making heavy use of paradox to manipulate the power
structure of the family. Beels and Ferber conclude by reminding us that
both groups exercise control in their own particular way. The conductors
implement their control in obvious direct ways, reactors in indirect paradoxical ways. As for where Beels and Ferber fit into their own classification,
I see them both as reactors, Ferber in a style inherited from Carl Whitaker,
Beels in the style of a reasonable professor who clarifies, negotiates, and
interprets the family's group process.

Today Beels and Ferber's study is useful in helping family therapists in
training get a sense of how their basic style of operating with a family fits
with that of others. Beginning family therapists inevitably go through stages
in which they mimic the styles of the masters. Only if this remains a fixed
phenomenon does it become an obstruction to the development of the
therapist as a clinician. It is my belief that a well-defined open-ended theory
does allow a family therapist to evolve his or her personal style of operating
with a family.

For example, as a family supervisor I was watching one of our trainees
work with a family. This is a talented and creative lady, outgoing, forceful,
totally irreverent, and never at a loss for thoughts or words. She has a
significant degree of clinical experience and competence. Of late she has
been getting into family systems theory more and more. She sat at the point
of a triangular seating arrangement, leaning back in contemplative fashion,
asking very carefully worded, measured questions, cooling affect on her part
and on the part of the couple, and carefully directing the flow of conversation through her. As I watched, I asked myself, "Does theory set limits on
style and confine it to a certain repertoire of behavior? Shouldn't theory, if
it's valid, free a therapist or agent of change to have multiple and widely
variant stylistic ways of movement with a family?"

There should be many stylistic ways to approach the same clinical
situation. Perhaps one therapist with a flamboyant, unmeasured, provocative, affectively-charged style might lean toward the father of the family,

place his hand on his arm, and say, "Where are you going, man? You gun shy? All your wife has to do is get upset and you head for the hills. How come you're so surprised your son stands in better than you do? Well, I guess she isn't doing any better dealing with your distant reasonableness. Maybe you two deserve each other." Another therapist, who is quiet and reserved, might ask a series of measured and balanced questions in the same situation: "How much of your being away from home a lot is tied into the pull of those outside things, and how much is it connected to your getting out from under trouble in your relationship with your wife? When she gets upset and you get bugged, how would you go about managing to stay around?"

If either therapist can avoid blaming, labeling a victim or a villain, becoming judgmental of the family, and adding his or her emotional reactivity to the stew, he will be fulfilling his responsibility to the family as an agent of change and his responsibility to himself to be himself. A valid theory should not confine the therapist's repertoire of behavior; otherwise only those people with a particular style of behavior would be able to use a particular theory, and that theory is then doomed to become a rationalization for a way of doing things.

Styles as such should not be disconnected from theory; but neither should theory dictate the personal style of a therapist. If a theory is valid, it will free its practitioners to use various styles that are natural to them.

Partly because of this belief of mine, and partly in reaction to the antitheory trend in the field, I set out to classify family therapists according to their theoretical persuasion. I divided family therapists into two basic groups, psychoanalytic and systems. The analytic category is subdivided into individual, group, experiential, and Ackerman-approach categories.

Some analytic therapists see families only when it is necessary to deal with situations in which a member or members of the family of their individual patient were undoing the progress that was taking place in the individual therapy. As a result of these family interviews, often other members of the family would be referred for individual therapy with other therapists. Others however, focus intensively on the family as a series of interlocking dyads, and in their work define process along the lines of interlocking intrapsychic processes. They try to salvage the concept and clinical tool of transference, alternately focusing on the aspects of transference observable between individual family members and therapists, and/or between family members themselves, particularly marital pairs. This method is especially effective with highly motivated neurotic level families; however, in times of extreme stress, therapists who do this often withdraw from a family model and revert to individual therapy for one or more family members.

Today more and more traditional therapists are beginning to see families. Many psychoanalysts with a wealth of clinical experience and a large investment in individual thinking are becoming interested in the systems approach to the family, and trying to deal with the ideological differences in these two approaches. Others are first seeing families and then adapting their own ideologies and techniques to fit the shift in clinical context. There is also significant interest in the adaption of general systems theory to work with families.

Probably most of what goes on throughout the country that is called *family therapy* is practiced on a group model. Bell was one of the original clinicians to embark on group family therapy; Lyman Wynne and Chris Beels are other well-known family therapists using primarily a group theoretical stance. Basically they define the family as a natural group as opposed to an artificially formed T-group. Operationally the family unit is approached in a way similar to a T-group. The family members are encouraged to interact with one another. The therapist assumes an observer position, and moves in to direct or clarify process or to make process or dynamic interpretations.

In the past few years this group has also shown an increasing interest in general system concepts and in the structures of transactional analysis as they apply to working with families clinically. Alger has combined group, general systems, and confrontational use of video playback in his version of family and multiple family therapy.

By 1968 there was a strong experiential thrust in the field. The experiential therapist defines his operating clinical territory as the time and space of the therapy session. The therapist sets several rules as to what will or will not happen in the session. Some of these rules are explicit, others are communicated on a meta level. One of the forbiddens is reporting on the goings on between the sessions. The therapist attempts by use of his or her feeling level barometer to monitor the family for feeling-level issues. Picking up an issue the therapist then moves to engage the family in an "experiential happening." The idea is that if the family could experience themselves in the therapist's presence in a different way on a feeling-level, change for the better—that is, a more open feeling-oriented family—would occur. The most widely known proponents of this position once were Carl Whitaker and Andy Ferber; but Whitaker has since shifted his focus from attempting to stage an experience for the family to attempting to set up an emotional experience for himself. His premise is that rather than trying to force the family to have an experience, if he as the therapist has an experience in craziness, the family will automatically benefit from their experience of him.

I expected when I first moved from Washington to New York that Ackermanian family therapy would be the prevalent form. Experience didn't bear this out. Ackerman in person and on film showed himself to be a crafty experienced clinician, at ease in the clinical situation involving the whole family. The theoretical threads running throughout his work were dependency, sex, and aggression. Ackerman remained closely tied to his position as a psychoanalyst, and it interfered with the development of a clearly delineated family theory in his work, as a result of which he had difficulty evolving a reproducible method of clinical family intervention.

Norman Ackerman, Nat's cousin and also an accomplished and experienced psychoanalyst and family therapist, is strikingly similar in his clinical operations. In recent years Norman has moved more and more toward systems as a theoretical base for working with families. Two other senior clinicians in the family movement also strongly influenced by Ackerman are Israel Zwerling and Salvador Minuchin. A videotape of a Zwerling family interview shows this influence, as Zwerling skillfully moves the family to a clear definition of the problem. Zwerling also has remained strongly wedded to psychoanalytic theory; at the same time he functions as perhaps the most important and effective administrative protector of developing family systems concepts. Minuchin shows the influence of Ackerman in his clinical artistry; he also reflects the theoretical influence in recent years of Jay Haley. Minuchin has somehow combined these influences and added his own considerable clinical experience and skill. Since 1970 Minuchin has clearly moved from an analytic theoretical base to a system base. In fact, he may well end up by bridging the ideologies in such a way that it will allow therapists to move more comfortably back and forth between them.

In 1970, the systems view was clearly a minority point of view. There were two major foci of its development in the field—the work of the California communications theorists, derived from Bateson, and the work of Murray Bowen.

Bateson's communications project, which was further developed by Jackson, Haley, and Satir, used a communications and structural model to define family process dysfunction. What has grown out of the original work is twofold; strategic therapy, and family structural therapy. Strategic brief systems therapy combines a communication systems approach, the use of paradox, and the strategic wizardry of Milton Erickson. Together these provide a framework for bringing about change in a system. The focus is directly on the presenting symptoms; the reality of the problem is defined as narrowly as possible, and strategies of intervention are planned.

A basic premise is that reality is defined as we choose to define it. In people's attempts to deal with life, their solutions most often become the problem. The hope is that intervention will bring about an alteration and redefinition of "reality" in the form of a more functional solution. This method appears to differ from that of Minuchin's in that in addition to communication, symptom focus, and paradox, Minuchin takes into consideration the characteristics of families, boundaries, and structural concepts such as triangulation. Minuchin's work is thus broader than the strategic therapists', but considerably narrower in scope than Bowen's.

The family systems theory developed primarily by Bowen originally centered around concepts closely tied to psychoanalysis and schizophrenia. Since the 1950s, however, Bowen has consistently moved to develop an extensive, all-encompassing system-based theory of emotional dysfunction. His working field is a three- to four-generational view of the family, in which he pays special attention to the triangulation, marital fusion, and reciprocity.

Each systems-based ideology differs in the scope of its focus, philosophy of what is possible in life via therapy, and definition of education. Both the strategic and structural approaches are pragmatic and context determinant in their philosophy; their focus is symptom oriented, and their belief is in the implicit education of experience. Their outlook is more pessimistic than Bowen's. The Bowenian model is cautiously idealistic and optimistic about the inherent human potential for growth and change. It is strongly based on a philosophy of free will. Education at its best is seen as a combination of the implicit knowledge of experiences, solidified and reproduced by cognitive appreciation of its form. The differences in philosophy and outlook are probably due to a combination of the personal characteristics of the people involved, the characteristics of the majority of their patient populations, and the context limitations of each.

In the years since I first published this classification, the systems approach has moved from the periphery to the center of the field. Different people mean different things by the word *systems,* however. As I see it today, there are basically four kinds of systems orientations present: general systems; structural family therapy; strategic family therapy; and Bowenian family systems theory and therapy.

The best psychoanalytic thinkers, like Otto Kernberg, frequently speak of general systems applications to the larger social context both in order to understand human behavior and to mobilize forces to alter the context. On an interventional level, however, they move back to cause-and-effect individual theory and the corresponding techniques. Other general systems thinkers such as Scheflen are heavily into the study of context determinants, sociology, and anthropology. Since this type of general system abstraction has not as yet been translated into clinically relevant terms, these people assume a position of interventional nihilism.

Another possible way to classify family therapists cuts across theoretical positions. Some use family interventions in all or most of their clinical work, but when faced with emotional dysfunction at home seek an individual therapist for that person. Others seek intervention on a family level for their personal system as well.

The men and women who have been largely responsible for creating, thinking through, and sustaining interest in the field of family therapy over its first quarter century developed their own base lines and fought a guerilla war. Those who follow in these second twenty-five years may not fully appreciate the context in which they operated. A useful paradigm for understanding the development of family movement as a conceptual revolution might be the struggle of Sigmund Freud as he tried to convince the established medical community of his own time that his ideas were not the ramblings of a madman.

The future of the family movement will be determined by many things. Two major influences will be the course of research, and clinical work. Another influence will be the future relationship between family therapy and the field of psychotherapy at large. Will it be able to move more into the mainstream without becoming absorbed and dissipated? It is inevitable that the restless minds of a new generation will seek new approaches to understanding human emotional functioning. If family theory does become conventional and orthodox, it will, like other human systems, draw up its own lines of resistance to change. Time will tell; and it will be fun to watch and participate.

CHAPTER 2

Chronicle of a Struggle to Establish a Family Unit Within a Community Mental Health Center

James L. Framo, Ph.D.

In June of 1972, three years after application, the first Family Therapy Unit as an independent service within any community mental health center in the nation was officially funded by NIMH. The community mental health center (hereafter referred to as CMHC) was part of a major medical university in the city of Philadelphia. I will document here the sequences of events surrounding this experiment in establishing a family unit in this setting, and describe the frustrations, difficulties, and satisfactions that were part of this attempt to integrate a systems service model with one based on the conventional model of individual psychiatric disorder. In doing so I am, of course, expressing only my own point of view.

Since 1957 I had been working with Ivan Boszormenyi-Nagy at the Eastern Pennsylvania Psychiatric Institute; our theoretical and clinical work with families was reported in *Intensive Family Therapy*. Preliminary discussions were begun in 1967 with Dr. Daniel Lieberman and Mr. Jerry Jacobs, the Director and Assistant Director of a Philadelphia CMHC which was in the process of being organized. Without their support, the enterprise would not have been possible. Indeed, without the support of the director of a mental health organization, no family unit anywhere has a chance. Dr. Lieberman had already established some innovative programs in California and Delaware, and is the sort of person who is receptive to new ideas. We discussed the possibility of having an independent family unit within the Center, and although it was not possible to include the project in the initial staffing grant request, it was decided to prepare a later proposal to NIMH as an expansion grant. I came on board in 1969, after the Center had been established, but without official status. In that same year, at the American Psychological Association annual meeting, Edgar Auerswald, Frederick Duhl, Matthew Dumont, Alan Levenson, Daniel Lieberman, Marshall Minor, and myself presented a symposium on "The systems approach to community mental health."

The Family Transactional Approach as a Central Integrative Model for Community Mental Health Services: "A Bold, New Approach." This was the title of my grant proposal to NIMH. Its grandiosity is immediately apparent. "Bold, new approach" is President Kennedy's phrase, used when he presented to Congress his proposal for the establishment of nationwide comprehensive CMHCs for "the prevention and treatment of the mentally ill and retarded in their home communities." The rationale of CMHCs was that all services for the mentally ill—emergency, outpatient, partial hospitalization, community, diagnostic, rehabilitative, pre- and after-care services, training, research, and evaluation—were to be placed under one umbrella in each local community. A considerable amount of planning and thinking was done in each state; I served on a task force that was planning CMHCs for the state of Pennsylvania. By 1971, about 450 CMHCs had received grants; 304 were in operation throughout the country, serving areas inhabited by some 65 million people. Great progress was made in meeting financial, administrative, staffing, and physical facility problems, but much confusion existed concerning the basic philosophy or theory of the community approach. As Gerald Caplan (4) stated, "The first problem which confronts the community psychiatrist, who wishes to guide his professional operations in a consistent and meaningful way, is the need for new theoretical models." Most CMHC literature dealt with organizational and empirical matters. Some articles described specific models for particular community situations, but only a few were devoted to the fundamental question of basic rationale and concepts (1, 6, 11, 14, 18, 21, 22). Furthermore, the Centers had an enormous mandate which was probably impossible to fulfill.

Some mental health workers had moved toward dealing with problems of living and functioning in the life situation; however the helping professions still put their major emphasis on central illness processes inside individuals. The possibility was very real that CMHCs would operationally become just a continuation and redistribution of traditional practices. As Reiff (20) observed, "The concepts of community mental health have the potential for introducing revolutionary innovations, but a sober look will reveal that institutionalized community mental health under the federal programs tends to become an extension of professional ideology over that part of society from which it has been hitherto alienated." Yolles (23, 24) then director of NIMH, sounded the call for "creative generalists" from all the behavioral sciences to develop "new departures in looking at problems of mental health" and "flexible, innovative programs" in order to meet the unique challenges of community mental health.

That challenge was clearly there for me. As one of the early workers in family theory and therapy, I envisioned the profound implications of a systems approach as an organizing principle for delivery of mental health services. As I saw it then, and still do, the family model deals with the real problems of people, instead of the symptomatic consequences of family disturbances. Moreover, the family approach offers the opportunity for secondary and tertiary prevention, helps avoid duplication of services, and delivers more efficient and rapid help at reduced cost. Take, for instance, the experience of a family crisis unit in Colorado (17, 19): they found that by treating whole families in crisis they were able to avoid hospitalization of a "psychotic" member over 85 per cent of the time, at one-sixth the cost of hospital treatment. Follow-up several years later showed that these "psychotic" patients were functioning in a way far superior to a control group of patients who had been admitted to the hospital.

Many aspects of family theory and therapy are relevant to community mental health. Developments in psychoanalytic ego psychology, child development, group dynamics, social-psychological theory, communication theory, cultural anthropology, general systems theory, social psychiatry, and family sociology coalesced in the 1950s into a family transactional approach which promised to lead to a revolution in psychopathological thought. Don Jackson (12) explicitly recognized the movement when he wrote: "We are on the edge of a new era in psychiatry and the related disciplines of psychology, social work, anthropology, and sociology. In this new era we will come to look at human nature in a much more complex way than ever before. From this threshold the view is not of the individual *in vitro* but of the small or larger group within which any particular individual's behavior is adaptive. We will move from individual assessment to analysis of contexts, or more precisely, the *system* from which individual conduct is inseparable." The view that psychiatric illness, craziness, odd disordered behavior is a socially intelligible response orchestrated to an odd, crazy, or disordered context marks a significant and momentous shift from demonological thinking.

I emphasized in my grant application that the family approach was not just another form of treatment that would take its place along with other therapies, such as individual, group, child, and other treatment methods. I tried to explain that it is a new philosophy and orientation to the human condition. I suggested that a family therapy unit could provide a meaningful service for members of the community, not only where they lived physically, but where they lived emotionally. That is to say, that while such social systems as the school, the work situation, and the neighborhood are important, the effects of family emotional systems on people are much more powerful. (I remember once a man in family therapy told how he had been in a concentration camp in Germany during the war. When I said that that must have been pretty rough, he replied, "As bad as it was, it doesn't even compare to the damage my family did to me.") Even the layman knows that when someone is manifesting a problem, that person's difficulties are usually related to what is going on in his or her family. However, although everyone in the mental health professions agrees that family relationships are important and highly influential, in actual practice only "sick" individuals are usually treated.

In my application I also pointed out that a systems viewpoint had many practical implications for community mental health. For instance, the symptoms of one or more family members may involve many community agencies and professional helpers, each dealing with a limited sector of the family process, leaving the system untouched. A marital difficulty, for example, may spill over into the children's presenting problems in school or in the community; it may involve the police, juvenile court, domestic relations court, social service agencies, psychiatrists, visiting nurses, Alcoholics Anonymous, religious organizations, and medical hospitals. In essence, the helping professions deal only peripherally with the effects of pathological family processes. Because they lack awareness of the total family situation, there is inefficient duplication of services, and sometimes the various agencies and helpers work at cross purposes: one family I know of had various family members simultaneously involved with eighteen agencies. By treating whole families, furthermore, contact can be made with asymptomatic people who bring others into treatment; these people may never seek treatment for themselves, and yet have great pathological impact on their intimates. The family approach, then, could move the helping professions into a heretofore unreachable part of the population. Moreover, since problems in families tend to repeat themselves from one generation to the next, treating the whole family gives us a chance to abort the problems in this generation—a truly preventative method. Rather than perceiving the family as an interference in the treatment of a "patient," or as a noxious influence, we can recognize it as needing help itself, and as containing the potential for possible change.

The mental health professions have traditionally dealt with emotional problems through programs set up for different population groups—children, adolescents, adults, aged—and for various diagnostic categories—schizophrenia, learning disabilities, drug abuse. As a matter of fact, NIMH is organized in this way, and funds its programs along these fractionated dimensions. By its very nature, family therapy cuts across population groups by simultaneously treating the several generations of the family; and since family therapists regard a "patient's" symptoms as an indication of a family-wide disturbance, diagnostic categories become somewhat irrelevant. Consequently, a Family Unit within a CMHC requires autonomy and a clear self-identity, since it serves across all the services of a Center.

I proposed the following programs as functions of the Family Unit:

Family Diagnostic Intake Evaluations. Family therapy experience has indicated that mental health professionals cannot rely on the school's, or the court's, or the family's, or even on a referring professional's definition of what the problem is, and who the patient is who alone needs evaluation or treatment. When a child is brought in for help, or an adult comes in for help, family therapists regard that person as the representative of the family group. He or she is the symptom-bearer, the consequence of the balance of forces in the family at any given time. A longterm, continuous, often hidden, dynamic family struggle has preceded the outbreak of that person's symptoms. Symptoms are formed, selected, faked, shared, perpetuated, carried vicariously for someone else, or extinguished on the basis of the family relationship struggles. Symptoms may be bribes, manipulations, games, the result of genuine intrapsychic conflicts, blackmail efforts, nonspecific attempts to introduce excitement or variance into a rigid, dead family, tactics in achieving a family advantage, and so forth (7). Unless the whole family is observed interacting together, it is very difficult to tell what the symptoms mean and who or what needs changing. Not the psychiatrist who does a consultation, or the clinical psychologist who administers tests, or the social worker who interviews a relative is in a position to understand the meaning of the presenting symptoms he is called upon to diagnose or treat.

Sometimes the dynamics of a particular family situation may require that one of its members be put out of the family. For example, a mother, married a second time, is forced to choose between her child and her second husband who can't stand her child. Not wanting to lose her second chance at happiness, yet not being able just to give up her child, she focuses upon some disability in the child, who is then taken to a professional for diagnosis and possible placement "for the child's sake." It is a bit frightening to realize how often mental health professionals officially certify the family's process of designating a patient. One wonders how many psychiatrists, clinical psychologists, and social workers have lent themselves to family extrusion processes, the rejects of which populate our institutions for mentally ill children, delinquents, and aged, and our mental hospitals, boarding schools, prisons, and military academies. Family diagnostic evaluations were proposed as the best way to determine what really produced the manifest symptoms in one or more family members, and indeed, whether there is a "patient" as such. Some behaviors are labeled by the family as mental illness which to outsiders are clearly not abnormal, and may even be adaptive. Other behaviors which are clearly disordered or dangerous from a psychiatric or social adjustment point of view, are denied, blocked out, or minimized by the family. Parents may be disturbed by their child's stealing, and remain oblivious to his suicidal gestures, or to the consequences of the child's being their marriage counselor when they fight. Or, a husband may prefer to see his wife's depression as her "illness," rather than as her response to his extramarital affairs or his refusal to talk with her.

In order to provide more efficient service which could lead to lasting and fundamental change, I claimed, practitioners must widen their conceptions of the problems they are called upon to treat, and consider how they do influence and could influence the decisive intrafamilial struggles fought just behind the manifest front of clinical symptomatology. A number of advantages for CMHC purposes in evaluating whole families, including the so-called "well" siblings, on initial consultation, were cited.

1) By evaluating whole families, more patient-community needs are met, not only because more people are seen, but because treatment and remedial efforts can be aimed intelligently and consequently given more rapidly than by traditional methods.

2) Family evaluations help avoid the "sickness-patient-diagnosis-treatment" sequence for one person. They also help other family members to take responsibility for the process in which they all share, so that these other members no longer have to expiate guilt through a variety of maneuvers.

3) Some people, especially adolescents and asymptomatic spouses, are often resistant to psychotherapeutic exploration. However, the involvement of the family increases motivation in truly symptomatic individuals, and may avoid desperate acting out or graver symptomatology as a means of forcing relatives to do something. Scapegoated family members then no longer have to feel that everything is being dumped on them.

4) Family evaluations help avoid hospitalization or institutionalization. This means there is no need to label someone a "mental patient," which can mark or scar a person for life and help make the problems irreversible. Occasionally a disturbed person thrusts forward someone else in the family as the patient, who, because it suits the family system, accepts the designation. Some "well" siblings have been found to be more disturbed than the labelled patient. And when the siblings are healthier, their presence in sessions is vital because they can usually give objective views of family events.

5) Caplan (4) has stated that the goal of community psychiatry "demands the smallest possible intervention in each instance, consonant with getting the sufferer back onto the track of adjustment and adaptation in the world of reality." Whenever a family is seen for evaluation, diagnostic and therapeutic functions overlap. Sometimes opening up family communica-

tion in just one session can unfurl a process that afterwards makes it unnecessary for the family to return. Even small system changes, such as involving the father more in the family, can make a great difference in total family functioning. Insistence on seeing fathers fills a gap in the traditional approach which tends to exclude them from participation.

What if the rest of the family, other than the symptomatic one, refuses to come in for family sessions? Although this does happen, in my experience it is rarer than one might think. If the professional has convictions about the family approach and presents it as "This is the way we work," most families will come in. Those professionals who have mixed feelings and doubt convey their uncertainty; or they apologize, rather than offering the session as a real opportunity. Most families are willing to come in, if for no other reason than to express their concern about the "patient." The family is defined, for these purposes, as those members of the immediate, extended, or psychological family who exert a demonstrable influence on the family system.

Short-Term Family Crisis Therapy. The practice of seeing families as soon as possible for emergency situations may mean well-aimed therapeutic intervention in families who are in the midst of an acute crisis. Acute crises develop around such events as suicide attempts; sudden personality changes in a family member; a death in the family or a successful suicide; an adolescent who has been arrested, run away from home, been truant, been taking drugs, or has become pregnant out of wedlock; someone's dropping out of school; premarital conflicts with in-laws; marital conflict where separation or divorce is imminent; post-divorce crises; squabbles about a will; the institutionalization of an adolescent or an aged grandparent; a parent is going to prison; situations where a parent is out of work or cannot take care of the house or children. Shortterm family therapy (one to ten sessions) can help resolve such emergencies because families in crises are usually more open to exploration and change. Therapeutic intervention is being introduced at a decisive time and in ways which can critically influence the later course of the family.

Clinical experience with brief family therapy shows that alleviation or removal of disorganizing stress situations usually results in a continued process of improvement, even in the absence of prolonged psychotherapy. Family sessions frequently break chronic cycles of uncommunicativeness and start a process of snow-balling whereby the family can come to rely on its own self-corrective mechanisms. Kaffman (13) evaluated the results of seventy families seen in shortterm family therapy, and found that in 75 per cent of the families there was a high degree of improvement as shown by disappearance of symptoms and referral problems, with only 5 per cent showing no change; follow-up checks revealed that the changes were sustained. Changes in family dynamics may ameliorate individual disturbances even in the absence of individual therapy; on the other hand, prolonged individual psychotherapy may fail to bring about clinical improvement due to the absence of parallel changes in the family system. Short-term therapy methods, moreover, fit into the expectancies of the great number of people who have no sophistication about psychotherapy, and are often surprised that more than one session may be necessary to help solve their problems.

Multiple Family and Couples Group Therapy. Multiple family therapy (MFT), consisting of the simultaneous meeting of several families together, has a number of advantages. Laqueur *et al.* (15, 16) and Davies *et al.* (5) are among those who have reported on their experiences with MFT. This treatment method has been found to be especially helpful with disorganized families who could not tolerate the intensity and depth of single family therapy; the presence of other families and consequent diffusion often enables them to participate more freely, especially when there are common problems. And there are almost always common problems. Every family has to deal with parent-child relations, marital conflicts, who does what around the house, disciplining of children, relationships with extended family, expression of feelings, privacy, and similar matters. MFT enables each family to compare itself to other families, and they do learn from each other, by pointing things out to each other and by identification. Mothers, fathers, teenagers, smaller children, and grandparents have an opportunity to share and compare the ways other families handle conflict. Broken, one-parent families are especially helped by being with other families, especially if a father from one family is present as a model for fatherless children in other families. These "sheltered workshops in family communication" have been so successful that families who have been through the process have referred other families from their neighborhood or circle of friends— a circumstance which certainly has implications for a community mental health center.

Couples' group therapy (9) is based on the principle that several married couples meeting together, usually with a male-female cotherapy team, can improve their relationship or get help in terminating the marriage. Couples get honest feedback from others, and benefit by observing how other couples work out their problems. Since there is a direct relationship between marital problems and problems in the original families of spouses, treatment sessions involving these adults and their families of origin can be held for motivated people (10).

Family Outreach Program. This sort of program may help the families in the catchment area who are either unable or unwilling to come to the Center. These are the indigent, unmotivated, often fragmented families who do not ordinarily seek professional help, cannot keep regular therapy hours, and are culturally unable to be treated by the usual psychotherapy techniques. Yet, this is also the population which has proportionately high rates of delinquency and crime, drug and alcohol addiction, infant mortality, unemployment, admission to state hospitals, and physical illness. All these disadvantaged families share, in common, poverty, despair, powerlessness, anomie, transiency of marital bonds with high rates of desertion, separation, and illegitimacy.

Nonprofessional indigenous family counselors were to be trained to see these families in their homes and help them with the emotional issues surrounding their real problems—housing, jobs, food, truancy, legal problems, public assistance, and marital conflicts.

Training and Research Programs. In addition to the foregoing clinical programs, we planned to institute training programs in family and marital therapy for CMHC personnel, and a program of evaluative research on the effectiveness of the clinical programs.

The projected training program was to be on two levels. One level of training in family dynamics and everyday family life problems was designed for pre- and nonprofessionals in the Center—medical students, residents, psychology and social work students, indigenous family workers, and nurses—and others outside the Center such as GPs, police, pastoral counselors, teachers, and others involved with family problems. The second level of training was designed for CMHC professionals with prior experience in individual or group therapy. These professionals were to be trained in family and marital therapy, utilizing, in addition to other training methods, the observation of family therapy sessions through the oneway mirror.

An important part of any program is its research function, because without systematic evaluation there is no way to determine whether a program is doing what it is supposed to do (8). Accordingly, a research plan was formulated to study, codify, and evaluate the clinical programs of the family unit in order to appraise their effectiveness.

Out of my enthusiasm for what the family approach had to offer, and being unaware of the truly formidable difficulties involved in such an undertaking, in the proposal I recommended a daring concept. I proposed that CMHCs become family centers, and that diagnostic family evaluations, where possible, become a routine part of the admission procedure to a CMHC, no matter how the problem was presented or who presented it. I was not suggesting that family therapy be done in all situations, since that would be unfeasible and at times inappropriate. Rather, on the basis of several family evaluation sessions, once the symptom-in-its-context was better understood, a team would be in a better position to determine which of a variety of treatment modalities was indicated and for whom; and referrals could be made to the various services of the CMHC—whether individual psychotherapy, conjoint marital therapy, peer group therapy, partial hospitalization, drug or alcoholic services, or family therapy. The family evaluation might also reveal that a psychiatric problem was not present; or that referrals were needed for specialized services like vocational guidance, homemaker service, remedial reading, parent effectiveness training, speech therapy, halfway house, employment services, homes for unwed mothers, or medical care. Family diagnostic evaluations, in other words, would constitute the primary admission procedure.

Governmental recognition of all the obvious (to me) truths contained in this proposal, I fantasized, would precipitate an immediate call from Washington to come down there and help reorganize the entire CMHC movement. The only official message I got from Washington, however, for three long years was silence. It was the beginning of my education on the mysterious workings of governmental and medical organizations. What now follows is a personal account of what actually happened later.

When I joined the Center in 1969, having no official standing (I was hired on paper, I believe, as a psychiatrist in mental retardation), I had to make do with makeshift quarters in the out-patient service. I had no staff or even a secretary, and started seeing families alone. In a short while I was able to get a secretary, and about a year later was moved to an old building which turned out to be a blessing in disguise. The building contained a large room with a fireplace that could be used as a treatment room; it looked more like a living room than an office—much better for family sessions. The Director managed to find some money for installing a one way mirror and for swivel chairs for treatment families. But we had no office furniture; so my secretary and I borrowed, expropriated, and scrounged around for old file cabinets, a typewriter, and a couple of desks. The Women's Auxiliary Board of the hospital, after I gave them a hard sell about the value of the work we were doing, kindly donated money for drapes and decorations, so that the place looked fairly livable and not so bare. By writing to department stores in the city, we were able to get them to donate rugs. The Director also squeezed money out of somewhere to set up a sound system and tape recorder so family sessions could be observed as part of a training program. In addition, a way was found for me to hire two staff members, a family therapist and a nonprofessional family counselor by letting them occupy unfilled slots from other services. We were nearly in business. Those days of having to get by on a shoestring were difficult, but nonetheless challenging and exciting. At the same time, I wished I had the plush quarters and video equipment they had in the medical college.

Having been used to the pace of a research and training institute for many years, I was unprepared for the rapid pace of a community mental health center. Memos, guidelines, announcements crossed my desk by the hundreds; written reports were constantly requested, and there were innumerable meetings with various services and agencies for sundry purposes. There was even a meeting once on why we had so many meetings. In any event, I got to know the people at the Center better, came to like many of them, and was learning how a CMHC worked. During meetings on delivery of services, when I would bring up the value of seeing whole families, I was listened to politely, but not heard. A curious dual attitude existed on the part of most of the professional staff: on the one hand, they were fascinated by family therapy and what it could do; and on the other hand, they continued to treat patients as they always had. In the Children's Unit, they operated from a child guidance model of treating the child, with the social worker seeing the parents, usually only the mother. Now and again some therapists would come over to observe family sessions, and this created interest in starting the training programs. I pretty much had to bootleg families to treat; because of my reputation some families were referred from agencies in the community. We rarely got fresh crisis situations, and frequently had to deal with families whose problems had calcified and who shopped professionally for help. Marital problems had usually been handled by treating the partners separately, but when the advantages of conjoint treatment became more apparent, we started getting couples referred to us.

During this period several informal messages came down from NIMH that if I rewrote the grant and oriented it toward the treatment of children or drug abuse, money might be available. I ignored these hints, determined to stick to my convictions. I got caught up in that syndrome familiar to those awaiting the outcome of a grant application—I anxiously followed the newspapers and newletter reports on how much Congress would appropriate for NIMH and on whether the President would cut NIH funds, and I worried about whether the application would get lost in the bureaucracy. The Vietnam War was still on, and I remember thinking bitterly that the Family Unit could be funded for the cost of one army tank. After an on-site visit from an NIMH committee, who were handled quite gingerly, we received word from the feds that the project was funded for an eight-year period for a million and a half dollars overall.

I had not, however, anticipated the roadblocks thrown up by the state and city mental health offices who were required to give matching funds. The state informed us that they didn't know if they could support a project that seemed to violate the CMHC act, which requires treatment for psychiatric illness. In other words, a married couple technically could not get help from a CMHC for their marital relationship; each partner needed a psychiatric diagnosis, and if they were not "sick" they were not eligible for treatment. By treating people without symptoms the Family Unit would technically be breaking the law. Luckily, the Director of the Center knew the then Commissioner of Mental Health for the state, and after repeated phone calls to him, we got state approval. The Deputy Health Commissioner for the city office of mental health was a friend of mine, so I was surprised when he seriously questioned the value and even the legal status of a family unit. He wanted to know, why have an independent unit for family therapy in a CMHC? If they gave matching funds for a family unit, why not set up units for group therapy or other treatment modalities? Somehow I was able to communicate that the family approach was not just another form of treatment; and eventually, with the assistance of the Regional Director of NIMH, who saw the merits of the proposal, the city office gave final approval. It should not have been necessary to use the help of friends.

Now we were legal! We could hire staff, put all the programs into operation, and, wonder of wonders, even get a videotape recorder—one of the most effective training devices and therapeutic tools via videotape playback to families. I discovered however that I could not hire staff until I prepared job descriptions. Job descriptions for family therapists did not exist, and so far as I could find out, they didn't exist anywhere in the country. So I had to devise job descriptions of various levels of responsibility: for my job of Chief, for Assistant Chief, Senior Family Therapist, Family Therapists II and I, and Indigenous Family Counselors II and I. Since family therapy is an interdisciplinary approach, I felt that family therapists should be paid according to their training, experience, and competence as family therapists, and not according to their basic professional designation. This idea was completely contrary to state regulations and salary practices of the medical school. Psychiatrists had to be paid more than psychologists, who in turn were paid more than social workers. I couldn't fight City Hall and had to give in to that hard reality, but I did resent the fact that my assistant chief, a psychiatrist, with far less experience, got $3000 more a year than I did.

It was not easy to recruit experienced family therapists. And many applicants, who would never have applied for individual or group therapy positions without prior training, felt sure they could treat families; after all, they grew up in a family. Eventually a staff of eight was recruited, including my former secretary who had left to get training and a master's degree, and returned to the Unit.

The next hurdle was the requirement, which also exists with insurance companies, that we give an official APA diagnosis to every member of the family. CMHC regulations prescribed that these statistics be kept by the research section of the Center. We developed the practice of labelling babies as having "infant adjustment reactions," and adults were fairly routinely diagnosed as suffering from "anxiety reactions." After all, who does not have to adjust and who is not anxious in this world?

One cannot escape a numbers game in a CMHC. All the services had to report monthly how many patients they saw, and it was impossible not to compare the patient census of each service when we had our chief-of-service meetings. Although accountability in a CMHC is a worthy endeavor, nonetheless this procedure fostered competition among services to see the largest number of patients. It also accounted for the territoriality syndrome; that is to say, patients, with some exceptions, tended to get the kind of treatment which was available wherever they happened to enter the system. The various services tended to hold on to the patients they got in order to build up their census, except for the "impossible" patients they would try to unload. There seemed to be no way of evaluating quality or appropriateness of treatment. I too pushed my staff to see as many people as possible.

In the early days, we used to insist that the entire family come in. Several times we followed the usual family therapy practice of refusing to see, say, a mother who came in alone to complain about a child or husband. Then one day we learned that one of these clients called the city office of mental health to complain that we were denying treatment. After that experience, we started family therapy with whoever showed up for sessions, and built up to the whole family from there. There are certainly things you can do in private practice that you cannot do in a public agency.

Families and couples were usually seen by heterosexual cotherapy teams, an inefficient procedure by CMHC standards since it cut down on patient-staff ratio times, but a most effective therapy procedure that produced change. It was difficult to get referrals from within the Center, so we established relationships with, and got referrals from, schools, the clergy, nonpsychiatric physicians, the courts, and so forth. In our first year we saw over 200 families containing over 500 individuals; however, I was always more interested in high treatment standards than numbers. The outreach program worked out fairly well because we had a dedicated nonprofessional team. Some problems did come up: some families did not want to be seen in their homes, because they did not want neighbors to know that people were coming to their home to help them; other families objected to getting help from those who were not "real doctors."

The other services of the Center seemed to have mixed feelings about the family unit. Perhaps they were responding to my earlier efforts to sell the family approach—efforts I learned that created defensiveness. Perhaps they resented the specialness of the unit or our relative opulence, because many of the services had to struggle for staff and equipment. (The Center at one point nearly closed down due to insufficient funding). On the other hand, those who observed treatment sessions, and came to see psychopathology in an entirely different light, did request training. The training programs turned out to be very successful for the pre- and nonprofessionals; but very rarely did the professionals enroll, especially the psychiatrists. Some of the Center's professional staff started seeing couples and families conjointly, but lacking specific training, some of them did family therapy inappropriately; bringing the family together to talk only about the patient is not family therapy. I came to understand that these professionals felt that to come to the Unit's training program would have constituted some loss of face. Many of the difficulties of the Unit would have been obviated had I been a physician or psychiatrist.

Being in a medical setting had some advantages, because we were able to get involved with that vast, untapped area of family problems associated with medical wards. The family therapist-physician on the Unit became a consultant to pediatrics, the dialysis ward, OB-Gyn, and even to physicians dealing with families when someone died. Medical hospitals have not yet recognized the enormous potential of family work in the practice of medicine. I found the medical students in the training programs to be more receptive than the psychiatric residents, who by that time were firmly grounded in the individual view of mental illness. Another productive training program was one I gave for a group of policemen, who spend the majority of their time, I was surprised to learn, dealing with family disturbances.

The number of reports I had to write increased; there were progress reports, research reports, one-year plans, and five-year plans. Meetings with outside agencies and other services of the CMHC proliferated; we were seeking out sources of clients, coordinating services, monitoring continuity of care, and so forth. I frankly got the feeling that we spent so much time writing and meeting about what we were doing and were going to do that there wasn't enough time in which to do it. Never had I been so tired at the end of the day. One observation I've made about mental health organizations, not just CMHCs, is that when the census goes down and there is pressure of service to justify professional existence, the staff get more anxious, have more meetings, and end up treating each other.

After four years at the Center, a series of circumstances led to my leaving the CMHC and accepting an offer to enter academic life. Those circumstances are another story, but one contributing factor was the opportunity it gave me for more time in which to practice, teach, develop concepts, and write.

As I look back on my efforts to set up an independent family therapy unit within a CMHC, the perspective of time makes it possible to evaluate the whole experience. Firstly, I have serious question as to whether a systems model of therapy can be mixed or integrated with an individual-illness model. I do not intend to denigrate individual therapy. There are proper indications for individual treatment, and there will always be a need for it. But I believe that the premises, philosophy, and orientation of the two models are too different for a marriage to occur. Family therapy, I am sure, is now probably being done at most CMHCs; but I can understand why no other independent family therapy units have been set up in any CMHC in the country (to my knowledge). When some of the full implications of the systems viewpoint become apparent—in terms of their effects on diagnosis and treatment procedures, admission policies, status, and so forth—establishment mental health finds it too threatening. Various people around the country, when they heard about the unit, got in touch with me and asked how they could do the same thing; I was not able to be too sanguine about their prospects, and promised that someday I would publish the reasons. A combination of this difference in philosophy with the way the laws are written, the bureaucracy of NIMH, the rules and regulations of CMHCs, not to mention the traditions of medical settings, add up to an awe-inspiring set of obstacles.

I do not know to what extent my own shortcomings led to less than striking success. My inexperience as an administrator was apparent in the way I felt I had to monitor everything myself, and had difficulty delegating duties. I discovered how easy it is to blame things on the boss until you yourself are the boss. For instance, I had great difficulty bringing myself to fire people. Possibly I could have been less doctrinaire and more tolerant of traditional ways of helping people, and not so imbued with a self-defined sense of revolution.

I also do not mean to criticize the Center, which in many ways was a fine model CMHC when compared to others. Nor do I wish to fault the sincere, conscientious, and competent people at the Center, the great majority of whom worked very hard to help the residents of the community they served. Indeed, statistical evidence exists that they ameliorated much human distress. However, most mental health professionals are bound by the concepts by which they were trained, and CMHCs are limited by ill-defined conceptual foundations. I emphasize that, as in a family, CMHCs are not "bad" systems, and no one, really, is to blame. People get caught up in organizational structures with their rules and guidelines, and these systems develop a life of their own, with their own regulatory powers. In any event, for me, overall, it was a good go, and I don't regret the experience.

Since I left the Center, I have learned that the CMHC has decentralized. The catchment area has been divided into five districts, each with its own team of specialists and generalists. Apparently decentralization has been found to be more effective in the delivery and volume of services. For example, whereas in the past only 20 per cent of therapists' time was spent in face-to-face contacts with patients, with decentralization this figure has increased to 50 per cent. The Family Therapy Unit has continued in modified form, and the previous training programs must have had some effect, because many more people are now doing family therapy. I had apparently left some imprint after all.

REFERENCES

1. S. Blackman and K.M. Goldstein. "Some Aspects of a Theory of Community Mental Health," *Commun. Mental Health Journal,* 4 (1968), 85–90.
2. W.M. Bolman. "Theoretical and Empirical Bases of Community Mental Health," Community Psychiatry. Supplement to *Amer. J. Psychiat.,* 124 (1967), 8–13.
3. I. Boszormenyi-Nagy and J. Framo (eds.). *Intensive Family Therapy.* New York: Hoeber, 1965.
4. G. Caplan. "Community Psychiatry—Introduction and Overview," in S.E. Goldston (ed.). *Concepts of Community Psychiatry.* Bethesda, Md.: U.S. Dept. of HEW, NIMH, 1965.
5. I.J. Davies, G. Ellenson, and R. Young. "Therapy with a Group of Families in a Psychiatric Day Center," *Amer. J. Orthopsychiat.,* 36 (1966), 134–46.
6. S. Feldman. "Ideas and Issues in Community Mental Health," *Hosp. & Comm. Psychiat.,* 22 (1971), 325–29.
7. J.L. Framo. "Symptoms from a Family Transactional Viewpoint," in N.W. Ackerman, J. Lieb, and J.K. Pearce (eds.). *Family Therapy in Transition.* Boston: Little, Brown, 1970.
8. _____ (ed.). *Family Interaction: An Encounter Between Family Researchers and Family Therapists.* New York: Springer, 1972.
9. _____. "Marriage Therapy in a Couples Group," In D. Bloch (ed.). *Techniques of Family Psychotherapy.* New York: Grune & Stratton, 1973.
10. _____. "Family of Origin as a Therapeutic Resource for Adults in Family and Marital Therapy: You Can and Should Go Home Again," *Family Process.* In press.
11. L.P. Howe. "The Concept of the Community: Some Implications for the Development of Community Psychiatry," in L. Bellak (ed.). *Handbook of Community Psychiatry and Community Mental Health.* New York: Grune & Stratton, 1964.
12. D.D. Jackson. "The Individual and the Larger Contexts," *Family Process,* 6 (1947), 139–47.
13. M. Kaffman. "Short Term Family Therapy," *Family Process,* 2 (1963), 216–34.
14. D.C. Klein. "The Community and Mental Health: An Attempt at a Conceptual Framework," *Commun. Mental Health Journal,* 1 (1965), 301–08.
15. H.P. Laqueur, H.A. Laburt, and E. Morong. "Multiple Family Therapy," in J.H. Masserman (ed.). *Current Psychiatric Therapies, IV.* New York: Grune & Stratton, 1964.
16. H.P. Laqueur. "Multiple Family Therapy: Questions and Answers," in D.A. Bloch (ed.). *Techniques of Family Psychotherapy.* New York: Grune & Stratton, 1973.
17. D.G. Langsley, D.M. Kaplan, F.S. Pittman, P. Machotka, K. Flomenhaft, and C.D. DeYoung. *The Treatment of Families in Crisis.* New York: Grune & Stratton, 1968.
18. C. Mayo and D.C. Klein. "Group Dynamics as a Basic Process of Community Psychiatry," in L. Bellak (ed.). *Handbook of Community Psychiatry and Community Mental Health.* New York: Grune & Stratton, 1964.
19. F.S. Pittman, D.G. Langsley, D.M. Kaplan, K. Flomenhaft, and C. DeYoung. "Family Therapy as an Alternative to Psychiatric Hospitalization," in I.M. Cohen (ed.). *Family Structure, Dynamics, and Therapy.* Psychiatric Research Report #20, The American Psychiatric Association, 1966.

20. R. Reiff. "Mental Health Manpower and Institutional Change," *Amer. Psychol.,* 21 (1966), 540–48.
21. M. Sabshin. "Theoretical Models in Community and Social Psychiatry," in L.M. Roberts, S.L. Halleck, and M.B. Loeb (eds.). *Community Psychiatry.* Madison, Wisconsin: Univ. of Wisconsin Press, 1966.
22. H.G. Whittington. "The Third Psychiatric Revolution—Really?" *Commun. Mental Health Journal,* 1 (1968), 73–80.
23. S. Yolles. *The Role of the Psychologist in Comprehensive Community Mental Health Centers: The NIMH View.* Paper presented at the Conference of State Chief Psychologists and Psychologists in USPHS, Chicago, 1965.
24. _____. "Community Mental Health Services: the View from 1967," Community Psychiatry Supplement to the *Amer. J. Psychiat.,* 124 (1967), 1–7.

Part II

THEORY

CHAPTER 3

Theory in the Practice of Psychotherapy

Murray Bowen, M.D.

There are striking discrepancies between theory and practice in psychotherapy. The therapist's theoretical assumptions about the nature and origin of emotional illness serve as a blueprint that guides his thinking and actions during psychotherapy. This has always been so, even though "theory" and "therapeutic method" have not always been clearly defined. Primitive medicine men who believed that emotional illness was the result of evil spirits had some kind of theoretical notions about the evil spirits that guided their therapeutic method as they attempted to free the person of the spirits. I believe that theory is important now even though it might be difficult to define the specific connections between theory and practice.

I have spent almost three decades on clinical research in psychotherapy. A major part of my effort has gone toward clarifying theory and also toward developing therapeutic approaches consistent with the theory. I did this in the belief it would add to knowledge and provide better structure for research. A secondary gain has been an improvement in the predictability and outcome of therapy as the therapeutic method has come into closer proximity with the theory. Here I shall first present ideas about the lack of clarity between theory and practice in all kinds of psychotherapy; in the second section I will deal specifically with family therapy. In discussing my own Family Systems theory, certain parts will be presented almost as previously published (1,2). Other parts will be modified slightly, and some new concepts will be added.

BACKGROUND TO THEORY IN PSYCHOTHERAPY

Twentieth-century psychotherapy probably has its origin in Freud, who developed a completely new theory about the nature and origin of emotional illness. Before him, mental illness was generally considered the result of some unidentified brain pathology, based on the structured model used by medicine to conceptualize all disease. Freud introduced the new dimension of functional illness which dealt with the function of the mind, rather than brain pathology. His theory was derived largely from patients as they remembered details of early life experiences and as they communicated this detail in the context of an intense emotional relationship with the analyst. In the course of the analysis it was discovered that the patients improved, and that the patient's relationship with the analyst went through definite, predictable stages toward a better life adjustment. Freud and the early analysts made two monumental contributions. One was a new theory about the origin and nature of emotional illness. The other was the first clearly defined theory about the transference relationship and the therapeutic value of a talking relationship. Although counseling and "talking about problems" may have existed before, it was psychoanalysis that gave conceptual structure to the "therapeutic relationship," and that gave birth to the profession of psychotherapy.

Few events in history have influenced man's thinking more than psychoanalysis. This new knowledge about human behavior was gradually incorporated into psychiatry, psychology, sociology, anthropology, and the other professional disciplines that deal with human behavior, and into poetry, novels, plays, and other artistic works. Psychoanalytic concepts came to be regarded as basic truths. Along with the acceptance there were some long term complications in the integration of psychoanalysis with other knowledge. Freud had been trained as a neurologist. He was clear that he was operating with theoretical assumptions, and that his concepts had no logical connection with medicine or the accepted sciences. His concept of "psycho" pathology, patterned after medicine, left us with a conceptual dilemma not yet resolved. He searched for a conceptual connection with medicine, but never found it. Meanwhile, he used inconsistent models to conceptualize his other findings. His broad knowledge of literature and the arts served as other models. A striking example was the oedipal conflict, which came from literature. His models accurately portrayed his clinical observations and represented a microcosm of human nature; nonetheless, his theoretical concepts came from discrepant sources. This made it difficult for his successors to think in concepts synonymous with medicine or the accepted sciences. In essence, he conceptualized a revolutionary new body of knowledge about human functioning that came to exist in its own compartment, without logical connection with medicine or any of the accepted sciences.

The knowledge was popularized by the social sciences and the artistic world, but few of the concepts found their way into the more basic sciences. This further separated psychoanalysis from the sciences.

There have been some clear evolutionary developments in psychoanalytic theory and practice during the twentieth century. Successors to Freud have been more disciples than scientists. They lost contact with the fact that his theory is based on theoretical assumption, and they have tended to regard it as established fact. The more it is considered to be fact, the less it has been possible to question the theoretical base on which it rests. Very early the disciples began to disagree with certain details of the theory (predictable in human relationship systems), and to develop different "theories," concepts, and "schools of thought" based on the differences. They have made such an issue over "differences" that they have lost sight of the fact that they all follow Freud's broad assumptions. The different branches of the tree spend their lives debating the proclaimed "differences," unaware that all spring from the same basic roots. As time passes and the number of branches increase, so do the differences.

The number of differences about the therapeutic relationship are even greater. Freud defined a basic theory about the therapeutic relationship. Beyond that, each practitioner is on his own in developing methods and techniques for applying the theory. There is more flexibility for developing "differences" about therapeutic method and techniques than about theory. Psychoanalysts maintain a strict interpretation of the "transference," which is considered to be different from the popular notion of the therapeutic relationship. There are differences, but the focus on differences obscures the common denominators. Group therapy is a good illustration of the trend. It sprang primarily from theory about the therapeutic relationship, and secondarily from basic psychoanalytic theory about the nature of emotional illness. The growing multitudes of mental health professionals who use all the different theories and therapies still follow two of the basic concepts of psychoanalysis. One is that emotional illness is developed in relationship with others. The second is that the therapeutic relationship is the universal "treatment" for emotional illness.

There are other evolutionary trends that illustrate the separation of theory and practice. It has to do with psychological research. The basic sciences have long been critical of psychoanalysis and psychological theory as nonscientific and based on shifting hypotheses that defy critical scientific study. There is validity to this criticism. The psychoanalysts and psychologists have countered that the field is different, and the same rules do not apply. They have coined the term social "sciences," and much research has gone into proving that they are scientific. There is some support for the proposition that social sciences are scientific. The major change has been in the development of the scientific method designed to study random and discrepant data in a scientific way. If the scientific method is pursued long enough, it should eventually produce the data and facts that are acceptable to the basic sciences. This has not occurred. The debate has gone through the century with the psychologists accepting psychoanalytic assumptions as fact and believing that the scientific method makes the field into a science, while workers in the basic sciences are still unconvinced. This is where research in the mental health field is today. The directors of research and experts who control the funds for research are schooled in the scientific method, which tends to perpetuate fixed postures. My own position on this is that, "There is no way to chi square a feeling and make it qualify as a scientific fact." This is based on the belief that human behavior is a part of all nature, so that it is as knowable and predictable and reproducible as other phenomena in nature; but I believe that research should be directed at making theoretical contact with other fields, rather than applying the scientific method to subjective human data. This has been a long-term conflict I have had with research in mental illness. To summarize, I believe that research in emotional illness has helped to contribute to the separation of theory and practice, and to the notion that psychological theory is based on proven fact.

There are trends in the training of mental health professionals that support the separation of theory and practice. Early in the twentieth century the popularity of psychoanalysis was increasing, but overall, psychiatry, and also the public, was still negative about it. By the 1940s and 1950s, psychoanalytic theory had become *the* predominant theory. By that time the psychoanalysts had developed so many superficial "differences" among themselves that the new trainees of the 1940s and 1950s were confronted with a spectrum of different "theories" all based on basic psychoanalytic concepts. They learned psychoanalytic theory as proven fact and the therapeutic relationship as *the* treatment for emotional illness. The trainees from that period are now the senior teachers in the field. The number of superficial "differences" have increased. Starting in the 1950s and increasing into the 1960s, we have heard much antipsychoanalytic talk by people who use basic psychoanalytic concepts in theory and practice. In the present era we have the "eclectic," who tells us that there is no single theory adequate for all situations and he chooses the best parts of all the theories to best fit the clinical situation of the moment.

I believe that all the differences belong within the basic framework of psychoanalysis, and that the eclectic shifting may be more for the needs of therapist than the patient. The average training programs for mental health professionals contain a few didactic lectures on theory appended to the basic training. An overwhelming amount of time goes to tutorial training, which emphasizes the therapeutic relationship, learning about one's own emotional problems, and the management of self in relation to the patient. This produces professionals who are oriented around the therapeutic relationship, who assume they know the nature and origin of emotional illness, who are unable to question the theoretical base on which the field rests, and who assume the therapeutic relationship is the basic treatment for emotional problems. Society, insurance companies, and the licensing bodies have come to accept this theoretical and therapeutic position, and have become more lenient about providing payment for psychotherapeutic services. Counselors, teachers, police, courts, and all the social agencies that deal with human problems have also come to accept the basic assumptions about theory and therapy.

Mental health professionals relate to theory in a spectrum. At one extreme are the few who are serious students of theory. A larger group can state theoretical positions in detail, but they have developed therapeutic approaches discrepant with the theory. A still larger group treats theory as proven fact. These last are similar to the medicine men who *knew* that illness was caused by evil spirits. Professional expertise becomes a matter of finding more ingenious techniques for externalizing the bad spirits. At the other extreme are the therapists who contend there is no such thing as theory, that theoretical efforts are post hoc explanations for the therapist's intuitive actions in the therapeutic relationship, and that the best therapy is possible when the therapist learns to be a "real self" in relation to the patient.

In presenting these ideas about the separation of theory and therapy in the mental health professions, I have inevitably overstated to clarify the issues. I believe that psychoanalytic theory, which includes the theory of the transference and talking therapy, is still the one major theory to explain the nature and origin of emotional illness, and that the numerous different theories are based more on minor differences than on differences with basic concepts. I believe Freud's use of discrepant theoretical models helped make psychoanalysis into a compartmentalized body of knowledge that prevented successors from finding conceptual bridges with the more accepted sciences. Psychoanalysis attracted followers who were more disciples than scholars and scientists. It has evolved into more of a dogma or religion than a science, with its own "scientific" method to help perpetuate the cycle. I believe it has enough new knowledge to be part of the sciences, but the professionals who practice psychoanalysis have evolved into an emotional ingroup, like a family or a religion. Members of an emotional ingroup devote energy to defining their "differences" with each other and defending dogma that needs no defense. They are so caught up with the ingroup process that they cannot generate new knowledge from within, nor permit the admission of knowledge from without that might threaten the dogma. The result has been a splintering and resplintering, with a new generation of eclectics who attempt to survive the splintering with their eclecticism.

THE THERAPEUTIC RELATIONSHIP IN BROADER PERSPECTIVE

Family research has identified some characteristics of emotional systems that put the therapeutic relationship into broader perspective. An emotional system is usually the family, but it can be a larger work group or a social group. The major characteristic to be examined here is that *the successful introduction of a significant other person into an anxious or disturbed relationship system has the capacity to modify relationships within the system.* There is another characteristic of opposite emotional forces, which is that the higher the level of tension or anxiety within an emotional system, the more the members of the system tend to withdraw from outside relationships and to compartmentalize themselves with each other. There are a number of variables that revolve around the characteristic in focus. The first variables have to do with the *significant other.* Other variables have to do with what is meant by *successful* introduction. Other variables have to do with the *introduction* of the significant other and how long he remains a member of the system. Still other variables have to do with what it means to *modify* a system. I have chosen the term *modify* in order to avoid the use of *change,* which has come to have so many different meanings in psychotherapy.

An individually oriented psychotherapist is a common *significant other.* If he can manage a viable and moderately intense therapeutic relationship with the patient, and the patient remains in viable contact with the family, it can calm and modify relationships within the family. It is as though the therapeutic relationship drains the tension from the family and the family can appear to be different. When the therapist and patient become more intensely involved with each other, the patient withdraws from emotional contact with the family and the family becomes more disturbed. Therapists have intuitive ways of dealing with this situation. Some choose to intensify the relationship into a therapeutic alliance, and to encourage the patient to challenge the family. Others are content with a supportive relationship. There are a number of other outside relationships that can accomplish the same thing. A significant new relationship with a friend, minister, or teacher can be effective if the right conditions are met. The right degree of an outside sexual relationship can calm a family as much as individual psychotherapy. When the affair is kept at the right emotional level, the family system can be calm and blind to evidences of the affair. The moment the outside affair becomes emotionally overinvested, it tends to alienate the involved person from the family and increase tension within the family. At this point the other spouse becomes a suspicious detective, alert to all the evidence previously ignored. This phenomenon, which has to do with the balance of relationships in a family, applies to a broad spectrum of relationships.

A set of variables revolve around the qualities that go into a significant other relationship. One variable deals with the importance of the family member to the rest of the family. The family would respond quickly to the outside emotional involvement of an important family member who is relating actively to the others. It would respond slowly to a withdrawn and inactive family member unless the outside relationship was fairly intense. The most important variable has to do with the assumed, assigned, or actual importance of the significant other person. At one extreme is the significant other who assumes or is assigned magical or supernatural importance. This includes voodoo experts, leaders of cults, great healers, and charismatic leaders of spiritual movements. The significant other can pretend to represent the diety and to have supernatural power. He pleads for the other to "believe in me, trust me, have confidence in me." The assuming of great importance and the assigning of importance is usually a bilateral operation, but there probably could be situations in which the importance is largely assigned, and significant other goes along with it. These relationships operate on high emotionality and minimal reality. When successful, the change can come rapidly or with instantaneous conversion.

At the other extreme are the situations in which the evaluation of the significant other is based largely on reality, with little pretense, and with little of the intense relationship phenomenon. The principal ingredient is knowledge or skill. Examples of this might be a genetic counselor, an estate planner, or a successful professor who has the ability to inspire students in his subject, more through knowledge than relationship. In between these two extremes are relationships with healers, ministers, counselors, physicians, therapists of all kinds, and people in the helping professions who either assume or are assigned an importance they do not have. The assuming and assigning of importance is clearest in its extreme forms in which the pretending of importance is sufficiently grotesque for anyone to notice. Actually, the assigning and assuming of importance, or unimportance, is present to some degree in all relationships, and present enough to be detectable in most relationships on careful observation. A clear example is a love relationship in which each has an overvalued image of the other. It is also easy to recognize the change in a person who is in love. Overall, the degree of assigning and assuming overimportance in the therapeutic relationship is on the high side. Psychoanalysis has subtle techniques to encourage the development of a transference, which is then dealt with in the therapy. Other methods do even more of this, and efforts to correct the distortion are even less.

Another set of variables revolve around the way the significant other is introduced into the system. At one extreme, the significant other pleads, exhorts, advertises, evangelizes, and makes promises of the great things if he is invited in. At the other extreme, the significant other enters the system only on unsolicited invitation and with a contract either verbal or written that comes closer to defining the reality of the situation. The rest fall somewhere between these two extremes. Other variables have to do with the length of time the significant other is involved in the system. The successful involvement depends on whether or not the relationship works. This involves the family member devoting a reasonable amount of thinking-feeling energy to the relationship without becoming too emotionally preoccupied.

An important set of variables revolves around what it means to modify relationships within the family. I avoid using *change* here because of the loose way this word is used within the profession. Some speak of an emotional conversion, a shift in mood, a shift in attitude, or a shift from feeling sad to happy as being "change" or emotional "growth." The word *growth* has been so misused during the past decade, that it has become meaningless. In contrast, other people do not consider change to have taken place without basic, documentable, structural alteration in the underlying situation that gave rise to the symptoms. Between these two lie all the other manifestations of change. It is common for mental health professionals to consider the disappearance of symptoms as evidence of change.

The more the relationship with the significant other person is endowed with high emotionality, messianic qualities, exaggerated promises, and evangelism, the more the change can be sudden and magical, and the less likely it is to be long term. The lower the emotionality and the more the relationship deals in reality, the more likely the change is to come slowly and to be solid and long lasting. There is some degree of emotionality in any relationship, especially in the helping professions where the principal ingredient is services rather than materials, but it is also present around those who deal in materials, such as supersalesmen. The emotionality can exist around the charismatic person who attracts the assignment of importance from others. Emotionality may be hard to evaluate with public figures who attain their positions from superior skill and knowledge, in which emotionality is low, and who then operate on reputation, in which assigned importance is high. The doctor-patient relationship encompasses a wide range of emotionality. At one extreme it can be almost all service and little relationship, and at the other extreme the emotional component is high. The physician who operates with a posture which says, "Have no fear, the doctor is here," is assuming great importance, and also using it to calm anxiety. The physician who says, "If doctors could only be half as important as their patients think they are," is operating with awareness and less assumption of importance. Emotionality is sufficiently high in medicine that the placebo effect is routinely built into responsible research to check the emotional factor.

Psychotherapy is a service that deals in a higher level of emotionality than the average doctor-patient relationship. The level of assumed and assigned importance is on the high side. The well-trained therapist has techniques to encourage the patient to assign him an overimportance which he interprets to the patient as part of the therapy. He is aware of transference "cures," and of the unhealthy aspects of countertransference when he becomes emotionally overinvolved with the patient. He may have operating rules to govern the right kind of therapeutic relationship: trying to match the patient with the therapist's personality, avoiding working with a patient he does not "like," or recommending a male or female therapist for particular kinds of problems. The psychotherapist does not get into emotionality that is in the spiritual range, but he deals constantly in a high level of emotionality. The well-trained therapist does well with these emotional forces, but the rapidly enlarging field of psychotherapy includes many who do not have this expertise. The training of therapists may involve the selection of trainees who have the right personality for a good "therapeutic relationship." The level of emotionality in the field makes it difficult to evaluate the results of psychotherapy.

I go into this much detail about the therapeutic relationship because concepts about the therapeutic relationship and the notion that psychotherapy is *the* treatment for emotional illness are basic teachings in the training of mental health professionals. The orientation is probably greater for non-medical people who do not have to learn the medical part of psychiatry. Mental health professionals are so indoctrinated in these basic concepts they have difficulty hearing another way of thinking. That is why my own theory is incomprehensible to those who cannot think through their early basic teaching and practice. Early in my professional career I was a serious student of the therapeutic relationship. In the psychotherapy of schizophrenia much effort went into eliminating the assumed and assigned importance from the therapeutic relationship. The more I was successful at this, the more I could get good results after others had failed. It was usual for others to consider these good results as related to some undefined personality characteristic in me, or to coincidence. A good result could be followed by a comment such as, "Some schizophrenics come out of their regression automatically." Successfully managing the transference in schizophrenia made it easy to automatically manage the milder transference in the neuroses. The change to family research provided a new dimension for dealing with the therapeutic relationship. It became theoretically possible to leave the intensity of the relationship between the original family members, and bypass some of the time-consuming detail. I began to work toward avoiding the transference. When I started to talk about "staying out of the transference," the usual response was, "You don't mean you stay out of the transference; you mean you handle it well." That is, my statement was countered by another even more dogmatic, and pursuit of the issue only resulted in polarized emotional debate.

The prevailing opinion of therapists who operate with the therapeutic relationship is that I handle the transference well. However, a therapist with knowledge of the facts inherent in systems theory, and especially a knowledge of triangles (discussed below) can deal largely in reality and facts and eliminate much of the emotional process that usually goes into a transference. Indeed, it is possible to routinely reproduce an operational version of the same expertise in a good percentage of professional trainees. This is in contrast to usual training methods in which the result of training depends more on the intuitive and intangible qualities in the trainee than on knowledge. One never reaches the point of not being vulnerable to automatically falling back into the emotionality of transference. I still use mechanisms to reduce the assumed and assigned overimportance that can get into any relationship. When one acquires a reputation in any field, one also acquires an aura of assigned overimportance that goes beyond reality. Among the ways I have dealt with this is by charging average fees, which helps avoid the emotional pitfalls inherent in charging high fees. The therapeutic effort is so different from conventional therapy that I have developed other terms to refer to the therapy process; for instance I speak of "supervising" the effort the family makes on its own behalf, and "coaching" a family member in working with his own family. It is accurate to say there is some emotionality in any relationship, but it is also accurate to say that the emotionality can be reduced to a low level through knowledge about emotional systems.

THE THERAPEUTIC RELATIONSHIP IN FAMILY THERAPY

The separation between theory and therapy in most family therapy is far greater than with individual therapy. The vast majority of family therapists started from a previous orientation in individual or group therapy. Their family therapy descends almost directly from group therapy, which came out of psychoanalytic theory with an emphasis on the theory of the transference. Group therapy led to far more differences in method and technique than individual therapy, and family therapy lends itself to more differences than group therapy. I have referred to this as the "unstructured state of chaos" in family therapy.

Family therapists deal with the therapeutic relationship in a variety of ways. Some great family therapists, who were adept at dealing with transference in individual or group therapy, continue their adeptness in family therapy. They use psychoanalytic theory for thinking about problems in the individual, and transference theory for thinking about relationships. There are those who speak of "getting into and getting out of" intense relationships with individual family members. They are confident in their skill and ability to operate freely within the family. They operate more on intuition than any special body of knowledge. Their therapy is difficult for trainees to imitate and reproduce. Most therapists use some version of group therapy in their effort to keep relationships "spread out" and manageable. Another group uses cotherapists, usually of the opposite sex; their rationale is derived from psychoanalytic theory that this provides a male-female model for the family. The cotherapist functions to keep some degree of objectivity when the other therapist becomes emotionally entangled in the family.

Others use a team approach in which an entire mental health team meets with a family or group of families in a problem-focused group therapy method. The team, or "therapeutic group," is composed of members of the various mental health professions. The team-group meetings are commonly used for "training" inexperienced professional people who learn by participation in the team meetings, and who can rather quickly gain the status of "family therapist." Trainees begin by observing, following which they are encouraged to become part of the group by expressing their "feelings" in the therapy meetings. These are people who have never had much training in theory, or in the emotional discipline of learning the intricacies of transference and countertransference. Theory is usually not explicit, but the implicit format conveys that emotional illness is the product of suppressed feeling and poor communication, that treatment is the free expression of feelings and open communication, and that a competent therapist is one who can facilitate the process. Family therapy has also attracted therapists who were never successful at individual therapy, but who find a place in one of the numerous kinds of group therapy methods being used in family therapy. These admitted overstatements convey some idea of the many kinds of family therapy methods and techniques that are in use.

Group therapy has long acted as though it did not have a theory. I believe the reasons for this are that family therapy for the most part is a decendant of group therapy, that family therapy has started variations in method and technique that were not possible in group therapy, and that the separation between theory and practice is greater in family therapy than any of the other therapies. All these circumstances may account for the fact that few family therapists have much awareness of theory.

My approach differs from the mainstream of family therapy. I have learned more about the intricacies of the therapeutic relationship from family research than from psychoanalysis or the psychotherapy of schizophrenia. Most of this was learned from the study of triangles. The automatic emotional responsiveness that operates constantly in all relationships is the same as the therapeutic relationship. As soon as a vulnerable outside person comes into viable emotional contact with the family, he becomes part of it, no matter how much he protests the opposite. The emotional system operates through all five senses, and most often through visual and auditory stimuli. In addition, there is a sixth sense that can include extrasensory perception. All living things learn to process this data very early and to use it in relation to others. In addition, the human has a sophisticated verbal language which is as often used to deny the automatic emotional process as to confirm it. I believe the automatic emotional process is far more important in establishing and maintaining relationships than verbal language. The concept of triangles provides a way of reading the automatic emotional responsiveness so as to control one's own automatic emotional participation in the emotional process. This control I have called detriangling. No one ever stays outside, but a knowledge of triangles makes it possible to get outside on one's own initiative while staying emotionally in contact with the family. Most important, family members can learn to observe themselves and their families, and to control themselves while on stage with the family without having to withdraw. A family member who is motivated to learn and control his own responsiveness can influence relationships in the entire family system.

The effort of being outside the family emotional system, or remaining workably objective in an intense emotional field, has many applications. Family relationships are remarkably different when an outsider is introduced into the system. A disturbed family is always looking for a vulnerable outsider. It would be healtheir if they worked it out among themselves, but the emotional process reaches out for others. For a quarter of a century there has been a debate in family research about ways to do objective observations of the family, free from outside influences. Well-known research investigators such as Erving Goffman and Jules Henry have insisted that objective observations be made in the family's native habitat, the home, by a neutral observer. Based on my experience with emotional systems, I am sure any such observers were fused with the family as soon as they entered the home, that the family automatically became different, and that their belief they were being objective was erroneous. Complete objectivity is impossible; but I believe the best version of objectivity is possible with significant others who know triangles. There was a recently publicized movie-television study of a family done by a movie crew who went into the home to film the family as it really was. From my viewpoint, the movie crew automatically became a significant other which helped propel the parents toward divorce. This situation might have found another triangle that would have served the same triangle force.

THEORY IN THE DEVELOPMENT OF FAMILY THERAPY

The family movement in psychiatry was started in the mid-1950s by several different psychiatrists who worked independently for several years before they began to hear about each other. I have described my version of that in other papers (1, 2, 6). Among those who started with family research on schizophrenia was Lidz and his group at Johns Hopkins and Yale (7), Jackson and his group in Palo Alto (3), and Bowen and his group in Bethesda (4, 8). The psychoanalytic principle of protecting the privacy of the patient-therapist relationship may account for the family movement's remaining underground for some years. There were strict rules against the therapist's contaminating the transference by seeing other members of the same family: the early family work was done privately, probably to avoid critical colleagues who might consider this irresponsible until it was legitimized in the name of research. I began formal research in 1954 after several years of preliminary work. During 1955 and 1956 we each began to hear about the others and to meet. Ackerman had been thinking and working toward family concepts in social service agencies and clinics (9). Bell, who remained separate from the group for some years, had a different beginning. His first paper was written some seven or eight years after he started (10). There were others mentioned in the earlier summaries.

For me, 1955 to 1956 was a period of elation and enthusiasm. Observing entire families living together on a research ward provided a completely new order of clinical data never before recorded in the literature. Only those who were there could appreciate the impact of the new observations on psychiatry. Other family researchers were observing the same things, but were using different conceptual models to describe their findings. Why had these findings, now so commonplace, been obscured in previous observations? I believe two factors to account for this observational blindness. One was a shift in the observing lens from the individual to the family. The other is man's failure to see what is in front of him unless it fits his theoretical frame of reference. Before Darwin, man considered the earth to have been created as it appeared before his eyes. He had stumbled over the bones of prehistoric animals for centuries without seeing them, until Darwin's theory permitted him to begin seeing what had been there all the time.

For years I had pondered the discrepancies in psychoanalytic theory without finding new clues. Now I had a wealth of new clues that could lead to a completely different theory about emotional illness. Jackson was the other of the early workers who shared the theoretical potential. Lidz was more established in his psychoanalytic practice than Jackson and I, and he was more interested in an accurate description of his findings than in theory. Ackerman was also established in psychoanalytic practice and training, and his interest lay in developing therapy and not theory. I had built a method of individual therapy into my research design for studying the families. Within six months there was evidence that some method of therapy for family members together was indicated. I had never heard of family therapy. Against the strong theoretical and clinical admonitions of the time,

I followed the dictates of the research evidence and after much careful planning started my first method of family psychotherapy. Later, I heard that others had also thought of family therapy. Jackson had been approaching on one level and Ackerman was approaching on another. In 1956 I heard that Bell had been doing something called family therapy, but I did not meet him until 1958.

The first family section at a national meeting was organized by Spiegel at the American Orthopsychiatric meeting in Chicago in March, 1957. He was Chairman of the Committee on the Family of the Group for the Advancement of Psychiatry and he had just heard about the family work in progress. That was a small and quiet meeting. There were papers on research by Spiegel, Mendell, Lidz, and Bowen. In my paper I referred to the "family psychotherapy" used in my research since late 1955. I believe that may have been the first time the term was used in a national meeting. However it happened, I would date the family therapy explosion to March, 1957. In May, 1957, there was a family section at the American Psychiatric meeting, also in Chicago. In the two months since the previous meeting, there had been an increasing fervor about family therapy. Ackerman was secretary of the meeting, and Jackson was also present. Family ideas generated there led to Jackson's book, *The Etiology of Schizophrenia,* finally published in 1960 (4). At the national meetings in 1958, the family sessions were dominated by dozens of new therapists eager to report their family therapy of the past year. That was the beginning of the family therapy that was quite different from the family research of previous years. The new people, attracted by the idea of family therapy, had been developing empirical methods and techniques based on the psychoanalytic theory of individual and group psychotherapy. The family research and the theoretical thinking that gave birth to family therapy were lost in the rush.

The rush into family therapy in 1957 and 1958 produced a wild kind of therapy which I called a "healthy, unstructured state of chaos." There were almost as many different methods and techniques as there were new therapists. I considered the trend healthy in the belief the new therapists would discover the discrepancies in conventional theory, and that the conceptual dilemma posed by family therapy would lead to new concepts and ultimately to a new theory. This did not occur. I did not realize the degree of therapeutic zeal that makes psychiatrists oblivious to theory. Family therapy became a therapeutic method engrafted onto the basic concepts of psychoanalysis, and especially the theory of the transference. New therapists tended toward therapeutic evangelism, and they trained generations of new therapists who also tended toward simplistic views of the human dilemma and family therapy as a panacea for treatment. Family therapy not only inherited the vagueness and lack of theoretical clarity from conventional psychiatry, but it added new dimensions of its own. The number of minor differences and schools of thought are greater in family therapy than in individual therapy, and it now has its own group of eclectics who solve the problem through eclecticism.

Jackson and I were the only two from the original family researchers with a significant interest in theory. Jackson's group included Bateson, Haley, and Weakland. They began with a simple communication model of human relationships, but soon expanded the concept to include the total of human interaction in the concept. By the time Jackson died in 1968, he had moved toward a rather sophisticated systems model. I believe my theory had a sounder base to connect it with an instinctual motor; Jackson was operating more on phenomenology, but he was moving toward a distinctly different theory. One can only guess where he would have emerged had he lived.

In the past decade, there has been the slow emergence of a few new theoretical trends. It is not possible to stay on a broad conceptual level and do justice to the work of individuals, and at this point it is not possible to do more than survey the field in broad concepts. The notion of systems theory started gaining popularity in the mid-1960s, but the the use of systems in psychiatry is still in a primitive state. On one level, it is no more than the use of one word to replace another. On another level, it has the same meaning as a transportation system or circulatory system. On a more sophisticated level, it refers to a relationship system, which is a system in human behavior. On a broad level, people believe that "system" is derived from general systems theory, which is a system of thinking about existing knowledge. In my opinion, the attempt to apply general systems theory to psychiatry, as psychiatry is presently conceptualized, is equivalent to the effort to apply the scientific method to psychoanalysis. It has a potential, longterm gain if things work out right. However, the slow emergence of something that goes in a systems direction is one of the new evolutions in the family field. There have been some fascinating innovations in concepts that still retain much basic psychoanalytic theory. Among these is Paul's concept (11) concerning unresolved grief reactions which has a therapeutic method that fits the theoretical concept, and effectively taps the basic emotional process. Boszormenyi-Nagy is one of the theoretical scholars in the field (12). He has a rather complete set of theoretical abstractions that may one day provide a theoretical bridge between psychoanalysis and a different family theory. One of the more unique new orientations is Minuchin's (13). He carefully avoids the complex concepts of theory, but he uses the term *Structural Family Therapy* for a therapeutic method designed to change the family through modification of the feedback system in relationships. His focus is more on therapy than on theory.

FAMILY SYSTEMS THEORY

The evolution of my own theoretical thinking began in the decade before I started family research. There were many questions concerning generally accepted explanations about emotional illness. Efforts to find logical answers resulted in more unanswerable questions. One simple example is the notion that mental illness is the result of maternal deprivation. The idea seemed to fit the clinical case of the moment, but not the large number of normal people who, as far as could be determined, had been exposed to more maternal deprivation than those who were sick. There was also the issue of the schizophrenogenic mother. There were detailed descriptions of schizophrenogenic parents, but little to explain how the same parents could have other children who were not only normal, but who appeared supernormal. There were lesser discrepancies in popular hypotheses that linked emotional symptoms to a single traumatic event in the past. This again appeared logical in specific cases, but did not explain the large number of people who had suffered trauma without developing symptoms. There was a tendency to create special hypotheses for individual cases. The whole body of diagnostic nomenclature was based on symptom description, except for the small percentage of cases in which symptoms could be connected to actual pathology. Psychiatry acted as if it knew the answers, but it had not been able to develop diagnoses consistent with etiology. Psychoanalytic theory tended to define emotional illness as the product of a process between parents and child in a single generation, and there was little to explain how severe problems could be created so rapidly. The basic sciences were critical of psychiatric explanations that eluded scientific study. If the body of knowledge was reasonably factual, why could we not be more scientific about it? There were assumptions that emotional illness was the product of forces of socialization, even though the same basic emotional illness was present in all cultures. Most of the assumptions considered emotional illness as specific to humans, when there was evidence that a similar process was also present in lower forms of life. These and many other questions led me to extensive reading in evolution, biology, and the natural sciences as part of a search for clues that could lead to a broader theoretical frame of reference. My hunch was that emotional illness comes from that part of man that he shares with the lower forms of life.

My initial family research was based on an extension of theoretical formulations about the mother-child symbiosis. The hypothesis considered emotional illness in the child to be a product of a less severe problem in the mother. The hypothesis described the balancing forces that kept the relationship in equilibrium. It was a good example of what is now called a system. Very quickly it became apparent that the mother-child relationship was a dependent fragment of the larger family unit. The research design was modified for fathers and normal siblings to live on the ward with mothers and the schizophrenic patients. This resulted in a completely new order of observations. Other researchers were observing the same things, but they were using a variety of different models to conceptualize findings, including models from psychoanalysis, psychology, mythology, physics, chemistry, and mathematics. There were some common denominators that clustered around the stuck togetherness, bonds, binds, and interlocking of family members with each other. There were other concepts for the balancing forces, such as complementarity, reciprocity, magnetic fields, and hydraulic and electrical forces. Accurate as each concept might be descriptively, the investigators were using discrepant models.

Early in the research, I made some decisions based on previous thinking about theory. Family research was producing a completely new order of observations. There was a wealth of new theoretical clues. On the premise that psychiatry might eventually become a recognized science, perhaps a generation or two in the future, and being aware of the past conceptual problems of psychoanalysis, I chose to use only concepts that would be consistent with a recognized science. This was done in the hope that investigators of the future would more easily be able to see connections between human behavior and the accepted sciences than we can. I therefore chose to use concepts that would be consistent with biology and the natural sciences. It was easy to think in terms of the familiar concepts of chemistry, physics, and mathematics, but I carefully excluded all concepts that dealt with inanimate things, and studied the literature for concepts synonymous with biology—that is, I used biological concepts to describe human behavior. The concept of symbiosis, originally from psychiatry, would have been discarded except for its use in biology where the word has a specific meaning. The concept of differentiation was chosen because it has specific meanings in the biological sciences. When we speak of the "differentiation of self," we mean a process similar to the differentiation of cells from each other. The same applies to the term *fusion*. *Instinctual* is used exactly as it is used in biology, rather than in the restricted, special meaning of its use in psychoanalysis. There are a few minor exceptions to this overall plan, which will be mentioned later. In the period when I was reading biology, a close psychoanalyst friend advised me to give up "holistic" thinking before I got "too far out."

Another longterm plan was directed at the research staff, and was based on the notion that the clues for important discoveries are right in front of our eyes, if we can only develop the ability to see what we have never seen before. Research observers can see only what they have been trained to see through their theoretical orientations. The research staff had been trained in psychoanalysis, and they tended to see confirmation or extensions of psychoanalysis. On the premise there was far more to be seen if they could get beyond their theoretical blindness, I devised a plan to help us all open our eyes to new observations. One longterm exercise required investigators to avoid the use of conventional psychiatric terminology and to replace it with simple descriptive words. It was quite an exercise to use simple language instead of terms such as "schizophrenic-obsessive-compulsive-depressed-hysterical-patient." The overall goal was to help observers clear their heads of pre-existing ideas and see in a new way. Although much of this could be classified as an exercise or a game in semantics, it did contribute to a broader viewpoint. The research team developed a new language. Then came the complications of communication with colleagues, and the necessity of translating our new language back into terminology others could understand. It was awkward to use ten words to describe "a patient," when everyone else knew the correct meaning of "patient." We were criticized for coining new terms when old ones would be better, but during the exercise we had discovered the degree to which well-trained professional people use the same terms differently, while assuming that everyone understands them the same way.

The core of my theory has to do with the degree to which people are able to distinguish between the *feeling* process and the *intellectual* process. Early in the research, we found that the parents of schizophrenic people, who appear on the surface to function well, have difficulty distinguishing between the subjective feeling process and the more objective thinking process. This is most marked in a close personal relationship. This led to investigation of the same phenomenon in all levels of families from the most impaired, to normal, to the highest functioning people we could find. We found that there are differences between the ways feelings and intellect are either fused or differentiated from each other, and this led us to develop the concept of differentiation of self. People with the greatest fusion between feeling and thinking function the poorest. They inherit a high percentage of life's problems. Those with the most ability to distinguish between feeling and thinking, or who have the most differentiation of self, have the most flexibility and adaptability in coping with life stresses, and the most freedom from problems of all kinds. Other people fall between the two extremes, both in the interplay between feeling and thinking and in their life adjustments.

Feeling and *emotion* are used almost synonymously in popular usage and also in the literature. Also, little distinction is made between the subjectivity of truth and the objectivity of fact. The lower the level of differentiation, the more a person is not able to distinguish between the two. The literature does not clearly distinguish between *philosophy, belief, opinion, conviction,* and *impression.* Lacking guidelines from the literature, we used dictionary definitions to clarify these for our theoretical purposes.

The theoretical assumption considers emotional illness to be a disorder of the *emotional system,* an intimate part of man's phylogenetic past which he shares with all lower forms of life, and which is governed by the same laws that govern all living things. The literature refers to emotions as much more than states of contentment, agitation, fear, weeping, and laughing, although it also refers to these states in the lower forms of life—contentment after feeding, sleep, and mating, and states of agitation in fight, flight, and the search for food. For the purposes of this theory, the emotional system is considered to include all the above functions, plus all the automatic functions that govern the autonomic nervous system, and to be synonymous with instinct that governs the life process in all living things. The term *emotional illness* is used to replace former terms, such as mental illness and psychological illness. Emotional illness is considered a deep process involving the basic life process of the organism.

The *intellectual system* is a function of the cerebral cortex which appeared last in man's evolutionary development, and is the main difference between man and the lower forms of life. The cerebral cortex involves the ability to think, reason, and reflect, and enables man to govern his life, in certain areas, according to logic, intellect, and reason. The more experience I have had, the more I am convinced that far more of life is governed by automatic emotional forces than man is willing to acknowledge. The *feeling system* is postulated as a link between the emotional and intellectual systems through which certain emotional states are represented in conscious awareness. Man's brain is part of his protoplasmic totality. Through the function of his brain, he has learned many of the secrets of the universe; he has also learned to create technology to modify his environment, and to gain control over most of the lower forms of life. Man has done less well in using his brain to study his own emotional functioning.

Much of the early family research was done with schizophrenia. Since the clinical observations from those studies had not been previously described in the literature, it was first thought that the relationship patterns were typical of schizophrenia. Then it was discovered that the very same patterns were also present in families with neurotic level problems, and even in normal families. Gradually, it became clear that the relationship patterns, so clear in families with schizophrenia, were present in all people to some degree and that the intensity of the patterns being observed was related more to the anxiety of the moment than the severity of the emotional illness being studied. This fact about the early days of family research conveys some notion of the state of psychological theory twenty years ago that is not appreciated by those who were not part of the scene at that time. The family studies in schizophrenia were so important that they stimulated several research studies of normal families in the late 1950s and early 1960s. The influence of the schizophrenia research on family therapy was so important that family therapy was still being considered to be a form of therapy for schizophrenia as much as ten years after the family movement started. The results of the early studies on normal families might be summarized by saying that the patterns originally thought to be typical of schizophrenia are present in all families some of the time and in some families most of the time.

My work toward a different theory began as soon as the relationship patterns were seen to repeat over and over, and we had achieved some notion about the conditions under which they repeated. The early papers were devoted mostly to clinical description of the patterns. By 1957, the relationship patterns in the nuclear family were sufficiently defined that I was willing to call a major paper, "A Family *Concept* of Schizophrenia." Jackson, who was reasonably accurate in his use of the word *theory,* had coauthored a paper in 1956 called, "Toward a Theory of Schizophrenia" (3). He urged me to use the term *theory* in the 1957 paper, which was finally published in 1960 (4), but I refused on the basis that it was no more than a concept in a much larger field, and I wanted to avoid using *theory* for a partial theory or a concept. The situation in the late 1950s was an absolute delight for me. It satisfied my theoretical curiosity that schizophrenia and the psychoses were part of the same continuum with neurotic problems, and that the differences between schizophrenia and the neuroses were quantitative rather than qualitative. Psychoanalysis and the other theoretical systems viewed psychosis as the product of one emotional process, and the neuroses as the product of another emotional process. Even today a majority of people in psychiatry probably still hold the viewpoint that schizophrenia and the neuroses are qualitatively different. It is usual for mental health professionals to speak of schizophrenia as one thing, and the neuroses as another type of problem; they also still speak of "normal" families. However, I *know* they are all part of the total human dimension, all the way from the lowest possible level of human functioning to the highest. I believe that those who assume a difference between schizophrenia, the neuroses, and the normal are operating from basic psychoanalytic theory without being specifically aware of it, and that they base the difference on therapeutic response rather than on systems theory. I believe psychiatry will some day come to see all these conditions as parts of the same continuum.

The main part of this family systems theory evolved rather rapidly over a period of about six years, between 1957 and 1963. No one part was first. A concept about the nuclear family emotional system and another about the family projection process had both been started in the early descriptive papers. They were both reasonably clear by the time it was possible to compare the patterns in schizophrenia with the total range of human problems. The notion that all human problems exist on a single continuum gave rise by the early 1960s, to the concept of differentiation of self. The notion of triangles, one of the basic concepts in the total theory, had been started in 1957 when it was called the "interdependent triad." The concept was sufficiently developed to be used in therapy by about 1961. The concept of multigenerational transmission process started as a research hypothesis as early as 1955, but the research that brought it to reasonable clarification had to wait till 1959 to 1960, when there was a larger volume of families for study. The concept of sibling position had been poorly defined since the late 1950s, but it had to wait until Toman's *Family Constellation* (14) in 1961 provided structure. By 1963, these six interlocking concepts were sufficiently defined that I was willing to put all six together into family systems theory, which satisfied a fairly strict definition of theory. It was not included in *Intensive Family Therapy* by Nagy and Framo (5), which was published in 1965, because they had specifically asked for a chapter on schizophrenia. The six concepts were finally published as a coherent, theoretical system in 1966 (1). After 1966, there were numerous changes in therapy, but the theory as presented in 1966 has remained very much as it is today, with some extensions and refinements. Finally, in 1975, two new concepts were added. The first, the emotional cutoff, was merely a refinement and a new emphasis of former theoretical principles. The last and eighth concept, societal regression, had been rather well defined by 1972, and was finally added as a separate concept in 1975. Also, the name *family systems theory* was formally changed to *the Bowen theory* in 1975.

Any relationship with balancing forces and counterforces in constant operation is a system. The notion of *dynamics* is simply not adequate to describe the idea of a *system*. By 1963, when the six interlocking concepts were defined, I was using the concept of system as a shorthand way to describe the complex balancing of family relationships. This idea was finally presented in some detail in the 1966 paper on theory. By the mid-1960s, the term *systems* was being used more frequently; some therapists picked it up from my writings, and others picked it up from general systems theory, which was first defined in the 1930s. In the past decade, the term has become popularized and overused to the point of being meaningless. Family systems theory has been confused with general systems theory, which has a much broader frame of reference and no specific application to emotional functioning. It is very difficult to apply general systems concepts to emotional functioning except in a broad, general way. My family systems theory is a specific theory about the functional facts of emotional functioning.

It is grossly inaccurate to consider family systems theory as synonymous with general systems, although it is accurate to think of family systems theory as somehow fitting into the broad framework of general systems theory. There are those who believe family systems theory was developed from general systems theory, in spite of my explanations to the contrary. At the time my theory was developed, I knew nothing about general systems theory. Back in the 1940s, I attended one lecture by Bertalanffy, which I did not understand, and another by Norbert Wiener which was perhaps a little more understandable. Both dealt in systems *of* thinking. The degree to which I heard something in those lectures that influenced my later thinking is debatable. In those years, I was strongly influenced by reading and lectures in aspects of evolution, biology, the balance of nature, and the natural sciences. I was trying to view man as a part of nature rather than separate from nature. It is likely that my systems orientation was patterned after the systems in nature, and unlikely that systems of thinking played any part in the theory. However it developed, family systems theory as I have defined it is a specific theory about human relationship functioning that has now become confused with general systems theory and the popular, non-specific use of the word *systems.* I have long opposed the use of proper names in terminology, but in order to denote the specificity that is built into this family systems theory, I am now calling it the Bowen theory.

Emotionality, feelings, and subjectivity are the principal commodities which the theoretician has to conceptualize, which the researcher has to organize into some kind of structure, and which the clinician has to deal with in his practice. It is difficult to find verifiable facts in the world of subjectivity. Conventional psychiatric theory focuses on the why of human behavior. All members of the mental health professions are familiar with why explanations. The search for why reasons has been part of man's cause and effect thinking since he became a thinking being. Once the researcher starts asking why, he is confronted by a complex mass of variables. It was the search for reliable facts about emotional functioning that led toward systems thinking early in the family research. From this effort came a method of separating the functional facts from the subjectivity of emotional systems. Systems thinking focused on what happened, and how, when, and where it happened, insofar as these observations could be based on observable facts. The method carefully avoids why explanations and the discrepant reasoning that follows. Some fairly efficient formulas were developed for converting subjectivity into observable and verifiable research facts. For example, one such formula might be, "That man dreams is a scientific fact, but what he dreams is not necessarily a fact," or, "That man talks is a scientific fact, but what he says is not necessarily factual." The same formula can be applied to almost the whole range of subjective concepts, such as, "That man thinks (or feels) is a scientific fact, but what he thinks (or feels) is not necessarily factual." The formula is a little more difficult to apply in the intense feeling states, such as love and hate, but as long as the researcher stays on the facts of loving and hating and avoids the content of these intense emotions, he is working toward systems thinking.

The effort to focus on the functional facts of relationship systems is a difficult and disciplined task. It is easy to lose sight of the fact and become emotionally involved in the content of the communication. The main reason for making this effort was for research purposes. The main concepts in the Bowen theory were developed from the functional facts of relationship systems. In this disciplined research effort, it was discovered that a method of therapy based on the functional facts was superior to conventional therapy. It is so difficult for most therapists to shift from conventional therapy to this method of family systems therapy that no one ever achieves more than partial success at it. When anxiety is high, even the most disciplined systems thinker will automatically revert to cause and effect thinking and why explanations. However, it is possible for therapists to keep perfecting their ability to think in systems concepts. The more I have been able to shift to thinking systems, the better my therapy has become. The shift to systems thinking requires the therapist to give up many of his old concepts. A recent exchange with a therapist involved in psychoanalytic research illustrates the dilemma in making such a shift. He said he could hear the notion of trying to find facts in subjectivity, but he simply could not give up the therapeutic contributions of dreams and analyzing the unconscious. I replied that I could respect his conviction if he could respect mine about the ultimate advantage of a total systems approach. A major advantage of systems theory and systems therapy is that it offers options not previously available. The young professional has the choice of continuing conventional theory and therapy, or of incorporating a few systems concepts, or of trying to go all the way toward systems thinking. I believe a few systems concepts are better than none.

The Bowen theory contains no ideas that have not been a part of human experience through the centuries. The theory operates on an order of facts so simple and obvious that everyone knew them all the time. The uniqueness of the theory has to do with the facts that are included, and the concepts that are specifically excluded. Said in another way, the theory listens to a distant drumbeat that people have always heard. This distant drumbeat is often obscured by the noisy insistence of the foreground drumbeat, but it is always there, and it tells its own clear story to those who can tune out the noise and keep focused on the distant drumbeat. The Bowen theory specifically excludes certain items from individual theory that are equivalent to the foreground drumbeat. The concepts we learned in individual theory all have their accuracy within one frame of reference, but they tend to nullify the unique effectiveness of the simple story told by a broad systems perspective. The Bowen theory is very simple to those who can hear, and the simple approach to therapy is determined by the theory.

THE BOWEN THEORY

The Bowen theory involves two main variables. One is the degree of anxiety, and the other is the degree of integration of self. There are several variables having to do with anxiety or emotional tension. Among these are intensity, duration, and different kinds of anxiety. There are far more variables that have to do with the level of integration of the differentiation of self. This is the principal subject of this theory. All organisms are reasonably adaptable to acute anxiety. The organism has built-in mechanisms to deal with short bursts of anxiety. It is sustained or chronic anxiety that is most useful in determining the differentiation of self. If anxiety is sufficiently low, almost any organism can appear normal in the sense that it is symptom free. When anxiety increases and remains chronic for a certain period, the organism develops tension, either within itself or in the relationship system, and the tension results in symptoms or dysfunction or sickness. The tension may result in physiological symptoms or physical illness, in emotional dysfunction, in social illness characterized by impulsiveness or withdrawal, or by social misbehavior. There is also the phenomenon of the infectiousness of anxiety, through which anxiety can spread rapidly through the family, or through society. There is a kind of average level of differentiation for the family which has certain minor levels of difference in individuals within the family. I shall leave it to the reader to keep in mind there is always the variable of the degree of chronic anxiety which can result in anyone appearing normal at one level of anxiety, and abnormal at another higher level.

Three of the theory's eight concepts apply to overall characteristics of the family. The other five focus on details within certain areas of the family.

A. *Differentiation of Self.* This concept is a cornerstone of the theory, and if my discussion becomes repetitive, I beg the reader's indulgence. The concept defines people according to the degree of *fusion,* or *differentiation,* between emotional and intellectual functioning. This characteristic is so universal it can be used as a way of categorizing all people on a single continuum. At the low extreme are those whose emotions and intellect are so fused that their lives are dominated by the automatic emotional system. Whatever intellect they have is dominated by the emotional system. These are the people who are less flexible, less adaptable, and more emotionally dependent on those about them. They are easily stressed into dysfunction, and it is difficult for them to recover from dysfunction. They inherit a high percentage of all human problems. At the other extreme are those who are more differentiated. It is impossible for there to be more than relative separation between emotional and intellectual functioning, but those whose intellectual functioning can retain relative autonomy in periods of stress are more flexible, more adaptable, and more independent of the emotionality about them. They cope better with life stresses, their life courses are more orderly and successful, and they are remarkably free of human problems. In between the two extremes is an infinite number of mixes between emotional and intellectual functioning.

The concept eliminates the concept of *normal,* which psychiatry has never successfully defined. It is not possible to define *normal* when the thing to be measured is constantly changing. Operationally, psychiatry has called people normal when they are free of emotional symptoms and behavior is within average range. The concept of differentiation has no direct connection with the presence or absence of symptoms. People with the most fusion have most of the human problems, and those with the most differentiation, the fewest; but there can be people with intense fusion who manage to keep their relationships in balance, who are never subjected to severe stress, who never develop symptoms, and who appear normal. However, their life adjustments are tenuous, and, if they are stressed into dysfunction, the impairment can be chronic or permanent. There are also fairly well-differentiated people who can be stressed into dysfunction, but they recover rapidly.

At the fusion end of the spectrum, the intellect is so flooded by emotionality that the total life course is determined by the emotional process and by what "feels right," rather than by beliefs or opinions. The intellect exists as an appendage of the feeling system. It may function reasonably well in mathematics or physics, or in impersonal areas, but on personal subjects its functioning is controlled by the emotions. The emotional system is hypothesized to be part of the instinctual forces that govern automatic functions. The human is adept at explanations to emphasize that he is different from lower forms of life, and at denying his relation with nature. The emotional system operates with predictable, knowable stimuli that govern the instinctual behavior in all forms of life. The more a life is governed by the emotional system, the more it follows the course of all instinctual behavior, in spite of intellectualized explanations to the contrary. At higher levels of differentiation, the function of the emotional and intellectual systems are more clearly distinguishable. There are the same automatic emotional forces that govern instinctual behavior, but intellect is sufficiently autonomous for logical reasoning and decisions based on thinking. When I first began to present this concept, I used the term *undifferentiated family ego mass* to describe the emotional stuck-togetherness in families. Although this phrase was an assemblage of words from conventional theory, and thus did not conform to the plan to use concepts consistent with biology, it fairly accurately described emotional fusion. I used it for a few years because more people were able to hear the concept when it was put into words they understood.

As I began to present the concept of a well-differentiated person as one whose intellect could function separately from the emotional system, it was common for mental health professionals to hear the intellectual system as equivalent to intellectuality which is used as a defense against emotionality in psychiatric patients. The most common criticism was that a differentiated person appeared to be cold, distant, rigid, and nonfeeling. It is difficult for professional people to grasp the notion of differentiation when they have spent their working lives believing that the free expression of feelings represents a high level of functioning and intellectualization represents an unhealthy defense against it. A poorly differentiated person is trapped within a feeling world. His effort to gain the comfort of emotional closeness can increase the fusion, which can increase his alienation from others. There is a lifelong effort to get the emotional life into livable equilibrium. A segment of these emotionally trapped people use random, inconsistent, intellectual-sounding verbalization to explain away their plight. A more differentiated person can participate freely in the emotional sphere without the fear of becoming too fused with others. He is also free to shift to calm, logical reasoning for decisions that govern his life. The logical intellectual process is quite different from the inconsistent, intellectualized verbalizations of the emotionally fused person.

In earlier papers, I presented this as a Differentiation of Self Scale." I did that to convey the idea that people have all gradations of differentiation of self, and that people at one level have remarkably different life styles from those at other levels. Schematically, I presented a scale from 0 to 100, with 0 representing the lowest possible level of human functioning and 100 representing a hypothetical notion of perfection to which man might evolve if his evolutionary change goes in that direction. I wanted a spectrum broad enough to cover all possible degrees of human functioning. To clarify the fact that people are different from each other in terms of emotional-intellectual functioning, I did profiles of people in the 0 to 25, the 25 to 50, the 50 to 75, and the 75 to 100 ranges. Those profiles are still amazingly accurate ten years later. In that first paper, I also presented the notion of functional levels of differentiation that can shift from moment to moment, or remain fairly constant for most of a life. Some of the major variables that govern the shifting were presented as a way of clarifying the concept and categorizing the apparent complexity of human functioning into a more knowable framework. The schematic framework and the use of the term *scale* resulted in hundreds of letters requesting copies of "the scale." Most who wrote had not grasped the concept nor the variables that govern the functional levels of differentiations. The letters slowed down my effort to develop a more definite scale that could be used clinically. The theoretical concept is most important. It eliminates the barriers between schizophrenia, neurosis, and normal; it also transcends categories such as genius, social class, and cultural-ethnic differences. It applies to all human forms of life. It might even apply to subhuman forms if we only knew enough. Knowledge of the concept permits the easy development of all kinds of research instruments, but to attempt to use the scale without knowledge of the concept can result in chaos.

Another important part of the differentiation of self has to do with the levels of *solid self* and *pseudo-self* in a person. In periods of emotional intimacy, two pseudo-selfs will fuse into each other, one losing self to the other, who gains self. The solid self does not participate in the fusion phenomenon. The solid self says, "This is who I am, what I believe, what I stand for, and what I will do or will not do," in a given situation. The solid self is made up of clearly defined beliefs, opinions, convictions, and life principles. These are incorporated into self from one's own life experiences, by a process of intellectual reasoning and the careful consideration of the alternatives involved in the choice. In making the choice, one becomes responsible for self and the consequences. Each belief and life principle is consistent with all the others, and self will take action on the principles even in situations of high anxiety and duress.

The pseudo-self is created by emotional pressure, and it can be modified by emotional pressure. Every emotional unit, whether it be the family or the total of society, exerts pressure on group members to conform to the ideals and principles of the group. The pseudo-self is composed of a vast assortment of principles, beliefs, philosophies, and knowledge acquired because it is required or considered right by the group. Since the principles are acquired under pressure, they are random and inconsistent with one another, without the individual's being aware of the discrepancy. Pseudo-self is appended onto the self, in contrast to solid self which is incorporated into self after careful, logical reasoning. The pseudo-self is a "pretend" self. It was acquired to conform to the environment, and it contains discrepant and assorted principles that pretend to be in emotional harmony with a variety of social groups, institutions, businesses, political parties, and religious groups, without self's being aware that the groups are inconsistent with each other. The joining of groups is motivated more by the relationship system than the principle involved. The person may "feel" there is something wrong with some of the groups, but he is not intellectually aware. The solid self is intellectually aware of the inconsistency between the groups and the decision to join or reject membership is an intellectual process based on careful weighing of the advantages and disadvantages.

The pseudo-self is an actor and can be many different selfs. The list of pretends is extensive. He can pretend to be more important or less important, stronger or weaker, or more attractive, or less attractive than is realistic. It is easy for most people to detect gross examples of pretense, but there is enough of the impostor in all of us so that it is difficult to detect lesser degrees of the impostor in others. On the other hand, a good actor can appear so much for real that it can be difficult for the actor or for others without detailed knowledge of how emotional systems function to know the dividing line between solid self and pseudo-self. This also applies to therapists, mental health professionals, and researchers who may attempt to estimate the level of differentiation in themselves or in others. The level of solid self is stable. The pseudo-self is unstable, and it responds to a variety of social pressures and stimuli. The pseudo-self was acquired at the behest of the relationship system, and it is negotiable in the relationship system.

Based on my experience with this concept, I believe that the level of solid self is lower, and of the pseudo-self is much higher in all of us than most are aware. It is the pseudo-self that is involved in fusion and the many ways of giving, receiving, lending, borrowing, trading, and exchanging of self. In any exchange, one gives up a little self to the other, who gains an equal amount. The best example is a love relationship when each is trying to be the way the other wants self to be, and each in turn makes demands on the other to be different. This is pretending and trading in pseudo-self. In a marriage, two pseudo-selfs fuse into a we-ness in which one becomes the dominant decision maker or the most active in taking initiative for the we-ness. The dominant one gains self at the expense of the other, who loses it. The adaptive one may volunteer to give up self to the dominant one, who accepts it; or the exchange may be worked out after bargaining. The more that the spouses can alternate these roles, the healthier the marriage. The exchanging of selfs may be on a short or longterm basis. The borrowing and trading of selfs may take place automatically in a work group in which the emotional process ends up with one employee in the one-down or deselfed, position, while the others gain self. This exchanging of pseudo-self is an automatic emotional process that occurs as people manipulate each other in subtle life postures. The exchanges can be brief—for instance, criticism that makes one feel bad for a few days; or it can be a longterm process in which the adaptive spouse becomes so deselfed, he or she is no longer able to make decisions and collapses in selfless dysfunction—psychosis or chronic physical illness. These mechanisms are much less intense in better levels of differentiation or when anxiety is low, but the process of people losing and gaining self in an emotional network is so complex and the degree of shifts so great that it is impossible to estimate functional levels of differentiation except from following a life pattern over long periods.

Profile of Low Levels of Differentiation. This is the group I previously described as 0 to 25, the lowest level of differentiation. The emotional fusion is so intense that the variables extend beyond the undifferentiated family ego mass into the undifferentiated societal ego mass. The intricacies of fusion and differentiation are much clearer in people with moderate levels of fusion in whom the various processes are more easily defined. There are some striking overall characteristics of the low levels of differentiation. People at the lowest level live in a feeling-dominated world in which it is impossible to distinguish feeling from fact. They are totally relationship oriented. So much energy goes into seeking love and approval and keeping the relationship in some kind of harmony, there is no energy for life-directed goals. Failing to achieve approval, they can spend their lives in withdrawal or fighting the relationship system from which they fail to win approval. Intellectual functioning is so submerged that they cannot say, "I think that . . ." or, "I believe. . . ." Instead, they say, "I feel that . . ." when it would be accurate to express an opinion or belief. They consider it truthful and sincere to say, "I feel," and false and insincere to express an opinion from themselves. Important life decisions are made on the basis of what feels right. They spend their lives in a day-to-day struggle to keep the relationship system in balance, or in an effort to achieve some degree of comfort and freedom from anxiety. They are incapable of making longterm goals except in vague general terms, such as, "I want to be successful, or happy, or have a good job, or have security." They grow up as dependent appendages of their parents, following which they seek other equally dependent relationships in which they can borrow enough strength to function. A no-self person who is adept at pleasing his boss may make a better employee than one who has a self. This group is made up of people preoccupied with keeping their dependent relationships in harmony, people who have failed and who go from one symptomatic crisis to another, and people who have given up in the futile effort to adapt. At the lowest level are those who cannot live outside the protective walls of an institution. This group inherits a major portion of the world's serious health, financial, and social problems. Life adjustments are tenuous at best, and when they fall into dysfunction, the illness or "bad luck" can be chronic or permanent. They tend to be satisfied with the result if a therapy effort brings a modicum of comfort.

Profile of Moderate Levels of Differentiation of Self. This is the group previously presented as 25 to 50. There is some beginning differentiation between the emotional and intellectual systems, with most of the self expressed as pseudo-self. Lives are still guided by the emotional system, but the life styles are more flexible than the lower levels of differentiation. The flexibility provides a better view of the interplay between emotionality and intellect. When anxiety is low, functioning can resemble good levels of differentiation. When anxiety is high, functioning can resemble that of low levels of differentiation. Lives are relationship oriented, and major life energy goes to loving and being loved, and seeking approval from others. Feelings are more openly expressed than in lower-level people. Life energy is directed more to what others think and to winning friends and approval than to goal-directed activity. Self-esteem is dependent on others. It can soar to heights with a compliment or be crushed by criticism. Success in school is oriented more to learning the system and to pleasing the teacher than to the primary goal of learning. Success in business or in social life depends more on pleasing the boss or the social leader, and more on who one knows and gaining relationship status than in the inherent value of their work. Their pseudo-selves are assembled from an assortment of discrepant principles, beliefs, philosophies, and ideologies that are used in pretend postures to blend with different relationship systems. Lacking solid self, they habitually use, "I feel that . . ." when expressing their pseudo-self philosophies; they avoid, "I think," or "I believe," positions by using another person or body of knowledge as their authority when making statements. Lacking a solid self-conviction about the world's knowledge, they use pseudo-self statements, such as, "The rule says . . ." or "Science has proved . . ." taking information out of context to make their points. They may have enough free-functioning intellect to have mastered academic knowledge about impersonal things; they use this knowledge in the relationship system. However, intellect about personal matters is lacking, and their personal lives are in chaos.

The pseudo-self may be a conforming disciple who pretends to be in harmony with a particular philosophy or set of principles, or, when frustrated, he can assume the opposite posture as a rebel or revolutionary person. The rebel is lacking a self of his own. His pseudo-self posture is merely the exact opposite of the majority viewpoint. The revolutionary person is against the prevailing system, but he has nothing to offer in its place. The sameness of polarized opposites in emotional situations has led me to define revolution as a convulsion that prevents change. It is relationship-oriented energy that goes back and forth on the same points, the issue on each side being determined by the position of the other; neither is capable of a position not determined by the other.

People in the moderate range of differentiation have the most intense versions of overt feeling. The relationship orientation makes them sensitive to others and to the direct action expression of feelings. They are in a lifelong quest for the ideal relationship with emotional closeness to others and direct, open communication of feelings. In their overt emotional dependence on others, they are sensitized to reading the moods, expressions, and postures of the other, and to responding openly with direct expression of feeling or impulsive action. They are in a lifelong pursuit of the ideal close relationship. When closeness is achieved, it increases the emotional fusion to which they react with distance and alienation, which can then stimulate another closeness cycle. Failing to achieve closeness, they may go to withdrawal and depression, or to pursuit of closeness in another relationship. Symptoms and human problems erupt when the relationship system is unbalanced. People in this group develop a high percentage of human problems, including the full range of physical illness, emotional illness, and social dysfunctions. Their emotional illness includes neurotic-level internalized problems, depression, and behavior and character disorder type problems; they get involved in the increasing use of alcohol and drugs to relieve the anxiety of the moment. Their social disorders include all levels of impulsive and irresponsible behavior.

Profile of Moderate to Good Differentiation of Self. This is the group in the 50 to 75 range. These are the people with enough basic differentiation between the emotional and intellectual systems for the two systems to function alongside each other as a cooperative team. The intellectual system is sufficiently developed so that it can hold its own and function autonomously without being dominated by the emotional system when anxiety increases. In people below 50, the emotional system tells the intellectual system what to think and say, and which decisions to make in critical situations. The intellect is a pretend intellect. The emotional system permits the intellect to go off into a corner and think about distant things as long as it does not interfere in joint decisions that affect the total life course. Above 50, the intellectual system is sufficiently developed to begin making a few decisions of its own. It has learned that the emotional system runs an effective life course in most areas of functioning, but in critical situations the automatic emotional decisions create longterm complications for the total organism. The intellect learns that it requires a bit of discipline to overrule the emotional system, but the longterm gain is worth the effort. People above 50 have developed a reasonable level of solid self on most of the essential issues in life. In periods of calm, they have employed logical reasoning to develop beliefs, principles, and convictions that they use to overrule the emotional system in situations of anxiety and panic. Differentiation between the emotions and the intellect exists in subtle gradations. People at the lower part of this group are those who *know* there is a better way; but intellect is poorly formed, and they end up following life courses similar to those below 50.

People in the upper part of this group are those in which there is more solid self. Persons with a functional intellectual system are no longer a prisoner of the emotional-feeling world. They are able to live more freely and to have more satisfying emotional lives within the emotional system. They can participate fully in emotional events knowing that they can extricate themselves with logical reasoning when the need arises. There may be periods of laxness in which they permit the automatic pilot of the emotional system to have full control, but when trouble develops they can take over, calm the anxiety, and avoid a life crisis. People with better levels of differentiation are less relationship directed and more able to follow independent life goals. They are not unaware of the relationship system, but their life courses can be determined more from within themselves than from what others think. They are more clear about the differences between emotion and intellect, and they are better able to state their own convictions and beliefs calmly without attacking the beliefs of others or without having to defend their own. They are better able to accurately evaluate themselves in relation to others without the pretend postures that result in overvaluing or undervaluing themselves. They marry spouses with equal levels of differentiation. The life-style of a spouse at another level would be sufficiently different to be considered emotionally incompatible. The marriage is a functioning partnership. The spouses can enjoy the full range of emotional intimacy without either being deselfed by the other. They can be autonomous selfs together or alone. The wife is able to function more fully as a female and the husband more fully as a male without either having to debate the advantages or disadvantages of biological and social roles. Spouses who are more differentiated can permit their children to grow and develop their own autonomous selfs without undue anxiety or without trying to fashion their children in their own images. The spouses and the children are each more responsible for themselves, and do not have to blame others for failures or credit anyone else for their successes. People with better levels of differentiation are able to function well with other people, or alone, as the situation may require. Their lives are more orderly, they are able to cope successfully with a broader range of human situations, and they are remarkably free from the full range of human problems.

In previous papers I have described a level of 75 to 100, which is more hypothetical than real, and which conveys an erroneous impression of the human phenomenon to concretistic thinkers who are searching for another instrument to measure human functioning. Rather than pursue the hypothesis about the upper extremes of differentiation, I shall instead make some general comments about differentiation. A common mistake is to equate the better differentiated person with a "rugged individualist." I consider rugged individualism to be exaggerated pretend posture of a person struggling against emotional fusion. The differentiated person is always aware of others and the relationship system around him. There are so many forces and counterforces and details in differentiation that one has to get a broad panoramic view of the total human phenomenon in order to be able to see differentiation. Once it is possible to see the phenomenon, there it is, operating in full view, right in front of our eyes. Once it is possible to see the phenomenon, it is then possible to apply the concept to hundreds of different human situations. To try to apply it without knowing it is an exercise in futility.

The therapy based on differentiation is no longer therapy in the usual sense. The therapy is as different from the conventional therapy as the theory is different from conventional theory. The overall goal is to help individual family members to rise up out of the emotional togetherness that binds us all. The instinctual force toward differentiation is built into the organism, just as are the emotional forces that oppose it. The goal is to help the motivated family member to take a microscopic step toward a better level of differentiation, in spite of the togetherness forces that oppose. When one family member can finally master this, then other family members automatically take similar steps. The togetherness forces are so strong in maintaining the status quo that any small step toward differentiation is met with vigorous disapproval of the group. This is the point at which a therapist or guide can be most helpful. Without help, the differentiating one will fall back into the togetherness to get emotional harmony for the moment. Conventional therapy is designed to resolve, or talk out, conflict. This does accomplish the goal of reducing the conflict of that moment, but it can also rob the individual of his budding effort to achieve a bit more differentiation from the family togetherness. There are many pitfalls in the effort toward differentiation. If the individual attempts it without some conviction of his own, he is blindly following the advice of his therapist and is caught in a self-defeating togetherness with the therapist. I believe that the level of differentiation of a person is largely determined by the time he leaves the parental family and he attempts a life of his own. Thereafter, he tends to replicate the life-style from the parental family in all future relationships. It is not possible ever to make more than minor changes in one's basic level of self; but from clinical experience I can say it is possible to make slow changes, and each small change results in the new world of a different life-style. As I see it now, the critical stage is passed when the individual can begin to know the difference between emotional functioning and intellectual functioning, and when he has developed ways for using the knowledge for solving future problems in a lifelong effort on his own. It is difficult to assess differentiation during calm periods in a life. Clinically, I make estimates from the average functional level of self as it operates through periods of stress and calm. The real test of the stability of differentiation comes when the person is again subjected to chronic severe stress.

It is reasonably accurate to compare the functioning of the emotional and intellectual systems to the structure and function of the brain. I conceive of one brain center that controls emotions and another that controls intellectual functions. The fusion suggests centers that are side by side with some degree of fusion, or grown togetherness. Anatomically, it would be more accurate to think of the two as being connected by nerve tracts. In poorly functioning people, the two centers are intimately fused, with the emotional center having almost total dominance over the intellectual center. In better functioning people, there is more functional separateness between the centers. The more the separateness between the centers, the more the intellectual center is able to block, or screen out, a spectrum of stimuli from the emotional center, and to function autonomously. The screening process, which might be biochemical, operates best when anxiety is low. The emotional center controls the autonomic nervous system and all other automatic functions. The intellectual center is the seat of intellect and reasoning. The emotional center handles the myriads of sensory stimuli from the digestive, circulatory, respiratory, and all the other organ systems within the body, as well as stimuli from all the sensing organs that perceive the environment and relationships with others. In periods of calm, when the emotional center is receiving fewer stimuli from its sensing network, the intellectual center is more free to function autonomously. When the emotional center is flooded by stimuli, there is little intellectual functioning that is not governed by the emotional center. In some areas, the intellect operates in the service of the emotional center.

There are many clinical examples that illustrate emotional dominance over the intellect in determining a life course. The intellectual center is either appended to, or is directed by, the emotional center. In the various psychotic and neurotic states, the intellect is either obliterated or distorted by emotionality. There may be an occasional situation in which there is an island of reasonably intact intellectual activity, such as in the psychotic person with a computer mind. In the various neurotic states the intellect is directed by emotionality. There is the intellectualizing person whose apparent intellect is directed by the emotional process. There are the behavior problems in which automatic impulsive action is directed by emotionality, and the intellect attempts to explain or justify it after the action. This can vary from childish misbehavior to criminal action. The parents and the social system ask why, pretending there is a logical answer. The organism responds with an instant excuse that appears most acceptable to self and others. In the same category falls the mass of emotional center-dominated behavior that is often called self-destructive. This behavior is designed to relieve anxiety of the moment, and the impulse for immediate relief over-rules awareness of longterm complications. It is at its worst in alcohol and drug abuse. There are situations in which the intellect aids emotionally-directed behavior—as, for instance, intellectual planning that helps emotionally directed crime. A large group of people choose their philosophies and ideologies because of emotional system pressure. In another group, a section of the intellect functions well on impersonal subjects; they can be brilliant academically, while their emotionally-directed personal lives are chaotic. Even in people who exhibit some degree of separation between emotion and intellect, and in whom the intellect can hold its own with the emotional system in certain areas most of the time, there are periods of chronic stress in which the emotional system is dominant.

B. *Triangles.* I began work on this basic concept in 1955. By 1956 the research group was thinking and talking about "triads." As the concept evolved, it came to include much more than the meaning of the conventional term *triad,* and we therefore had a problem communicating with those who assumed they knew the meaning of triad. I chose *triangle* in order to convey that this concept has specific meaning beyond that implied in triad. The theory states that the triangle, a three-person emotional configuration, is the molecule or the basic building block of any emotional system, whether it is in the family or any other group. The triangle is the smallest stable relationship system. A two-person system may be stable as long as it is calm, but when anxiety increases, it immediately involves the most vulnerable other person to become a triangle. When tension in the triangle is too great for the threesome, it involves others to become a series of interlocking triangles.

Sophie's choice

In periods of calm, the triangle is made up of a comfortably close twosome and a less comfortable outsider. The twosome works to preserve the togetherness, lest one become uncomfortable and form a better togetherness elsewhere. The outsider seeks to form a togetherness with one of the twosome, and there are numerous well-known moves to accomplish this. The emotional forces within the triangle are constantly in motion from moment to moment, even in periods of calm. Moderate tension states in the twosome are characteristically felt by one, while the other is oblivious. It is the uncomfortable one who initiates a new equilibrium toward more comfortable togetherness for self.

Mistresses children

In periods of stress, the outside position is the most comfortable and most desired position. In stress, each works to get the outside position to escape tension in the twosome. When it is not possible to shift forces in the triangle, one of the involved twosome triangles in a fourth person, leaving the former third person aside for reinvolvement later. The emotional forces duplicate the exact patterns in the new triangle. Over time, the emotional forces continue to move from one active triangle to another, finally remaining mostly in one triangle as long as the total system is fairly calm.

When tensions are very high in families and available family triangles are exhausted, the family system triangles in people from outside the family, such as police and social agencies. A successful externalization of the tension occurs when outside workers are in conflict about the family while the family is calmer. In emotional systems such as an office staff, the tensions between the two highest administrators can be triangled and retriangled until conflict is acted out between two who are low in the administrative hierarchy. Administrators often settle this conflict by firing or removing one of the conflictual twosome, after which the conflict erupts in another twosome.

A triangle in moderate tension characteristically has two comfortable sides and one side in conflict. Since patterns repeat and repeat in a triangle, the people come to have fixed roles in relation to each other. The best example of this is the father-mother-child triangle. Patterns vary, but one of the most common is basic tension between the parents, with the father's gaining the outside position—often being called passive, weak, and distant —leaving the conflict between mother and child. The mother—often called aggressive, dominating, and castrating—wins over the child, who moves another step toward chronic functional impairment. This pattern is described as the family projection process. Families replay the same triangular game over and over for years, as though the winner were in doubt, but the final result is always the same. Over the years the child accepts the always-lose outcome more easily, even to volunteering for this position. A variation is the pattern in which the father finally attacks the mother, leaving the child in the outside position. This child then learns the techniques of gaining the outside position by playing the parents off against each other.

Each of the structured patterns in triangles is available for predictable moves and predictable outcomes in families and social systems. A knowledge of triangles provides a far more exact way of understanding the father-mother-child triangle than do the traditional oedipal-complex explanations. Triangles provide several times more flexibility in dealing with such problems therapeutically.

Knowledge of triangles helps provide the theoretical perspective between individual therapy and this method of family therapy. An emotionally involved relationship is unavoidable in the average two-person, patient-therapist relationship. Theoretically, family therapy provides a situation in which intense relationships can remain within the family and the therapist can be relatively outside the emotional complex. This is a good theoretical premise that is hard to achieve in practice. Without some special effort, it is easy for the family to wrap itself around the therapist emotionally, install the therapist in an all-important position, hold the therapist responsible for success or failure, and passively wait for the therapist to change the family. I have already discussed ways other therapists have dealt with the therapeutic relationship, as well as my continuing effort to operate from outside the family emotional system. Initially that included making the family members responsible for each other, avoiding the family tendency to assign importance to me, and promising no benefits except from the family's own effort to learn about itself and change itself. Most important was a longterm effort to attain and maintain emotional neutrality with individual family members. There are many subtleties to this. Beyond this effort, it was knowledge of triangles that provided the important breakthrough in the effort to stay outside the emotional complex.

One experience, above all others, was important in learning about triangles. That was a period in which much of my family therapy was with both parents and behavior problem adolescent child. It was possible to see the workings of the triangle between parents and child in microscopic detail. The more I could stay outside the triangle, the more clearly it was possible to see the family emotional system as it operated on well-defined emotional circuits between father, mother, and child. Therapeutically, the family did not change its original patterns. The passive father became less passive, the aggressive mother less aggressive, and the symptomatic child would become asymptomatic. The average, motivated family would continue for 30 to 40 weekly appointments and terminate with great praise for the "good result." In my opinion, the family had not changed, but I had learned a lot about triangles. It was possible to observe a family and know the next move in the family before it occurred.

From the knowledge of triangles, I hypothesized the situation would be different by excluding the child and limiting the therapy to the two parents and the therapist. Rather than dealing in generalities about staying out of the family emotional system, I was then armed with specific knowledge about the parents' triangling moves to involve the therapist. Therapeutically, the results were far superior to anything before that time. This has remained the one basic therapeutic method since the early 1960's. On a broad theoretical-therapeutic level, if the therapist can stay in viable emotional contact with the two most significant family members, usually the two parents or two spouses, and he can be relatively outside the emotional activity in this central triangle, the age-old fusion between the family members will slowly begin to resolve, and all other family members will automatically change in relation to the two parents in the home setting. This is basic theory and basic method. The process can proceed regardless of content or subject matter discussed. The critical issue is the emotional reactiveness between the spouses, and the ability of the therapist to keep self relatively detriangled from the emotionality. The process can proceed with any third person who can keep self detriangled, but it would be difficult to find such an outside relationship. The method is as successful as other methods in short-term crisis situations. In the early years, I was active in engaging the family emotionally in consultations and short-term crisis situations. A calm, low-keyed, detriangling approach is more effective with a single appointment or with many.

3 C. *(Nuclear Family Emotional System.)* This concept describes the patterns of emotional functioning in a family in a single generation. Certain basic patterns between the father, mother, and children are replicas of the past generations and will be repeated in the generations to follow. There are several rather clear variables that determine the way the family functions in the present generation, which can be measured and validated by direct observation. From a careful history, in connection with knowledge of the details in the present generation, it is possible to do a rather remarkable reconstruction of the way the process operated in past generations. From knowledge about the transmission of family patterns over multiple generations, it is possible to project the same process into future generations, and, within limits, do some reasonably accurate predictions about future generations. No one person lives long enough to check the accuracy of predictions into the future, but there is enough detailed knowledge about some families in history to do a reasonable check on the predictive process. Based on

experience in family research, the predictions of ten to twenty years ago have been rather accurate.

The beginning of a nuclear family, in the average situation, is a marriage. There are exceptions to this, just as there have always been exceptions, which is all part of the total theory. The basic process in exceptional situations is similar to the more chaotic pattern in poorly differentiated people. The two spouses begin a marriage with life-style patterns and levels of differentiation developed in their families of origin. Mating, marriage, and reproduction are governed to a significant degree by emotional-instinctual forces. The way the spouses handle them in dating and courtship and in timing and planning the marriage provides one of the best views of the level of differentiation of the spouses. The lower the level of differentiation, the greater the potential problems for the future. People pick spouses who have the same levels of differentiation. Most spouses can have the closest and most open relationships in their adult lives during courtship. The fusion of the two pseudo-selfs into a common self occurs at the time they commit themselves to each other permanently, whether it be the time of engagement, the wedding itself, or the time they establish their first home together. It is common for living together relationships to be harmonious, and for fusion symptoms to develop when they finally get married. It is as if the fusion does not develop as long as they still have an option to terminate the relationship.

The lower the level of differentiation, the more intense the emotional fusion of marriage. One spouse becomes more the dominant decision maker for the common self, while the other adapts to the situation. This is one of the best examples in the borrowing and trading of self in a close relationship. One may assume the dominant role and force the other to be adaptive, or one may assume the adaptive role and force the other to be dominant. Both may try for the dominant role, which results in conflict; or both may try for the adaptive role, which results in decision paralysis. The dominant one gains self at the expense of the more adaptive one, who loses self. More differentiated spouses have lesser degrees of fusion, and fewer of the complications. The dominant and adaptive positions are *not* directly related to the sex of the spouse. They are determined by the position that each had in their families of origin. From my experience, there are as many dominant females as males, and as many adaptive males as females. These characteristics played a major role in their original choice of each other as partners. The fusion results in anxiety for one or both of the spouses. There is a spectrum of ways spouses deal with fusion symptoms. The most universal mechanism is emotional distance from each other. It is present in all marriages to some degree, and in a high percentage of marriages to a major degree.

Other than the emotional distance, there are three major areas in which the amount of undifferentiation in the marriage comes to be manifested in symptoms. The three areas are marital conflict; sickness or dysfunction in one spouse; and projection of the problems to children. It is as if there is a quantitative amount of undifferentiation to be absorbed in the nuclear family, which may be focused largely in one area or distributed in varying amounts to all three areas. The various patterns for handling the undifferentiation comes from patterns in their families of origin, and the variables involved in the mix in the common self. Following are general characteristics of each of the three areas.

Marital Conflict. The basic pattern in conflictual marriages is one in which neither gives in to the other or in which neither is capable of an adaptive role. These marriages are intense in the amount of emotional energy each invests in the other. The energy may be thinking or action energy, either positive or negative, but the self of each is focused mostly on the other. The relationship cycles through periods of intense closeness, conflict that provides a period of emotional distance, and making up, which starts another cycle of intense closeness. Conflictual spouses probably have the most overtly intense of all relationships. The intensity of the anger and negative feeling in the conflict is as intense as the positive feeling. They are thinking of each other even when they are distant. Marital conflict does not in itself harm children. There are marriages in which most of the undifferentiation goes into marital conflict. The spouses are so invested in each other that the children are largely outside the emotional process. When marital conflict and projection of the problem to children are both present, it is the projection process that is hurtful to children. The quantitative amount of marital conflict that is present reduces the amount of undifferentiation that is focused elsewhere.

Dysfunction in One Spouse. This is the result when a significant amount of undifferentiation is absorbed in the adaptive posture of one spouse. The pseudo-self of the adaptive one merges into the pseudo-self of the dominant one, who assumes more and more responsibility for the twosome. The degree of adaptiveness in one spouse is determined from the longterm functioning posture of each to the other, rather than from verbal reports. Each does some adapting to the other, and it is usual for each to believe that he or she gives in more than the other. The one who functions for long periods in the adaptive position gradually loses the ability to function and make decisions for self. At that point, it requires no more than a moderate increase in stress to trigger the adaptive one into dysfunction, which can be physical illness, emotional illness, or social illness, such as drinking, acting out, and irresponsible behavior. These illnesses tend to become chronic, and they are hard to reverse.

The pattern of the overfunctioning spouse in relation to the underfunctioning spouse exists in all degrees of intensity. It can exist as an episodic phenomenon in families who use a mixture of all three mechanisms. When used as the principal means of controlling undifferentiation, the illnesses can be chronic and most difficult to reverse. The sick or invalided one is too impaired to begin to regain function with an overfunctioning spouse on whom he or she is dependent. This mechanism is amazingly effective in absorbing the undifferentiation. The only disadvantage is the dysfunction in one, which is compensated for by the other spouse. The children can be almost unaffected by having one dysfunctional parent as long as there is someone else to function instead. The main problem in the children is inheriting a life pattern as caretaker of the sick parent, which will project into the future. These marriages are enduring. Chronic illness and invalidism, whether physical or emotional, can be the only manifestation of the intensity of the undifferentiation. The underfunctioning one is grateful for the care and attention, and the overfunctioning one does not complain. Divorce is almost impossible in these marriages unless the dysfunction is also mixed with marital conflict. There have been families in which the overfunctioning one has died unexpectedly and the disabled one has miraculously regained functioning. If there is a subsequent marriage, it follows the pattern of the previous one.

Impairment of One or More Children. This is the pattern in which parents operate as a we-ness to project the undifferentiation to one or more children. This mechanism is so important in the total human problem it has been described as a separate concept, the family projection process.

There are two main variables that govern the intensity of this process in the nuclear family. The first is the degree of the emotional isolation, or cutoff, from the extended family, or from others important in the relationship system. I will discuss this below. The second important variable has to do with the level of anxiety. Any of the symptoms in the nuclear family, whether they be marital conflict, dysfunction in a spouse, or symptoms in a child, are less intense when anxiety is low and more intense when anxiety is high. Some of the most important family therapy efforts are directed at decreasing anxiety and opening the relationship cutoff.

Family Projection Process. The process through which parental undifferentiation impairs one or more children operates within the father-mother-child triangle. It revolves around the mother, who is the key figure in reproduction and who is usually the principal caretaker for the infant. It results in primary emotional impairment of the child; or, it can superimpose itself on some defect or on some chronic physical illness or disability. It exists in all gradations of intensity, from those in which impairment is minimal to those in which the child is seriously impaired for life. The process is so universal it is present to some degree in all families.

A composite of families with moderately severe versions of the projection process will provide the best view of the way the process works. It is as if there is a definite amount of undifferentiation to be absorbed by marital conflict, sickness in a spouse, and projection to the children. The amount absorbed in conflict or sickness in a spouse reduces the amount that will be directed to the children. There are a few families in which most of the undifferentiation goes into marital conflict, essentially none to sickness in a spouse, and relatively small amounts to the children. The most striking examples of this have been in families with autistic, or severely impaired, children in which there is little marital conflict, both spouses are healthy, and the full weight on the undifferentiation is directed to a single, maximally impaired child. I have never seen a family in which there was not some projection to a child. Most families use a combination of all three mechanisms. The more the problem shifts from one area to another, the less chance the process will be crippling in any single area.

There are definite patterns in the way the undifferentiation is distributed to children. It focuses first on one child. If the amount is too great for that child, the process will select others for lesser degrees of involvement. There are families in which the amount of undifferentiation is so great it can seriously impair most of the children, and leave one or two relatively out of the emotional process. There is so much disorder and chaos in these families, it is difficult to see the orderly steps in the process. I have never seen a family in which children were equally involved in the family emotional process. There may be some exceptions to the process described here, but the overall patterns are clear, and the theory accounts for the exceptions. There are suggestions about the way children become the objects of the projection process. On a simplistic level, it is related to the degree of emotional turn on or turn off (both equal in emotional systems terms) the mother feels for the child. This is an automatic emotional process that is not changed by acting the opposite. On a more specific level, it is related to the level of undifferentiation in the parents, the amount of anxiety at the time of conception and birth, and the orientation of the parents toward marriage and children.

The early thoughts about marriage and children are more prominent in the female than the male. They begin to take an orderly form before adolescence. A female who thinks primarily of the husband she will marry tends to have marriages in which she focuses most of her emotional energy on the husband, and he focuses on her, and symptoms tend to focus more in marital conflict and sickness in a spouse. Those females whose early thoughts and fantasies go more to the children they will have than the man they will marry, tend to become the mothers of impaired children. The process can be so intense in some women that the husband is incidental to the process. Spouses from lower levels of differentiation are less specific about marriage and children. The children selected for the family projection process are those conceived and born during stress in the mother's life; the first child, the oldest son or oldest daughter, an only child of either sex, one who is emotionally special to the mother, or one the mother believes to be special to the father. Among common special children are only children, an oldest child, a single child of one sex among several of the opposite sex, or a child with some defect. Also important are the special children who were fretful, colicky, rigid, and nonresponsive to the mother from the beginning. The amount of initial special emotional investment in such children is great. A good percentage of mothers have a basic preference for boys or girls, depending upon their orientation in the family of origin. It is impossible for mothers to have equal emotional investment in any two children, no matter how much they try to protest equality for all.

On a more detailed level, the projection process revolves around maternal instinct, and the way anxiety permits it to function during reproduction and the infancy of the child. The father usually plays a support role to the projection process. He is sensitive to the mother's anxiety, and he tends to support her view and help her implement her anxious efforts at mothering. The process begins with anxiety in the mother. The child responds anxiously to mother, which she misperceives as a problem in the child. The anxious parental effort goes into sympathetic, solicitous, overprotective energy, which is directed more by the mother's anxiety than the reality needs of the child. It establishes a pattern of infantilizing the child, who gradually becomes more impaired and more demanding. Once the process has started, it can be motivated either by anxiety in the mother, or anxiety in the child. In the average situation, there may be symptomatic episodes at stressful periods during childhood, which gradually increase to major symptoms during or after adolescence; intense emotional fusion between mother and child may exist in which the mother-child relationship remains in positive, symptom-free equilibrium until the adolescent period, when the child attempts to function on his own. At that point, the child's relationship with the mother, or with both parents, can become negative and the child develop severe symptoms. The more intense forms of the mother-child fusion may remain relatively asymptomatic until young adulthood and the child can collapse in psychosis when he attempts to function away from the parents.

The basic pattern of the family projection is the same, except for minor variations in form and intensity, whether the eventual impairment in the child be one that leads to serious lifelong dysfunction, or one that never develops serious symptoms and is never diagnosed. The greatest number of people impaired by the projection process are those who do less well with life and who have lower levels of differentiation than their siblings, and who may go for a few generations before producing a child who becomes seriously impaired symptomatically. This theory considers schizophrenia to be the product of several generations of increasing symptomatic impairment, with lower and lower levels of differentiation, until there is a generation that produces schizophrenia. In clinical work, we have come to use the term *the triangled child* to refer to the one who was the main focus of the family projection process. Almost every family has one child who was more triangled than the others, and whose life adjustment is less good than the others. In doing multigenerational family histories, it is relatively easy to estimate the family projection process and identify the triangled child by securing historical data about the life adjustments of each sibling.

Emotional Cutoff. This concept was added to the theory in 1975 after having been a poorly defined extension of other concepts for several years. It was accorded the status of a separate concept to include details not stated elsewhere, and to have a separate concept for emotional process between the generations. The life pattern of cutoffs is determined by the way people handle their unresolved emotional attachments to their parents. All people have some degree of unresolved emotional attachment to their parents. The lower the level of differentiation, the more intense the unresolved attachment. The concept deals with the way people separate themselves from the past in order to start their lives in the present generation. Much thought went into the selection of a term to best describe this process of separation, isolation, withdrawal, running away, or denying the importance of the parental family. However much *cutoff* may sound like informal slang, I could find no other term as accurate for describing the process. The therapeutic effort is to convert the cutoff into an orderly differentiation of a self from the extended family.

The degree of unresolved emotional attachment to the parents is equivalent to the degree of undifferentiation that must somehow be handled in the person's own life and in future generations. The unresolved attachment is handled by the intrapsychic process of denial and isolation of self while living close to the parents; or by physically running away; or by a combination of emotional isolation and physical distance. The more intense the cutoff with the past, the more likely the individual to have an exaggerated version of his parental family problem in his own marriage, and the more likely his own children to do a more intense cutoff with him in the next generation. There are many variations in the intensity of this basic process and in the way the cutoff is handled.

The person who runs away from his family of origin is as emotionally dependent as the one who never leaves home. They both need emotional closeness, but they are allergic to it. The one who remains on the scene and handles the attachment by intrapsychic mechanisms tends to have some degree of supportive contact with the parents, to have a less intense overall process, and to develop more internalized symptoms under stress, such as physical illness and depression. An exaggerated version of this is the severely impaired person who can collapse into psychosis, isolating himself intrapsychically while living with the parents. The one who runs away geographically is more inclined to impulsive behavior. He tends to see the problem as being in the parents and running away as a method of gaining independence from the parents. The more intense the cutoff, the more he is vulnerable to duplicating the pattern with the parents with the first available other person. He can get into an impulsive marriage. When problems develop in the marriage, he tends also to run away from that. He can continue through multiple marriages, and finally resort to more temporary living together relationships. Exaggerated versions of this occur in relationship nomads, vagabonds, and hermits who either have superficial relationships or give up and live alone.

In recent years, as the age-old cutoff process became more pronounced as a result of societal anxiety, the emotional cutoff has been called the generation gap. The higher the level of anxiety, the greater the degree of generation gap in poorly differentiated people. There has been an increase in the percentage of those who run away, and who become involved in living together arrangements and communal living situations. These substitute families are very unstable. They are made up of people who ran away from their own families; when tension builds up in the substitute family, they cutoff from that and move on to another. Under the best conditions, the substitute family and outside relationships are poor substitutes for original families.

There are all gradations of the emotional cutoff. An average family situation in our society today is one in which people maintain a distant and formal relationship with the families of origin, returning home for duty visits at infrequent intervals. The more a nuclear family maintains some kind of viable emotional contact with the past generations, the more orderly and asymptomatic the life process in both generations. Compare two families with identical levels of differentiation. One family remains in contact with the parental family and remains relatively free of symptoms for life, and the level of differentiation does not change much in the next generation. The other family cuts off with the past, develops symptoms and dysfunction, and a lower level of differentiation in the succeeding generation. The symptomatic nuclear family that is emotionally cut off from the family of origin can get into cyclical, longterm family therapy without improvement. If one or both parents can re-establish emotional contact with their families of origin, the anxiety level subsides, the symptoms become softer and more manageable, and family therapy can become productive. Merely telling a family to go back to the family of origin is of little help. Some people are very anxious about returning to their families. Without systems coaching, they can make the problem worse. Others can return, continue the same emotional isolation they used when they were in the family, and accomplish nothing. Techniques for helping families to re-establish contact have been sufficiently developed so that it is now a family therapy method in its own right. This differentiation of a self in one's own family has been presented in another paper (15). It is based on the experience that a spouse who can do a reasonable job at differentiating self in his parental family will have accomplished more than if he was involved in regular family therapy with self and his spouse.

ᐧ *Multigenerational Transmission Process.* The family projection process continues through multiple generations. In any nuclear family, there is one child who is the primary object of the family projection process. This child emerges with a lower level of differentiation than the parents and does less well in life. Other children, who are minimally involved with the parents, emerge with about the same levels of differentiation as the parents. Those who grow up relatively outside the family emotional process develop better levels of differentiation than the parents. If we follow the most impaired child through successive generations, we will see one line of descent producing individuals with lower and lower levels of differentiation. The process may go rapidly a few generations, remain static for a generation or so, and then speed up again. Once I said it required at least three generations to produce a child so impaired he would collapse into schizophrenia. That was based on the notion of a starting point with fairly good surface functioning and a process that proceeded at maximum speed through the generations. However, since I now know the process can slow down or stay static a generation or two, I would now say that it would require perhaps eight to ten generations to produce the level of impairment that goes with schizophrenia. This is the process that produces the poorly functioning people who make up most of the lower social classes. If a family encounters severe stress in perhaps the fifth or sixth generation of a ten-generation process, it may produce a social failure who is less impaired than the schizophrenic person. The degree of impairment in schizophrenia comes from those poorly differentiated people who are able to keep the relationship system in relatively symptom-free equilibrium for several more generations.

If we followed the line through the children who emerge with about the same levels of differentiation, we see a remarkable consistency of family functioning through the generations. History speaks of family traditions, family ideals, and so on. If we follow the multigenerational lineage of those who emerge with higher levels of differentiation, we will see a line of highly functioning and very successful people. A family at a highest level of differentiation can have one child who starts down the scale. A family at the lowest level can have a child who starts up the scale. Many years ago I described schizophrenia from a phenomenological standpoint as a natural process that helps to keep the race strong. The weakness from the family is fixed in one person who is less likely to marry and reproduce and more likely to die young.

Sibling Position. This concept is an adaptation of Toman's work on the personality profiles of each sibling position. His first book in 1961 (14) was remarkably close to the direction of some of my research. He had worked from an individual frame of reference and only with normal families, but he had ordered his data in a way no one else had done, and it was easy to incorporate them into the differentiation of self and the family projection process. His basic thesis is that important personality characteristics fit with the sibling position in which a person grew up. His ten basic sibling profiles automatically permit one to know the profile of any sibling position, and, *all things being equal,* to have a whole body of presumptive knowledge about anyone. His ideas provided a new dimension toward understanding how a particular child is chosen as the object of the family projection process. The degree to which a personality profile fits with normal provides a way to understand the level of differentiation and the direction of the projection process from generation to generation. For instance, if an oldest turns out to be more like a youngest, that is strong evidence that he was the most triangled child. If an oldest is an autocrat, that is strong evidence of a moderate level of impaired functioning. An oldest who functions calmly and responsibly is good evidence of a better level of differentiation. The use of Toman's profiles, together with differentiation and projection, make it possible to assemble reliable presumptive personality profiles on people in past generations on whom verifiable facts are missing. Knowing the degree to which people fit the profiles provides predictive data about how spouses will handle the mix in a marriage, and how they will handle their effort in family therapy. Based on my research and therapy, I believe that no single piece of data is more important than knowing the sibling position of people in the present and past generations.

Societal Regression. This eighth and last of the concepts in the Bowen theory was first defined in 1972, and formally added to the theory in 1975. I have always been interested in understanding societal problems, but the tendency of psychiatrists and social scientists to make sweeping generalizations from a minimal number of specific facts resulted in my interest's remaining peripheral except for personal reading. Family research added a new order of facts about human functioning, but I avoided the seductive urge to generalize from them. In the 1960s, there was growing evidence that the emotional problem in society was similar to the emotional problem in the family. The triangle exists in all relationships, and that was a small clue. In 1972 the Environmental Protection Agency invited me to do a paper on human reaction to environmental problems. I anticipated doing a paper on assorted facts acquired from years of experience with people relating to larger societal issues. That paper led to a year of research, and a return to old files for confirmation of data. Finally I identified a link between the family and society that was sufficiently trustworthy for me to extend the basic theory about the family into the larger societal arena. The link had to do, first, with the delinquent teenaged youngster, who is a responsibility for both the parents and society, and secondly, with changes in the way the parents and the agents of society deal with the same problem.

It has not yet been possible to write this up in detail, but the overall structure of the concept was presented in outline form in 1974 (16). The concept states that when a family is subjected to chronic, sustained anxiety, the family begins to lose contact with its intellectually determined principles, and to resort more and more to emotionally determined decisions to allay the anxiety of the moment. The results of the process are symptoms and eventually regression to a lower level of functioning. The societal concept postulates that the same process is evolving in society; that we are in a period of increasing chronic societal anxiety; that society responds to this with emotionally determined decisions to allay the anxiety of the moment; that this results in symptoms of dysfunction; that the efforts to relieve the symptoms result in more emotional band aid legislation, which increases the problem; and that the cycle keeps repeating, just as the family goes through similar cycles to the states we call emotional illness. In the early years of my interest in societal problems, I thought that all societies go through good periods and bad, that they always go through a rise and fall, and that the cyclical phenomenon of the 1950s was part of another cycle. As societal unrest appeared to move toward intensification of the problems through the 1960s, I began to look for ways to explain the chronic anxiety. I was looking for concepts consistent with man as an instinctual being, rather than man as a social being. My current postulation considers the chronic anxiety as the product of the population explosion, decreasing supplies of food and raw materials necessary to maintain man's way of life on earth, and the pollution of the environment which is slowly threatening the balance of life necessary for human survival. *nuclear*

This concept proceeds in logical steps from the family to larger and larger social groups, to the total of society. It is too complex for detailed presentation here. I outline it here to indicate that the theoretical concepts of the Bowen theory do permit logical extension into a beginning theory about society as an emotional system.

SUMMARY

Most members of the mental health professions have little interest in, or awareness of, theory about the nature of emotional illness. I have developed a family systems theory of emotional functioning. For some ten years I have been trying to present the theory as clearly as it is possible for me to define it. Only a small percentage of people are really able to hear it. In the early years, I considered most of the problem to be my difficulty in communicating the ideas in ways others could hear. As the years have passed, I have come to consider that the major difficulty is the inability of people to detach themselves sufficiently from conventional theory to be able to hear systems concepts. In each presentation, I learn a little more about which points people fail to hear. I have devoted almost half of this presentation to some broad background issues which I hoped would set the stage for people to hear more than they had heard before, and to clarify some of the issues between my family systems theory and general systems theory.

I have never been happy about my efforts to present my own theory. I can be perfectly clear in my own mind, but there is always the problem of restating it so others can hear. If it gets too brief, people hear the theory as too static and too simplistic. If I try to fill out the concepts with more detail, it tends to get wordy and repetitive. Ultimately, I hope to present it so that each theoretical concept is illustrated with a clinical example, but that is a long and complex book. I believe that some systems theory will provide a bright new promise for comprehending emotional illness. Whether the ultimate systems theory is this one or another remains to be seen. After some twenty years of experience with this theory, I have great confidence in it. It does mean that the therapist must keep the whole spectrum of variables in his head at once; but, after some experience, knowing the variables well enough to know when one is out of balance becomes automatic.

REFERENCES

1. M. Bowen. "The Use of Family Theory in Clinical Practice," *Comprehensive Psychiatry,* 7(1966), 345–74.
2. _____. "Family Therapy and Family Group Therapy," in H. Kaplan and B. Sadock (eds.). *Comprehensive Group Psychotherapy.* New York: Williams and Wilkins, 1971.
3. G. Bateson, D.D. Jackson, J. Haley, and J.H. Weakland. "Toward a Theory of Schizophrenia," *Behavioral Science,* 1 (1956), 251.
4. M. Bowen. "A Family Concept of Schizophrenia," in D. Jackson (ed.). *The Etiology of Schizophrenia.* New York: Basic Books, 1960, 346.
5. _____. "Family Psychotherapy with Schizophrenia in the Hospital and Private Practice," in I. Boszormenyi-Nagy and J. Framo (eds.). *Intensive Family Therapy.* New York: Harper and Row, 1965, 213.
6. _____. "Family Therapy After Twenty Years," in J. Dyrud and D. Freedman. *American Handbook of Psychiatry,* Vol. V. New York: Basic Books, 1975.
7. T. Lidz, S. Fleck, and A. Cornelison. *Schizophrenia and the Family.* New York: International Universities Press, 1965.

8. M. Bowen. "Family Psychotherapy," *American Journal of Orthopsychiatry,* 30 (1961), 40.

9. N. W. Ackerman. *The Psychodynamics of Family Life.* New York: Basic Books, 1958.

10. J. E. Bell. "Family Group Therapy," *Public Health Monograph 64,* United States Department of Health, Education, and Welfare, Washington, D. C., 1961.

11. N. Paul and B. Paul. *A Marital Puzzle.* New York: W. W. Norton, 1975.

12. I. Boszormenyi-Nagy and G. Spark. *Invisible Loyalties.* New York: Harper and Row, 1973.

13. S. Minuchin. *Families and Family Therapy.* Cambridge, Mass.: Harvard University Press, 1974.

14. W. Toman. *Family Constellation.* New York: Springer, 1961.

15. M. Bowen. "Toward the Differentiation of Self in One's Family of Origin," in F. Andres and J. Lorio (eds.). *Georgetown Family Symposium Papers,* I. Georgetown University Press, 1974, 77.

16. _____. *"Societal Regression as Viewed Through Family Systems Theory.* Paper read at the Nathan W. Ackerman Memorial Conference, Venezuela, February, 1974.

CHAPTER 4

Theoretical Aspects and Clinical Relevance of the Multigenerational Model of Family Therapy

Philip J. Guerin, Jr. M.D.

Katherine Buckley Guerin, M.A.

By using a three- to four-generational model, it is possible to remain relevant to a family's presenting symptom, and at the same time go beyond it to the underlying patterns of the multigenerational system.

Families can present in many ways. One way is with the symptoms in the child, either a physical symptom like asthma, or an emotional symptom like depression. On the other hand, a family may present with a marital focus—open conflict on the verge of divorce, or just a communicational breakdown. A family may present with emotional or physical symptoms in one or the other spouse. In rare instances a family will present with an extended family problem. And in these days of having to deal with aging and death perhaps more often than in the past, we also see families whose major concern is with an aging parent and whether or not to institutionalize.

Most of the time, however, the symptoms are presented to family therapists clinically as isolated to the nuclear family. Only after tracking and uncovering, and elaborating on the boundaries of the system is it possible to understand how the nuclear family conflicts tie into the remainder of the system. Most frequently the place that the symptom presents in the family is where it seems to be safest for a symptom to reside. For instance, in some families in which symptoms present in the child, it is evident in the first interview that it isn't safe for that family to have a problem in the marriage.

There is a lot of anxiety that if the therapist looks too closely at the marriage, it is going to rupture or break apart in some way. Other families come in with a marital problem, yet symptoms are obviously leaking down a generation to the kids, and if you begin to investigate the parenting function, they get very skittish about that. Every family has safe and unsafe areas, and very often there is one generational level the family finds it difficult to let the therapist in on. Research and clinical experience seem to indicate that most often this is in the extended family. Many families don't see the clinical relevance of the grandparent generation to their specific problem, and it's up to the art of the therapist to make the three- to four-generational model relevant.

The family we shall discuss here started out originally as a child-focused family. They have three adopted children, two boys and one girl. The parents are both in their late thirties. The problem presented originally in the daughter. The parents were concerned about her social behavior, considering it sometimes inappropriate. They also worried about whether or not she had a learning disability. The parents were seen by themselves; with just their daughter; and with all the kids together. The parents are both Catholic and originally from New York City. The husband is of Slavic origin; the wife is Irish. The husband, a very effective and successful businessman, was clearly an object-oriented overfunctioner. His wife, on the other hand, was a relationship-oriented emotional overfunctioner. She was tied into and anxious about the kids and their functioning, and about her mothering. He was the distant critical expert, especially in relation to the job she was doing with the children. He was very much into his own business and projects around the house, whereas she was underfunctioning and really distant from a lot of the family busy work. There was some activity with the kids on his part, more with the boys than with his daughter.

In a child-focused family it is important not to fall into the trap of trying to sell the parents the idea that what they really have is a family problem or a marital problem. Any such attempt will only trigger already primed feelings of parental guilt and responsibility, and the result will be an increase in the family's anxiety level, and a reinforcement of denial and projection.

Whenever I see a child-focused family, I automatically assume a set of four potential triangles: the central nuclear family triangle of mother, father, and symptomatic child; two auxiliary nuclear family triangles, one involving a parent, the symptomatic child, and an asymptomatic sibling, the other an intersibling triangle among three of the children; and finally, a triangle over three generations involving a grandparent, a parent, and the symptomatic child. There are many other possibilities, but these are the most frequently encountered clinically. As I evaluate the family, I try to search for the active existence of any one or more of this set of potential triangles. Once I locate the existence and spell out the process, I am ready to intervene. In this family the initial intervention was a two-stage process. The central nuclear family triangle of father, mother, and symptomatic child was clearly spelled out. The father was in the distant critical position, the mother emotionally overinvolved with her daughter and reactively distant from her husband. Since the daughter was exquisitely sensitive to her father's criticism of her, and especially tuned in to her mother's anxiety level, an increase in either one predictably exacerbated the daughter's symptomatic behavior.

In order to set the stage for structurally shifting the process in this triangle and thus shifting the symptom, a detoxification of father's critical expert position had to take place. Therefore, stage one was to instruct father to increase his coaching of mother until she gets it right and daughter shapes up. This was meant to exacerbate the problem to the point where father had to concede this method of proceeding was useless—after which the stage was set for move two.

The second intervention was to encourage mother to move out of her present position and become more interested in some extrafamilial things. She was also instructed to decrease her degree of responsibility for daughter's functioning and well-being. The father was instructed to move into the space vacated by mother. If these steps are carried out by the family, they are engaged, and a shift in the process usually occurs. In this particular family, mother moved out, father moved in, and father began to question whether his distance wasn't something that was affecting the family. As his wife moved out, he began to find that he had a lot of difficulty dealing with her being outside his radar. As long as she was where she was supposed to be when she was supposed to be there, he could go off and do his thing around the house or elsewhere and be calm about it. As soon as she was out somewhere doing something, and her bleep wasn't appearing on his radar screen, he began to get anxious. He developed some somatic symptoms and became somewhat depressed and concerned about himself. The little girl in the middle of this process responded to the attention from her daddy and the decrease in pressure from her mother by showing marked improvement in her functioning. The primary shift had thus occurred. The process had shifted, and the problem been redefined and systematized with the relocation of the symptom in the marriage.

As the marriage is worked on, and the marital fusion unfolds, the process inevitably involves a tie into the extended family. The interlocking character of the three generations comes into view. Pieces from all three of those generations must be worked on at different times, depending on what's going on in the present time frame with the family. Success and progress don't mean that the symptoms and the dysfunction just disappear; instead symptoms will reappear over time in all three generational levels of the family. For instance, as you get close to the core of the difficulty in the marital fusion a child may pop up symptomatic again in response to the rising anxiety level. In sorting out the nuclear family process, grandmother's part in it may move the focus to the extended family. Working with a family over a long period of time reinforces the view that there is a transgenerational flow, and that isolating an emotional problem inside the nuclear family makes no more sense than isolating it inside an individual's head. The whole three-generational structure of the system, with all of its interconnections, becomes ever clearer. Change is measured in terms of a decrease in the intensity and duration of the reoccurring predictable dysfunction as the process inevitably recycles itself.

Not all families embark on a long term course. Some fail to engage at all, and sabotage interventions with "I can't," or "I won't do that," or some version of "You've got it all wrong, Doc," or "You wouldn't suggest that." Other families will buy the initial intervention; with symptomatic relief, they then gratefully withdraw lest the therapist in his zeal for further change mess it up all over again.

The term *fusion,* in a systems-relationship framework, indicates a blurring of self boundaries. This blurring of boundaries carries with it a constantly fluctuating, momentarily changable reactive state in the relationship. On one end of the spectrum is the time-limited comfort of relationship refuge. On the other end is the discomfort of the furnace-refrigerator phenomenon of active and open conflict. Every married couple I have studied exhibit complementary operating principles and reciprocal functioning. That is to say, people with opposite operating principles marry each other, and these differences in their operating principles provide an attraction and a balancing stability to the relationship. As their interdependence grows, each relies on the other for emotional balance, so that reciprocity of function evolves. The husband, let us say, is the objective overfunctioner, and the wife is the emotional overfunctioner; these characteristics form a complementary bond which operates like a seesaw: if one spouse's functioning is up, the other's must be down.

In this marriage, for instance, the husband is the reasonable, object-oriented emotional distancer. He responds to upset and crisis with rational thought; emotionally he operates on an even keel, only blowing up after long build ups. He keeps active and busy, deplores small talk, and likes to spend his relationship time discussing important nonpersonal issues, or participating in some invigorating activity like tennis, handball, or sex. His wife, on the other hand, is the relationship-oriented emotional pursuer. She reacts intensely to upset and crisis; her facial expression is a mirror of her inner thoughts and feelings. She deposits the byproducts of her inner turmoil into a relationship with anyone who will listen. She explodes easily, but then the fire and smoke dissipate quickly. She likes activity, but likes just sitting and talking best of all, especially when it involves small talk and juicy gossip. Both spouses are competent adults. His distant, reasonable reserve provides a balance for her in the same way that her talkative emotional tolerance for people provides a balance for him. So how come they don't live happily ever after? Well, a lot of funny things happen in human relationships. One of them is that people become more like themselves when stress hits a relationship. Distancers reason at feeling; and when this fails, they seek refuge in nontalking-back objects. Pursuers express their feelings from the soul and seek refuge in togetherness; then they wonder why everyone is moving away from them. The balance becomes the itch. So if you ask someone what he or she likes best and what least about the spouse, the answers could be the same, depending on the emotional climate of the moment.

The build up of dependence on the operational attributes of one's spouse atrophies the development of those same parts of one's self. In time of crisis, if a call is made to that part of the self, there will then be nothing there to respond; and the dependence on other to fill that void becomes further intensified. This increasing interdependence builds to the point of producing a reciprocity of functioning, so that when one spouse functions well, the other functions poorly. This may move back and forth like a seesaw, or it may become relatively fixed. The fixed states produce the most emotional symptoms.

A clear definition of the relationship reciprocity is therapeutically important because it educates people to the process they are caught up in, and produces a hope for change. Establishing the way reciprocal functioning swings back and forth over time can validate the emotional experience of the present underfunctioner, and perhaps serve to motivate an attempt at change on his or her part. It should be kept in mind, however, that it is the one in the overfunctioning state at the time they are seen clinically who will have the easiest time changing his or her part in the process.

The issue of self-boundary—how people define themselves and their personal space in relation to others—is another aspect of marital fusion. Emotional pursuers are boundary invaders, always moving into another's personal space. They want to know what everybody else is thinking, and feeling; they also want to take responsibility for helping others. The emotional pursuer's own boundaries usually tend to be nonselective, that is he tends to invite almost anyone in, and lets them know about rather personal matters. This nonselective boundary may foster a state of chaos in which the emotional pursuer feels quite at home. The emotional distancer tends to invade only on object-oriented issues; only rarely does he ask anybody into his own personal space. Even when he seems to want to, his tightly-drawn boundaries make it difficult. Order and quiet, and a mildly cool emotional climate are preferred.

Taking responsibility for others is also central to the emotional marital fusion. In this family, for example, both spouses monitored each other's public image. The husband was extremely tuned in to how his wife appeared in social groups, and whether she was making a fool of herself or not. Responsibility for changing the other is something that all of us get into. We get uptight in a situation; our insides put the problem outside of ourselves into the other; and the automatic programmed response is to change the other. A close look at the situation shows each spouse is doing a fine job of being critical of the other's areas of responsibility while not doing his or her own jobs well or at all. Furthermore, each spouse assumes that his or her own behavior can't be helped, but that the other's behavior is on purpose.

This transcript is from the fifth session of therapy with this family. The beginning of the shift in the central nuclear family triangle has already happened. I am trying here to dissect the elements in the marital process and to relabel them, and also trying to define the positions of each of the spouses in reference to listening and hearing, with subsequent directives to get into one position or the other. The central issues in this first segment, for the husband, are productivity, organization and public image. For the wife the issues are their relationship, togetherness, and obtaining approval. Some of the component parts of the marital fusion are elicited.

[*Parents at session without children have just reported that their daughter is much improved. I take that opportunity to broaden the focus of the therapy to include the marriage.*]

Dr. G.: Suppose the kids were perfect? Then life would be——

Ann: Oh, hell, we had six years of that with no children around, and it wasn't—

Jim: It wasn't what?

Ann: We had six years, and we didn't have a peaceful relationship.

Jim: What do you expect?

Ann: Then the animal has to come out, all the nastiness, all the—everybody is human.

Jim: You mean you have some statements about the first six years? You can look back and say they weren't a good six years?

[The husband shows his reluctance to view the marriage as anything but normal and good.]

Ann: I'm not saying that they weren't a good six years.

Jim: They were a six years that had a few problems.

Ann: What I am saying is your disposition hasn't changed, it was rotten then and it still is.

Jim: What? What? What? *(laughter)*

Ann: He was a lousy. . . .

Dr. G.: Was he born like that or did his mother give it to him?

[Therapist participates in the banter, without getting caught up into trying to mediate.]

Ann: Well, not any more but I think she was very difficult when she was young, according to his sister.

Dr. G.: All you gotta do is wait it out. He'll mellow as he gets older.

[Therapist continues banter]

Ann: Well, I am not waiting until he is eighty-four years old, though.

Dr. G.: You're going to change him now?

[Therapist labels efforts at changing other; wife shows evidence of assuming her husband's motivation. His toxic behavior is on purpose; hers, she can't help.]

Ann: Yeah, absolutely, I am not going to change him. But he is too intelligent, he is not a dummy, there is no reason, because I think a lot of it is his will, you know, I think he—

Dr. G.: You think he could be nicer if he really wanted to be?

[Therapist picks wife up on her assumption of his motivation.]

Ann: Absolutely, I am really convinced of that, I really am, I really feel that.

Dr. G.: Well, if he didn't have the kids to get bugged at you about, what would he get bugged about?

[Therapist attempts to focus the conflictual process around issues, to get away from the attack-defense pattern and sharpen the focus on the relationship process.]

Ann: He can't pick on my weight any more, or my eating habits, because they're together.

Dr. G.: You changed all that for him?

Ann: No.

Dr. G.: You just changed it for you, and he happened to like it?

Ann: Yeah, and he happened to like it. I am not very good at changing things just for him, because he is not pleased even when I do it.

Dr. G.: No matter how you do it, he is not pleased?

Jim: Oh, that's—come on, come on.

Ann: Bullshit, then you try something else. You are going to give me a two-week reprieve here, until you start with the cigarettes, and then you are going to start on that.

Dr. G.: Two main complaints about Jim here would be his criticalness of you and the kids, and your being unable to get underneath his expertise to the real him.

[Therapist tries a process hypothesis, focusing on the husband's tendency to criticize his wife's mothering, and the way her reactiveness to his critical expert makes it difficult to bypass it and get to the real him behind it.]

Ann: Number one is right. Number two, you might be right, but I haven't ever really given it much thought.

Dr. G.: Well, you're talking about his moving around on the table the stuff you put out there, instead of putting out his own stuff.

[Therapist pushes hypothesis.]

Ann: Yes, I would sense you are very right on the second one, but I never really thought about it. There was a thought that went through my mind last week about how I rely on Jim and his expertise, and how much I need his strength. You know, I need his approval of things I do, there's no question about it.

[Wife responds by talking about herself for the first time, describing the other side of the marital fusion—the degree to which she depends upon the parts of him that at other times she labels as toxic and willfully destructive to the relationship.]

Jim: Expertise in what? By the way, that's not true. You have really shown over the last couple of years that you handle the most difficult situations with great expertise, even better than I.

[Husband continues to counter wife's position even in this.]

Dr. G.: Now, when things get wound up between the two of you, both of you have trouble assuming the listening position. You sort of get into buttal, rebuttal.

[Therapist moves to stay in control of of the flow of the therapy session.]

Jim: Yeah, there's a lot of that.

[Husband's first validation of marital conflict.]

Dr. G.: How responsible do you think Jim feels for your happiness?

[Moving quickly back to wife and her reactivity, therapist asks a question aimed at the marital fusion—responsibility for other's feelings—in an attempt to detoxify wife's anxiety, and to get her to on to a new thinking track.]

Ann: That's a question to ask me tonight. I would say not too much.

Dr. G.: You don't think it bugs him when you look unhappy?

Ann: He claims it does. I would say that would be a difference in the past few weeks. For the first time in fourteen years I have had a feeling that he might care whether I am happy or not.

[Wife proceeds to describe beautifully the movement in their relationship which has led to a fixed distance between them. The husband, in response to thoughts developed in an earlier session about his distancing behavior, has attempted to move toward his wife. The resulting process is one in which the wife, from her position of reactive distance, mistrusts her husband's moves toward her, and gets caught in a fixed expectation that once he attempts a change he'll never fall back into old ways.]

Dr. G.: What would give you that impression?

Ann: Telephone calls from the office.

Dr. G.: He calls to see how you are?

Ann: Yeah, tells me he is sorry, how much he loves me but he can't do it in person.

Dr. G.: He is moving towards you, and you are complaining about the way he does it. He calls you on the telephone and makes contact with you, and you say he can't do it in person.

[Therapist labels this process in both instances.]

Ann: But then he walks in the house and has a complaint, and I can't see why he bothered calling me.

Dr. G.: You expect that when things get a little better between you, they are going to remain better? You don't expect him to become his old self again?

[Therapist labels fixed expectation.]

One of the things brought out in this segment is that the husband has made an effort to change things, to which the wife has responded from her position of reactive distance with the resentment built up over time and stored in her bitter bank. He attempts to move toward his wife in an effort to connect with her; she criticizes him for the way that he does it. That's the kind of thing that happens all the time, and is a significant roadblock to change. The emotional pursuer has pulled back in frustration to a position of reactive distance; the distancer, sensing the empty space, moves in and runs into some version of, "You weren't there when I was looking for you, so buzz off." It's seen as too little too late. The distancer usually then pulls back with a confused, "What can I do, I tried?" and a fixed distance sets into the relationship, which is then set up for triangulation.

Another point of importance is that the therapist validated what's important to different family members, and the differences in what's important to each of them. The wife talks about her social network. True, she is sidestepping the issue of closeness. However, the husband is also invalidating its importance by putting down her interest in the social network. It is more comforting to his insides if he can isolate her and have her orbit around him, and function as she is supposed to in the house. But that also indicates how her network functions for her: it helps to keep her insides calm in the presence of his distance. Also touched on is the issue of safeness —that is, whether it is safe to put your insides out into the relationship and what will happen if you do.

What about the issue of the therapist taking sides? Have I been triangulated into the relationship in any way? Some may consider that I am obviously on her side and seeing things her way, because I spend so much time talking to her to the exclusion of him. Being triangulated means being emotionally locked into the process in the family in such a way that you see a victim and a villain. It means that the issues being raised by the family trigger something in you so that you behave vi-sà-vis the family or one member of the family in a way that demonstrates you are reactive to their toxic behaviors. As far as the process in this particular session, the husband was more reluctant about being in therapy and about attempting to redefine the problem as a family problem. He is more the distancer; you never chase a distancer, but rather engage him while leaving him a lot of room. The therapist has to watch lest he get reactive to the wife's blatant attacks, or become infatuated with her amusing descriptions; at the same time, he has to assist her providing information.

If the therapist can stay detriangulated, the family is then going to have an experience different from what usually happens to it, for whenever this couple would sit with any one else, or whenever one of them would move unilaterally toward someone else, that person would quickly lose neutrality and choose sides. In addition to staying detriangulated, the therapist has to label the dysfunctions present in the relationship, and challenge the patterns. This is done by pointing out the pattern and asking individual family members what they can do to change it. Or, what would it take to change it? Challenging the pattern gives the family at least a hint that the therapist expects change, and a hope that change is possible. Then the therapist can try to guide them as they form a plan for trying to change things.

How can the therapist deal with his or her personal triggers so as to avoid being triangulated? I stay tuned into my own reactivity by observing what the triggers are for me with a particular family. Is it someone talking too much? not talking at all? contradicting everyone in sight? or invalidating what I think is going on? Having isolated the triggers that tend to activate emotional response in me and set me off on a punitive or reactive course toward the family, I try to pick them up and feed them back into the family. If I pick up something that the husband does that bugs me— let's say, being vague—then I feed that back into the system by asking her, "What do you do when faced with your husband's vagueness?" or, "How does your husband's slipperiness affect you?" That is a very effective way of freeing myself from being pulled into reactivity to that behavior. I assume that if the behavior is bugging me there's a good possibility it also bugs some family members. One good indication that you have been caught in the system is that you notice you don't have any more questions, or any more thoughts, or any sense of where you want to move with the family. Then you know you are incorporated into it somehow, and you are effectively paralyzed.

This next segment begins with my turning to Jim. While I was spending a lot of time talking with Ann, I told Jim to assume the listening position; therefore I had to return to him and ask him what he heard, what was going on with him while he was listening.

Jim begins to concur with the relabeling—that is, he agrees that there appear to be some problems in this marriage. I challenge the pattern by asking what it would take for him to decrease his criticism and get out of his predictable ways of behaving toward his wife. That begins to register with him; then the wife interrupts, and he quickly jumps back to the kids. His jump is a result of her incendiary remark and my having challenged his pattern and tickled him to change. This is a frequent pattern in therapy; as progress is being made in sensitive areas, the anxiety level rises sufficiently to retrigger the presenting complaint. Ann doesn't want to go back to the child focus, and offers evidence that there really are other problems in the family apart from the ones around the kids. At the end of the segment the issue of control in the relationship and how it is exercised comes into view.

Dr. G.: Have you been listening, Jim? what are your thoughts about it?

Jim: I am sad. I guess that there is a problem between us.

Dr. G.: What has you sad?

Jim: I don't know. I am sad because I guess over the last fourteen years or so we have had our share of arguments and fights and all, but I relate, I always relate to a feeling that I have towards Ann. There isn't an altercation that we've had, nor that we ever will have that will change my opinion of her.

[Husband describes his hurt at being criticized, and describes his persistence in caring for his wife.]

Dr. G.: So you care for her, and there are a lot of things about her that you think are A number one. [Therapist recognizes and reinforces positive factors, and then moves to process and asks how often they are communicated to wife.]

Jim: Yeah, something like that.

Dr. G.: How often would you communicate those things?

Jim: Occasionally, not a lot.

Dr. G.: So a larger percentage of your communication would be of the shape up kind.

Jim: Yes, I guess the sexual part of it is the time that I reveal this, or talk about this, or just convey the feeling.

[Husband validates his difficulty in communicating tenderness and positive responses, except in conjunction with sex.]

Dr. G.: So when you are making love you let her know about the positive things about her?

Jim: I think so, I try.

Dr. G.: Is that hard for you to do?

Jim: For me? No, it's not hard.

Dr. G.: Is it hard for you to do when you are not making love to her, just come up to her when she is slopping around the kitchen or something?

[Therapist presses for an expansion of the positive feedback to other nonsexual times.]

Jim: Hard, no. Maybe I have been neglectful of it. I wouldn't find it hard, no.

Dr. G.: What would it take for you to be less critical?

[The press continues.]

Jim: Work.

Dr. G.: What kind of work?

Jim: Hard work.

Dr. G.: You mean you would really have to sit on it?

Jim: Yeah, I would really have to work on it. I would have to have a reminder, I would have to have a string around my finger.

Ann: I could get you some flash cards.

[Wife tosses in a provocative barb.]

Dr. G.: Isn't Ann enough of a reminder when she starts bristling at your criticism? Or is that a red flag to bring the bull on?

[Therapist labels it as red flag.]

Jim: It's funny, but most of these situations occur when the children are involved. I would say that most of it, I disagree—

[Husband reacts, and takes problem focus back to the children.]

Ann: Oh, Jim.

Jim: I am telling you right here and now.

Ann: What about when we go out to dinner?

Jim: Those are situations that occur earlier, they are not the situation at dinner time.

Ann: I am talking about times when we are away from the children when they occur.

Dr. G.: Ann says she senses you are being critical even when the kids aren't involved.

Ann: When we are out with people.

[The pattern has been defined and established as repetitive, and successfully kept within confines of marital fusion.]

Jim: Under certain circumstances, yeah, if you tend to monopolize the discussion or get on the religious situation.

Ann: You're always telling me something that I shouldn't do.

Dr. G.: Could you get less responsible for the way she behaves, and let her be responsible for herself?

[Therapist challenges the pattern by questioning the husband on his ability to change his predictable part in the process.]

Jim: Well, it depends on the circumstances. There are certain people that might be interested in whatever she has to say, and others that are definitely not interested.

Dr. G.: Next time your wife is making an ass of herself in your opinion, why don't you leave her responsible for herself?

Jim: Regardless? Yeah, I'd need work on that.

[After several times around the bush, the husband agrees to give it a try.]

Dr. G.: Otherwise you end up responsible for her. Then she ends up feeling responsible for you as a critical husband who makes negative statements about his wife in public. Suppose she, suppose you left her out there to catch her own left hooks?

Jim: I would really have to work at that.

Dr. G.: Would she take her own lumps?

Jim: I think she would take her own lumps.

Dr. G.: Why don't you try letting her take her own lumps and see what happens? [Therapist pins down the prescribed change.]

Jim: O.K. Then she is going to take her own lumps.

Throughout most of the next segment the issue of control is the focus as it relates to the marriage itself; eventually the issue of control is tied into the process of the therapy. In relation to the marriage the issue of control is there in every relationship. We all know that people control by different kinds of behavioral variants. At one extreme, being controlled can be a controlling behavior. In most relationships both people are struggling for some semblance of control, and going about it according to their own operating styles. Each sees his or her own behavior from the "I can't help it" position, but assumes the other's actions are on purpose. The issue of control in this particular family was not being verbally expressed. The therapist's thinking-system and feeling-system radar has to remain active to pick up the toxic and invisible issues that are not being talked about, so that he can introduce them into the discussion of family process in such a way that they can hopefully be heard and detoxified. In the process of bringing the issue of control to the surface, Ann and Jim get into a chaotic dance, bouncing off each other and interrupting each other's statements. Since I believe the therapist must not get locked into a position of being the referee, I give them a brief reverse communication—"Could they continue this chaos, and escalate it for the rest of the week?"—they agree they can, and the tension and bickering dissipate. That maneuver on my part is an effort to retain control of the session.

Dr. G.: Would it be important to you to be in control of what is going on around you?

Jim: In control? Not completely, no. I think I have relinquished a lot of control in Ann's area.

Dr. G.: Control has been an issue then. It's gotten better, but it is an issue in the relationship? [Issue re-emphasized.]

Ann: Never a voiced one. [Invisibility of issue validated.]

Dr. G.: Would you get anxious inside if you sensed yourself losing control of the situation?

Jim: Out of personal control of the situation, yeah, I guess so.

Dr. G.: You are comfortable when you know what's coming. If things get unpredictable you would start spinning around inside?

Jim: Yeah, but that doesn't happen very often. When it does happen I do get upset but I think my reaction is pretty sound.

Ann: You made a comment that you don't have as much control over me as you used to, what do you mean by that?

[Control and oppression are triggers for the wife, and now that they are visible, she zeroes in.]

Jim: No, no, we are not talking about control over you—

Ann: No, before didn't you say something about that?

[A tiny bit of chaos gets in.]

Jim: Control over you?

Dr. G.: I believe you said you relinquished a lot of control in Ann's area, She wants to know what you mean?

[Therapist clarifies.]

Jim: I meant from the standpoint of functioning as a married couple with a family, with a house, with this and that.

[Husband normalizes.]

Dr. G.: You mean telling her how she had to live her life, that kind of stuff?

[Therapist escalates.]

Jim: No, no.

Ann: That's a feeling I have that we get into this every once in a while and never get down to the core. But you ask me, what are you complaining about? What are you talking about? You do what you want, and I don't stop you in any way, you have all the freedom that you want, you finally reached it.

[Wife opens up the issue more widely.]

Jim: All the freedom, no, no. Why do you always say all, everything has to be all.

[Husband complains about wife's all-or-none positions.]

Ann: O.K. most of the freedom. You have relinquished control with regard to me. When we first got married you would come home and tell me what was expected of me.

Jim: You came from a family with a very hip-shooting attitude towards spending of money and—

[The issue around which control is exercised by the husband surfaces.]

Ann: There is something tied up with this money and my attitude and feelings about money?

Jim: Of course.

Ann: You said that money is no problem.

Jim: Ann, if we had urinated our money away, instead of pissed away, we wouldn't have had certain things that we have today and maybe these things aren't important, I don't know, I don't want to get into that.

[A flurry of reactive process emerges around money, control, and who dictates how proper behavior is defined.]

Dr. G.: What's the difference between urinating it away and pissing it away?

[Therapist playfully encourages flurry to run its course.]

Jim: She would punch your fucking heart out and I would just—

[Husband and wife continue banter.]

Ann: That's awful to say that. You fucked yourself around the whole house yesterday, you used that word every two seconds, but that's all right. Jim, I am going to say punch out your fucking heart. I am not vindictive and I don't like to expend energy in getting even, but I am going to say it, I enjoy saying it, I don't feel there is anything wrong with it and I am not going to stop saying it because you tell me it's a dirty word, when you use it all the time yourself.

Jim: No, no, I don't use it all the time, in fact I don't use it much at all.

Ann: You use it towards me.

Dr. G.: Can the two of you continue this kind of thing for the rest of the night, if you really try?

[Therapist moves to regain modular control of session.]

Ann: If we really try, yeah.

Dr. G.: I think you ought to practice ping-ponging it back and forth with one another.

Jim: I think she's ready, I think she really has her guns out.

[Wife proceeds to make a clear statement of her feeling state. She protests her helplessness to control it, while holding husband responsible for doing his toxic numbers on purpose.]

Ann: I told you before it's not something I work at, it is something that takes place within me that disturbs me, and I get very hurt and very upset and I don't get over it easily. I never used to be this way. It gets worse and worse all the time, and it's not something I'm in complete control of. I got up this morning and I decided, it's not going to bother me. Before a quarter to nine, the kids were out of the house. You know, even before they left at ten after eight I was all stirred up inside, and then after they left, I said it's not going to bother me. By a quarter to nine I had all this to face, and boy, if you were there I would have told you it was on my mind. I couldn't get it off my mind. I had a pit in my stomach all day, I felt shitty all day, you know, it's something I have no control over. I can't turn it on and off like you do.

Dr. G.: Do you think his criticism is more on purpose than your being upset the way that you are now?

[Therapist attempts to refocus with a balancing question, giving wife responsibility for her own behavior.]

The eventual goal here is to work toward the development of one-to-one personal relationships with as many people in the family as possible, in the hope of being able to provide the individual members of the family a degree of emotional freedom from their reactive triggers. That way they won't continually be in a responsive position, caught up in the reactive flow of the family process and behaving like predictable robots; instead, they will have some initiative to move in many different ways within the context of the relationship system.

Ann and Jim did a fine job of getting self-focus and beginning to define themselves in relation to one another. Ann got a sense of the way she operated, the triggers that pulled her into performing her toxic behaviors, and the reflexive character of her blaming those behaviors on Jim so that she held him responsible for her unhappiness. Jim became much less critical; he developed a sense of his tendency to distance from feeling, and saw how much his attempts to control Ann's movements were tied into his internal comfort. They both began to change their own behaviors, and found ways to remain in charge of themselves when their anxiety rose.

The process of defining marital fusion eventually goes back to the family of origin. A focus will develop on each spouse's primary parental triangle. Marriages of grandparents and siblings will be compared. Sometimes there is a very proximate and obvious connection between nuclear and extended family processes so that the transition to extended family focus becomes automatic. Other times something in the extended family will affect the nuclear family, and thus bring the third generation's part in the process into sharp focus. A mother-in-law's input, or a wife's special relationship with her brother will be perceived as increasing the uptightness in the nuclear family; it may be coming out in the marriage, or even have moved down another generational step to the children. A child's functioning must be viewed not only in relation to parents, but also in relation to the extended family. Very often a grandmother and a mother and child are involved in a fairly intense triangle which demonstrates itself by dysfunction in the child.

The last segment of transcript occurs after six months of work. The wife is beginning to give some serious consideration to her relationship with her mother. I am trying here to get Ann to focus on extended family relationships. The tracking process starts with the demonstration of triangulation over three generations as related to the issue of the favorite child, and brings out the ambivalent feelings that Ann has for her mother. Sometimes extended family exploration produces a totally bastardized version of a parent. "You wouldn't even ask me to get into that if you knew my mother." Or it may produce an overidealized whitewashed version—"They were great folks"—but without any detail. Asking a family member to paint a family landscape may help to bypass some of the denial. If denial persists, and layers of semigloss continue to hide the view, then an artful dissection and elaboration by the use of a set of questions developed from clinical experience and theory is most helpful.

Nodal events in this family's life cycle—Ann's sister's marriage, and her stepfather's heart attack—are discussed. Ann talks about her relationship with her mother, and how it shifted so that she became her mother's mother. Questioning her about that experience pinpoints the nodal events around which it happened. Focusing in on these nodal events allows other pieces in the historical process to fall into place so that other occurrences over the years that relate to that particular nodal event begin to make more sense, and the past comes into perspective in relation to the present.

Dr. G.: You said your mother works hard on keeping it impersonal and general with you?

Ann: Hmmmm, yes, especially with Bill around. When Bill's around she has to create this intellectual type of climate.

[This emphasizes the importance of getting each parent alone if anything is going to develop. Otherwise the field is contaminated, and the other people present are easy ways to detour working on the relationship.]

Dr. G.: So she is out to impress Bill?

Ann: Yes.

Dr. G.: And when he is not around, what?

Ann: Oh, well, then she is more herself I guess. She is more on a personal level.

Dr. G.: What would be in the content of the communication then?

Ann: Well, she'll ask how the children are, and I'll start to tell her. Then she gets to talk about things like she tells me how Richie is her favorite, and that she really can't help it, and then I ask her to please try and keep that to herself and not show it to the other two children. I don't think it's a good idea to have a favorite grandchild when you have three, and she knows that I definitely disapprove of something like that.

[Ann begins to develop one aspect of the three-generational triangulation in this family.]

Dr. G.: Do you have some kind of principle that your kids should be equal in the eyes of their grandmother?

[Therapist challenges Ann's position.]

Ann: But, you don't realize, it's not practical.

Dr. G.: Are you trying to protect your kids from not being the favorite or from being the favorite?

Ann: Well, because I was the favorite in my house over my sister, and then I was faced with the same problem myself with the boys and Susan, and I kind of feel it's not a good thing.

[The generational repeat surfaces.]

Dr. G.: How is she going to go around pretending that Richard is not her favorite?

[Therapist continues to challenge.]

Ann: Well, she said it Saturday night in front of him. I kind of appreciated it as something she has been feeling for a long time; and usually she sneaks it in without directly saying it. So Saturday night when she said it, I said, "Why?" She wants to take Richie to the ballet for Christmas, and she doesn't want to take the other two anyplace, and I won't let her do that because I don't feel it's fair. She hasn't taken any of them any place in eight years, and I know that they would really be hurt. So I suggested if you take one someplace that you take the other two too, not necessarily to the same thing, but that you follow up with Eddie and Susan some place. Then she takes Eddie into it and completely leaves Susan out. Then I go through the same thing nicely, you know, I really think it's better to take all three, some time at least. It doesn't have to be all the time.

Dr. G.: What would happen if she took Richard, the kids would start complaining?

[Therapist moves to concretize the process.]

Ann: Yes.

Dr. G.: Eddie and Susan would start complaining that Richard is going on a trip with Grandmother, and she likes Richie better?

Ann: She told Richie that.

Dr. G.: If they complain, tell them to go to your mother. Would they like that?

[Therapist suggests surfacing the process in the family.]

Ann: Susan would.

Dr. G.: What would your mother say if one of them said, hey I hear you like Richie better?

Ann: And she'd say, "Now Ann, you know I didn't mean that. I just felt that Richie is more sensitive, and I can't help that I relate to him a little bit more. He was the first in the family, you know," and all that.

Dr. G.: You tell her, tell Susan that?

Ann: But she really doesn't see him very often. That would really be something, I would really like to see that.

Dr. G.: How are the kids going to get a relationship with their grandmother if you are in the middle directing traffic? Maybe it makes you anxious to get out of the middle, and out of the directors' position?

Ann: I don't know, I'm so confused, I really don't know. After the past couple of weeks, I even thought, how much do I really like my mother? It's the first time, no it's not the first time I ever thought about it, I've thought about it for the past five or seven years. I really don't know how I feel about my mother.

[Ann moves off the kids and into the process between her mother and herself.]

Dr. G.: How much time do you spend just you and her?

Ann: None.

[Therapist concretizes time and space aspects of Ann's relationship with her mother.]

Dr. G.: So there is always somebody else around. How would you work it just to get the two of you alone?

Ann: Well, I'd go out to dinner with her.

Dr. G.: What would that be like?

[Reinforces the idea.]

Ann: I really don't know, I haven't done it, I haven't been alone with my mother I guess for fourteen years.

[More information on distance between Ann and her mother.]

Dr. G.: That's a long time. Is that about how long you've been her mother too functionally?

[The dissection process continues.]

Ann: No.

Dr. G.: How long have you been functionally her mother?

Ann: Five years, six years, maybe something like that.

Dr. G.: How are you going to switch that back?

Ann: I know that's what I started to think about.

Dr. G.: Why did you pick this time to start to think about it?

Ann: I came up with the idea of just how I feel about my mother, and like do I really have deep feeling for her? Do I really? Maybe not. Am I clouded by the last six years or so, if I am being too caring at times and guilty because I don't care enough, don't put myself out enough.

Dr. G.: So it brought in a whole flood of feelings and thoughts and questions.

Ann: Uh huh.

Dr. G.: Have you got the last five or so years put together as to what's going into the thing where you ended up her advisor and counselor and taker-care-of? What's that all about?

Ann: Well, I think it really happened when my father had his first heart attack. Maybe it could even be seven years. It could also be around the time my sister got married and she left. My mother didn't have Jane around once Jane was married. She battles with her all the time, but she didn't have her around as much. She didn't have Jane depending on her as much, maybe it could be that.

[The nodal events surface, and are connected by Ann to the relationship process with her mother.]

Dr. G.: So you would connect it to your stepfather's coronary, and your sister's getting married?

Ann: Yes, I think I could.

Dr. G.: Which happened first?

Ann: Jane's getting married.

Dr. G.: How long after that did your stepfather have his coronary?

Ann: Do you remember, Jim?

Jim: No, I'm very bad about dates and things like that.

Dr. G.: You never connected those two events?

Ann: No.

Dr. G.: Does your stepfather have trouble dealing with your mother when she gets upset?

Ann: I really don't know.

Dr. G.: How would you find out if you wanted to?

[The challenge to continue on the track.]

Now that Ann's thoughts have moved from her children, to her mother's relationship with her children, on to her relationship with her mother, it is time for her to begin to define a self in relation to her family of origin. The goal for the work in the extended family is the same as for the nuclear family—a sense of emotional freedom from her own and her family's automatic emotional responses. To do this Ann must set out to get a one-to-one relationship with each important family member. In her family Ann is the older of two girls. Her mother and father were divorced five years after they were married, when she was five and Jane was four. Her mother then married Bill, and since that time Ann hasn't seen her father. Her mother is the younger of twin girls, followed by a younger sister and then a brother.

First, of course, she had to define what the problems were, and where she and her sister fit into them. How did her mother relate to her and to her sister? Were they adopted by Bill? Did they take his name? What was their relationship with mother and biological father? I found that he had been an alcoholic. I asked Ann what would happen if she looked him up after thirty years. She said that first of all she couldn't do it, because of all the negative stuff. Secondly, it would be disloyal; she wouldn't be able to handle the responses by mother or aunts or sister, and especially by stepfather because of his poor heart. It took several months before she was willing to consider the possibility of connecting with her biological father.

One of the effective questions I asked was, how was she going to get her mother to be her mother again? How could they have an adult-to-adult relationship unless she did manage to get to where her mother was her mother again? I coached her to go to see her stepfather directly when her mother wasn't there, talk about the issue of her biological father, and tell him she was upset about being seen by him as disloyal and ungrateful for all that he had done for her. She did it. Bill said, "I told your mother she hasn't been responsible in not making sure that you knew your father better. So, I think it's a great idea. But expect trouble from your mother and her siblings." Now, the easiest thing in the world when somebody asks you for permission is to say "It's okay with me, but watch out for those other guys." But at least Ann had made meeting her father an open issue.

Then she finally got to the point where she was able to call her father and make a date with him for lunch. They met in a restaurant in midtown Manhattan. Who showed up in the restaurant while they were there? Her mother. Nobody had told her about the meeting. She didn't know Ann was there. She works in Manhattan, but not in the same area. She came into the restaurant, looked around, saw there was a long waiting line, and while Ann sat with her heart in her mouth, then walked out. If you study enough families, you begin to appreciate the power of emotional systems. Crazy things like this happen all the time.

Ann thus had connected with her father; he is a reformed alcoholic who's been married three times. The biggest complication, however, is that he's rich. How was he going to make it up to his two kids?

The response to Ann's contact was negative all around. Furthermore, she learned from her father that her parents had had a clandestine relationship off and on over the thirty years. By connecting with her father, she'd blown this clandestine relationship out into the open. The whole family began to relate to the long-absent father, who became specially close to the younger sister. So Ann, after having done all the work, ended up on the outside. But her mother began to treat Ann as she had when Ann was an adolescent: lots of criticism, lots of shape up. So Ann is definitely no longer her mother's mother.

The issue of sex in their relationship was a problem that Jim defined as Ann's problem, and that she defined as her problem. I touched on it off and on, but she wasn't ready to tie into it and grab hold. When she wouldn't take a direct symptomatic approach to the sexual issue, I tried to get her into the programmatic approach, asking her where her programming came from about sex, and how it tied into her sexuality in her marriage. She said she didn't know, since her mother was a swinger, still a beautiful woman at 58, who still sees herself as desirable, and who is still active sexually. So it wasn't a hang up from mother. Then she began to wonder if it had to do with grandmother and grandfather. Well, grandfather was called the Colonel, and was a compulsive gambler, which led to the premise that her mother was the counter-positioner to her grandmother's strict position about sex. In fact, grandmother even counter-positioned her as an adolescent into marrying Ann's father. Since Ann had lived in the home with the grandparents, she supposed she had picked up and complied with her grandmother's position about sex.

The older of the twins, Aunt Margaret, had in many ways been the functional mother in Ann's family. She was the responsible older twin; Ann's mother was one who flitted around. She lived off in the midwest, married to a man with a couple of kids from a former marriage. She married only after the grandmother had died, and everybody else in the family was settled except one sister who never married.

Aunt Margaret had been a heavy smoker all her life; she had chronic lung disease, and had also had pneumonia many times. She got sick again and it became clear that her lungs had run their course, and she was dying. Ann went to the midwest and connected with her aunt. She opened up these issues of her father and her relationship with her mother; she also tried to get some information about her grandmother and how that might tie into the sexual thing she was struggling with in her marriage. Margaret got a little bit better, and Ann came home, but a few months later Margaret again ended up in intensive care, and the doctor said that it was probably for the last time. Ann went to see her again, this time with other members of her family. She connected with Margaret in the intensive care unit, and began after that visit to remember how important Margaret had been to her when she was a kid, how when her mother was off having a good time Margaret was always there. Margaret and she were the only ones in the family who open talked about the fact that Margaret was going to die, and they reviewed her life together. Ann went through a difficult time with the other members of her family because of her aunt's obvious response to her as somebody special. Margaret died. Ann came home.

After she was back, she felt different. She felt sexually freer, but she didn't quite understand what it was. Two weeks later, she dreamed she was involved in homosexual activity with a beautiful friend of hers; in the middle of the dream, the friend changed into Aunt Margaret. She woke up in a fright and a cold sweat. In the next three days there was a breakthrough in her sexual relationship with Jim. It was fantastic. He came into the next session with a big smile on his face, and when I said "What's the matter?" he replied, "Wait till we tell you."

What Ann's story has to teach us is how important it is to connect with those who matter to us. However, the people who are moving in have to be in control of their own anxiety, and know what they are doing. If not, they'll raise the anxiety level of the whole system so high there will be a blow up, with all kinds of ensuing havoc. They must have a carefully thought out plan; otherwise the family system will chew them up and spit them back out in the automatic, predictable response to anyone who behaves in a different way, crosses a family boundary line, or breaks some family taboo. As soon as one family member is able to begin to change, it opens up new sets of pathways and new options for the whole system of relationships. Again, any change will be resisted by the system, which will try to push the changing member back into his old position. If you're an overfunctioner, and you begin to underfunction on purpose, the reaction you'll get will be that there's something wrong with you; you don't understand the way things really are, and you had better change back or else. If you're a distancer and begin to move in, you'll be invalidated. If you're an emotional pursuer and you move back and stop your demands, you'll be accused of making those demands anyway, even though you know positively you aren't. That's the way emotional systems operate. And if you can get people to understand their own responsiveness to the system some way, then you make it possible for them to change.

CHAPTER 5

Communication Theory and Clinical Change*

John Weakland

I. "THE READER IS WARNED"—JOHN DICKSON CARR

Titles, like other labels, are often best met with critical wariness, including this one. "Communication Theory and Clinical Change" is accurately descriptive, since I will indeed discuss both communication theory and clinical change—here taken as purposeful intervention into problems on an individual and family scale, although the view involved is also more broadly applicable to human behavior and change. The apparently insignificant little word *and,* however, is perhaps the most important and potentially troublesome part of the title. It indicates, but probably does not adequately caution, that I will here be fundamentally concerned with the relationship between theory and practice. Since family therapy is increasingly a field of *practice,* and theorists and practitioners are, ordinarily, two different and separate breeds, discussion focused on this relationship may seem labored and beside the main point to many family therapists. The matter may be made still worse by the fact that "Communication and Clinical Change" is a large subject to cover in a small compass, requiring severe selection and condensation. Accordingly, detailed information and illustrative examples will be minimal here—though amply available elsewhere (1, 2, 3); rather, I will outline the ideas and relationships I see as most basic, because they are general—not in the sense of "vague," but of "broad relevance."

My aim here, that is, is not to get down to cases, but to get down to basic ideas and how they relate to getting down to cases. But since very different conceptions of communication and family therapy co-exist today, what

---

*Note: The views expressed in this article are the formulation and responsibility of the author individually. Nevertheless, it is certain that they reflect long experience at Mental Research Institute and it is probable that most of the author's Institute colleagues would generally agree with them.

seems basic and clear to the author and some of his colleagues may seem to others interested in theory to be on the wrong track, or to oversimplify complex and serious matters.

In short, the communicative task proposed here, even if it is possible, may be rather fruitless. But let us get on with the attempt, and since the going will be difficult in any case, start with the relationship of theory and practice in general.

II. THEORY AND PRACTICE

Theory has various meanings. As used here, in a broad but particular way, theory refers to whatever general concepts and principles a person holds in connection with some area of knowledge and action—in essence, a view or mental model of some matter. A theory, in this sense, may be less explicit, comprehensive, and systematic than the scientific ideal; indeed, people may even claim their ideas and behavior are atheoretical. Yet even in such cases, a general view or model, often quite systematic and consistent, can usually be readily inferred from a reasonable amount of observation of their behavior—that is, specific actions and related statements. And such a model is always important in understanding the area of behavior to which it relates. It outlines what is taken as important or not important, logical or illogical, to be pursued or to be avoided, even what is possible or impossible. That is, we do not think and act in direct relation to reality, but in relation to some theory, view, or model—the term chosen is not important —of reality. Accordingly, any theory held, whether it is explicit or implicit, simple or complex, neatly organized or a melange of bits and pieces, has important practical consequences. To take an obvious example, if a therapist believes pathology is located within an individual, he may prescribe drugs or do analytic work, but he will not practice family therapy; this would not "make sense." And despite common complaints about the illogicality of human behavior, it seems more generally the case that people, including therapists, do behave logically in terms of their own premises— often, when the premises are questionable, all too logically, whatever the outcome.

It is, of course, common knowledge that theory can and has obscured as well as clarified, has caused difficulty as well as been helpful. Many and varied examples of this exist in history generally and the history of science in particular. In our own field, the family therapy movement itself has in considerable part arisen out of criticism of theories of individual psychopathology and treatment.

It would appear, though, that theory is apt to promote difficulty or error in practice not because of its inherent nature—and in any case practice necessarily involves theory as defined here—but primarily under certain circumstances: 1) When theory is neglected—usually by being left largely implicit. Then it is more difficult to make any critical examination of the kind of premises held, or of their consistency, or any comparison of expectations with observable events. 2) When theory is exalted—taken not as a useful view and tool, but as "reality" or at least a close approach to this ideal goal. Then theory tends to become an ultimate standard according to which all else must be decided, done, and judged. 3) It is curious to note that these two apparent opposites are both likely to occur in relation to the same situation—the downgrading of the immediate data of observations and statements from primary to secondary importance, and a corresponding elevation of interpretation, as the means to some deeper and more profound knowledge. In the one case, this usually involves emphasis on the clinician's empathy or intuition; that is, special personal insight that is not open to being challenged. In the other, theory reached via elaborate constructs and chains of inference becomes so grand and complex that if any discrepant data appear, these often are easily explained away or incorporated by further theoretical elaboration of similar kind, rather than revising and simplifying the theory (4).

On the view of theory stated earlier, no theory can be complete or perfect. A theory by this definition is a simplification, a tool for use in facilitating understanding and action (including transmission of ideas and techniques to others), and therefore is to be judged only by the results of its use. Generally, however, it appears best to have one's theory made as explicit as possible, and as simple and as closely related to data of direct observations as the subject of interest permits. The basic ground for this preference is that the terms and implications of such a theory, and its results in use, can be most readily subjected to critical survey.

In the more specific situation where one is involved, as we all are, in acting in some field as a practitioner, the importance of considering the relationship between theory and practice only becomes intensified—since professional work specifically implies deliberate behavior and operational expertise based on some general understanding. And what this understanding is, the view held of the field, largely determines what actions will be taken, the results of these actions, and even their evaluation.

Our own field, for instance, might be most broadly defined as concerned with dealing professionally with human events and actions that—being seen as strange, deviant, or destructive—present problems either to others, or to the actor himself. The corresponding basic questions are: What is the nature of such situations? What is their cause? What should be done about them? Historically among laymen and professionals there have been two main lines of explanation for such difficult or puzzling human situations, both for individuals and for groups of persons seen collectively—general views, with variations on each theme. On the one hand, human events and especially problems have been seen as the consequence of powerful impersonal forces, external to the realm of human behavior. Such forces may be supernatural, physical, or even social in so broad a sense as to be not personal—fate, God's will or demons, climate or geography, the economic system. To this class of large and powerful forces, in our day might be added certain minute but powerful factors, such as microbes and drugs.

Alternatively, human problems have been seen as the consequence of inherent personal factors—physical, mental, or moral attributes character-istic of an individual, or of a group of individuals, that determine their bad or mad behavior. And in some instances, such as with climate and racial character, or genetic theories of behavior, these two broad lines of interpre-tation may overlap.

These broad theories have correspondingly broad implications and ex-pectable consequences which often are similar despite the apparent polarity of the two views. On the *nature* of human problems, both are concretistic. That is, they lead to seeing problems in an external and isolated way, apart from the viewer and from the flow of his ordinary life, as separate phenomena, existing in themselves. Correspondingly, the nature of such a problem is apt to be seen as rather plain or self-evident. The important question is then not its *what,* but its *why.* As to *cause,* such isolated and external viewing of problems is naturally accompanied by simple linear cause-effect theories; at the extreme (but a common extreme), "What is *the* cause of this problem?" Also, the cause is predefined as external to the person or persons defining the problem. The cause is "out there" in the external world, or in someone else, except—which is hardly a real exception —when it is in me, but not of me: I am doing something, but only involun-tarily. Finally, there are corresponding implications about the *handling* of problems. To the idea of a single ultimate cause, there corresponds a search for overall or final solutions. The impersonal forces view leads either toward resigned acceptance—"Nothing can be done"—or to a call on some other external and higher power—God, a leader or science—for a major coun-tereffort. The "someone is bad or mad" view may also lead to helpless pessimism, but it is more apt to lead to some combination of blame plus attempts, either hostile or supposedly benevolent, to change that other someone or ones, usually in a major way.

Of course there are human difficulties for which one of these views may be most appropriate, such as the kinds of concrete and practical difficulties immediately consequent on storm or earthquake, economic depression, accident, or sudden physical illness. But the problems people typically bring to psychotherapists are not like these. Clinical problems may arise out of such concrete difficulties, although more often no striking or dramatic origin is apparent; but in either case what is characteristic is helplessness, manifested either by inaction or confused activity, in the face of persisting difficulties that are escalating or have reached an impasse.

Here a model of problems based on the idea of communication and interaction may be more appropriate. Certainly such a model is fundamentally different in focus and implications from both of the views outlined above. From such a view, problems are seen as primarily involving ongoing behavior and interaction between persons in some system of social relationships. The relevant questions concern *what* is going on, which is not taken as self-evident; *how* does this continue when people want things to be different; and *how* can the functioning of the system be altered for the better, though no solution will be final or perfect? All this is abstract and general, but has profound human implications. Problems are not conceived as separate, but on a human scale related to everyday behavior, and as interactive, a matter of joint responsibility: "All in it together" rather than "sick versus well" or "bad versus good" or "wrong versus right." While this spreads the burden of dealing with problems, it also implies a spreading of any gains. A joint enterprise has potential mutual benefits, rather than winners versus losers.

But this is only a broad outline of a view, a conception to be tested by its usefulness. In order even to approach such critical appraisal, it is necessary next to pursue matters much further—to indicate, at the least, how this view developed, to spell out its terms in more detail, and to state more specifically what such a view leads to in practice.

III. COMMUNICATION THEORY—DEVELOPMENT AND DELINEATION

Even the very general communicative view just sketched, let alone the specifics to be added shortly, did not spring into being fullblown, like Venus from the sea-foam. Rather, the view being presented here represents a distillate of a long developmental process involving a variety of interrelated observations and ideas. A brief account of this development may be useful in two ways. For a more extensive account, from a somewhat different viewpoint, see (5).

In the first place, a view of the circumstances out of which this view of communication and interaction arose may help clarify and delimit what we are talking about more concretely than formal definition alone can. Communication has become a catchword and a catch-all. It means one thing to people interested in the mass media. It means another to communications engineers, who are largely concerned with clear and economical transmission of rather simple messages. And it means a variety of different, usually ideal, things to patients who complain about "poor communication" as a family problem—or even to various family therapists hoping to promote "good" communication. All these are different from our primary concern with the nature of observable face-to-face communication, verbal and non-verbal, among members of a family or other ongoing social group, and its significance for the shaping of actual behavior.

In the second place, a developmental account gives further perspective on the relation of practice and theory by presenting a concrete example of how the interaction of a few basic ideas and a variety of exploratory observations led to the present view of communication, problems, and their handling, which is quite different from the view of problems and therapy held originally, and may be expected to alter further in the future. This developmental summary may appear somewhat disorderly. In this also it reflects an actual relationship between theory and practice, rather than the fitting of events to a myth. In a view common among scientists as well as laymen, science develops according to an orderly scheme, involving the formulating of hypotheses based on existing knowledge, testing these out empirically, affirming or altering the hypothesis in line with the results, and repeating the process. This may be so somewhere. It is not how communication theory and family therapy grew up in close relationship, at least in Palo Alto, to which this account mainly refers. One thing did lead to another, but not in so orderly and planned a way. Certainly at times, theory—a systematized view—was distilled from practice *post facto,* rather than leading to it, although the converse did occur at other times, if often not altogether clearly and deliberately.

The beginning of this present view of communication and interaction may be referred—as always, somewhat arbitrarily—to Gregory Bateson's research project on communication. This began in late 1952, and involved Jay Haley, John Weakland, William F. Fry, Jr., and later Don D. Jackson. Initially, there was nothing specifically clinical about this research, though it was housed in the Palo Alto VA Hospital. Rather, it was broadly concerned with communication in general, and especially with communicational paradoxes. For example, Epimenides the Cretan says, "All Cretans are liars." If he is telling the truth, he must be a liar, and vice versa. Drawing on the idea of Logical Types, which Whitehead and Russell had developed and used in *Principia Mathematica* to explain certain contradictions in mathematics, such paradoxes were seen as related to the existence of multiple levels of abstraction in language. This simple but basic idea was kept in mind while examining a wide variety of actual communication, ranging from the conversation between a ventriloquist and his dummy to the play of otters observed in the zoo. The otter studies led to the conclusion that even animals must be able to give classificatory or framing messages equivalent to "What I am doing is play," and this led from the original idea of multiple levels of abstraction to the view that, in human communication especially, there is no such thing as a simple message. Instead, people are always sending and receiving a multiplicity of messages, by both verbal and nonverbal channels, and these messages necessarily modify or qualify one another.

That is, not only must all messages be interpreted, but the significance of any message singled out for attention cannot be determined from that message alone. It always depends also on how it is qualified—modified, reinforced, contradicted, specially framed ("When you call me that, *smile!*"), or whatever—by other simultaneous, preceding, or following messages. These (along with the setting, the relationship between the communicating parties, and so on) form part of the *context* which must be considered in interpreting any such message.

Moreover, the significance of a message is not just a matter of meaning, in the sense of information, but of behavioral influence. There is some message that indicates whether it is a serious bite or a playful nip, but this also largely determines whether more play or a fight will be the response. It is, of course, no discovery to note that messages can affect behavior; this is only common knowledge. It is an important further step, however, to insist that rather than *some* messages being informative and some directive, *all* messages have the two aspects labeled in the earlier work of Ruesch and Bateson (6) as report and command. This key idea has been elaborated and discussed in other terms as well, including the expressive and effective aspects of messages, information and influence, and content and process in communication. Regardless of the specific terminology, this served to focus attention on the pervasiveness of communicational influence, which may be most important to note and understand precisely when it is complex, subtle, indirect or covert, rather than obvious. Another important idea was the recognition that unlike physical influence, in which a passive object is moved by and in proportion to the magnitude of an external force, communicational influence operates by activating and directing the energy of the receiver of a message. Therefore, small signals may easily have large effects, and still further multiplication of effect can occur when one signal frames the interpretation of many others, as often occurs. For these two reasons, then, the potential importance of communicational influence on behavior is great, and should never be neglected.

The project next took its first step from concern with communication in general toward involvement with clinical matters, by beginning to examine the communication of schizophrenics, being surrounded by this fascinating material in our VA Hospital setting. Schizophrenic speech (like their "crazy" behavior) was then generally thought to be incomprehensible nonsense. But the matter began to look quite different when actual samples were tape-recorded for repeated study and examined in context, with attention not just on the schizophrenic's words in isolation, but also on those of the interviewer, and the institutional environment as well. A new view was also promoted by having in mind our prior insight that most communication does not consist of simple declarative statements (an ideal of normality to which schizophrenic talk ordinarily was implicitly compared), but of a complex of mutually qualifying messages, including some which indicate how others should be interpreted—again, whether as a serious bite or a playful nip. This, too, is not really a new idea. Everyone knows that there are humorous, ironic, sarcastic, playful, and other kinds of messages as well as simple factual statements. But this knowledge had not been applied to schizophrenic communication, presumably because this, defined as "crazy," was viewed as separate and different in kind. Once we began to examine it in the same way as other communication, using the same general ideas, it appeared that if regarded as metaphoric in style—only lacking in the usual signs of metaphor, such as "It's like . . ." or the use of conventional, familiar metaphors—much schizophrenic speech, otherwise unintelligible, made comprehensible sense. Even this lack of clear interpretative signs might be explained by considering that hospitalized patients could well be cautious and defensive, like members of the underworld relying on their private argot.

These notions received further support when we found that if we responded to patients' statements as metaphorical—instead of the common response of taking them literally, and trying to get the patient to acknowledge their illogic or unreality, a covert form of arguing with the patient—they then spoke more plainly. Different communication led to different communication. Somewhere along the line we began to see, perhaps aided by our prior insight that report and command are matters of analytic distinction rather than separate kinds of messages, that communication and behavior are not separate and different, but essentially the same thing viewed from different perspectives. Communication occurs only through the observation and interpretation of behavior, while all behavior in the presence of another is potentially communicative. (As a special case, one person can be both sender and receiver.) Which aspect is emphasized or seen as primary is only a matter of the point of view and purpose of the observer at a given moment.

In short, one thing had led to another until at this stage the research was already pursuing the study of the relationship of communication and behavior into the realm of "pathological" communication and behavior. But it was doing so on the basis of the same ideas about the complexity of communication, and its related ubiquitous, powerful, and complex behavioral influence as before, and with similar methods of close observation and study. That is, we were conceptually treating the abnormal the same as the normal, and moving progressively toward explaining things positively by inclusion—how does schizophrenic speech make sense in relation to speech in general—rather than negatively and by exclusion—how is it "illogical." Although this is a basic principle in scientific explanation, the principle is often breached in dealing with the abnormal, which is set apart, beyond the pale. In avoiding this, we were helped by the anthropological background of some of the research team. Anthropologists have traditionally been involved in the task of making sense out of apparently strange or bizarre behavior by viewing it in relation to other behavior, building up a view of a patterned whole within which each item has an understandable place and function. In any event, although many of our basic ideas were not novel, we were now involved in pursuing them toward wider limits: Just how much and what kinds of behavior (in the widest sense, including speech, actions, feelings, even bodily functioning) might be understood and accounted for on a basis of communicational influence, before having recourse to other avenues of explanation such as instincts or other genetic factors, biochemistry, early childhood events, or whatever? This line of inquiry, in fact, is still far from exhausted.

With our new view of the nature of schizophrenic communication, we next approached the question, "How is it that patients communicate in this fashion?" One part of our answer to this is implicit in what was said about the hospital context—quite possibly, such speech serves a defensive or protective function. Our other concern was with how schizophrenics might *learn* to communicate in such a way—essentially, "To what pattern of communication would such speech be an appropriate response, in some sense?" This also arose naturally out of our anthropological background, since by training and experience anthropologists commonly look for how behavior is learned in structured contexts of social interaction.

This inquiry about learning was pursued in part speculatively, by applying general knowledge about learning principles and multiple levels of messages to our characterization of schizophrenic speech; and in part by further empirical study. Since we had no way to reliably observe the past communicative background of our subjects, we started with what was directly observable, the communication of currently schizophrenic patients with their family members, especially young adult patients and their parents. Again this involved tape-recording and repeated close study. Out of such work came the concept of the "double-bind" (7), which described schizophrenic speech and other symptomatic behavior as a response to incongruent messages of different levels, within an important relationship, and where both escape from the field and comment on the incongruity were blocked. In the present context, the details of this formulation are less important than its general nature (8), which is an attempt to produce a communicational explanation of crazy behavior by relating it to an identifiable pattern of communication within the family system from a functional view—that is, how the patient's behavior fits in and makes a certain kind of sense within a certain peculiar but observable communicational context.

In fact, things seemed to fit together so well in the here and now that we felt little need to move back toward the preschizophrenic days of the patient and family. Rather, our focus on the present system increased as we studied the interaction of schizophrenics and their families. Up to this stage, we had mainly studied dyadic interaction. Even in this, it had soon become evident that ordinary distinctions between "sender" and "receiver," or "stimulus" and "response" were also analytic artifacts, essentially a matter of imposing punctuation on an ongoing system of communicative interaction. Since we describe and explain mainly by means of language, which involves discrete units and linear structure, such punctuation may be analytically useful or necessary. Certainly, it is important to recognize that the participants in any system of interaction regularly impose similar punctuation (which could also be seen as a larger scale example, applied to sequences, of that interpretation which is always involved in communication), and in ways that can be of major practical importance. For instance, many clinical problems involve punctuation directly paralleling that very commonly seen in children's quarreling: "You started it!" ("I'm only reacting to what you did.") "No, you started it first!" From a broader viewpoint, however, such punctuation, as well as being a source of conflict, is inaccurate and inappropriate. There is no "starting point" in an ongoing stream of interaction; the simple linear model of cause and effect is not appropriate. When we began to examine the more complex, yet highly patterned and repetitive interaction occurring in families, it became even clearer that the relevant epistemological model is one derived not from mechanics, but from cybernetics, where the focus is on the structure of interaction within some ongoing system.

Rather than pursuing our family studies into the preschizophrenic past, then, if this were possible, we concentrated on present functioning, and rapidly also became involved in looking toward the future. That is, motivated both by positive hopes, and by feeling the danger of being engulfed into their system while interviewing such families, we began attempts to change the going system in schizophrenic families for the better. These attempts were also promoted by observations that hospitalized patients who improved with individual treatment and were sent home often soon reappeared for further hospitalization, as well as by some early experience of Dr. Jackson with various members of patients' families.

This, then, was the beginning of family therapy in Palo Alto based on a communicational view of behavior (9). (At about the same time, of course, various others were also beginning to work with families from a variety of backgrounds in experience and viewpoint.) While neither our ideas nor our related techniques were fully and clearly formulated at this point, they appeared promising. And it was only a modest and natural next step—especially since schizophrenia was both a most difficult problem and one whose varied manifestations seemed to include much that was also characteristic of other kinds of clinical problems—to explore the relevance and use of family therapy as a general treatment approach. Where this has led, in terms of clinical practice and related theory, can now be described.

IV. PROBLEMS, PERSISTENCE, AND CHANGE

The communicational view of behavior and related ways of dealing with problems developed gradually, with one thing leading to another, and action at times preceding formulation. In addition, some ideas—and certainly many specific terms—that were important or necessary as part of this development in retrospect no longer have the same importance. Put bluntly, a sizable part of our work on communication now appears related to digging ourselves out of individual-centered, depth-psychological views of behavior, problems, and therapy in which we originally were imbedded, rather than to any elaborate creation of new views. Once perceived, the ideas about communication and behavior basic to a communicational approach to treatment appear as rather few and rather simple, if not obvious. This, of course, is not to say there are no difficulties involved in sticking to these ideas in areas where one has learned well to understand matters in another way, or in applying them in specific, often apparently chaotic or confusing situations.

The two central ideas—of equal importance and closely interrelated—from which all else logically flows are: 1) that specific behavior of all kinds is primarily an outcome or function of communicative interaction within a social system; and 2) that "problems" consist of persisting undesired behavior.

On this view, unless there exists clear and clearly relevant evidence—not just a possibility, or ambiguous signs—of some other significant causal factor such as organic pathology, observed behavior should be considered as structured and maintained primarily by current communicative interaction within some ongoing system of social relationships. This means *all* behavior, good or bad, voluntary or involuntary, normal or pathological. Indeed, if anything, this view should be applied most deliberately to unusual or abnormal behavior, for it is behavior labeled as such that most needs explanation—as a therapist once told an inquisitive patient, "Neither you nor I need to explain what is normal"—and that is most apt to be explained by different and special means. The relevant system of interaction is usually the family, but other systems such as school or work organizations may be important in some cases.

Clearly, this view puts an emphasis on observable communication—statements and actions—in the here and now. Similarly, the kinds of problems that people bring to therapists are seen as matters of currently persisting (or worsening) difficult, deviant, or symptomatic behavior. (Transient behavior may be unpleasant, but nothing need be done about it; by definition, it will pass.) Two closely related but distinguishable elements are involved in this: the more or less objectively observable behavior, and how it is judged and labeled by the patient or others associated with him. This distinction is important because in some cases—for instance, parents' overanxious concern about ordinary childish mischief—the judgment, more than the behavior it labels, makes the problem. In either case, though, we see the problem as one of interpersonal behavior—what is being done, or how something is being labeled—neither as something more internal and personal, nor more external and impersonal.

This view of the nature of behavior and problems has several immediate and profound implications for treatment. First, the question, "What is wrong with this particular patient?" is largely irrelevant. This question is based on an individualistic view of problems, while from a communicational viewpoint the relevant question is, "What is going on in the system of interaction that produces the behavior seen as a problem?" or "How does this behavior fit in?"

Second, the concern common in many treatment approaches, "What is the *underlying* problem?" also is not relevant. If behavior is seen as primary, this "tip of the iceberg" idea no longer makes sense. Rather, the behavior complained of (or perhaps, as mentioned, its labeling as something requiring change) is the primary focus of treatment. This is not to say that other related behaviors may not need attention from the therapist. In fact, the communicational view clearly implies that the problem behavior must be considered in relation to other behavior. Nor does it mean that feelings, or past traumatic experience, for example, are simply to be neglected. It does mean that such factors are to be considered in relation to present behavior, not as somehow deeper or more fundamental, and are to be dealt with by appropriate changes in present behavior.

Somewhat similarly, the search for a root or original cause of any problem is foreign to the communicational view. This presumes a linear view of causality: A causes B, which then causes C. Such a view also subtly influences one to seek a cause corresponding in magnitude to the eventual problem. For instance: Schizophrenia is a dread syndrome, so somewhere behind it there must be great trauma, genetic deficiencies, biochemical abnormality—something big. But the picture is quite different on a cybernetic epistemology, which a view based on communication and interaction directly implies, and which indeed constitutes the most basic and general difference between interactional and individualistic approaches. From a cybernetic view, attention is focused on the structure of the system of interaction, and especially on its feedback loops. And where there is positive feedback—more of A leads to more of B, which leads to more of A, and so on—large effects can readily arise from minimal initial events. In more ordinary terminology, problems arise by snowballing, or vicious circles (10, 11). Similarly, though this has received less consideration and investigation, the cybernetic epistemological view also raises the possibility that there may be no necessary or close relationship between the origin of a problem and its particular nature as ordinarily conceived—that is, the "diagnosis." For both size and shape of problems, any original precipitating event or difficulty may be of minor importance, and how it was dealt with in the environing system the main thing.

From this point of view, for the fullblown problems that reach therapists' offices, the central question is not one of origins, but one of organization and persistence: "What behaviors in the ongoing system of interaction are functioning, and how, to maintain the behavior seen as constituting the problem?" This also fits with the idea that problems consist of behavior; that is, a problem is not something that simply exists in itself, a passive concrete object, but something that exists only in continuous or repeated performance. Furthermore, such a view centers on matters open to current inquiry, with a minimum of inference about unobservable past or intrapsychic events. For example, if a person says "isolation" is a problem, it is highly pertinent to consider how he behaves to avoid other people and to keep them from making contact with him, and to inquire, of course judiciously, about this.

Finally, at this general level, the resolution of problems correspondingly appears as primarily requiring a change of the problem-maintaining behaviors so as to interrupt the vicious positive feedback circles, and the therapist's main task as promoting such changes. Such alternative behaviors are always potentially open to the patient and other members of the system, but ordinarily it is not possible for them to change their usual but unsuccessful problem-solving behaviors on their own; those who can, do so, and therefore do not reach our offices. The therapist's job, accordingly, is to find and apply means of intervention that will help them make such changes, and the test of both specific interventions and the general approach is highly pragmatic: Do beneficial changes occur?

This outlined interactional approach to problems and treatment is clearly different from that of individual psychodynamic therapy, but the principles stated are still broad and general. A number of rather different views of family interaction and techniques of family therapy, involving different explicit or implicit emphases on structure, on good versus bad communication, on process versus content, and so on could largely fit with these principles. Discussion of such variants would be too lengthy here, and perhaps confusing. Instead, only the particular approach developed by MRI's Brief Therapy Center will be specifically described. The members of the Center see this particular approach as exemplifying a further refinement, boiling-down, and direct application of the most essential principles of the communicational view—though others, of course, may see it as a departure from the classic mold of family therapy.

Two further specifications of views already stated are important in the Center's approach and practice. First, while the origin of problems is not a vital question on the communicational view, one important aspect of the genesis of problems seems related to the crucial question of problem maintenance. In our experience, it appears that the problems brought to therapists commonly arise from difficulties of everyday life that have been mishandled by the parties concerned. Although such difficulties may at times involve special or unusual events—accidents, sudden illness, unexpected job loss— most commonly they involve adaptation to an ordinary life change or transition, such as marriage, childbirth, entering school, and so on. The mishandling involved may range from ignoring or denying difficulties on which action should be taken, to attempts to actively resolve difficulties that need not or cannot be resolved, with a wide area between where action is needed but the wrong kind is taken. Bad handling certainly does not correct, and usually increases, the original difficulty, which is then apt to be relabeled as a "problem," which is usually met by more of the same or similar inappropriate handling, leading to exacerbation or spread of the difficulty —and so on and on. That is, instead of viewing the cause and the nature of any problem as separate and different, we see the same essential process involved in problem formation as in problem maintenance. Rather similarly, we do not sharply separate chronic from acute problems, but see chronic ones as merely involving mishandling for a longer time. In short, the central focus of this view is not on difficulties as such—life is full of these, even for the most normal—but on their handling, for better or for worse.

Second, though quite consonant with the first point, our clinical observations indicate that usually it is precisely the ways people are trying to handle or resolve their problems that constitute or include those behaviors which are maintaining the problem in question. This of course is unrecognized by the participants in a problem situation. While we recognize that there are some payoffs from any system of interaction, even one full of problems, we do not see these as central in problem maintenance, nor as any major obstacle to change. The situation is not that bad—though in a way it is worse. Rather, our view is that people generally are well-intentioned and trying to improve things as best they know how; but what they see as the right and logical thing to do in the circumstances—often the *only* right thing and often supported by prevailing cultural views—is not working. The therapist's job, then, is apt to be the unenviable task of getting people to change that which they are apt to be clinging to most strongly. Correspondingly, to produce beneficial results, the therapist may have to promote remedies that might appear quite illogical to those most immediately concerned, and perhaps to many others as well.

Our overall treatment plan and procedures follow directly from these basic principles. Since our treatment focus is symptomatic, in a broad sense, we want first to get a clear statement of the presenting complaint, in terms of the specific, concrete behavior involved, and how this constitutes a problem. We attempt to get this information primarily by simple means such as direct questions, requests for clarification and examples, and asking for order of importance if a number of complaints are mentioned. Where more than one person is present, we ask each to state the main problem as he sees it, assuming their views may differ.

Next, we ask in a similar concrete way what the patient and any involved others are doing to try to handle the problem, based on our view that problems only persist if somehow maintained by other behavior, and that the locus of this ordinarily lies in peoples' efforts to deal with or resolve the problem. In our experience, when specific information on problem handling is obtained, and is considered in this light, problem-maintaining behavior often appears rather evident. For instance, it does not take any special skill, but just some objectivity and perspective, to see that the person with a sexual problem who works at performance is likely to make things worse rather than better by seeking to do the spontaneous voluntarily; or that the parents who tell a truant child what a wonderful experience and opportunity school offers are producing alienation rather than compliance. In some cases, of course, problem-maintaining reinforcements may be more difficult to perceive. They may be more complex or subtle; they may involve contradictory messages by the same or different persons; or the therapist's own accepted views about sensible behavior may obscure his observation of actual interaction and its effects.

Third, we ask all parties involved to state their minimal goal of treatment—that is, what observable behavioral change, at the least, would signify some success in the therapy. This is a difficult question for most patients to answer concretely, but an important one. Just to pose it conveys that change is possible, that it should be judged by observable behavior, and that small changes can be significant. According to our cybernetic view, if a small but significant change can be made in what appeared a major and hopeless problem, this is likely to initiate a beneficial circle and lead on to more progress. In contrast, pursuing vague or global goals is apt to lead only to uncertainty and frustration.

In addition to these three specific questions, two other matters are important from the outset, although information on these is gained more from close attention than direct inquiry. It is important to decide who is the main client—the "customer" for treatment. This means the person who most wants to see real change in the problem situation, usually because he or she is most concerned or hurting from it. This need not be the identified patient, or the person who makes the initial contact with the therapist. A wife may call to arrange an appointment for a drinking husband, or parents bring in a child who is failing in school. In such cases, unless the identified patient clearly indicates he personally is seriously concerned about the behavior in question, which often is not the case, we would if possible arrange to work primarily with the complainant—the wife or the parents. If one takes the idea of interaction in systems seriously, it follows that effective intervention can be made through any member of the system. Family therapy in this view does not consist of having everyone present in the therapist's office (although this may at times be desirable for information gathering or strategic purposes), but in working from an interactional *viewpoint*. And usually intervention can be most effectively made with the chief complainant, the person concerned enough to do something different.

For a similar reason, we attempt as soon as possible to grasp each client's "language"—the ideas and values that appear central to him. If people are to be moved to change their behavior, especially rapidly and in regard to behavior they believe is already logical and right, the therapist must perceive and utilize existing motivations and beliefs. Otherwise, his advice, however good, is likely to be ignored or opposed.

Once these inquiries and observations have been made, the therapist plans a related treatment strategy. That is, he concisely formulates the main presenting problem, and judges what behaviors are most central in maintaining it. He decides on a goal of treatment, estimating what concrete behavior would be the best sign of appropriate positive change. In all of this he of course takes full account of what the patients and others have said. But since on this view the therapist is an active and deliberate change agent —someone being paid to exert influence expertly and beneficially—the responsibility for final decision is his. Even if his formulations agree with the patient's, it is the therapist who is deciding to proceed on this basis.

Once the goal of treatment is determined, the therapist must consider intermediate steps, and the means to achieve them. What changes in the behavior of the patient, or others involved in the problem, are needed to approach the goal; and what interventions might be effective in promoting these changes? In general, the therapist will aim to interdict the problem-maintaining behaviors he perceives. The substitution of opposite behaviors for these will often be promoted, both to insure appropriate and adequate change, and because it is difficult for anyone just to stop doing something.

And since patients are already doing what they consider right, such changes can only rarely be accomplished by giving direct behavioral instructions on what to avoid or what to do. Instead, effective intervention usually requires reframing. That is, the problem situation must be redefined in such a way that the original motivations and beliefs of the persons involved now lead toward quite different behavior.

Beyond this, intervention rapidly becomes too particular a matter to be pursued further here. There is no "good intervention" as such; what is effective and useful always depends on the circumstances of the particular case. Of course this is true of every aspect of actual practice. One must get down to particulars, and often in difficult circumstances, with people who are confused, anxious, angry, or dogmatic. Even in the first and simplest matter of inquiring what the problem is, practical difficulties may arise, and special techniques or interventions may be needed just to get necessary basic information.

More has been said about the practice of change elsewhere (2, 12), and despite its importance, this is not the main focus here. Rather, I have outlined a communicational view of behavior and problems, to show how certain general principles and procedures relate to this view—a framework for guiding and evaluating the more specific thought and action that practice necessarily involves.

REFERENCES

1. Paul Watzlawick, Janet H. Beavin, and Don D. Jackson. *Pragmatics of Human Communication: A Study of Interactional Patterns, Pathologies, and Paradoxes.* New York: Norton, 1967.
2. Paul Watzlawick, John H. Weakland, and Richard Fisch. *Change: Principles of Problem Formation and Problem Resolution.* New York: Norton, 1974.
3. Paul Watzlawick, and John H. Weakland (eds.). *The Interactional View: Studies at the Mental Research Institute, 1965–1974.* In press.
4. Thomas S. Kuhn. *The Structure of Scientific Revolutions.* Chicago: University of Chicago Press, 1962.
5. Jay Haley. "Development of a Theory: The Rise and Demise of a Research Project," in Carlos E. Sluzki and Donald Ransom (eds.), *Double Bind: The Foundation of the Communicational Approach to the Family.* New York: Grune and Stratton, 1976.
6. Jurgen Ruesch, and Gregory Bateson. *Communication: The Social Matrix of Psychiatry.* New York: Norton, 1951.
7. Gregory Bateson, Don D. Jackson, Jay Haley, and John H. Weakland. "Toward a Theory of Schizophrenia," *Behavioral Science,* 1 (1956), 251–64.
8. John H. Weakland. " 'The Double-Bind Theory' by Self-Reflexive Hindsight," *Family Process,* 13 (1974), 269–77.
9. Don D. Jackson, and John H. Weakland. "Conjoint Family Therapy: Some

Considerations on Theory, Technique, and Results," *Psychiatry,* 24 (1961), 30–45.

10. Magoroh Maruyama. "The Second Cybernetics—Deviation Amplifying Mutual Causative Processes," *American Scientist,* 51 (1963), 164–79.

11. Paul H. Wender. "Vicious and Virtuous Circles: The Role of Deviation Amplifying Feedback in the Origin and Perpetuation of Behavior," *Psychiatry,* 31 (1968), 309–24.

12. John H. Weakland, Richard Fisch, Paul Watzlawick, and Arthur M. Bodin. "Brief Therapy: Focused Problem Resolution," *Family Process,* 13 (1974), 141–68.

CHAPTER 6

A Theoretical Framework for Family Group Therapy

John Elderkin Bell, Ed.D.

INTRODUCTION

I have been trying to think sensibly about family therapy for a long time, and am still at it, as my ideas and family work change. Now I see family therapy as a primary option available to me when I want to use direct intervention with a family like the majority, where most interpersonal problems are solved within the family, but where occasionally a point of critical difficulty in taking a next step into the future is reached. At such time, I use a family group therapy method, first formulated twenty-five years ago, and in development ever since. I conceive of this therapy as a structured effort, made by the family and me as the therapy group. Our joint aim is to establish interrelations within this therapy group so as to achieve functional social adaptations within the family. My model for this approach is drawn from two sources—direct experiences in family group therapy, and social-psychological experiments and thought about how small groups develop.

BACKGROUND

From my earliest days in family group therapy, I have tried to summarize my experiences for myself, and to some extent for others. In the beginning I did this privately. I was acutely conscious that the ideas I was trying to formulate challenged previous central ideas about psychotherapy. After I had established my own confidence in the feasibility and functional value of family group treatment, I initiated some efforts to acquaint the professional community with the methods of family therapy.

Soon I began to be confronted by experienced psychotherapists and theoreticians, who disapproved of my practice and were uncomfortable with my concepts. I learned that these critics were not to be won over easily by simple endorsements of working with the whole family, and usually answered their arguments by saying I would take their comments into account, as I did; but I also learned I could not fit older theories to my new experiences. I realized that, fundamentally, I had to find the rationale for family therapy from my own experiences, in private reflections on the actions of which I was a part. As a result, more and more I found myself avoiding the ideas and language of individual therapy and traditional group therapy. I found, also, that the formulations and terms mastered for my university teaching on personality and abnormal psychology had little pertinence to my new activities.

Recognizing the tentativeness of my theories, I kept pointing out to myself the gaps, confusions, irrelevancies, repetitions, pretensions, and many other deficiencies in my efforts at systematization. Continual self-criticism of my theoretical work and recognition of its difficulties also made me uncertain about the adequacy of others' theories, especially those expressed in highly authoritative manners. These doubts still remain, particularly when I hear advocates of certain theoretical positions turning their ideas into the shibboleth to differentiate the "true" family practitioners and believers from adherents to "faulty" notions.

There is no intrinsic validity in including any specifically-designated group in family therapy. There is no preeminent set of therapeutic techniques. There are no particular therapy goals that all therapists should promote. There is no theoretical system for exclusive use in interpreting the experiences within family therapy. Family therapy is based on selection of techniques, goals, and ideas. Because of the selectivity behind any so-called system of family therapy, the assertion of prescriptions for therapy methods, goals, interpretations, and evaluations must remain open to question, especially on the level of the personal factors behind a therapist's selection. So also, concepts to explain what is taking place in the therapy must continue to be subjected to rigorous criticism, and must be expanded continually toward sufficiently comprehensive statements to integrate immediate and process observations of individuals, families, therapists, and social and physical settings.

I am particularly critical of magnifying the importance of concepts relating to part-processes when, arbitrarily or unconsciously, such partial concepts are presented as full-blown theories of family therapy. I can illustrate how elevation of part-process concepts to a general theory of family therapy fails, by citing my previous position (1,2) that in family therapy we are primarily dealing with family communication, an idea, of course, with roots in individual therapy. There, in accordance with my training and common practice, I gave a great deal of attention to analyzing the content of what a patient was communicating to me. Generally accompanying the content analysis was analysis of the interrelations between the patient and me. Content analysis always seemed easier than relational analysis, because the content of what a patient was reporting in psychotherapy was out of the time-frame of the present—that is, it was either retrospective, looking to the past, or anticipatory, in looking to the future. Only what was said directly between the therapist and the patient was in the immediate present; and since the therapist was directly engaged in those interrelations, analyzing them required dropping out for reflection, and re-entering the relations for action.

In contrast, in family therapy, the content of functional speech within family action seemed immediate in its reference, in the here and now, and current in its purposes. It had a liveliness for me that made understanding seem especially cogent, and it continued even when I retreated into reflection. Accordingly, I borrowed and adapted from individual therapy the practice of making interpretations, especially about the content of what the family members were saying to one another. This seemed a functional method, appropriate for explaining and modifying the communication within the family and therefore I engaged in efforts to analyze the content of family communications, and to generalize from them.

Interesting as these therapeutic interpretations and theoretical reflections were to me, and, to some extent, to other professionals, they proved therapeutically unproductive. Also, communication analysis was a disappointment as a basis for fruitful generalizations about families. Any conclusions it led to were largely incapable of characterizing the families who were in therapy, or differentiating them from those outside therapy. The statements could not separate those families who succeeded in family therapy from those who failed; nor did they discriminate between families with similar or different compositions, identical or unusual problems, common or unique modes of interaction, and varying behaviors in therapy sessions. Without denigrating the importance of communication, I came to realize that it was not the primary process.

It was only when I had been working in family therapy for a long time that I came to use the term *functional action* for what I was observing within a family, and to stress the operation of purposes or motivations, evaluations, resolutions and decisions, interpersonal adjustments, rehearsals, and other elements of the total action processes. I then recognized communication as a part process within the extensive action framework, a mediational process of great importance as such, but not an end for the family. That is, for most families communication is not primarily a goal for its own sake; it is sought as a tool for the reaching of the family's distinctive end goals. Similarly, I came to see that dramatic as the explosions of hostile feelings and revelations of affection are during the course of the therapy, their exposure is only a step within the action toward family-directed goals.

A comparable change occurred in the development of techniques. In the beginning, I was inclined to value family therapy extremely highly, and to regard its future as dependent on its power to solve all family problems. Increasing technical skill allowed me to be more effective in treatment, but did not insure the success I expected. I learned from my successes, but I was instructed by my failures; therapeutic successes are emotionally satisfying, but in the long run not nearly as productive or clarifying as study of therapeutic failures.

When I began to be realistic about failures, and free to search for effective methods to overcome difficulties with some families, I began to look elsewhere for methods to help families. In my family work, I have traveled to Europe, Asia, Africa, the Pacific Islands, and the countries of North America (3). Everywhere I met families in both casual and planned encounters, learning from them directly that they cannot be defined by a narrow set of specifications. Indeed, quite the opposite is true—the units to which the name *family* is applied vary immensely in composition and behavior, and are changeable over time. Even to communicate about family requires precise description of the unit and the members who compose it at this time and in this place. Generalizations otherwise are panoramic, and thus somewhat indeterminate.

Families in all these many parts of the world taught me the intensity and pervasiveness of problems within them. All are exposed to many vicissitudes, and all, except those severely debilitated by poverty, hunger, disease, and disabilities, seem engaged in efforts to comprehend and overcome the problems they confront.

In addition to internal pressures that may move any specific family toward new actions, ever-new external forces move families toward change, destructive or positive. Some of these forces are accidental, nonpurposive. Some are derivative, the result of physical and social change that are deflected on to families. Some are direct. These last may be nearly global, as in programs for population control; national, as in governmental programs involved in health, education, welfare and housing; or local, as in programs for family life education, planned parenthood, sexual education, nutrition, housing, home decoration and furnishing, and child rearing.

I came to see that family therapy has its place within this general setting of family interventions. Once I placed family therapy within many functional alternatives, I was able to examine it more dispassionately, assess its processes and values more realistically, apply it more selectively, and invent alternatives to it when family therapy could not be the intervention of choice. Out of this background, my present work and ideas have been shaped. I do not present the ideas as a theory, but as a body of concepts, primarily descriptive in form but capable of generating operational procedures for family therapy. The concepts include statements about the processes in therapy, the goals, and the role of the therapist. Specifically excluded are ideas about how families solve their problems. I regard the information available in that respect to be so diffuse that meaningful generalizations cannot yet be achieved, except by the dubious practice of overaccentuating the importance of what is observable in family processes in therapy.

A CONCEPTUAL POSITION FOR FAMILY THERAPY

I now see family therapy as an outgrowth of psychotherapies, using a medical model for its efforts toward change. In contrast, though, I see it as distinctive, in that it aims beyond the treatment of individuals to the treatment of families, and beyond the treatment of the individuals who make up a family to the treatment of the family as a unitary group. The therapist's relations are with the family; the locus of the problems (the center of the pathology) is placed in the family; and the outcomes are to be evaluated in terms of family wellbeing.

I once assumed that the fundamental explanation of how family therapy works would be found in family processes, in information specific to a family in treatment, and in techniques used to deal with the family and promote change. Later, as I struggled to explain how the therapy process could be so similar from family to family, when there were such evident differences among the families I was treating, I came to the insight that the therapy group is not the family, but the larger group made up of the therapist and the family. Furthermore, I recognized that this therapy group —the therapist *plus* the family—is a newly-constructed entity, and therefore I look for parallels with the social psychological study of constructed groups. There I keep finding many ideas that relate to my conceptions of the processes of family therapy, more than are available from sociological and psychological studies of the family. Indeed, the emergent processes in family therapy parallel in striking ways scientific findings about small-group developmental processes.

The Stages of Family Therapy

The therapy group appears to progress through stages comparable to those found in ongoing groups of strangers who are brought together to engage in some common project. I shall list the stages first, then describe them in some detail. The identification of these stages comprises a framework for describing the family therapy. The framework has technical implications; each stage requires practiced therapy methods, which I will not describe here.

1. *Initiation.* In this stage persons—the family and the therapist—are brought together, they explore their individual and group expectations, begin to form relations, and define rules, permissible behaviors, and prohibitions, within which the therapist, the family, and the therapy group as a whole will relate and act.

2. *Testing.* The parameters of the defined social situation are probed, to determine how much and in what ways the participants will adhere to and depart from the definitions of the group membership and modes of functioning.

3. *Struggling for power.* In this stage, individuals and coalitions of persons fight for dominance. They refine their understandings of the circumstances under which persons will assert, capture, and use power.

4. *Settling on a common task.* This is the task toward which the group as a whole, as well as individuals, will concentrate their energies with optimal involvement and purposiveness.

5. *Struggles toward completion of the common task.* With the goals of accommodating the purposes of all, and arriving at a livable resolution of respective goal-demands of each group member, the group as a whole play out their struggles with one another in speech and action.

6. *Achieving completion.* The task is finished and inclusive conciliation is reached among the group participants.

7. *Separating.*

Initiation. The initiation of the therapy group begins with the separate availabilities of the participants. The therapist, through public knowledge of his or her professional competence and general availability, is seen as accessible to a family, even though he or she does not take primary steps to involve them. Most typically, the initiative is taken within the family, commonly by one member, sometimes by more than one, and seldom by the whole family group.

Implicit in a family's seeking, or, under pressure, agreeing to enter therapy, is some expectation that the therapist has skills and methods to enable a family to overcome obstacles to reaching objectives on their own. In a way, then, the admission to therapy is an acknowledgment of diminished or nonexisting capacities, techniques, and resources to solve problems or reach family goals.

The initiative is sometimes provoked or promoted by persons outside the family; ultimately, however, it must be adopted by at least one person within the family in order to lead to a face-to-face meeting with the therapist. Once this happens, a series of steps follow, some taken by the family members, some by the therapist, and most taken jointly. All steps are oriented toward establishing a structure and determining the modes by which the therapy group may interrelate. Typically, the therapist and the family representatives together determine who shall attend group sessions. The therapist provides the basic definition of his or her role and functions, and, with the assurance derived from experience, sets forth the rules for the therapy. Some of the rules are directive for the family as well as the therapist. Some are restrictive, and close off content, modes of relating within the family, the therapy group, and with outsiders. The family, for their part, introduce the therapist to their expectations, usually through spokesperson(s), commonly parents, who voice some of the family aims, colored by the personal perspectives of each speaker.

The initiation ends with a modest commitment to proceed as a group.

Testing. The second major step involves testing the commitments to participate, and testing the firmness of the definitions, rules, control of content, and direction of energy. Not all conceivable or ideal dimensions of relations and actions are possible among the group members, who include the therapist, individual family members alone, family subcoalitions, and the family as a whole.

The mode of testing includes a range of behaviors, from a major attack on the group and its specifications, to a full withdrawal from it. Most difficult to identify, but essential to confront, are the scarcely conscious and mostly indirect assaults on the therapist, or within the family—often in the name of fostering the therapy.

Struggle for Power. As the relevant parameters of the group become more certain, and the group is contained and functioning, an inevitable power struggle ensues. At issue is not so much the group organization as the assurance that each individual has a place, has functions compatible with the immediate interrelations and the anticipated end goals, and has power to move the group or portions of it. This is often a period of explosive hostility. Total group organization, operation, duration, and accomplishments are at stake. The struggle, seen wrongly by some therapists as centered in the family, and an end in itself—an exorcism by which the family demons are driven out—is instrumental to total group development and consolidation. The enterprise and creativity of each of the family members is released and made available for choosing the family problem(s) on which to work, and mobilized for family action toward solving these problems. Expressed another way, the family group becomes functional toward selecting and reaching family goals. These goals are strongly influenced by culture: for example, it is especially American "to deal with problems"; European, "to be," in an existential sense; and British, "to cope."

The power struggle also confirms that the therapist's role is that of a process leader, and that he or she will function fully and exclusively in that role, and not allow a slip into the in-family roles of the family members. The therapist demonstrates, often in response to tests by family members, that he or she will take certain stands.

Among these may be that the therapist will relate to the family as a whole. The therapist will not join the family. The therapist will not cling to identity with individuals—even though inadvertently slipping into that identity on occasion. The therapist will not take over family roles from individuals. The therapist will not impose potential end goals for the family, but will allow the family to choose their own, even though at the moment they may be dimly recognized, or not even known at all. The therapist aims to convey in advance the idea that he or she will defer consistently to the family in evaluating the extent to which they have reached their expectancies.

Behind the therapist's capacity to act appropriately as group process leader is his or her own stance on a common moral issue for therapists—that is, whether or not to impose on the family efforts to solve problems that the therapist sees, but which are not perceived by the family as problems to work on. The therapist weakens the capacity to lead if he or she demands solutions to problems that may be solvable, but which are not given priority for action by the family. The therapist-leader accepts as critical the family's prerogatives to live toward their own goals, and solve those problems to which they give precedence.

It took me years to learn to overcome my ambitions for families, and to center on their own objectives. During those years, results were often achieved by the family that convinced me at first that my own goals for them were desirable. The families accommodated my ambitions for them, but when my relations with them were over, they did not persist with what they had "gained" (to my mind), unless it also expressed their own major purposes. Thus I have knowingly adopted the process of intermediary leadership, and restrained my impulses to improve, educate, direct, and dominate families. This position has had important implications for the struggle for power within the family, because the therapist who acts as leader cannot be used as an alternate family member; nor can he be pushed by an individual or coalition of family members in a power move to displace one of them.

The therapist maximizes therapy power by limiting his or her behavior, a paradox made understandable by the pressures this exerts on the family to mobilize themselves. These pressures begin to be acknowledged when the family, with the therapist's help, gain a new balancing of power among themselves—a reflection of the balancing within the total therapy group. The power balance allows each family member to participate in the therapy group interaction at a level that can be accepted by self and all others. The modes of interrelating have been compromised and articulated.

Selecting a Common Task. The family as a whole becomes free to select a common task that is sufficiently important to keep each family member engaged, and symbolic enough that working on the task promises to spread accomplishment into other unnamed tasks.

In this respect, the family group, because of its future, differs somewhat from many other groups drawn together to accomplishe a task. An *ad hoc* group organized to work on a particular project may not be concerned that their task, their ways of relating, and their manner of completing their work will set precedents for future relations and later tasks. Brought together to do one job, and with the expectation of dissolving their association at its completion, they function by methods they deem relevant to reaching a project goal. The family, in contrast, works on an immediate task in the context of having to live with the results, with their implications, and with the residual complications from the methods they use.

Because of these considerations, the family may spend a great deal of time on the selection of a common task, with the individuals or subgroups proposing a problem to solve, a goal to work toward. The selection is not an intellectual exercise, but rather a focusing of the attention of the family through emotionally strong challenges. It directs the family to take action toward some desired end, such as solving this particular problem, getting rid of this annoyance, or reaching this accomplishment or state.

It must not be feared that selection of a common task represents a running away from family problems. I have found, rather, that failing to achieve a consensus on what problem to tackle represents the running away. Making the effort to achieve a common choice seems to imply, in part, that the chosen problem or aim will represent a range of other significant family problems. Action toward solving the chosen problem can be seen, then, as action toward also solving the other problems it symbolizes.

During the task selection, the therapist keeps alert to the interactions taking place, especially to the evidences of persons' withdrawals from interchanges with others. This is done so that the therapist can intervene to restore or promote an operating level of mutual engagement among the participants.

Struggles toward Task Completion. The therapist continues concentration on the involvement of family members, while their group tackles the accepted common task, and struggles creatively toward its completion. The creative work is undertaken primarily through the action of speech, colored by expressions of feeling. In a sense these efforts may also be described as an interactive struggle played out by the family in their efforts to solve their problems, or to reach the goals they have foreseen for the family. The struggle here differs from the group-formative power struggles mentioned above, for this struggle is within the agreement that all family members will participate. It takes place in a longer time-frame, binding present action with future consequences.

The struggle may be described in various ways. It may be said to release the creativity of each family member. It also involves evaluating decision-making and trial action, for pertinence to each person's moves toward a common goal; overcoming the lassitude or withdrawal that follows failed efforts to reach an end; removing blocks to action, including reopening of communication, or widening its scope and intensity; redefining expectations; and holding a fracturing family together.

Many kinds of struggles may intrude on progress toward completion of the agreed task. Such intrusions are not introduced by the therapist, but occur because of the interactions within the family in the therapist's presence. The therapist is present both visibly and in action within the therapy situation and in the intervening periods between sessions. When the family goes home to continue their common task, the therapist continues to be taken into account, because they know they must face the therapist at the next session. This allows the family to practice relating present actions to future consequences. They act in the microcosm of the therapy time frame, relating the family's immediate efforts at home to the family's future work at the next therapy session. Later, the relating of efforts to the family's long-range future follows some of the patterns exemplified in the task struggles.

Completion of the Task. The completion of the family's task is marked by their reaching agreement that they no longer need to work on the particular problem, that their goals for the therapy have been reached, and that their dependence on the inclusion of the therapist in the working group is no longer necessary. Such a decision involves a consensus that they can take future leadership in problem-solving within the family, that they have gained a successful outcome in their own terms, and that the therapy group is now irrelevant to them.

Associated with such conclusions is harmonizing conciliation, usually shown in mundane ways. Within the conciliation, each family member is in effect provided the evidence of acceptance within the family, and group consideration and appreciation of his or her insights, aims, rights, and contributions to the family group.

Separation. The final stage is the separation of the family group from the therapist. This stage is frequently marked by struggles about the separation. Demonstration that separation is needed and possible may be accomplished through symbolic gestures by individuals in the family, where they separate themselves from the family group—especially when it meets with family approval. Sometimes the separation is accompanied by a purging of residual hostility within the family, which is used to sharpen the break with the therapist. Or, at the opposite extreme, the separation may become possible only when there is a tentative compact by which the door to the therapy room is kept open for the family. Most typically the family members tighten the boundaries around their family by accentuating the strength and importance of family initiatives, communication, decisions, and other actions.

The therapist, too, must separate from the therapy group. Some residual emotional ties may remain, and lead him or her to recall and think about the family at later times. The bond with the family may reveal itself more abstractly, too, in reflective analysis and conceptual efforts—just as the writing of this sentence has been accompanied by fleeting images of some families with whom I worked.

The Therapist

That the therapist is relevant to therapeutic progress is unquestionable; why, leads to many speculations. I am not satisfied that we have yet formulated a satisfactory theory to explain the impact of the therapist in the therapy group. Part of our difficulty has been that we have concentrated overmuch on the family.

Behind my participation in therapy are a number of goals that I know and use for myself. I do not tell them to the family in explicit ways. Rather, they are communicated implicitly in how I act with the family throughout the therapy.

My goals are subsumed in the efforts I make to induce changes in interrelations to make them functional for the family. For me, the primary word in that sentence is "functional." I am concerned that the family "works." In a sense this is a moral commitment, with deep roots in my upbringing and adult development. It is a passion that drives me in spite of the knowledge that fulfillment can never be wholly attained. If there is success, it will always be partial; and if there is failure, I knew in advance it might occur.

My functional orientation is reflected in both process and end goals for the therapy and for the family. The goals of the process I regard as my province, although I share them to some extent with the family. These process goals operate during and up to the end of the therapy. The end goals I see as essentially in the province of the family. They may be partly reached during the therapy, but perhaps they are not fully won until long after it is over. The end goals depend on the family members, and on the private and collective demands that grow out of their individual and family histories; they are shaped by the flow of their lives in past and present, within changing social and physical environments. Like all goals, they are directed toward the future.

The Therapist's Process Goals. The goals of the therapist for the therapy process, simply stated, are to provide personal and environmental impacts and resources for the family. In theory and in practice, the process goals shape many of the techniques that the therapist uses in the treatment. Since I have described them fully elsewhere (3), I shall focus my attention here on the therapist's purposes. As I see them, these are as follows:

1. The family will gain release from constrictions that bind them into nonfunctional activities and relations.

2. The family will have had therapist-supported experience in exploring and developing among themselves their creativity, some innovative steps for advancement toward explicit family-designated goals (often expressed as solving certain problems), and other goals that are not made explicit.

3. The family will not be diverted into working on low-priority family concerns, or trying to solve existing problems on which they do not choose to work.

4. The family will have been so protected by the therapist from therapy-disrupting intrusions from beyond family boundaries that the family will have gained increased experience and knowledge about the nature and consequences of acting together as a family.

5. The therapist will have imposed no therapist-constructed model of how family members should interact.

6. The family will have been permitted to experience successful problem-solving, and will have received some solid gratifications from having solved at least one problem chosen by them from among the many they confront.

7. The family will stay independent of the therapist, so that they do not attribute success in problem-solving to the therapist, nor assume that to solve problems the family must seek a therapist's help.

8. The family will be able to generalize from a successful problem-solving effort, so that they can tackle some problems beyond those identified in the therapy with greater confidence.

9. The therapist will leave the family with increased autonomy, and will not have promoted either family dissolution or solidarity as an objective; but he or she will have allowed the family, during the therapy and at the end, to determine their own objectives in regard to continuity of the family.

10. The way will be left open for resumption of the therapy, if family experience demonstrates the need for further work with the therapist.

11. The therapist will have become emotionally free enough in his evaluation of the family and its ways of acting to be able to avoid imposing this family's patterns and values on any future clients.

12. The therapy process will be accomplished as economically as possible in terms of therapist and family time.

To achieve these objectives, I work on process interventions that will have the effect of engaging the family and moving them through the stages of the total group development. Within each stage, the therapist's interventions are chosen for their ability to facilitate progress through the stage.

The Therapist's Leadership. Sometimes in final summary of the therapy, the family members give glimpses of why they think the therapist has been helpful. These remarks have seemed superficial to me, though they contain some truths that have stimulated my thinking about the therapist's impact. The family's suggestions contrast with the breadth and intensity of my personal experience as I participate and make therapeutic interventions.

I see myself engaged in leading the group process by: 1. *stating and legitimizing a leader role,* in which I aim for clarity in family understanding of my therapist role, and for relevant adaptability within a prevailing consistency of behaviors; 2. *concentrating my attention* on what is going on in front of me by observations at the center of the family—focusing my gaze on what is going on between and among family members, rather than by them as individuals (and by inference within them); 3. *directing my private analyses* of what is happening with the family (including the content of what is spoken) to the meanings of what I perceive for characterizing the total group interactions. In effect, I hope to reduce the internal (private) components of my relations and accentuate the action (social aspects); 4. *bridging gaps between family members,* by relational centering, and by mirroring, when I comment under selected circumstances and without interpretation, on some of what I *see* going on *among* the family. I comment only on what observant family members might also be able to see, and I initiate this action only when behavior of at least one family member suggests that the person needs to extend his or her participation, or seems to be showing progressive withdrawal from family action; 5. *modeling the act of listening,* by actually listening intently, as shown by my posture, and by comments that show I am listening; 6. *distributing opportunities* for family members to speak—not so much by coercing a person to speak and others to listen, as by helping them all to reflect on an interaction as I mirror it; 7. *confining the content* in most stages to intrafamily matters, and by so doing, reduce the individual's chances to escape from family interactions; 8. *firming up the boundaries around the family* in a related way, not only by content specification, but by limiting my interactions with the family to those that take place when the whole family is present; 9. *adapting the pace of development of the group* to that which emerges with each particular family; not arbitrarily pushing toward precipitate emergence of interaction stages in the group, while, at the same time staying alert to where the family is, and whether my techniques are relevant; 10. *affirming the importance of each individual and of the family as a whole,* by attempting to make sure that my functions do not deprive any family members of initiative, opportunities to act, experience of themselves in actions, and evaluations of the results of their actions; and, by the same token, not becoming so ego-involved that I lose my own consistent attention to the process tasks that I have to do. I release myself from the burden of choosing the family goals and thrust this task on the family, affirming thereby that they know best the resources they have available, that they can comprehend best the complex intrafamily factors that need to be watched and reconciled to make ends right for the family, and that they have learned the problems and handicaps that they cannot overcome; 11. neither by my actions nor intentions promoting the notion that a family should assume that all existing relations must be revised; rather, by regarding the family as operating with a stock of expertise for relating and problem-solving, I *assist them to explore what will now work,* out of what they know how to do; 12. *encouraging trials* of new interactions, regarded as promising by the family members, in fantasy, in communication, protected by the presence of the therapist, and at home between therapy sessions, so they may use these trials as a basis for future decisions; 13. *facilitating termination* of the therapy and dissolution of the therapy group by gestures toward ending the treatment.

Separating these concepts has made me increasingly aware of the similarities between the therapist's group leadership and leadership in other kinds of small task-oriented groups. This awareness has helped me develop new leadership techniques, which I test, retain, or discard. But no overall explanation of the therapy-induced change in families has emerged; nor have we yet formulated satisfactory explanations of creativity.

I feel I have not lost sight of the complexity of the processes involved in therapy. I have tried to keep in mind the inadequacy of our understanding and language, and of the narrow observations which family theorists have made. I do not anticipate that we can avoid to-be-expected difficulties in observing and analyzing actions. I recognize that flexibility in attitude, action, and thought will be required for a long time before we reach a sufficiently comprehensive theory of family therapy.

In general, the therapy process is limited. It is shaped by what a therapist can do within the limits of a particular setting and schedule in working with a particular family who come as clients. Some patterns of family therapy seem especially distinctive, because the interventions are narrowly defined so that the techniques fall in a narrow range. Other patterns are more diffuse, but not necessarily less valid. Many interventions beyond those now being applied could be conceived, and probably will be. The techniques I have learned about seem to range between emphasis on the therapist's asserting himself or herself, and emphasis on the therapist's affirming the family and facilitating their use of their own strategies toward problem-solving and attaining their own goals. My own approach clearly leans toward the latter point of view, but I recognize that to assume any helping role in therapy is an assertion.

No family therapist can use all suggested or conceivable ways to affect a family's position. Any such comprehensive program of techniques would lead to confusion and inefficient leadership. Many of the variations among family therapists occur because certain constituent process elements that they have developed or adopted fit their own personal styles of relating, and because he or she has had success in using them. Some formulate their methods in semiabstract statements, passing them on to others. These statements may take on authority because of their sources; but this authority interferes with the attempts to arrive at general theories about family therapy, and prevents the consensual validation that would allow a comprehensive paradigm. Our field is fortunate, however, in having recently attracted the interest of logicians and philosophers (5, 6) who are working to clarify and order the statements that family therapists are making about the therapy process. I recommend for their consideration an examination of what has been and should be said about the processes of the unitary therapist-family group.

REFERENCES

1. John E. Bell. "Family Group Therapy," *Public Health Monograph No. 64.* Washington: U.S. Government Printing Office, 1961.
2. _____. "A Theoretical Position for Family Group Therapy," *Family Process,* 2 (1963), 1–14.
3. _____. *The Family in the Hospital: Lessons from Developing Countries.* Washington: U.S. Government Printing Office, 1970.
4. _____. *Family Therapy.* New York: Aronson, 1975.
5. Wertheim, Eleanor S. "Family Unit Therapy and the Science and Typology of Family Systems," *Family Process,* 12 (1973), 361–76.
6. _____. "The Science and Typology of Family Systems II. Further Theoretical and Practical Considerations," *Family Process,* 14 (1975), 285–309.

CHAPTER 7

System Concepts and the Dimensions of Self

Thomas F. Fogarty, M.D.

INTRODUCTION

I believe enough is presently known to formulate a barebones systems theory about the family as a unit, and about the individual person as a member of the family, a theory general enough to allow for the uniqueness of each person and family, yet specific enough to be relevant and useful. Any theory about the family must include a map of the relationships between people—the external system—and the processes that go on inside a person —the inner system. Both exist and form a continuum. When we see families clinically, we start with the external system. Relationships between people are observable, accurately reportable, and easily defined; and to that extent, they are scientific. Within this framework provided by a study of the external system, we can study the inner system, and make one consistent with the other. In explaining the theory I am proposing here, however, I will reverse this order, starting with the dimensions of the self, and leading into the relationships.

In this theory, there are four dimensions of self: depth, object, personal, and time (1). There are three systems that link one person to another: thinking, emotional, and operating (2). And there is a triangle dimension that develops when a two-person system becomes overloaded with tension. Thus there are four systems involved: the three that link one person to another, and a triangle when the tension in a two-person system becomes overloaded.

THE DIMENSIONS OF SELF

The depth dimension includes all the elements that are in a person. The spiritual and mystical search for completeness are part of it; so are abstract and concrete thinking, and the ability to make a choice. It contains feelings, such as fear of flying, and deeper emotional processes that are often converted into physical symptoms, and that link the cognitive with the physical. Physical characteristics, sexual instincts, body image, and genetic make-up are included, as are the factors that lead to physical desires to touch, to drink, to take drugs. The depth dimension contains fantasy, imagination, and psychosis, memories, experiences, creativity, beliefs, viewpoints, goals, purposes, values, perceptions, and misperceptions. Though it involves potential, it has no movement in it. All these elements may either be tapped or ignored. Each of us divides them into those he believes he knows, those he is unsure of, those he could get to know if he were interested, and those that remain dark and unknowable.

All people have a variable amount of emptiness inside themselves (3) in their depth dimension. Emptiness is a feeling-emotional process consisting of loneliness, a feeling of being a nothing, confusion, hopelessness and helplessness, a sense of not belonging, sadness, and of being uncared for. It includes a sense of failure, shame, and emotional death. There is paranoia and the urge to flee to a happier, more fulfilling existence. There is a horrible, overwhelming feeling that something vital is missing. People can be acutely aware of these feelings, or totally unaware of them; or awareness can fall anywhere on the spectrum in between.

The second dimension of self involves movement toward objects. Movement toward objects is necessary for survival—the first law of nature. Watching TV or reading a newspaper is pure object movement. If someone goes to a bar to have a drink and to talk to people, he is involved in object-person movement. Other objects people commonly move toward are work, sports, drugs, food, housecleaning, community activities, and social causes. Object movement represents 25 per cent of the person.

The third dimension of self involves movement toward people. This is the dimension of the personal relationship. We move toward other people or away from them, get connected or grow distant. The personal dimension also accounts for 25 per cent of the person—that is, it is as important as the object dimension. What I do is a part of my self and my self is more than what I do.

Time is the fourth dimension of self. It is an always present part of the person, yet we place little emphasis on it. If we move or stand still, are impatient or patient, think slowly, or react spontaneously, change or preserve the status quo, we are involving the time dimension. If we move toward objects more than toward people, we are giving more time to one than the other. Time helps us to describe and locate any event within our physical world. Some people live in bitter memories of the past or in the fantasies of the future, others in the present where change can occur. Some move rapidly and others slowly. A person who operates in the past will fail to connect with another who operates in the present. One may talk rapidly and another slowly. Impatience and distance will creep into their relationship.

There is another aspect of self and systems—the natural incompleteness of everything—that cannot be pictured by the mind. Some people believe that a person, a system, a new idea, a new therapy, a divorce, a marriage, or a family will deliver the fantasy of complete fulfillment. But completion does not exist. A good rule is to avoid aiming for this impossibility, since the possible is difficult enough to attain.

SYSTEMS BETWEEN PEOPLE

To become connected, people use three types of systems—the thinking system, the emotional system, and the operating system. To get a relatively complete picture of himself, a person must define his self in terms of the context of both people and objects, in terms of his "I" and his relationships. The person and the systems between people form a necessary, inseparable continuum.

The thinking system tries to define facts, make judgments and opinions based on knowledge, perceived reality, and experience. It is apt to make mistakes and suffer problems in direct proportion to limited knowledge, distorted reality, biased experience, and, most of all, by the confusion of thought that results when fact is confused with feeling.

Emotional systems are neither rational nor irrational. They form the undifferentiated background of awareness, apart from any identifiable sensation, perception, or thought. They are like the color in a picture, the setting in a play. They provide the longing for closeness between people, and at the same time are the major source of problems in developing personal relationships. An emotional system is neither true nor false, right nor wrong. An emotional system is rated by function. It either works or it doesn't.

The operating system defines the action, the movement, the method that people use to connect within a system. It defines the "how" of the interconnections between people. If one person is angry, does he convey it by silence, withdrawal, open fury, sarcasm, or the tone of his voice?

OPERATING PRINCIPLES

We can study these three systems between people, in particular the operating system, and observe over time what it is that does not work. From these observations, a therapist may derive operative principles or beliefs that do work. These form the basis of structural family therapy, and can be used to rearrange the external structure in the relationships between people. Action in the family is rapid and complex, and there is not enough time for the therapist or members of the family to analyze each and every facet of what is happening. A clear understanding of some universal principles for functioning will serve both the therapist and the family as tools to help them deal with the infinite number of situations that occur in life every day. Many of these principles are known to all experienced family therapists. For instance: there is no such thing as an emotional problem in one person; never pursue a distancer; except for small children, don't tell the other what to do; everyone assumes responsibility for his own feelings; avoid triangles. All of these are structural ideas. They can be used to introduce new processes into external relationships, and thus produce change.

CLOSENESS, FUSION, AND TRIANGULATION

One of the basic assumptions of systems theory is that all people seek closeness. As people move closer to one another, the level of emotionality between them rises, and so does the level of expectation. Each person finds it difficult to remain close, and at the same time maintain a space between himself and others. People tend to fuse, to blend into each other (4). The force behind fusion is the desperate hope of filling one's emptiness by uniting with or taking something from the other. Emptiness expects to be filled by emptiness.

Fusion is marked by conflict between the two people, or by the development of symptoms in one. Over the lifetime of the relationship, the identity of each person is blurred. One may speak for the other, or make decisions for the other, and the boundaries of both people overlap. Confusion arises about what one should get from himself, and what from others, with loss of identification and differentiation. The reaction to fusion is distance; the twosome ping-pong back and forth between fusion and distance. Over time, the emotional climate tends to deteriorate. Islands of sensitivity develop; once these have become fixed, behavior can be triggered in predictable fashion. Often, one becomes the pursuer, trying to fill his emptiness from the other, and the other will distance, moving his personal dimension away from the pursuer and toward work or a girlfriend. To maintain the relationship system, the twosome will form a triangle. Rather than face the sensitivities, the increasing distance between them, the emptiness in each of them, they will displace their emotional tensions onto a third party or issue. Thus the twosome avoids a personal confrontation by discussing difficulties in terms of a third party. But the dry rot of creeping distance, unfilled emptiness, and unfulfilled expectations continues to spread. The person and the personal relationship continue to deteriorate. Fusion may become diffused throughout the family, so that it is difficult to tell where anybody begins and ends, or who is saying what about whom; when this happens, we have the undifferentiated family ego mass (5).

THE FORCES OF TOGETHERNESS AND INDIVIDUALITY

People can tolerate large imbalances inside themselves and in the family; how large depends greatly on their level of expectation of life. After some point, imbalances in self or in the system become uncomfortable, and are called "problems." This point will vary from person to person and from family to family. There are no absolute standards of function. There is no normality. When one or more members of a family say over time that there is a problem, then by definition, there is a problem.

Once a problem has been acknowledged by a family, they will move to place it either in one person, or between people in the family relationship system. But no matter where the problem shows up, imbalances in self or in the system cannot exist alone. If one imbalance is there, the other must be there too. Once a problem has been identified by the family, the forces of individuality and togetherness will be mobilized; but when there is little understanding of emotional systems, the "solution" may often become a second and larger problem.

One member of the family may, for example, become a pursuer, and represent the forces of togetherness. Armed with ideas of sharing, unity, and agreement, the pursuer will move in and become embroiled in relationship problems. After he becomes tired and frustrated, he will pull back out of hopelessness, and often develop symptoms in his inner system. The distancer, on the other hand, represents the forces of individuality carried to the extreme. Unsure of himself, he depends on privacy for self-protection, and tries to prevent others from intruding on his turf. To preserve self, he avoids emotional involvement, and symptoms will be related to his way of maintaining distance. If he uses alcohol, his symptoms will be regarded as an individual problem. If he uses a girlfriend, he will be seen as having a marital relationship problem. When triangles are used by the family to deal with a problem, symptoms show up all over the place, both inside and between members of the family.

Different solutions by different members of the family thus often increase and obscure the problem. When this happens, the struggle between individuality and togetherness becomes aggravated. After such either-or solutions in the family have obviously failed, the family will either continue to deteriorate or will seek outside help.

A MODEL OF FUNCTION

Systems theory has made a major contribution to our understanding of the family by giving us a model of the functioning family—a clear, definite, pragmatic concept of what it is to have a functional family, and what it is to be a functional person in such a family.

A functioning family has the following characteristics: (1) It has the kind of balance that can adapt to and even welcome change. This balance is different from homeostasis, which acts to maintain the status quo in the presence of change. (2) Emotional problems are seen as existing in the unit, with components in each person. There is no such thing as an emotional problem in one person. (3) Connectedness is maintained across generations with all members of the family. (4) There is a minimum of fusion, and distance is not used to solve problems. (5) Each twosome in the family can deal with all problems that occur between them. Triangulating onto a third person who is used to arbitrate or judge or solve the dispute is discouraged. (6) Differences between people are not only tolerated, but encouraged. (7) Each person can operate selectively using both thinking and emotional systems with other members of the family. (8) There is a keen awareness of what each person gets functionally from himself, and what he gets from others. These are the areas of identification and differentiation. (9) There is an awareness of the emptiness in each member of the family, and each person is allowed to have his own emptiness. There is no attempt made to fill it up. (10) The preservation of a positive emotional climate takes precedence over doing what "should" be done and what is "right." (11) Function in the family is determined by each member saying that this is a pretty good family to live in over time. If one or more members say there is a problem, there is a problem. (12) Members of the family can use others in the family as a source of feedback and learning, but not as an enemy.

Systems theory also allows us to describe where the family is at any given moment. By following the flow of movement through the four dimensions, through the systems, and into triangles, we can see where the imbalances in the person, in the family, and in the interconnecting systems exist. This tells the therapist where and with what to intervene in the family. When a wife says that she misses her husband who plays golf all the time, we can see the emptiness in her depth dimension, how she moves her personal dimension toward her husband to fill the emptiness and how he moves toward the object (golf) to avoid her, keeping his depth dimension and the feelings in it away from her. We can see how golf serves as the third leg of a triangle, allowing the husband and wife to avoid the distance, emotional tension, and emptiness in their relationship. As the husband talks about how important golf is to his business, he deals with his wife via the thinking system. She, on the other hand, is talking about her feelings, about missing him, and is in the emotional system. The systems never meet, and the two never meet.

The wife must learn to deal with the emptiness in her depth dimension, the emptiness responsible for the emotional push that turns her into a pursuer. She has to learn that one can never pursue a distancer. He has to learn that distance is useful as a way to get his head together, but that distance never solves a problem. He must learn to use his depth dimension in a personal relationship with his wife, and not to protect it by triangulating onto golf. Both must learn to get close without fusing. We know that fusion is present, because of the distance that exists between them. The wife fuses by trying to accumulate self from her husband. She rates her personal significance by how much he moves toward her. His movement away from her decreases her sense of her own self.

If a therapist can identify where the family is during any specific episode, then often he can answer questions that the family asks. An effective answer depends on fitting the episode into the picture of the family. In the example cited, anything that would stop the wife from moving after her husband would be helpful; however, if the family system changes over time, that answer may no longer be helpful. The therapist must be able to track the flow of movement at any given moment and know the position of significant members of the family. When he compares that picture to the model of function, he can identify the gaps between dysfunction and function. Therapy is the business of closing these gaps.

SYSTEMS LANGUAGE

The complexity of a family, the many observations possible on each one, the great number of combinations among ones, twosomes, and threesomes in each family, and the way symptoms are shifted from one member of the family to the other make it impossible to use standard, individual psychodynamic terminology if we want to achieve a clear picture of the family. Instead, we need and have developed a systems terminology general enough to include all human phenomena and knowledge, and specific enough to be useful.

This systems language includes the concepts of time and space. In this language, a person is described in terms of position—helpless, overresponsible, uncommitted. Movement is described in terms of direction (toward or away from the other person or into self), speed (patient or impatient), amplitude (labile, or flat and calm), and nature (angry or tender). Movement may also be described in terms of resonance (empathic, compassionate, or critical); movement toward objects or people; and thinking or emotional movement. The time always involved in movement has to do with birth, death, the past, present, and future.

The spatial configuration of members of the family is described in terms of the amount of closeness or distance between people, and the presence or absence of triangles. The interrelationship between positions in the family is described in terms of empty spaces between people, who creates them and who fills them, how much space a person keeps around himself as his own turf, and the bridges that establish connectedness between people. (If a husband has sexual bridges toward his wife, and she has emotional bridges toward him, ne'er the twain shall meet.) The spaces between people are filled with an emotional climate that may be understanding or bitter. Combinations of positions in the family are described in terms of the one (the self); the twosome (the personal relationship); the threesome (three simultaneous twosomes); and single or interlocking triangles. The core problem in all relationship systems is called fusion.

The development of this language has been an extraordinarily important contribution of systems thinking to the understanding of the family. It allows therapists, teachers, and students to communicate with each other in brief, clear, and relatively complete terms. The language is comprehensive enough so that no knowledge has to be excluded. Understanding derived from psychoanalysis, behavior therapy, and transactional analysis can be included. Yet the words are specific enough so that it is possible to state what changes should be made in the family. If pursuit does not work, try distance. If overresponsibility does not work, try helplessness. And perhaps most important of all, these words and ideas can readily be understood and appreciated by the people and families that therapists talk to.

OPERATING PRINCIPLES

Systems theory has also contributed a great many universal operating principles that may be applied to function in the family. Naturally, any one episode may involve many principles, some of which come in conflict; when they do, you have to decide which one takes precedence. For example, one principle is to avoid triangles, but a therapist who sees a big man beating a small child will intervene, since the principle of survival for the child is more important than the functional principle of avoiding triangles. Some examples of operating principles have already been given. Others include: Don't use right, wrong, fault, or blame in an emotional system; never reason with a feeling; defense invites attack, so never defend yourself unless in court; the only change one can make is a change in self. Don't try to change others, including patients.

Not all principles are this obvious. More controversial examples, for instance, would be: people in an emotional system deserve each other—not in a moralistic way, but in the sense that a hand fits a glove and a glove a hand; the only differences between men and women are biological; adults are large children, and children are small adults, and aside from this physical fact, there are no differences between them; there are no needs, only wants, with one exception. Connectedness is a need. Connectedness is defined as the ability to stay in the presence of those people who are closest to you, and keep your level of expectation of them at or near zero.

A SYSTEMS DEFINITION OF SELF

Individual theories start by focusing on the individual person and his various facets, then go inside the person to explain his motivations. Systems theory starts by taking at least a three-generational overview of the person and the family, and by considering the external structure of the relationship system of the members of the family. The person and his motivations are a component of this system, and they are defined in terms of what we know to exist in the external system.

In defining the person from a systems viewpoint, there is no "real self." There are parts of self that a person believes in so strongly that he carries them around with him from situation to situation; but to a far larger degree, self depends on context. Different contexts bring out different aspects of self. Everyone knows that different parts of his self come out when he is with his family, when he is at work, or when he is in a social situation. Someone who defines his "I" in the presence of a therapist comes up with a "therapeutic I," a picture of himself colored by what is normal and what is abnormal. If he defines his "I" in the presence of a group, it will be a "social I," in the presence of his family, a "family I." The "family I" is a person in a system who must remain a person but do whatever is necessary to make the system function for everybody. It is a compromised "I," but has rewards of closeness that make the compromise well worth while. Analysis, then, focuses on the individual, often to the detriment of the family system; systems theorists, however, sometimes run the opposite risk, and focus on the system to the detriment of the individual. It is critical to remember that systems are strongly influential, but not determinative. Problems occur in systems when they run the people in them, and restrict the individual.

The four-dimensional concept of the self presented here is a systems definition of the "I." It stays away from all terms like the "average" person, the "normal" person, the "abnormal" person, the person who is "acceptable" to society and culture. The self is an ever-changing person balanced within his own four dimensions and within his family; and he is undoubtably different in different families, different situations, and different times. The search for balance in the self and in the relationship system, and the use of the family as the working context for the balance have striking implications for the definition of one's own person.

Systems thinking, of course, is only one of many ways to approach human phenomena. Like all other theories, it is not magic. It does deal with the fact that people want to change, to be different. Furthermore, it does ask, How do you want to define your self? Do you want to be defined by a psychiatrist? by your peers? by your family? In the long run, whom do you trust to do the best by you? A family therapist believes that even with all the emotional blinders that are always there, each of us must rely on his family. For in the long run, they care more than anyone else.

REFERENCES

1. T. Fogarty. *Systems Therapy, A Four Dimensional Concept of Self.* J. Bradt and C. Moynihan (eds.). Washington, D.C.: Groome Child Guidance Center, 1971.
2. ———. "The Family Emotional Self System," in *Family Therapy.* New York: Libra Publishers, 1975, 79–97.
3. ———. *The Family, Emptiness and Closeness.* New Rochelle, N.Y.: The Center for Family Learning, 1975.
4. ———. "Fusion in the Family System," in *Georgetown Family Symposia,* F. Andres and J. Lorio (eds.). Washington, D.C: 1972, 45–52.
5. M. Bowen. "The Use of Family Theory in Clinical Practice," *Comprehensive Psychiatry,* 7 (1966), 345–74.

CHAPTER 8

The Hindrance of Theory in Clinical Work

Carl Whitaker, M.D.

I have a theory that theories are destructive—and I *know* that intuition is destructive. Isn't it sad? and no excuses will be accepted. Bert Schienbeck says,

> *Kyk.*
> *('t is vell erger)*
> *(dan je denkt)*
> *als je denkt*
> *is 't nog erger*

Look. It's worse than you think. And if you think, it's much worse.

THEORIES

Theory is the effort to make the unknowable knowable. It's trying to work out a method for forcing the left brain to control the right brain. The process was defined many many years ago: "It's not given to man to see the face of God except through a glass darkly." Theory is also, of course, one of the ways of trying to understand the impossible. It's been theorized, for instance, that we are all conceived in sin. It has also been hypothesized that we are all born innocent. Tillich says Being is Becoming, and that we avoid being by trying. We keep doing to avoid being. My theory is that all theories are bad except for the beginner's game playing, until he gets the courage to give up theories and just live. Because it has been known for many generations that any addiction, any indoctrination tends to be constrictive and constipating.

Success in psychotherapy with neurotic patients leads to a theory that developing the capacity to "comment upon" the double binds we use to entrap ourselves is curative. This escape hatch is not often available in psychotherapy with seriously disturbed persons, and is probably never available in working with families. However, psychotherapists are very susceptible to the disease of metacommunication. We talk about talking so successfully or think about thinking so effectively that we are in danger of losing our freedom to talk or think.

Furthermore, the combination of metacommunication and professional objectivity tends to bring about a loss of caring. We talk about the "love object," or the development of techniques for "social manipulation." It's like talking about "body counts." Dependency on theory is often increased by the discovery that many patients get well. Some neurotics get well from even a research investigation of their etiology and psychopathology. (The fact that psychotics do not get well from this kind of research is merely viewed as a matter of unresolved additional data.) But technical approaches do not seem to succeed for second generation therapists. Rogerian theory, which worked so well for Carl Rogers, did not work as well for those people who learned to follow him; eventually many of them gave up Rogers' theory and became themselves, rather than carbon copies of the master. This same thing occurred with Lazarus, who moved from copying Wolpe's theoretical structure to being a real person, and even wrote a book called *Beyond Behavior Therapy*.

THE SYMPTOM THEORY

Medical practice teaches the serious danger of relieving symptoms as though they were the disease to be treated. Every medical student is warned not to treat a lower right quadrant abdominal pain as a *sui-generis* problem. Doing so may lead to a ruptured appendix. Yet in psychotherapy much effort is expended to relieve the symptom as such. Success at this maneuver may indeed be of great relief—but what if the symptoms arise because of an adaptation to a pathological cultural and family situation? Aiding the patient to adapt may be at least a disservice and at most an abortion of the central striving for growth and integration. The symptom may be an exquisite experience of regression in the service of the ego, and if it is, a comforting therapist may reverse an existential shift (Eisenberg) that would not only yield a two-week "peak experience" (Maslow), but change the person as both person and teammate. Mayhap relieving the pain will prevent the formation of a pearl.

The chilling effect theory has on intuition and creativity in general is highlighted by the fact that it tends to make symptom relief the objective of psychotherapy—adaptation to culture, to family, to situational stress. Psychiatric symptoms, like abdominal pain in the lower right quadrant, must not be relieved, lest it disguise the appendicitis so that the patient dies from generalized peritonitis. The patient whose symptom is relieved while his effort to integrate the conflicting forces in his own life experience is destroyed is an example of an operation being successful, although the patient dies.

An example? Joe went psychotic. His Christlike efforts to show his terrified mother that her fearful nightmares should be suppressed worked. She became comfortable again, although, of course, worried about his terrible problem.

One of the objectives of psychotherapy of the family is to counter the culture bind. One demand made by our culture is like the demand of mother —that we feel a symbiotic belongingness, addiction, and enslavement to the culture pattern. This is enforced, like mother, by making it hypnotically important to not know that you're symbiotically enslaved. The family also uses the culture's demands that we be different from each other as substitute for being a self. If I am indoctrinated with the clear conviction that I'm not like you, I can believe that therefore, I must be me. Self discovery by denial is, of course, one of the basic understructures of attempted divorce. If I'm not part of that other person, then I must be myself. A very neat delusion to induce isolationism.

Zoroaster is supposed to have instigated the Western world's addiction to the god-devil dichotomy. People are labeled as good or bad; behavior becomes the basis for judgmental decisions even about life and death. Theory is used by its devotees to dichotomize patient and therapist patterns of interaction. Interpretations carry endless judgments; the freedom to interact exists only beyond the borders of the system, away from the tyranny of a right-wrong polarization.

One of the effects of a therapeutic orientation based on theory is that the therapist becomes an observer. In doing so, he not only avoids his chance of being a person, but he also tends to help the family avoid their courage to be. The resolution of Tillich's koan, "Being is becoming," turns into "Doing is to keep from being." Many families who are very busy use their busyness as a kind of reciprocal contract to be functional and thus avoid anxiety, and also to produce a paralysis of the integration that is wholeness. Each becomes an observer and presents a performance demand; each becomes distanced thereby and afraid of the performance failure. The pathology is a static, nonevolving groupness.

Young physicians very often find the anxiety-provoking experience of sharing a patient's life stress very hard to tolerate. Their failures leave a residue of impotence; their successes induce a euphoria which covers the phobic concerns about the next patient. Any shorthand label helps them neutralize some of these effects. At first their theories are simple—her mother was unloving, his father was cruel, the parents didn't want this third baby. As their three training years unfold, so do the concepts: play therapy should be designed to release aggression; physical touching is effective in resolving the affect hunger of the orphan syndrome; all women over thirty are neurotic, and all men over thirty are indifferent. They need to devise reasons why for their experiences.

The faculty of course are much more sophisticated, so that we can and do give them complex, all-inclusive explanations for why the patients are distressed. Courses in child development offer an endless series of parenting distortions, and failures are explained as due to excess permissiveness, the lack or excess of a generation gap, an authoritarian atmosphere, or lack of intimacy between the parents' unwanted children.

There must be a way. The poor resident is himself haunted. Is the answer Freudianism, Jungianism, or Rogerianism? Who is right? Adler seems to have something, but so do Rank and Reich. Maybe all psychology should be thrown out—isn't biology gradually taking over? If one drug won't solve it, two or three might. Or "they"—*Who are these they?*—will find a new drug to relieve their anxiety. As experience with patients grows, theories expand and become both more global and protected by subtheories: the patient wasn't ready for therapy; or, the etiology was oedipal, but father's death made resolution impossible. Sometimes the explanations are as tortuous as those of a theologian who has resolved his anxiety about the way with a theory, or two or five.

There are three usual resolutions of this dilemma of psychotherapy training. Each resident either gives up on psychotherapy, becomes a convert to one system of thought, or espouses a life style of endless searching. The half-life of his transference to each new theory varies, but in general their usefulness decreases as he is forced to recognize that there are as many spontaneous recoveries as there are theoretical. Part of the problem is the theoretical delusion that science is curative—that enough knowledge, enough information, the right kind of facts will bring about the resolution of life's doubts, the resolution of all distress. This point of view differs, of course, from most philosophical and therapeutic efforts in the East. Yoga is not really a method of therapy. It assumes that the individual's therapy takes place within the culture; yoga is then utilized for expansion of the person after he has become a well-adapted individual who knows how to utilize himself, and after he has lived through many of his growth struggles.

And in the West, too, therapy takes place in the culture, despite the fact that books on psychotherapy may assume that nonprofessional helpfulness is inadequate, nonexistent, or a mistake. There is no question but that a great many children headed for schizophrenia in their infancy happen to make contact with a loving-hearted lady next door, or even maybe with a friendly dog next door, and so learn how to love, learn how to be personal and intimate. This context is ordinarily just called friendship, but more honestly should be called social therapy. The grandmother who gives some little girl cookies whenever she comes to visit, the old carpenter who takes a neighbor's boy fishing, the boss who calls an employee in and rakes him over the coals, the supervisor who sits down to be straight with one of his workers may each be therapeutic. Our culture itself, however, seems to have grown less therapeutic over the recent decades. Family reunions used to bring people together for a Sunday celebration at Grandma's house, but this kind of community psychotherapy is not as common today.

Without theory, though, how is the young therapist to make decisions? Psychotherapy is an art. The development of that right-brain intuitive gestalt process not easy; the techniques emerges painfully from under the compulsive dominance of the anxiety-binding verbalizing authority of the left brain. Good supervision, and protection from the excess grief of raising one or more specially crippled children may help to develop sensitivity to the pain of caring. Gradually the toughness needed for the separation and the recurring emptynest syndrome will develop. If that toughness is not achieved, the young therapist will inevitably withdraw to a safe distance with almost every patient. The new mother needs the tender care of her husband and of her mother as she learns to feed and love her new baby; the new therapist needs a teammate and a nurturing elder statesman.

Nontechnical or nontheoretical family therapy has various components. One of the most valid is borrowed from Zen, which is structured around the effort to break the computer programming of the past by posing an impossible problem. Zen does not teach adaptation; it teaches increased courage and how to face impossible problems. It aims at helping or pushing the student to break through into a new integration by separating him from all logical, theoretical, disciplined patterns of understanding. It asks the student to answer an unanswerable question, a koan. The best known koan is, "If two hands clapped together makes a loud noise, what is the sound of one hand clapping?" To answer this may take many months of struggle and necessitate moving out of the ordinary framework of thought. One of the possible answers is that the sound of one hand clapping is *om,* the sound of the universe.

The process of nontechnical or nontheoretical family psychotherapy also uses a deliberate effort to increase anxiety. The therapy team establishes a pattern of caringness, so the family dares to be more anxious instead of escaping into protective, defensive patterns. The therapist models, with some member of the family, an I-thou relationship characterized by caring and flexibility, with the aim of pressuring the family into tolerating more anxiety. Much of the modeling is the freedom to share with the family the secret language that the therapist uses with himself, including metaphorical allegories, free association, and fantasies. Once, for example, a picture came into my mind of a fishing line that went through the lobe of each ear of a family's scapegoat and then around the room through each ear lobe of the other family members. Sharing this bit of fantasy with the family helped them to move toward a kind of togetherness that they had dreamed of but had become hopeless about.

The initial phase of family therapy is a struggle to see whether the family can depend upon this foreign person to maintain their stability while they reorganize their system to cure the scapegoat or make for better individuation. Once the battle for structure, or the battle to establish the generation gap between the patient and the therapist is settled, the subsequent tendency is to demand that the therapist give rules for life, take over the family, say what's right and what's wrong. If the therapist is dedicated to a theory, or even if he himself believes a theory of psychotherapy, he tends to make it into a theory for change and a theory for growth, or even a theory for living. And once that is imposed, no matter how subtly and no matter how carefully, the patient or family becomes dependent and rebellious, and the generation gap ends with less than ideal results.

Ideally then, there should be a reversal of roles so that once the therapist has been established, he denies all theory and forces the family to establish its own theoretical or systematic organizational way of living. He insists that just as his life is inexplicable to him, their life must be inexplicable to them, but it is nonetheless something they must make decisions with, for, and about. This reversal of roles, which may look like paradoxical intention, is really an active parenting with a reverence for the identity of the individual and the unique identity of this family. Just as one person is intrapsychically unique, the family is interpersonally unique. Once this fact has been settled and the family is clear that they have their own structure and the therapist does not know what is best for them, he becomes able to join the family as the consultant, to move into and to individuate from the family. By making it clear that his living is his own affair and must be handled in his own way, he moves out of the family.

The therapist thus becomes a model. The modeling may be done using a purely technical style. Typical is the good mother whose breast is always available. At its worst, this induces symbiosis; at its best it results in increasing dependency and a psychopathic manipulation for more milk at less need. It is, in essence, a kind of addiction, in which the patient or family becomes addicted to the therapist. In this kind of all-giving approach, in which the therapist forces the patient into dependence, the therapist himself becomes mechanical and bored, someone who is living in the world of metacommunication and doesn't communicate. The performance demand from the family is also massive, for they must conform or leave.

Mastery of a theoretical approach often results in an effective technique that is able to induce the family into therapy. When the process is not successful and the family stays dependent, or becomes rebellious and breaks out of therapy, the therapist's fear of failure may lead him to take up the observer role. He's then stuck with a loss of intimacy, and co-opts the patient by his own self-denial. That is, he becomes a kind of technical prostitute.

The nontechnical psychotherapist or the therapist who is not addicted to a theory operates in a much less rigid manner. He demythologizes himself to the family by modeling his own unpredictability. This modeling takes the form of uniting with the family at one moment, and separating from them at another moment. His caring for them is clear both when he's joined and when he's separated; but he also exposes the fact that he cares more for himself than he does for them. They sense that his reason for working with them is to expand his own capacity to care and to expand his own person. In defining with them the usefulness of craziness—that is, compulsive non-compulsiveness—he teaches them to individuate and be creative as individuals, as subgroups, and as a whole. He extols the group craziness of the family who go off on a crosscountry automobile trip together, or the individual craziness of the psychiatric resident who one day a month puts on a clown costume and wanders around the city playing silly tricks and being somebody else, or the group of teenagers who go off on their own as a whole group leaving the parents to struggle with their twoness. In modeling playfulness, the therapist by his own regression induces the family to regress in the interview. They may have a whole interview which has no purpose.

One of the other functions of the therapeutic modeling role is to break the cultural mythology of psychotherapy. When therapy has been well-structured, the therapist can bring in a cotherapist, a consultant, or one of his own children. He can become the patient and struggle with one of his own problems, or bring in other patients or even another family. The sharing of his own slivers of pathology, remnants and fragments of his undisciplined, unintegrated person, or vignettes from his family of origin are all grist for this midphase stage of family therapy which should be free of any theoretical structure and intensely involved in the process of disrupting all ingrained, imprinted patterns.

One of the most useful aspects of this kind of nontheoretical approach is the therapist's freedom to not demand or even push for progress. The freedom to be involved in the current "beingness" of the family, the freedom to invite the family to be involved in his current "beingness," helps establish a break with their theory of change, as well as with their theory of hope for the future or threat of the past. Finally, the therapist should be able to reverse roles in such a way that he exposes his own hunger and thereby allows himself to be co-opted by the family system as its new scapegoat; he can then prove that he can break his way out, as the individual family members are hoping to do. They don't really want to stay out of the family. They do want to be free to go in and out as they choose.

We have to have some way to decide what the object of psychotherapy is in order to talk about it. We presume that families come because of their inability to be close and the resulting inability to individuate. They come to recover their capacity to care, to discover that people can be symbiotically close without being bound, vulnerable, or victimized. We assume that they're also coming in hopes of getting their anger resolved so that they can be more free to care.

The objective of family therapy is to become part of a group which has such role flexibility that anyone can take any role under the proper circumstances. We assume the normal family grants a freedom to subgroups in any way—that is, father-daughter and mother-son can play at being partners without evoking jealousy in the other parent or in the other children. Mother and father can each become a child in the family set without disrupting the group belongingness. Father can come home with a headache from work and feel comfortable in asking his little son or daughter to be his mama; and mother can come home from a hard day and comfortably be a little girl to her own child.

However, any family must also establish a clear generation gap. Although the parents are a subgroup of the family as a whole, their role is differentiated by their generation. We assume the triangles within the family are comfortable and mobile, and that if father and daughter gang up against mother, or mother and daughter gang up against father, this is temporary and exciting, not static and painful. The normal family casually revels in the present. The ghosts of the past and the hopes of the future do not bedevil the present. Each person has an I-position and is an integrated, that is, focused, unidirectional person. All members are clear that the center of each person's life is in himself even though the family is part of his expanded self. It's enriching that the nuclear family has an intimate connection with mother's family of origin and father's family of origin. In essence, then, the normal family is a genuinely mutual and loving family; struggles for individuation and separateness are acceptable and exciting, and despair is not the affective undercurrent. Their freedom to regress in the service of individual egos is exciting, and their fun as a group is childlike, open, and free of the metacommunicational heaviness of an intellectual orientation to life.

Masters and Johnson have reduced sexual problems to two basic patterns: the fear of performance, and the distancing process of the spectator role. This simple formulation may be an excellent place to start an effort to move away from fifty years of evolving theories, each of which has had some serendipitous therapeutic success. Is it possible that our theoretical efforts are a head trip to avoid our fear of impotence?

The objective evaluation of pathology and the deliberate effort to correct deviation cannot be applied to the family. Theories about the etiology of psychopathology are abstractions relating to infantile character and personality development: they cannot be superimposed on the development of a family system and its pathology.

Family pathology requires an operational theory that includes family myths and cultural myths. Indeed, the therapist lives by his unconscious operational theory based on the family myths and cultural myths of his own upbringing. Whereas research into the pathology of an individual patient with neurotic problems can many times result in the correction of the pathology, it's very clear that in family therapy this process is not sufficient. The essential therapeutic defect seems to be a lack of power in the therapist. He is impotent. One of the bases for this impotence is that he has been trained in linear causology, whereas study of the family system shows very clearly that causology is circular. There's no way of saying where the pathology is in a family, just like there's no way of saying what caused World War I. Although theories are valuable in explaining processes and are important as a preliminary to work of any kind, a good blueprint does not guarantee a good house.

Good therapy must include the therapist's physiological, psychosomatic, psychotic, and endocrine reactions to a deeply personal interaction system. The freedom to move in shaman-like primary process responses must be defended by a professional cotherapist or a professional cuddle group. Psychotherapy is a counterculture process, and if the therapist is not protected, the community will wither him.

Dedication to theory in family therapy work is essentially a copout, a disguise that will eventually conceal even the process of therapy. It's an emergency escape hatch from the powerful stress that exists between the therapeutic team and the family itself. It is assumed by many that the intellect provides a structure that makes involvement possible without abnormal entanglements. I do not believe this is true. Theory is a left-brain abstraction of a two-brained operation. Theory supports an objectivity in order to prevent countertransference—more truly, transference—and as such it's as fallacious as the theory of unconditional positive regard, which is to say that love conquers all.

Exactly how little effect theory may have on the actual practice of psychotherapy is well illustrated by the story of group therapy done with members of the 8th Air Force during World War II. The group therapist in charge had thirty group therapists under him. They were struggling to keep the bomber pilots who flew each day to bomb Germany from becoming psychotic. More particularly, they were trying to keep the navigators sane, since with nothing to do on the missions except sit, they went crazy at a much higher rate. Among these therapists were people who were trained

—Freudians, Sullivanians, Kleinians; therapists who were pediatricians who'd been given a ninety-day emergency course; and doctors who had only taught. During the two years he ran this intense group therapy, he observed that success and failure seemed related exclusively to the person of the psychotherapist. That is, people who were expertly trained, people who had had long group therapy experience, and people who had no group therapy experience all seemed to succeed or fail largely to the degree to which they were human beings with their groups. Effectiveness, in other words, seemed to be independent of technical expertise. He also decided that the inexperienced people could be used provided that supervision was available to protect them against recurrent countertransference problems.

What can we use as a substitute for theory? The accumulated and organized residue of experience, plus the freedom to allow the relationship to happen, to be who you are with the minimum of anticipatory set and maximum responsiveness to authenticity and to our own growth impulses. We must also recognize that the integrity of the family must be respected. They must write their own destiny. In the same sense that the individual has a right to suicide, the family has the right to self-destruct. The therapist may not, and does not, have the power to mold their system to his will. He's their coach; but he's not playing on the team.

The fact that patients—and especially a family—declare themselves impotent by asking for help does not imply weakness. The weakness that becomes apparent early in therapy is a transference syndrome; in no way does it indicate any need for the kind of tender, passive listening. Instead, the caring therapist can trust his own empathy and the strength of the family to make direct interchange useful and valuable.

The therapist must develop the kind of power necessary to invade the family, and do battle with them. Simultaneously, he must develop the courage to be himself, and to share his own irrelevancies and free associations. He must expand his own person, thus modeling for the family their own growth. Family therapy is like psychotherapy with the psychotic—long-circuited thought processes will activate the "it's phony" switch, which is as sensitive in the family as in the psychotic. Breaching the programmed family mind must be induced by the therapist's deprogramming himself, and advancing his own growing edge. The only personal response to primary process communication is primary process—that is, free association—by the therapist. Free association has an instantaneous response time that forces an intimacy in the relationship very difficult for even the hypermanic or sophisticated paranoid schiz to parry or repress. Sharing intrapsychic responses induces first a symbiotic sane/crazy we-ness, and soon thereafter a reversible role teaming. This role switch leads to individuation of the therapist and the patient, after which the step to independent lovingness completes the repair cycle. Crucial to the intimacy is a freedom to be vulnerable—the exposure of personal value systems, codes, and even slivers of the therapist's pathology. As Barbara Betz said, many years ago, "The dynamics of psychotherapy is in the person of the therapist." Why should the family expose their tender underbelly if the therapist plays coy and self-protective?

The medical ethos insists that the physician's unswerving devotion to science and humanity is enough reason for being. Those who choose to be physicians therefore very often become workaholics and coronary victims; psychotherapists seem to elect suicide as their early resolution. My personal opinion is that either a coronary or suicide is better than drying up. But there is an alternative—a set of rules that will help to keep the therapist alive.

1. Relegate every significant other to second place.

2. Learn how to love. Flirt with any infant available. Unconditional position regard probably isn't present after the baby is three years old.

3. Develop a reverence for your own impulses, and be suspicious of your behavior sequences.

4. Enjoy your mate more than your kids, and be childish with your mate.

5. Fracture role structures at will and repeatedly.

6. Learn to retreat and advance from every position you take.

7. Guard your impotence as one of your most valuable weapons.

8. Build long-term relations so you can be free to hate safely.

9. Face the fact that you must grow until you die. Develop a sense of the benign absurdity of life—yours and those around you—and thus learn to transcend the world of experience. If we can abandon our missionary zeal we have less chance of being eaten by cannibals.

10. Develop your primary-process living. Evolve a joint craziness with some one you are safe with. Structure a professional cuddle group so you won't abuse your mate with the garbage left over from the day's work.

11. As Plato said, "Practice dying."

Part III

CLINICAL ISSUES

Section A

MEMBERSHIP

CHAPTER 9

Including the Children in Family Therapy

Donald A. Bloch, M.D.

Children are the same as everybody else, only more so. Their involvement in family consultations may be as primary patients; or their involvement may be secondary to disorders elsewhere in the family system. Whatever the apparent reason for therapeutic involvement, there is always significant expression at the family level. One may pick up the ball of twine at any point and follow the thread back to the same configuration.

Although their orientation is to the entire family as a functionally integrated system, it is not always true that family therapists direct their efforts to the entire unit. When the presenting problems are found in adult members of the family, children are rarely included. On the other hand, when the family comes for treatment because of child-related problems, it is desirable to include the symptomatic child in initial sessions. My impression is, however, that many experienced and dedicated family therapists as quickly as possible arrange formats in which they are dealing with adult children—that is, parents in regard to *their* families of origin (again excluding siblings)—and pay little direct attention to minor children.

This state of affairs is particularly puzzling, since concern with the psychiatric problems of childhood was one of the major factors leading to the development of family therapy. Child therapists observed that changes in the psychosocial functioning of children could not be achieved or maintained unless associated changes were achieved in the family system. Each day's careful therapeutic knitting up was unraveled at night in the home. The natural conclusion was that therapeutic intervention must take into account the reciprocal impact of child and family system on each other. This concept soon gave way to more sophisticated notions of homeodynamic equilibria, where child and adult members of the family system were accorded equal importance. The logical next step was to implement these notions with therapy formats that involved the entire family.

Montalvo and Haley (17) bring this issue full circle. They analyze the interpersonal structure of the conventional pattern of child psychiatric care, in which the child is defined as "sick" and treated by individual psychotherapy, and show how this mode of treatment can produce changes *in the family system* commensurate with the theoretical position of family therapists. Therapy is seen as a directed learning experience for the child in new behaviors—a definition markedly in contrast to the theories of child analysts. (Strean (24) looks at Freud's Little Hans from a family perspective.) Montalvo and Haley's view is that the symptom-focused modes of therapy are related to traditional child therapy.

I shall discuss here the place of minor children in family psychotherapy conducted for whatever purpose, and deal with child membership in family therapy sessions; the nature of resistance to their inclusion in sessions; modes of relating to them so as to maximize their useful involvement; and the particular benefits that can be had from their participation.

MEMBERSHIP ISSUES

Today, diagnostic and therapeutic consultations with families are used to deal with the widest possible range of human disorders, including problems of a drug addiction, coronary illness, schizophrenia, delinquency, obsession, depression, and phobias, to mention just a few. The presenting problem may be located in an individual; generally it is in the family system (4). Generational strife, marital discord, the consequences of divorce, issues associated with nonstandard—single parent, homosexual, and multilateral —families, among others, commonly lead to family consultation. Malfunction originating at any systems level must have expression at the family system level; conversely, the structural dynamic aspects of family functioning must correspond to phenomena at other systems levels. Issues of economy and efficiency may sharply delimit the scope of therapeutic involvement, but the tactics or practical necessities of therapy should not be mistaken for its conceptual base.

Attention to the membership to be included in the actual therapy sessions has been an early and persistent concern of family therapists. Thus Sonne *et al.* (23), writing in 1961, speak of the "absent member maneuver"; and Friedman (7) says, "Out of our experience with conducting family therapy on the spot, in the home, we furthermore learn the importance of including as an integral part of the therapy unit, not only all siblings, but grandparents, close relatives, and others who share the twenty-four hour living experience under one roof. These individuals are inevitably a part of the emotionally meaningful organization of family relationships. . . ." Absence from sessions is considered to be "acting out of a secret alliance with, and a resistance for, another family member who is physically present," a point Sonne makes as well.

Those who think in terms of family systems vary as to how they set the limits of that system, both conceptually, in defining who shall be thought of as being effectively within the family system, as well as operationally, in defining those to be included in the therapeutic work. In addition to the fact that there is no standard practice, there is, of course, no standard family. Nor is there a typology of families that would allow us to speak with any confidence of meaningful categories, each warranting its own treatment arrangements. Individual children vary importantly as to sex, age, and developmental stage, psychobiological characteristics, character structure, and ordinal position in an unknown number of siblings. Finally, therapeutic goals and purposes do not fall easily into rational categories, so that the objectives of the work for both therapist and family will vary widely and in ways that are hard to categorize. It is tempting to put the matter down as unmanageably complex.

Despite this, my experience has been that routinely inviting all children in a family to join in the session is workable and productive; moreover, failing to do so is often costly to the work. I recognize that this is considerably at variance with what is done by many others. Many family therapists do not include any minor children in their therapy sessions, or limit their involvement to older children or to the index patient if such be a child. But in the following instance, the youngest child present at a family session contributed mightily to an understanding of the family dynamics.

The initial consultation with the Tartaglia family was delayed so that their fifth child, two week old Adorée, could attend. The infant had been held in hospital with a postpartum infection. The basis for the consultation was to review a persistent pattern of marital discord. There had been three separations, spaced more or less evenly among the births of the four older children, the oldest of whom, seven-year-old Gino, was leading his siblings in a mad race around the interview room. In this romp the principal obstacle being leaped over was Adorée, lying unprotected in a baby carrier on the floor, unnoticed by her parents, but the object of anxious parental attention by myself and my male cotherapist. A few minutes later Gino hugged eighteen-month-old Lisa roughly to him and forced a bottle into her mouth, which she sucked on eagerly while trying to prevent her brother from bruising her lips with his harshness.

These vignettes set the thematic motifs for this family, deeply and painfully ambivalent in its organization around parenting. This was the father's second marriage; his first wife had died shortly after the birth of daughter Judy. He had decided to marry his present wife after an incident that indicated clearly to him what a good mother to Judy she would be. While on an outing this second wife to be had inadvertently slammed the car door on the youngster's hand, and had been overcome with remorse immediately afterward. This showed him her affection for children. A few years after the marriage, Judy died mysteriously under circumstances that seemed to spell severe neglect.

It is my practice to include all members of a household, together with all minor children, particularly in the early phases of the work. Starting with the presenting complaint, a series of linked, open-ended, therapeutic contracts are negotiated; after that the membership of sessions is determined by the goals of that phase of the work. When subsystems of the family are excused from later sessions, it is done symmetrically and in keeping with structural principles. Most commonly this means that attendance is limited, for example, to members of one generation, or one sex; or that all spouses of adult children will, or will not, be included.

Generally speaking, there are three initial goals: the reduction of scapegoating of the identified patient; the elimination of symptomatic behavior; and the establishment of the family system as the locus of the malfunction to be treated.

A principal reason for advocating the inclusion of *all* the children in the initial sessions with a family is to facilitate the progress of this sequence. If only the symptomatic child comes, the serious disadvantage is that scapegoating is abetted. This makes it more difficult to orient the family away from individual pathology and toward considerations of family system functioning. A strategy of linked therapeutic contracts leaves open the question of child membership in sessions after the initial phases. As an aside, we may note that, for some therapists, the establishment of the family system as the locus of malfunction is often taken to be equivalent to defining the problem as malfunction of the *marital* pair, so that family therapy goes forward as marital therapy—not infrequently in a couples group. I believe that any such automatic program is unduly limiting. All options should be kept open, and to give up including children in the sessions may be unnecessary and misleading.

A recent development of great importance in family therapy has been the use of short-term approaches; these seem, among other things, to dictate a different attitude toward children. The hallmark of these strategies is the effort to rapidly secure behavioral change in the index patient. Characteristically such therapeutic effort is restricted to six to ten sessions, or, on occasion, limited by discrete interest in one target behavior. The therapist relies heavily on creating an atmosphere of compliance with professional authority, and on the use of such techniques as prescribing the symptom, and paradoxical injunction. Therapeutic task assignments that break up, or override, established symptom-maintaining properties of the family system are almost always employed, frequently with great imagination and creativity: see Haley (8), Palazolli *et al.* (19), Watzlawick *et al.* (25), and Weakland *et al.* (26). Milton Erickson (5) has been influential in this area; the following case of his illustrates these short-term techniques:

> The patient is the eight year old son of a divorced mother who also has two daughters aged six and nine. The son becomes enormously rebellious and destructive, apparently in relation to his mother's having male friends. In a single session, a procedure whereby the boy "will change his behavior himself " is outlined. The mother is instructed to provide herself with refreshments and reading matter and then literally sit on the boy for an uninterrupted session of several hours. She is advised that all of her strength, dexterity and alertness, in addition to her weight, will be required to master the situation and is further advised not to accept surrender because of pity. When blandishments and temper tantrums do not avail, the youngster eventually surrenders and a permanent behavior change ensues at home and outside as well.

Orthodox behavior modification techniques within families bear some resemblance to the methods just described, in that they are oriented entirely toward change in one or a few target behaviors, and tend to be short term in duration. Rarely are any children other than the identified patient included in sessions; they are never part of sessions aimed at adult problems, such as marital discord.

It does not seem to me that there is any useful way at this time to decide the relative merits of these widely differing approaches. Indeed, I think it more likely that therapeutic theorizing in the future will address itself to complex systems that include the therapist and her/his theory, technique, and personal style as essential elements. More and more we will assess a treatment plan as to its suitability in the hands of specific practitioners. Thus, therapists should work with children who are amused and energized by them, whose sensibilities are enlarged by the young, and who are reasonably at peace with their special way of ordering and relating to things and people. It should be said that the therapist may be mistaken in his ideas about himself in this respect. If he has the notion that he cannot work with children, he ought to test this by exposing himself to the possible rewards of so doing.

RESISTANCE TO INCLUSION OF MINOR CHILDREN

The reluctance of therapists to work with young children is understandable. Family interviews under any circumstances are strange and difficult information environments. A large number of data must be attended to, and in a fashion quite different from that to which individual psychotherapists are accustomed (4). Many of the issues raised by work with families in general are accentuated as the age of children decreases and their number in the interview room increases. Little ones do not talk; they spill their food, they need their diapers changed, and they will not (should not) stay in one place. More importantly, they activate response patterns in therapists that are often intense and troublesome re-experiences of issues in their own lives as parents or children.

The therapist may find him/herself painfully participant in an overcontrolled situation:

Suzie, aged three, came to the interview exquisitely dressed, as was her four-year-old sister. Her chubby legs peeped out from layers of flouncy petticoats; her two meticulously braided pony tails quivered as she managed to sit "like a lady" on the edge of her seat. Finally she eased off, wandered around the room daintily, watching the therapist and her parents keenly for the slightest sign of disapproval, only to trip over an electric cord she was too preoccupied to notice. Her father pounced on her angrily, sending her into panic.

Or the therapist may find him/herself present at a primitive and uncontrolled, albeit therapeutically productive, riot:

At an initial interview there were three children present, two boys aged two and three, and a six-year-old girl. The parents were both mental health professionals. Within a very short time the children systematically dismantled my relatively childproof office. The most extreme excess was avoided by my intervention when a clock was held overhead about to be dashed to the floor. As this mayhem went on, the parents alternated between ineffectual efforts to halt it and attacks on each other as being responsible for it. After a bit the children organized themselves into a marching line with basket masks over their heads, tramping endlessly around the adults who sat in the middle of the room. Without warning the six-year-old asked, most surprisingly, "What's a graveyard?" Before anyone could speak, she answered her own question, "I know. That's where they bury the people and the flesh rots off them," which she graphically illustrated by pulling at her cheek. Shortly after I learned that the parents were both concentration camp survivors.

There is a balanced spirit with which we can best approach such resis-tance in ourselves. Little profit is to be had from romanticizing the problems of working with children in family therapy; it may not be right for us, or for them. What may be harder to resist is the tendency to build ideological positions that rationalize personal preferences.

TECHNICAL MANEUVERS THAT DEPEND ON THE PRESENCE OF CHILDREN

Plainly it makes a difference if something is done in the presence of others. The refusal of therapist to become involved in detailed examination of the index child's malfeasance speaks eloquently. If she or he pays atten-tion to the asymptomatic children, is concerned with the distress of the scapegrace, solicits help from the underdog, he or she is making powerful statements *in action* for the orientation of the family to itself as a system. These become something other than pious declarations.

A classic article on structural approaches to family therapy by Aponte and Hoffman (3) reports on the way nonsymptomatic children—Jill, age 12, and Stephen, age 10—together with Laura, the index patient, age 14, were used in therapy. They were particularly important in the early phase of the interview where the therapist, Minuchin, made alliances with the kids and thereby helped to establish generational boundaries. The presence of the children in the interview also permitted an exploration of the general theme of enmeshment throughout the family in regard to *all* of the youngsters, as exemplified by the huddling and cuddling that went on with the father in the parental bedroom. Finally, it was possible to explore this lack of differ-entiation by the failure of the parents, and even of the therapist, to distin-guish the two older girls from each other as to person and age. A pattern in the family that kept children young and prevented them really from entering puberty was related to the presence of symptoms of anorexia in Laura.

THE CHILD IN THE THERAPY SITUATION

The unique aspects of the child's experience of the family therapy situa-tion stem, among other things, from his or her powerlessness, and, for a younger child, from the absence of an adequate cognitive frame. The devel-opmental stage of the child influences its perception of the situation. It behooves the therapist to take particular note of these issues. One of the very few articles in the literature directly dealing with these matters was published in 1970 by Ackerman (1).

Ackerman asks, "What is the child's perception of the family encounter? What do they imagine? What do they expect? What are their anticipatory images, their needs, desires, suspicions, fears and resentments?"

He notes that at first meeting the therapist is another stranger, and "should keep his distance. In the meanwhile the child's autonomy and initiative call for respect . . . children do not just come to the interview, they are brought, and anxious parents often engage in deceit, manipulation; they mislead the child." Parents, too, are worried that the child will expose them and "often adopt an insincere posture as the therapist's assistant." Thus, the child may receive mixed messages, including an open message to talk with the concealed message to be quiet.

Ackerman pays particular attention to the child's "surge of tension" expressed through such means as the need to eat, or go to the bathroom, and relates this to the importance of involving the child. The child's nonverbal disagreement with the parents may be expressed by a sour face or restless squirming; the therapist must indicate that it is safe to speak out, that he "has the confidence and power to counteract the threat of punishment." If the child is frightened or intimidated by parental constraint, he isolates himself.

The parents' fears of the child and of their own helplessness, as well as their anxiety and rage are emphasized; so is the importance of the therapist's being able to show he is not afraid, and can control the child if need be. I have observed Ackerman physically restrain an out-of-control youngster. (Safer (20) and Erickson (5) also report on this.) Throughout, the emphasis seems to be on rebalancing. If "one is dealing with a scapegoated terrorized child, the therapist must side with the child . . . if at the other extreme the child turns into a destructive monster and terrifies the patient, the therapist must again equalize the relationship."

A few additional comments about the conduct of the therapist in such sessions. The therapist's attention should be equally available to large and small alike. Each child, as well as each adult, should be attended to in each interview, touched by hand or eye, and by direct speech. The powerlessness of children is maintained by many subtle social conventions; they are condescended to, talked about in their presence, talked over, as if their comments were of little value. The counterattack is often very funny. I recall the barely audible singsong comment of a superbright six-year-old as his parents were explicating their liberal racial views: "Nixon's my man." Could one ask for a better cotherapist?

The parents, as Ackerman notes, are equally entitled to the protection of the therapist. In this regard a particular danger comes from our competitive efforts to show that we can be better parents, an effort often rooted in unresolved issues in our own families. At times we are drawn into subtly currying favor with the symptomatic child in an effort to create a tradeoff that will persuade reluctant parents to permit the work to continue. It is a hazardous gambit.

PHYSICAL SETTING AND SPECIAL TECHNIQUES

While interviews involving young children can be conducted in almost any kind of a setting, it is helpful to have a room that is spacious, allowing youngsters to move freely in and out of the main action center. Depending on the age of the child and the general degree of tension present in the interview, as well as the specific place in the family constellation each child occupies, there will be varying movement in and out of the field.

It is practical in my office to leave the outer office door open because the children can safely wander in and out. Other settings might not permit this, and it would be foolish to expose the child to risk, or the interview to interruption. Consultation rooms should be reasonably childproof, although it does not seem necessary to go to extremes; and they should, of course, be safe places for children as well. Perhaps the biggest hazard in this regard is the one-way mirror; understandably, they fascinate toddlers, who seem to like banging on them.

A box of simple toys is about all that is needed in the way of special equipment. Some therapists establish a doll play corner in the room, and use the productions of the child there much as they would be used in play therapy. While this seems useful to me, I have not tried it. Instead I make available a basket of miscellaneous toys and construction materials that can both amuse the child and serve as expressive vehicles. Given the choice, it is reasonable for the therapist to opt for quiet, soft, nonstaining toys. Other special techniques that hold promise are family art sessions (12) (22), and family sculpting.

THE CHILD IN FAMILY THERAPY SESSIONS

What do we hope to accomplish by including young children in family therapy sessions? Why bother? what benefits will offset the obvious difficulties? To answer these questions, I will cite sequences from two videotapes of work with one family. Treatment was sought because of marital discord. The family is plagued by emotional dishonesty and marginal criminality. There are four children: one 16-year-old girl, April; George, the 12-year-old; and fraternal twin boys age 8, David and Alan. In these sequences, the children had been told that they were coming to see the therapist to wish him a happy holiday, a somewhat unusual pretext for a consultation.

Father: Last night when we told the kids they'd be going with us here today, that's right you did say that.

George: I knew we were going to have a discussion.

Mother (covering up for the parental lie): I explained, whether I explained that to all of them.

David (scapegoat and family truth teller): You didn't 'splain that to me.

Mother (attacking as the best defense): Well, the trouble with you, David, is that usually you're talking so that when someone says something to you, you don't listen, and I'd explain that to you also.

David (protesting): I wasn't even with you.

Mother (overtalking him): It would be nice if you would do a little more listening than all the talking.

George (making an alliance with mother): David, we're here for a reason. *(He turns his head sharply to check mother first before going on.)* If you're going to sit there playing and talking, the reason's not going to work, right?

We can see here much about the use of circumlocution and deceit to gloss over such painful matters as the reason for the family interview. The functional position David occupies as family scapegoat and truth teller is evident, as is the ambiguity in George's position, first attempting to gain power by knowing what is going on, and then caving in and joining his mother in the attack on his brother.

There are no irrelevant or trivial behaviors. Many things determine the degree to which a behavior can be understood, including, of course, the sensitivity of the observer. The child's gift for metaphor and vivid expressiveness can be touched simply and directly by the therapist, often with results that are moving and meaningful. During the following interchange in the same family, it was evident that the boy involved, David, was fully in touch with the nature of the therapeutic work.

Therapist: Did your Mommy give you the reason that you were coming here to wish me a happy holiday?

David: Yep.

Therapist: Uh-huh.

David: I never heard of having a discussion over our life. If we're gonna do that. . . .

Therapist: Yeah, if we're having a discussion over your life, we're really talking about something quite different, aren't we?

David: This is part our life.

Therapist: Right, this is part your life.

David: It's like talking about our life.

Therapist: Well, how is your life?

David (heavily): Bad.

Therapist: Yeah, well . . .

Alan (the other twin, who up to this point gave no sign even of hearing this conversation, provides the metaphor): Like the apple last night . . .

David: Like eating out of a broken apple.

Therapist: Eating out of a broken what?

David: A bad apple.

Therapist: Well, that kinda says a lot. Could you spell that out and tell me more about that? How is it a bad life?

David: I don't like it.

Therapist: Yeah.

David: We have too many fights.

Therapist: Yeah, O.K.

David: Not including me.

Therapist: Yeah?

David: When I say fights, it's the people in my family.

Therapist: That's what I mean, David. You mean, even if you're not in the fights?

David: Sometimes I'm in the fights, yeah.

Therapist: It could be a fight that you're not in.

David: Fights that I'm not in, that doesn't involve me.

Therapist: Does it make you unhappy still?

David: Yeah

George (back at his invalidating position): I don't think he knows what you're talking about.

David: I know.

Therapist (openly supporting the truth teller): I think he knows exactly what I'm talking about.

The therapist is obliged to consistently and evenly scan all persons in a family interview. Learning how to do this is a difficult task; we are coerced by those who talk or act dramatically into paying them a disproportionate amount of attention. The family therapist has little real interest in the details of what is being told him; sequences and patterns are his concern. Yet the pressure of the family system is enormous, and its ability to induce congruent patterns in the therapist despite his or her best intentions must be respected.

Silent children need to be paid attention to fully as much as articulate and active ones. On one videotape Alan, the silent, less mature twin, sits quietly in the corner of the room in a chair. As the conversation swirls around him, he silently leans his head against his father's arm in an obvious effort to nestle up close to him. The father pays no attention and raises his arm, pushing the boy away. The boy subsides in his chair for a few seconds more, then gets up and sits in the little chair next to the mother. Meanwhile, David, the older twin, has nestled himself firmly in the therapist's lap. Alan is not being noticed by anybody at this point. Alan next sits down near his mother and pushes his arm onto hers; she pays no attention. While the conversation goes on animatedly around him, he turns, faces the one-way mirror and begins to wave at it and gesticulate in a bizarre fashion. Turning back he makes several efforts to break into the conversation, commenting on points that his sister is making. Nobody pays any attention. He calls his sister by name again and again, after which he begins to clap and to throw his head backward in an exaggerated posture, finally getting her attention. While he is talking to her, his mother talks right over him, also to the sister, and flatly eliminates him from the conversation, whereupon he looks back at the mirror again, then holds his mother's arm and finally says to her "Look in my eyes, look in my eyes." At first she pays no attention, until he almost climbs in her lap and begins to pull her lower lids down to make her look in his eyes; she permits it, but still pays no attention.

A few seconds later, Alan leaves her and sits next to the therapist.

Alan: Can I say something?

Therapist: Yes *(slapping knee and leaning forward over enthusiastically)!* Yes, by golly, now listen, we've got to clear a little room for this guy *(putting an arm around Alan)*.

Alan: About my sports—

Therapist: O.K., get cranked up and say it, let's have it.

Alan: I need a hand on bowling.

Therapist: You need a hand on bowling *(David walks to the middle of the room, imitating a bowling ball)*.

Therapist (holding hand up for silence): Who's the best person to give you a hand on bowling?

Alan: Um, um, um, Rod Stewart, I saw him do 300 on television.

Therapist: No, no, I mean who is the best person in the family to give you a hand on bowling?

Mother: He's big on sports, this kid. *(David, comes over and begins tickling the back of Alan's head.)*

Therapist (puts an arm in between to ward David off): Now, now, now, come on. Who do you want to go bowling with? *(David continues to play with the back of his head, but Alan answers the question.)*

Alan: April.

As the discussion continues, the whole family breaks into animated conversation, and the therapist weakly chirps "Who do you—who do you —who do you" and then can be seen to subside, lean back in his chair, and turn his face away. Alan turns away from the therapist, faces the mirror, and begins vehemently pointing at it, gesticulating and carrying on a silent tirade to his own reflection in the mirror. In the midst of this, there is one poignant moment when he looks at the therapist, the therapist looks at him unseeingly, turns away, and Alan continues making faces at his reflection in the mirror.

The therapist can use him or herself in a playful way that will activate emotionally meaningful configurations in the family session. In the following sequence the discussion had been centering around the efforts of April, age sixteen, to isolate herself from the family. Just before the exchange, mother has been complaining that the daughter would not do anything with the family. The father said that really she would not do anything with him.

Daughter (pointing to therapist): He's wearing red socks to match his shirt and I'm wearing green socks *(she bends forward and shows her socks)*.

Father: They clash.

Therapist (sticking a foot out): Do you want to put your socks next to my socks?
Daughter: A Christmas tree, isn't that nice? Anybody in blue and white? (*leans to her right to examine socks of one of her brothers*).
Father: I'm wearing red, white, and blue underwear.
Therapist: Daddy's getting right in there. You and I, we're just playing footsie, but he wants to show us his underwear.
Father: If it weren't for the TV camera, I'd take my pants off and show you.
Daughter: I see it all the time (*points at her father's crotch*).
Therapist: You see his underwear all the time?
Mother: Oh yes, he walks around the house all the time in his underwear.

In examining these sequences it is instructive to consider among other things, the therapist's use of himself, somewhat more evident on the video tape but discernible in the transcript as well. He aids the family truth teller, protecting him from his mother and older brother ganging up on him, and dealing gravely and quite directly with his distress and unhappiness. His effort to work against the flow of the family system fails with the immature twin, actually the more dysfunctional of the two. Finally, by his adopting a playful and flirtatious role with the sixteen-year-old daughter, essential aspects of her position in the family are made evident.

Our view is that children add immeasurably to the rewards of family therapy for the family and for the therapist. All ages can join in the work and both add to it and benefit from it. From the therapist's point of view their presence enriches and makes more vivid his grasp of the complex multigenerational sweep of family life. The struggle to understand and deal with children and oneself in relation to them is frustrating, growth enhancing, funny, and painful. It sharpens the intellectual challenge of the work and offers ready access to those data essential to increasing our knowledge of human behavior. Finally, it is true to the holistic, contextual spirit of family therapy. Certainly, it is worth trying.

REFERENCES

1. N. Ackerman. "Adolescent Problems: A Symptom of Family Disorder," *Family Process,* 1 (1962), 202.
2. _____. "Child Participation in Family Therapy," *Family Process,* 9 (1970), 403.
3. H. Aponte and L. Hoffman. "The Open Door: A Structural Approach to a Family With An Anorectic Child," *Family Process,* 12 (1973).
4. D. Bloch and K. LaPerriere. "Techniques of Family Therapy: A Conceptual Frame," *Techniques of Family Psychotherapy: A Primer,* Donald Bloch (ed.), New York: Grune and Stratton, 1973.
5. M. Erickson. "The Identification of A Secure Reality," *Family Process,* 1 (1962).
6. R. D. Freeman. "The Home Visit in Child Psychiatry: Its Usefulness in Diagnosis and Training," *Journal of the American Academy of Child Psychiatry,* 6 (1967), 1–4.

7. A. Friedman. "Family Therapy as Conducted in the Home," *Family Process,* 1 (1962).
8. J. Haley. *Uncommon Therapy: the Psychiatric Techniques of Milton H. Erickson, M.D.* New York: W. W. Norton, 1973.
9. E. Irwin, and E. Mallory. "Family Puppet Interview," *Family Process,* 14 (1975), 179–91.
10. M. Kaffman. "Family Diagnosis and Therapy in Child Emotional Pathology," *Family Process,* 4 (1965).
11. _____. "Short Term Family Therapy," *Family Process,* 2 (1963), 216.
12. H.Y. Kwiatowska. "Family Art Therapy," *Family Process,* 6 (1967), 37.
13. M.S. Martino, and M.B. Newman. "Intrapsychic Conflict, Interpersonal Relationship, and Family Mythology," *Journal of the American Academy of Child Psychiatry,* 14 (1975), 422.
14. J.E. Meeks and J. Martin. "Teaching the Techniques of the Post Diagnostic Family Conference," *Journal of the American Academy of Child Psychiatry,* 8 (1969).
15. D.R. Miller and J. C. Westman. "Family Teamwork and Psychotherapy," *Family Process,* 5 (1966), 49.
16. _____. "Reading Disability As a Condition of Family Stability," *Family Process,* 3 (1964), 66.
17. B. Montalvo and J. Haley. "In Defense of Child Therapy," *Family Process,* 12 (1973).
18. J. W. Osberg. "Initial Impressions of the Use of Short Term Family Group Conferences," *Family Process,* 1 (1962), 236.
19. M.S. Palazzoli, L. Boscolo, G. F. Cecchin, and G. Prata. "The Treatment of Children Through Brief Therapy of their Parents," *Family Process,* 13 (1974), 429.
20. D. J. Safer. "Family Therapy for Children With Behavior Disorders," *Family Process,* 5 (1966).
21. R.S. Shellow, B. Brown, and J.W. Osberg. "Family Group Therapy in Retrospect: Four Years and Sixty Families," *Family Process,* 2 (1963).
22. C. Sherr, and H. Hicks. "Family Drawings As a Diagnostic and Therapeutic Technique," *Family Process,* 12 (1973), 439.
23. J.C. Sonne, R.V. Speck, and J.E. Jungreis. "Absent Member Maneuver As a Resistance in Family Therapy of Schizophrenia," *Family Process,* 1 (1962), 44.
24. H.S. Strean. "A Family Therapist Looks at 'Little Hans', " *Family Process,* 6 (1967), 227.
25. P. Watzlawick, J. Weakland, and R. Fisch. *Change: Principles of Problem Formation and Problem Resolution.* New York: W.W. Norton, 1974.
26. J. Weakland, R. Fisch, P. Watzlawick, and A. Bodin. "Brief Therapy: Focused Problem Resolution," *Family Process,* 13 (1974).

CHAPTER 10

A Family is a
Four-Dimensional
Relationship

Carl Whitaker, M.D.

Twenty years of play therapy with children, relationship therapy with delinquents, mothering of neurotic self-doubters, and depth therapy with chronic schizophrenics was coming to a grinding halt. Couples therapy became more and more boring. How could one aging therapist stay alive? Even co-therapy, the twenty-year model for patient parenting, felt sterile and stereotyped. It became clear that my personal growing edge must become my central objective in every relationship—if experiential therapy was for my experience, then patient modeling could be for real. If I could change, they might try to. I am time limited; my marriage is deep, long, and wide coursing; but the family lives, and has a forever-extended time dimension.

THE NECESSITY OF THREE GENERATIONS

M. J., a man of forty, with three children, left his wife to live with another woman and her two sons. He'd always done "whatever gave him fun." Marriage didn't make any difference in his sexual life. He had lived for a year in a European village with this girlfriend—a hooker with two children, whose husband "hadn't supported her in four years." When her boyfriend had doublecrossed her, M. J. took her on to help her "get herself back together." The endless struggle to keep the two women in his life happy required lies and all sorts of cheating, although he always stayed inside the law. Jealous of each woman, he kept convincing each that he was faithful. M.J. had occasional fantasies of suicide: he'd tried hypnotherapy and marital counseling, but he still felt "terribly insecure."

He has a brother and two sisters, all much older than he; his parents are still together. They are "good people," and he reports that life with father was "rugged." His wife is not exciting sexually. His girlfriend always has twenty ways to increase his sexual excitement, while his wife can't think of any way to satisfy. However, when he told her to go off on her own, she made a life for herself without him, which threw him into an acute panic.

The plan for treatment: "Those two women you're sleeping with are catching on to you. They should both come into the interviews. I'll need a cotherapist. We would try to help solve the problem all three of you share. Each of them is suffering like you're suffering. Each is as dishonest with you as you are with them. Read the *Mask of Sanity* by Hervey Cleckly; listen to the record of George Bernard Shaw's *Don Juan in Hell.* Don Juan thought *all* those women loved him. Call me when you've thought about it!"

If M. J. does bring in his two women and all five children, my cotherapist and I will then insist on at least one consultation with his parents and his siblings. Without the additional stress of facing his family of origin, he might still avoid an integrating experience, continuing to wear this mask of sanity that enables him to make believe he's two separate people in two separate places. The third generation would escalate the pressure, and therefore might evoke the psychotic-like episode needed to put him together into a single person who is not self-destructive one minute and pseudo-stimulated the next.

My engagement with two-generation families began in 1945. I decided I didn't believe in individuals. They seemed more and more like fragments of a family. Then, as time went on, I heard the ghost of grandmother knocking on the door. Each dad was apparently trying to restructure his own family of origin, using his wife and children as puppets. Each mom was also pushing to rekindle her at-home security by using the same nuclear family group. Why not get the three-generation system together and at least begin an accommodation to the introjected reality of the entire two-family system? Homogenizing that dual set of family myths might make the nuclear family myths less enslaving to the grandchildren. It might even allow the grandparents to dump their thirty-year child raising hangup, and begin to live. I don't believe in the individual or free will at all any more. I'm tempted to say over the phone before the first visit, "Bring three generations or don't bother to start."

Many people question the grandparental visits to the interview and the purpose it serves. Should they be patients? should they be a place for the identified patient or spouse to express affect or confront old myths? The most basic reason for having the parents in is to get their implicit permission for the therapist to become the object of transference.

In individual therapy, transference takes place in the framework of an implicit and sometimes explicit disloyalty to the parents. Psychotherapy is basically countercultural, and as such involves breaking with the parental model. If we get the parents in for the first interview, it helps the patient feel less disloyal and the therapist feel less responsible for moving in an direction antagonistic to the parental model. The content of that interview may be purely social, or merely supportive: it certainly need not involve content of any significance. It need not, for example, result in the parents' discovering that the patient is homosexual, or has had an affair, or is suicidal. It merely serves as a time when the parents meet this man who's going to replace them, and develop some willingness to turn over to him the care and nurturing of their child.

Jim and Mary came about two things: the question of a divorce, and how to discipline their three-year-old. Mary wanted the divorce because Jim had a terrible mother. She said mother still kept the bluechip stock left him by his father, and also kept Jim's army savings from the two years before they married. Her fury had grown during the last three years because mother had sent such chintzy Christmas and birthdays gifts to their child. After several weeks of listening to this, I insisted they bring mother from a distant city for a consultation visit.

As the consultation got going, Mary confronted her mother-in-law about the chintzy gifts. Mother said she thought the gifts were merely symbolic, since she also sent a hundred-dollar check each time. She also had sent money for the new piano they had asked for, after rejecting her offer to rent one for a year.

The values of this consultation were that I was able to rectify my image of that mean old mother-in-law who sent chintzy gifts and kept the husband's savings account; Jim developed the courage to stand up to his wife's attack on his mother; I was free to tease the wife about the projected bitterness she carried toward her own mother; the grandmother and her son resolved the bank account remnant of their premarital affair; and the grandmother achieved a new freedom, released from the triangular war that had been heating up within the group.

The family ended treatment soon after and a five-year follow-up indicates that all goes well.

Mrs. W. M. divorced her husband one year after marriage because he beat her up. She was then six months pregnant. Subsequently she had several years of good psychotherapy, and was referred to me by her therapist so that I could monitor the relationship between her and her ten-year-old son. I had from between one and 5 triangle interviews each summer for the next six years. These interviews helped maintain the separation between the generations—that is, the identity of mother and son as two separate persons, and a two-generation, one-parent unit.

When her son was seventeen, the mother asked to bring in her own parents, so she could work on that relationship. She arrived with her mother, but without her father. When asked why her father hadn't come, she said he wasn't needed, and anyway he didn't want to come. She was refused the interview, she came back a week later with son and both parents, and within twenty minutes she and her father were in a physical fight. After this had been resolved, father explained to the therapist that he thought her assault was a fake. I suggested that it looked like a husband-wife fight. The identified patient immediately flared into a blistering attack on the missing husband, whom she hadn't seen in eighteen years, as "a horrible person" for beating her. I insisted that it was necessary for her to get him and bring him in. She called him. He arrived from across the continent three days before the next interview; they met, and she beat him up within 36 hours. We had three subsequent good appointments, and did a great deal to resolve all three generations of chaos. Oh, if only I'd done this six years earlier.

This reactivation of the bilateral paranoia between the patient and her exhusband resolved the identification of father and exhusband. It also helped rectify the disorganized family introject in the seventeen-year-old son. He finally knew how it was with his mother and her parents, and with "that man who had once been his father."

Looking back to individual therapy, I wonder how and if I really changed anybody. Did couples therapy change the relationship or the people? or was it time that healed, and role expectations that shifted? Is therapy any different with three generations on the first visit? Why try it? and how does it help?

Sixteen-year-old Sue had failed school, had been out all night and now was surly and bitter. Her little brother was withdrawn, mother was depressed, and father was furious, tightlipped. He demanded that Sue conform with school, and also with home rules. Since grandmother was visiting at the time, she was invited to the interview. Asked about the family, she said, "I never put my nose into my daughter's family life." Asked about grandfather, she said, "He died eight years ago." "How?" "A motorcycle accident." "Had he been suicidal?" "Well, now that you speak of it—I hadn't thought of it, but he'd had lots of motorcycle accidents." "Were you afraid of him?" "Oh, yes. He beat me several times."

From there it was easy to help the father see how his wife expected him to beat her. He agreed that he was afraid of his temper, and then recalled a violent fight in high school when he almost killed a classmate. That led to the daughter's getting family credit for teaching mother how to fight with dad, and helping dad enjoy his temper without becoming suicidal or beating his wife.

The hidden agenda: Twenty-four-year-old Ezra had been referred after five years of psychotherapy that hadn't helped his "schizophrenia." Mother phoned asking an appointment for son, and was told, "I don't see patients, I just see families." She said, "Well, I'll come." "How about your husband?" "Well, we're getting a divorce." I explained to her that I would not see them without the father, and she said, "OK, I'll bring him." "Who do you live with?" "My parents." "Well, let's bring them." "They aren't related to my son's problem." "OK, go see someone else." "But I want to see you." "So bring your parents." "OK, I'll bring them." "How about your husband's parents?" "Well, they live in Montreal." "That's okay. Just have him call me if they won't come."

All arrived for the three-hour consultation except father's mother, who had suddenly developed arthritis. I took a history about the family's life together, first from father's father, then mother's father, then mother's mother, then father, and finally from mother. The whole story was pseudo mutual sweetness. There was nothing wrong with this family. Exhausted, I turned to the "schizophrenic." "Listen, they're all nuts. You're a crazy grandson in the middle of all this family who are so ideal. It's impossible." He answered, "I'll tell you the story in five minutes. Mother's mother is father's father's big sister. And she made her little brother force my father to be a rabbi, and now they're all forcing me to be a Hasidic scholar." Without this third generation, I could have spent four years treating the nuclear family, and still never discovered the problem in the grandparents.

We all realize that in a large percentage of marriages the family of the bride and the family of the groom stay covertly or overtly hostile for years. Those mother-in-law jokes are not funny. They're real. "There's something eerie about that guy who stole our daughter." "Mother, don't you think Edna is awful snooty to Jim?"

The initial therapy visit of a three-generation system resolves several issues. It establishes the fact that this is a network, and that it is concerned with the problem at hand, even if it's just the nuclear couple's effort to grow. There is a group that each person belongs to, and that whole group is involved. Secondly, the implicit contract in the visit does settle a mantle on the therapist. The responsibility for the pain and the operation has been transferred to him. If the hour goes well, and first one and then another tries to express doubts, fears, and hopes, there may even be a new warmth between the two sets of grandparents. However, if the isolation walls are left intact, the members of the nuclear family are able to see quite clearly that they are truly responsible for their own destiny.

Mary was just out of a state hospital after four months of serious psychotic behavior. The husband was a profound square, and the three children, six, eight, and ten, were having great difficulty readapting after their mother's long absence. The two sets of grandparents had not seen each other or talked to each other since the marriage eleven years before. Each set had been unhappy about their child's choice. The two hours of consultation seemed to be quite superficial—chitchat about the usual family tension systems, but without the courage to get into serious matters. Nobody was able to face the fear of another psychotic break, and the consultation as a whole seemed like a fairly inadequate experience. At the next interview, however, Mary said almost immediately, "Now I know why my husband is such a compulsive. I'd never met his mother. She's just like him. She even made me be careful about my behavior. I had thought he was just an old maid."

As a result of the consult, the wife forgave her husband some of his covert hostility and pathological "sanity"; his parents, who had not come to the wedding, became friendly with her parents; the husband-wife war about which family of origin system would be copied in this new family system was resolved in a relative compromise; the children were less constrained by stress about which set of grandparents they should be loyal to. They did not have to choose either father or mother; both sets of grandparents could back away from their parental responsibilities and enjoy the relaxed play quality possible between grandparents and grandchildren; and finally, hope of preventing another psychotic break was increased, because there were two sets of grandparents ready to support the nuclear family's effort to build a healthy family system.

Does it make any difference if you have already started with a two-generation unit? I think it's wise to establish the symbolic significance of the third generation on that first visit. Then a visit from one or the other, or even both sets together, can serve as a consultation. The therapist need not reveal secrets nor even ask for data about childhood problems. The fact that this family reunion has a purpose, plus "that family therapist and his x-ray eyes" make the meeting significant. Even a casual history of the early relationship of grandma and grandpa will turn up loaded topics for the parents, and often for the grandchildren as well. Let the group carry the ball. They know how much they can stand, and what topics are poison.

What if there has been a divorce or two? Invite 'em all! Re-opening old doors with the idea that parenthood is forever always seems useful, and I have never seen it harmful. What if they refuse? Keep pushing, and ask the symptom bearer to urge them to come as consultants to the therapist. "I don't want more patients. I don't want to be a judge. I'd just like help with my therapy job." What about the aunts and uncles and cousins? The more the merrier. I've worked with a family of thirty for three full days together; many times I've worked with fifteen to twenty. A large group demands much less of the therapist. Such a family system needs none of the leadership that makes network therapy or group therapy so arduous. One spark in the extended family usually strikes tinder; and it's a rare family that doesn't have flint and steel available, just waiting to strike each other.

When family therapy has reached an impasse, and the therapist decides to increase the therapeutic power either by adding another member or inviting a consultant, it's equally helpful to add one or many team members from the extended family. They should be invited as assistants to the therapist, not as patients. Otherwise, if it is the grandparents, for example, who are invited in, they assume they're going to be assaulted, made guilty, made responsible for what's gone wrong. But if the cotherapists, in setting the stage for this consultation, tell the couple or the family, "We want your grandparents in to help us; we are failing," then the grandparents can come in as assistants to the therapist. Once in the interview, it's explained to them that the therapy *is* failing. "We're not doing our job in helping these people become more satisfied and more alive to their own living process, and therefore we'd like any help we can get." If this does not start anything going, the therapist can ask if they're willing to share any of their perceptions of the family, either about the past or the present, and maybe their fears or hopes for the future. If this does not succeed, the therapist can ask if they would reveal some of *their* problems in marriage, or their successes, and tell what caused them in hopes that this information might be helpful in the current family struggle. Should they come back once this consultation hour is completed? I usually invite them to visit if and whenever they like; I also offer them a chance to come every week if they feel they would like to.

This kind of consultation interview serves many symbolic purposes. The therapist does not see the grandparents as ogres. This may be a surprise to the parents. The grandparents are able to agree that their children are adults. The parents usually discover in this real-life confrontation that the grandparents are much different from their introject of twenty or thirty years earlier, which may enfeeble the control residing in that introject. The parents may discover that the grandparents are capable of running their own life. Thereby they are freed of that reverse parental responsibility they've been carrying. The couple may discover their grandparents don't object to their independence, don't object to their belonging to the younger generation, and will allow them to discipline their own children. Thus both the parents and the grandparents become freer to live their own lives in their own way. The two families become free to separate and thus free to belong.

I must stress here that in many years of utilizing this extended family consultation I have never seen it harmful, although occasionally grandparents are angry afterwards. Also, I've never seen it fail to be useful. Many times I can't understand why, but I grow more and more convinced that it's always helpful.

Jim, the father, had been in personal psychotherapy for four years, without losing his retiring shyness. His wife, a schoolteacher, then began psychotherapy because of psychotic episodes related to stress over her four adopted children. After a year of treatment her psychiatrist turned gay and left town. She was referred to me, and I asked the father's therapist to be cotherapist and help treat the family. Mother had three psychotic episodes in the next year. In one of them, she jumped in front of a car, breaking several bones, and was in the hospital for weeks. During this time the cotherapist forced the father's father and the mother's mother into psychotherapy, as well as father's sister. For the next two years treatment included husband, wife, four children, two grandparents, and one adult sibling. No interview was allowed unless all were present.

The essence of this therapeutic process was the gradual emergence of the grandparents out of their isolated retreat from life. The father's psychotic understructure also surfaced and was integrated. The children matured from belligerent, chaotic little animals to creative human beings, and the extended family group interaction became alive and vivid. Mother had more psychotic episodes, progressively less serious, and the entire three-generation system became more cohesive.

Including the third generation increased the power of our intervention in resolving the identified patient's symptom, as well as helping with the multiple family problems. Having the three generations present also allowed the therapists operational freedom to move in and out of the family structure. This was vital, since if the cotherapists ever become enmeshed, the game is lost. The three-generational process brought about the rehabilitation of all the individuals in the family: four children, two parents, a sibling of one parent, and two grandparents. Three-generation therapy also prevented the total failure of the previous treatment of the two individuals, the couple and their children.

How does one start such a three-generation group cooking? I usually begin by defining my impotence in detail. "Family systems are powerful groups. Like the Green Bay Packers, any change must be a group decision. This family seems to be losing games; I'd like to coach them to victory, but I feel pretty feeble. I'm not even on the field of play—just a new coach. How can I help you most? What did you grandparents do when you had similar problems in your younger days? Did you see this trouble coming on?" I always invite them back at any time they can come, and every week if it's feasible. Sometimes they keep coming, and it becomes a revolution *in situ.* If they cannot come in regularly, I ask for the right to use them as consultants at a later period, either as a group or as subgroups at their convenience or my need.

Much of the progress in psychotherapy has been serendipitous. Professionals tend *not* to be innovative until they are pushed into it by their caring and the creativity of their patients. I moved into couples because of my insecurity in working with individuals, and then into families as a way of breaking out of impasses with couples. I'm now discovering what one patient can do to bring about the reunion of an entire family. One symptom carrier instigated a massive number of telephone calls that resulted in 35 out of 45 available family members arriving to meet with a psychotherapist for a three-day family war. Objective—the cauterization of family bleeding.

One of the characteristics of family network therapy is that the more people who are present, the less pressure there is on the professional therapist. His function is mainly to be a time and a place; it's not even necessary for him to be a moderator. The anxiety and the preplanning that have already occurred in each person's head, as well as between members of the group, guarantee a meeting loaded with secret agendas. The only question is, who will have the courage to start? The therapist may structure the situation by giving them some idea of systems theory; he may also destructure their fantasies about what he will contribute. But once the reunion has begun to move, usually with the senior people firing the first guns, the battle is on; the therapist need only sit still and watch. Many times there is so much stress that he will not be able to even add perspective because things are too hot for him to touch. The traditional multiple-impact approach, or recurrent meetings are generally not necessary, since the family reunion has its own dynamics; another meeting may also be difficult to arrange because of time and space. It is possible, however, to use one, two, or three days of fulltime meeting, and accomplish a remarkable release of affect, discovery of new realities, detriangulation of some of the family structurings, remobilization of groups that were previously intimate, and cooling off some of the wars.

The objective of such a conference is to resolve rifts in the family subgroups, and, almost as important, the discovery of who the other family members are, how they live, and the way they operate. Like resolving intrapsychic ambivalence, it's an integrative process. If you ask me whether this effort is supposed to reorganize the entire family, my answer is, I have no intention of trying for that. However, the discovery that one belongs to a family, and can call on blood connections makes a great deal of difference to people who feel isolated in a socially manipulative, cold, urban community.

When the family group becomes convinced that I really do believe that people know more than anybody, a kind of serendipity may develop. The group may bring the minister who was their first counselor; or they may recall what the family physician said during that last asthmatic attack. One family brought mother's newly acquired stepfather, who had been accused of killing the father in a brawl. Still another extended family brought a neighbor who was invited by the family to spread the dirty linen on the table, and did so to everyone's benefit.

Many times the therapist is well advised to keep a low profile, except to ask forgiveness for his own personal circumstances: "Sorry, I'm not Catholic," or "Wish I could speak Dutch."

One almost universal fallout residue of the three-generation approach is a sense of dignity in the family as a whole—a sense that "We are the John W. Does." This perspective and historical awareness make possible a feeling of continuity which is not present at the ordinary family parties, weddings, or funerals. Often the discovery of the grandparents by the grandchildren may evoke forgiveness and a group esprit, which have the long-range effect of healing that kind of stir-crazy stress so usual in the isolated nuclear family. A suburban mother's battle fatigue, or the workaholic addiction of a successful father are really massive problems; they are difficult to resolve with the limited facilities of the nuclear group and their therapist.

One further spinoff from the use of the family as consultant is an empathic sense of wholeness which serves as an excellent counterforce to the cultural alienation so neatly defined by Kiser as the "delusion of fusion," and which also increases each individual's readiness to face his own aloneness and his time-measured finiteness.

Interaction within the three-generation group may neatly define and lubricate the interface between the generations. The therapist can easily stimulate them to talk about the good old days which allows the grandchildren to picture family rituals and enjoy biographical tidbits. Each generation group may come to admit that it is only possible to belong to one's own generation, so that role expectations are eased, and new roles are developed. The interface between the sexes—flirtation between grandma and grandson, between grandfather and granddaughter—may often serve to relieve much oedipal guilt in the nuclear family, and turn love and sexuality into an integrated, rather than a dissociated recreation.

The interface between the two families of origin is especially benefited. Each family of origin secretly claims all the adapted offspring, and parenthetically attributes to the other family all misfits, either real or imagined. The jealousy thus induced may escalate and spread. A family conference often burns away this dissonance by the warmth of visual introjection. This recognition of otherness further induces in the individuals a sense of self-esteem unrelated to the self-respect derived from the drive for success. Every individual has his own I-position in his family of origin; and it's given a third dimension by increased belonging to the three-generation group.

Covertly, and at times overtly, the individual sees himself twenty-five years ago and twenty-five years from now, and this sense of projected time redefines the present in right-brain wholeness in a way not possible by any episode of therapeutic working-through. Some members may even begin to make tentative forays into a new adulthood. Roles become flexible. Teenagers can contribute wisdom, oldsters can dare to be irresponsibly childlike, men can be tender, and couples freshly loving. Grandparents may become fun playmates for the first time.

When the three-generation system has been assembled, whether as a preventive experience, a healing force, as consultant to the frustrated therapist, or to mediate a three-generation civil war, the long-range benefits may outweigh the immediate ones. Increased flexibility in role demands are almost automatic; frequently loyalty debts and covert collusions are altered. Involvement in the metagame of change allows new visual introjections of individuals and subgroups, thus altering each person's intrapsychic family. Discovering that one belongs to a whole, and that the bond can not be denied, often makes possible a new freedom to belong, and of course thereby a new ability to individuate.

CHAPTER 11

Family Therapy with One Person and the Family Therapist's Own Family

Elizabeth A. Carter, M.S.W., and Monica McGoldrick Orfanidis, M.S.W.

This article is based on the theoretical concepts of Dr. Murray Bowen, which have been fully elaborated in his writings and are therefore only cursorily outlined in this paper (Refs. 1, 2, 3). It should be noted that this theoretical framework, family systems theory, provides a way of thinking and intervening in the full spectrum of social and emotional functioning. Family thereapy in this framework is not considered to be a specific treatment modality among many, with indications and contraindications. Rather, this orientation provides a way of thinking about people in the context of their family emotional system, in response to any variety or degree of dysfunctioning in any family member. Based firmly on the systems idea that if one person changes, all others in emotional contact with him will have to make compensatory changes, family therapy is not defined by or restricted to the number of family members who attend therapy sessions.

THE HISTORY

This article will describe two variations of what is basically the same process: the "coaching" of an individual in his efforts to change himself in the context of his nuclear and parental family system. The different designations in the title relate chiefly to the context in which such coaching is done, the former referring to "treatment" cases in which only one family member

193

is seen by the family therapist; the latter to the same work undertaken by family therapy trainees as part of their professional training to become family therapists. Both were initiated by Murray Bowen during the early 1960's.

At a time when the majority of family therapists still used a combination of group therapy techniques to work with families, and interspersed these with traditional individual therapy for the "sickest" or most dysfunctional member of the family, Bowen developed a systems approach that excluded working in the transference or doing supportive therapy with individual family members. He developed a way of doing family therapy with one person which grew out of his personal efforts to apply his theory to himself in his own family and his subsequent discovery that his trainees made significantly more progress when he coached them to change relationships in their own families than when he focused exclusively on their clinical work. In Bowen's clinical practice, when only one member of a family was available or motivated, or when highly conflictual spouses used therapy to attack each other or excuse themselves, he would work with the available or most motivated individual alone, teaching family concepts and the operation of emotional systems. The goal was to help the individual stop complaining about or trying to change other family members and to start defining himself in his emotional system by observing, controlling, and changing the part he played in the family process.

Since 1967 a number of family therapists have published reports of their systematic efforts at defining themselves in their families of origin following Bowen's example and the principles of his theory (Refs. 4, 5, 6, 7, 8, 9, 10, 11).* Several training programs have set up groups and seminars specifically devoted to the trainee's emotional functioning in his own family, after this was begun by Bowen at Georgetown. Such professional seminars vary in size, length of time and depth of exploration of the subject. Some groups meet for a weekend or for several sessions and simply introduce trainees to the general idea of looking at themselves in the way they look at "patients", while other such seminars meet in a small structured group format initiated by Dr. Philip Guerin for the coaching of trainees in serious long-term personal family work.

At The Center For Family Learning, where both authors teach, the study and work on the family therapist's own family is a mandatory part of the curriculum and is interwoven with clinical seminars and supervision of the trainees' clinical work. In our experience there and at other training centers where our staff teaches or has taught, there appears to be a relationship between work done by a therapist in his own family of origin and his clinical proficiency as a family therapist. Such a connection

---

*In addition, at least one such presentation can be heard each fall at the Georgetown Symposium on Family Psychotherapy in Washington, D.C.

has long been reported by Bowen, but is still by no means universally agreed upon in the field. Nor is it generally agreed that working with extended family is a necessary or even relevant part of family therapy for "patient" families. The structuralist therapists, led by Salvador Minuchin, strategic therapists such as Jay Haley, and advocates of brief problem-focused therapy such as Watzlawick, Weakland, and Fisch in Palo Alto, all work only on nuclear family problems in the here and now, including extended family members only if they are directly involved in the household and in the current crisis. Training in these methods of family therapy does not include work on the therapist's own family, which is considered professionally irrelevant. Bowen, at the other extreme, considers that intense emotional problems cannot be resolved within the nuclear family process and advocates ignoring the current crisis and focusing therapeutic work on the families of origin of one or both spouses. At the Center For Family Learning, Philip Guerin and Thomas Fogarty, both trained by Bowen, tend to work back and forth on similar patterns in both nuclear and extended families (whether working with one or more family members). The majority of other family therapists do not take an exclusively family approach in their therapeutic work with individuals, Norman Paul being a notable exception.

FAMILY THERAPY WITH ONE INDIVIDUAL AND TRADITIONAL INDIVIDUAL THERAPY: SOME DIFFERENCES

In the family systems approach, discussion focuses on overall patterns, and not on the individual's intraphsychic processes; the "patient" of choice is the most motivated and functional one in the family, rather than the "sickest"; emphasis is on the who, what, when, where, and how of family patterns and themes, rather than on the why of individual motivation; feelings are preferably talked *about* and related to family emotional patterns, rather than escalated in direct expression to the therapist; the main work of the therapy is conducted outside of therapy sessions in the relationships with actual family members, rather than during sessions in the relationship with the therapist; teaching, thinking, planning, and other intellectual processes are given priority over interpretation, insight, or emotional catharsis and support; emotional functioning is viewed in the context of universal reciprocal processes ranging in degree from family to family. This does not discount the impact of the internal psychological or physiological system on a persons functioning. Rather, the internal and external systems are seen as having significant impact on each other. In fact, recent research has begun to indicate correlations between the internal and external systems. (13, 14)

Because the goal of the systems method is to coach the individual in work to be undertaken in his actual natural family group, the direct therapeutic importance of the relationship between therapist and patient is greatly diminished. Emotional issues and expression of feelings are steered toward the natural relationship where they belong, rather than being displaced into the therapy session or the therapy relationship. It follows that in family systems therapy, even with only one member, transference phenomena will be actively discouraged, and the therapist, in the posture of consultant, will try to keep himself from being pulled into the family emotional field, or from entering it intentionally, while developing a reality-oriented, open, and hopefully friendly relationship with the individual who is consulting him.

BASIC FAMILY SYSTEMS ASSUMPTIONS

The assumptions of family systems therapy are based on the idea that the family is the primary, and except in rare circumstances, the most powerful emotional system we ever belong to, which shapes and continues to determine the course and outcome of our lives. As in any system, relationships and functioning (physical, social, and emotional) are interdependent, and a change in one part of the system is followed by compensatory change in other parts of the system. Such primary impact makes the family our greatest potential resource as well as our greatest potential source of stress.

Family relationships tend to be highly reciprocal, patterned, and repetitive, and to have circular rather than linear motion. In other words, cause and effect thinking, which asks why, and looks for someone to blame for a problem, is not useful in identifying patterns and tracing their flow, since all family patterns, once established, are perpetuated by everyone involved in them, including their so-called "victims". If any one of the participants changes, his predictable emotional input and reactions also changes, interrupting the natural flow. Other family members will be jarred out of their own unthinking responses, and in the automatic move toward homeostasis that is inherent in all systems will react by trying to get the disrupter back into place again. In two-person sub-systems, such as married couples or a parent-child relationship, the element of reciprocity of emotional functioning can be striking, as in the enduring marriages of the villain and the saint, the master and the slave, the dreamer and the doer, the optimist and the pessimist, or in the involvement between nagging mother and dawdling child. From a systems point of view, there is no blame or causality on either side of these patterns; instead there is active participation of both in order to perpetuate them, with ramifications for the rest of the family and antecedents in previous generations.

The emotional forces of interdependence tend to lead to a kind of fusion, or stuck-togetherness of family members within the system. Family members fail to develop themselves or they give up part or most of their autonomy because of their perception that otherwise they will disturb other family members. The effort of family therapy with one person is to help this person to define his own individual beliefs and life goals apart from the family's presumption of shared positions, policy, and goals. The measure of emotional maturity is thus that an individual is able to think, plan, know, and follow his own beliefs and self directed life course, rather than having to react to the cues of those close to him. Such a person does not spend a great deal of his life energy on winning approval, attacking others, or maneuvering in relationships to obtain emotional comfort. He can move freely from emotional closeness in person-to-person relationships to work on his personal life goal and back, at will. He can freely take "I-Positions," which are calm statements of his beliefs or feelings without having to attack others or defend himself. In his person-to-person relationships, he can relate openly, without needing to talk about others or to focus on activities or impersonal things in order to find common ground.

The basic stable unit of an emotional system is the triangle, which occurs in every two-person system under stress. Few people can relate personally for very long before running into some issue in their relationship that makes one or both anxious, at which point it is automatic to triangle in a third person or thing as a way of diverting the anxiety in the relationship of the twosome. It is dysfunctional in the sense that it offers stabilization through diversion, rather than through resolution of the issue in the twosome's relationship. Thus, a couple under stress may focus on a child whose misbehavior gives them something to come together on in mutual concern. Repeated over time triangling will become a chronic dysfunctional pattern, preventing resolution of differences in the marriage and making one or more of the three vulnerable to physical or emotional symptoms, because stabilization with dysfunction, although problematic, is experienced as preferable to change.

In a triangle, the three relationships are interdependent; they are not three separate person-to-person dyads. Any dyad in a triangle is a function of the other two. The more distance there is between spouses, the closer one spouse will be to the third point of the triangle, for example, to a child or a grandparent. The closer one parent and one child are to each other, the more distant both will be from the other parent. If the child attempts to change this by moving toward the distant parent, he will disturb his current relationship with the close parent and also that parent's relationship with the distant parent. De-triangling, in family systems parlance, is the process whereby one of these three frees himself from the enmeshment of the three, and develops separate person-to-person relationships with each of the other two. Involvement in triangles and interlocking triangles which span the generations is one of the key mechanisms whereby patterns of relating and functioning are transmitted over the generations in a family.

The concepts of fusion and reactive distance, or total cutoff, are central to systems theory. The pull for togetherness in a relationship can be pictured as exerting a force like that of two magnets. When the pull becomes too strong and threatens to engulf individuality and blur separateness, there will be a reactive pulling away on the part of one or both. Much of the emotional interaction between spouses, and between parents and children, consists of the jockeying of both parties for an optimal position in relation to the other, in which the emotional bond will be felt as comfortable, rather than too close or too distant. Since each is highly likely to have a different comfort range, the shifting back and forth is continuous. When the emotional intensity in the system is too great, the pull toward fusion too strong, family members frequently try to cut off the relationship entirely.

Cutting off a relationship by physical or emotional distance does not end the emotional process: in fact it intensifies it. If one cuts off his relationships with his parents or siblings, the emotional sensitivities and yearnings from these relationships tend to push into new relationships, with a spouse or with children, seeking all the more urgently for resolution. The new relationships will tend to become problematic under this pressure and lead to further distancing and cutoffs.

Since distancing and cutting off primary relationships does not work, something different must be done. First, a person has to define clearly to himself, and then to the others, where he stands on all important issues in the family. He will have to take responsibility for his own beliefs, feelings, and actions, and distinguish this sense of personal responsibility from tendencies either toward overresponsibility or its opposite. An overresponsible person may fear disclosing an important personal stand on some matter to his parents, "because it would hurt them." The opposite stance involves his forcing his thoughts on others in an attempt to prove himself right or as a way of punishing the other for lack of agreement or approval. Both approaches are irresponsible and show he is not clear about the support he needs to give to himself in life, and what he may legitimately ask or expect of others. He must think about what is entailed in being responsible for oneself and responsible to but not *for* others. A person's characteristic sense of personal and interpersonal responsibility is usually related primarily to his sibling position and to the structure and expectations of his family of origin. (Ref. 12)

All these assumptions underlie the idea that if one person changes his emotional functioning in his family of origin, the system will change; previous patterns will tend not to repeat themselves, and the person will be able to function more freely in his current and future relationships, whether these be family, social or professional.

BASIC OPERATIONS

The ideal goal of family work according to Bowen is to get a person-to-person relationship with each living person in your extended family. The process of working out personal relationships occurs at different levels, and the work on each level depends on each person's individual timing.

The most intimate level is the nuclear family: spouse and children. This area is often the most intense because of the high level of present involvement. However, for most people it is also the area of highest motivation. The next level is that of the family of origin. The most difficult relationships to work out here are also the most important: the triangle with one's parents, and then the relationships with one's siblings. Aunts, uncles or grandparents are at a somewhat greater distance. But these relationships may prove extremely fruitful for an understanding of some of the closer relationships and for reversing the repetitive patterns. At a still greater distance are the cousins, and the family history and genealogy. The payoff for work at these distant levels is least immediate, but it can give a rich perspective on one's origins or on certain highly significant family patterns which may flow over many generations.

If you can change the part you play in your family, and hold it despite the family's reaction, while keeping in emotional contact with the system, the family will change to accommodate your change. Any change thus involves a minimum of three steps: (1) The change, (2) The family's reaction to the change, and (3) Dealing with the family's reaction to the change.

Most of us do a two-step much of the time: we attempt to change, but when someone says "Change back," we do it. Successful change involves going beyond this, and planning how to deal with the predictable reaction to the initial effort. This intense and automatic reaction of the system to maintain homeostasis and resist change has led to the development of various paradoxical strategies.

Humor

Among the most significant of these techniques is humor. Humor is one of the most effective ways to detoxify a situation. Part of the very nature of triangles, ruts, labels, and rigid patterns is that we feel stuck, and take the situation too seriously. Surprise and a gently humorous redefinition of a situation may jostle that inflexibility in such a way that the challenge is softened by an element of sharing. After a long story about mother's "unbelievable intrusiveness," for instance, a coach might smile and ask, "How come you don't appreciate her great love for you?"

Carrying a situation to the point of absurdity may often help people gain perspective on their overly intense involvement in a rigid position, and reduce what was threatening and serious to triviality. After long complaints about a husband's conversational style at a party the therapist may say, "I really don't think you ought to take him anywhere with you until he learns how to behave right."

Furthermore, the very act of sharing a laugh can help to reduce the tension and restore some of the commonality that has been cut off by bitterness. By suddenly disorganizing the established social situation, humor creates a surprising new arrangement and opens new possibilities. "Just think," one therapist remarked, "of the wonderful opportunity that impossible woman is giving you to learn patience!" Humor relabels a situation and thus allows one to gain power over a system in which he had previously been caught.

Reversals

A number of techniques are specifically useful for shifting family patterns. A primary strategy here is the reversal, an attempt to change a habitual pattern of relating by saying the opposite of what you usually say or do in response to someone else. The reversal expresses the unspoken and unacknowledged other side of an issue, and tends to break up rigid, predictable, repetitive communication patterns. A wife who ordinarily gets angry when her husband gets sick, and calls him a hypochondriac reverses her pattern and plays Florence Nightingale, a man who usually can't talk to his father because he's so dictatorial, asks for advice.

It is important to realize that strategies such as reversals are not to be undertaken lightly. They only succeed when the person doing them has the emotional control to edit his feelings of hurt, anger, sarcasm, and vengeance out of such communications, and when they are done in a manner consistent with the style of the doer. Such techniques are not a substitute for, or part of, person-to-person intimacy. In disciplined hands they can substitute for the existing destructive emotional games and repetitive interchanges that are part of every relationship, and thus reduce some of the distance or repetitious conflict that stands in the way of intimacy.

De-Triangling

Detriangling is frequently accomplished with the use of reversals. Detriangling is shifting the motion of a triangle. Reversals can be used which refer to the recurring pattern in the triangle, but which place the speaker in a different position in the triangle. For example, a son who has an overly close relationship with his mother and a distant relationship with his father might detriangle by going to his father with the confidences his mother has shared with him, and say, "Your wife seems terribly upset and I hope you can help her out. I don't know why, but she came to me with her worries, and said. . . ."

Opening up a Closed System

In trying to get family members to talk about important but buried issues, there are several ways to proceed. Sometimes it can be done merely by contacting family members who have been cut off from the family; or it can be done by carefully raising the loaded issues with various family members. A more complex operation for a system not in current crisis is what Bowen calls setting up a tempest in a teapot: magnifying small emotional issues in such a way that old dormant triangles are activated and can be dealt with in a new manner. Tactics that stir up, without attacking, an emotional system that is not currently in a state of tension are necessary because emotional patterns are not clear when the system is calm. The triangles and other patterns are dormant, available for use in the next family crisis.

It might be necessary to activate a dormant triangle, for example, if a person cannot move directly toward his father without the father's withdrawing. In such a case it may be necessary to move toward those people with whom the father has relationships, perhaps the father's siblings or his parents. Such moves not only can provide a wealth of information and perspective on the father, but may also activate the triangle between the father, his brother, and their mother. Once the father realizes that his brother is giving family information, he may feel himself impelled to open up with his side of the story. If the father felt like the outsider in the relationship with his mother and brother, he is likely to fear being the outsider again if his own child moves toward his brother. If the direct contact with the uncle is not enough to create a shift, the son may want to raise a toxic issue with the uncle, on the theory that the uncle may then take a different move with the father and thus open the system. If the system is very closed, the son may have to magnify a small issue, or spread a "rumor" with the uncle in order to push the system to react.

Taking an "I-Position"

An I-position is a clear statement, neither offensive nor defensive, of one's thoughts or feelings on a subject. Ultimately one hopes to be able to relate by stating clearly his I-Positions, but there are many times when other ways of communication are more useful for opening up the system. This is especially true in tight triangles, where I-Positions may create a negative reaction and tend to close down the relationship.

For example, take the situation in which a mother-in-law tells her son negative things about his wife, which the son then repeats to the wife. A reactive confrontation would be for the wife to blow up at the husband about his mother's behavior and then to blow up at the mother directly. If the wife takes an I-Position instead, she may say to the husband, "I wish you wouldn't tell me negative things your mother says about me." She may then say to the mother-in-law directly, "Your son told me what you said about me, and I was upset and hurt by your saying that to him. In the future I wish you would tell me directly what you think of me." Hopefully one does arrive at the point where one can deal with thoughts and feelings directly; but this is usually possible only when the system is relatively open and anxiety free. When it is not, I-Positions may further raise the level of tension. In this situation, therefore, the wife was advised to detriangle by use of a reversal. She told her mother-in-law, "Your son told me some of the things you've been saying about me, and I'm so pleased to know, because I was so worried that you would not like me or would wish your son hadn't married me." When the wife did this she felt a sense of immediate relief as she told her mother-in-law of her real anxiety about not being acceptable to her. The mother-in-law immediately shifted toward her, and began reassuring her about her feelings. Subsequently the husband reported that his mother had completely stopped her negative comments about the wife.

There are a number of useful rules of thumb in this work.

(1) Keep your own counsel. Don't try to share efforts with others in the family. At times there is a strong pull to differentiate together, with a spouse, for example, or a favorite sibling; but obviously differentiation is an individual process and talking about it with others in the family is likely to raise their anxiety and lead to efforts to get you to stop, or at least do it their way.

(2) Keep clearly in mind that your changes are for yourself. The work cannot be undertaken for the coach, or for anyone else but yourself; nor can it be an effort to change others in the family.

(3) Don't underestimate the family's reaction to your efforts. The family's reactiveness will be intense, and will take you off guard if you are not prepared.

(4) Have a plan. Schematizing and hypothesizing ahead of time, as well as thinking out very clearly what you want to be and do, will be very helpful in avoiding getting caught up in the family's emotional process and becoming reactive to them, rather than relating the way you want to.

(5) Use strong feelings of anger or hurt as signals. When you start to see villains or victims in the family or to feel that you are one yourself, examine your own feelings to get a better perspective on the circular processes of the system.

(6) Distinguish carefully between planned and reactive distance. It is often useful to distance from an intense emotional field in order to gain objectivity. In particular, it is useful for people who tend to move toward others to plan instead to back off. However, it is important that this move be intentional and based on flexibility, so that when the other starts moving in, you are free to come back also, rather than keeping the distance fixed.

(7) Expand the context. It is often useful, when anxiety is high, to bring up the problem with members of the larger family system in order to increase the realm in which it can be dealt with and absorbed.

(8) Keep family visits time-limited in order to maintain your focus, relate to people individually when possible, rather than at large, ritualized family gatherings.

(9) If someone is blocking the way to a distant family member, if, for instance your sister-in-law monitors all your efforts to deal directly with your brother, it is usually futile to try to find a way around such interference. It makes much more sense to deal directly with the person who is blocking, even though he or she may seem peripheral to your efforts.

(10) Writing letters is a useful way to open difficult emotional issues without having to deal immediately with the reactivity of the system. By predicting the response in the letter itself, some of the intensity can also be deflected. In general, writing individualized letters, that is, not writing to both parents together, and taking up only one emotional issue in each letter will help to focus your efforts.

THE PROCESS OF COACHING

The process of coaching a single family member in work on his family of origin, whether he be patient or family therapy trainee, appears to break down into at least five not completely distinct phases: The engagement of the client in the process; the teaching or planning phase; the re-entry; the work; and the followthrough.

ENGAGEMENT

Engagement consists of helping the client to shift his focus from self or others to an overview of self-with-others. If a patient, he may be concerned with what others are doing to him in his life or with his own upset feelings or poor functioning; if a trainee, he may be prepared to look at and "understand" others, and to discuss his feelings and judgments about them. Talk about self generally produces commentary about personal feeling states: in those who have had previous experience in individual therapy may offer long, logical, cause-and-effect explanations directed at answering the question, "Why?" Initial family histories often abound in good guys and bad guys. The individual is frequently portrayed as a victim or rescuer, with very little attempt at objective, nonjudgmental reports of emotional or behavioral transactions among family members.

At this stage we find it useful to broaden the perspective on the presenting problem or the central relationships by asking about similar issues at various levels of the system, by inquiring about various members' views of central issues, and by gradually introducing systems concepts into the discussion. We have found it helpful to recommend the reading of professional articles, especially personal family stories, to help orient those who are interested, to a family systems point of view.

During the initial phase of engagement and history taking, it is important to set a calm, matter-of-fact tone to help defuse the intensity of emotion aroused by a current crisis, or by the opening of anxiety-producing material. The approach emphasizes thought about overall patterns rather than direct communication of reactive emotional states. It is also useful to introduce family systems concepts as soon as the anxiety is low enough for them to be heard including ideas about emotional interaction, reciprocity, triangles, changing self, effects of sibling position on relationships, and the transmission of relationship patterns from one generation to the next.

PLANNING

Planning is usually an indistinct continuation of the initial stage of engagement; it is reached when the client's anxiety has diminished and he begins to discuss how his thoughts and feelings fit into family patterns, and to give some consideration to possible changes he might make and their effects. He may ask; "If I were to try to get to know my father better, how would I go about it and how would that help me with my current problem?" Understated questions designed to elicit in detail the tone and history of this relationship and the main triangles in which it is embedded are often better than suggestions for concrete actions which may shoot his anxiety up again.

The first real step in planning is to ask the person to draw up a genogram. This is a map of the family structure over at least three generations, showing family relationships with factual data on names, births, deaths, marriages, divorces, geographical location, and all significant physical, social, and psychological changes or dysfunctioning.

We also ask for a family chronology, which is like a time map, as the genogram is a structure map. It shows in chronological order the major family events and stresses, and is especially useful for understanding the motion of family patterns over time. This is important due to the relationship of major family events is often obscured within the family because of the anxiety caused by stress.

Some people have a difficult time figuring out the family issues or themes that are important to them even after they have become intellectually committed to the idea of working on themselves in their families. This is especially true for trainees who are not experiencing a current family crisis; with people who are part of a cohesive, calm family, where politeness and civility are experienced as closeness and openness; and with people who are emotionally distant or cut off from their families for vague rather than explosive reasons. In such cases we have found it extremely beneficial to have the person sculpt his family in a group setting.

The technique of family sculpting was developed by Peggy Papp, who brought it to its present usefulness in therapy and training. Family sculpting is a technique whereby a person arranges people who represent his family members, in a tableau that shows their emotional relationship to each other. It is a graphic way to demonstrate family systems concepts, and to engage a person so that he can appreciate the relevance of the family relationship system to his personal emotional experiences. In the sculpting, the person arranges and shifts other people who represent his family members in their emotional and spacial relationship to each other over time. The transmission of family relationship patterns over generations, and the impact of major stressful events and changes, such as births, moves, and deaths are graphically conveyed by this technique. When the tableau is set in motion, it can become very clear how the subject is emotionally caught in the family system, and his characteristic patterns for trying to cope with this position.

Although we do not suggest concrete moves in a family at an early planning stage, there is actually no such thing as no move if there is any contact with the family. People frequently report rather dramatic reactions in the family in response to requests for information to fill out the genogram. Their own awareness and thinking about themselves may be altered just by making up the genogram or the family chronology. In addition, the very process of looking at the family this way shifts the focus from guilt and blame to a more objective researcher position. As the client begins to observe and listen at a family gathering, instead of participating as usual, shifts may occur; these should be carefully noted and incorporated in the planning.

Gaps in the genogram or family chronology are obvious places to start the work of learning about the system and changing one's relationships. The assumption is that the more facts you know, the better position you are in to evaluate what has happened in your family and thus to understand your own position and to change it if you wish. In terms of gaining a preliminary focus on the family patterns, for example, one could look at the similarity between the central triangles over three generations: self, mother, father, and each parent with his or her parents; the effects of sibling position on the family process and triangling in each generation; and the stress on the family at crucial points in the family history, such as just before the marriage, and around the birth of each of the children. Other things that may be examined are the patterns of reciprocity in the marriages in the family: who overfunctions and who underfunctions; who tends to move in, and who tends to move out; and what the toxic issues are in the family that tend to be avoided. All of these are of primary importance.

The authors favor holding off on concrete moves in a family at least long enough for the person to get a general notion of how the emotional system operates, what the central issues are, and what the person's own agenda and motivations are. If he wants to make someone else happy, save someone, change someone, tell someone off, get someone's approval, or justify and explain himself, the effort will fail, and will in any case not be worth the struggle, since it will represent either no change, or at best the other side of the coin, as when the victim becomes the bully.

RE-ENTRY

The process of differentiating can be rather simply defined: It consists of developing personal relationships with each member of the family, particularly with each parent: and of detriangling oneself, or changing one's part in the old repetitious, dysfunctional emotional patterns that involve multiple family members, particularly when family tension is high. This sounds so simple that it is difficult to convey the anxiety that is aroused each step of the way, even in those most committed to the work. The first moves to be recommended by the therapist will depend on what kinds of relationships the client currently maintains with family members, and what kind of motivation he has for changing these relationships. A relationship which has been intense and conflictual will require a more gentle re-approach than one which is characterized by a distancing.

Mary, a middle aged wife who had not seen her parents for many years, had spent several sessions describing her current marital and in-law conflicts. She had not corresponded with her mother since an angry exchange of letters several years before. She had not heard from her father since her parents divorced at about the same time. She considered them "hopeless" and irrelevant to her current life and problems. After looking over and discussing the striking patterns of marital conflict, in-law problems, and emotional cutoffs on her genogram, she wrote a letter to her mother in which she referred briefly to their last argument, and then went on in a rather chatty, friendly way to bring her up to date on general family news. To her father, for whom she had fewer conflictual feelings, she was encouraged to write in more depth about her life, and to propose a meeting with him in the near future.

If the person is involved in a conflictual relationship with a parent, and the issue has been displaced onto some specific concrete explosion, such as a falling out over some long past insult, or onto some abstract issue such as religion or politics, we frequently recommend that the person "let go of the rope" as a first step, so that the personal emotional issues can have a chance to emerge. In other words, the person is asked to drop his stubborn hold on the issue so that the relationship can move on to other more important issues.

Kathy came from an Irish Catholic family. She was the only member who had left the Church and married a Protestant. Since her marriage she had had little contact with her mother because, she said, her mother kept bringing up religion and they would get into fights. She was convinced there was no way to talk to her mother about anything else, because her mother was such a fanatic that everything in her life was colored by her religion. After some discussion, Kathy wrote to her mother that she was coming to appreciate her mother's strong faith, and although she wished she could share it, she could not. She said she admired her mother's inner peace, which seemed to be related to her faith, and that she felt somewhat lonely and cut off from her family as a result of not being able to share their faith. To her great surprise, her mother responded warmly, saying she had been very touched by the letter, was surprised that Kathy thought she had such inner peace because at times she indeed felt troubled, and that she was sorry that Kathy felt isolated. From here Kathy was able to move into dealing with her own important personal issues with her mother.

If a person maintains routine, dutiful contact with the family through general letters addressed to both parents or phone conversations with mother, who acts as the central switchboard relayer of family news, it is suggested that the person establish direct contact with father and other family members. This shift alone may bring many buried issues to the surface.

Harold, a forty-year-old executive, described his family as "friendly and close." He saw no connections between the state of his family relationships and the problem for which he sought help: dealing with the effects of his wife's serious physical illness. He called his mother weekly for an exchange of general family news. He saw his father, brother, and sister on holiday get togethers a few times a year. When asked how difficult he thought it would be to talk directly with each family member, he shrugged and said there would be no difficulty in that, but it would make no real difference. However, when he started to do it, he found that he became intensely nervous after a few minutes of talk with his father because he could find nothing to say; that his brothers quickly turned the phone over to their wives; and that his sister responded to a letter from him with an angry attack about his having left responsibility for their aging parents entirely to her. These responses in himself and his family enabled him to recognize that he had been emotionally pulling away from his wife in her illness as he had pulled away from his family and their concerns. He embarked on restoring his family relationships with the initial motivation that they could offer each other support.

If the person has an over close relationship with one or both parents that is not overtly conflictual, a first step might be to break off routine patterns such as daily phone calls or weekly visits on a certain day, making contacts less frequent and more unpredictable.

Such initial contact steps are usually followed with brief visits, during which the person's main task is to observe and listen to family interaction in a new way. This information is then incorporated into further planning sessions during which tentative hypotheses are developed concerning the role the person plays in the family process; and predictions are made about the reactions of others to any changes in posture or behavior on his part.

THE WORK

Once the client has begun to think about himself and his family in systems terms, and to take initial moves to shift his position, he may begin to put a lot of work into this endeavor, often focused around one or two major issues in the family. This work is so individualized and depends so much on the particular family situation that it can best be described by example.

Alison, a twenty-five-year-old family therapy trainee, became interested in family systems after hearing a professional presentation in which the possibility and value of establishing person-to-person relationships with one's family was suggested. Alison became very anxious at the idea, particularly in terms of her relationship with her mother. This had been stormy and negative as she grew up, and had become somewhat more distant and tenuously calm after four years of individual therapy. She had "realized" that her mother was a woman with her own problems, limited in what she could give to her daughter; and that the best thing to do was to keep things calm and not get too involved, focusing instead on marriage and friends.

In her work with other families Alison was competent and clear-thinking when things went well, as was also true of her in her own family. But when things bogged down she would begin to react in ways that led to her becoming more stuck. She would become an overresponsible do-gooder, placating and making everything "nice" in the nuclear family system. She would say, "Let's just all work together and we'll make everything fine." Meanwhile, Alison was the one "working together," and the family was becoming more and more passive or even negative about change. Or Alison might try to reason them into changing. She had a lot of faith in logic. "If I can just talk them into understanding each other, things will get better." Under greater stress she would become the advocate of the "victim" in the system, perhaps a withdrawn son or a passive, overworked father. She would thus move into being the blamer of the "villain," frequently a bossy, nagging mother or wife. If there was a silence she tended to move in and fill it. Even under the best of circumstances she tended to work for a kind of romanticized closing off of the nuclear family, with the idea that the family that talks together stays together. It was as though she believed that talking would cure anything.

As Alison listened to the presentation, she realized acutely how much she missed having a positive relationship with her mother, although the relationship was no longer as negative as it had once been. The distance from her mother involved a triangle with her father in which Alison was his favorite and would talk to him about how difficult her mother was. There was also a triangle involving her husband, her mother, and herself in which she tried to mediate between them. Alison began to think there might be a great deal to be gained from getting to know her mother in particular and other family members as well.

Several months later, when her mother came to visit for the first time since Alison had been married two years previously although they lived only fifty miles apart, Alison took the opportunity to discuss with her mother some issues about the mother's family. Alison said she was interested in understanding herself better, and thought some of her mother's family experiences might help her do that. Mrs. Connor became very defensive and said that absolutely nothing from her miserable childhood had been carried over to the way she had raised her own children. Alison continued to push for discussion of her mother's background, and her mother accused Alison of "trying to destroy" her by bringing up unpleasant subjects. Alison dimly sensed that her mother's difficulty talking about issues was not a withholding behavior meant personally against her, but she couldn't think of any way to proceed in the face of this difficulty.

At this point Alison began systematic coaching sessions, in which it was suggested that pushing her mother was no way to get either the information or the relationship she was looking for. Alison's initial coaching sessions occurred about every two weeks for the first year, once a month during the second year, and a couple of times during the third year: they helped to clarify some of the general family patterns, as well as some things Alison would have to change if she wanted a different relationship with her family.

The women in the family were generally dominant, smart pushers, often seen as villains. The men were seen as victims: intelligent, kind, loving introverts who had to put up with their nagging wives. The family generally related on the basis of keeping the peace and trying to agree about everything. No one in the family ever made a scene. The rule was, you didn't talk about problems. No one ever got sick, divorced, arrested, became alcoholic, or had therapy. In fact, using Jay Haley's definition of a normal family as one in which no member has ever had therapy or been arrested, this family was normal until Alison took them over the brink by entering therapy.

Alison, known in the family as "Daddy's girl," the "Philadelphia lawyer," and the "family psychologist," was the middle of three daughters from a Boston Irish family. However, the family kept no ethnic connections. In fact, the predominant family pattern was to close off the nuclear family in a nice, no-conflict set up, concentrating on friends—who, after all, you could choose—and maintaining only the most superficial contact with relatives on rare holiday visits. Alison's father, Mr. Connor, called "Sweetie" by his wife, a shy, warm, humorous, intellectual lawyer, was the oldest of three in his mother-dominated family of origin, in which all the children were overprotected, and from which none of them ever really escaped. He married his wife at forty-two and formed with her a mutual caretaking relationship. Mary Connor, called "Boss" by her husband, an attractive, dynamic, talented go-getter, was the youngest of three daughters, very attached to her self-educated, quiet father, while she disliked and felt rejected by her mother, whom she described as exquisitely beautiful and utterly vain. Alison's older sister was known as the "princess," and her younger sister as the "strong arm."

Alison was somewhat of an over-functioner in her family: the mediator, the caretaker of the emotional system, even-tempered, although at times much too persistent and judgmental.

Some of the difficulties of Alison's role in her family of origin began to surface when she married a very introverted Italian scientist. The difficulties of highly reciprocal, rather stereotyped roles soon became apparent. Alison became the pusher in the marriage, but her husband fought back, a reaction very different from the patterns in her own family. Integrating the two systems was quite difficult, and had led her to thoughts of cutting off completely from her own family in order to work out a relationship with her husband and fit into his world.

Alison's first attempts in her family were directed at changing the relationship with her mother. She made a concerted effort not to ask questions about her mother's family; to find out as much as possible about mother and her family from aunts, family friends, and any other source she could find; to tell her mother about herself—her work, marriage, thoughts, fears; and to make positive comments about her mother's side of the family, and to play down her father's side, with whom she had always been identified.

The first move was to contact her mother's oldest sister, Aunt Frances, whom Alison had not seen in fifteen years. Though the aunt seemed astonished to hear from her, and a bit suspicious, she invited Alison to visit. Alison discovered that it was quite easy to talk to her about the family background. Aunt Frances told her many things about Alison's mother Mary and their parents, including a description of the night Alison's mother was born. This impressed Alison particularly, because she had always imagined her mother as a full-grown, imposing, overpowering mother and never as a baby. The experience gave Alison many new perspectives on her mother.

The trip to see Aunt Frances was made without notifying Alison's mother, who soon heard about it from Frances. Mary then began volunteering considerable information about her family, perhaps to make sure that Alison was getting the "correct story." The two sisters, who had maintained only superficial contact for twenty-five years, began to contact each other regularly, spent several holidays together, and made a vacation trip together to the homeland of their ancestors.

Soon after this visit, Alison gingerly asked her mother if she could discuss something about her family which Aunt Frances had mentioned. Her mother replied, "Alison, if there is anything I can do to help you understand more about yourself, I'll be more than willing." Alison was shocked at the reference to their first conversation, because she had assumed she had not gotten through to her mother. From that point on, Alison and her mother moved slowly toward a more open relationship. She began telling family stories and giving Alison family pictures to keep for an archive, and discussing many personal experiences in a more open way.

Alison then visited her mother's middle sister, Aunt Kate, from whom her mother had been totally cut off since their mother's terminal illness, when they had a falling out over the care of the mother. This sister, Kate, had been her mother's favorite and also very close to Mary as a child. Alison had known so little about her mother's family that she had not realized that this cut off existed. She thought the families had little contact because they lived in distant cities and did not like to write. That was how this particular system operated. Negative feelings were not expressed or dealt with, but went underground, and a quiet cutoff of the emotional relationship would occur. Contact with Aunt Kate was harder to achieve because Kate associated Alison with Mary and went through several blatant evasive maneuvers before finally agreeing to a luncheon date.

Alison and Kate had a pleasant lunch, during which Alison heard many family stories from yet a different point of view. For example, Alison's mother had always said that Alison's grandmother had no "useful" activities in life. Mary would reply to questions about the grandmother in an annoyed tone. "She did nothing, she thought about nothing. She just went shopping." Aunt Frances, however, had spoken of grandmother's difficult life, full of worry about her husband who had a very dangerous and time-consuming job which left her frequently alone. Aunt Kate had yet another view on Alison's grandmother. "Oh, my mother had the most fabulous taste! She used to go shopping, and she had the most incredible eye for beauty. She could go into a junk shop and come out with the one exquisite antique in the whole town." Alison almost burst out laughing as she suddenly realized that her own mother had the same knack, and was in fact an antique dealer who spent her life shopping for interesting and beautiful things.

Getting to know her aunts and learning from them more about her mother's family background gave Alison a strong appreciation of her mother's experience and enabled her to relate much more flexibly to her mother.

Over the first year of her work, Alison also worked in other areas: to delabel her father as the "poor victim" of her mother's dominance, for whom Alison should feel sorry, and protect with nonverbal signals; to delabel herself as "the defensive psychologist-lawyer," who probes everyone else's psyche and reveals nothing about herself. This was accomplished primarily by making frequent references to her own feelings and problems, and by making jokes about herself; to find out as much factual information as possible about both sides of the family by contacting relatives and doing research in libraries; to stay out of her husband's problems with his family by focusing on her own instead; to deal with her sisters' injunctions to stop her probing and leave them alone in much the same way as she had dealt with her mother's—that is, by taking responsibility herself for problems in their relationship, where previously she had continuously tried to get them to "gain insight" into their "defensiveness and unresponsiveness."

Alison's father was rather severely impaired by a stroke. This had left him with a serious speech difficulty which tended to exacerbate his habitual silence in the family. Since the stroke Alison had begun to avoid her father and not talk to him much, because of her discomfort at his obvious frustration when he could not find the words he sought to express himself. Finally Alison summoned the courage to tell her father she wanted to have a conversation with him about his life and several personal things. She was astounded when he not only readily agreed, but began the conversation quite dramatically by saying, "Well, you see, the first thing about my family is that my mother was a very lonely woman." They went on to discuss a number of very personal issues which Alison had always wanted to ask about but had not, for fear of making him unhappy with "unpleasant" reminiscences.

Alison's work with her husband involved a great many moves, since in such an intimate relationship there are many complex issues to work out. One of the most difficult involved her feelings and actions when her husband's mother was diagnosed as having terminal cancer. Although Alison had learned by this time not to push in too much on her husband, or probe him when there was stress, the intensity of this experience was very difficult. Being an "expert" in family relationships, she kept wanting to give him advice about what he should do, predicting doom if he did not express and deal with his feelings by a show of emotion and a lot of talk—that is, in her style. The more she talked to him and gave advice, the less responsive he became. It was with enormous difficulty that Alison pulled back and began to deal with her own feelings about death, including her many worries about the future death of her own parents.

Alison also stopped mediating between her husband and her mother. If they were unpleasant to each other or made snide comments she just let them do it and pretty soon they became friends, to the point that they began seeing each other occasionally even when Alison wasn't around. If Alison and her husband had a disagreement in front of her parents, she would joke about how she had managed to hook up with such an "uncouth" type. The first time this happened, her mother said, "You have no idea how many times I wished your father would fight or disagree with me."

Alison also made many contacts with her extended family to learn about the family history. She took a trip back to the country from which her family had emigrated, and discovered their homesteads, with relatives still living there. All these efforts gave her a greatly enriched sense of who she was.

Alison's work on her family relationships enabled her to gain an enormously more positive attitude about her own ability to work out her life as she wishes, and she was able to appreciate and relate to her family in ways she never imagined possible. She no longer works herself into such intense frustration over attempts to solve problems that instead only make them worse.

There has also been a marked difference in her clinical work. She now finds it much easier not to get locked in with a difficult family. She can back off and let them decide what they want to do, where previously she would get caught up in an overresponsible, messianic effort to make them keep working. She can express hopelessness if this is useful, where previously she thought she always had to be positive. She can more easily shift gears and go around by an indirect route if she comes to an impasse, rather than trying to hammer away at a bolted door. Previously she questioned everyone else and said nothing about herself. Now she is freer to make use of stories and jokes about herself, to go at things nonverbally, such as by sculpting, to get around the difficulties in verbalization with some families. She is able at times to suggest to family members that they not talk to each other, where previously she always suggested that they have "deep" conversations and get everything into the open. Most importantly, because she does not feel that she has to do all the work herself, she and the families are freer to work together.

FOLLOW THROUGH

The length of time that a person will devote to intensive work in his family varies with the degree of motivation and the felt impact of the results in his own life. Although Bowen reports consistent cases of continued intensive work for four or five years, it has been our experience with most patients that after some degree of change is accomplished and the presenting symptoms or crises have subsided, motivation is reduced until a new crisis appears. Family therapists and trainees may work with varying degrees of intensity over a longer period, which perhaps is related to their additional professional goals and their immersion in the ideas.

Even small changes may be experienced with considerable relief, a resurgence of hope, and, sometimes, elation. Such results may paradoxically reduce rather than increase motivation to continue. There is a great tendency at this point to slide along, until the stress on the system increases the urgency for another move. The immobilization may be strongest after a very positive shift in a system which has been severely stressed over a long period of time.

Once a person has decided to "try it," there is often a period of considerable enthusiasm. People tend to begin work around some central problematic focus: a parent, a spouse, a significant family secret, or a cutoff. After the initial impetus, some get bogged down enough to say, "I tried and it didn't work. I give up. My family's hopeless." This point may come after a single precipitous move which was not clearly thought out, and which scared the person and his family into a standoff. The thought of giving up may also occur after a well-planned move which did in fact shift the system.

However, if the person has been caught up in the family's reactions, he may see the shift as negative, and his move as unsuccessful. Sometimes, during work on a relationship that mistakenly ignores an important triangle in which the dyad is imbedded, the intensity of the third person's reaction is seen as a new and startling problem which may confuse and overwhelm the person working. This is particularly likely to occur when a sibling has not been taken into account in the planning of work with a parent.

It is interesting the extent to which the importance and the potential of sibling relationships is denied or overlooked by many people. Although siblings have participated in more of our primary experiences than anyone else in our lives, it is frequently stated about them that, "We have nothing in common."

Everyone seems to work in phases interspersed with periods of inactivity, and to vary in the ability to work at certain levels. For example, some people work very well for a time in the nuclear family, but have great difficulty moving into the extended family. Some will work well and hard in the parental generation, but resist dealing with a spouse. At times a coach may recommend shifting some particular issue to another level of work as a way around an impasse at the present level.

Those who work in a systematic way over an extended period of time can have very positive results in the form of relief or reversal of immediate stress, and an ability to deal differently with future stress.

Coaching sessions, or therapy appointments, may begin at regular weekly or biweekly intervals; but these intervals will usually be lengthened as the focus shifts from learning and planning to doing the work. A systems therapist rarely terminates a case, in the traditional sense of a mutual decision that the work is finished. Rather, appointments gradually become spaced at longer intervals; and even when it is agreed that a major piece of work is accomplished, there is usually the understanding that the person will continue on his own trying to apply the principles in family, work, and social relationships, and that further appointments with the therapist can be sought if he gets stuck, or sees himself heading into a potential crisis. It is not uncommon for a client, after one or two years' absence to request a couple of appointments to help him get back on course. Family therapists trained in this method frequently incorporate it as a lifelong approach to all relationships, and openly check with each other when they realize they are stuck in some situation involving family or work systems.

THE COACH

Since family systems theory does not view change as something brought about through an extra family relationship, such as a corrective relationship with a therapist, concepts such as transference and therapeutic relationship are not part of the approach. The family systems therapist works to avoid direct emotional involvement with his client, while still establishing a working relationship with him. Such a posture is better described as "coach" or "consultant," than as "doctor" or "therapist"—terms derived from the medical model upon which psychiatry has been based.

A family systems coach, then, must have enough of a relationship with his client or trainee to permit open discussion of intensely personal and sensitive material, without himself becoming emotionally involved and reactive to the material. He will try to avoid taking sides emotionally with any family member and instead see all parts of the process. As he listens to his client's accounts of situations, or expressions of personal feelings and reactions, the coach mentally places these into his growing picture of the patterns of the family emotional system, and will direct the client's attention toward those patterns through questions, comments, or summaries. He will not limit himself to responding to the client's focus.

The coach will expect automatic moves on his client's part to triangle him into the process—for example, by getting him to agree that another family member is "hopeless," "crazy," or "wrong." He will work to keep himself detriangled, using many of the same techniques that he is teaching his client to use in his family. He will expect and resist attempts to get him to provide direct emotional support, approval, or reassurance. The coach will not want to become emotionally more important to a client than his family members are, nor to be more concerned or responsible for the client's life decisions and actions than the client is himself. The coach will clearly label his teachings as his own personal and professional beliefs, and not as "the truth." Rather than accuse his client of "resistance," he will take I-Positions such as, "I am not willing to continue to spend my time in this way, because I don't think it is productive or helpful." The coach will keep the emotional tone of the sessions in a low key, both to enable the client to think, and to forestall the client's directing to him emotional expressions that belong in a family relationship. When the client's anxiety is low and he is able to think objectively about his family patterns and his own part in them, the coach may help to stimulate ideas about ways to proceed by giving direct suggestions, or relating examples of how other clients, or the coach himself, handled similar situations in their families.

Paramount in the coach's task is the assessment of the intensity of emotion aroused in the client by actual or suggested moves in his family relationships, and his ability to control and modify his emotional reactivity to family members. In this regard, the importance of the coach's work in his own family becomes clear. If the client is extremely reactive to the rearrousal of the old emotional pulls, and expresses fear of going on because "she's really too old for this now," or "You don't know my father: this could give him a heart attack," the anxiety in the coach may rise also. If he has not done this work himself, it may be extremely difficult for him to evaluate the situation objectively, and to pace the work accordingly. A therapist who has not worked in his own family may tend to collude in the client's resistance, or send him ahead rashly or ill-prepared.

Beyond the basic family systems concepts, which can be taught didactically, the details of the work, the context, cultural factors, pace, timing, moves, and family reactions all offer a wide variety and style of ways to proceed. Once they have begun to grasp the basic principles and have learned to control their own reactivity in the families, most clients seem to produce a natural flow of ideas that are consistent with their own and their family's styles. When they become stuck and are pulled back into the emotional process, or if they become too anxious during predictable family efforts to get them to stop changing, a coach who is able to control his own anxiety can help reduce the client's tension to the point that he will be able to hear the coach's suggestions again and to resume his flow of ideas. It has been our experience that therapists who have not been coached through work in their own families are generally not successful in coaching others past the initial re-entry steps.

SPECIAL CIRCUMSTANCES

Although space does not permit an expanded discussion of the techniques which may be used for coaching in special circumstances, we may mention some of them briefly:

When one or both parents are dead, the client can achieve some degree of self-definition in relation to them by talking about them with their siblings or close friends, trying to get as objective a picture as possible of what they were like as people, rather than just as parents. The more objective information one can gain, the more one can evaluate oneself realistically.

When individuals were not raised by natural parents it is generally prescribed that they work to define themselves in the adoptive or foster system, since people are formed in the emotional system in which they are raised. Search for and discovery of natural parents, if the adoptee wants to do so and proceeds responsibly, will enrich the work and add depth and solidity to it. In instances where the ghost of a natural parent has been evident in the person's life, such a search for the reality of the natural parent may be a necessary part of the work. (Ref. 6)

Coaching in groups, as in professional training seminars or supervision groups, can be a very useful method. It allows trainees to move at their own pace, and to learn by displaced material from the experiences of others things that might be too emotionally charged for them to recognize immediately in their own families. However, the coach must be clear that the work is to proceed in the family process of each individual and not in the group process, which exerts a strong pull. There is often a point at which trainees working in groups will seek individual coaching appointments in addition to the group sessions. This may stem from anxiety about a family crises or difficult move in the family, or from reluctance to share some personal issues with professional peers. Following the model of training seminars, several systems therapists have reported successfully coaching single clients in groups, using the same careful structuring of the sessions to avoid slipping into group process.

Coaching by mail can be successfully accomplished if the initial planning and starting of the work has been done face-to-face.

REFERENCES

1. M. Bowen, "The Use of Family Theory in Clinical Practice," *Comprehensive Psychiatry,* 7 (1966), 345–74.
2. _____ "Toward the Differentiation of a Self in One's Family of Origin," in F. Andres and J. Lorio (eds.), *Georgetown Family Symposia: A Collection of Selected Papers,* I. Washington, D.C., 1974.
3. Anonymous. "Toward the Differentiation of a Self in One's Own Family," in J. Framo (ed.), *Family Interaction.* New York: Springer, 1972.
4. Anonymous. "Taking a Giant Step: First Moves Back Into My Family," *The Family,* 2 (1974).
5. C.F.L. Staff Member, "A Family Therapist's Own Family," *The Family* 1, (1973).
6. F. Colon, "In Search of ONe's Past: An Identity Trip," *Family Process,* 12, (1973), 429–38.
7. W. Erickson, "Reconnecting: A Therapist's Own Family," *The Family,* 2 (1975).
8. E. Friedman, "The Birthday Party: An Experiment in Obtaining Change in One's Own Extended Family," *Family Process* 10 (1971).
9. C.M. Hall, "Efforts to differentiate a Self in My Family of Origin," *Georgetown Family Symposia, A Collection of Selected Papers,* F. Andres and J. Lorio (eds.), 1. Washington, D.C., 1974.
10. Ferber et al. (eds.), *The Book of Family Therapy,* New York: Science House, 1972.
11. P. Guerin and T. Fogarty, "The Family Therapist's Own Family," *International Journal of Psychiatry,* 10 (1972).

12. W. Toman. *Family Constellation.* New York: Springer, 1969.
13. T. Holmes & M. Masuda, "Life Change and Illness Susceptibility," *Separation and Depression: Clinical and Research Aspects,* American Association for the Advancement of Science (Publ. 94), Washington, D.C., 1973.
14. Dohrenwend, B.S. and B.P. Dohrenwend, eds., *Stressful Life Events Their Nature and Effect,* John Wiley & Sons, N.Y. 1974.

CHAPTER 12

Social Networks as the Unit of Intervention

Carolyn L. Attneave, Ph.D.

By comparing clinical sessions with the excitement and behavior associated with a wide variety of other settings—such as a Preservation Hall Concert, a tribal healing ceremony, an alternate life style group meeting, a wedding, a bar mitzvah, or a class reunion—Speck and Attneave have stimulated many family therapists to become interested in family networks. They have described the energy flow in large tribal assemblies using a rationale and a number of techniques that do not depend upon pathology as a basis for intervention. Their ideas open up sessions to a range of participants that includes friends, neighbors, and colleagues, as well as conventionally identified family members.

For some therapists this idea is disturbing, or even vaguely threatening. These therapists would prefer to work within the family as a well-defined unit. Others, however, are readily able to transfer the technical aspects of their work with families to work with groups that include all significant persons in their client's lives. Indeed, working with people who share significant relationships, whether family or nonfamily, seems more logical than working with groups of "intimate strangers." It saves time and often induces changed behavior more efficiently than merely discussing the projections and fantasies about these others. It seems advantageous to utilize the social network as the unit of intervention, and to select persons to be included in sessions from the full range of relationships operative in real life.

Social network intervention builds its techniques from this rationale. It presumes that in addition to the family, people have natural social relationships which can be mobilized as natural support systems. The therapist's role is often seen as defining the sources of stress within or around the family in terms of concrete problems and human needs, and mobilizing the natural social resources and supports to solve the problems and meet the varied needs. Emphasis is on restoring control of function to the natural system rather than a professional's assuming complete responsibility.

HISTORICAL USAGE OF THE SOCIAL NETWORK CONCEPT

To understand what social networks are, and how they function, it is helpful to understand the history of the concept.

The observation that human beings who are not familially related are held together by bonds of association that are sometimes the simple result of contact and proximity, and sometimes seemingly mysterious and multidetermined, is as old as the literature about human behavior. The Book of Proverbs points out, "Better a near neighbor, than a far brother." In Greek mythology, these apparent patterns of life were associated not with any human ability to manipulate and construct relationships, but with the idea that the Fates wove a predetermined tapestry. Later on, the interrelationships between members of neighborhoods, communities, and larger political units were seen as subject to human design. The nineteenth-century novelists—for instance, Hardy, Dickens, Stendhal, and Tolstoy—all give excellent descriptions of social networks, although they are not labelled as such. Even today, although the struggles and the perceptions of the individual are important to most contemporary writers, many best sellers still tend to be meticulous descriptions of these larger networks of relationships. Popular attention certainly still finds concepts and descriptions of social networks in the criminal world attractive—for example, the Mafia (1,2) or radical groups, like the Manson family (3,4). This literature reflects the fact that American idealization of the family as a model has influenced efforts to compress all extrinsic relationships into a family context. Kinship terms thus are used in many social efforts; "soul brothers" by the black reformers, and "sisters" by the members of the women's movement.

Before it was defined, several insightful behavioral scientists used the concept of social networks metaphorically. The concept of a network has always been part of literary usage and the more poetic social scientists use it in this way. Leighton introduces the Sterling County Studies thus (5): "Through all this land are people dispersed in isolated farms and fishing coves, a living network of individuals suffused with happiness and misery, moving, meeting, leaving and meeting again, a network that ever remains while ever replaced by birth, growth, migration, death, and new birth. If one asks what can produce happiness or misery in this multitude of exchanging individuals, he will see at once that there is an infinity of possibilities involving questions of depth and quality as well as members."

The British author Delderfield uses the term *network* in his Swann trilogy (6), both in the classic transportation/communication sense and the social relations sense. American writers have not yet become so comfortable, but a New York *Times* headline, "13 NOW Leaders Form a Dissident 'Network' " (7), suggests that the concept and usage are becoming viable outside clinical and social science works in the U.S.

DEFINITIONS AND DESCRIPTIONS

Social network and its related term, *family network* imply a set of principles that relate to the noninstitutionalized channels of social exchanges and communication within a given society. There are three levels of networks. The most abstract encompasses all the possible relationships of a given group, and is probably only limited by the number of people in the whole world. At the other extreme is the family network that is defined in terms of the relationships to members of a particular nuclear family at a particular time; its approximate limits are between 50 and 1,000 persons, depending on the culture, the circumstances, and the personalities of the family members. In between are personal networks—people related through a common identity, as for instance, loosely structured collegial contacts, or closely related social units that share many of the same characteristics. For the purpose of this discussion, *social network* will be used for family-centered relationships.

Barnes, the English anthropologist, first defined the term twenty years ago (8). In 1972 he redefined a social network thus (9): "Every individual in society is seen as linked to several others by social bonds that partly reinforce and partly conflict with one another; the orderliness or disorderliness of social life results from the constraints these bonds impose on the actions of individuals."

Following Barnes' early work, many other anthropological and sociological studies have been published, most of which utilize data from European and African populations. These articles, with varying degrees of rigor, attempt to specify, quantify, and comprehend the relationships of people within social networks, using mathematics derived from topology, graph theory, and systems analysis. Boissevain in his *Friends of Friends* (10) is the least mathematical of the Europeans; Mitchel *et al.* (11) have made attempts to measure characteristics of social networks in their natural habitat as opposed to sociologists who try to reconstruct social nets in laboratories. In her second edition, Elizabeth Bott (12) detours from clinical work into a review of anthropological research.

Only two American therapists have as yet attempted to apply this rigorous approach to network definition and description: Mansel Pattison

(13, 14) of the University of California at Irvine, and W. D. Ratliffe (15) at the University of Alberta. In a more easily grasped and naturalistic manner, Mary Howell describes (16) the constituent types of social and family networks, giving a particularly good picture of open and closed families, as well as the kin, friends, and neighbors that make up a family network.

The stance Howell adopts relative to the potential competence of people in families and networks, and their abilities to solve many of their day-to-day problems, as well as crises, is typical of most persons who begin to utilize the concepts of social network in their thinking and professional delivery of services. The basis for this orientation seems to be an expanding awareness of the social resources available, a desire to return responsibility for family members back to an appropriate (not necessarily professional) source, and a sense that repair of network relationships will restore orderliness and balance to disordered lives and unbalanced individuals.

Something of the same burst of exploratory energy that accompanies the dissolution of any artificial boundaries is shared by the family therapist, who is thus freed to include nonfamily members in family therapy sessions. There is a sense of greater freedom when one thinks in terms of this larger, more heterogeneous social grouping. Some of the discomfort expressed about taking this step is undoubtedly due to a lack of a clear vision of who makes up the social network in any given case.

VISUALIZING THE FAMILY NETWORK

To make social networks more visible to both therapists and clients, Attneave has developed a guide for mapping the family network (17) which permits not only an orderly inquiry into social space, but also provides a graphic display of some of its relationships. Designed to lead the individual into discussion and discovery, this instrument can be completed by family members as young as junior or senior high school age.

The network map is the culmination of a series of steps outlined in the instrument. The first task is to order relationships into lists in four degrees of comparative intimacy and emotional significance: (1) people in your household; (2) those who are emotionally significant; (3) casual and functionally-related persons; and (4) persons geographically distant or seldom seen. These lists are then arranged spatially on a map in relationship to one another. Space on the map is made for listing both positive and negative relationships. People who are disliked are often as important to the eventual solution of problems as those for whom affect is neutral or positively valanced. This is true of all levels of intimacy.

Finally, individuals who know one another are connected with lines, which gives the map a characteristic spider web appearance. The resulting patterns can then be analyzed for emerging substructures. Focal individuals who know many people are designated as *nexus individuals*. A cluster of such people is called a *plexus*. Isolates and cliques, both open and closed, are identified. Attention can be directed to the distribution of sex, family, nonfamily, as well as to the roles of pets in these relationships. The result is a more complete picture of the social matrix than a genogram which only includes kin.

Although it can be done singly or in groups, the task of mapping one's own network almost always arouses intense emotions, and should not be done by network members in isolation. There should be someone else available, usually the therapist, with whom the feelings and resulting information can be discussed. The actual task itself usually takes about 45 minutes to an hour. An equal length of time to discuss the material evoked is probably an adequate allowance for debriefing in the preliminary therapeutic session. A longer time or second session will be needed to utilize the information for selecting participants in sessions or developing other therapeutic applications.

CLINICAL INTERPRETATIONS OF NETWORKS

A number of topics familiar to all clinicians can be raised with regard to their impact on the network as well as on individuals or families. For instance, geographical moves may result in very significant people being displaced outward from the center of the map, and the emergence of new significant individuals. Other events with similar impact are changes that result from completing a stage in the life cycle, completing an education, or being promoted to a new level of job responsibility. Illness may constrict a social network because it restricts mobility and also because it creates demands upon the intimate circle. Death may tear the fabric of relationships in ways that affect more than just the bereaved individual.

Of course, these events are frequently dealt with in individual and family therapy; but looking at the ways they effect the social network may lead to new insights, as well as give the persons involved clues about how they might control, reconstruct, or repair their social contexts.

Some configurations of relationships seem to go hand in hand with the kinds of stress that lead to pathology or to seeking out therapeutic assistance. One such configuration is marked by a depletion of the number of people in the circle of significant emotional relationships. Sampath (18) has described a syndrome common in the Arctic or other remote areas among persons suddenly transported away from their accustomed haunts for periods of intensive work, which he calls being "bushed in the bush." For those individuals who are working in arctic resource development, the hollowness of casual, shallow social relationships, in conjunction with separation from home and family, leads to agitation, physical weakness, depression, withdrawal, and paranoid behaviors. According to Sampath, individuals who have some unconscious insight into the origins of their problems make every effort to return home, where their usual social interactions can exert a restorative effect. Suggested preventive measures for avoiding this syndrome focus on more effective ways to keep the network relationships intact, both through planned frequent returns and more effective communication. Normal Paul (19) describes a somewhat similar syndrome in Eskimo children who have been hospitalized in Alaska, and suggests the use of tape recorders as one way to keep family relationships active. Speck's work with schizophrenics (20) convinced him that the families of the index patients depleted their own resources by withdrawing from contact with friends and family while caring for the disturbed member.

Systematic collection of family network data may uncover other trends and characteristics that might serve as useful diagnostic signs. One thing already seems clear: there is not as much variety in patterns in any culture as one might suppose. There are some indications of ethnic patterns; patterns also tend to shift according to stages of the life cycle between adolescence and old age. The map of a network makes available a summary of the current social matrix within which the individual or family lives. In this sense it is an orienting principle which does not need precise quantification to be clinically useful, although further research would be helpful.

DECIDING WHO TO INCLUDE

One of the obvious ways to use the network concept is to help decide who might appropriately be included in the therapy sessions. When the map is employed for this purpose, the debriefing session will be geared to the question of whom to invite. Family discussions almost always involve negotiating the inclusion of persons who hold significant relationship to some members, but who are unknown to or disliked by others. This matter may evoke considerable tension in situations involving adolescents, since parents almost invariably disapprove of many of their teenager's friends. Sometimes it is also a problem between spouses, or between siblings.

Negotiation and some form of contractual agreement will generally solve these differences of opinion. The therapist may need to decide arbitrarily how many people each member of the family may equitably invite to a network assembly, in addition to mutually agreed upon persons. When there are gulfs between family members, network assembly situations that include the presence of emotionally supportive friends of each often make the whole meeting less threatening. In many situations where the attributed negative valence of some members of the network has been unrealistic, agreement to include them in the sessions along with supportive persons from the rest of the network may allow for confrontation of fantasies, and developing some sense of being able to cope rather than being powerless. In actual practice, such persons, when invited, often lose their advocacy roles and become general members of the network as they gain recognition and find a role in the total social group. This reduces the feelings of estrangement in the fragmented nuclear family.

In a few instances, such as the assembly of partial networks of residents in halfway houses (21) or in prison settings (22), a frank discussion of persons in the negatively valenced sector of the map, as well as of the possible impact of others still attached to a life style involving drugs and crime, is probably imperative. The therapist and the index patient may then, if it seems desirable, include in their contract of mutual help the goal of changing the social network in which the individual was previously enmeshed.

One powerful advantage of using a network map is that the total network membership is shared with the therapist before any discussion about whom to include in the sessions. To be sure, families and individuals will think of others to add; but the basic network structure is available for the therapist and members of the family. This often prevents premature exclusion; or unproductive piecemeal collection of information.

INVITING THE WHOLE NETWORK

The techniques of large-scale assembly of networks of forty to one hundred persons have been well described in the literature (23, 24, 25). Uri Ruveni (26) has been conducting training sessions for teams of network interventionists, and has videotaped actual sessions; these are available for workshops and inservice training. The Groome Clinic at Sibley Hospital, Washington, D.C. has videotaped a simulated session involving a teenager in conflict with parents and society.

Since the assembly of a network is usually prompted by crisis, and has as its goal the loosening of the binds and strengthening of the bonds between members, it is inclusive rather than exclusive. The more varied the people participating, the more chance for channeling the energies of the network into practical problem solving.

The professionals involved exert their control of the group and its internal processes in ways that are often quite different from those employed in more traditional clinical encounters. Some writers try to make network a verb to express this activity. As Garrison (26) points out, "network" is a noun referring to entire social or family network as the unit of intervention or conceptualization. The techniques developed by Speck and described by Speck and Attneave (27) are those of *assembling* the social network, which they prefer to call a process of *retribalization* rather than "networking."

SELECTING PARTS OF THE NETWORK

Interaction on such a large scale is dramatic, but not always necessary. However, conceptualizing the total social matrix, not only family but also other significant persons, permits a wide latitude in the choice of whom to incorporate into various intervention sessions. Subgroups, often the plexi from the mapped network, may be relevant and efficient combinations to involve in partial network interventions. Garrison (28) uses intimate friends as well as family members in a screening-linking-planning process at the time of emergency, usually a crisis involving admission to a psychiatric inpatient facility. Building on closely related techniques developed by Hansell (29) as a triage model for emergency rooms and psychiatric intake, Garrison has found that working with a small group of the most intimate persons around a decompensating person can definitely shorten, if not eliminate, the need for hospitalization. Working with a partial network from the beginning also circumvents the stage of patient dependency upon a therapist which is typical of other modes of treatment.

In staging the intervention, Garrison elicits a "laundry list" of complaints from each of those affected by the distressed person's behavior: boyfriend, roommate, children, parents. He then positively reinterprets this behavior as a striving for one or more of the basic values or needs in life. The concreteness of this demystifying process allows the development of practical problem formulations and solutions, which in turn sets the stage for behavior change both by the index patient and by the network members.

Two therapists have attempted similar interventions with persons already resident in inpatient facilities: Callan, *et al.* (20) with residents of a halfway house for drug abuse offenders, and Blackford (30) at a community psychiatric inpatient facility. Both have found that inclusion of staff as well as persons from the life space network of the patient is essential if the intervention is to succeed. These sessions seem to link institutional experience and the patient's real world in functional and fruitful partnership.

CARETAKERS AS PART OF THE NETWORK

The inclusion of other caretakers is also cited by Fine (31), who worked among the residents of a black ghetto of Philadelphia. He found that network concepts greatly facilitated a clearer understanding of the social matrix of the patients at a pediatric facility. The staff was able to deal more realistically with problems than when they relied on the traditional stereotypes developed by research limited to fragmenting descriptions of the family. Much of Fine's work, as well as that of Taber (32), who worked in the same community, was directed at discovering positive ties between people in the community that could be used to focus self-stabilization during therapy, and as resources after the crisis had passed. The active inclusion of pediatricians, nurses, social workers, and paraprofessionals as team members in working with families gave Fine an opportunity to bring together the caregivers with the previously unrecognized plexus of social supports available to their clientele.

The use of network concepts has also been developed by Curtis (33, 34); he utilizes volunteers from the community who spend at least half a day a week for a year as staff members of a Community Mental Health Center which he directs. After a training period, these lay persons meet with small plexi from the network of individuals calling upon the services of the Community Mental Health Center. They and the network together develop treatment strategies to solve the "patient's" problems. Staff members, both professional and volunteer, soon become proficient in dealing with the myriad of relationships within the community, and are consequently able to handle a highly diverse caseload using a smaller professional staff than more traditionally organized community mental health centers.

ADAPTABILITY TO CROSS CULTURAL SETTINGS

The usefulness of the inclusion of caretakers as members of a network or partial network becomes apparent whenever the clientele being served has an ethnic or cultural background different from that of the caretakers. Social distances are eliminated and much more open communication is possible between agencies, as well as more effective deployment of community resources. In many instances Fine did not find it necessary to assembly the network at all. After they had explored their social world, family members and selected others made or renewed contact with a viable larger network. As Fine says (30), "Broad family-like ties were fundamental among the people in this neighborhood; in fact they were sought. . . . Examples of these groups from the neighborhood served by our program included Moslems, black Jews, Protestant sects, radical cells and block groups. Each provided structure, leadership, role definition and continuity similar to those in an extended family. Differing in form, they were helpful in function, especially in developmental and psychiatric situations, as transmitters of social values and group supports."

This comment emphasizes how adaptable the concept of the family network is. The therapist can include relationships not usually considered part of a conventional family—as, for instance, those therapists who work with Spanish-speaking populations whose culture includes the roles of *compadrismo* that are not present in the Anglo-American repertoire. A paper by Burrel and Chavez (35) describes the establishment of La Frontera as a mental health unit to serve the barios of Tucson on this basis. Another description of applying these concepts without utilizing the assembly technique is given by Attneave (36), who compares therapy with American Indians with therapy done with middle-class populations of the eastern seaboard.

Social network concepts have also proved helpful for people in difficult or sensitive positions, such as clergy. They offer a useful way to explore the social difficulties that pastors face, allowing them to talk freely and frankly about all aspects of their social needs and roles. Discrepancies between clergymen's expectations of themselves and their perceptions of parishioners often cause tension. One or more of the conventional modes of therapy may be helpful in reducing such tension; but when the initial appraisals of the situation include the use of a family network map, it allows for an exploration of the context in terms that are nonjudgmental, yet theologically acceptable. Clergy of many faiths have also found it useful to think of the seasonal and life-cycle celebrations and rituals of their liturgies as examples of spontaneous assemblies of family networks. They report that it deepens their appreciation of the processes involved within a congregation at times of personal celebrations like weddings, bar mitzvahs, or of seasonal festivals, and holy days.

PREVENTIVE APPLICATIONS

Network concepts are also useful as preventive mental health practice. In a preretirement seminar at a community college, for example, couples completed maps of their present network. This sparked a discussion of what changes might occur in their relationships at retirement. This anticipation of losses of relationships with friends seemed to add a dimension of reality testing to the dreams of moving to Florida or retiring to a simple life in the country. Sharing these perceptions seemed to bring couples closer.

Another retirement related application involved a plexus of school staff whose principal was retiring after forty years in the same community (38). Construction of the principal's network not only ratified widespread participation, but vitalized the ceremonial aspects of the retirement. It also facilitated handling many instances of separation anxiety which might otherwise have gone unrecognized.

Still another preventative application of network concepts is reduction of intergenerational conflicts. Katz (38), working with adolescent girls referred by a pediatrician, found that by including all relevant persons in the discussion she could help the girls become effective change agents within their own families. Many of the examples cited earlier also contain illustrations of this theme. At least one alternative school on each coast, and a number of day care centers are finding network concepts similarly useful.

A FINAL WORD: Y'ALL COME

The variety of therapists and the many applications of the concept of the social network or family network as the unit of intervention range widely over the files of family therapy. Perhaps most of the persons cited use a systems approach to therapy, although not all of them are rigorous theorists. Few therapists have found that the inclusion of nonfamily members distorts their basic methods of dealing with families. From the social network point of view there is no problem about who should or should not be included in a family session. The freedom to include those whom the family members feel are appropriate is just as adventurous, and no more apt to get out of hand, than the number of guests who turn up at a party in the South in response to the constantly repeated invitation, "Y'all come!"

REFERENCES

1. M. Puzo. *The Godfather,* New York: Putnam, 1969.
2. ———. Dark Area, New York: Dell, 1969.
3. E. Sander. *The Family.* New York: Dutton, 1971.
4. V. Bugliosi and C. Gentry. *Helter Skelter.* New York: Norton, 1974.
5. A. Leighton. *My Name Is Legion.* New York: Basic Books, 1959.
6. R. F. Delderfield. *God Is an Englishman;; Theirs Was the Kingdom; Give Them This Day.* New York: Simon and Schuster; 1970.
7. *New York Times,* November 15, 1975.
8. J. A. Barnes. "Class and Committees in a Norwegian Island Parish," *Human Relations,* 7 (1954), 39–58.

9. _____. "Social Networks," *Anthropology Module* #26. Reading, Mass.: Addison Wesley, 1972, 1.

10. J. Boissevain. *Friends of Friends Networks, Manipulators, and Coalitions.* New York: St. Martin's Press, 1974.

11. J. C. Mitchell, ed. *Social Networks in Urban Situations: Analyses of Personal Relationships in African Towns.* Manchester University Press, 1971.

12. A. Bott. *Family and Social Network.* London: Tavistock, 1968.

13. M. Pattisson. "Psychosocial Systems Therapy," in R. G. Herschowitiz, ed., *Handbook of Community Mental Health Practice.* New York: Spectrum Publications, 1975.

14. _____. "A Psychosocial Kinship Model for Family Therapy," *American Journal of Psychiatry,* 1975.

15. W. D. Ratcliffe and H. F. A. Azim. Paper presented at Canadian Psychiatric Association, September 1975.

16. M. Howell. *Helping Ourselves: Families and the Human Network.* Boston: Beacon Press, 1975.

17. C. Attneave. *Family Network Map.* Available from 5206 Ivanhoe N.E., Seattle, Washington, 1975.

18. H. M. Sampath. *The "Bushed Syndrome"—Environment and Mental Health in the Canadian Arctic.* Paper presented at the Canadian Psychiatric Association, September, 1975.

19. N. Paul. Unpublished. Report to Indian Health Service. 1969.

20. R. V. Speck. Personal communication.

21. D. Callan, J. Garrison, and F. Zerger. "Working with the Families and Social Networks of Drug Abusers," *Journal of Psychedelic Drugs,* 7; 19–26.

22. D. Trimble. Personal communication.

23. R. Speck, "Psychotherapy of the Social Network of a Schizophrenic Family," *Family Process,* 6 (1967), 208–14.

24. R. Speck and U. Ruveni. "Network Therapy—Redeveloping Concept." *Family Process,* 8 (1969), 182–90.

25. R. Speck and C. Attneave. *Family Networks: Retribalization and Healing.* New York: Pantheon, 1973.

26. U. Ruveni. "Network Intervention with a Family in Crisis," *Family in Process,* 1975.

27. J. Garrison. *Network Methods for Clinical Problems.* Paper presented at American Group Psychotherapy Association, Boston, 1976.

28. _____. "Network Techniques: Case Studies in the Screening-Linking-Planning Conference Method," *Family Process,* 13 (1974), 337–51.

29. N. Hansel. "Casualty Management Method: An Aspect of Mental Health Technology in Transition," *Archives of General Psychiatry,* 22 (1968), 462–67.

30. V. Blackford. Personal communication.

31. P. Fine. "An Appraisal of Child Psychiatry in a Health Setting," *Child Psychiatry,* 11 (1972), 279–93.

32. R. Taber. "Providing Mental Health Services to a Low Income Socio-Economic Black Community without Requiring that People Perceive Themselves as Patients," *J. Orthopsychiatry,* June, 1970.

33. W. R. Curtis. *Annual Report,* Taunton Lakeville Mental Health Center. 1971.

34. _____. "Community Human Service Networks: New Roles for Mental Health Workers," *Psychiatric Annals* 3 (1973), 23–42.

35. G. Burrel and B. Chavez. "Relevant or Irrelevant to Mexican Americans," in A. Tulipan, C. Attneave and E. Kingstone, eds., *Beyond Clinic Walls.* University of Alabama Press, 1975.
36. C. Attneave, "Therapy in Tribal Settings and Urban Network Intervention," *Family Process,* 8 (1971), 192–210.
37. E. Paul. Unpublished paper. 1975.
38. A. Katz and A. Gutherie. "Pediatric Paradox—Adolescents as Change Agents in the Community," in Tulipan, Attneave, and Kingstone, eds., *Beyond Clinic Walls.* University of Alabama Press, 1975.

Useful videotape materials on family networks are available from:

Groome Child Guidance Center, 5225 Loughboro Road N.W., Washington, D.C. 20016. Tape shows the process of introducing the network assembly process to a family. Attneave. Contact Charles Padduck, Training Director.

Eastern Pennsylvania Psychiatric Institute, Philadelphia. Several network assemblies filmed live. Uri Ruveni and staff. Usually require therapist to accompany tape and lead discussion.

ETL, Inc., Videopublishers, 1170 Commonwealth Avenue, Boston, Mass. 02134. Mapping the Family Network. Attneave as workshop leader. Contact Fred Duhl, M.D., Director.

Section B

SYMPTOM-FOCUSED FAMILIES

CHAPTER 13

THE CHILD-CENTERED FAMILY

Mariano Barragan, M.D.

INTRODUCTION

During the last decade, an emerging trend in child psychiatry has been taking place at child clinics, that of moving away from intrapsychic ways of formulating and treating children's difficulties. New conceptualizing frames are provided by systems theory and interpersonal formulations of conflict. A body of theory is emerging based on new concepts: the descriptions of child-centered families, ways to identify them, and techniques to treat them.

Interest in these families stems from evidence that the very same processes producing their dysfunctional structure are the ones that interfere with the emotional growth of the family as a unit, and, again, the same ones that produce important developmental deviations in children. Developmental deviations in turn give rise to symptomatic adaptation. In spite of their importance as producers of a wide variety of emotional difficulties in children, these families are all too frequently overlooked by mental health professionals. Sometimes, even when they are recognized, they are ignored and left out of the treatment situation. When this happens, the therapist actually reinforces the dysfunction of the family by focusing on the child and defining him as "the problem."

Since child centeredness beyond the stage of dependency for survival is exclusive to the human animal, and since the problem seems to be expanding with the increasing complexities of our civilization, we must start putting together some basic knowledge about the child-centered family, and derive some treatment guidelines from it.

A number of questions must be answered, first. We have to know what child-centered families are; how they function; what their origins are; what their consequences are; what keeps them frozen in such a pattern; what their main forms of expression are; how we can identify them; what our goals are when we try to change them; and how we go about reaching those goals.

DEFINITION

Just as personality is not a stable entity, but a continuously changing phenomenon, in the same fashion families are not static units. It follows, then, that a child-centered family is not a type of family, but rather, an expression of deviant family development (11). This is obvious, since we know that at some point in the family life cycle, child centeredness is not only characteristic, but strictly necessary for the survival of the totally dependent child. Normal family development in functional families is that this trait decreases as children grow and their needs become less. Keeping the above in mind, we may define child-centered families, then, as dysfunctional structures. By use of child-focusing mechanisms, they produce developmental difficulties with varying degrees of impaired emotional functioning in children, leading in most cases to symptom production. Some forms or outside appearances of the child-centering process have been defined by Bradt and Moynihan (3), who state that family members "become preoccupied with one of its members as if life and the limits of life depend upon the definition of a child." They also note that, "The child-concerns of parents supersede reality, self-functioning, responsibility to each other, to the extended family and to the community."

The agents and factors involved in this developmental deviation, and the ways that they combine to produce it occur over time. They are in *past or predisposing* elements, those that existed before the problem of child centeredness is manifest, and whose unfolding processes culminate within its establishment. And they are in *present or perpetuating* elements, those that secure the prominence of child centeredness day by day. Together, these form the function of the deviant structure, insofar as preventing change represents the maintenance of the continuous circular process of a stagnant family development being responsible for the child centering, and simultaneously the child centeredness producing the lack of growth in the emotional life of the family.

Two systems principles explain how the causative agents behave in establishing and maintaining a child-centered structure. The first is that behavior of parts is different when studied in isolation or within the whole. This is because an isolated part is not under the influence of forces, such as organization and order, that act on it only within the interaction of the total system. It follows that attempts to understand child centeredness on the basis of personality traits of mothers, fathers, or children in isolation would be futile (2).

The other systems postulate is the Non-summativity principle, that describes this type of family not as the end result of the sum of the causal agents involved, but rather as rising from interrelations between them. This is why they transcend individual qualities (20).

As an example that illustrates these principles, suppose we see a family that shows excessive preoccupation with an eight-year-old boy who is an only child and who comes to the clinic with a problem of agressiveness and disobedience. In traditional child psychiatry, the case presentation would elaborate on the "significant elements" involved in the production of impulsivity. An exhaustive study would be done of each one of these; however, each would be studied not only in isolation, but in fact by different professionals.

Accordingly, the psychologist describes this child as an anxious, somewhat depressed little boy with a low normal intelligence. The social worker explains the parents' main personality traits, stating that the mother is possessive, overprotective, and obsessive compulsive and the father is weak, passive, and himself overprotected by his own mother, the domineering grandmother who still lives in the house. The child psychiatrist then explains the little boy's development; tainted by overprotection and by the lack of an assortment of desirable identifications, he has inevitably developed a weak Ego. This case presentation is then followed by a variable period of discussion in which each participant makes some kind of criticism about the way in which the history was presented, until at last the training director sums up the problem, stating that the child in fact has had faulty development, and that indeed this leads to a rather weak Ego; and since one of the functions of the Ego is impulse control (there are seven or eight more for variations in diagnostic formulations), it is quite obvious why this child is aggressive. The treatment prescription is then individual play-therapy, in some lucky cases supplemented by counseling of the parents by the social worker. Notice that this reinforces focus on the child and therefore worsens the dysfunction.

The same case conceptualized on the basis of systems principles would stress the relationship between the different elements within the context of the total family. We then see that the paternal grandmother, being a domineering woman, has achieved a higher place in the household hierarchy than the mother. The unhappy and frustrated wife consequently nags her husband constantly about his mother, boring him with a detailed account of all the things she does to her. Besides being tired from work, the husband is impotent to do anything about the situation, because he himself is lower in the pecking order than his mother, who keeps him that way by babying him at every opportunity. Subordinate to her mother-in-law, and resentful of her husband for being such an idiot, mother is left with no other source of satisfaction than to be a "good mother." To avoid loneliness, she spends most of her time with the little boy, putting all her energy into raising the "perfect" child.

On the other hand, the child cannot go beyond his intelligence capabilities, and thus cannot comply with his mother's demands for excellence. He reacts to this situation with chronic anger and irritation, behaving as any angry and irritated child does, that is, by being aggressive and disobedient. His disobedience is checked by neither the father nor the grandmother. The father does not stop him because he enjoys reading the newspaper or watching TV quietly, without his wife's nagging him; so, as long as the child keeps her busy, he is safe. The grandmother does not correct her grandchild because he gives her everyday living proof of her daughter-in-law's incompetence, which helps her maintain her own position as first lady of the house.

Formulated in these terms, the problem would have to be treated with family therapy. Even though this example is oversimplified, it does illustrate the importance of the systems view in formulating a problem and treating a child-centered family.

Without attempting to explore the relationships between the different factors that produce a child-centered family, since obviously their combinations vary in each case, let us now consider them in some detail. Three factors are outstanding in the group of past or predisposing elements. First, the families of origin of the parents-spouses, with their cultural traditions and idiosyncracies. Second, the individual histories of each of the parents —their biological and temperamental endowments, the way their personalities were shaped by different interpersonal experiences and life circumstances, and so on. And third, and by far the most important, the process of mutual accommodation shared by the couple before the arrival of children.

In the families of origin of the parents, we find the transmitters of the cultural traits (14) and with them, the degree of child centeredness for each cultural group. This certainly poses wide variations. Also, the families of origin maintain values as far as generation boundaries are concerned, which have a decisive influence on the independence of the young couple. Such independence is absolutely necessary if the couple is to create its own problem-solving mechanisms.

Of interest as far as the parents' individual histories are concerned would be their temperamental traits, and their degree of proficiency in interpersonal relationships that will directly affect nurturance patterns. Frequently, we find parents centering on their children in an attempt to provide them with what they themselves lacked, but strongly wished to have. Most of these deficits are products of early interactions with their own families that were either insufficiently nurturant or distorted in a variety of ways. Lack of one or both parents almost invariably produces an irresistible tendency toward child centering in the orphan's future parental behavior.

Prominent among the elements of the past are those derived from the couple's interactions before the arrival of children. Rossi (17) expresses the concept very clearly. "The balance between individual autonomy and couple mutuality that develops during the honey-moon stage of such a marriage may be important in establishing a pattern that will later affect the quality of the parent child relationship." Hannah Gavron (7) says that "Only in the context of a growing egalitarian base to the marital relationship can one find a tendency for parents to establish some barriers between themselves and their children." The same author describes this as "a marital defense against the institution of Parenthood."

Before the arrival of children, a couple should ideally have a workable and mutually satisfying situation that according to Berman and Lief (1) encompasses three critical dimensions. *Power:* Who is in charge? *Intimacy:* How near, how far? *Inclusion-exclusion:* The dyadic limits, and who or what else is considered to be part of the marital system—for instance, in-laws, careers, activities? The same authors say that in healthy relationships the solutions are not static, but instead are in continuous flux; whereas dysfunctional couples tend to erect more static and rigid solutions.

Optimal conditions for child centeredness will occur when the couple has not adequately dealt with power, intimacy, and inclusion-exclusion. The young couple has to adapt to each other's ways, at the same time that they are separating from their families of origin. The separation may bring adequate or faulty limit definition; failures at this level are characterized by the excessive intrusion of parents-in-law, frequently by way of financial or emotional support.

The intimacy of the young couple is fragile because of the lack of rules; the same is true of power. Minuchin (16) offers some concrete examples: "They must develop routines for going to bed and getting up, for having meals together, for setting and clearing the table. There must be a routine for being naked and for having sex, for sharing the bathroom and the Sunday paper . . . for going out to places that both of them enjoy."

Crucial to the negotiations of the rules is the fluidity of the mechanisms used to resolve conflicts (16). Adequate mechanisms lead to rules, and to clear definitions of what is desirable and allowed and what is prohibited or undesirable. These mechanisms may be interfered with by avoidance patterns—prolonged silence (days and even weeks), long working hours even when they are not required, newspaper reading, TV watching, and so on. Such faulty procedures are at the core of dissatisfaction, with or without overt fighting between the spouses.

No symptom, structure, or system can survive without a function. What present or perpetuating elements offer are gains in terms of equilibrium, change prevention, or need satisfaction—that is to say, the gains that families and individuals derive from the process of child centering.

Anybody in a dual role tends to compensate for dissatisfaction with one of the roles by perfecting or overdeveloping the other. In the nuclear family, the two adults have the dual role of being spouses and parents at the same time. The arrival of children affords an opportunity for dissatisfied spouses to develop as parents; satisfaction in this role may compensate for their unhappiness with the other. Since success and satisfaction as a parent are often measured by how successful the children are, unhappy spouses may set forth on the task of raising children as close to perfection as they can get them to be. The pattern has another advantage in that the "good father" or "good mother" can justify their deficiencies as spouses with the noble excuse that they are sacrificing themselves for the future happiness of their children.

At the same time, the more a couple centers on their children, the easier it is to avoid marital confrontations, because there is always something to worry, criticize, correct, or complain about with the children. This also explains the dependency on the children's symptoms that these families exhibit, and the tenacity with which they resist giving them up to therapy. Vogel and Bell (19) say that it is a common phenomenon to achieve group unity through the scapegoating of a particular member. This is actually only one of the ways to do it.

Secondarily, lonely spouses with no expectations from their mates seek company and satisfactions from their children. They want to be with them at all times, and have high expectations about their social and economic success. As children grow, these parents overvalue alliance patterns with them, just as they overvalue their opinions and value judgments. Elements in the children themselves are part of the child centering processes, but they are not always present. The main ones are physical illness in the child; temperamental traits of "difficult children" (4); and adoption. Sibling order also has an influence; first and last-born children are more vulnerable to being focused on (3).

EXTERNAL APPEARANCE OF THE FAMILY UNIT

Once all the elements are present in the appropriate combination, and the child-centered structure is established and secured by perpetuating patterns, what we see from the outside is a family always together around the children, or focused on issues that involve the children. They are over-concerned most of the time that they function well, although there are exceptions to this, such as child-centering through scapegoating. The parents relate to the surrounding community much more as parents—they are apt to be notorious for their active participation at PTA meetings—than as spouses, seldom socializing as couples with other couples. Recreational activities most of the times are with the children, and seldom or never as a couple. Family finances are based on disproportionately large priorities and allocations for children's needs: the kids usually have excessive amounts of clothes and toys, go to private schools at the expense of other family needs, and so on. Education is overvalued in many ways; the parents' choice of living quarters is subordinated to the availability of excellent educational facilities, regardless of whether this may mean the father's driving forty or fifty miles to work every day. Religion and religious duties are stressed for the children; the order of preference for friends and relatives is decided also in terms of who is beneficial or better for the kids. The child emphasis is constantly reinforced by phrases like, "There can be exspouses and exjobs, but not exchildren"; "Their happiness is important, ours is not"; "We are old and our time is past"; and, "We've already had our share."

Because the children's success is extremely important, its indicators are watched anxiously. Every measurement, every word said by the pediatrician is carefully registered, not to speak about the amount and balance of food, hours of sleep, dental care, and of course, very high on the list, progress in school.

CONSEQUENCES FOR THE FAMILY

Developmental defects in the family thus produce the focus on the child; this emphasis in turn hampers further family growth, establishing a closed mechanism that usually feeds on a symptomatic child.

The marital dyad cannot continue to redefine its allocations of power, intimacy, and limits, since these are all now centered on the children. The couple may fall into one of the various types of dysfunctional patterns described by different authors. Cuber and Harroff (5) identify three types: the conflict-habituated marriage, which is an unpleasant, tense, conflict-loaded relationship held together by fear of aloneness; the devitalized marriage, where the relationship is characterized by numbness and apathy. Externally it is conflict free, but devoid of zest. Most of the times these marriages are held together by moral and legal bonds, and by the children. The passive congenial marriage is a "pleasant" but uninvolved type of interaction. The principal social supports come from outside the marriage, and interests are with other people. The partners tend to feel that "every marriage is like that."

Bradt and Moynihan (3) describe other, more specific types: the "peace-agree"; "conflict-disagree"; "silence-distance"; "nurse-caretaking"; "just-like pattern"; "child-spouse substitute"; and "isolation from other social units." All these are deviant interactional patterns that give rise to child centeredness and depend on it for permanence.

CONSEQUENCES FOR THE CHILD

The focus on the child invariably results in symptomatic children with an ample variety of defects in their emotional development. They clearly show impaired independence and autonomy, and inadequate handling of the triangular situation with mother and father. A large number of these children suffer the consequences of overprotection, and some of them the unshielded impact of parental aggression. Levy (13), in his classic study of maternal overprotection, has said its effects on the children are that they show dependency, submissiveness, and shyness. Also, many are demanding and disobedient children. We can easily identify maternal overprotection as a frequent component within the child-centered family structure.

The children's symptoms can be viewed as having a double function. One is that the symptoms are a protest against being focused on, because this is indeed stressful on an everyday level. The other is that symptoms serve as targets for the maintenance and perpetuation of the dysfunctional pattern. In other words, the child not only responds to the child-centered family, but activates it as well (15), restoring the status quo in the event of any attempts to change (12). Thus, most symptomatic children are definitely the products of disturbances or disruptions in intrafamilial relationships and interactions, rather than the products of intrapsychic conflict (18).

Symptom choice is determined by two factors. The first is the form with which the parents express their child centeredness; the other is the way with which the child becomes involved in the parental conflict. In regard to the first, we know that parenting has two broad sections or functions, the instrumental and the expressive (17). The first is concerned with efficiency, limit setting, reinforcement of rules, and so on. The other has to do with care taking, nurturance, affection expression, and warmth. Child-centered parents who emphasize the instrumental functions tend to raise children with passive types of symptoms, such as shyness, oversensitiveness, and fears. When the focus is exerted mainly through the expressive function, the child tends to exhibit active types of symptoms—aggressiveness, rebelliousness, and all the range of undesirable behavior type of disorders.

Minuchin (16) has identified these observable patterns in the ways in which a child becomes involved in parental conflicts. *Triangulation:* Each one of the parents, who are in conflict, asks for the child's loyalties, making it impossible for the child to get close to one of them without betraying the other. *Stable coalitions:* There is spouse conflict, but the child is allied to one of the parents, more commonly the mother. Two variations are possible here, depending on the behavior of the excluded parent. In one variant, the parent keeps asking for the child's loyalties with no results; in the other, the parent gives up relating to the child, and steps out of the situation. *Detouring-attacking:* Although conflict exists, the couple handles it by uniting against the child, who is defined as "bad" or "the family problem." *Detouring-supporting:* The parents get together in overprotecting and being overconcerned with the child, who is defined as "weak" or "sick" rather than bad.

In our experience, triangulations and stable coalitions tend to produce symptoms of anxiety or their equivalents—hypochondriasis, obsessions, phobias, and so forth. Detouring-attacking seems to predominantly produce behavior disorders, delinquency, and learning difficulties. Finally, detouring-supporting produce shyness, insecurity, and psychosomatic disorders. We stress here that there is no absolute specificity between patterns and symptoms. We can only say that increases in the frequency of certain symptoms are apparently connected with certain interactional patterns without excluding other possibilities.

IDENTIFYING CHILD-CENTERED FAMILIES

Detecting a child-centered family in the early stages of treatment is not difficult, because the emphasis on the children is so evident. However, some families with this structure may come for treatment reluctantly, referred by school or courts. Resistance to treatment may be expressed as "having more important things to do"; or, the problem is regarded as being of "no consequence." This attitude may give the impression of lack of concern for the child; but these families focus on the child usually through the use of hostility and aggression. We therefore need other ways to identify besides the overt appearance of focus on the child to avoid being misled.

Two basic aspects of the family have to be carefully studied, namely, content and process. Content may be defined as "that which is said by the family members"; it can be transcribed by a stenographer recording the sessions. Process, in simple terms, is everything else that is going on in the room, and includes the places the family members sit in, any changes of place, distances between people, body language, tone of voice, amount of participation, controlling maneuvers, and so on. The totality of process cannot be entirely perceived by the therapist, even if he is an experienced observer, probably because the number of message units in the process is larger than our capacity to register, and this disproportion grows even greater in terms of our ability to decode them. The small amount of process that we can assimilate has to be simultaneously compared with the content for consistency. Consistency is one of the main things to rely on in assessing the accuracy of observations. Inconsistencies should always put us on guard about possibly being intentionally or inadvertently misled by the family. Inconsistencies should also be used to evaluate the line of exploring, so if it is wrong we can change it and find the right track.

We can artificially divide content and process into three dimensions, and observe what is occurring with each one of them. One dimension involves what is happening between the parents, including interactions with other significant adults; the second, between the parents and the children; and the third, between the children themselves. Obviously, also, we keep observing everybody's interaction with us.

Content and process between the parents may show that they avoid talking to each other, and sometimes about each other; and that they have difficulties communicating if we block the topic of children, and force them to go to other contexts. Avoidance behavior may become evident if we introduce or focus on the conflict within the marital dyad itself; if we keep them interacting around the definition or the resolution of a problem, we find that they seldom achieve either. There is an almost irresistible force always bringing content and process back to the children, regardless of any attempts to stop it. This is how these parents manage to always place the problem on the children.

Interaction between parents and children is heavily colored by overprotective behavior and statements. In sharp contrast, fury and concentrated aggression may be centered on the child. The children may exhibit behavior that is consistent with intrusion between the parents. They may exhibit geographic interference—that is, they sit between the parents, they share the same bedroom, and sometimes sleep between them. Parents allow and foster this interfering behavior. They may also interfere by monopolizing the time of one or both parents so they have no time left for themselves. As far as importance in the family is concerned, several content and process clues may indicate that the child is more important than either parent. As for the siblings, child centeredness fosters a fierce competition between them. This exacerbated rivalry produces an atmosphere of hostility. Furthermore child focus enhances whatever roles are assigned: the obedient brother is an "angel," the rebellious one is the "bastard," the well-behaved sister is the "princess," the ill-behaved one the "witch"; good students are called "geniuses," tinkerers become "mechanical wonders," and so forth.

THERAPEUTIC GOALS

Goal definition is not difficult in the treatment of these families. Therapy must aim at pulling the children out of the focused attention of the parents, so that they may associate with peers and reintegrate themselves into their own generation. To do only this would make the parents feel like turtles whose shells have been stolen; consequently, treatment should identify faulty conflict-resolution mechanisms and correct them. All avoidance behavior must be removed. The marital dyad should then be guided into exploring issues of power, intimacy, and limits. Careful supervision of this process by the therapist puts the parents back on the road to developing as a couple. In the terminal stages of treatment there should be a parental dyad capable of resolving their marital difficulties without having to include the children. As for the children, they should be asymptomatic, with succesful and varied interpersonal contacts with peers, and of course also able to resolve competently their own developmental difficulties. Finally, the family as a whole should have undergone a process of diversification from which they have emerged with a variety of interests, and behave accordingly. There should, for instance, be a vacation period and place for parents and children together, but also arrangements made by the parents for themselves. Diversity should be confirmed in a variety of different contexts.

THERAPEUTIC TECHNIQUES

Once we have defined the therapeutic goals clearly, we have to describe how to achieve them. Early in the treatment contract, we have to define the issue of membership in the therapy group. Ideally, all the family should be part of the treatment process; however, it is not necessary to have the whole group in every session.

We are essentially trying to change ways in which family members deal with one another (8); as long as we are pledged to changing the family system of interaction (6), problems such as who is in the room with the therapist at any given moment are subordinate to the primary undertaking. Thus it is valid to see the child alone for one or more sessions, without having to collide with the family's belief that the child is the problem, which has the advantage that we do not too obviously threaten to change the system. Besides, seeing the child alone affects the family structure and organization in ways that have been described by Haley and Montalvo (10). They state, for instance, that "some families report that their most determined efforts to modify their behavior towards the child came from fear of what the child was telling his therapist about them." The same reasons we give for seeing a child alone also can be used to justify having one or several sessions with different parts of the family—for instance, mother and child, father and child, spouses, or grandmother and parents. Sessions with part of the family are particularly useful for prescribing individual behavioral changes that will have an impact in the total family.

It is important to break our final goal down into workable subgoals; otherwise we will find ourselves trying too hard to defocus the child early in the treatment process. This may mean losing the family to some enthusiastic fan of play therapy. Joining the family and engaging it in therapy is the first objective. Drawing on his extensive work with child-centered families, Minuchin (16) states that "joining and accommodation" are "the processes by which a therapist creates a therapeutic system and positions himself as its leader."

In the early stages, tracking occupies a central position as a technique for joining and accommodating. Tracking is synonomous with accepting the family as it is, approaching it without threatening to change it. This is usually the first step in any successful therapy. To challenge some of the deviant family relations at the beginning would be the same as arousing suspicion in a paranoid patient by disagreeing with his delusions. We have to accept what he says, and join him by telling him that we had better think of some way to help him out of his very dangerous situation.

Joining and tracking moves with child-centered families means then that we agree with and accept their concern for the child, and with their definition of him as the problem. Haley (10) points out that some family therapists may object to this on the grounds that focusing on the child reinforces the deviant family ways; but he also points out that "different approaches have different advantages." In regard to joining, remember that the efficacy of maneuvers of paradoxical intention is directly related to how closely one agrees with and reinforces the presenting situation from the very beginning.

Assuming that we have positioned ourselves within the effective therapeutic range, we must then proceed with the engineering of the necessary changes. We must take into consideration the relationships between all the factors participating in the production and perpetuation process of child centering. Each family situation is unique in this regard, and we must approach it as such. Special attention should be paid to the function of the symptom as a homeostatic agent in the family system. Haley had a useful although not by any means a conclusive shortcut for identifying the symptom function—he asked each one of the family members what the situation would be if the symptom became worse. Their answers were often very revealing in terms of clarifying its function. For instance, a mother might state that if her child became more scared of the dark, she would be forced to sleep with him. The mother-child binding function of the symptom and the exclusion of the father thus become obvious, and so do the symptom's intimacy-interfering properties.

Another important section of the therapeutic reshaping deals with identifying the avoidance devices used by family members to evade confrontation with a variety of issues. This leads to the area of faulty conflict-resolution mechanisms. All the changes to be made hinge on changing the relationship between the various components that contribute to the emphasis on the child; a list of these changes should be drawn up based on the plausibility of change, which is then redrawn to fit each unique family situation. At this point we are ready to design strategies to implant each step of our sequence. Order of changes and number of them are highly specific to each family.

What are some of the features of the changing maneuvers, and how do we move to achieve them? A crucial point to consider is that actions, relationships, and interchanges are defined by the context in which they occur. Context identifies a male hand upon a woman's breast as a highly indecent form of aggression, an expression of love and/or passion, or a routine professional gesture that is part of a physical examination. The nature of an interaction and its relationship to the context in which it takes place allow us to effect change by use of two different types of maneuvers. The first is concerned with directly changing the nature of the relationship; the second tries to alter consequences by modifying the context in which the relationship occurs. Both types may of course be applied to the same situation.

Suppose, for example, that the interaction of a mother and her child is characterized by coldness, indifference, and overcriticism on the mother's part, and resentful withdrawal on the child's part. A direct maneuver would be to persuade the mother to become warm, supportive, and affectionate, and to encourage the child to respond to this. To complement this persuasive move, we might prescribe specific changes in the interaction; for instance, we could ask the mother to bring in her pocketbook something that the child considers a favorite treat for the next session, and then arrange for the child to discover it while we tell him that his mother thinks of him often. We may repeat this maneuver in a variety of ways, usually suggested by the particular style of the family.

As for modifying context, we might program mutually enjoyable behavior and togetherness under different circumstances, like games, or trips. More specifically, we might ask the mother and the child to enact a story about a loving mother who could not be warm and nice to her child because she thought she might spoil him. Her child was a quiet little boy who could not express his need for warmth and affection, and instead acted sulky. (Of course, this story would differ depending on the specific situation.) This kind of therapeutic intervention changes the context because they are asked to enact a story that contains all the actual elements of their stereotyped interchange, but which is different from reality. Besides, the "it's just a story" excuse gives the participants an opportunity to try different behaviors without the fear of some awful confrontation. The number of these treatment devices is limited only by the therapist's creativity in the design of new contexts, and by his capacity for adapting them to each family's situation and style.

One of the most frequent findings in a child-centered family structure is the existence of one or more overinvolved dyads, one of which usually including the symptomatic child. Haley (9) describes three ways to handle the overinvolved dyad: first, by acting on the relationship between the child and his mother; second, by modifying the relationship between father and child; and thirdly, changing the relationship between the spouses. In all three cases, changes are directed to the interaction and the context in which it occurs.

I would like to stress here that we are not after changing the family values as such to replace them with our own; but rather that we are trying to bring back functionality and growth to a family characterized by stagnation and dysfunction. Knowledge about the existence, the features, and the poor functioning of child-centered families will hopefully allow us to identify their structures and separate them from healthy parenting. We must also be aware of what techniques can be used to change them, so that we can restore them to adequate functioning. All of us concerned with children's emotional growth must learn to spot these families and to treat them early in the course of their difficulties. This will help us to meet the dual tasks of preventing and treating troubled children.

REFERENCES

1. E.M. Berman and H.I. Lief. "Marital Therapy from a Psychiatric Perspective: An Overview," *Amer. J. Psychiatry*, 132 (1975), 583–92.
2. L.V. Bertalanffy. *General System Theory*. New York: George Braziller. 1968.
3. J.O. Bradt and C.J. Moynihan. "Opening the Safe: A Study of Child-Focused Families," Washington, D.C. in J.O. Bradt and C.J. Moynihan (eds.), *Systems Therapy*.
4. A. Thomas, S. Chess, and H.G. Birch. *Temperament and Behavior Disorders in Children*. New York: New York University Press, 1969.
5. J.F. Cuber and P.B. Harroff. *Sex and the Significant American*. Baltimore: Penguin Books. 1966.
6. A. Ferber and C.C. Beels. "Family Therapy: A View," *Fam. Prog.*, 8 (1969), 280–318.
7. H. Gavron. *The Captive Wife*. London: Routledge & Kegan Paul, 1966.

8. J. Haley (ed.). *Changing Families: A Family Therapy Reader.* New York: Grune and Stratton. 1971.

9. _____. "Strategic Therapy When a Child is Presented as the Problem," *J. Am. Acad. Child Psychiatry,* 12 (1973), 641–59.

10. J. Haley and B. Montalvo. "The Mystery of Child Psychiatry." Unpublished.

11. J. Haley. *Uncommon Therapy.* New York: W.W. Norton, 1973.

12. D.D. Jackson and J.H. Weakland. "Conjoint Family Therapy: Some Considerations on Theory, Technique and Results," *Psychiatry,* 24 (1961), 30–45.

13. D.M. Levy. *Maternal Overprotection.* New York: Columbia University Press, 1943.

14. T. Lidz. *The Person.* New York: Basic Books. 1968.

15. S. Minuchin and J. Haley. "Broadening the Unit of Intervention." Unpublished.

16. S. Minuchin. *Families and Family Therapy.* Cambridge: Harvard University Press. 1974.

17. A.S. Rossi. "Transition to Parenthood." Paper presented at the annual meeting of the American Orthopsychiatric Association, Washington, D.C. 1967.

18. J. Stachowiak. "Psychological Disturbances in Children as Related to Disturbances in Family Interaction," *J. Marriage Fam.,* 30 (1968), 123–27.

19. E.F. Vogel and N.W. Bell. "The Emotionally Disturbed Child as the Family Scapegoat," in *A Modern Introduction to the Family.* Glencoe, Illinois: Free Press, 1961.

20. P. Watzlawick, J.H. Beavin, and D.D. Jackson. *Pragmatics of Human Communication.* New York: W.W. Norton, 1967.

CHAPTER 14

Family and Social Management of Schizophrenia

C. Christian Beels, M.D.

My experience with the family and social management of schizophrenia began in 1962 at the Westchester Square Day Hospital, where as a resident I learned from Israel Zwerling and Harris Peck how to keep patients out of the hospital by working with their families (1). It continued at the Adult Psychiatry Branch of the National Institute of Mental Health, where I learned that the "family" theory of the etiology and treatment of schizophrenia is a very complicated matter indeed. When I returned to the Bronx to work with Israel Zwerling, Andrew Ferber and Marilyn Mendelsohn in the Family Studies Section (2) of what is now called Bronx Psychiatric Center, I organized and for two years headed the Family Service. That Service attempted, for the first time as far as I know, to base the treatment of a whole catchment area's population of chronic and remitting schizophrenics on a family model. Further, it undertook to do so as a permanent service to that population, not just as an experiment to see what could be done with the families of a few selected cases. It is important to note that what we learned together, we learned the hard way; we winnowed out in the case conferences, supervisions, and planning meetings what I present here without reference to the misery and confusion involved in its discovery.

The Family Service organization is the treatment of last resort for the chronic patients who live in the Northeast Bronx, which has a population of 210,000. The acute psychiatric needs of this area are met by the nearby Bronx Municipal Hospital Center; we have pressed the Hospital Center to take patients with first psychotic breaks, for reasons I will go into later. Its outpatient department also sees a certain number of the chronic patients we regard as "ours." They will in fact become "ours" the next time they decompensate; we have an understanding that if a patient presents for a second hospitalization, we will handle the case if the city hospital refers it. Meanwhile, to avoid some confusing shuttling back and forth, we work to keep those patients who are already ours—about 700 on the rolls at any time —away from the emergency room and outpatient department of the Municipal Hospital. We have the same budget and line allotments as the other geographic units of the hospital, and we have to contend with the same hiring freezes and civil service regulations that afflict the rest of the New York Department of Mental Hygiene. We are special only in the enthusiasm that we generate from our own resources, of which I will say more below.

THE SCHIZOPHRENIC AND HIS FAMILY

A number of fascinating publications mostly recent and mostly American have tried to show that families cause, or help to cause, one of their members to be schizophrenic, and some of these have claimed to show the mechanisms by which that terrible subjugation takes place.

Frieda Fromm-Reichmann (3) attributed it to the schizophrenogenic mother, Gregory Bateson (4) to the family's double-binding communication, Theodore Lidz (5) to the narcissistic egocentricity of the parents and the schism or skew in their marriages, Lyman Wynne and Margaret Singer (6, 7) to the parents' fragmented or amorphous style of communication; and so on through an impressive list of very perceptive writers in this tradition.

An etiology so elegantly worked out should lead eventually to a basis for treatment, but as Henry Massie and I showed in an earlier paper (8), the family therapy of schizophrenia has neither been well developed in practice nor had much demonstrable success. There is almost nobody writing today who advances family therapy by itself as the treatment of choice for schizophrenia. On the other hand, an entire generation of psychotherapists, taught by the above writers, have come to understand that something must be done about the family of the schizophrenic if the therapy is to succeed.

The question is, What is to be done? The quarantine of the noxious family from the patient does not seem to work—even when the patient is in the hospital, they seem to have a way of getting back together. Performing a sort of sanitizing "therapy" on family members to turn them into a better "environment" for the patient also does not work, if for no other reason than that the family cannot stand the guilt. They are often in an agony of self-reproach over the patient's breakdown to begin with, and to be told by the professional staff that the very manner of their love and concern is what caused it is too much. Further, that position will not form the basis of a therapeutic relationship with the family, since it implies a conspiratorial split with the good staff and the treatable patient on one side and the bad family on the other.

In thinking about schizophrenia, we have had to arrive at models or descriptions with a three-way fit so that we can 1) talk to patients about it, 2) talk to families about it, and 3) talk to each other about it. Each of these three presentations must be essentially the same. It is contradictory if we say to the patient that he has "special difficulties in living" that do not have a medical name (though he knows he has a diagnosis because he is in a hospital); if we say to the family that it is true that he has schizophrenia, but it is not a hereditary condition, and there is nothing wrong with his head —it is a "functional illness"; and if we say to each other that he is acute, paranoid, and has a delusional thought disorder and auditory hallucinations. It does not solve the problem to say in a family session with everyone present that the problem lies in the family's pattern of communication. Surely, in doing this we are subjecting the customers and each other to the same sort of mystification that—depending on one's theory—produces, or sustains, or results from the thought disorder in the first place. The problem becomes pressing when we meet, as we often do, with large groups containing patients, family members, and staff-multiple family groups, where the focus is on understanding and coming to grips with the problem, not just in one family but in general. There we see the models in active conflict: the patients behaving as if they are being patronized or put down for some mysterious reason; the families acting as if the patients need "help" (medicine, therapy) for their sickness; and the staff talking in obscure terms about it all and then going to a separate meeting afterward where, it is understood, they talk in scientific language to each other about what they *really* think.

In approaching this problem of a viable model, we have taken note that the nature of schizophrenia is still much debated among the leading authorities and that all ways of talking about it are metaphors taken from medicine, psychology, art, religion, or what-have-you. Inevitably, each metaphor carries its distortions as well as its truth. We nevertheless need to talk descriptively about schizophrenia, and we try to use metaphors that are as consistent, communicative, and truthful as possible.

We begin by saying that schizophrenia is constitutional, something between a talent and a handicap.[1] It is a talent in the sense that people who have it are able to notice things that others cannot, but a handicap in that they notice too much and are inclined to react to and worry about it all. It is in some sense physical, judging from its genetic component (9) and its physiological concomitants (10). To the extent that it is a disease, schizo-

---

[1] I am indebted in this section to Brian Stogoll.

phrenia is like epilepsy, in that it is mainly manifested in alterations of behavior and consciousness. Historically it is also like epilepsy, in that it was once thought to be mysterious and threatening but is now, with the appearance of appropriate medication, coming more under control and understanding. Again like epilepsy, it requires intelligent planning with the family for its management more than it does medical treatment. What we want to avoid are the *illness* connotations of the disease model—the social role of a sick person incapacitated until properly treated. We want instead a disease model that implies retraining and rehabilitation and the avoidance of situations that lead to recurrence. This can be more potential than actual, as in epilepsy or well-managed diabetes. And like diabetes, it is a syndrome with an outcome that can be affected by many factors and can take different final forms. The analogy with diabetes is useful in talking to patients and their families because they can usually perceive from their own experience the parallels that:

Schizophrenia gets worse as a result of stress;

You can live with it and hardly know you have it;

Some forms of it are managed by longterm and relatively benign medication;

It manifests itself in different ways at different times of life; and

Its heredity is not a simple matter.

It may come as a surprise that a family approach to schizophrenia can embrace a disease model, considering how long such family theorists as Laing and Esterson (11) and Murray Bowen (12) have labored to take the diagnosis and the labeling, or in their words the scapegoating of the patient, out of the process of treatment. Laing and others have been careful to call it "madness," a kind of derangement common among us all from time to time, connoting outrage and protest and perhaps a deeper sanity than the insensitive normality of the average person.

I have several reasons for talking in terms of a disease that appears in certain constitutionally disposed people when the conditions are right: 1) It is close to the way in which the culture has come to think of such people —they are "crazy," which is a way of being "sick," and that is how many of the patients, as members of the culture, think of themselves. 2) There is a great deal of medical experience and research—the use of medication, for instance—which suggests that concept; this medical model would be almost impossible to deny or discontinue; but it can be moderated in some important ways. 3) The medical model of a constitutional predisposition is not so pejorative today as it was in Kraepelin's time; we no longer speak of "degenerate stock" as he did, but rather of *tendencies,* such as a constitutional predisposition to collagen disease, diabetes, allergy, or hypoglycemia, or of inborn errors of metabolism and differences of temperament. 4) If the family therapist can relax about calling schizophrenia a disease, he is better able to talk in social-process terms with the patient and family. He will have their respect, since they will not see him as defending a dubious position, and they will be better able to model their attitude after his.

What are the characteristics of this disease? It appears under stress. It is a special way of responding to *change*. Everyone's life contains occasions of stressful change in which the customary supports for our sense of who we are become especially uncertain—or unavailable. Adolescence, moving, going to a new school, courtship, marriage, childbirth, job change, death, or the threatened loss of a family member—any of these experiences can make any of us lose heart, become depressed, be uncertain of what to do next, and appear distracted or preoccupied to our fellows. They require movement into a new life with a new group or an altered sense of who one is in the old one. Sometimes it is not a definite environmental event or a real change of role. The most devastating change can be the loss of an illusion —the realization, for example, that one is no longer young, or respected, or that a loyalty or promise on which one was secretly counting will never be made good.

Our culture has endorsed several ways of responding to these crises of self-confidence. One healthy reaction that middle class people have learned, for example, is to see the change as a challenge to personal growth and career, to seek the company and support of others who have been through it, and to consult experts for technical advice. Other cultures arrange rites of passage in which the role change is ceremonially recognized. In some of these the person going through the upheaval is ritually encouraged to withdraw into a special nonfunctional status for a while. He is allowed to "retreat." So American adolescents "drop out," and since that withdrawal has a name, social status, and probable duration, it is tolerated by parts of the society.

Some people cannot respond to these crises, experiencing them as a rejection of themselves by a new group or by the old group as newly reorganized. They sense this rejection as a personal failure of a very radical nature, what Sullivan called a "rebuff," from which they do not recover. Sullivan said (13):

> We find that the stricken individual, following the peculiar and characterizable failure to react to rebuff, has lost a great part of the confidence in the integrity of the universe, the goodness of God, and so on, which is our common human heritage from infancy; and that from thence onward he goes on feeling decidedly uncertain about life. Apparently, if one is sufficiently uncertain about life, one loses the cognitive assets which serve us in distinguishing products of autistic or purely subjective reverie from products which include important factors residing in so-called external reality; and when one has lost this

ability to distinguish between such reveries and such objects having more external points of reference, one begins to sink into mental processes significantly like those that we experience when we are asleep.

With the appearance of a partition in which considerable waking time is spent in a condition in which one is without the ability to tell what has true, genuine, and consensually acceptable, external references, and what instead is purely personal fantasy, there appears a peculiar disorder of social activity (and I might say even of nonsocial activity), and it is these peculiarities that seem to constitute the essence of schizophrenic behavior.

In having difficulty responding to rebuff, schizophrenics are clearly like the rest of us—they are "more simply-human than otherwise," as Sullivan said. But they do have a great difficulty in responding, some part of which is a constitutional intolerance for change of this kind. They tend to respond awkwardly to strangers and new situations, to fail to learn or to misapply the social forms that the group provides for handling, in Sullivan's terms, the "integration" of new situations. And so their symbolization of the nature of the change—their thinking about what is going on—will be different from that of the primary group that might help them through the trouble. They withdraw, their thinking becomes private and specialized, and they fail to communicate or understand. The emotional and gestural signals by which they indicate their place in the social process—for instance, the eye movements and the timing of speech—all are "off" (14) and are seen as "alien" by others.

A crucial event then takes place within the group (the family, school, clan, or village). The group decides that the person who was hitherto one of them, in that they all shared a common set of meanings about what was happening, is now not one of them, is alien, and is crazy. This means that the person cannot be dealt with by "reason"—that is, by the usual social forms of control—but must submit to some special process of control and reintegration into the group, which in our society is called psychiatric treatment.

We can now look back at the writings on the family etiology of schizophrenia and see that they were describing the *social process* of the family group as it "drives the person crazy" (15), and that it would be a mistake for us to locate the impetus for this in either the family or the patient—it is an interaction in which both participate. And we can now also describe the social setting in which schizophrenia takes place in a way that will lead to a rational treatment program.

The Social Setting of The Schizophrenic and His Family

This social setting can be looked at as a series of concentric rings surrounding the patient in which the innermost one is the family.

Certainly what has been said about the family of the schizophrenic has been borne out by our experience. The secrets (16), the unresolved narcissistic dependencies, the covert communications, the double binds, the projections, and the whole nightmare of repetitive cycles within the cohesive isolated group (17) are all to be found. But these observations do not necessarily lead to a plan for change. It is not enough to uncover secrets or to straighten out communications. The attitude of the family members toward their predicament must be changed by offering them an alternative *structure,* by giving them a positive way of dealing with it in the form of new opportunities and new people with whom to interact.

The family members have failed to see the psychosis as a developmental crisis, and have instead projected their doubts and ambivalences onto the patient. They see him as having a "screw loose" that some doctor or hospital has got to tighten, or they see him as in need of special efforts on the part of the family caretaker—usually the mother—to encourage him to greater willpower and determination. The family members have to be encouraged to see the psychosis of one of them as part of a process of change that they are all going through, each one responding differently—one with psychosis, others with headache, insomnia, flight, unemployment, or exhaustion. The end result will be that they all must live in some new relationship—the next plateau in their lives, where the caretaking of everyone will be different.

The schizophrenic and his family usually lack a network of connections with society. In order to establish such a network, it is usually necessary to experiment with new relations between the family and others—the extended family, the professional "family" of the treatment team, and other families in the same trouble. Typically, the families of schizophrenics are isolated from their environment in a number of ways (18); they are often ashamed of having a chronic patient living in the house, or their relatives and neighbors find them difficult and unrewarding. The family members close themselves off and restrict their lives, so that the futility and repetitiveness of their behavior and thinking feeds on itself.

Schizophrenics are often further immured in their families or in their private rooms by the judgment of the outside world that they are not congenial or productive workers. In a society in which much of one's sense of self comes from being either publicly congenial or productive or both, this is a large setback. Getting and keeping a good job is often the worst kind of terror for schizophrenic people, since it involves meeting strangers, making an impression, and dealing with the coldness, ambiguity, and bureaucracy of the society's larger structures.

Once schizophrenics have been classified as unproductive, and thus at one with the poor, the crippled, the criminal, and the children, then the largest units in the society, the great superagencies of government, bring to bear on them the merciless subjugation that is called "social service," "psychiatric treatment," or "welfare." For anyone who is frightened by ambiguity, uncertainty, and mixed messages, this is the ultimate experience of a rejecting parent who cannot be labeled as such. Protecting patients and their families from the bureaucracies that are set up to care for and control them is the hardest part of our job.

Looking at these concentric social rings around the schizophrenic, we can see that we are not dealing just with a disordered "thought process" or even with a disordered family communication system. These are only the most centrally identifiable parts of a career, a life in social context. There are indeed several possible careers, and probably as many "schizophrenias." But still speaking of them as one, we can say in general that the job of treating this disease requires the marshaling of an organization that will address itself to the whole life of the person, and not just to a part of it.

It is no accident that for so many centuries our production-conscious society locked schizophrenics up in asylums—it was an expression of the fact that the life and career of the patient *as a whole* was an affront to the society, and vice versa. It was for this reason that in mercantile 17th-century France they were first herded, together with the poor and the criminals, into the empty leprosaria (19).

Now that ever larger numbers of patients are living outside the asylums in a society that is often still unwilling to tolerate them, and knows well how to drive them back into the crazy house if they get out of line, the job of the treating organization becomes twofold: first, teaching both patients and their families and others to tolerate each other in all their idiosyncrasies—making life possible in whatever odd places the patient's career can fit in with the careers of others; sometimes creating new places for people to live and work. And second, anticipating and preventing or smoothing over the crises of confidence, the changes that produce acute psychotic episodes in families where things were previously stabilized. This has been called "crisis intervention," and it is a large part of our work.

Those tasks dictate the design of the treating organization. It is further dictated by some features of the natural history of schizophrenia as we understand it.

The patient is the person in the social system least able to bear the strain and responsibility for making changes. In fact, as we said, our definition of schizophrenia is that it is a constitutional intolerance for certain kinds of change, and therefore it requires more tolerance from others.

A primary condition for a schizophrenic's stabilization is clarity concerning what is happening in his intimate social world. The encounter between that world and the therapeutic team, along with everyone's comments about it, is presumed to promote that clarity. The idea is to create clear opportunities for change—openings in the thicket—without leaning too hard on the patient.

A tolerant environment peculiarly suited to the patient's life and development may look very strange to others; it should involve as few dogmatic assumptions as possible and no bureaucratic formulas—just lots of opportunity. The family and patient sense that their predicament may last a lifetime. They are not helped by a plan to fix them up and then leave them on their own, because they know there will be more trouble.

From the above needs of schizophrenics and their families, we arrived at the initial design of our family service:

It had to be small enough to be unbureaucratic. The Service is staffed by about fifty people, and the work groups are not larger than ten.

It had to be large enough to do everything for its population, while providing continuity of care. We set up three crisis intervention teams, a day center, an in-patient ward with three shifts, and a foster care unit. We started therapy groups, multiple family groups, activity groups, and drop-in medication clinics.

It would be generally nepotistic in that there were social friendships and personal trust among many of the founding members. No one was accepted because of trade union or civil service credentials such as seniority or having passed examinations. From the start we had the benign patronage and protection of the director of the hospital and the top business officer, without whom we would not have had the almost complete administrative freedom that the enterprise needed.

We would be flexible and unhierarchical, so that novel solutions to peculiar problems could be undertaken without straining anyone's dignity, job description, or place in the organizational chart.

As part of a permanent care delivery system in the State Department of Mental Hygiene, which is set up to give care forever to this population, rich or poor, we could, in sincerity, make a lifetime contract with our patients; we would not have to turn them away for lack of funds or insurance.

Thus we would be able to provide in the atmosphere of the Service, from its general design to the individual attitudes of its people, the note of hope that in my reading of studies of the treatment of schizophrenia appears to be the indispensable—and sometimes the only effective—ingredient.

The family and social system approach permits us to focus on the world around the patient, rather than grappling with him alone in his isolation and despair and ambivalence. As we cheerfully work away at the configurations of people who surround the patient in his life in the family and on the ward, the patient often gets better while nobody is looking at him so intently. This, more than anything else, is the theory behind the treatment approach of the service.

This treatment approach is as much oriented to the morale of the family and of the treatment team as to the condition of the patient.

TYPES OF SCHIZOPHRENIA

Kraepelin originally introduced the idea, still in use, that the way to classify schizophrenics is by their *course.* He thought that symptoms and other discrete phenomena were important, which we have come to doubt. But we distinguish different *types of social career,* a sort of interaction of temperament and opportunity that produces several different kinds of *lives.* This is close to the original "psychobiology" concept of Adolph Meyer (20). We can best develop the concept of the patient's course or career in the context of the different types of patients.

First Breaks

People who are becoming psychotic for the first time in a rather definite and dramatic way, especially if they are young and have had "good pre-morbid" lives of fair social adjustment beforehand, have attracted special interest ever since Sullivan (13) pointed out that they sometimes have a good prognosis. He noted that this is especially true if the catastrophe is reshaped as an opportunity, a crisis in development, and if the family is somehow kept at bay. His special ward at The Sheppard and Enoch Pratt Hospital in Towson, Md., was designed to treat the break as a human phenomenon leading to a reorganization of the personality, perhaps a useful one. Loren Mosher (21) has advanced these ideas in the design of his Soteria House, an experimental treatment facility in the San Francisco Bay area where young and accepting staff members who have this view of psychosis work with the patient. A number of reports (22) and our own experience indicate that if the patient is an adolescent, intensive conjoint family therapy is contraindicated in most cases.

If the patient is older and is having a psychotic reaction to adult life—such as a reaction to divorce, a postpartum psychosis, or a midlife or involutional crisis—the phenomenology may be similar, but the indications for family therapy are positive, as I will show later in the story of Edna. The point I want to make is that the first psychotic episode requires special handling; there is evidence that if this is provided, the break need not be repeated. Moreover it can change the patient's career in a decisively positive sense (23). Such successful outcome depends on positively influencing the attitude of the family and patient toward the meaning of the crisis for the future.

Periodic Patients

If there is a second break, we may be heading for a different kind of experience and a different career. Patients with the definite and dramatic onset of schizophrenia described above may reach a social adjustment and then go through the experience of psychosis all over again. When this becomes a pattern, we note that these patients are still different from other repeating patients, the chronic ones. Periodic patients are more out of the hospital than in—that is the most objective definition of their careers. They may also be better able than chronic patients to work, to live with their families, or to live alone, as many of them do. They have an interest in becoming more skilled in both public and private life and a cautious interest in learning to recognize and cope with *change*. They and their families are interested in forestalling the next crisis or the one after that, and they sometimes succeed.

Chronic Patients

These patients are more in the hospital than out. Many of them had the kind of slow, early, and insidious onset which is described for process schizophrenia. Many had a poor premorbid history. Some have organic difficulties as well. They are less likely to be married, generally have a poor work history, and their families, when they are on the scene, find living with them less manageable than do families of periodic patients. All these things no doubt feed into one another, but we see no evidence that the more chronically hospitalized the patient, the more rejecting the family; we think we can distinguish between these chronic patients and another group of patients whose careers were like those of periodic patients up to a certain point in their lives. At that point, however, their families decided they were through with them, and the patients got into a power struggle to influence the families to take them back. The result is a standoff, with the patient making his combat headquarters in the hospital. These patients are in the hospital for years, not because of their own requirements but because of a shift in the family's expectations.

CAREERS IN SCHIZOPHRENIA—SOME STORIES

The cases I shall now discuss are not real cases—they are fictional combinations of aspects of cases that seem to me to fit together, assembled to make some of the points I want to present. They should not be read as the usual case conference or report, or as scientific accounts of what worked and what did not. It is difficult to talk about effectiveness in the treatment of schizophrenia. The criteria of success rarely have to do with cure or change, but more with stabilization and placement. We cut the number of beds used by our catchment area in half, and likewise halved the admission rate, in our first two years of operation. But the question remains—what should we expect to be able to do for these people?

Ralph Melzer: A First Break

When we first saw him, Ralph was 17, a slender, intellectual high school senior who apparently had always been rather anxious and retiring. In the special New York school where he majored in physics, however, he had recently experienced an increase in self-confidence as a result of joining a group of Marxist student activists. He had an older sister, Miriam, 20, an English major at a city college. His mother was a school guidance counselor and his father worked long hours as the owner of a small manufacturing concern in the Bronx.

Mr. and Mrs. Melzer were both communists when they met in their youth, but Mr. Melzer was now disillusioned with the prospects of the revolution. He and Ralph had been speaking even less since Ralph became a Marxist—their occasional conversations resulted in angry political shouting matches from which Ralph would finally retreat. Miriam and Mrs. Melzer, though more in agreement with Ralph, felt torn between the two men. Ralph would have long, unsatisfactory talks with his mother and sister about politics, and avoided talking about his personal life. On rare occasions he revealed to Miriam a largely fantasied relationship with a girl in his student group.

One day after the group had finished a sit-in lasting several days, Ralph disappeared for a week. He showed up disheveled, mute, and terrified, at Miriam's college. She got him home with much difficulty. When he saw his father, he became rigid with fear.

With the help of neighbors the family brought him to the municipal hospital emergency room, where they were regretfully told there were no beds, and so he was committed to the State hospital. He arrived on the ward of the Family Service in the middle of the night, stuporous and dehydrated. He was given Thorazine, and the next day the inpatient staff began to coax him to eat and drink and talk a little. The crisis team then met with the family, including Ralph himself.

The crisis team consisted of Mildred, a psychiatrist, Ellen, a social worker, and Mike, who was an assistant therapy aide (ATA). This group was selected to work with the case mainly because Ellen, the social worker, was on call that day; Mildred, the psychiatrist, was needed for evaluation of the new case; and Mike, the ATA, was a man that Ellen liked to work with. Ellen knew she would probably be managing this case; she had a hunch she would need a man to help the team relate to this catatonic young male patient.

The family meeting lasted 2 hours. Ralph kept running in and out, and Mike walked with him and reassured him as he paced the halls. Mildred and Ellen, having gotten the story, tried to get Ralph and his father to talk to each other, but Ralph ran out of the room again. The meeting ended with a plan to contact the leader of the student group and to meet again with the family, perhaps without Ralph.

Ralph was quite upset after the meeting and paced the floor that evening with Art, an ATA on the evening shift. He told Art he was sure his father wanted to kill him or at least castrate him because he was a homosexual. Art told him that was a very common fear among people going through a psychosis for the first time. Ralph also talked with Art about his fear of the other patients in the hospital.

That evening Ralph was visited by some members of his student group and talked a long time with them. He seemed much calmer after the conversation and went to bed. The next afternoon, though he was under escape precautions (meaning he was in pajamas), Ralph disappeared from the ward. A day later his mother called Mildred and told her she had heard from the leader of the student group that Ralph was with them. He was about the same, still fearful, but eating and drinking and talking with them. The group had some ideas, from reading Ronald Laing and seeing "Wednesday's Child," about how such situations should be managed. They didn't want to bring Ralph home or to the hospital, but wanted to assure the family that he was all right.

The crisis team of Mildred, Ellen, and Mike, plus Art and the head nurse of the inpatient service, arranged to meet with two members of the student group and the family to decide what to do. The meeting lasted 3 hours, during which many things happened. There was an exchange between the student group's leader and Mr. Melzer that revealed, in a way that Mr. Melzer could hear, that Ralph wanted to get in touch with his father but could not. Mildred, by sympathetic questioning of the students, brought out their ambivalence about managing Ralph. Opinions about the danger of suicide or further decompensation were discussed. The students said that Ralph really wanted to stay with them, and that they would consult with Mildred if they needed advice. Mr. Melzer argued for going after him with the police. Mildred, after much hesitation, decided to send Ralph a letter about the meeting, signed by everyone present. It urged him to call Mike or Art if he got into something he couldn't handle, but endorsed his staying with the group for a while if he thought that would help. The letter explained that the team would go on meeting with the rest of the family. Mildred persuaded the group members to take some Thorazine with them for Ralph, and they agreed to give it to him in spite of their prejudices against it. It was agreed that Mildred would be consultant to the group.

During the next weeks Ellen met with the three family members a few times and, by getting Miriam to talk to her father about Ralph, prepared them for the idea that Ralph, if he returned to the family, might be quite a changed person. The meetings dealt with the father's identification with Ralph, and with his disappointment and sense of loss.

Meanwhile the student group was getting tired of looking after Ralph. They were taking turns staying home from school, but sometimes he was alone at the apartment of the older brother of one of the group, where he slept. Mildred and the student leader agreed it was time to meet with Ralph again and make new plans. Ralph agreed to meet with Miriam and the team, but not with his parents.

When he "surfaced," Ralph was bearded, strangely dressed and had lost some weight. But he was articulate in a very slow and cautious way. He had decided he was not a homosexual after a conversation with the girl of his prebreak fantasies. He had also decided his father was not out to kill him, but still did not want to talk with him. He had begun work on a written explanation of what had happened to him, viewed in terms of Marxism and astrology.

In the course of the meeting, Ellen began to work on plans for the future. The next weeks were busy for Ralph—they included a return home, a readmission, a final settling into a halfway house, sporadic attendance at the day center, and the beginning of individual therapy with a psychologist interested in working with this kind of problem. None of these arrangements went smoothly, but after much difficulty a program was patched together. Thereafter Ralph had a very rocky course, but he was not rehospitalized. The parents continued to see Ellen to discuss their adjustment to their son's strange new way of life and his alienation from them.

Here, with the case unresolved but with the elements of treatment in place, I will stop and present some of the points this story raises:

1. Ralph's case should never have come to us, but there is no good place in the Bronx for his kind of problem. The area does not have a really sequestered, receptive place like Soteria House. In retrospect, the student group functioned as such an environment for him, accepting him in his changing identity.

2. The team managed the crisis of Ralph's escape by calling a meeting of his network and working out plans with everyone present. They did this rather than reacting to Ralph's "absence against medical advice" by trying to recapture him, which would have been the correct response under hospital policy.

The emphasis in the meeting was on having everyone present, on getting ideas from everyone, and on coming to a conclusion, all of which maximized and clarified the communication. The letter to Ralph, telling him everything about the meeting and letting him know who was in charge and who was going to be meeting with whom, was very important. It was the best way to guard against escape and panic. It also validated Ralph's only positive communication, which was that he wanted to stay with the student group. It was a move that dealt with the *immediate* problem of what to do but that also left the door open for a number of later developments. It thus followed Jane Ferber's rule of crisis management: "Think about what has to be done next."

Most of the adjustment was expected from the parents and the leader of the student group, so they received strong support in coping with new developments through meetings with Ellen and Mildred. Miriam (the well sibling) and the student group leader were used as spokesmen for Ralph in the family system, since the father could not face him directly.

Family therapy of an intensive type is not indicated in this kind of situation because the emotional responses of fear, disappointment, and despair are so strong that the family group can only with difficulty see the first schizophrenic break as an opportunity. The adolescent patient is in the midst of a transition with little group support, either from the past or from the society that is to be his future. He has to develop some of his new personality with the help of other, non-family therapy; some time must pass before this happens and a meeting with the family is possible. Until then, work with the parents is useful for preparing them for the change.

For contrast, I will tell the story of a first break we handled well with family therapy.

Edna Hogan: A First Break

Edna, 24, a stenographer, is the youngest child of a "professional" family with three other children—Jane, a nurse; Mary, a teacher; and John, who is a lawyer like his father. Everyone in the family is married and successful except Edna.

When she came to us, Edna was the only one still at home with her parents. For 2 years after graduating from college, she had a job in a law firm as secretary to one of her father's law school classmates. She was quiet and respectful, and had made one friend in that office, another secretary.

Within the same month, both this office friend and Edna's next-oldest sister, Jane, were married, and Edna was a member of both weddings. Afterward she became somewhat depressed with a flu-like illness that kept her home from work. During the next 6 months she had a number of medical consultations, since she seemed to be very weak and could scarcely get out of bed. A neurological workup was negative. To one of her doctors, she confided that she thought her employer had a secret means of having intercourse with her as she lay in bed at home. She had never told anyone about this because it seemed very crazy to her; she begged the doctor not to reveal it to her family, but she did think it was the cause of her illness. She told a psychiatrist who saw her next that she now was not sure whether the person with whom she had the mysterious sexual contact was her employer or a rock star she had seen on television. The psychiatrist recommended hospitalization. At the hospital, Edna convinced the admitting resident that the whole thing was a mistake and that she would seek psychiatric help. She went home and went back to bed.

A neighbor put the family in touch with our Service. Two members of a crisis team, George, a psychologist, and Sue, a social work student, arranged with the parents to make a home visit. Edna would not speak with them on the phone, but she did get out of bed when they arrived and joined in the meeting.

The team made three visits over the next 2 weeks. Edna sat through these rather silently while George and Sue talked to the parents and whoever of the sisters and brother were able to join them. The family wanted the team to provide treatment for Edna, but George told Edna that he thought she was being silent because she had no reason to trust anyone yet, and it was all right with him if she listened in until she felt more comfortable. The team also made it clear that they were meeting with the family not because they thought the family was the cause of Edna's trouble, but because they knew from experience that the family might be the people who could help figure it out.

At the first meeting George and Sue, after some social pleasantries, began by making a *genogram,* a diagram of the family. This is a standard procedure in our first meetings, and is important for understanding what is happening; focusing attention on the family rather than on the patient; and arriving at a contract and plan. George put a large sheet of paper on the table where everyone could see it, took a marking pen, and asked for the family's help in making the diagram, which took about half an hour to complete.

During the course of this work, George and Sue noted the following:

1. Mr. Hogan (James) had had a bad year in 1950, when both his parents had died. That was also the year before Edna was born. Mr. Hogan said

the funerals were almost the last time he had seen his brother and sister in Boston. There was considerable coolness among them, which had partly to do with arguments about the parents' wills. Mr. Hogan vigorously denied grief or resentment.

2. Both Mr. and Mrs. Hogan are youngest children. Mrs. Hogan (Theresa) said she was once very close to her sister Angela in Buffalo, but had not seen her in many years, though Angela had offered several invitations. Angela looked after their mother, Marie.

3. Edna looked blank as her father detailed the professional accomplishments of the other children. When her mother said she had not seen her sister in 10 years, Edna reminded her that it was only 8 years since she had gone there. When Mrs. Hogan said her brother-in-law was a business man, Edna half-smiled and said "junk dealer." Her mother shared the smile. George and Sue noted the covert alliance between Edna and her mother and felt that though Edna said almost nothing else during the interview, she was not so acutely psychotic that she could not observe and make effective disagreement. A family's and a patient's best level of psychological functioning comes to the fore during a concrete task, like the genogram. They are grateful not to be attacked first on the salient aspects of their pathology.

4. There was an angry exchange between Jane and her father when they were talking about Jane's children. Following this, an exchange of glances between Jane and her mother led to an inquiry into how Mr. Hogan and his other children got along. The tension in the room mounted rapidly, and Mr. Hogan launched into a disconnected tirade against Jane and Mary. At several points he got their husbands' names confused.

5. As the interview went on, George and Sue referred frequently to the diagram for new areas to explore, and generally indicated that "the problem" was not Edna but was "in there somewhere."

6. At the end of the meeting, the diagram was used again to make a contract as to who would be willing to attend meetings and at each meeting the minimum membership the team would accept.

What emerged in the meetings did indeed clarify the problem. Mary, John, and Jane had each kept a very fixed distance from the family since their marriages, returning only to participate in stormy arguments with their father, who tried to interfere in many details of their lives. Their mother was paralyzed by these scenes, had been depressed since Jane's marriage, and had started to drink in secret. Everyone in the family had been worried about their mother; each confessed to the guilty thought that maybe Edna would remain to keep her company. The guilt was related to a "worry" about whether Edna would ever marry. No one had seen any of these problems as reflecting a difficulty in Mr. and Mrs. Hogan's relationship—that was strongly denied by all when Sue inquired about it.

After this, the team moved the meetings from the home to the Family

Service office. In time they got some of the fights between Edna's siblings and their father clarified, and encouraged Edna to comment on discussions in which she had an interest. Edna took a turn for the worse after the group talked about the parents' marital difficulties, but improved when the team urged her to realize that she was not responsible for her parents' happiness. The team asked her to spend a weekend with Jane and her husband to see what would happen if her parents were left alone, which she did. The following week Edna startled everyone by saying she was going to get a job in a place that had a typing pool. She had not liked the old job; she confirmed Sue's speculation that she had thought her former employer was a spy for her father. She agreed that it would be hard to go for a job interview feeling as shy as she did, so she had some private sessions with Sue at which she talked about, and practiced applying for, a job.

Edna's successful application for a job was accompanied by great tension in the family, a new round of discussions about whether she would ever get married, and detailed inquiries as to whether she would be bored or exploited. George and Sue amplified Edna's mumbled statements that she liked to be with other typists and didn't like the high-powered professional atmosphere the rest of the family claimed to enjoy. The team worked on the family's disappointment in Edna as being "different" from the rest of the family. During one of these discussions her mother cried and said that she had felt Edna was the only one in the family who understood her. This led to tears all around and more discussion of Mrs. Hogan's limited life, her drinking, and her need to talk to more people. Two weeks later, at the team's urging, Mrs. Hogan made her first visit in 8 years to her favorite sister in Buffalo. While she was away, Mr. Hogan got drunk and assaulted Jane's husband, after which a new atmosphere of candor appeared in the family sessions. Edna kept her job, and the other family members continued to talk about and accept their differences from one another, with Mr. Hogan protesting and filibustering all the way.

There are several points to be made about this successful case.

It was not easy. There were endless telephone negotiations throughout and many cancelled appointments. Edna's silences were maddening. Many times she diverted meetings by wanting to go back to bed or by refusing to come at all. Mr. Hogan was a skillful opponent, and he and the team had wearying power struggles as to who would run the meetings.

There are some important differences between Edna and Ralph as patients. She was older and had some good experiences with work and friends in her past. She was able to use "getting sick" to put herself in the way of help and had some insight that her problems might be psychological. But beyond this, there was the general sense that Edna's psychosis was not such a radical upheaval in the life of either the family or the individual as was Ralph's. In Edna's case, there was a large supporting network to work with.

Some of the factors that I think contribute to success are present in both cases: Both involved upper middle class, professional families that shared values with the team members, such as the power of communication and understanding in human affairs. Both families had some intellectual tolerance for individual differences, meaning that the teams could better work with their emotional dread of those differences that they saw as deviant. Both families had the financial reserves to take time off from work and to avoid, in general, the kind of panic, rage, or hopeless resignation that hits a lower class family when a crisis occurs and their small margin of resources has to be spent in adjusting to it.

Edna's family, once it settled down, required the attention of two team members about 1½ to 2 hours a week, including consultation and telephoning. This is unusually economical. The cases I will present in the rest of the paper required greater outlays of people and time, especially at the beginning. But the point I want to make is that George and Sue could not have undertaken the case without the backing of a large organization that could help if Edna had to be hospitalized. Small outpatient agencies regularly fail with cases like Edna's because the workers lose their nerve when the going gets rough, fearing they will lose the case to a hospital with which they have no connection.

Mae Franklin: A Periodic Case

Mae was 38 when she came to our Service as a hospital admission in the middle of the night. She was brought in screaming and battling two policemen, accompanied by her husband Arthur, who was very businesslike and aloof and who indicated to the staff that he had been through this a number of times before.

Mae's first hospital admission had been after graduating from high school in Jamaica, and her second followed the birth of her first child Ernest, now 16. Arthur said that during that episode he first learned from Mae's mother that she had been "sick" before, and that he felt he had been sold damaged goods. Neither Arthur nor Mae's mother was surprised, then, when Mae had to go to the hospital again after the birth of a second child, Annette, now 12, and after that, Arthur resigned himself to having a sick wife. He was also from Jamaica, and had no immediate family in the area. He drove a taxi which he had bought with his own savings and some money from Mae's mother. Thus he could arrange his hours to help care for the children. A natural alliance had developed between him and Mae's mother as Mae's two caretakers when she was "going off."

This she did every 2 or 3 years. She would begin with a flattening of her already rather restricted, polite range of affect; she would become very quiet and spend time staring at the wall. She would then announce a discovery —usually that a neighbor had told her Arthur was being unfaithful—and would then start to pester her mother, Arthur, the children, her married sisters, and finally the minister and the police for more information about her discovery. She would get angrier and more excited and demanding, and finally, after some sleepless nights, she would be brought to the hospital in the state in which we first saw her. She usually got better quickly on medication and left the hospital within 2 months.

She was in fact quiet, but still very guarded and suspicious, at the family meeting that was held on the 2nd day of her admission to our ward. Those present at the meeting were Arthur, the son Ernest, Mae's mother, and one of the sisters, and for the Service, Hal, a psychiatrist, and Arlene, a nurse on the ward who was also from Jamaica. The history was given in a very authoritative tone by Arthur and Mae's mother, speaking in turn. Efforts to get Mae to tell her story were met with sullen mutterings from her, at which her mother and sister would cluck their tongues reprovingly. In a side conversation with Arlene, however, Mae did say that it always made her mad when the family threw her in the hospital. What was happening was not her fault, since she was the victim of witchcraft. Arlene said she knew somethingabout witchcraft and asked if someone had put a spell on her. Mae confirmed that she had heard voices telling her through the television set that Arthur had a woman who was putting a spell on her to make the family hate her.

Hal and Arlene concluded from the meeting that the family had acquired a stereotyped way of responding to Mae's psychotic episodes, and that whereas she would probably again recover rapidly, it would help in the future if this break could be handled differently. At a second meeting with the same group, Hal and Arlene suggested that Mae be transferred to the day center. Hazel, a nurse who worked at the day center, was also present to talk with the family about the transfer.

Mae liked the idea of going to the day center, since she could be home evenings and weekends. She was worried about what was happening to her family and about the time Arthur was taking off from work. Arthur and her mother "reassured" her that the family was getting along just fine, and Arthur said ominously that he certainly didn't want Mae leaving the hospital until she was quite well and free of delusions.

Hazel explained that the same treatment and activities would be available to Mae in the day center as on the ward, with the added advantage that she would recover more rapidly because she would have more of a chance to practice responsible behavior again. After considerable dubious discussion with the family, a contract was worked out: The new treatment team would be Hazel, the nurse from the day center, and Ann, a dance therapist there. Mae, Arthur, and Mae's mother would meet weekly for a while with them. Mae would start doing whatever household work she could at home nights and weekends and would come to the day center weekdays. A few days after she transferred to the day center Mae chose the telephone switchboard as her job, and on the advice of Hazel, joined a women's group in addition to her regular group of 10-or-so patients who met with Hazel 3 mornings a week. This schedule of activity was drawn up in a written contract and signed by all parties, to run for 2 months and then be renegotiated.

Mae found the day center a friendly and businesslike place. It reminded her of a garment loft she had worked in the year before Ernest was born. She got involved in sorting and mending the clothes the center was collecting for its thrift shop. Her first weekend at home was quite tense, since it was clear to her that Arthur did not want her there. He and the children seemed to be walking on eggs, treating her with exaggerated consideration. Mae concluded that Arthur did not want her around because he wanted to be with the woman who had cast the spell. She decided to stay at home on Monday morning to see if she could force him into a revealing move. There was a shouting match in which Mae refused to go to the center and also refused to let Arthur leave the house. Arthur called the center to say that Mae was getting sick again and that he thought she should be in a full time hospital.

Hazel and Ann asked Hal, the psychiatrist, to join them in an extra meeting with Arthur and Mae that afternoon, agreed to after a long telephone exchange between Hazel and the couple. It was a stormy meeting, but Mae did not become assaultive and, as Hal pointed out, did not base her suspicions on hallucinations or delusions, but directly on her interpretation of Arthur's behavior. Hal gave a very professional talk to Arthur about the connection between his distant behavior and Mae's suspicions of infidelity. He said he understood that Arthur couldn't be aware of this, but that it was going to be an important thing to work on. Mae appeared relieved, and agreed to come to the center regardless of her suspicions. Hazel and Ann renewed their contract with the couple to work on the problems they were having with each other. Mae said it would be better to meet without her mother, and that was agreed to. At the end of the meeting Hazel and Sue emphasized that it was *behavior* they were interested in, not the craziness or sanity of anyone's ideas. They asked Arthur and Mae to think during the week about what each of them did that the other didn't like, and bring a list to the next meeting.

This training in focusing their anger continued in meetings with the couple for the next several weeks. In her women's group, Mae met two other black women with stormy marriages. In talking with them she realized that she had very little experience outside her family. She had been preoccupied with rearing her children, a task to which she had never felt adequate, and had accepted her mother's and Arthur's supervision and criticism. She had fewer friends than her sisters and, even when her children were independent, had a strange hesitation about getting a job. Hazel suggested to her, in a one-to-one talk, that she had had a very narrow life, in which "getting sick" had been the only breaking-out.

The following weekend there was an angry shouting match between Arthur and Mae and her mother. Mae appeared on Monday morning sullen and withdrawn, and only after much coaxing from Hazel told the morning group about the fight. She had no idea what started it, but it had been about all the old topics. Hazel and Ann decided to ask Mae's mother and the oldest sister to the next family meeting.

That meeting lasted two hours. With the help of the sister, the team defined Arthur and the mother as a caretaking coalition that had been protecting Mae most of her life. There was a hint that this had been the covert marriage contract—the mother would take care of Arthur if he would help take care of Mae. Mae's mother became angry and tearful at this. Ann and Hazel got the sister to join them in recognizing Mae's mother as the most important person in Mae's life in many ways. They refocused the meeting on the present: How did everyone feel about Mae's getting a job and having a life outside the house? The family expressed fears that she would get sick again. The team asked them all to think about how Mae had reacted to being at the day center, where she had taken on several jobs and been quite responsible. They ended the meeting with an empathic exchange with Mae's mother, telling her they understood her feeling about Mae's needing her special care.

Two weeks later, after the center had a clothing sale of which Mae was treasurer, everybody agreed that she could leave the center to look for a job. The meetings with Arthur and Mae had produced greater candor in their exchanges with each other, but they seemed to be stuck in a rather sterile, empty world. They agreed with some trepidation to join a couples group which was conducted once a week in the evenings by Ann, in cooperation with Alex, a photographer who was a volunteer on the Service.

During the next 6 months Mae got a part-time job as a cashier in a restaurant where one of the women in her women's group worked. Arthur and two of the other husbands in the couples group agreed that women's liberation was bad for their children. Ernest, Mae's and Arthur's son, was arrested for possession of marijuana and released. Arthur told the group he was surprised Mae did not "go off" as a result of this but, indeed, rose to meet the crisis. Mae had to visit Arthur at his garage one day and found him with another woman. This produced a major crisis. There were extra family meetings; Arthur refused to come to the couples group; Mae's mother went to bed with a mysterious illness, and Mae spent a week with her sister. At length, Arthur agreed to return to the couples group. At the meeting of the group to which they returned, Mae and Arthur told their story. There was a general discussion of infidelity and what it might mean or had meant to the several couples in the group. The group talked about it as something that happens sometimes but that is redeemable. Ann and Alex made the point that infidelity, like psychosis, appears in families at times of change and stress. Mae took some satisfaction in all this, and seemed to feel that a score had been settled. She and Arthur returned to living together in an uneasy truce.

A year after this, they had stopped attending the couples group and Mae appeared at the day center only for medication and for chatting with Hazel. One day Mae's sister called Hazel and said that Mae had quit her job and was sitting at home staring. Arthur and her mother were conferring about what to do. Hazel called a meeting of the whole family. Mae looked as she had at the first meeting on the ward almost two years before, but managed to say she had quit her job because she thought she had seen Arthur and one of the waitresses together. Exploration revealed that Arthur had been spending a lot of time away from home, but he insisted he had been working extra hours to pay off some debts. The team pointed out to him that he had not discussed this with Mae and that she had not asked him about it. Mae had also stopped her medication.

Another meeting was needed to get Mae started on medication again, back to her job, and attending the couples group with Arthur. The group was glad to see them, and there was an exchange of stories between the couples about patterns of relapse and how to handle them, the importance of medication, and the role of the spouse in the patient's illness. The group felt very expert in these areas since they had a great deal of experience, and Arthur told Ann there were some things about mental illness she would never understand because she had not been through it firsthand, as he had.

I have told the story of Arthur and Mae Franklin at length because it illustrates a number of points:

1. The Service was able to shift Mae quickly from the inpatient ward to the day center without bureaucratic hangups and loss of information or control—solely because it was the better treatment. This kind of rapid choice between treatment options is indispensable.

2. The day center design requires that counseling work with the family, the interaction between the patient and the family, and the patient's experience in the day center all be in progress at the same time and that they be presided over by the same clinical staff. This produces a maximum of information, the kind of clarification of the environment that I mentioned earlier in this article. Attendance at the day center cannot be fruitful, and will not last long, without concurrent family therapy, at least to the extent of keeping the staff informed of what is happening in the rest of the patient's world. Conversely, family therapy for a case like this without the additional

structure and experience of day center activities is a lost drop in the bucket.

3. The aim of this many-dimensioned therapy effort is to stabilize the patient's social environment by adding elements to it (day center, job, multiple family group) that can buffer the feedback circuits in the family. An example of such a feedback circuit is: Arthur is absent—Mae withdraws —Arthur consults her mother—mother visits to see if Mae is "going off" again—Mae feels another woman is plotting with Arthur—this contributes to Arthur's absence or distance from her, and so on. We arbitrarily designated this sequence as beginning with Arthur's absence because that was the easiest thing to identify and change, and Arthur was the easiest person to make responsible, not because that is where the cycle definitively started. We do not try to reverse or stop a sequence. We only want to damp its swings and avoid the next hospital admission that is part of its later and wider excursions.

4. More distant and stable members of the family, like Mae's sister, are brought in from time to time to reinforce the buffering effect and to implement the interventions of the team with overinvolved members such as Mae's mother. Note that it was Mae's sister who alerted the team for the second crisis intervention. This was the result of a carefully planned agreement with the whole family, an early warning system that ensured we would be called if *anyone* became apprehensive.

5. Hal, the psychiatrist in this system, was called in for the sparingly used exercise of medical authority. We have few psychiatrists on our Service, and they present themselves to the families mainly when someone needs to be impressed. Otherwise they help with the teaching, write prescriptions, and keep their powder dry.

6. The multiple family group is important to the maintenance of the system both before and after—but especially after—discharge. Families with a psychotic member feel freakish, isolated, and helpless, and the mere meeting with others in the same boat combats such feelings. The multiple family group provides an artificial network; a means of following patients' progress without subjecting them to interrogation on each visit; the feeling, for patients and families, of being expert about the problems of others; an arena for modest group and family therapy moves by the therapists; the demystification of the experience with psychosis; and perhaps most important, a context in which the staff can feel interest, pleasure, and genuine respect in their work with chronic and periodic schizophrenics. The multiple family groups constitute a subculture with values that are alternatives to the rejecting values of the larger culture.

Angelo Fiore: A Chronic Case

Angelo, the second child of five born to Mr. and Mrs. Anthony Fiore, is now 34. His father has been a bail bondsman for the last five years; before that he was a barber. Angelo's older brother, Jack, is a policeman, his younger sisters Maria and Louise are both married to construction workers, and his youngest brother Mario, 16, is in high school. Mr. and Mrs. Fiore live with Mario in a two-family house, the upper floor of which is occupied by Mr. Fiore's mother and father. All Mr. Fiore's children live within six blocks of this house—that is, all except Angelo who, when we first took over the Family Service, had already lived in Bronx State Hospital for the eight years since it was built. Mr. Fiore had him moved there to be close to the family. Before that, Angelo had been in Rockland State Hospital since he was 20.

Prior to his hospitalization in Rockland State, Angelo and his family had been through a long nightmare of psychiatric experiences. Before he went to school he was treated for what seemed to be *petit mal* seizures. He was slow to develop, sensitive, irritable, and withdrawn. In the first grade he was found to be retarded and was transferred to a special school. The diagnosis of retardation was dropped two years later, but he remained in the special school because of behavior difficulties that the regular school could not manage. It is not clear what these were, but Mrs. Fiore's recollection is that other children in the school and the neighborhood used to pick on Angelo. It was for this reason that she first started to keep him at home when he was 8. There followed a series of encounters with truant officers, school psychologists, and child care agencies, with many different recommendations. By the time he was 10, the family was reluctantly convinced that he was ill and needed treatment. He was spending most of his time in his room playing quietly. There were family battles over the long periods he spent in the only bathroom, and his mother became his primary defender as well as his caretaker.

Of several possible treatments, the Fiores chose the one recommended by the family doctor: visits to an aging psychiatrist with an office in the neighborhood. This doctor gave Angelo injections, probably of vitamins, once a month for the next three years. Angelo became his mother's cross to bear, and the other children were lectured by their father when they made fun of him or attacked his privileged status.

When Angelo was 14 he discovered movie magazines and pinups, of which he acquired a large collection. He spent a lot of time masturbating and began to make obscene remarks to his sister's friends. This resulted in a great deal of worry and argument and consultation with the psychiatrist, who administered two electric shock treatments.

Angelo would not return to that psychiatrist, but became much calmer and spent a lot of time watching television. He began to lose weight and appeared to be kneeling in prayer for an hour or two before going to sleep. One night in his 16th year, shortly after his younger brother Mario was born, he attacked his mother as if to strangle her, and after a long consultation with the whole family his father reluctantly presented him for the first time to the city hospital emergency room.

He was admitted, stayed for 3 months, and was discharged, having failed to establish any rapport with the resident who had tried to begin individual therapy with him. More of these "attacks" on his mother followed at intervals of a few months. They soon acquired an almost ritual character. Angelo would give warning by pacing the house and muttering, and his father and brother Jack would "watch" him, yelling instructions to each other. Angelo would eventually lurch at his mother, and the men would restrain him. There would be a hasty consultation, a trip to the emergency room with the mother in tears, and an injection of Thorazine after which everyone would go back home. Any suggestion that he be admitted was met with increased weeping from his mother and an explanation from Jack that the family "knew how to take care of him."

As we noted, Angelo was sent to Rockland State Hospital when he was 20. Both Jack and Maria were to be married that year, and Louise planned to become a nun. Mario, then 4, was home from the hospital after open heart surgery and was taking up much of his mother's attention. Angelo had another "attack," and this time when he informed the emergency room resident, as he often had before, that he wanted to kill his mother, the family saw the threat as real and asked that he be committed. His mother screamed and cried as before, but she had Mario to look after. Jack and her husband were very firm with her, and Angelo was shipped to Rockland the following week.

The next twelve years were monotonous for Angelo, both at Rockland and Bronx State Hospitals. He visited home about two weekends a year, but was brought back early if he or his mother showed any interest in his staying. He still spent a lot of time in the bathroom and paced the halls in a regular way. His main interest became the afternoon soap operas on television. He established a territory in front of the ward television set and fought off anyone who wanted to watch the quiz shows instead. He had a delusional love affair with one of the heroines and enjoyed talking to the staff about her. He read teen-love comics, which he bought in whatever quantity he could afford.

The Family Service acquired Angelo when it took over the catchment area in which his family lived. For him, as for all the patients we inherited, we held a series of conferences to assess the possibility of placing him in the community so that he could have some expectations of life larger than those which faced him in the hospital. In Angelo's case, the staff noted that he was no trouble to have around; he performed the routine of the ward with great punctuality, and even had a dim sense of humor, which he applied to the interactions of his fellow patients in terms from the teen-love comics.

Previous attempts to discharge Angelo were noted in his record; all had failed because the family protested that he would destroy his mother. It was observed, however, that he had never struck anyone in the hospital, although he sometimes behaved threateningly. Placement in a foster home had never been tried. The decision was made to explore placement in a foster home, to be supplemented with some kind of day activity, possibly in a sheltered workshop situation.

At this point I will have to edit Angelo's story very strictly, since it details an epic struggle over the following year and a half, and I want to concentrate on the "family" aspects of this battle. But a summary of some events from this period is relevant: A group of patients like Angelo was formed on the ward—patients who needed to learn new skills applicable to the outside world. They called themselves the "Gateway Group," and with the ward staff they practiced things like taking the bus, going to the Welfare Department to be interviewed, playing games, and making activity decisions for the day. Discharged patients already in foster homes were part of the group, and there was much charged discussion of "life outside." The mere setting up of such a mixed inside-outside group, and the planning and administrative politicking needed to keep it alive, occupied enormous amounts of staff time. Marjorie, a nurse, and Carol, a social worker, were managing this enterprise from the outside, and Evelyn, an ATA, was running the group and keeping the hospital staff informed from the inside. Marjorie and Carol did battle with city and state foster care agencies for control over the selection and monitoring of both the patients and foster families. Transportation, funding, and medical clearance—everything that had to cross the boundary between the hospital and the outer world—were ridden with bureaucratic mischief and frustration. It was as if some mysterious force was preventing anything from crossing that boundary, even as everybody was talking about "rehabilitation" and what a good idea it was.

To return to the Fiore family's role in this scenario, a meeting was called to discuss the prospect of Angelo's living outside the hospital. Present at this and at most subsequent meetings, were Angelo, Mr. and Mrs. Fiore, and Jack, now 36 and just promoted from patrolman to sergeant. Angelo, who before had been tentatively interested in the idea of placement, was unable to talk about it in the meeting and kept changing the subject by asking Jack irrelevant questions. Jack and his father were polite but evasive, and the mother started to cry just before the meeting ended on a note of postponement. The team (Carol, Marjorie, and Evelyn) had agreed to introduce the family to the prospective foster family as soon as one could be found.

The family they decided on, Mr. and Mrs. William Archer, were, like most of the foster families in our part of the Bronx, urban blacks who owned a well-kept house from which their older children had departed. There was a bedroom with two beds and a separate bath on the third floor; Harry Kraft, another patient from our ward and member of the Gateway Group, was already living in it. Evelyn recalled that Harry and Angelo had gotten along well together on the ward. Mrs. Archer had worked in a nursing home as an attendant before her last child, Winston, was born. Winston was now 14 and took up a large amount of her time because he was mentally retarded. He lived on the second floor of the house with his parents. Mr. Archer worked nights at the post office and slept until midafternoon, so that the house had to be quiet. Mrs. Archer took Winston out with her on errands on weekdays, and since she did not want to leave Harry at home it was essential that he have the Gateway Group's day program to attend. This was the household that Angelo, Evelyn, and Marjorie went to visit twice before the next family meeting with the Fiores.

Angelo surprised everyone by conducting a very businesslike discussion of the TV privileges—hours, programs. He had already talked with Harry about this matter, and it was clearly a potential source of conflict. The Archers seemed very gracious and obliging. Mrs. Archer laid down rules, mostly about meals and the use of the kitchen. At the second meeting it seemed that Angelo's main reservation was that he would be en route to the Archer's on the afternoon bus at the time of his favorite TV program.

At the family meeting that followed, Mr. Fiore protested at length that their doubts about the foster home idea had nothing to do with the Archers' color, but with the lack of professional staff present. He asked what would happen, for instance, if Angelo should get sick in the middle of the night. The Fiores patiently attended three more such meetings at which race, health, activity, violence, TV, and other issues were dealt with reassuringly by the team. The schedule of activities and hospital contacts was reviewed in detail. Angelo said less and less, and Mrs. Fiore wept at the end of each meeting and would not say why. It became clear to the staff that the Fiores were in polite ways comparing the Archer's home to their own and saying essentially, "These people could never take care of Angelo." Carol finally suggested that it would upset the Fiores if Angelo lived with another family when they had decided he couldn't live at home. Angelo promptly got up and lurched toward his mother; Jack restrained him, and his mother burst into tears. Mr. Fiore pointed to this as proof that Angelo was too sick to leave the hospital, Angelo said loudly that he didn't want to live with a bunch of niggers, and the meeting broke up.

Carol then met with Mrs. Fiore alone for a while, going over the history and talking over Mrs. Fiore's feelings about Angelo. Meanwhile, two State senators and the attorney general wrote the hospital director, objecting to

Angelo's proposed discharge. This required a lot of traffic with the hospital director's office, including a conference and a written report. The team psychiatrist telephoned Jack and told him the family's political tactics were not going to work and offered to discuss the problem with the family directly.

Meanwhile, the relationship between Carol and Mrs. Fiore progressed to the point where Mrs. Fiore was willing to meet with Mrs. Archer. Evelyn and Marjorie, who knew Mrs. Archer well, prepared her for the meeting. The two ladies talked about their sick children, Mrs. Archer was very reassuring, and Mrs. Fiore gave permission for Angelo to visit there for a weekend. Angelo, however, had stopped attending Gateway meetings, and the staff felt that he and Harry should first make contact again. They finally did so, and Harry escorted Angelo to the Archers' for a meal and an evening of TV.

A year later, Angelo was living at the Archers' and had just graduated from the Gateway Group to the hospital's sheltered workshop. The year had been marked by ups and downs in relations between the team, the Archers, and the Fiores, with Angelo being pulled toward the various corners of that triangle as he settled down to his new way of life. A typical sequence went like this: Angelo would go home for a visit; his mother would cry. Angelo would decide he wanted to live at home and would not return to the Archers'; Mr. Fiore would phone Marjorie to say Angelo was too sick to be out of the hospital; Marjorie would refuse to take him back into the hospital and would tell him over the phone to return to the Archers'; Jack would bring him to the hospital where the night physician would admit him; Angelo would escape and show up next morning to yell at his mother; Marjorie would make a hurried home visit and drive Angelo back to the Archers'; the team would smooth things over with the Archers, who were angry and frustrated; there would be a meeting of Carol, Marjorie, Mrs. Archer, Mrs. Fiore, and Angelo to rehearse again everyone's feelings about Angelo's living at the Archers'. The eventual ending of this tug-of-war was aided by the Archers' attending a multiple family group of foster parents run by the team, to which such parents could take their problems and where they could get mutual support and a sense of communal expertise. The Fiores refused to attend any meetings that were not specifically about Angelo, so they were not part of a multiple family group. Another intervention that may have been decisive occurred when Mr. Fiore's father died and his mother was alone in the upstairs apartment, bedridden with pneumonia. Carol got visiting nurse service to help Mrs. Fiore care for her mother-in-law at home and in various ways promoted Mrs. Fiore's status as a strong, indispensable person in time of trouble. This reduced her tearful anxiety over Angelo.

The routine of life finally settled down for everyone, with Angelo leaving the Archers' every day for the workshop with a brown bag lunch he made himself after breakfast and returning in time for the last soap opera of the afternoon. His mother visited him on Sunday afternoons, and he went to his family on holidays.

The story of Angelo's placement in a foster home is fairly self-explanatory, but some points should be brought out:

1. The objective here is *placement* in the literal sense of putting the patient in the best available context for his gradual development—that is, for the acquisition, at his own pace, of some of the social skills of an independent citizen. This is the most he can expect of life. That kind of judgment is made at the outset; repeated experience has told us that greater expectations for patients like Angelo lead only to frustration for everyone, especially for the patient himself. There is evidence that chronic patients like Angelo make better adjustments out of the family and out of a hospital, in sheltered, limited contact with both the world and the family. A good foster family provides guilt-free objectivity, along with warmth and consistency, for a balanced emotional environment (24).

The placement of patients like Angelo is no small trick, and I have tried to show here that it requires vigorous work with the family and with an extended network of others. The unstable triangle of family, patient, and foster family, if left to its own tendencies, will force the patient back into a hospital, where he will have little chance to develop, even slowly.

2. The job of our Service, then, is to construct in the interstices of the workaday community a *place* (25), a second, more tolerant community that consists of the sheltered workshop, the Gateway Group, the foster home, a halfway house (if we had one), the special floor of a hotel (if we had one of those)—a niche where people like Angelo can live and have some access to the opportunities of the open world, as the rest of us do.

Protecting this kind of inner-shell community from the ravages of the outer world is hard work. It is much harder than running a hospital, but it is better for everybody, since it keeps them—staff and patients and family —more alive to each other.

Clearly, all these services must be under the same administration and must be smoothly coordinated. To parcel them out to different agencies is simply to ensure their failure.

CONCLUSION

In each of these stories, families existed and were willing to be involved. The patients were not very threatening or forbidding people, though they each had quite different temperamental and social endowments. All the families were comfortably well-off. Each of the stories would have been different—with many of the gains far more difficult, or impossible—with violent patients, actively uninterested or absent families and poverty as part of the background.

Of all these complicating factors, I will say a word here only about uninterested families. We don't take a family's lack of interest at face value; sometimes it is necessary to discharge the patient to his home to find out how interested a family really is. And when a family is presenting a member for admission, we make a clear contract at the front door, stating what we will do for them and what we expect from them by way of participation and help. Our position as hospital of last resort gives us a wedge in these negotiations, but we have to expect a certain amount of political flak such as we had from the Fiores.

By now it should be clear to the reader that we regard the success of our operation as a complex interaction of the patient's constitutional endowment and the family and social context that has been provided for its development, of which previous psychiatric treatment is a very important part. There are ways of studying all these factors, of seeing how they fit together, that enable the constructing of a group of typical careers with many more examples than the four I have put together here. But there are only a finite number of *kinds* of stories.

In order to understand the factors in relation to the careers, we need to go beyond our present individual diagnostic approach to the classification of patients, and to classify instead the *lives* of patients in family, economic, and treatment contexts. It is a job for sociologists and cultural anthropologists with a bent for classifying people in terms of their interactions with the culture. The record keeping system of a service such as ours, if reorganized to provide systematic social information, would be applicable to this task. Anyone listening closely at our case conferences would soon discover that this is the information the staff actually uses to make plans and predictions about patients—they reserve the psychodynamic and diagnostic incantations for the charts and the professors.

A word about the staff of the Family Service, since there are thoughts about it that I want to underline for the reader—especially the legislative, administrative, and budgetary reader who determines the conditions of work and recruitment.

I have said throughout that many aspects of the lives of the patients and their families must be kept in mind if the treatment is to succeed. The same thing is true of the staff members and their lives and contexts. Treatment of this kind—perhaps all psychiatric treatment—is not limited merely to the hour or day during which the staff and patient are in contact. That contact is actually the touching of many tangent circles—whole lives in progress—

that are implied, though not seen, in the "treatment situation."

People in other fields often ask, "Why would anyone want to spend his life working with schizophrenics?" or "How do you keep from getting discouraged or going crazy yourself?" These are good questions—they imply a recognition that people do not go into this kind of thing as one might go into manufacturing or the Internal Revenue Service. And rather than speak of "motivations" for this kind of work (we have learned that "motivation" is a slippery notion in complex social fields), I prefer to continue to speak of careers in context, since those are much more observable, whether we are talking of patients or staff.

Unfortunately, many departments of mental hygiene treat the careers of our staff members as if they were just like any other jobs in a bureaucracy. I have said above that bureaucracy as a form of social organization is lethal in its effect on treatment organizations such as ours. This is interrelated with the bureaucratic individual's *career.*

A bureaucratic career in mental health is one in which the long-term expectations are those of bureaucratic careers in general—security, increasing hierarchical responsibility with increasing salary, job assignment on the basis of the Civil Service examination, and eventual retirement-with-pension from the highest possible place (salary) in the hierarchy. What has been called "custodial care" is essentially the routines that tidy-minded, security-conscious people have developed for living day in and day out with the world's most difficult, shy, distressed, and upsetting people and their families. It is a way of keeping patients and their lives at arm's length from the staff, and presentable to the outside world.

I have described the kind of imaginative risk taking, subversive politicking, minor rule breaking, and bending of conservative institutions that is required to do social and family management of schizophrenia. The kind of work we do is incompatible with the bureaucratic career, beginning with our most basic priorities.

There are nonbureaucratic careers that don't work, of course. The "angel of love and mercy" career, and the Laingian cultural revolutionary who thinks that "crazy is better" because the madman sees to the heart of things—these cannot survive contact with the real world of schizophrenia, and they burn out as they enter its atmosphere. But I want now to return to the question, What are the career expectations that enable people to work with schizophrenics and their social systems?

This is not easy to answer, because diversity is the first key to what I want to describe. People who work well in our organization are a very mixed lot. A good treatment team is an association of all sorts of men and women, respecting each other for the peculiar contribution each is able to make to interaction with the families and patients. We have had gay graduate students, stuffy suburban matrons, nonstuffy suburban matrons, black labor leaders, men and women with criminal records, exnuns, black and Puerto Rican State Hospital ATA's, and, of course, pipe-smoking psychologists. The important thing is that all are working together to make whatever contribution they can to this work, at this period in their lives, according to their talents and limitations.

However diverse these individuals, each of their careers is primarily a *personal quest.* I have never met anyone in this business who was not dealing, in one way or another, with his own private understanding of human hope and despair—often trying to deal with it as it has been reflected in his own life. The intensity of this work, the constant facing of defeat without becoming personally defeated, the finding of some way to redefine a situation to include the possibility of hope and constructive action is an exhausting personal encounter. One must be able to retreat sometimes. No one can do this work all week long or every year of his life. The working life of the staff must include times of rest and reflection. Otherwise they get "burned out"—permanently turned off from too much coping.

People who are really effective in this work are able to keep going because they see it as part of their own development. I don't mean just their professional development—although they do learn skills and get degrees that are useful later. The personal development is much more important. Most members of our staff—or at least those whom I have gotten to know well enough to talk with them about this—have had their own brush with psychosis, either in themselves, or in a relative, or in the way they look at the world, and they are trying to view the experience through that window which sometimes turns into a mirror. The therapist as a seeker, sometimes of himself, is a feature of most good therapeutic communities (26). I want to emphasize that this is not just a romantic description of us all. I mean that time for training, learning, reflection, meditation, and mutual teaching and encouragement is a necessary condition of this kind of work. It is more important to productivity than money.

Development implies change. Almost nobody works for more than five years at the same role without feeling he has outgrown it. Ten years is a very long time for any group to work together without a total change of both leaders and followers, teachers and learners. Being able to pass from learning to teaching, or on to more effective practice, and finally to the discovery of the real gift you can give to this kind of work, is the change everyone works toward. You may have to go somewhere else to discover your gift. In fact, people who have gone elsewhere are one of our most important products; we must not regard them as a loss to the organization.

To restate the above paragraphs in hard personnel policy terms: I have been talking about criteria of employment; salary levels in relation to qualifications; provision for time-off, study-leave, in-service training, and flexibility of job assignments; the funding of teaching and training items as part of the service budget; and leavetaking and pension practices that make it easy to come and go. Administrators usually think of these as "fringe benefits" or concessions they have to make to the staff; and they worry about the staff's becoming too lazy as a result of soft policies. I have been trying to make it clear that in professional work with schizophrenics these soft policies are the key to hard productivity.

To those uneasy administrators, I want to direct a final word about rigor. The things that hold this kind of organization to a high work standard are: 1) an exact idea of what we are trying to achieve; 2) the freedom to invent new ways to achieve it; 3) a precise record system to tell us how we are doing; 4) a research design that re-evaluates our work from year to year; and 5) theories or ideas that provide us with our own conscience as we test our experience. If we can be left alone with these tools, we will deliver as best as we can.

Leaving us alone, of course, is difficult for most administrators. What will make it easier is a reliable scoreboard that both we and the administrators can consult. That is what I mean by a precise record system, and by the call for research to develop classifications more precise and valid than those we now use. Such a scoreboard is the key to the accountability of this system.

When a staff generates its own accountability, deals successfully with its own and the patients' social and political problems, and contributes to its own personal growth, then it can do a commendable job of looking after patients and their families.

REFERENCES

1. I. Zwerling and M. Mendelsohn. "Initial Family Reactions to Day Hospitalization," *Family Process,* 4 (1965), 50–63.
2. A. Ferber, M. Mendelsohn, and G. Napier (eds.). *The Book of Family Therapy.* New York: Science House, Inc., 1972.
3. F. Fromm-Reichmann. "Notes on the Development of Treatment of Schizophrenia by Psychoanalytic Psychotherapy," *Psychiatry,* 11 (1948), 263–73.
4. G. Bateson, D. Jackson, J. Haley, and J. Weakland. "Toward a Theory of Schizophrenia," in D. Jackson (ed.). *The Etiology of Schizophrenia.* New York: Basic Books, 1960, 346–72.
5. T. Lidz. *The Origin and Treatment of Schizophrenic Disorders.* New York: Basic Books, Inc., Publishers, 1973.
6. L. Wynne and M. Singer. "Thought Disorder and Family Relations of Schizophrenics, I and II," *Archives of General Psychiatry,* 9 (1963) 191–206.
7. _____."Thought Disorder and Family Relations of Schizophrenics, III," *Archives of General Psychiatry,* 12 (1965), 187–212.
8. H. N. Massie and C. C. Beels. "The Outcome of the Family Treatment of Schizophrenia," *Schizophrenia Bulletin,* 6 (1972), 24–37.

9. D. Rosentahal and S. Kety. *The Transmission of Schizophrenia.* Oxford: Pergamon Press, 1968.

10. G. Gunderson, J. H. Autry, L. R. Mosher, and S. Buchsbaum. "Special Report: Schizophrenia, 1974," *Schizophrenia Bulletin,* 9 (1974), 16–54.

11. R. Laing and A. Esterson. *Sanity, Madness and the Family.* New York: Basic Books, 1971.

12. M. A. Bowen. "A Family Concept of Schizophrenia," in D. Jackson (ed.). *The Etiology of Schizophrenia.* New York: Basic Books, 1960, 346–72.

13. H. S. Sullivan. *Schizophrenia as a Human Process.* New York: Norton, 1962, 221.

14. A. Scheflen. *Communicational Structure: An Analysis of a Psychotherapy Transition.* Bloomington, Ind.: University of Indiana Press, 1973.

15. H. Searles. *Collected Papers on Schizophrenia and Related Subjects.* New York: International Universities Press, 1965.

16. N. L. Paul. "The Role of a Secret in Schizophrenia," in N. W. Ackerman (ed.). *Family Therapy in Transition.* Boston: Little Brown, 1970, 223–48.

17. J. Henry. *Pathways to Madness.* New York: Random House, 1971.

18. R. Speck. *Family Newworks.* New York: Pantheon Books, 1973.

19. M. Foucault. *Madness and Civilization.* Translated by R. Howard. New York: Pantheon Books, 1965.

20. A. Meyer. *The Commonsense Psychiatry of Dr. Adolph Meyer.* Edited by A. Lief. New York: Arno Press, 1973.

21. L. R. Mosher. "A Research Design to Evaluate a Psychosocial Treatment of Schizophrenia," *Hospital and Community Psychiatry,* 23 (1972), 229–34.

22. H. A. Guttman. "A Contraindication for Family Therapy: The Prepsychotic or Postpsychotic Young Adult and His Parents," *Archives of General Psychiatry,* 29 (1973), 352–55.

23. M. Bowers. *Retreat from Sanity.* New York: Human Sciences Press, 1974.

24. D. Mechanic. *Mental Health and Social Policy.* Englewood Cliffs, N.J.: Prentice-Hall, 1969.

25. D. H. Sanders. "Innovative Environments in the Community, A Life for the Chronic Patient," *Schizophrenia Bulletin,* 6 (1972), 49–59.

CHAPTER 15

Alcohol and the Family System

David Berenson, M.D.

Family therapists, along with their mental health colleagues, mostly do not like to treat alcohol problems. In a review of the literature about family treatment approaches to alcoholism, Steinglass points out that although alcohol specialists have found family therapy techniques extremely useful in their work, family therapists have shown remarkably little interest in the clinical and theoretical aspects of alcoholism especially when contrasted with such conditions as schizophrenia, delinquency, or psychosomatics (18). This author stumbled into the field of alcoholism by accident and somewhat reluctantly; but I have found working with alcoholics and their families to be clinically rewarding and theoretically fascinating. My goal here is to communicate some of the difficulties in working with alcohol problems, as well as some of the possible gratification and success.

The two most obvious difficulties that confront a family therapist in dealing with alcohol problems are lack of information and anxiety about drinking. There has been a torrent of information about alcoholism published since the formation of the National Institute on Alcohol Abuse and Alcoholism, and family therapy has been identified as "the most notable current advance in the area of psychotherapy" for alcoholism (13). The stereotypes of the alcoholic as a skid-row bum, and of the alcoholic's wife as a masochistic, immature individual have been demolished. Alcohol problems affect at least 9 million adults and their families, and alcohol is again the preferred drug of teenagers. These facts make it essential that a family therapist be alert for alcohol problems in his or her practice.

The anxiety about drinking on the part of the therapist has at least two components: concern about whether the therapist or members of his family might have a drinking problem, and difficulty in exposing oneself to intoxicated behavior by clients. I have found that desensitization of the therapist's anxiety about drinking and drunken comportment is necessary, and that the use of films and videotapes with discussion of feelings aroused by them, similar to techniques used in training sex therapists, is very helpful.

Even if therapists have accurate information about the facts about alcoholism, and even if they deal with their anxiety about treating alcoholics and their families, there remain at least five difficulties or paradoxes that must be recognized if one is to successfully treat alcoholism in a family system or other context. Once these difficulties are appreciated, my experience is that doing therapy with alcoholism becomes an interesting challenge with a considerable likelihood of success, and the therapist's approach to nonalcoholic problems is changed and clarified. These problems or paradoxes are not unique to alcoholism, but they are most evident when dealing with it.

THE TRAP OF CAUSE AND EFFECT THINKING

Bowen, among others, has warned about the problems of falling into cause and effect thinking in doing family therapy. Systems theorists, cyberneticists, and information theorists have pointed out that we are in the midst of a scientific revolution in which we are giving up our outmoded notions of causation. However, in the field of alcoholism many people are still looking for ultimate causes, trying to find out if alcoholism is a biological addiction, if alcoholics are oral dependent people, if the wife of an alcoholic causes his alcoholism, or if alcoholism is caused by basic disturbances in our society. As soon as the therapist falls into believing any of the above or any other cause and effect explanation for alcoholism, he is, in my opinion, incapable of effectively treating alcohol problems. At the same time he must be willing to allow clients to accept cause-and-effect thinking, such as the disease model of alcoholism, if that will assist them in helping to resolve their drinking problem. The therapist must, therefore, not commit himself to any causative notion of alcoholism but act as if he had one.

THE ISSUE OF LEVELS

At the same time that the therapist recognizes there is no ultimate cause for alcoholism, he also needs to recognize that there are factors that contribute to an alcoholic drinking pattern, and that these factors operate at different levels (8). For example, if an individual drinks a quart of whiskey every day, he will likely become biologically addicted to alcohol. If an individual comes from a family where many people are alcoholics, he is likely either to become alcoholic himself or to marry someone who is alcoholic. If someone lives in a society where alcohol is very important, such as the businessman who has a two-martini lunch, or the inner-city unemployed man or the suburban housewife who drink as a way of passing time, he or she is at risk to become alcoholic.

Factors on the biological, psychological, family, and social levels all contribute toward producing an alcoholic individual or alcoholic family system, but none in themselves can be said to cause alcoholism. The therapist needs to appreciate that alcoholism is not caused, and that it is important to respond to the most relevant system level that is perpetuating the drinking. For example, in the course of doing family treatment of alcoholism it may be necessary to biologically detoxify the alcoholic, deal with family systems issues within both the nuclear and extended family, and finally to help both the alcoholic and the spouse with social problems such as work or friends. Focusing on the wrong level at the wrong time will not make treatment impossible, but it will prolong it.

RESPONSIBILITY VERSUS WILL POWER

As Alcoholics Anonymous has demonstrated, will power is almost useless in stopping alcoholic drinking. The first and probably most important step of AA is "we admitted we were powerless over alcohol." At the same time both AA and other successful therapeutic approaches have emphasized the importance of being responsible for one's actions. This apparently unresolvable paradox, which the therapist must resolve for himself or herself to successfully treat alcoholism, will be indirectly addressed here.

THE USELESSNESS OF BEING A HELPER

A continuing problem is that alcoholics and mental health professionals often play complementary "games." The alcoholic position is, "Please help me, but I won't let you"; and the therapist's is, "Why won't you let me help you like I do all my other clients?" These positions, if not modified, can create a Game Without End (22) in which alcoholics or alcoholic families and therapists see each other over years, yet the drinking persists; or in which the alcoholic goes from one therapist to another in an unsuccessful attempt to achieve sobriety. The responsibility for ending the game rests with the therapist, since he is the one who is getting paid. If the therapist waits for the alcoholic to cure himself through insight or to be grateful for what help he gets, he is likely to wait forever.

HAVING A CLEAR OUTCOME

In most therapy the goals are very hazy. One frequently hears such terms as growth, self-actualization, increased differentiation of self, and better communication. In working with alcohol problems, one has a very simple measure of effectiveness. Is the problem drinker drinking or not, and is his behavior disruptive? If the alcoholic continues to be repeatedly hospitalized, if he is arrested for drunken driving, or loses his job, or if the couple is in and out of family court, it is pretty hard for the therapist to say that treatment has been successful. Thus, there are clearcut behaviors, easily measureable, which give the therapist an indication of how successful the treatment has been. At the same time the therapist must also be alert not to accept cessation of drinking as the only measure of outcome. AA has long recognized that there is a difference between "dry" and being "sober." The paradox remains: if the therapist does not directly deal with drinking and drunken behavior, he will be a failure as a therapist. If he only deals with drinking and drunken behavior, he will only be a partial success.

There is one further difficulty which is often mentioned as a problem, the differentiation between alcoholism and alcohol or drinking problems, both terms I have used in this paper. Clients often make a distinction between the two, and they may be joined by the therapist in debating the issue. The most effective position is one similar to that used by AA, that it is up to each individual to determine for himself or herself whether he or she is an alcoholic. I never get involved in labeling anyone alcoholic; but I also take the position that if any one in the family or myself as a therapist think there is an alcohol problem, by definition there is an alcohol or drinking problem.

Having mentioned some of the difficulties in treating alcoholism, it is appropriate to mention some of the possibilities and advantages in treating alcoholism. Paradoxically, the greatest advantage is the direct observation or reports about drunken behavior, which has been traditionally the reason most therapists have avoided treating alcoholism. In other words, the behavior of the alcoholic individual and the family while drinking is the key the therapist can use to help resolve the drinking problem.

The position I am advancing is not in fact either new or radical. People may refer to alcohol as "truth serum," or mention that they can only do certain things while they are drinking. And there is that old expression, *in vino veritas.* Bateson states that, "Surrender to alcohol intoxication provides a partial and subjective shortcut to a more correct state of mind" (2). Davis, *et al.* (9) point out that one of the "adaptive consequences of drinking" is that certain reinforcing behaviors are expressed when drinking that are not expressible when sober. MacAndrew and Edgerton (14) showed how drunken comportment is socially determined and encouraged, with drunken behavior having different rules in different societies, but serving the general function of "time out." Drunken behavior, therefore, can be seen as a clue that will help to resolve the problem, rather than being a problem that must be rigorously suppressed.

There is a tendency to consider behavior expressed when drinking as more correct or more adaptive or better than sober behavior. That seems to fly totally in the face of commonsense, which holds that drinking is self-evidently very bad for people. I believe there are two reasons that account for this confusion; the first is that drinking is often mistaken for drunken behavior, and the second being that people have an insufficient understanding of the nature of the drunk experience. I would like to emphasize first that drinking does not by itself cause drunken behavior. The behavior does not come out of the bottle. Rather, drinking provides physiological, psychological, familial, and social cues that elicit the drunken behavior. Merely taking away the alcohol and not allowing some of the behavior to be expressed when sober will usually have the result of either intensifying the desire for alcohol or establishing a "dry" state in which the individual or family has only a partial repertory of behaviors and feelings.

The second point has to do with the nature of the drunk experience. It is my belief that alcoholic individuals and family systems are the true split personalities or oscillating systems. In the majority of cases there is a rapid swing from the over-responsible, nonexperience of dryness to the under-responsible, intense experience of wetness. Table 1 sets forth some of the behaviors and feelings that I have seen associated with this switch. It shows neither set of behaviors or feelings is better or more correct, but that both are necessary if maximum functioning is to be achieved. The therapist has the strategic and tactical option of either getting "drunk" behavior expressed when not drinking, or "sober" behavior expressed when drinking, both by the alcoholic and other members of the family system. The ultimate goal is a synthesis of the two states.

Some consideration must also be paid to the issue of moving from an

Table 1   Differences Between the Dry and Wet States

Dry	Wet
Nonexperiencing	Overexperiencing
Objective	Subjective
Overresponsible	Underresponsible
Boring	Exciting
Reasonable	Irrational
Distant	Overclose or reactive distance
Polite, unassertive	Angry, aggressive
Use of willpower	Impulsive
No sex	Sex, or excuse not to have sex
Modest	Boasting
Stoical	Maudlin

individual to a family level. We tend to discuss alcoholism as if it were an individual problem, but in fact the alcoholic family system could be substituted for the alcoholic individual in this discussion, and what has been said would still be accurate. Steinglass has suggested that an alcoholic system is one that organizes itself around the issue of alcohol (18, 20). It makes little theoretical difference who is doing the actual drinking. In one couple I saw, whenever the husband would drink, the wife would act "drunk" by getting overanxious about her husband and acting out of control. In an alcoholic system the drinking may be said to be maintained by the behavior of all members of that system, and frequently also reflect long-standing behavioral patterns in the families of origin of the spouses. A particular family may be organized around alcohol in much the same way that another family is organized around money, sex, work, death or schizophrenia. Frequently a family is organized around alcohol *and* other issues. What is unique about an alcoholic system is not the intensity of pathology or lack of flexibility, but rather the oscillation from one set of behaviors and feelings to another. Alcoholic systems are no more mature or immature than other systems. When treated properly, individuals within the system have every possibility of being as prone to the entire range of function and dysfunction as do individuals living in nonalcoholic systems.

CLINICAL CONSIDERATIONS

Steinglass has pointed out that alcoholism is relatively unique in that symptoms occur in the parental subsystem. He states, "Family therapy historically developed in response to clinical conditions manifesting symptomatology in the childhood generation (schizophrenia, delinquency, school phobia, psychosomatics). The concept of the identified patient, the key concept in the development of family therapy, has traditionally been applied to situations in which a child in the family becomes symptomatic in response to a dysfunctional family system. Alcoholism in a family context perhaps represents the reverse situation; a parent becoming periodically symptomatic as an *adaptive* or *stabilizing* mechanism for the family system" (18).

I have found it clinically useful to divide parental drinking into two general categories, usually correlating with whether the individual or family has consulted me as a general family therapist and psychiatrist, or, on the other hand, as a specialist in alcoholism. In the first category, drinking is seen by family members as incidental to other family problems; frequently the extent of the drinking is not readily apparent unless the therapist specifically takes a drinking history. In the second category, one or both

Table 2
Two Categories of Family Systems With Alcohol Problems

	Category 1	*Category 2*
Perception of alcohol as problem	Family agrees that alcohol is not a problem, or minor problem	Agreement that alcohol is a problem, or intense conflict about it.
Duration of problem	Acute to subacute	Chronic
Family history of alcoholism	Occasionally	Usually
Relationship to other family problems	Secondary—alcohol recedes if other problems are resolved	Primary—makes other problems worse and unresolvable
Behavior change when drinking	Slight, infrequent	Intense, very common
Relationship between spouses	Symmetrical on surface, "we-ness"	Fluctuating, complementary, overt conflict
Amount and pattern of drinking	Variable	Variable

NOTE: Some types of periodic drinking fall between these two categories—for example, getting drunk and into a fight with spouse twice a year.

spouses come in with the complaint that alcohol is the problem, and the family system may be said to be triangulated or organized around the issue of alcohol, regardless of whether the actual drinking has reached addictive proportions. Table 2 summarizes the general differences I see between these two categories. It should be emphasized that these differences are not invariable, and that a system that presents apparently in one category may actually wind up in the other or as a mixture of the two.

A clinical example that illustrates the first category was a family whose identified problem was anorexia in the younger of two children. Within the first three sessions it was determined that both parents were symmetrically drinking at least six drinks a night, and then falling asleep. They both insisted that there was no behavior change in either while drinking, and also mentioned, in response to specific questions, that they had not had sex in over five years and that they for a time unsuccessfully tried alcohol as an aphrodisiac. The therapeutic approach that was used was structural family therapy, as described by Minuchin (17), with initial therapeutic efforts focused on the eating problem and including reframing of the other sibling as also a problem. The couple was also seen separately and given mild sensate focus instructions, as described by Masters and Johnson (16), with a specific modification that the couple was not to pleasure each other when one of them had been drinking. Subsequently, when the child relapsed and started losing weight again, the couple was told that giving up drinking would increase the chances of their child's regaining weight.

Other family problems involving alcohol that fall in the first category may present around a family life crisis (a mother may drink after her last child has left home), or may be viewed as family difficulties that have not yet become entrenched problems. Here strategic approaches and tactical interventions as described by Haley (12) and Watzlawick, Weakland, and Fisch (23) may be very useful. Once the family life crisis is resolved, or the therapist uses the proper paradoxical technique, the drinking problem either moderates or disappears.

In summary, when dealing with the drinking problems in the first category, the therapist makes sure to take a complete drinking history so as to desensitize talking about drinking; but he does not label alcohol as a problem. The therapist has at his disposal the entire range of family techniques. If after some weeks of treatment the presenting problem persists unchanged, or if the drinking becomes worse, the therapist has the option of redefining the problem to the family and moving his treatment approach into the second category.

I have previously described an approach to the second category of family alcohol problems that is derived from Bowen's family systems theory, and that also emphasizes the concurrent use of Alcoholics Anonymous and Al-Anon (3). This treatment approach has two phases; the first is to get the family system calmed down and the drinking stopped; and the second is the establishment of intimate behaviors by the couple that were previously only expressible in extreme forms while one or both spouses were drinking. The rationale behind the approach is that the family emotional system is so intense that any initial effort to change it by getting the spouses to express their feelings or to communicate to each other better will almost always perpetuate or increase the dysfunction of the system. Thus, Bowen's style of directing all communication through the therapist, the focus on thinking rather than feeling, and the option of seeing the more functional or responsible spouse individually are all appropriate techniques (5). I vary from Bowen's approach in that I do not regard alcoholism *per se* as reflective of a low level of differentiation within the family,[1] that I regard it as

---

[1]Bowen sometimes asserts that alcoholism reflects a low level of family differentiation, and other times seems to state the reverse, that intensity of drinking has no correlation with basic level of self.

unlikely that the "alcoholic" can resume social drinking, and that I consider direct expression of emotional feelings, such as anger and love, as well as specific sex therapy, as useful in the second phase of treatment (6, 7).

The main leverage in a system where one spouse drinks excessively is the nondrinking spouse. He or she is usually the one who is suffering more and is more motivated to make a change. The spouse is often also, in Bowen's terms, the more functional one, or, in Fogarty's terms, the emotional pursuer. The nonalcoholic is *not* the spouse who has the power in the relationship. I have found power an almost useless concept in working with alcoholic family systems, since both spouses feel powerless in their attempts to control each other, and are often involved in a futile, escalating, fluctuating attempt to gain power of control.

The focus is on the nonalcohol's becoming more responsible for self, rather than attempting to control the alcoholic. In alcoholic family systems with a low level of emotional intensity, the spouse may readily accept the operating principles proposed by the therapist, and relatively easily achieve some emotional distance or detachment. In systems with a higher degree of emotional intensity, the spouse may become quite depressed before he or she is able to take an I-position and decrease the reactive behavior, which is usually characterized by fluctuating between being overcaring and over-punitive in response to the alcoholic's drunken comportment. I have found Fogarty's ideas about getting people in touch with their emptiness before taking an I-position essential (11). The goal is for the spouse to hit bottom before the alcoholic does.

In systems with an even higher degree of intensity, where the spouse is worried about the alcoholic's literally killing himself if he or she stops being reactive to the drinking, a physical separation may be a necessary step toward achieving some degree of emotional separation. The therapist must be responsible for predicting the possible immediate and remote consequences of a separation, and also has to carefully avoid either pushing a spouse away from an alcoholic before she is ready, or keeping her locked in when she is prepared to differentiate. The anxiety generated in both spouse and therapist in these situations is usually quite high, and outside assistance may be necessary to control the anxiety. The assistance may take the form of the spouse going to Al-Anon, where she may receive both emotional support and practical tips; the establishment of a multiple-couples group, where some supportive network can be created; or the use of a consultant to allow the therapist to share the anxiety and retain objectivity. The consultant need only be seen a few minutes at a time by the therapist, or brought into only one therapy session.

Once the nonalcoholic spouse distances or detaches, the alcoholic usually becomes worse. If the spouse sticks to the plan and does not get pulled back into the fusion or homeostasis, the alcoholic will usually take his turn to hit bottom and then stop drinking. There is a particular therapeutic paradox that occurs here. The more a spouse takes a position for herself, the more likely the alcoholic is to stop drinking; the more the spouse takes a position in order to get the alcoholic sober, the more likely such a move is going to be a failure or transient success; or, if successful, the more likely there will be other family problems when the drinking stops. The more the spouse uses willpower, the more the move is likely to fail; the more the spouse takes responsibility for self, the more the eventual outcome is likely to be successful. Needless to say, in most situations the motivation to take responsibility for self, as opposed to controlling the spouse, remains mixed, and the therapist must remain prepared to handle the consequences when a reactive confrontation predominates.

In the theoretical and rare actual situation where a true I-position predominates, subsequent therapeutic work is relatively easy or unnecessary, and the couple can be said to live happily ever after, meaning that they experience only average difficulties with themselves and each other. Usually, however, further therapeutic work is indicated, since the couple is maintaining an artificial emotional distance, a walking on eggs state where both fear that the drinking will resume if either expresses a strong positive or negative emotion. The therapist's goals are now to decrease the emotional distance, allowing the couple to express behaviors and feelings that previously only came out while drinking in a more attenuated way while sober.

I have usually found it necessary to have some hiatus or interruption between the two phases of therapy. The hiatus gives the couple some opportunity to simmer down, and decreases their fear that a move toward togetherness will automatically set off the drinking again. When I have immediately tried to work on other problems after the drinking stops, such as using a Masters and Johnson style of sex therapy, I have found that the couples do not follow the instructions. There are two general paths that I employ during this interim period. The first is to encourage the spouses to continue in AA and Al-Anon with the understanding that if the problems of the walking on eggs state persist after 6 to 12 months, family treatment will resume with a different goal. The other path is to continue the couple in a multiple-couples group with the emphasis switching from the spouses taking I-positions to some beginning extended family work or coaching, as well as some mild encounter group exercises that encourage individuals in the group to learn to trust each other but do not directly touch on the uptightness within each family system. Transcendental meditation may also be a useful adjunct at this time. It is my impression that a multiple-couples group speeds up the process of therapy, but frequently there are logistical problems in establishing such a group.

SECOND PHASE OF THERAPY

The goal of the second phase of therapy is to decrease the emotional distance without having the drinking resume, and the preference is for conjoint sessions with the spouses. If the couple was previously seen in a multiple-couples group or conjointly with their children, sessions with just the couple are held either in addition to or instead of the other sessions. Therapeutic approaches that are useful to consider are sex therapy (16), "fighting therapy" (1), and viewing the adaptive consequences of drinking with video tapes that had been recorded sometime previously (9). Adjuncts to therapy at this time may be continued extended family work, or coaching, to free one or both spouses from continuing emotional input from the extended family that may serve to disrupt the nuclear family system.

During the second phase of therapy two issues frequently come up: conflict between the spouses about continued attendance at AA meetings, and discussion about whether the alcoholic can now become a social drinker. Both issues can serve as the third point on a triangle and prevent the couple from establishing a person-to-person relationship. AA may be a problem if the alcoholic has an impression that he can only share his thoughts and feelings at AA meetings or with his sponsor, not with spouse. The spouse may get reactive and angry at being left out, driving the recovered alcoholic further toward AA, and perhaps culminating in an affair with another AA member. Generally, I find this pattern more likely to occur when the nonalcoholic spouse's position prior to the alcoholic's stopping drinking had been more in the nature of a reactive confrontation than a true I-position. Thus, a possible therapeutic approach is to encourage spouse to get into her emptiness now if she had not done so before; the therapist takes a position with the alcoholic that in the first few months of sobriety it is almost impossible to attend too many AA meetings, but that continued, excessive attendance after some years is often a weapon against the spouse, similar to what the bottle had been before.

I handle the issue of resuming social drinking by making an analogy with smoking. Few heavy smokers are ever able to become social smokers who are able to smoke just a few cigarettes a day. In a similar way, if an alcoholic drinking pattern has been established by physiological, psychological, family, and social factors, it is unlikely that the system can be modified enough to permit the resumption of social drinking. Another paradox operates here: one can become a social drinker only when it is truly unimportant whether one drinks or not. If it is unimportant to drink, then there is no necessity to do so.

OTHER THERAPEUTIC ISSUES

Adolescent drinking may be also conceptualized as falling into two categories, the first when there is no significant family history of alcoholism, and the second when there are drinking problems in the parental subsystem as well as the sibling subsystem. In the first case, I have found that contingency, behavioral or reciprocal social contracting, similar to that described by Alexander (15) and Stuart (21) in their work with juvenile delinquents and their families, will work. Usually the family is at least as concerned about the adolescent's also using marijuana and other drugs, and there are frequently other discipline problems.

In contingency contracting, observable acceptable behaviors of the adolescent are rewarded, and unacceptable behaviors are discouraged by withholding of privileges. The parents are advised not to attempt to control their child's drinking out of the house, a usually undoable task, but to diminish disruptive behavior whether or not associated with the drinking. The goal is to diminish the overconcern about the drinking, set effective limits, and allow the teenager an opportunity to grow up and become a social drinker, someone whose behavior is seen as coming from within himself, not from a bottle. A clear distinction must be made by the therapist between behavior, thoughts, and feelings. Parents are responsible for monitoring aspects of their children's behavior, which are transactional, but not for their thoughts or feelings, which are personal and private.

When the adolescent drinking pattern reflects alcohol problems also existing in the parental subsystem, I prefer first to deal with the parental problems in the manner described above. Frequently, however, mother is more concerned about child's drinking than about husband's. In such a case the therapist might move either toward contingency contracting including contracts between parents, if possible, or first get mother helpless and hopeless about child's drinking rather than husband's.

Theoretically, there is no difference whether the alcoholic is the husband or the wife. However, many practical problems exist, including an increased tolerance and perhaps encouragement of the woman's drinking, since she is frequently not the breadwinner and may use drinking as a way of structuring her time. There also may be a physiological difference; drinking may seem to enhance the wife's sexual responsiveness, whereas it decreases the husband's sexual performance. In such cases the therapist may have to work initially with the alcoholic wife, the apparently more dysfunctional member of the couple, with the goal being to get the distant husband into the therapy as quickly as possible by coaching the wife in expressing either overpositive or overnegative feelings about the therapist to husband. Encouraging the wife to join a woman's group or to go to school or work may also be useful, with the understanding that it may lead to some of the same difficulties of triangulation that AA sometimes does.

When both spouses are drinking alcoholically, the difficulty for the therapist goes up geometrically. If the system is one where the spouses take turns drinking alcoholically, the therapist may get some leverage by working with the dry spouse, always being prepared to switch to the other spouse when the drinking switches in the system. Otherwise the position for the therapist is the extreme Bowen position of being a researcher who observes the family drinking patterns, asks questions about how the drinking ties into the family emotional functioning, and predicts patterns through time. If the therapist can restrain his desire to help by stepping in and changing the system, the couple may eventually get some perspective on their drinking pattern and take responsibility for changing it.

REFERENCES

The clinical approach described in this chapter was partially developed under the support of Grant 3 T15 AA00152-01S1 from the National Institute on Alcohol Abuse and Alcoholism, Department of Health, Education, and Welfare.

1. G.R. Bach, and P. Wyden. *The Intimate Enemy.* New York: Avon, 1970.
2. G. Bateson. "The Cybernetics of Self: A Theory of Alcoholism," *Psychiatry,* 34 (1971), 1–18.
3. D. Berenson. "A Family Approach to Alcoholism," *Psychiatric Opinion,* 13 (1976), 33–38.
4. M. Bowen. "The Use of Family Theory in Clinical Practice," *Compr. Psychiatry,* 7 (1966), 345–74.
5. _____. "Family Therapy and Family Group Therapy," in H. Kaplan, and B. Sadock (eds). *Comprehensive Group Psychotherapy.* Baltimore: Williams and Wilkins, 1971, 384–421.
6. _____. "Alcoholism and the Family System," *The Family, Journal of The Center For Family Learning,* (1973), 20–25.
7. _____. "Alcoholism as Viewed Through Family Systems Theory and Family Psychotherapy," *Annals of the New York Academy of Science,* 233 (1974), 115–22.
8. M. Chafetz, M. Hertzman, and D. Berenson. "Alcoholism: A Positive View," in S. Arieti and E.B. Brody (eds). *American Handbook of Psychiatry,* New York: Basic Books, 1974, III, 367–99.
9. D.I. Davis, D. Berenson, P. Steinglass, and S. Davis. "The Adaptive Consequences of Drinking," *Psychiatry,* 37 (1974), 209–15.
10. J.A. Ewing, and R.E. Fox. "Family Therapy of Alcoholism," in Masserman (ed.), *Current Psychiatric Therapies.* New York: Grune & Stratton, 1968, VIII, 86–91.

11. T. Fogarty. "On Emptiness and Closeness," *The Family, Journal of The Center For Family Learning,* in press.
12. J. Haley. *Uncommon Therapy: The Psychiatric Techniques of Milton H. Erickson, M.D.* New York: Ballantine Books, 1973.
13. M. Keller (ed.). "Trends in Treatment of Alcoholism", *Second Special Report to the U.S. Congress on Alcohol and Health,* 145–167. Dept. of HEW, Washington, D.C., 1974.
14. C. MacAndrew, and R. Edgerton. *Drunken Comportment.* Chicago: Aldine Press, 1969.
15. R.E. Malout and J.F. Alexander. "Family Crisis Intervention, A Model and Technique of Training," in R.E. Handy and J.G. Cull (eds.), *Therapeutic Needs of the Family,* Springfield, Illinois: Charles C. Thomas, 1974, 47–55.
16. W. Masters and V. Johnson. *Human Sexual Inadequacy.* Little, Brown and Co., Boston, 1966.
17. S. Minuchin. *Families and Family Therapy.* Cambridge: Harvard University Press, 1974.
18. P. Steinglass. "Experimenting With Family Treatment Approaches to Alcoholism, 1950–1975: A Review," *Family Process,* in press.
19. P. Steinglass, S. Weiner, and J.H. Mendelson. "A Systems Approach to Alcoholism," *Arch. Gen. Psychiatry,* 24 (1971), 401–08.
20. P. Steinglass, D.I. Davis, and D. Berenson. "In-Hospital Treatment of Alcoholic Couples," Paper presented at the American Psychiatric Association Annual Meeting, May, 1975.
21. R.B. Stuart. "Behavioral Contracting Within The Families of Delinquents", *Journal of Behavior Therapy and Experimental Psychiatry,* 2 (1971), 1–11.
22. P. Watzlawick, J.H. Beavin, and D.D. Jackson. *Pragmatics of Human Communication.* New York: W.W. Norton, 1967.
23. P. Watzlawick, J.H. Weakland, and R. Fisch. *Change: Principles of Problem Formation and Problem Resolution.* New York: W.W. Norton, 1974.

CHAPTER 16

Sexual Dysfunction and the Family System

Lawrence S. Jackman, M.D.

Sexual dysfunctions are significantly different from many other family problems because they include a somatic or bodily malfunction which then becomes the focus of the difficulty. Successful management requires not only alteration of the interactional system, but also the biological system.

Sexual problems are classified according to their biologic manifestations —for example, impotence, premature ejaculation, orgasmic dysfunction. In order to effectively restructure these derangements of the biological systems, it is useful to appreciate how the sexual apparatus functions under normal conditions, and how derangements in other systems produce biological system (bodily) effects.

The nervous system responds to sexual stimuli by increasing the blood supply and muscle tension of the sexual organs. The stimuli may be external sensations (sights, smells, touch), or internal stimuli (memories and fantasies). The responses to these stimuli are usually divided into four phases.

In the first phase, *excitement,* an increase in blood contained in the penis produces erection in the male, and an increase in blood in the tissues around the vagina produces lubrication in the female. These events occur within seconds after the stimulus is perceived. Persistance of stimulation over a period of time, called the *plateau* phase, produces further development of these effects, plus others, such as swelling of the testes and clitoris. In addition the vagina becomes longer and the testes and uterus are elevated from their unstimulated positions. All of these effects are associated with the subjective feelings of arousal and pleasure.

The third phase, *orgasm,* is controlled by a different portion of the nervous system. It is the portion which under other circumstances also controls the body's emergency responses (fight or flight), and is activated by anxiety regardless of its cause.

Orgasmic response is characterized by pelvic muscle contractions and is perceived as a feeling of intensely pleasurable release in both sexes. Ejaculation in males normally occurs at the time of orgasm and has no direct female equivalent. After orgasm in the male there is a period of time during which he cannot be sexually stimulated (refractory period), while females have the capacity to respond with multiple orgasms without a time delay. The most important determinant of the length of the refractory period is age.

The final phase, *resolution,* is a regression of all changes back to the unstimulated state.

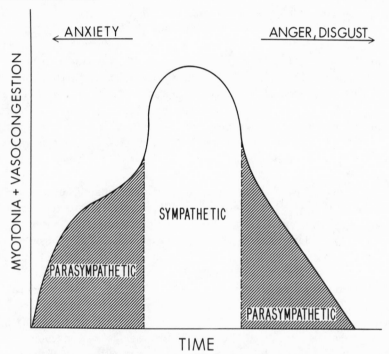

Figure 1.
A diagram of the sexual response cycle emphasizing the portions of the nervous system which control the biological system events.

The passage of control of the sexual response from one portion of the nervous system (parasympathetic) to another (sympathetic) is the physical event that is most reactive to emotional states, and therefore the interactional system. Anxiety, from whatever cause, disrupts the normal response by hastening this passage of internal nervous control. In males this produces several clinical problems, including premature ejaculation (men who usually ejaculate before they want to) and impotence (the inability to get or maintain a satisfactory erection). Other emotional states such as anger and disgust delay or prevent the passage of nervous system control; that is, they have the opposite effect from anxiety on the sexual response. In males there is extraordinary delay or total prevention of ejaculation (ejaculatory incompetence). The mechanism of male sexual dysfunctions which occur in response to emotional causes are therefore classifiable as either manifestations of too rapid passage of control, in response to anxiety; or delayed passage, in response to anger or disgust.

Female dysfunctions can be less clearly differentiated and classified. The most common problem is sexual arousal with delayed, absence of, or infrequent orgasm. This corresponds to ejaculatory incompetence in the male; that is, there is delay or absence of passage of internal nervous system control. This is referred to as orgasmic dysfunction. A different problem, the inability to become sexually aroused, corresponds to impotence in the male. It is virtually always a result of anxiety (as is impotence). Labelled orgasmic dysfunction in the past, it is better called inhibited excitement. Vaginismus is an involuntary spasm of the muscle surrounding the vagina which, when severe, makes vaginal penetration and intercourse difficult or impossible. There is no corresponding male dysfunction.

A chain of causality producing psychosomatic sexual dysfunctions can now be defined. The sexual response is dysfunctional because the nervous system's switching mechanism is functioning improperly. The nervous system functions improperly because a negative emotional state—anger, anxiety, and so on—disrupts the mechanism. The negative emotional state is activated in anticipation of, or during, the sexual behavior. The origin of these emotions may be uni- or multifactorial but they are characteristically self-reflexive. In other words, a positive feedback cycle invariably acts to perpetuate the dysfunction, often long after the original cause of the problem has been resolved. Because of this vicious-cycle phenomenon, the most useful approach has been to interrupt and restructure the present behavioral cycle, rather than dwell on an intensive investigation of the original cause.

Figure 2 depicts diagrammatically how physical illness and drugs, other family problems, and past learning can all result in sexual symptoms. It also shows the self-reflexive, vicious cycle which acts to reinforce and perpetuate the dysfunction in the present. Organic etiologies should always be considered, suspected, and referred for appropriate diagnosis and treatment. Reversible factors outside the vicious cycle, such as drugs and misinformation, which continue to feed it should be corrected as rapidly as possible.

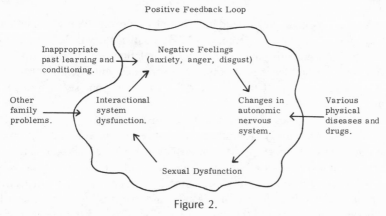

Figure 2.

How commonly are sexual symptoms a part of the constellation of problems in families? No statistically valid research data is available to answer this question, but Masters and Johnson have estimated that at least 50 per cent of all marriages have a clinically recognizable sexual dysfunction at some time. This suggests that a high index of suspicion is warranted on the part of the therapist, and that sexuality and sexual functioning are often related to the presenting complaints in a more or less important way.

SEXUAL HISTORY TAKING

Because we live in a fundamentally antisexual culture which inbeds its viewpoint deeply into our upbringing, even educated and sophisticated clients may find it difficult to reveal their true sexual concerns and responses. Therapists raised in the same or similar antisexual environments are often equally reluctant to probe in detail the specifics of client's sexual behavior, and are relieved when general questions like "How is your sex life?" fail to uncover any problems. Such reactions by therapists reflect the emotionally charged nature of sexual material, and serve to reinforce a collusion of the therapist in the conspiracy of silence or superficiality with the client.

Obstructions to frank communication of sexual information occur even more often at the nonverbal level. Pregnant pauses, stuttering, stumbling over specific words or phrases, blushing, and body language all convey the therapist's discomfort as easily as the clients. Therapists must evaluate their own ability to discuss sexual topics in frank, nonjudgmental ways which foster, rather than impede, useful communication.

Three kinds of sexual history taking are useful to the family therapist. Each is appropriate in different family therapy contexts.

A screening inventory should be a routine part of any family evaluation. "How often do you have intercourse?" "How satisfactory is that frequency for you?" "How satisfying is your sexual relationship?" "How do you handle your sexual feelings at other times, or when you are not satisfied?" "What would you most want to be different about your sexual relationship?"

Asking this series of questions is useful whether they are answered truthfully or defensively. Truthful answers give the therapist a quick overview of the sexual aspects of the relationship, as well as a background about how this family views sexuality. Even when the client answers defensively (or deliberately lies) a useful interchange has occurred. The client learns that the therapist is interested in this area, and that it is appropriate to talk explicitly about sex in the therapy setting. Not infrequently the client will raise the subject at a later time and be more open at that time than previously.

When the above or similar screening inventory uncovers a problem, or when the client spontaneously offers a sexual issue for discussion, the therapist may follow up the lead. This is best done through a sexual problem history. In such a history it is important to learn in detail as much as possible about the issue. In taking a sexual problem history the following aspects should be explored. (1) The circumstances of onset or identification of the problem. (2) Its duration and course. (3) The family's assessment of its cause and ownership—whose problem is it? (4) What has been learned from reading, friends, and other sources about this situation? (5) What previous professional help has been sought, and what were its results? (6) What self-help treatments have been tried, and what was their outcome? (7) Does the family want further help, and what would be the concrete goal of getting such help?

The only really important guide to sexual problem history taking is to get the specific details. I ask clients to paint a word picture, sufficiently detailed, so that I could direct an accurate movie scene of their sexual behavior from it. This serves several purposes. First, it identifies the level of the client's discomfort in talking about sexual topics, and gives the therapist a clue as to his/her/their general comfort or anxiety. A good rule of thumb is that if no one in the room is uncomfortable, you probably have not been explicit enough.

A second and obvious purpose of a detailed history is to ascertain the real nature of the client's concern and the events or feelings that trigger it. It is all too easy to make the common error of assuming to understand the euphemisms and evasions normally used to describe sexual behavior. Assuming that "sleeping together" means sexual intercourse is occasionally a grievous mistake. Similarly, "making love" may mean intercourse to one client, while to another it may be an evaluation of how much emotion is being shown: "We have sex every night, but he never makes love to me."

This kind of failed communication not only can exist between therapist and clients, but is often present between the partners themselves and significantly contributes to the muddle. I therefore find it most useful to obtain as much history as possible with both partners present. I will interrupt frequently to check out the partners' understanding of the complaints, "Did you know she thinks that when you turn your back it means. . . . ?" I direct them to address each other with me acting as referee. "You can't really tell her what she feels, only what you think she is feeling."

I find complete sexual history taking from a couple usually requires both joint and individual sessions. Not infrequently it is in the individual interviews that important past and present material which has significant effect on the problem will be forthcoming. This is particularly true of the most anxiety-producing feelings and behaviors, such as masturbation, homosexual feelings, or encounters and extramarital liaisons. Maintaining the strict confidentiality of the individual sessions and assuring the client of this promotes comfort, and facilitates these revelations.

Yet another purpose of a detailed and explicit sexual problem history is that it exposes the limits of the client's belief system and knowledge of sexual behaviors. Clinical experience has repeatedly taught me that making any assumption of knowledge about sexuality on the part of clients is so often erroneous that it is dangerous and counterproductive. The level of the client's general education, intelligence, and sophistication is rarely a valuable guide to his or her knowledge in the sexual sphere. Sexual ignorance may be a reflection of insufficient exposure to sexual education and limited experience with sexual behavior; or it may be, and often is, the result of selective avoidance of such material and experience. In either case an important missing ingredient is an understanding of sexual physiology, anatomy, and response; its lack prevents the formation of a foundation of knowledge on which satisfying sexual relationships can develop.

The next question, of course, is how can a family therapist make a useful intervention in a sexual problem? The answer to this question is not simple, but there are some guidelines.

It is worth pointing out that simply taking a detailed history, particularly if both partners are present during the interview, is in and of itself an important intervention. For many couples such an interview may represent their first effort at verbalizing their view of the situation to a disinterested (but not uninterested) third party, and in the presence of the partner. Clear communication is the goal, and explicitness is the rule. Areas of sexual anxiety, such as masturbatory behavior and sexual fantasy material, may be opened up for discussion, and sometimes the problem disappears like the bubbles in a soft drink when exposed to the air. In other words, there may be no substance to the problem when communication is open and clear.

Two interventions available to any knowledgeable family therapist are permission giving and education. Simplistic as such approaches may seem, they are useful first steps and may sometimes be all that a family requires.

Permission giving is essentially reassurance by an authority that what the clients are doing, or thinking, or feeling is normal, healthy, enjoyable, nonpathologic, and okay to continue. In American culture, where people exhibit a high level of sexual anxiety, authoritative permission to be sexual is sometimes sufficient to eliminate the client's concerns. The permission may also be permission not to respond or behave in ways the clients think they *should*. For example, permission not to try for simultaneous orgasms, not to think they should want sex more often or less often, and not to accede to a partner's advance when not personally motivated or interested often fall into this category.

Permission is usually combined with giving limited information. No attempt need be made to give a comprehensive course in sexuality. Instead, limited information can be focused at the specific concerns which have been identified. For example, middleaged couples are often concerned about failing male potency. Sometimes a male's need for direct stroking of the penis to initiate erection is misinterpreted by the couple as the first sign of waning ability to perform sexually. In fact, this is a normal physiologic change in sexual response among older men, and in no way heralds sexual senescence except if it is interpreted as such by the individual or couple. In that case, anxiety about future sexual inability supervenes and blocks the erectile response, and a self-fulfilling prophecy is completed.

Even the best educated clients sometimes lack simple knowledge of things sexual. Neither partner may actually know where the clitoris is located or how to stimulate it; or that its disappearance behind the symphysis pubis in late plateau phase is a sign of increased rather than decreased arousal.

Obviously, discussion, explanation, diagrams, models, and pictures are all useful in the education process. Permission to explore and become familiar with one's own and one's partner's anatomy and response can be directly given to reinforce the education.

Of course, many cases of sexual anxiety, anger, and disgust which result in difficulties for one or both partners in the relationship are not so easily managed. In such instances a complete sexual history may be the only means of defining the etiology of the negative feelings.

A complete sexual history should include a detailed discussion of the present sexual relationship, the context in which it began and continued, and all important changes and events which took place from the beginning to the present. Of particular importance are courtship experiences and feelings, the honeymoon (a well-known takeoff point for lifelong problems), pregnancies, both wanted and unwanted, labor and delivery, children, privacy, illness, drugs, and extramarital sexual relationships. Attention must also be directed at childhood experiences, early sexual learning, menarche, masturbation, homosexual experiences, religious upbringing, parental and peer influences, dating and petting, first intercourse, and, in summary, all the factors which may play a part in the sexual outlook and expectation of the couple. The goal of such exploration is to see how the interactional system contributed in the past to, and continues to perpetuate, the dysfunction in the biological system.

When sufficient history has been obtained, the family therapist must also evaluate the optimal way to proceed. A general list of options is:

1. Acknowledge the presence of the sexual difficulty, but avoid intervention for the present, and direct the therapy toward other issues.

2. Begin directly to intervene in the sexual behavior.

3. Interrupt the therapy and refer the clients to a "sex therapist."

4. Refer the clients to a "sex therapist" and continue family therapy concurrently.

The most appropriate choice in a given situation will depend on the family's agenda for therapy; the therapist's comfort and competence; and the family's situation, relationship, and current life problems.

In general, only couples genuinely interested in experiencing a change in their sexual relationship will benefit from direct intervention techniques. Often, one member of the couple is so inclined while the other is reluctant. With such couples, the outcome is quite good if the reluctant member comes to view the difficulty as a couple's problem from which he or she suffers no less than the dissatisfied partner because of the ongoing anger, anxiety, and frustration which results.

The comfort and competence of the therapist is no less important than the motivation of the clients. It is clear that the therapist's comfort with open explicit sexual discussion is a critical variable in determining outcome. Therapists experienced at monitoring their own emotional reactions will have no difficulty identifying their own discomfort, and should recognize that the family is then best served in this area by referral.

No less critical is the therapist's competence. A thorough understanding of sexual anatomy, autonomic physiology, possible organic etiologies, effects of drugs, and the specific behavioral techniques which have been found useful interventions in sexual dysfunctions is required, and must be mastered.

The decision whether to immediately intervene or defer is not always clear cut. In the past, deferring the issue was the most likely choice of psychotherapists. Most clients had other intrapsychic and interpersonal problems which, it was felt, must first be resolved. Until recently it was also true that most such problems were more amenable to therapy than a sexual dysfunction, and that *sometimes* the sexual problem did, in fact, resolve itself during the course of the therapy. It is now clear that neither of these considerations is necessarily true today. The techniques for direct intervention into sexual behavior have a high success rate when used with motivated clients, with outcomes far superior to spontaneous remission rates with or without other kinds of talk therapy.

Most types of direct intervention are more successful when couples are seen together as a unit. In view of this fact, it is consistent with family systems theory to initiate sex therapy for a couple whenever it is deemed both useful and possible to foster increased closeness between the partners. Families in crisis, in which the therapist strives to cool rather than stir up the situation, are therefore not candidates for immediate sex therapy. In less definitive situations, sex therapy may be begun as a kind of *in vivo* experiment: proceed as far as possible and until other issues obstruct the progress, then change strategy and deal with the obstruction. (I am repeatedly surprised, however, at how frequently theoretically anticipated obstructions fail to actually materialize.) Such an *in vivo* experiment serves another useful purpose. Often, interpersonal system problems are less well disguised in the sexual arena than elsewhere. The sexual interview may rapidly uncover the core of the maladaptive interactional system.

What intervention techniques can be usefully employed to foster significant change in sexual behavior patterns? To answer this question it must be kept in mind that the desired changes fall into two distinct categories: voluntary changes, and involuntary (autonomic) responses. It is not possible at present to consciously will (or teach) an autonomic response, although biofeedback techniques hold the promise of future development. Fortunately, in otherwise healthy adults the bodily responses occur naturally and are disturbed only when influenced by other factors. The therapist's main objective, then, is to structure the voluntary behavior of the clients in such a way as to eliminate the disturbing influences and allow the bodily response to occur.

The overall goal of direct intervention into sexual behaviors is to establish or re-establish pleasure as the operant emotion during sexual behavior. In order to achieve this, it is necessary to eliminate behaviors, at least temporarily, which are associated with negative emotional reactions, or to modify the client's emotional response, or both. That is, it has become common practice to prohibit certain behaviors early in the therapy, and substitute a series of pleasurable exercises to establish pleasure as the operant emotion. The starting point is determined by the clients. Many can begin with nude, general body (but not genital) touching exercises, in which the receiver controls the experience and must not permit himself to be touched in unpleasant ways. This forces both partners to be attentive to the receiver's pleasure, and the receiver must make his responses explicitly known. The couple needs the opportunity to experience the exercise three or four times; then their progress is reviewed in the next therapy session. The therapist must directly oppose any suggestions that the exercise can be done well or badly—that is to say, that it can be *performed.* Actually, it can only be *enjoyed,* and must be evaluated only in terms of the enjoyment and pleasure which result.

When one or both partners have not fully enjoyed the experience, attention must be paid to the details of what prevented full enjoyment. Often such blocks can easily be changed voluntarily. For example: "The kids might get up"—lock the door. "I'm exhausted by eleven o'clock"—try nine o'clock. "He always suggests it when I am busiest"—you be the initiator. Sometimes the blocks are involuntary: "It's disgusting to see an erect penis, it shows what animals men are." These difficulties are often bypassed by systematic imaginal desensitization techniques, with or without the partner's presence at the sessions.

If it is found that the anticipation of the exercise is producing anxiety, the exercise itself should be restructured to a simpler and less threatening one. I have started extremely anxious couples with hand holding at the table or on the couch, moving them through clothed caressing and kissing, undressing in semidarkness, undressing in the light, and so on. I always proceed at the pace of the slower partner.

Clients sometimes report that they fail to accomplish the exercise, usually because they couldn't find the time. This can be handled in several ways, but it is important *not* to try to convince them that they should do it. One useful approach is to offer the thought that they are free to improve rapidly or slowly as they choose, and that when they have found a way to have the experience three or four times, that will be soon enough to evaluate the exercise and suggest another. A second approach is to redefine their reluctance as cooperation, perhaps suggesting that they must very much want a really pleasurable experience to choose their times so carefully.

Most therapy sessions present some opportunity to re-educate people about their own bodies and their sexual responses. I take every opportunity to reduce misinformation and dispel mythology and make extensive use of models and pictures as aids in this process.

Some couples choose to continue other forms of therapy, others to suspend or terminate them while resolving a sexual difficulty. Few problems with either choice are encountered in practice, and are usually simply resolved when the therapists communicate with each other clearly.

SUMMARY

Sexual problems are a significant part of the difficulties experienced by families who seek help. They should be recognized and evaluated by family therapists. A number of interventions, including the establishment of open and clear communication, permission giving, and limited education are available to all therapists. Those who are secure in their knowledge and comfort in this area can incorporate more structured techniques, such as behavioral exercises and imaginal desensitization into ongoing family therapy to resolve biological system, as well as interactional system, dysfunctions.

CHAPTER 17

The Role of the Family in the Treatment of Chronic Asthma

Ronald Liebman, M. D.

Salvador Minuchin, M. D.

Lester Baker, M.D.

Bernice L. Rosman, Ph.D.

INTRODUCTION

Children who develop chronic, severe, relapsing asthma in spite of competent pediatric management are candidates for parentectomy: they improve after separation from the family, but may relapse after returning home (1–5). We believe that this syndrome, which Peshkin and Tuft (1) have labeled intractable asthma, represents a psychosomatic disorder in which the primary allergic disorder has been profoundly complicated by emotional factors, especially chronic unresolved conflicts in the family. These conflicts engender chronic stress, which precipitates acute attacks and perpetuates the chronicity of the illness. Therefore, the system of the family is the basic unit toward which therapeutic interventions should be directed (3,4,6).

We have identified patterns of family organization and functioning associated with psychosomatic illness in children, and developed a therapeutic approach designed to change these patterns (7). Our results suggest that structural family therapy represents a significant breakthrough in the treatment of this perplexing and frustrating illness.

A review of the literature indicates that children with intractable asthma constitute 10–12 per cent of children with asthma (8). Many investigators have reported on the importance of intrapsychic, interpersonal, and family factors in the precipitation of the acute attacks and in the development of chronic forms of the disorder (9–16). The success of parentectomy in alleviating the symptoms indicates the effect of the family on the clinical course of intractable asthma. The studies of Long *et al.* (2), which showed that 18 out of 19 hospitalized asthmatic children showed no evidence of respiratory distress following exposure to high concentrations of their own house dust, and of Owen (17), which showed that hospitalized asthmatic children responded to tape recordings of their mothers' voices with more changes in their patterns of respiratory activity than a control group, provide supporting evidence. Pinkerton's work presents excellent arguments for reducing intrafamilial stress in order to maintain clinical improvement (4,5,18,19). We will describe here a family oriented treatment program which has proved successful in the treatment of chronic severe asthma.

CHRONIC SEVERE ASTHMA IN THE FAMILY

We have observed that the parents of patients with chronic severe asthma tend to be people who are intrinsically overdependent, especially on physicians. Frequently, the parents imagine the doctor to be a powerful person possessing certain magical qualities which will enable him to cure their child. The family system exerts a powerful pull on the pediatrician, drawing him into a position of overinvolvement where his attempts to deal with the child's symptoms meet with little success. From the families we have treated, we have delineated events associated with the development of chronic severe asthma in the family.

A significant factor is the manner in which the family system, especially the parents, responds to the diagnosis of asthma. The quality of the relationship between the parents and the physician, and the intensity with which they respond to his suggestions concerning management also influence the course of the illness. The greater the dependency of the parents on the physician (plus the presence of certain family characteristics to be described below), the greater the possibility for the development of the psychosomatic syndrome of chronic, severe, relapsing asthma.

After the occurrence of significant allergic symptoms and/or an attack of wheezing, the family's pediatrician suggests to the parents that they see an allergist for a more thorough evaluation of their child. After taking a detailed history and obtaining the results of skin tests, cultures, blood studies, and x-rays, the allergist usually tells the parents that the primary problem is one of allergic hypersensitivity and hyperreactivity to offending allergens. It is common for the patient to be found allergic to house dust, certain foods, certain pollens and molds, and animal fur or dander. The importance of infection as a precipitating and perpetuating factor is stressed, and some comment is usually made to the effect that strenuous physical activity may precipitate an attack of asthma. The parents are cautioned that attacks frequently occur in the early morning hours after the patient has gone to sleep.

Following this introduction, all or part of the following therapeutic regimen may be outlined for the patient and parents: the house must be thoroughly cleaned and kept as dust-free as possible on a daily basis; certain foods must be avoided because of their potential allergenic nature; household pets may have to be given away; a program of desensitization is recommended to decrease the allergy to pollens and molds; the patient's peer group relations and extracurricular activities are curtailed; and it is recommended that the patient avoid competitive sports, including physical education classes in school (20).

Obviously, this regimen affects the entire family. The most significant effects are experienced by the parents. When the mother is told that her child might have asthmatic attacks during the night, she may decide to leave the bedroom doors open to insure that someone will hear the slightest wheeze. This open-door policy results in a loss of privacy and autonomy for all the family members. The tension and anxiety which arise at bedtime decrease the frequency and gratification of sexual relationships. The mother may become overinvolved with the patient to the extent of neglecting the needs of other family members, and her overinvolvement with the patient usually occurs at the expense of the marital relationship. If the family remains intact, significant conflict and stress develop between the parents, and between the patient and the more peripheral parent. The patient experiences guilt because he feels, in some way, responsible for the problems between his parents. However, because parents and siblings have been cautioned not to upset or overstimulate the patient, the hostility and resentment are submerged, to be acted out in covert, self-defeating maladaptive patterns.

The entire family becomes organized around emergencies associated with the symptoms of the patient in order to get him to the doctor or hospital as quickly as possible. As a result, the father's work record suffers and his future may be compromised. Family vacations and trips become significant problems because of the possibility of an acute attack. The parents rarely go away by themselves because they are afraid that the patient may become ill.

The siblings of the patient usually feel neglected. They harbor a great deal of resentment toward the patient, which is generally suppressed. Instead, the siblings tend to act out their resentment at home or school in order to get their parents' attention. There is an increase of sibling rivalry. The patient is usually excluded from the activities planned by the siblings.

The effects of the traditional regimen on the patient are significant. He is labeled a special, sick, weak child. This leads to the development of low self-esteem, a decrease in self-confidence, and a decrease in ability to cope with and solve problems. Significant secondary handicaps in the areas of educational underachievement, and emotional and behavioral maladjustment have been reported (21). As a result of parental overprotectiveness, his autonomy and independence are constricted. When he is restricted from age-appropriate activities, he suffers from partial isolation and alienation from his sibship and peer group. His interpersonal relationships at home, school, and in the community are impaired.

The patient's special role in the family depends on the presence of his symptoms, and he has tremendous power to manipulate the family through his symptoms. Frequently, he is not disciplined when he should be, because his parents are afraid to upset him. This has maladaptive consequences for the patient, the parents, the relationship between the patient and his siblings, and the relationship between the parents and the siblings. The family system that emerges is characterized by hostility, tension, frustration and anxiety. However, these feelings have to be avoided within the context of the family, in order to protect the patient from being overstimulated.

If asthmatic attacks continue, the physician may assume that the patient is not following the details of the treatment program, or that the parents, especially the mother, are not making the child follow the regimen. Consequently, a more vigorous attempt is made to get the family to follow the regimen. If acute attacks still occur, the physician may conclude that emotional factors are causing the child to fail to respond, and a psychiatric evaluation is recommended. At this point, the suppressed frustration, anger, and anxiety of the family are transferred to the child psychiatrist.

The traditional, one-to-one, dynamically-oriented approach may fail with the chronic asthmatic patient (3,22), because it intensifies the role of the patient as the sick member of the family, neglecting the roles of the parents and siblings in perpetuating the symptoms. It supports the patient's role as the symptom-bearer for the family. If traditional one-to-one psychotherapy fails, the child psychiatrist refers the family back to the pediatrician. Having tried everything, the pediatrician often concludes that it is contraindicated for the patient to remain with his family. He may suggest that parentectomy is the only remaining method that might reverse the chronic relapsing course of the illness.

The parents' feelings of impotence, frustration, and hopelessness result in their agreeing to parentectomy—the process whereby the sick family member is excised from the family and transplanted to a safe place where the family no longer has to deal with him or their ambivalent feelings toward him. At the same time, the family is given the message that it has a noxious, deleterious influence on the patient, which engenders more guilt and frustration on the part of the family. The patient is angry and resentful toward his family because of separation. Parentectomy amplifies the feelings of hopelessness and helplessness which pervade the entire family, and particularly the patient, who is now physically removed from his main source of security and nurturance. The process of excision crystallizes in the patient the formation of a profound, negative self-image: he perceives himself as a defective, inferior, sick, helpless, weak person who is so repulsive to his family that he has to be removed from them. This perception is unfortunately supported by the behavior of the family. The child has become a medical invalid who is crippled by his symptoms.

We view parentectomy as a process which is emotionally traumatic and deleterious to the family in general, and to the patient in particular. Our alternative to parentectomy enables the child with chronic severe asthma to stay at home with his family where he can grow and develop in an age-appropriate fashion. This alternative, structural family therapy consists of changing the structure and functioning of the family to eliminate the factors reinforcing the symptoms and perpetuating the chronicity of the illness.

THE CHARACTERISTICS OF THE PSYCHOSOMATOGENIC FAMILY

On the basis of our clinical studies (7), we have observed that the development of severe psychosomatic symptoms in a child is related to the presence of certain patterns of family organization and functioning, with the following interactional characteristics:

1. *Enmeshment.* Family members are overinvolved with and overresponsive to one another. Attempts by any member to change stimulate a chain of events to maintain the status quo and prevent change from occurring. Family members intrude upon each other's thoughts, feelings, activities, and communications. There is little autonomy and privacy for individual family members, and the generational boundaries between parents and children are weak and easily crossed. Interpersonal boundaries which define where one person leaves off and the other begins are also weak, resulting in a confusion of roles.

2. *Overprotectiveness.* The family members have a high degree of concern for each other; nurturing and protective responses are constantly being elicited and supplied. Parental overprotectiveness results in few extrafamilial relationships and activities for the patient. When the patient becomes sick, the entire family becomes organized around his care, often submerging intrafamilial conflicts in the process.

3. *Rigidity.* The family often presents itself as being completely normal

without any problems except for the patient's medical problems. Therefore, they deny the need for change within the family system, and they preserve accustomed patterns of interaction and behavior.

4. *Lack of conflict resolution.* There is a low threshold for overt conflict in these families. Confrontations involving differences of opinion and issues of autonomy and control are avoided or diffused. Consequently, there is a chronic state of submerged unresolved conflict, with associated stress and tension. The child with severe psychosomatic symptoms plays a vital part in the family's avoidance of conflict. The experience of being able to protect the family, especially the parents, from conflict by way of symptoms is a powerful reinforcement to the patient. In addition, the sibling subsytem may reinforce the symptoms as part of a protective and/or a scapegoating system.

5. *The patient is involved in parental conflict.* In these families, in which generational boundaries between the parents and the children are weak and easily crossed, the child's symptoms function as a conflict avoidance and detouring mechanism, especially in connection with the detouring of spouse conflicts. Submerged conflicts, which threaten the stability of the spouse dyad, the marriage, and the maintenance of an intact family system, remain submerged by total concentration on the symptoms of the patient. The patient is brought, and to a certain extent brings himself, into the spouse dyad to form a triad through which the conflict between the spouses can be detoured. Thus, the patient's symptoms protect the family structure and are reinforced by that structure.

In two of our families, for example, a pattern existed in which the patient would begin to develop symptoms Friday evening or Saturday morning. By Saturday evening, the parents would have to take the patient to the emergency room for treatment, which took several hours. Previously, when the parents had gone out Saturday evening, they had occasionally gotten drunk and returned home to verbally and/or physically abuse each other. The development of acute attacks which necessitated a trip to the hospital protected the parents. They could not go out, and they were preoccupied with the medical status of the patient. As long as the spouse's conflicts remained unresolved, the patient's symptoms would persist.

A typical consequence of this conflict-detouring process is the dysfunctional set. A dysfunctional set is a pattern of defective or ineffective communication between two or more people that results in a lack of resolution of disagreements, and the perpetuation of the existing stress and tension. Frequently, the dysfunctional set is a part of a family system in which there is a strong alliance between mother and patient, with an excluded, angry, peripheral father. In this system, the dysfunctional set consists of the father and the patient. The presence of a specific dysfunctional set is supported by other dysfunctional relationships in the family, particularly between the parents. It is manifested by the patient's becoming upset and developing an asthmatic attack when the father disciplines or criticizes him. The wheezing drives the father away, and calls the mother and siblings in to protect the child. Then the family organizes itself around the task of taking the patient to the hospital.

The characteristics of the psychosomatogenic family are important because they constitute the foundation and direction for family therapy aimed at correcting dysfunctional family patterns, and at disengaging the children from the arena of spouse conflict.

REVIEW OF PATIENTS

In twenty-five families with a chronic asthmatic child that were referred for evaluation over a period of four years, all of the patients had failed to respond to competent, adequate medical management over a period of several months to several years. All had significant severe asthmatic symptoms, and had been maintained on chronic steroids and IPPB treatments. They all had vigorous courses of allergic desensitization, and therapeutic trials of several different bronchodilators. Eight of the patients had individually oriented psychotherapy or counseling. The patients had lost significant amounts of time from school, and had had several acute attacks requiring emergency treatment and/or hospitalization. Several aspects of their physical and personality development had suffered because of their isolation from school and the peer group, and the effects of chronic illness and steroid administration. Prior to referral, several of the parents had been presented with the possibility of parentectomy in an attempt to alleviate the severe, crippling, asthmatic symptoms. In all cases, the referring allergist felt that a major factor contributing to the severity and chronicity of the asthma was emotional problems in the patient and/or within his family.

THE TREATMENT PROGRAM

General Principles

Treatment of the child within the context of his family frequently engenders a significant amount of anxiety in the family members; this can be used to motivate the family to enter therapy, in spite of the occasional occurrence of an initial period of resistance to therapy. There is a need to shift responsibility for the care of the patient away from the pediatrician and the hospital, and back to the family. Ultimately, the patient will then be able to assume more age-appropriate responsibility for the care of his illness.

Initially, the transfer of responsibility is met with resistance by the parents who try to increase their dependency on the pediatrician. These initial problems must be overcome in order for the family psychiatrist to gain entrance to the family system, where he will function as a catalyst to effect changes in the family system.

In our treatment of these families, we have been able to identify one consistently important factor—the willingness and ability of the pediatrician to transfer and share medical authority and responsibility with the family psychiatrist. The pediatrician must support the family psychiatrist and de-emphasize some of the aspects of previous medical management. This will enable the family psychiatrist to gradually return more responsibility to the parents. As the parents' dependency on the pediatrician decreases, there will be an increase in the ability of the patient and the parents to cope with the asthmatic symptoms, resulting in a significant reduction in emergency visits to the pediatrician or hospital.

Since the symptoms of the patient occur within the context of his family and are reinforced by the family, it is logical and appropriate to consider the family the basic unit which requires change. Specifically, the structure and functioning of the family system must be changed to enable the patient to change his role as the symptom-bearer of the family. Once this is achieved, the patient will have more freedom to establish meaningful peer group relationships and extrafamilial activities.

The general characteristics of structural family therapy (23) are as follows:

1. *Structural* refers to the concept of the family as a system consisting of various subsystems. In the treatment of psychosomatic illness in children, the parental and child subsystems and the generational boundaries which separate them are most important.

2. Its basic assumption is that the patient will not be able to give up his symptoms or change his role in the family unless the structure and functioning of the family system are changed.

3. Its therapeutic interventions are directed at correcting dysfunctional behavior patterns in the family.

4. Therapeutically, it is concerned with the present and immediate future, not the past.

5. It is based on observable, transactional, interpersonal processes between and among family members; it is not based on psychoanalytic concepts of the development of psychopathology.

The success of this structural family therapy approach is manifested by the clinical improvement of the asthmatic child as a result of therapeutic interventions aimed at changing the structure and functioning of the family. We consider a successful outcome to be characterized by: elimination or significant alleviation of severe symptoms, resulting in a significant reduction of emergency trips to the pediatrician or hospital; elimination of chronic dependency on steroids, IPPB treatments, or nebulizers; restoration of normal physical activity and age-appropriate peer group relations; a normal school or work attendance record; and the *alteration of dysfunctional family patterns that have reinforced and perpetuated the patient's symptoms.*

Goals of Treatment

Weekly outpatient family therapy sessions are organized into three phases, depending on the goals to be accomplished in each phase. Phase 1 is concerned with the alleviation of the symptoms of asthma to prevent the use of the patient as a means of detouring family conflicts. Once the symptoms are reduced, there is more freedom and flexibility available to promote change within the family. Phase 2 consists of identifying and changing those patterns in the family and extrafamilial environment that have tended to exacerbate and perpetuate the severe symptoms. Phase 3 consists of interventions to change the structure and functioning of the family system to promote lasting disengagement of the patient, in order to prevent a recurrence of the symptoms or the development of a new symptom-bearer.

The pediatrician assumes a significant role in the first phase of family therapy. It is important for the family psychiatrist and the pediatrician to discuss the treatment program, and to develop a co-operative working relationship with mutual support, respect, and confidence. The pediatrician should be present during the first family therapy session to state explicitly that medical management has not been successful in the past, and that, in the future, medical management will be de-emphasized. This will show the family that he supports and agrees with the family psychiatrist's desire to transfer more of the responsibility for the management of symptoms to the patient and the parents.

Early specific goals are: to desensitize the patient and the family to the problems of asthma, awakening the possibility for hope and for symptom improvement; to help the parents and the patient to avoid emergency treatments and/or hospitalizations by increasing their ability to cope with precipitating stressful situations; to change the role and status of the patient in the family, so that he becomes an equal, healthy, functioning member who receives no special treatment or privileges; and to enable the family to accept the patient as a more healthy, autonomous member.

Treatment Process and Techniques

The first step is to stop the patient's functioning as a detourer of family conflicts by helping him to decrease the intensity and frequency of acute attacks. This is accomplished by using different strategies and interventions. The work of Luparello emphasizes the importance of the patient's expectations, suggestability, and conditioning regarding the precipitation and the treatment of acute attacks (24–26). LaScola reported on the treatment of acute attacks by teaching the patient muscle relaxation exercises (27). The reports on the principles and use of behavior modification and biofeedback training raise the possibility for increased voluntary control of asthmatic symptoms (28–33). We have been able to utilize these principles by teaching the patient to use a series of deep breathing exercises at the first sign of bronchoconstriction, which is usually a "squeak" at the end of expiration. The exercises are done until the squeak disappears and the dyspnea is relieved. However, behavior modification and breathing exercises, while effective in decreasing the symptoms of the patient, do nothing to change the context of the patient's family where the symptoms originated and are reinforced. Therefore, behavior modification and biofeedback exercises *alone* will not prevent relapses from occurring after active therapy is stopped within the context of a dysfunctional family system.

We use the process of teaching the exercises to the patient as a technique for changing the structural relationships within the family system. For instance, in a family where the patient is closely allied with the mother, and the father is peripheral, with a dysfunctional set existing between father and patient, we assign to the father the task of practicing the breathing exercises with the patient on a daily basis. The mother is advised to help her husband learn to relate more effectively to the patient, but she is not to exclude or undermine him by taking this responsibility away from him. This decreases the coalition between the mother and the patient; it modifies the dysfunctional set between father and patient and between the parents; it changes the role of the father in the family by increasing his involvement in a constructive manner; and it shifts the relationship between the parents onto a more mutually supportive, goal-directed level.

The increased control of symptoms provides the patient and parents with hope and optimism. The changes in the family relationships increase the emotional distance between the patient and his parents, facilitating the disengagement of the patient from spouse conflicts. It also expedites the return of the patient to the child subsystem of the family, which prepares the patient for increased peer group activities in the future.

To provide the patient with an increased feeling of mastery and increased autonomy, one can establish an operant reinforcement paradigm in which increased accessibility to age-appropriate peer group activities is made contingent on progressive symptom reduction. This is an effective strategy, because symptom reduction will provide increased freedom and autonomy for the entire family.

The parents should be instructed on the emergency treatment of an asthmatic attack at home, and should be provided with adrenalin and syringes. If an acute attack fails to respond to muscle relaxation, the more peripheral parent is given the task of calling the pediatrician to get instructions on the administration of the appropriate amount of adrenalin. This precludes any emergency trip to the pediatrician's office or to the hospital. It is an effective strategy, because it increases the competence of the parents in dealing with their sick child and strengthens generational boundaries in the family. The parents are told that if they work together in a mutually supportive way, they will be successful in helping the patient master the symptoms. This uncovers pathogenic coalitions, power struggles, and dysfunctional sets, providing an opportunity to deal with them in the family therapy sessions.

Other general guidelines are:

Search for dysfunctional sets that produce stress and precipitate acute attacks, and convert them into functional sets.

Change pathogenic relationships which are maintained by the presence of symptoms in the patient.

Uncover concrete problems at school, or with peer group that involve the siblings of the patient. Frequently, these problems have not been attended to by the parents because of their preoccupation with the patient. Focus on one problem at a time, involving one sibling, and instruct the parents to organize a plan to help the sibling solve the particular problem. The parents must follow through with every detail of their plan, and they are advised to have private discussions each evening in their bedroom. This modifies the dysfunctional set between the parents. Although this problem-solving approach may appear superficial, it is effective in removing the patient as the sole symptom-bearer in the family, and decreases his centrality and power to manipulate the family. Furthermore, it renders the patient less deviant and less isolated from his siblings, because all of the children now are seen to have problems which demand the equal attention of the parents. It forces the parents to work together in a mutually supportive way, preventing the patient's symptoms from splitting the spouse dyad. The parents' experience of effectively helping their children cope with their problems increases their self-esteem and self-confidence as the executive heads of their family.

Return the patient to the child subsystem, and strengthen the boundaries between the parental and child subsystems. Confront the parents about special treatment of the patient, which allows him to avoid household responsibilities and appropriate discipline. The patient must not be treated any differently from his siblings, and must be regarded as an equal, responsible member of the child subsystem.

Disengage the parents from an enmeshed, over-protective relationship with the patient. Begin by having the parents plan to go out one evening a week by themselves, leaving the children home with a babysitter. The next step is to have the parents plan to go away overnight or for a weekend. It is most important to clarify and organize a plan of action should an emergency develop when the parents are not home, in order to decrease parental anxiety. If the parents have an open-door policy with respect to the bedrooms, they are encouraged to secure privacy by keeping the doors closed. Simultaneously, enlist the support of the parents to encourage the patient to develop age-appropriate peer group and sibling relationships and activities. The parents are given the task of arranging with the school authorities for the patient to resume taking physical education classes, and to encourage the patient to participate in extracurricular activities.

There is a constant redefinition of the problems, so as to move away from the scapegoating, conflict-detouring process which previously centralized and reinforced the patient's asthmatic symptoms, and toward family involvement in and concern about interpersonal transactional issues within the family system. Eventually the emphasis must shift to activities outside of the family involving the school and peer group. A broad-based flexible approach is needed in order to promote constructive changes in the system constituted by the patient, his family, and the extrafamilial environment.

As the patient's symptoms decrease, there is a gradual increase in the stress between the parents associated with the surfacing of long-submerged marital conflicts. At this point, the therapist must shift his emphasis to the spouse dyad to resolve chronic conflicts which previously have been detoured through concern with the symptoms of the patient. By working to resolve or alleviate the problems of the spouse dyad, the therapist helps to prevent a recurrence of symptoms in the patient.

RESULTS

The results of our treatment program can be summarized as follows:

1. Family therapy has been successful in alleviating the intensity and frequency of acute attacks of asthma. Although some of the patients have occasional attacks of wheezing, the patients and their families are more able to cope with the symptoms, so that there are fewer hospitalizations and emergency visits to the pediatrician.

2. The patients are no longer medical cripples, and are less dependent on the daily use of steroids, IPPB treatments, or desensitization programs

to control the symptoms. Periodically, however, medications are used to treat acute seasonal attacks of wheezing associated with specific allergies.

3. The patients have more normal life styles, associated with normal school attendance records, increased peer group involvement, and increased physical activities.

4. Associated positive changes have occurred in the functioning of the siblings and the parents, and in their interpersonal relationships.

We conclude that family therapy should be considered a necessary and effective modality in the treatment of chronic severe asthma in children.

PREVENTION OF THE DEVELOPMENT OF CHRONIC SEVERE ASTHMA

From our experience, the pivotal person in the prevention of the development of chronic severe asthma is the pediatrician or allergist. Specifically, and of equal importance, is the way that he presents himself and the illness to the family following the initial diagnosis. It is helpful *not* to present asthma as a "black box disease" with unknown etiological factors. Instead, the various etiological factors, such as climate, infection, allergy, emotional problems, and family conflict should be discussed. It should be stressed that in most situations some combination of these factors causes the clinical presentation of asthma. It is important to explain the details of medical management in a simple direct way, emphasizing that it *will* be successful in preventing acute asthmatic attacks and in controlling the allergic symptoms. It is helpful to keep the family from becoming dependent on him in an exaggerated maladaptive way. He should be alert to the presence of dysfunctional family patterns that might interfere with treatment.

The family and patient will function better if they are told that they can learn to cope with the symptoms. One way to achieve this is to limit, as much as possible, the restrictions placed on the patient and family. This will encourage the continuation of normal family life despite the presence of the diagnosis of asthma in one of its members. In addition, the patient will not become isolated from siblings and peers. This prevents the development of a negative self-image, with its associated emotional, behavioral, and school problems. If the patient is not labelled as someone who is special or different, he will not be able to split the spouse dyad and manipulate the entire family system. Visits to the pediatrician should be kept to an adequate minimum. The chronic administration of medication, especially steroids and IPPB treatments, should be avoided whenever possible. Teaching the patient techniques of muscle relaxation to abort acute attacks can be extremely helpful. An important goal is to teach the parents and the patient methods to prevent the development of an acute asthmatic attack that will require emergency hospitalization. Responsibility for this, initially, is to be shared equally by the physician, the patient, and the parents, with the patient ultimately being able to take more age-appropriate responsibility.

It is helpful for the allergist to educate the family and patient about asthma in a factual, simple, positive fashion. It is important not to overemphasize the risks associated with asthma, such as the possibility that the patient may go into respiratory arrest and die following an acute attack.

We are not saying that the allergist should be deceptive or deny the realities of asthma. We are saying that it is helpful if he emphasizes the positive, constructive aspects of management, and de-emphasizes the negative aspects. Asthma does not have to become a disease crippling to the patient and family.

The goal is to have a child who is normal, except for the coincidental occurrence of allergies or asthma with which he can effectively cope. Too often, we hear the patient say that he or she is "an asthmatic," or hear the parents say that one of their children is "an asthmatic." The child's identity as a person has been replaced by a disease entity within himself, and within the context of his family. This must be avoided, if we are to decrease the medical and psychiatric morbidity of this illness.

REFERENCES

1. M.M. Peshkin and H.S. Tuft. "Rehabilitation of the Intractable Asthmatic Child by the Institutional Approach," *Quarterly Review of Pediatrics,* 11 (1956), 7–9.
2. R.T. Long, J.H. Lamont, B. Whipple, *et al.* "A Psychosomatic Study of Allergic and Emotional Factors in Children with Asthma," *Am. J. Psychiatry,* 114 (1958), 890–99.
3. M. Sperling. "Asthma in Children: An Evaluation of Concept and Therapies," *J. Am. Acad. Child Psychiatry,* 7 (1968), 44–50.
4. P. Pinkerton. "Pathophysiology and Psychopathology as Co-determinants of Pharmaco-therapeutic Response in Childhood Asthma," in *Psychotropic Drugs in Internal Medicine,* A. Pletscher, and A. Marino (eds.). Amsterdam: Excerpta Medica Foundation, 1969, 115–27.
5. P. Pinkerton and C.M. Weaver. "Childhood Asthma," in *Psychosomatic Medicine,* O. Hill (ed.). London: Butterworths, 1970, 81–104.
6. L. Grolnick. "A Family Perspective of Psychosomatic Factors in Illness: A Review of the Literature," *Family Process,* 11 (1972), 457–86.
7. S. Minuchin, L. Baker, B. Rosman, *et al.* "A Conceptual Model of Psychosomatic Illness in Children," *Arch. Gen. Psychiatry,* 32 (1975), 1031–38.
8. F.M. Rackemann, and M.D. Edwards. "Asthma in Children, A Follow-up Study," *New Eng. J. Med.,* 246 (1952), 815–23.
9. P.H. Knapp and S.J. Nemetz. "Personality Variation in Bronchial Asthma: A Study of 40 Patients," *Psychosomatic Med.,* 19 (1957), 443–65.

10. J.E. Weblin. "Pathogenesis in Asthma: An Appraisal with a View to Family Research," *Brit. J. Med. Psychology*, 36 (1963), 211–25.

11. J.A. McLean and A.Y.T. Ching. "Follow-up Study of Relationships Between Family Situation and Bronchial Asthma in Children," *J. Am. Acad. Child Psychiatry*, 12 (1973), 142–61.

12. T.M. French. "Psychogenic Factors in Asthma," *Am. J. Psychiatry*, 96 (1939), 87–101.

13. T.M. French and R. Alexander. "Psychogenic Factors in Bronchial Asthma," *Psychosomatic Med. Monograph IV*. Washington: Nat. Res. Council, 1941.

14. J.L. Coolidge. "Asthma in Mother and Child as a Special Type of Intercommunication," *Am. J. Orthopsychiatry*, 26 (1956), 165–78.

15. S.I. Cohen. "Psychological Factors in Asthma: A Review of their Etiological and Therapeutic Significance," *Postrad. Med. J.*, 47 (1971), 533–40.

16. C.J. Mohr, H. Tausend, S. Selesnick, *et al*. "Studies of Eczema and Asthma in the Preschool Child," *J. Am. Acad. Child Psychiatry*, 2 (1963), 271–91.

17. F.W. Owen. "Patterns of Respiratory Disturbance in Asthmatic Children Evoked by the Stimulus of the Mother's Voice," *Acta Psychother.*, 11 (1963), 228–41.

18. P. Pinkerton. "Correlating Physiologic with Psychodynamic Data in the Study and Management of Childhood Asthma," *J. Psychosomatic Research*, 11 (1967), 95–99.

19. P. Pinkerton. "The Psychosomatic Approach in Pediatrics," *Brit. Med. J.*, 3 (1972), 462–64.

20. W.E. Nelson. *Textbook of Pediatrics*. Philadelphia: W. B. Saunders, 1964, 1471–75.

21. I.B. Pless and K.J. Roghmann. "Chronic Illness and its Consequences: Observations based on 3 Epidemiologic Surveys," *J. Pediat.*, 79 (1971), 351–59.

22. K. Purcell, K. Bernstein and S.C. Bukantz. "A Comparison of Rapidly Remitting and Steroid-dependent Asthmatic Children," *Psychosomatic Med.*, 23 (1961), 305–10.

23. S. Minuchin. *Families and Family Therapy: A Structural Approach*. Boston: Harvard University Press, 1974.

24. T.J. Luparello, H.A. Lyons, E.R. Bleecker, *et al*. "Influences of Suggestion on Airway Reactivity in Asthmatic Subjects," *Psychosomatic Med.*, 30 (1968), 819–25.

25. T.J. Luparello, N. Leist, C.H. Lourie, *et al*. "The Interaction of Psychologic Stimuli and Pharmacologic Agents on Airway Reactivity in Asthmatic Subjects," *Psychosom. Med.*, 32 (1970), 509–13.

26. T.J. Luparello, E.R. McFadden, H.A. Lyons, *et al*. "Psychologic Factors and Bronchial Asthma," *New York J. Med.*, 71 (1971), 2161–65.

27. R.L. LaScola. "Hypnosis with Children," in *Clinical Hynotherapy*, D.B. Cheek and L.M. Lecron (eds.). New York: Grune and Stratton, 1968, 201–11.

28. N.E. Miller. "Learning of Visceral and Glandular Responses," *Science*, 163 (1969), 434–45.

29. K. Gaarder. "Control of States of Consciousness, I and II," *Arch. Gen. Psychiatry*, 25 (1971), 429–41.

30. A.B. Alexander. "Systematic Relaxation and Flow Rates in Asthmatic Children: Relationship to Emotional Precipitants and Anxiety," *J. Psychosomatic Research*, 16 (1972), 405–10.

31. A.B. Alexander, D.R. Miklich, H. Hershkoff. "The Immediate Effects of Sys-

tematic Relaxation Training on Peak Expiratory Flow Rates in Asthmatic
Children," *Psychosomatic Med.,* 34 (1972), 388–94.
32. E. Heim, A. Blaser, E. Waidelich. "Dyspnea: Psychophysiologic Relationship,"
Psychosom. Med, 34 (1972), 405–23.
33. "Biofeedback in Action," *Medical World News,* March 9, 1973, 47–60.

CHAPTER 18

Marital Crisis

Thomas F. Fogarty, M.D.

One of the most common areas where a problem rises to the surface in a family is in the marital relationship. In 1974 there were almost one million divorces in the United States. There are many social, religious, legal, economic, and cultural reasons for all these divorces, but whatever the reasons, the situation has forced family therapists to pay particular attention to marital stress and strain, and to develop theory and practice that will allow us to deal with these problems.

When family symptoms appear in the marriage, many family therapists will refuse to get involved with the family unless both husband and wife agree to come. Certainly all therapists would like to have the cooperation of husband and wife; but the fact is, that in many situations only one spouse is willing to come. The other spouse has little confidence in psychiatry; or will be afraid of blame or abuse in the therapy hour; or will be trying to protect his or her own guilt and shame. One of the big advantages of using a systems approach to human problems is that not all members of the family need be present and working on the problem. While no one member of the family can determine what others will do, the intense emotionality present in all families makes what one member does strongly influential on the others; therefore, it is possible to work with one spouse and coach that spouse about the marriage.

If the other spouse is determined not to appear, it is a mistake to have the one in treatment pressure him or her to come. It will not work. Efforts to change are most productive when the therapist is dealing with those and only those members of the family who want change. If a wife is going to suggest to her husband that he accompany her, she can best do it by stating that the doctor wants to see him so that he can help the wife with her problems. The husband may be so astonished to discover his wife thinks she has a problem that he may come. If he does appear, he should be generally ignored during the first few sessions except for politeness, and for asking him what he thinks about his wife. The more the heat is taken off him, the more he will want to express his own opinions. If he does not come, the therapist can proceed to coach the wife according to the details of the problem.

PURSUIT AND DISTANCE

When two people marry, they start moving toward each other. Over time, problems develop and adjustments or change will be called for. One of the most common adjustments used involves a pattern of distance and pursuit. One spouse becomes the distancer in a certain area, and the other the pursuer. The wife may pursue her husband emotionally, wanting him to listen to her, to understand her, and to sympathize with her feelings. The husband may become the pursuer sexually, longing for the comfort of her physical presence and touch. The pursuer in one area may become the distancer in another.

When problems arise, the pursuer tends to blame, accuse, and attack, and the distancer to defend. The pursuer is invariably avoiding an inner emptiness, and can be taken for granted, since he is always moving toward his spouse. A pursuer has to be taught the operating principle, "Never pursue a distancer." The more anyone goes after a distancer, the more he will distance. The therapist should take the pursuer into his own inner emptiness by asking him questions like, "What would it be like inside you if you lost your spouse?" In effect, the pursuer must learn to get from himself many of the things he is hoping to get from his mate. In other words, the pursuer must learn to distance; and since he is living with a walking textbook on the subject, if he can stop complaining about the distancer long enough to study her, he can learn from his spouse and stop trying to change her. The therapist will do well to keep his own prescription in mind, and not pursue the distancer in the family. The distancer must come in under his own steam. Eventually, he must learn that distancing is a useful way to get his head together, but that it never solves a problem. When the distancer sees that nobody is chasing him, he will get in touch with his own loneliness and his fears of losing his spouse. Ordinarily, the therapist uses his time most productively if he concentrates his efforts on the pursuer. The pursuer is the one who is most anxious and uncomfortable, and therefore most apt to change.

When the pursuer gets tired of chasing, he will often stage a revolution. He comes into therapy saying, "I have no feelings for my wife anymore. The marriage is dead. I want a divorce." At this point, the distancer suddenly comes alive, grows frantic over the impending loss, makes every effort to appease, and to do what the other wants. The therapist will want to work mainly with the rebellious party, since he or she has the power in the family.

The one being moved toward is always the effective person.

It is a waste of time to try to abort the revolution. The therapist has to expose the emptiness in the rebellious person, show that he or she is only reduplicating patterns that existed in the extended family, and that getting a divorce is not changing anything. If both people played a part in the development of the problem, then the one who leaves the marriage will carry his portion of the problem with him. The one who is rebelling must learn about his past mistakes before he leaves the marriage. This also affords the distancer a chance to change, so that perhaps the marriage can reform on new ground. Once past a certain point of frustration, bitterness, and resentment, the revolution will be unmanageable; the marriage will inevitably break up, and the therapist can only hope to salvage as much of each person as is possible.

OPEN CONFLICT

We are all familiar with the openly conflictual twosome. They fill the air with charge and countercharge. One issue leads into another and nothing is ever resolved. Each sees the problem as being in the other. Therapists often make a mistake the minute they meet such a couple. It is important for the therapist to be in control with every family, but especially so with the conflictual family. And if this control is not set up at the beginning, it will be difficult to enforce later. If the therapist is an observer who watches what the family does and then intervenes, he will be at a disadvantage, because conflict, once started, is difficult to stop. If the family continues to argue and fight in the office, they are only duplicating what they do so well and with such futility at home, and any such experience will only confirm their belief that change is impossible.

The operating principle to use in such a situation is to avoid overloading the system. A conflictual relationship needs only a spark to set it off. The topic for discussion and the direction of the movement should be away from the relationship between the husband and wife. The therapist can do this by underscoring the idea that both people brought problems to the marriage, and then directing each one to explore his understanding and connectedness with his own extended family. Besides being a productive experience all by itself, this move takes their attention away from each other and cools the system off. Talking about events of their lives that happened before they knew each other depersonalizes the discussion, and they can begin to listen to each other. The therapist can also take the discussion into the network by examining work or the children, if this will have the same effect. Sensitive areas in the marriage can be explored later. If it proves impossible to cool the system down, the therapist must consider seeing them separately. Seeing people separately does not invalidate family therapy, since the theory applies to all emotional problems and has little or nothing to do with the number of people in the room.

Marital crises can present with one or both partners having an affair. This situation involves particular difficulties for the therapist. It is clearly a triangle, and every family therapist knows that means real trouble. A triangle takes the emotional tension that is present between two people and displaces it onto a third party. This focus on the third party prevents the twosome from dealing with the issues inside and between them. If the focus remains on the third party, the husband and wife relationship will continue to deteriorate. Yet the therapist will have trouble moving toward either spouse without alienating the other. The spouse—let us say, the wife—who is not having an affair will alternately feel hurt or want the marriage to be perpetuated. If the therapist asks her about her part in the family problem, it will activate her self-righteousness. The husband, on the other hand, who is having the affair will often be unable to make any stand. The affair looks good to him because it is a relief from his wife; it has built-in distance since it is a sometime thing; and it is different. He will be unable to make a cool, unbiased decision about it.

The therapist can tinker with this process for any length of time, but it always comes down to the same thing. The spouse having the affair must begin to realize that he or she cannot operate simultaneously in two systems that are mutually incompatible. It is trying to do the impossible, and is characteristic of an uncommitted position. It is generally a useful idea for him to leave both his wife and his mistress for an unspecified period and prove to himself that he can live by himself. Once he has done this, he can begin to make some sound evaluation of his marital state. Few people, however, will do it. The therapist also gets into the bind if he feels unwilling to take a position because he may be accused of moralizing. It is perfectly possible and absolutely necessary to take a position about triangles and two systems. It has nothing to do with moralizing; it is soundly based in theory.

In dealing with the husband who is having the affair, the therapist cannot talk to him effectively about his marriage. He will be mostly interested in his inner self. The therapist can deal with him as if he were in analysis. On the other hand, the wife who has been left will be very interested in the marriage, and so the therapist must talk to her about it, and about the external system between the couple. They can talk about her inner self later on. She must come to realize that if the system is dead, it should be buried. On the other hand, if it is alive, she must learn how to distance from her husband. The therapist must remember that no system is dead until it has been tested out in therapy.

Sometimes the distance in a marriage gets so great that one spouse leaves. The husband may take off to be with his girlfriend, to do his own thing, to be by himself away from his wife's attacks. After he is out in that big wide world, he may get in touch with his loneliness and discover that he really wants to be home, and that he misses his wife and family.

Nobody in a family perfectly balances his or her many positions. A man will be more husband, father, or worker. A wife will be more mother, wife, or homebody. When the husband returns home, he will have to face the anger, self-righteousness, and hurt of his wife. He will tend to try to do and be what she wants him to be in order to impress her. She will fill his mind, and yet he will often be rebuffed by her; so he may try to be more husband than anything else. He does not appreicate that his wife is really more mother than wife, in the sense that her worry, concern, and empathy go predominantly toward her children, and so he will invariably fail.

First of all, he has to learn that being what she wants him to be will make him a nonperson. She may like it, but she will not respect or believe it, and respect comes before liking. Secondly, if he really wants to impress her, he should do it by being the best father that he knows how to be. Because her major concern goes toward the children, she will be more impressed by his fathering than by his husbanding. I therefore teach the husband to make a move toward his children every time his wife enters his head. If he is thinking about doing something nice for her, I tell him, do it toward the children instead. This will often work a seeming miracle. If he can begin to take his "I" positions, instead of trying to please the wife, he may be back in business.

In dealing with these situations, it is important for the therapist to remember that there is no such thing as an emotional problem in one person, no matter how it looks. The scoundrel is not the entire problem. It is difficult to get behind the self-righteousness of the wife and into her emptiness and hurt, but it can be done sometimes by taking her continually into her inner system and back into her extended family. This direction moves her away from her husband, and therefore away from the object of her anger.

MARRIAGE COUNSELING

It is a common experience for family therapists to hear one story from the husband, and another story from wife. Each one blames the other and then they look to the therapist to be the judge, the giver of truth. No matter how much experience he has, the therapist can never really decide factually when he first meets the couple if a marriage has enough caring left in it. The emotional connectedness between the twosome must be tested over time by stretching, by examination, by efforts to change. Only then will it be clear whether the marriage will continue or stop.

There are some general guidelines. First, there should be one therapist for the couple, regardless of whether they are seen together or separately. If each spouse goes to a different therapist, it is almost possible to guarantee a break in the marriage.

Secondly, a dead system, tested so everyone knows it is dead, should be buried. People do not really stay together for the sake of the children, nor is such staying together of any value to the children. If one spouse wants to break the marriage, the other spouse should not fight against it, because the effort will be futile. The one who wants to break the marriage has to be responsible for initiating the legal action. If the husband tries to keep his wife against her will, what does he really have? He doesn't even have his own self-respect. In some relationships, the divorce issue may be used as a smokescreen by the couple to avoid the real issues inside each one of them and in the relationship, and the "marriage" becomes the third leg of a triangle, as if it had an existence of its own. One wants to keep it and the other to break it up; or they may reverse positions and keep it going that way. Nothing useful is accomplished by discussion in such cases. The therapist can test this by saying, "Perhaps you should get a divorce. What do you think about that?" This will get him out of the marriage counseling business, and his reading of their reaction will allow him to begin to move forward. If they say that they can't divorce because of the children, or the economics, or other reasons, then he knows that they mean to stay together, but are not dealing with their insides and their personal relationship.

Lawyers are sometimes involved in a marriage at the same time as the family therapist. Some lawyers are positively malignant in their zeal for their client, and increase and feed the anger, bitterness, and blame already present in surplus amounts. On the other hand, many lawyers will refer those marriages that they think have some life left in them. The therapist should always inquire about the type of information that is being fed into the problems by the lawyer. He should feel free to take a position against any advice that is destructive to either partner in the marriage. He cannot be an advocate and side with husband or wife at the same time. If called to court, he can appear as a witness for the family and not for any one party.

There is one particular situation in which the use of an attorney is particularly effective. Let's say that the wife has been very helpless with her husband. For years she has threatened him with leaving or taking some position, but he overwhelms her and pays no attention to her. They are stuck. Then she enters therapy with the desire to do something about herself. She works on herself, and decides that she no longer wants to stay married unless her husband changes himself. He does not believe her. If she can go to an attorney and have a letter sent stating that she has approached the attorney for a separation, then her credibility gap with the husband may vanish, and she becomes believable. It should be stressed that this tactic should be applied with caution, after thought, and with due regard for the risks. The husband may welcome the letter. But at the least it can clarify the situation, and often it may bring him running in to "save" the marriage.

The triangles present in every family and every marriage have been aptly described as the building blocks of the immature family. They are omnipresent phenomena. It is important for the therapist to have a clear picture of the nature and forms of triangles. He must be able to teach this to the married couple, or they will go from episode to episode and issue to issue looking for a separate solution in each situation. If the couple understand the nature of triangles, they can apply this knowledge independently to all situations. It is also important that the therapist be aware of triangles for his own sake. If he is not, he will become a member of the triangle with the husband and wife. He will tend to side with one or the other, make a judgment based on his own bias for one and against the other, or be afraid to answer any question. If he does become triangled into the marriage, then he is not only neutralized, but he is actually participating in and fostering the perpetuation of the marital problem.

In every marital difficulty, there is a great deal of bitterness, resentment, and hurt. One will often try to forgive and forget the real or imagined injustices of the other, but this never really works. The lingering memory of the hurt will persist even though it is not mentioned anymore. There is only one way for someone to deal with his own hurt, and that is, to realize that there is no such thing as an emotional problem in one person. If the husband has had an affair, the wife cannot forget it. She must realize that she played a part in it. She did not encourage him to have the affair. She is not responsible for his affair. However, she did play a 50 per cent part in the distance that grew up between the two of them prior to the affair. She must realize and understand this part that she played, so that it will not recur when they get together. If the injured spouse can understand her own part, then she will not feel so hurt. After all, it is not reasonable for one bankrobber to accuse another of robbing a bank.

When a husband and wife dispute, it is positively amazing how often the words *should, ought to, fairness, right, wrong, fault,* and *blame* are used. These words indicate that the spouses do not realize the nature of an emotional system. They evaluate feelings in some imaginary world of fairness and justification, as if such a world really existed; and they deal with feelings as if there were a right and wrong to them. It is a bastardized use of responsibility to blame and accuse the other and to excuse oneself, and it is critical for the therapist to teach that this is not a fair world, whether it should be or not. It is equally important to teach families that emotional systems have nothing to do with right or wrong. Emotional systems respond purely to function. Does what I am doing work or not work? Is it functional? The *shoulds* and the *ought tos* have to be traced back to their origins in the extended family, and re-evaluated. Is something right if it does not work in the family? Ultimately, it is necessary to test right and wrong by testing a principle in the family and seeing if it does work.

THE LARGER VIEW

In the long run, there is no such simple matter as a "marital crisis." The more one looks at it, the more complicated it gets, and the more people are seen to be involved. There are, so to speak, at least three, and usually more than three, people in a bed. One cannot examine the marriage without investigating the extended family. The relationships that a person has with his father and mother vitally influence the kind of marriage he will have. All people, usually without knowing it, try to improve on the family they came from. They incorporate what they perceive to be good, and eliminate what they saw as bad in their extended family. Much of what they do, much of what they aspire to, much of what they believe in will depend on how accurately they perceived their parents. All unresolved difficulties in the extended family thus influence the marriages in the next generation.

A personal re-evaluation therefore demands that someone go back at least one generation and take a look at his parents in a different light. If there has been an emotional cut off, if he has not seen his father for some time, for example, then the connection must be re-established. If he sees one parent as good and the other as bad, then he must work on that picture until he can see them as being emotionally equal, fitting each other like a hand fits a glove. If he sees his parents as having done him in, then he must begin to wonder what he has ever done for them. All perceptions that come from the extended family significantly influence the expectations that he brings to his own marriage. A child who pays little attention to his father will wake up some day with a son who pays little attention to him. Anyone who disavows his extended family will often put so high a level of expectation into his nuclear family that it must be doomed to fail. Generally, every marriage must be put into a three-generational overview to make episodes and emotional overloads understandable.

In some families, marital conflict is thinly masked by the problem's showing up in one or more of the children. When a father and mother in such a situation are asked about their relationship, they may state that the child is the problem, and that their marriage is average, normal, or fine. The therapist may almost sense from their description that they are being defensive and protective. Many family therapists tend to move into the marriage to take the heat off the child, in an effort to take the label of "problem" off the child and distribute it around the family. This can be a mistake if it is done too rapidly. The marital relationship in such a child-centered marriage is the most sensitive and difficult relationship in the family. If the therapist moves in to challenge it or shake it up too soon, the chances are that the emotional system in the family will be overloaded, and that the family will not return for more visits. The therapist does have to get to the marital relationship in a child-centered family, but it should be done slowly and with the utmost delicacy. After the family is more comfortable and can put more trust in the therapist, they may be willing to challenge their greatest sensitivities.

All marital conflict is marked by an increased emotionality, at least until distance sets in as a fixed solution. In each person there are two sets of feelings. The first kind are feelings that are reactions to the other person— I am angry at you, I miss you. The second are feelings about himself, feelings he would have if he never knew the other person—I am ashamed of myself, I feel that I am a failure. Married people often get into a reciprocal relationship that is out of balance. So, too, with feelings. One spouse seems to be full of feelings that are reactions to the other spouse. They start out in self, but rapidly move to focus on the other person: I feel angry at you, because you. . . . This spouse must learn to express his own feelings about himself. The feelings of the other spouse will be reciprocal: I feel that I can't talk; or, I have no feelings. This spouse must learn to abandon his self-centered preoccupations with his own feelings. The therapist might ask him questions to take him away from himself, such as, "How do you think your wife feels? What do you think is happening inside her?" This should help move the twosome into better balance.

Feelings of emptiness exist in everyone; only the degree and the details of the emptiness vary. Emptiness is feelings of loneliness; of being uncared for; of not belonging; of insignificance, failure, shame, and sadness. It is as though there were some degree of emotional death inside the person. Each spouse will, to varying degrees, try to fill self from the other. The result may be conflict between them, or the appearance of symptoms. Any discussion of marriage must deal with these issues of emptiness if it is to be something more than merely a band-aid approach to solving problems; otherwise the relationship will remain sharply delimited and vulnerable to minor stress.

To deal with emptiness, each person must stop running from it, and get in touch with his own emptiness. Once he does, he will realize that these feelings invariably take him back to his extended family. Emptiness in the nuclear and extended families is used to enlarge the picture of the emotional state inside self. Initially, each spouse keeps these feelings to himself, and change at this stage is truly a lonely business. Later, when he knows he can survive them, and is able to look at them without bitching to others or expecting others to fill him up, he can communicate them. When someone discovers that emptiness exists in all members of the nuclear and extended families, strange things happen. He develops an inner peace and a compassion for others. Sensitivities disappear, and events are taken less personally. Emptiness is turned into an asset and there is no longer any need to fill it by using others, or to run from it. When such a person gives of himself, he does so without needing any response or reaction from the other. An emotional climate is created that allows for the freedom of self in the context of a relationship system. That is a marriage.

CHAPTER 19

Family Reaction to Death

Murray Bowen, M.D.

Direct thinking about death, or indirect thinking about staying alive and avoiding death, occupies more of man's time than any other subject. Man is an instinctual animal with the same instinctual awareness of death as the lower forms of life. He follows the same predictable instinctual life pattern of all living things. He is born, he grows to maturity, he reproduces, his life force runs out, and he dies. In addition, he is a thinking animal with a brain that enables him to reason, reflect, and think abstractly. With his intellect he has devised philosophies and beliefs about the meaning of life and death that tend to deny his place in nature's plan. Each individual has to define his own place in the total scheme and accept the fact that he will die and be replaced by succeeding generations. His difficulty in finding a life plan for himself is complicated by the fact that his life is intimately interwoven with the lives about him. This presentation is directed to death as a part of the total family in which he lives.

There are no simple ways to describe man as part of the relationship around him. In another chapter in this volume, I have presented my own way of conceiving of the human as an individual and, also, as part of the emotional-social amalgam in which he lives. According to my theory, a high percentage of human relationship behavior is directed more by automatic instinctual emotional forces than by intellect. Much intellectual activity goes to explain away and justify behavior being directed by the instinctual-emotional-feeling complex. Death is a biological event that terminates a life. No life event can stir more emotionally directed thinking in the individual and more emotional reactiveness in those about him. I have chosen the concept of "open" and "closed" relationship systems as an effective way to describe death as a family phenomenon.

An "open" relationship system is one in which an individual is free to communicate a high percentage of inner thoughts, feelings, and fantasies to another who can reciprocate. No one ever has a completely open relationship with another, but it is a healthy state when a person can have one relationship in which a reasonable degree of openness is possible. A fair percentage of children have a reasonable version of this with a parent. The most open relationship that most people have in their adult lives is in a courtship. After marriage, in the emotional interdependence of living together, each spouse becomes sensitive to subjects that upset the other. They instinctively avoid the sensitive subjects and the relationship shifts toward a more "closed" system. The closed communication system is an automatic emotional reflex to protect self from the anxiety in the other person, though most people say they avoid the taboo subjects to keep from upsetting the other person. If people could follow intellectual knowledge instead of the automatic reflex, and they could gain some control over their own reactiveness to anxiety in the other, they would be able to talk about taboo subjects in spite of the anxiety, and the relationship would move toward a more healthy openness. But people are human, the emotional reactiveness operates like a reflex, and, by the time the average person recognizes the problem, it can be impossible for two spouses to reverse the process themselves. This is the point at which a trained professional can function as a third person to work the magic of family therapy toward opening a closed relationship.

Chief among all taboo subjects is death. A high percentage of people die alone, locked into their own thoughts which they cannot communicate to others. There are at least two processes in operation. One is the intrapsychic process in self which always involves some denial of death. The other is the closed relationship system. People cannot communicate the thoughts they do have, lest they upset the family or others. There are usually at least three closed systems operating around the terminally ill person. One operates within the patient. From experience, every terminally ill patient has some awareness of impending death and a high percentage have an extensive amount of private knowledge they do not communicate to anyone. Another closed system is the family. The family gets its basic information from the physician, which is supplemented by bits of information from other sources and is then amplified, distorted, and re-interpreted in conversations at home. The family has its own carefully planned and edited medical communique for the patient. It is based on the family interpretation of the reports and modified to avoid the patient's reactiveness to anxiety. Other versions of the communique are whispered within the hearing of the patient when the family thinks the patient is sleeping or unconscious. Patients are often alert to whispered communications. The physician and the medical staff have another closed system of communication, supposedly based on medical facts, which is influenced by emotional reactivity to the family and within the staff. Physicians attempt to do factual reports to the family which are distorted by the medical emotionality and the effort to put the correct emphasis on the "bad news" or "good news." The more reactive the physician, the more likely he is to put in medical jargon the family does not hear or to become too simplistic in his efforts to communicate in lay language. The more anxious the physician, the more likely he is to do too much speechmaking and too little listening, and to end up with a vague and distorted message and little awareness of the family misperception of his message. The more anxious the physician, the more the family asks for specific details the physician cannot answer. Physicians commonly reply to specific questions with overgeneralizations that miss the point. The physician has another level of communication to the patient. Even the physician who agrees with the principle of telling the patient "facts" can communicate them with so much anxiety that the patient is responding to the physician instead of the content of what is being said. Problems occur when the closed communication system of medicine meets the age-old closed system between the patient and the family, and anxiety is heightened by the threat of terminal illness.

My clinical experience with death goes back some 30 years to detailed discussions about death with suicidal patients. They were eager to talk to an unbiased listener who did not have to correct their way of thinking. Then I discovered that all seriously ill people, and even those who are not sick, are grateful for an opportunity to talk about death. Over the years I have tried to do such discussions with seriously ill people in my practice, with friends and people I have known socially, and with members of my extended families. I have never seen a terminally ill person who was not strengthened by such a talk. This contradicts former beliefs about the ego being too fragile for this in certain situations. I have even done this with a spectrum of comatose patients. Terminally ill people often permit themselves to slip into coma. A fair percentage can pull themselves out of the coma for important communications. I have had such people come out long enough to talk and express their thanks for the help and immediately slip back. Until the mid-1960's, a majority of physicians were opposed to telling patients they had a terminal illness. In the past decade the prevailing medical dictum about this has changed a great deal, but medical practice has not kept pace with the changed attitude. The poor communications between the physician and the patient, and between the physician and the family, and between the family and the patient are still very much as they were before. The basic problem is an emotional one, and a change in rules does not automatically change the emotional reactivity. The physician can believe he gave factual information to the patient, but in the emotion of the moment, the abruptness and vagueness in the communication, and the emotional process in the patient, the patient failed to "hear." The patient and the family can pretend they have dealt clearly with each other without either being heard through the emotionality. In my family therapy practice within a medical center, I am frequently in contact with both the patient and the family, and to a lesser extent with the physicians. The closed system between the patient and the family is great enough, at best. I believe the poor communication between the physician and the family and between the physician and the patient is the greatest problem. There have been repeated situations in which the physicians thought they were communicating clearly, but the family either misperceived or distorted the messages, and the family thinking would be working itself toward malpractice anger at the physician. In all of these, the surgical and medical procedures were adequate, and the family was reacting to terse, brief speeches by the physician who thought he was communicating adequately. In these, it is fairly easy to do simple interpretations of the physician's statements and avert the malpractice thinking. I believe the trend toward telling patients about incurable illness is one of the healthy changes in medicine, but closed systems do not become open when the surgeon hurriedly blurts out tense speeches about the situation. Experience indicates that physicians and surgeons have either to learn the fundamentals of closed system emotionality in the physician-family-patient triangle, or they might avail themselves of professional expertise in family therapy if they lack the time and motivation to master this for themselves. A clinical example of closed system emotionality will be presented later.

FAMILY EMOTIONAL EQUILIBRIUM AND THE EMOTIONAL SHOCK WAVE

This section will deal with an order of events within the family that is not directly related to open and closed system communications. Death, or threatened death, is only one of many events that can disturb a family. A family unit is in functional equilibrium when it is calm and each member is functioning at reasonable efficiency for that period. The equilibrium of the unit is disturbed by either the addition of a new member or the loss of a member. The intensity of the emotional reaction is governed by the functioning level of emotional integration in the family at the time, or by the functional importance of the one who is added to the family or lost to the family. For instance, the birth of a child can disturb the emotional balance until family members can realign themselves around the child. A grandparent who comes for a visit may shift family emotional forces briefly, but a grandparent who comes to live in a home can change the family emotional balance for a long period. Losses that can disturb the family equilibrium are physical losses, such as a child who goes away to college or an adult child who marries and leaves the home. There are functional losses, such as a key family member who becomes incapacitated with a long-term illness or injury which prevents his doing the work on which the family depends. There are emotional losses, such as the absence of a light-hearted person who can lighten the mood in a family. A group that changes from light-hearted laughter to seriousness becomes a different kind of organism. The length of time required for the family to establish a new emotional equilibrium depends on the emotional integration in the family and the intensity of the disturbance. A well integrated family may show more overt reactiveness at the moment of change but adapt to it rather quickly. A less integrated family may show little reaction at the time and respond later with symptoms of physical illness, emotional illness, or social misbehavior. An attempt to get the family to express feelings at the moment of change does not necessarily increase the level of emotional integration.

The "Emotional Shock Wave" is a network of underground "after shocks" of serious life events that can occur anywhere in the extended family system in the months or years following serious emotional events in a family. It occurs most often after the death or the threatened death of a significant family member, but it can occur following losses of other types. It is not directly related to the usual grief or mourning reactions of people close to the one who died. It operates on an underground network of emotional dependence of family members on each other. The emotional dependence is denied, the serious life events appear to be unrelated, the family attempts to camouflage any connectedness between the events, and there is a vigorous emotional denial reaction, when anyone attempts to relate the events to each other. It occurs most often in families with a significant degree of denied emotional "fusion" in which the families have been able to maintain a fair degree of asymptomatic emotional balance in the family system. The basic family process has been described in another chapter in this volume.

The "Emotional Shock Wave" was first encountered in the author's family research in the late 1950's. It has been mentioned in papers and lectures, but it has not been adequately described in the literature. It was first noticed in the course of multigenerational family research with the discovery that a series of major life events occurred in multiple, separate members of the extended family in the time interval after the serious illness and death of a significant family member. At first, this appeared to be coincidence. Then it was discovered that some version of this phenomenon appeared in a sufficiently high percentage of all families, and a check for the "shock wave" is done routinely in all family histories. The symptoms in a shock wave can be any human problem. Symptoms can include the entire spectrum of physical illness from an increased incidence of colds and respiratory infections to the first appearance of chronic conditions, such as diabetes or allergies to acute medical and surgical illnesses. It is as if the shock wave is the stimulus that can trigger the physical process into activity. The symptoms can also include the full range of emotional symptoms from mild depression, to phobias, to psychotic episodes. The social dysfunctions can include drinking, failures in school or business, abortions and illegitimate births, an increase in accidents, and the full range of behavior disorders. Knowledge of the presence of the shock wave provides the physician or therapist with vital knowledge in treatment. Without such knowledge, the sequence of events is treated as separate, unrelated events.

Some examples of the shock wave will illustrate the process. It occurs most often after the death of a significant family member, but it can be almost as severe after a threatened death. An example was a grandmother in her early 60's who had a radical mastectomy for cancer. Within the following two years, there was a chain of serious reactions in her children and their families. One son began drinking for the first time in his life, the wife of another son had a serious depression, a daughter's husband failed in business, and another daughter's children became involved in automobile accidents and delinquency. Some symptoms were continuing five years later when the grandmother's cancer was pronounced cured. A more common example of the shock wave follows the death of an important grandparent, with symptoms appearing in a spectrum of children and grandchildren. The grandchild is often one who had little direct emotional attachment to the grandparents. An example might be the death of a grandmother, a daughter who appeared to have no more than the usual grief reaction to the death but who reacted in some deep way, and who transmitted her disturbance to a son who had never been close to the grandmother but who reacted to the mother with delinquency behavior. The family so camouflages the connectedness of these events that family members will further camouflage the sequence of events if they become aware the therapist is seeking some connectedness. Families are extremely reactive to any effort to approach the denial directly. There was a son in his mid-30's who made a plane trip to see his mother who had had a stroke and who was aphasic. Before that time, his wife and children were leading an orderly life, and his business was going well. His effort to communicate with his mother, who could not speak, was a trying experience. Enroute home on the plane, he met a young woman with whom he began the first extramarital affair in his life. During the subsequent two years, he began living a double life, his business was failing, and his children began doing poorly in school. He made a good start in family therapy which continued for six sessions when I made a premature connection between his mother's stroke and the affair. He cancelled the subsequent appointment and never returned. The nature of the human phenomenon is such that it reacts vigorously to any such implications of the dependence of one life on another. Other families are less reactive and they can be more interested in the phenomenon than reactive to it. I have seen only one family who had made an automatic connection between such events before seeking therapy. This was a father who said, "My family was calm and healthy until two years ago when my daughter was married. Since then, it has been one trouble after another, and the doctor bills have become exorbitant. My wife had a gall bladder operation. After that, she found something wrong with each house where we lived. We have broken three leases and moved four times. Then she developed a back problem and had a spinal fusion. My son had been a good student before my daughter married. Last year, his school work went down and this year he dropped out of college. In the midst of this, I had a heart attack." I would see this as a family with tenuously balanced emotional equilibrium in which the mother's functioning was dependent on her relationship with the daughter. Most of the subsequent dysfunction was in the mother, but the son and father were sufficiently dependent on the mother that they too developed symptoms. The incidence of the emotional shock wave is sufficiently prevalent that the Georgetown Family Section does a routine historical check for it in every family history.

Knowledge of the emotional shock wave is important in dealing with families on death issues. Not all deaths have the same importance to a family. There are some in which there is a fair chance the death will be followed by a shock wave. Other deaths are more neutral and are usually followed by no more than the usual grief and mourning reactions. Other deaths are a relief to the family and are usually followed by a period of better functioning. If the therapist can know ahead of time about the possibility of an emotional shock wave, he can take some steps toward its prevention. Among the deaths most likely to be followed by a serious and prolonged shock wave are the deaths of either parent when the family is young. This not only disturbs the emotional equilibrium, but it removes the function of the breadwinner or the mother at a time when these functions are most important. The death of an important child can shake the family equilibrium for years. The death of the "head of the clan" is another that can be followed by a long-term underground disturbance. It can be a grandfather who may have been partially disabled but who continued some kind of decision making function in family affairs. The grandmothers in these families usually lived in the shadow of their husbands, and their deaths were less important. The family reaction can be intense following the death of a grandmother who was a central figure in the emotional life and stability of the family. The "head of the clan" can also be the most important sibling in the present generation. There is another group of family members whose deaths may result in no more than the usual period of grief and mourning. They may have been well liked, but they played peripheral roles in family affairs. They are the neutral ones who were neither "famous nor infamous." Their deaths are not likely to influence future family functioning. Finally, there are the family members whose deaths are a relief to the family. This includes the people whose functioning was never critical to the family, and who may have been a burden in their final illness. Their deaths may be

followed by a brief period of grief and mourning, which is then followed by
improved family functioning. A shock wave rarely follows the death of a
dysfunctional family member unless that dysfunction played a critical role
in maintaining family emotional equilibrium. Suicides are commonly followed by prolonged grief and mourning reactions, but the shock wave is
usually minor unless the suicide was an abdication of an essential functional
role.

THERAPY AT THE TIME OF DEATH

Knowledge of the total family configuration, the functioning position of
the dying person in the family, and the overall level of life adaptation are
important for anyone who attempts to help a family before, during, or after
a death. To attempt to treat all deaths as the same can miss the mark. Some
well functioning families are able to adapt to approaching death before it
occurs. To assume that such families need help can be an inept intrusion.
Physicians and hospitals have left much of the problems about death to
chaplains and ministers with the expectation they know what to do. There
are exceptional clergymen who intuitively know what to do. However,
many young chaplains or clergymen tend to treat all death as the same.
They operate with their theology, a theory about death that does not go
beyond the familiar concepts of grief and mourning, and they tend to aim
their help at the overt expression of grief. This may provide superficial help
to a majority of people, but it misses the deeper process. The popular notion
that expression of grief through crying may be helpful to most complicates
the situation for others. It is important for the physician or therapist to
know the situation, to have his own emotional life under reasonable control
without the use of too much denial, or other extreme mechanisms, and to
respect the denial that operates in the family. In my work with families, I
carefully use direct words, such as death, die, and bury, and I carefully
avoid the use of less direct words, such as passed on, deceased, and expired.
A direct word signals to the other that I am comfortable with the subject,
and it enables others to also be comfortable. A tangential word may appear
to soften the fact of death; but it invites the family to respond with tangential words, and the conversation soon reaches the point that one wonders
if we are talking about death at all. The use of direct words helps to open
a closed emotional system. I believe it provides a different dimension in
helping the family to be comfortable within themselves.

The following is a clinical example that illustrates an effort to open the
communication with a terminally ill patient, her family, and the medical
staff. As a visiting professor in another medical center, I was scheduled to

do a demonstration interview with the parents of an emotionally disturbed daughter. Enroute to the interview room, I learned the mother had a terminal cancer, that the surgeon had told the father, and the father had told the family therapist, but that the mother did not know about it. In my own practice, it would have been automatic to discuss this issue with the family, but I was reluctant to take this course when follow-up interviews would not be possible. A large group of professional people and trainees observed the interview. I elected to avoid the critical issue. The beginning of the interview was awkward, difficult, and sticky. I decided the cancer issue had to be discussed. About ten minutes out, I asked the mother why she thought her surgeon, her family, and the others had not told her about her cancer. Without the slightest hesitation, she said she thought they were afraid to tell her. She calmly said, "I know I have cancer. I have known it for sometime. Before that, I was afraid of it, but they told me it was not cancer. I believed them for a time, thinking it was my imagination. Now I know it is cancer. When I ask them and they say "No," what does it mean? It either means they are liars or I am crazy, and I know I am not crazy." Then she went into detail about her feelings, with some moderate tears, but with full control of herself. She said that she was not afraid to die for herself, but she would like to live long enough to see the daughter have a life for herself. She hated the responsibility of leaving the daughter the responsibility of the father. She spoke with deep feeling but few tears. She and I were the calmest people in the room. Her therapist wiped away tears. The father reacted by joking and kidding about the mother's vivid imagination. To prevent his reaction from silencing her, I made a few comments to suggest he not interfere with his wife's serious thoughts. She was able to continue, "This is the loneliest life in the world. Here I am, knowing I am going to die, and not knowing how much time I have left. I can't talk to anyone. When I talk to my surgeon, he says it is not a cancer. When I try to talk to my husband, he makes jokes about it. I come here to talk about my daughter and not about myself. I am cut off from everyone. When I get up in the morning, I feel terrible. I look at my eyes in the mirror to see if they are jaundiced and the cancer has spread to my liver. I try to act cheerful until my husband goes to work, because I don't want to upset him. Then I am alone all day with my thoughts, just crying and thinking. Before my husband returns from work, I try to pull myself together for his sake. I wish I could die soon and not have to pretend any longer." Then she went into some background thoughts about death. As a little girl she felt hurt when people walked on graves. She had always wished she could be buried above ground in a mausoleum, so people would not walk on her grave. "But," she said, "we are poor people. We can't afford a mausoleum. When I die, I will be buried in a grave just like everyone else." The technical problem in this single interview was to permit the mother to talk, to keep the father's anxiety from silencing her, and to hope the regular therapist could continue the process later. It is impossible to do much toward opening an emotionally closed relationship of this intensity in a single session, although the father said he would try to listen and understand. The patient was relieved to be partially out of the closed system in which she had lived. The therapist said she had known about the cancer but had been waiting for the mother to bring it up. This is a common posture for mental health professionals. The therapist's own emotionality had prevented the wife from talking. At the end of the interview, the mother said, smiling through her tears, "We have sure spent an hour walking around on my grave, haven't we?" As I said goodbye to them in the hall, the mother said, "When you go home tonight, thank Washington for sending you here today." The less expressive father said, "We are both grateful." There were a few minutes with the audience who had observed the interview. Part of the group had been moved to tears, most were silent and serious, and a few were critical. The criticism was expressed by a young physician who spoke of hurting the wife and having taken away her hope. I was pleased at having decided to take up this issue in this single demonstration interview. Enroute home, my thoughts went to the differences in audience response and the problems of training young professional people to contain their own emotionality sufficiently to become more objective about death. I guessed it would be easier to train those who cried than those who intellectualized their feelings. This is an example of a good result in a single session. It illustrates the intensity of a closed relationship system between the patient, the family, and the medical staff.

THE FUNCTION OF FUNERALS

Some 25 years ago, I had a clinical experience that illustrates the central point of the next section of this chapter. A young woman began psychoanalysis with, "Let me bury my mother before we go to other things." Her mother had been dead six years. She cried for weeks. At that time, I was practicing within the framework of transference and intrapsychic dynamics. The patient's statement was used later as a way of describing systems theory about the unresolved emotional attachments between people that remain viable for life, that attach to significant future relationships, and that continue to direct the course of a life. There is a way to utilize the funeral to more completely "bury the dead at the time of death." Few human events provide as much emotional impact as serious illness and death in resolving unresolved emotional attachments.

The funeral ritual has existed in some form since man became a civilized being. I believe it serves a common function of bringing survivors into intimate contact with the dead and with important friends, and it helps survivors and friends to terminate their relationship with the dead and to move forward with life. I think the best function of a funeral is served when it brings relatives and friends into the best possible functional contact with the harsh fact of death and with each other at this time of high emotionality. I believe funerals were probably more effective when people died at home with the family present, and when family and friends made the coffin and did the burial themselves. Society no longer permits this, but there are ways to bring about a reasonable level of personal contact with the dead body and the survivors.

There are numerous present-day funeral customs that function to deny death and to perpetuate the unresolved emotional attachments between the dead and the living. It is most intense in people who are anxious about death and who use the present form and content of funerals to avoid the anxiety. There are those who refuse to look at a dead body because, "I want to remember them as I knew them." There is the anxious segment of society that refers to funerals as pagan rituals. Funeral custom makes it possible for the body to be disposed of from the hospital without the family ever having personal contact with it. Children are commonly excluded from funerals to avoid upsetting them. This can result in a lifetime of unrealistic and distorted fantasies and images that may never be corrected. The private funeral is another custom that avoids the emotionality of death. It is motivated by family anxiety to avoid contact with emotionality in others. It prevents the friendship system an opportunity to terminate their relationship with the dead, and it deprives the family of the supportive relationships from friends.

I believe that professional support to a family at the time of death can help the family members toward a more helpful funeral than would be possible if they listened to advice from anxious relatives and friends. In 20 years of family practice, I have had contact with several thousand families, and I have been in the background "coaching" families through hundreds of deaths and funerals. I urge family members to visit dying family members whenever possible and to find some way to include children if the situation permits. I have never seen a child hurt by exposure to death. They are "hurt" only by the anxiety of survivors. I encourage involvement of the largest possible group of extended family members, an open casket, and the most personal contact that is possible between the dead and the.living, prompt obituary notices, and the notification of relatives and friends, a public funeral with the body present, and the most personal funeral service that is possible. Some funeral services are highly ritualized but it is possible to personalize even the most ritualized service. The goal is to bring the entire family system into the closest possible contact with death in the presence of the total friendship system and to lend a helping hand to the anxious people who would rather run than face a funeral.

The following is an example of coaching friends from the background. It involved neighbors rather than people in my professional practice. The young parents in their early thirties and their three children ages ten, eight, and five, had come to live with her widowed mother in preparation for the husband's going overseas on a prolonged assignment. On a Sunday one month before his scheduled departure, the young mother died suddenly of a heart attack. The entire community was shocked. That evening, I spent some three hours with the father. He and the wife had been very close. He had dozens of questions about how to handle the present emergency, the funeral, the future of the children, and his own life. He wondered if the children should go to school the next day, what he should tell the teachers, and if he should seek release from his overseas work. In the afternoon, he had tried to tell the children about the mother's death, but he started to cry and the children responded, "Please don't cry, Daddy." He said he simply had to have another mother for the children, but he felt guilty saying this only eight hours after his wife had died. During the visit, I outlined what I would consider to be the ideal course of action for him. I suggested he take as many of the ideas as were consistent with himself, and if they made sense to him, to use them as far as he could go. I suggested that the ability of children to deal with death depends on the adults, and the future would be best served if the death could be presented in terms the children could understand and they could be realistically involved in the funeral. I warned him of adverse emotional reactions of friends and to be prepared for criticism if he decided to involve the children. In the first hours after the death, the children had been responding to his emotionality rather than to the fact of the mother's death. In this kind of a situation, it is common for the children to stop talking and deny the death. I suggested that he get through this block by mentioning the death at frequent intervals during the coming days, and, if he started to cry, to reassure the children that he was all right and not to worry about him. I wanted to keep the channel open for any and all questions they might have. I suggested that the children decide whether or not they wished to go to school the next day. On the issue of involving the children with the dead mother, I suggested that he arrange a time before the funeral to take the children to the funeral home, to remove all other people from the room, and for him and the children to have a private session with their dead mother. I reasoned that this would help the children adapt to the reality of the mother's death, and that it could work if anxious members of the extended family were excluded. On Tuesday evening, I spent an hour in the bedroom, with the father in a chair and the three children in his lap. He could cry, and they could cry, and the children were free to ask questions. He told them about the plan to go to the funeral home the following afternoon. The five-year-old son asked if he could kiss mommie. The father looked to me for an answer. I suggested that would be between the son and his mother. Later, in the living room, I announced to the relatives and friends that the father would take the children to the funeral home the next afternoon, that it was to be private, and that no one else could be present. Privately, I considered it unwise to expose the children to the emotionality in that family. The father's mother said, "Son, that will be too hard on you." The father replied, "Mother, shut up. I can do it." On Wednesday evening, I visited the funeral home. The entire family-friendship system was present. The maternal grandmother, who had been calm through these days, said, "Thank you very much for your help." The father did a detailed account of the children's visit in the afternoon. The children went up to the casket and felt their mother. The five-year-old son said, "If I kissed her, she could not kiss back." All three spent some time inspecting everything, even looking under the casket. The eight-year-old son got under the casket and prayed that his mother could hold him in her arms again in heaven. Some family friends came while the father and children were in the room. The father and children withdrew to the lobby while the friends went into the room. In the lobby, the youngest son found some polished pebbles in a planter. He was the one who found objects to give his mother as "presents." He took a small pebble into the room and placed it in his mother's hand. The other children also got pebbles and put them into their mother's hand. Then they announced, "We can go now, Daddy." The father was much relieved at the outcome of the visit. He said, "A thousand tons were lifted from this family today." The following day I attended the funeral. The children did well. The ten-year-old daughter and eight-year-old son were calm. During the service, the eight-year-old whispered to the father, "Daddy, I sure am going to miss Mommie." The five-year-old clung to the father with some tearfulness.

There was some criticism about the father involving the children in the funeral, but he did well with it and the criticism turned to admiration after the funeral home visit. I was in close contact with the family the following year. The father continued to mention the mother's death. Within a week. the children were talking about the mother in the past tense. The children stayed with their grandmother. There were none of the usual complications usually seen after a death of this kind. The father took an assignment closer home, so he could return if he was needed. The following year, the father remarried and took the children with him and his new wife to another city. It has now been 12 years since the death and the family adjustment has been perfect. I am still in periodic contact with the family, which now includes three grown children from the first marriage and younger children from the second marriage. Some years after the death, the father wrote his version of the experience when the first wife died, entitled, "My God, My Wife Is Dead." He described his initial shock, his efforts to get beyond self-pity, his resolution to make his own decisions when anxiety was high, and the emotional courage that went into his plan in the critical days before the funeral and burial. This illustrates what I would consider an optimum result from a traumatic death that could have had lifelong sequelae; but this father had more inner strength than any other relative I have seen under stress of this intensity.

SUMMARY

Family systems theory provides a broader perspective of death than is possible with conventional psychiatric theory, which focuses on death as a process within the individual. The first part of this chapter deals with the closed relationship system between the patient, the family, and physicians, and family therapy methods that have been helpful in overcoming some of the anxiety that creates the closed system communication. The second section deals with the "Emotional Shock Wave" that is present to some degree in a significant percentage of families. Knowledge of this, which is the direct result of family research, provides the professional person with a different dimension for understanding emotional interdependence and the long-term complications of death in a family. The final section deals with the emotional impact of funerals and ways the professional person can help surviving relatives to achieve a better level of emotional functioning by calmly facing the anxiety of death.

Section C

THERAPY

CHAPTER 20

Brief Therapy with Couples Groups

Peggy Papp, M.S.W.

This is a description of a brief therapy format for a couples group that is designed to produce accelerated change through planned strategy. The change begins in the session and is carried over into daily living through tasks. By *accelerated change* is meant an immediate change in behavior in relation to a spouse. A prescription for the change is given by the therapist, aimed at reversing the self-defeating, repetitive transactional pattern between the couple.

The conceptual framework for this therapy is based on the following premises:

1. People change by acting differently. An emotional system responds to action, not interpretation.

2. Change can be immediate. Although the reverberations and assimilation of change takes place over time, change can take place immediately.

3. Results of immediate change can be as long lasting as those of gradual change. They are self-reinforcing, and amplify themselves over time.

4. The rate of change is related to the therapist's expectations. The therapist's belief that immediate change is possible and desirable influences the rate of change.

Brief therapy, by its very nature, must be highly structured, intensely focused, and directive. It is a therapy of precision; its goals are limited to isolating and intervening in the presenting problem. The format itself becomes a vital element in influencing the process of change. The format for the couples group is designed to produce change through the use of an artifice. The artifice alters the form of the problem by changing the system from the outside. The form that problems take becomes rigidified through repetition, and they are inaccessible to change as long as they remain in their predictable form. Through the use of artifice the problems are cast into a new and more flexible form which renders them accessible to change. The problem changes as the form changes.

Three techniques are used as artifices for changing the form of the problem. They are family choreography (a derivative of family sculpturing); prescribed tasks; and a group setting. They are combined in such a way as to compel the couples to define their problems differently, relate to one another differently, and conceive of change differently. The choreography redefines the problems symbolically through the use of metaphors in action; the tasks carry the redefinition pragmatically into daily living; and the group setting sustains and amplifies the redefining process. A new experience is thus structured into the lives of the couple from outside the world of their perceived reality. It is orchestrated by the therapist, based on his knowledge of the interlocking system which keeps the problem constant.

When a couple comes for therapy, they seldom have a clear idea of what the problem is between them. Because marital relationships are extremely complex, the basic conflict is usually buried under a morass of irrelevant details, accusations, projections, denials, defensiveness, and vague statements such as "We don't communicate." Often this is expressed through trivial arguments such as who should close the garage door. Choreography quickly penetrates confusing verbiage by changing the medium of communication from words to space, movement, time, and physical positioning. Robbed of their familiar verbal cues the couple is compelled to define their relationship differently, using new images and associations. The true nature of a relationship can be seen only in terms of movement as it is always in flux. Its reality lies in action. Language, being linear, is limited to description capable of expressing only one thought at a time followed by another in a straight line. Choreography, being multi-dimensional, is capable of picturing relationships spatially, physically outlining the vital sequence of behavior which keeps the problem perpetually in motion. In order to eliminate the superficial details in which this sequence is embedded, the relationship is choreographed metaphorically rather than literally. As in dreams and poetry, metaphors abstract the essence of everyday events and distill them into simple and eloquent images.

In an attempt to tap into this poetic precision of dreams, the following procedure is utilized. During the first session the couples are asked to close their eyes and have a dream about their partner—not a dream from the past, which would confuse the issue, but a conscious dream from the here and now. They are then asked to see their spouse in whatever form he or she would take in a dream, to see themselves in whatever form they would take in relation to the form of the spouse, and to visualize how he or she would move in relation to the other. This is actually a controlled fantasy rather than a dream; however, the word *dream* is used because of its symbolic connotations. Asking the couples to visualize their own form and movement in relation to that of their spouse assures that the dream will be systemic rather than individualistic. As the forms move toward one another in larger than life images, the circularity of their predicament is caricatured. The contradiction in the predicament is condensed and magnified into a parody of their relationship. This parody is the focus of change.

The tasks used are based on perceiving the contradiction in the parody, and counteracting this by reversing or exaggerating the contradiction. It is the contradictory aspect of the predicament which keeps it forever a predicament. The-more-he-does-this-the-more-she-does-that-and-the-more-she-does-that-the-more-he-does-this syndrome is interrupted by prescribing complementary actions that reverse the syndrome. The new process which is set in motion creates a new experience and consequently changes the shape of the problem.

After the first session in which the relationships are choreographed, the couples are divided into husbands and wives groups which meet separately for the purpose of assigning tasks without the knowledge of the other spouse. This creates an element of surprise, an invaluable asset in bringing about change. The tasks are timed and coordinated to set change in motion on several different levels simultaneously. While each partner is changing his own behavior through the tasks, he is also reacting spontaneously to the change in his partner's behavior, and at the same time speculating on the source of change which is taking place. Is it being prescribed by the therapist, initiated by the partner, or is he himself creating it? An atmosphere of curiosity, humor, and intrigue replaces the grim determination and hopelessness which had previously surrounded the problem. The terms of the struggle are changed.

The tasks are presented in such a way as to stimulate the imagination and encourage the fantasy and playfulness of each partner. The use of the idiosyncratic resourcefulness of each person is considered of prime importance and is carefully cultivated.

Conceiving and giving tasks requires great skill on the part of the therapist. If the task is not aimed at changing the basic contradiction in the relationship, it is superficial and will reap superficial results. Changing the contradiction in the relationship usually involves changing each person's goal in some way and mobilizing him to move in a counter direction. As this is bound to upset the homeostasis of the relationship, it must be made palatable and is usually better done indirectly. The failure to follow through on tasks may be due to the therapist's failure to make the tasks seem fruitful and appealing. On the other hand, the task may be executed well but will have little effect if it has been aimed at a side issue rather than the central conflict. One of the major benefits of tasks is that they are concrete. They put the tools for change into a person's hands and give him a sense of accomplishment and purpose. When a couple come for therapy, although they may not want to change themselves, they want desperately to change their situation. Too often they are not shown how by the therapist, who then blames the lack of progress onto their resistance.

A group setting is used to dramatize the process of change. There is a theatrical power in a group that, when properly channeled, propels people in a new direction. Everything that happens in a group happens before an audience. This audience has expectations that are nearly always in the direction of change. These expectations heighten awareness and influence all of the proceedings. Since the choreography and tasks require shifting conventional thinking, the group is used to create an atmosphere of challenge and experimentation. Group interaction is kept focused on the marital relationships, even when husbands and wives meet in separate groups. Group feedback is confined to a discussion of formulating and carrying out the tasks. Relationships between unrelated group members are not allowed to become confrontational or interpretive, as this will interfere with taking action.

The criterion for inclusion in a couples group is solely that the presenting problem is a marital problem rather than one focused around a child. The couples meet for twelve sessions, four couples to a group. The first session is devoted to choreographing their relationships. They are then divided into separate husbands and wives groups in order to assign each a task without the knowledge of the other spouse, since surprise and unexpectedness are important elements in change. Periodically, the couples are brought together for a joint session when the therapist feels the need to test her speculations regarding the effect of the task on their relationship. The final session is used to summarize their experience and suggest directions for the future.

The following discussion illustrates how the choreography, tasks and group process are integrated. A wife saw her husband as King Kong and herself as Fay Wray in her dream. She portrayed herself as being totally within his power. "He is holding me in the palm of his hand and carrying me to the top of the Empire State building. If he dies I go with him, as he won't let me go." She was then asked to choreograph the ways in which she had tried to cope with her predicament. She had tried to fight him physically, throw dishes at him, argue at him, hide from him, leave him— all of which incited him to clutch her more desperately.

The husband, in his dream, also saw himself as an ape—but an impotent ape. "I see myself as this huge hulking ape. The bizarre thing is the ape is helpless. It's a dark street and I see her on the ground, but when I try to lift her up she fights me. It's a total feeling of frustration in not being able to communicate with her." He was then asked to enact the various ways he had tried to rescue her: standing her on her feet, shaking her, embracing her, pushing her away—all of which spurred her efforts to escape. The more he tried to rescue her, the more she tried to escape; and the more she tried to escape, the more he tried to rescue her. Enacting the problem and the solution in sequence telescoped time, and outlined the circularity of the interaction. To break this cycle, each would have to move in a different direction. This meant changing goals.

The couple was then asked to try a different solution to their dilemma in terms of position and movement. This is how choreography provides a way in which to experiment with various alternatives. Although a person can seldom see the way out of a dilemma by himself, his attempts do give the therapist a better understanding of his coping style. In this case, the husband, instead of approaching his wife aggressively, knelt by her side and indicated his willingness to try a more equal approach: "Working on the same level, maybe we can get it together." This was seen by the therapist as only a half solution. Although he was giving up his King Kong position, he was still moving toward her preoccupied with lifting her up. His method had changed, but his goal remained the same. Reversal here would mean a change in the established goal. This was done through the task prescribed in the husband's group.

After replaying the tape of the choreography, which re-emphasized the futility of his actions, a discussion followed as to the exact manner in which this was carried out in everyday life. He maintained his King Kong position in the home by constantly giving his wife advice about how to run her life. This was intended to be helpful and constructive advice; but when she refused to follow it, he became critical and flew into a rage. Discussion centered around his changing his goal from rescuing her to leaving her on the ground and walking away. It was suggested he do this by having no answers to her problem, and that whenever he was tempted to give her advice about how to run her life, he was to ask her for advice about how to run his life instead. He responded to this with a burst of laughter. A reversal always seems absurd, as it changes the premise under which one is operating, "You mean—you mean, *I* should ask *her* how to run *my* life?" was his incredulous and humorous response. The very absurdity of the task helped to create a spirit of curiosity and intrigue, which is essential in attempting the difficult business of changing one's course of behavior. The other members of the group who were not caught up in this particular emotional system immediately saw the paradoxical logic behind the task, and became supportive and challenging. An atmosphere of camaraderie and competition developed, which helped to propel the husband into action.

Discussing the difficulties and pitfalls that can occur in the execution of a task is essential. It acknowledges the strength of the system, and provides an opportunity for rehearsing a change in a protected setting. The first thought that occurred to the husband was that his wife would give him bad advice, and he would end up giving her advice about her advice. As absurdity upon absurdity unfolded, he began to see the ludicrousness of his advice-giving position.

The tasks of husband and wife were coordinated and complementary, to match their complementary metaphors. While the husband was being helped to back up and give his wife more room, the wife was being helped to move toward her husband in a new way. It was suggested she change her stance from one of resisting his help to one of soliciting it. She was to keep asking him for his advice until he got tired of giving it to her. This moved both husband and wife in counter directions, and broke the repetitious, predictable cycle of reactivity between them. It created a new pattern of interaction full of surprises, new negotiations, and unexpected consequences. Since neither was able to do a complete about-turn, they met in a more balanced ground in the middle.

Besides breaking a circuit of interaction, a reversal produces a new experience through role change. It is impossible to act differently without experiencing something different. The husband described his experience as follows. "I saw her doing something wrong, and I started to get uptight inside and wanted to correct her. Instead, I stopped myself and just mechanically—it was very mechanical at first—told her about a problem I was having at work and asked her advice. Her advice wasn't bad, wasn't great, but wasn't bad; but then she said, "No matter what decision you make, I know you will do the right thing," and that made me feel great. She's never said anything like that to me before. After that I didn't feel the need to correct her." Only by moving forward can one look back on where one has been. If one never moves from one's position, one can never gain perspective.

The metaphors provided a road into the private world of the individual, and permitted solutions to be posed in the couples' own language. The metaphors were used in various ways; for example, after the wife's first task, her metaphor was used to further release her from her helpless victim position. Since she posed as her life's predicament, "How to live with King Kong?" the question was taken seriously. How do you go about living with King Kong? Do you fight him? Since she weighed 98 pounds and he weighed 190, this did not seem profitable. Do you hide from him? He'll always find you. Do you try and argue with him? He'll always win. The suggestion was then made that it is only when you are in the position of a tamer that you can hold your own with a beast. Had she ever thought of trying to tame him? She burst out laughing. It was a new idea, but she thought she might try it. As a matter of fact, she did know how to make him melt. She was instructed not to tell the group how she did this, but to go home and try out different ways during the week. Since there were probably thousands and thousands of women across the country who lived with King Kongs and had no idea how to handle them, she was instructed to write down all her ideas in case she ever decided to write a book on *How to Live with King Kong*. She was instructed to try three different ways of taming him she had never thought of before—ways that the therapist would not have thought of. This put her in a position of authority, not only with her husband and other wives, but also with the therapist.

Reversals do not work with couples in which one or both of the partners is covertly resistant to therapy, as they depend on conscious cooperation with the therapist. A paradoxical injunction is the most effective way of dealing with resistance, as it is based on a person's not being aware of the process of change. In one case, a reversal boomeranged because of the wife's covert resistance, which the therapist had failed to clearly calculate. In this couple, the husband was a dry alcoholic. In a first evaluation interview, before being placed in a couples group, the wife had launched a bitter attack on her husband for all the suffering his drinking had caused over the years, making him responsible for all her difficulties, including her high blood pressure and migraine headaches. The husband sat looking properly contrite, and pleading guilty for the sake of the therapist.

In their choreography, the husband placed himself kneeling on the ground praying to his wife, who was positioned as an angel, wings spread, wearing a beautiful white flowing gown—all knowing, all powerful, always right. She then became Mother Nature, pointing her finger at him accusingly, and turning him into a "helpless little boy intimidated by her anger." "You don't fuck around with Mother Nature." He meant this literally, as they hadn't had sex for nearly a year. The wife placed her husband on the floor, folded over like a clam. She then went through a series of frustrating attempts to open him up, all of which served to close him tighter. The choreography in and of itself had a powerful effect on this couple. The husband reported in the next session: "Somehow the relationship got defused by the session last week. I had a very powerful reaction to the session—in ways I cannot describe.

"I don't know what there was about it, because I think that if my wife had given me a multiple choice about what I was going to be, and a clam was among a few things, I would have said 'She is going to make me a clam.' That didn't surprise me. I think this angel thing coming through to her was something new. She has had a difficult time dealing with that, so we both —I ended up feeling nothing going home, she cried all the way home, and then I really felt frightened. The next day I was hypermanic and I didn't know it until a colleague of mine told me; and then I said, you know, "That session must have just scared the shit out of me." And yet I can't tell you what it was, but when I get scared I—I tend to approach my wife more, and I told her how frightened I was, so I think that the relationship changed, and that it wasn't all anger but it got more volatile in ways, so that there was lovemaking and fights, and it was really—yeah—and instead of being in a horror house the whole time, we were on the roller coaster, and it went through the horror house and it went through the tunnel of love. You know, it was really bananas, but I liked it a helluva lot better."

It sometimes happens that simply dramatizing relationships through the choreography causes a temporary reversal of positions—Mother Nature became helpless and cried all the way home, the clam became manicky. Tasks were used to solidify this change. To continue the opening up of the clam, the husband was instructed, among other things, to surprise his wife with three unexpected expressions of feeling during the coming week—any kind, as long as they surprised her. This gave him control over his actions and her reactions. One of the ways he chose to accomplish this task was to ask her to accompany him on a professional trip by telling her how much he needed her to be with him, how anxious he felt about giving his lecture, and how comforting it would be to have her there. This was indeed a surprise to the wife, who was usually invited to go with a curt, "Are you coming?" Although they experienced some tensions and problems on their trip, both reported it was the best time they had had together. They had sex for the first time in eleven months. He chose to handle his fear of her anger by embracing her when she exploded, rather than withdrawing. She reacted to this with a mixture of consternation, humor, and pleasure.

The wife had been shaken by her husband's image of her as the angel, or, as she put it, "Mrs. Right." In order to get her off her pedestal, she was advised to become "Mrs. Wrong," to find ways of becoming helpless and bumbling, and to ask her husband for help. However, her unresolved bitterness got mixed up in this, and she used her tasks as a means of getting back at her husband—burning his dinner, and scorching his shirts. When the husband reported positive changes in a joint session, she negated these by saying that they wouldn't last, and she didn't trust him. The therapist then realized that the wife resented her husband's looking good, and could not give him any credit for any change in their relationship. It then became clear that neither husband nor therapist could succeed until her bitterness over past issues had been dealt with. Rather than attempting to counteract her bitterness, the decision was made to give it credence.

A ritual was devised aimed at alleviating both her bitterness and his guilt. The husband was to perform an act of penance to expiate himself from his past sins. It was explained that this was necessary in order for him to be relieved of his guilt, and for her to be able to forgive him. The wife was to choose the penance. She requested her husband take over the handling of the family finances, a job which he loathed and had left entirely to her, to her eternal resentment. Their equation for rigidifying their Mrs. Right-Mr. Wrong position was that he would spend with abandon, she would try to balance the checkbook, and then they would end up fighting.

During the first week that the husband took over the accounts, the wife broke down in tears as she observed him under a pile of bills struggling with a mountain of figures. She offered to relent, but he refused. During the next session she said she felt that he had had enough, as after all he knew nothing about accounts and figures. The therapist then asked the wife if she felt his suffering was equal to hers, she agreed it was not, and the husband was instructed to continue. A homeostatic tendency always goes hand in hand with a desire for change. Although both husband and wife were obviously accruing some emotional gratification from their Mrs. Right/Mr. Wrong equation, they were also extremely uncomfortable with the consequences. In being compelled to experience something different, they finally opted for change. The wife began to realize that she was greatly relieved at having this burden removed. The husband experienced a feeling of competence and took pleasure in having robbed his wife of a weapon.

The co-ordination of the therapeutic move requires that the therapist be aware of the other-side-of-the-coin phenomenon. Each spouse has within him the potential of his partner's stance. The more extreme, the greater the potential. As Jung has described the phenomenon, "Every psychological extreme secretly contains its own opposite, or stands in some sort of intimate and essential relationship to it." In activating these opposites through countermoves, the therapist must be able to predict them and balance them. In another case, the couples' presented problem centered around sex. The wife described her husband as a sex maniac; she felt constantly pressured by him, and had consequently lost all sexual desire. The husband, on the other hand, described his wife as a "little girl, not a woman," and declared that he did not want to go through life with a wife who could not respond to him sexually. All his efforts through their six years of marriage to turn her on were to no avail. The husband had been in individual therapy; he understood that sex was related to his self-esteem, and was somewhat of an obsession, but this did not deter him. They had also been seen in couples therapy for a year. Their relationship had improved in other ways, but their sexual problem remained unchanged. Both felt pessimistic about ever resolving it. The wife felt that her husband, while obsessed with sex, did not care about affection or closeness which for her were prerequisites of sex. She loved to caress and be caressed; but this only aroused her husband, who became frustrated and angry if sex did not follow.

In her choreographing, the wife saw herself in a beautiful landscape. She was cold and wanted to get warm. Her husband looked like a horse. She wanted to ride the horse to explore the countryside and warm herself up, but every time she tried to mount him, he turned into a mule and either kicked her or bucked. The husband saw his wife as a cactus plant with a beautiful, perfumed flower at the center. He kept trying to reach the flower, but the prickly spears kept him away. No matter how he approached the plant, the spears stuck him.

The first task given to the husband aimed at interrupting his cycle of stung pursuer. This needed to be done in a special way. In the past he had tried not pursuing his wife, but had done so by withdrawing into angry silence, waiting and watching for her to approach him. When she didn't, he grew more angry than ever. The husband was told that his situation was extremely difficult, if not impossible, and that therefore his task would be difficult if not impossible to accomplish. He assured the therapist that he would try anything, since nothing else had worked so far. He was then instructed to satisfy his wife's desire for fondling by inundating her with caresses to the point where she asked him to stop. He was never to follow through with sexual intercourse, and if she requested it, he was to gently refuse by saying he didn't feel like it. As usual this brought forth a burst of laughter, followed by an incredulous, *"I'm* to tell *her* I don't feel like it?"* A response of humor is the best indication that a task will be done successfully, as it suggests an ability to become playful with a grim problem.

The first step with the wife was to extricate her from her rebellious pupil role, in which she felt inadequate, defensive, and resentful, and give her a better sense of control over her situation. She was asked if she had ever taught her husband how to make love to her. She replied with astonishment "What could I teach him?" It was explained to her that the reason her husband had never been able to turn her on was because he obviously did not know how, and she needed to teach him. Since every woman has unique sexual responses, her husband needed to know what hers were before he could do anything about them. Her choreography had indicated she wished to explore a lush landscape. What kind of landscape would she choose as a setting for love? A beach? A bedroom? Would she like to be surrounded with flowers, perfume, music, candlelight? She had no idea, she had never thought about it. Her first task was simply to think about it all week, and come back with a picture of her ideal setting for love.

At the next session, she reported she had been unable to think of anything, so she had asked her husband how he would treat a mistress. He told her he would send her flowers, take her to dine at the Plaza, order champagne, and shower her with lavish compliments. She then told him that that's what she would like him to do for her—which he proceeded to do. She was still wary of having sex, but felt more and more warmth and closeness toward him as he continued to be "loving and kind." She found herself becoming more aggressive with him in other than sexual ways. She began teaching him to play the guitar, from which she derived unexpected satisfaction. "I never thought I could teach him anything."

The husband, in the meantime, reported that he had lost his sexual desire for his wife. He didn't know what was happening, but he was concerned and ambivalent about the change. On the one hand, it was a great relief not to be under the power of a compulsion; on the other hand, it made him feel like a new person. "I have to get acquainted with my new image. I'm a different person. I don't know—I guess I rather enjoyed being a sex maniac." Then he expressed his real worry. "Wouldn't it be funny if my wife became a passion flower, and I became impotent?" It was important at this point to arrange for a new experience to occur that would counteract his fear of total eclipse.

The wife, on learning that her husband had lost his sexual desire for her, was filled with consternation. The therapist sympathized with her concern, and wondered if she thought she could seduce him. She wasn't sure, and even if she could, she worried that she might get her old feelings of revulsion back in the middle of it. Since she wasn't sure what really turned either her or her husband on, it was suggested she ask her husband to participate in an experiment with her in order to find out. Since experiment vanquishes imperative, both were released from a sense of duty or obligatory performance. At the last session, they stated they were enjoying their first honeymoon.

Most changes in brief therapy do not depend on a single task, but on a series of interdependent tasks, each emerging from the other. Timing is crucial in reversing the problematic sequences. Certain situations call for an experience to be tested over a longer period of time than the twelve weeks of the brief therapy. One of these situations is a trial separation. A couple was removed from a group after several sessions as it became clear that the husband's ambivalence over his commitment to the marriage hindered any progress. A prerequisite for carrying out a task is the desire to improve the marriage, and this husband could not make up his mind whether to improve the marriage or leave it. A situation of this sort does not respond to cooperative intervention, as the ambivalence itself is used as resistance. This Hamlet syndrome usually ends up with one spouse endlessly obsessing over whether or not to leave, the other spouse obsessing over the other's obsession, and the therapist obsessing over their joint obsession. Often this obsessing covers a secret or unrealistic fantasy which keeps the system forever teetering on the edge of a cliff.

In this case a paradoxical ritual was used to uncover the fantasy. The husband was an actor aspiring to a glamorous career in the theater. He felt trapped into domesticity by the demands of his wife and baby. On the one hand, he yearned to be free to follow the Bohemian life of an artist; on the other, he felt genuine affection for his wife, and their home provided him with a sense of security. The wife reacted to his distancing by withdrawing from him sexually, and moving closer to her circle of family and friends, which served to further alienate him.

The husband's fantasies of a free life were elicited, which proved to be highly romanticized. On the premise that only by experiencing them would they ever be dispelled, he was encouraged by the therapist to live them out.

The therapist agreed with him that since he was a creative person, it was important he not put limits on himself that might possibly stunt his creative development. He must go all the way and experience life to its fullest. Since artists were different from other people, he had the right to embrace life fearlessly and passionately, giving into every impulse. As the therapist began to elaborate on his fantasies, he began to equivocate—at which point the therapist pressed the need for him to totally abandon himself to the exotic. He then confessed that he had been toying with the idea of moving into a friend's vacant apartment for the summer, but had been afraid to tell his wife. He was planning, however, to see his wife and baby every day. The therapist discouraged this, on the basis that he would never know whether or not he wanted to separate until he had tested it out in a way that was totally free and unfettered. He was not to see his wife during this time, and arrangements were to be made for him to pick up the baby from the babysitter, so that he would not have to have any contact with his wife.

The therapist then said that since they were both experiencing sadness at the thought of this separation, they should share this sadness at a pre-scribed farewell dinner. It was explained how important it was for them to share their mourning, rather than experiencing it separately. Since the husband had a flair for the dramatic, he was put in charge of producing and directing this auspicious occasion. He was to choose a restaurant which held special memories for them. She was to wear his favorite dress, he to order their favorite wine, and they were to spend the evening reminiscing over the memories of their relationship—all their pleasant and unpleasant hopes, dreams, disappointments, expectations, and yearnings. They were then to make love for the last time. Since their lovemaking had been unsatisfactory, this would give them a memory with which to compare future partners favorably. The husband sat with tears streaming down his cheeks, as the therapist described the procedure. "You're making it sound like Napoleon's farewell speech to his troops, or something."

Prescribing a paradoxical ritual of this sort which tests the marital system to its limits also tests the therapist's dedication to change. It requires not only a commitment to the operating principle of the paradox, but a willingness to take the risk and responsibility involved in what must always be experimental by its very nature. A paradoxical intervention is not an intervention of safety or convenience; there are no tried and true formulas to follow. It requires time-consuming planning on the part of the therapist, an ability to judge the operation of the marital system accurately, a willing-ness to follow through with a speculative strategy, and an ability to predict the outcome. Beyond these professional skills, it requires a sense of the absurdity of life that encompasses the belief that the therapist as a mere mortal can never devise a strategy as divinely absurd as life itself.

The temptation at this point in the therapy would have been for the therapist to waver along the way with the husband, which would have vitiated any possibility for true change. Instead, she instructed them not to meet until three months hence, on their anniversary. They were to meet at the same restaurant for an anniversary reunion, but were not to come back together. A definite time was set for both the farewell dinner and the reunion. The therapist was to call them at the end of the summer to find out how they both felt about the new arrangement. When the therapist called, the husband answered the phone. He had not been able to stick it out until their anniversary, and had moved back home after six weeks. They were "managing" and felt they no longer needed further help. The husband stated he realized how important his wife and baby were to him, and never wanted to leave them again. The wife reported the separation had proved extremely valuable to her, as she began to think more about herself as a separate person. She had begun to write again, an activity she had given up when she married, and she felt less dependent on her husband. The door was left open for a follow-up session if needed. A year later they were still successfully managing.

SUMMARY

The format for brief therapy for a couples group described here was designed to structure change through choreography and tasks in a group setting. The therapist sets the stage for change through planned action. The first step is considered the most important in this change process; it unsticks the couples from their repetitious and predictable pattern of interaction, and sets them moving in a new direction. The rapidity of the change creates hope and produces a momentum which is self-reinforcing.

Tasks are based on different concepts, each designed specifically for each situation. This lends an experimental atmosphere to the group, and becomes an important element of the therapy.

The results, as always, varied with the individuals, and depended not so much on the chronicity or severity of the problem, but on their motivation and the therapist's imagination. The maintenance of the rapid change also varied greatly, depending mainly on the expertise of the therapist in coordinating and reinforcing the forward thrust. The one thing that remained invariable was the initial rapid improvement in each relationship. This in and of itself is considered significant, because once the couple has experienced it, they know it can be achieved again.

BIBLIOGRAPHY

J. Haley. *Strategies of Psychotherapy.* New York: Grune and Stratton, 1972.
_____. *Uncommon Therapy.* New York: Ballantine Books, 1973.
P. Watzlawick, J. Weakland, R. Fisch. *Change.* New York: W.W. Norton, 1974.
P. Watzlawick, J. Weakland, R. Fisch, A. Bodin. "Brief Therapy; Focused Problem Resolution," *Family Process,* 13 (1974) 141–67.
M. Palazzoli, L. Boscolo, G-F. Cecchin, G. Prata. "The Treatment of Children Through Brief Therapy of Their Parents," *Family Process,* 13 (1974), 429–42.
M. Palazzoli. *Self-starvation.* London: Chaucer Publishing.
C. Whitaker. "Psychotherapy of the Absurd, With a Special Emphasis on the Psychotherapy of Aggression," *Family Process,* 14 (1975), 1–16.
S. Minuchin. *Family and Family Therapy.* Cambridge: Harvard University Press, 1974.
M. Bowen. "Family Therapy and Family Group Therapy," in H. Kaplan and B. Sadock (eds.), *Comprehensive Group Psychotherapy.* Baltimore: Williams and Wilkins, 1971.

CHAPTER 21

Multiple Couple Therapy

Ian Alger, M.D.

INTRODUCTION

As our theoretical understanding of human behavior has expanded to include a systems approach, the focus of therapy has shifted from the individual to the family. It is not surprising that the therapeutic format has also moved from the dyadic to the group mode. In traditional treatment the individual patient was the subject of the therapy, and classically the spouse not only was never seen in consultation with the partner, but the therapist often would refuse any discussion with the spouse.

Family therapy holds that the behavior of one individual cannot be understood outside the context in which it is occurring. While one person can still be seen in therapy with this overall system approach, none of the others in the system is excluded. Indeed, the practice of assembling family members has the particular advantage of allowing some immediate experience of the family behavior in the presence of the therapist, so that distorted secondhand reporting is not the only source of data. Therapy with couples thus fits easily into the family therapy framework. Actually, in families where the designated patient is a child, the course of family therapy frequently evolves to an identification of serious difficulties in the parent relationship, and the family therapy itself becomes couple therapy.

In this approach, family problems or dysfunctions are identified as system problems. Family therapy has incorporated this concept, and its techniques have to a large extent involved a group approach. Family groups, whether a marital couple, or a larger family group with children and extended family members, are natural groups. Multiple couple therapy obviously finds roots from this family therapy source (8), but its second source of origin is from group therapy. This latter discipline also has been greatly influenced by systems theory and communication theory, and although individuals in group therapy seek help with their own lives, the dynamics of the group become powerful influences in clarifying the contextual significance of any individual's behavior, and in providing motivation and assistance in changing attitudes and behavior.

The therapist who uses multiple couple therapy, or couples group therapy, needs to be experienced in the theory and practice of family therapy as well as of group therapy. The multiple couple group provides a blend of natural family groups, and the heterogeneity of a mixed group of previous strangers. Its uniqueness and effectiveness lie in this blend; workers such as Framo (4) have described the method as the most effective way of treating couples.

Peterson (14) has stated that couples therapy was established as early as 1942. Certainly couples have experienced problems in their relationships as far back as history records, but earlier classical therapy usually treated each individual as an isolate. Other methods of treating marital problems eventually were introduced, however, including concurrent therapy, with each partner seeing the same or another therapist separately; conjoint therapy, with one therapist seeing both partners together; and combined therapy with each partner having individual therapy, and then meeting together either with another therapist, with one of their own therapists, or in a four-way session with both partners and both therapists.

The group marital approach is more recent, and although articles on it have been appearing for over two decades, Lebedun (9) in 1970 reported that to that time only 39, including books, had been published. The interest in the method and publication about it have recently increased. Gurman (5) notes that the interest in the therapy of couples in groups has significantly increased over time, while the writings about other methods of couple therapy have been diminishing in the literature.

Here I examine the nature of multiple couple therapy; some of the indications for its use, and the particular advantages it may offer; a consideration of the stages of evolution in the group, and of the therapist's role; a review of some specialized techniques that are useful in the group process; and finally some comments on the evaluation of results.

BASIC CONSIDERATIONS

Selection of Couples

The causes of dysfunction and subjective suffering in couples are manifold, and careful evaluation is important to determine if a workable therapeutic relationship is possible. Factors to be considered are the presenting problems as defined by the person(s) bringing the complaints; the reality factors in the life of the couple; the quality of relationship and communication between the partners; the understanding and expectation the partners have of therapy; and the willingness of the partners to engage in an effort for some resolution involving emotional, financial, and other personal sacrifices.

Couples or families may arrive for consultation through pressure from the courts or from schools. One member of the family may have engaged in delinquent or criminal behavior; or marital strife may have brought the police and courts into the picture. Such situations may serve to convince the family that outside help is necessary; or, the family may focus on the problem member and an evolution in understanding the systems problem may be the first stage in the development of therapy. Whether the family seeks help through its own concern about one member, or whether it is coerced by school or court, the focus of family therapy in the first stage should be around the immediate crisis. This should become the concern of the therapist(s), because the family cooperation can best be achieved by working with them through that current anxiety. As interventions are made in the operation of the system, a new juncture will occur when the parental couple, if the member in crisis was a child, or the marital pair, if the crisis focused around marital strife with a court-ordered consultation, is ready to consider other aspects of their relationship as basis for work in therapy. The couple then has a new opportunity to make a commitment to therapy, and the introduction of this couple into a multiple couple group is feasible.

The most frequent call for consultation is still from one or the other spouse, and although the marriage may be talked about, the focus is often on personal symptoms, from anxiety and depression, to psychosomatic complaints. It is easy to see that with a therapeutic approach which focuses on individual pathology, and which utilizes a one-to-one therapeutic relationship, the dynamics of the marital system may be grossly neglected or seriously distorted. When a joint consultation is suggested, the idea is often opposed, and the opposition can represent a collusion by both partners in avoiding confrontation with serious problems in their marriage. Again, a therapeutic evolution is needed to enable both partners to move through the focus on the behavior of one of them, to a sense of the system's dynamics. At this point a decision may be possible in which marital therapy is seen as a choice, and this couple too may then be introduced to a multiple couple group.

As marital therapy has become more accepted, and concepts of relationship and communication have become part of everyone's understanding, couples are increasingly seeking joint therapy for problems they face as a couple or as a family, or for dissatisfaction they feel in the quality of their married life together. The specific problems may be identified within a particular stage of the marital cycle, while other difficulties may appear at any stage (1).

A brief survey will help to identify the content of couples' concerns as they engage in group therapy, and define the breadth of the group's capacity to deal with a wide spectrum of difficulties. Problems in early marriage often are related to the adaptation to a new family system. Each partner came from his own family, and each had a particular place in that constellation. Rules and roles were familiar and well-practiced, if not necessarily happily accepted nor satisfying. In the new marriage new rules must be developed, even though this process of development may go on almost entirely out of conscious awareness. Issues of power and dependency may be important; one spouse who was the dependent child in his family of origin may suddenly find himself in charge of his new wife whose dependency overshadows his. The specific areas around which struggle may occur include money, sex, friendships, and allocation of time. The changing relationship to families on both sides also may become a large problem.

With the loosening of the extended family, and the greater fragmentation of family support systems in our post-industrial society, the effect of the closed nuclear family unit is constricting and limiting for many people, and tends to produce heavy demands on individual partners. When children arrive, the pressures and the limitations of the system are increased, and this new stage in the marital system signals an increase in the dissatisfactions and symptoms of the partners, now parents. Economic pressures usually increase; time limitations are severe, more often on the mother, who may have little support from extended family, and little support from other helpers because of economic limitations. The phase of childrearing may last for two or three decades of the couple's life together. During this period the children are often triangulated in the system as an expression of dysfunction and unhappiness in the basic operational effectiveness of the family. It is also during this phase that husband or wife may develop symptoms, and it is clinically important to view these in the framework of the family context if the patient member is not to become the scapegoated member.

During the childrearing stage the career development of the father, and increasingly the simultaneous career development of the mother, are important concurrent issues. The teenage crises, which create turmoil in the family balance as the growing members attempt to break out into a new way of life for themselves, frequently coincide with the middle-age crises of the parents. The father's career may be at the point where earlier expectations are now seen to be unrealistic, and compromises may be very painful. The disappointment generated may find its focus in the family, and the husband may look for personal validation in new relationships, and a new marriage. Women in this stage of marriage may also realize that as the children move out, their roles as mother must undergo change, and new career choices may be necessary. Awareness of some of the emptiness in the marriage may then become agonizingly apparent. Those women who have already undertaken careers in addition to the tasks of the home may now find new time and energy to devote to their work; but this may unbalance the marital relationship, and lead to new problems over power, and new competitive struggles over dependency issues.

Frequently one spouse seeks consultation, sometimes out of desperation, at other times at the insistence of the partner. The therapeutic task is to first create a possibility of exploring and defining the family system, and offering the opportunity of assessing the potential of each member of the partnership, and of the relationship as well. When the couple arrives with a definite decision to divorce, or when divorce is arrived at during therapy as the best resolution, the therapy can then at times be useful in creating a transition to new agreements which support the growth not only of the partners, but also of children, and other relatives and friends in the system. In my experience the placement of a couple who are decided on divorce into a group of couples is not indicated, because of the disruptive effect. On the other hand, when a couple is undecided, their presence in a group can be very constructive, and if during the course of the group a decision for divorce is made, all members of the group can integrate this process in a useful way.

Older couples who seek help may be troubled by problems of illness in one of the members; with difficulties in creating new life after the retirement of one or both partners; with continuing problems in the triangulation of children, and now grandchildren; with worries about finances, difficulties in sexual relations, or fears about death; and with a gradual seepage, or sudden explosion of years and years of hidden resentments, accrued bitterness, and disappointments. The fact that older couples are now seeking help in solving some of these painful situations is a reflection of the changing cultural realization that learning and personal growth can be a renewing continuation no matter what the age.

Other couples seeking help are those involved in a second marriage. Frequently there may be an age difference, but this in itself is not usually the core of the problem. Often couples of the same age marry again, and although many second marriages avoid problems that were part of the first, many still encounter difficulties which, possibly because it *is* the second marriage, lead the partners to seek an early resolution.

There is enough variety in this list to raise the question about criteria for selection of couples for a particular group. In my own practice I have experimented with various formats. I do not introduce a couple who has decided on divorce into a group, other than to a group of couples who have arrived at a similar decision. I have never made the age of a member a factor of decision. The stage of the marriage, however, has entered into my selection at times, and I have assembled groups of recently married couples, groups of new parents, groups of couples with teenaged children, and groups who are facing the problems of retirement. Economic level also has not been a factor, except that in private practice it operates as a selective force.

Although groups of couples who have certain common features have operated in a useful therapeutic way, I have more and more come to appreciate the value of intermixing couples at different stages of the marital cycle. Problems of communication and goal determination run through all stages; difficulties which emerge because of the very structure of modern marriage, with its nuclear constellation, lack of extended network, and resulting constrictiveness are also experienced through all stages of the marital system. From the point of view of group dynamics, the presence of members representing different marital stages offers the possibility of greater empathy, better clarification of role expectations, and the inclusion of the wisdom of experience freshened by the excitement and hope of younger couples. Issues of parent-child interaction are more readily identified, and a perspective on the marriage and life cycle is attained which facilitates the growth of each individual, and the resolution of disagreements.

Size of the Group

My own experience has been similar to most of that reported in the literature: namely, that optimal size is three or four couples. The fact that in addition to the individual members of the group there are ongoing dyadic relationships adds to the richness of the material presented, and for this reason enlarging the group produces a limitation on the useful work that individual couples can initiate in the group and then carry away with them for further work by themselves. This last factor is extremely important, because it highlights one of the most valuable attributes of the multiple couple group, which is that the natural family unit is able to continually apply and practice learning which has come from the group activity.

Various reasons may prevent one or more members from attending any particular session. No rule is made which excludes one partner if the other does not attend. Such a rule would provide one member with an unfair coercive and restrictive leverage over the other. Absences are considered as in any group, and may be reflective of the group process, of tension between the couple, of anxiety in one partner, or of extraneous reality factors.

Time

Time includes frequency of sessions, length of sessions, and duration of course of treatment. The duration of treatment is related to group goals. Time-limited groups may run from six to ten sessions, to periods of six months, or one year. A definite number of sessions with a defined goal may be selected, with the provision for renewal of the contract. Time-limited groups are effective when specific goals can be identified; for example, communication impasses, sexual dissatisfaction, money management, and assessment of the quality of life in the marriage.

Marital groups also can operate in an open-ended way, and this is the method I use most often in my practice. With this mode, couples leave and new couples enter the group, and the process of exploring and assisting has a continuity, so that the group has a life beyond the particular constellation at any moment. Such an arrangement also facilitates the re-entry of a couple if they wish to engage later in additional work.

Some workers hold two or three meetings a week for a few weeks at the beginning of a group in order to establish group cohesion, but I hold weekly meetings. The usual length of meetings is one and one-half hours; with four couples in a group, this may be extended to two hours. I do not recommend alternate or leaderless sessions for the multiple couple groups, but there is no rule against social activity together, and couples may often join for dinner or cocktails following a meeting.

COTHERAPY

Practical, clinical, and theoretical arguments are offered in the debate over the indication for a male-female cotherapy team (12). Some workers (11) advocate a marital pair as therapists, believing that the actual resolution of problems that the therapists have achieved in their own lives is a powerful therapeutic force, serving not only as a model, but as a continuing demonstration of problem-solving in a couple. Other workers state that a single therapist is not able to empathize with both men and women in the group, and that biased triangulations and alliances are frequently missed or dealt with inadequately because of the therapist's personal distortions and prejudices.

On the other hand, workers such as Haley (6) believe that cotherapists complicate therapeutic efforts, and the most effective interventions can be made mostly directly by one therapist. In his view, it is also likely that multiple couple therapy would be seen as a complicating organization, and that optimum therapy would be attained by working with one family system at a time.

The practical consideration is an economic one. In hospital and clinical settings, especially where training programs are operating, it is feasible to assign two therapists to a group; but in private practice the cost factor may make the treatment so expensive that most couples are excluded. In my own practice I have worked with a cotherapist with some groups, and as a single therapist in others. There have been advantages in both experiences. Work with the other therapist requires more conference time between regular sessions. This time, however, can be extremely valuable in evaluating the process and in determining therapeutic strategies. On the other hand, as Haley says, the additional relationship between therapists does complicate the situation, and may take up group time for its resolution.

I believe the cultural attitudes regarding power relationships and role assignments concerning men and women may emerge so powerfully in some groups that a single therapist's own bias creates alliances that cause hostility and impasse. A cotherapist of the opposite sex can be extremely helpful in these situations. One way to clarify these issues is to make a contract in the group that an additional therapist will periodically join the group for two or three sessions of consultation. This method allows the regular therapist to step back from his usual role, and for the entire group as newly constituted to make a fresh evaluation of process.

INITIATING THE GROUP

Evaluation

The couple first makes contact with the therapist through an individual session. At times this may be with only one partner because of the reluctance of the mate to attend a session, but if at all possible both partners are encouraged to attend together for the first meeting. My standard procedure is to schedule from four to six sessions for evaluation. The first meeting is structured for the couple to tell their own story of why they are seeking help, and an attempt is made to leave the format open so they can demonstrate their own method of such decision making. Frequently this session is videotaped, the use of which adjunct I will discuss below.

In the second and third sessions, each partner has a chance to go over his or her own history in the presence of the other, and often things are heard by each for the first time. The following sessions are used to define some of the problem areas, and to set at least some tentative goals. At this point, the couple may be invited to join a group. Questions may be raised as to the relevance of this approach, because many couples feel their problems are so intimately their own that they cannot see why others should be involved. Some people feel the importance of privacy, and also are reluctant to share secret family information with others. Couples who have become isolated, have little family connection, and very little network with close friends may at first be very reluctant to break old codes which encourage family members to keep family business within the family. However, because of the isolation that is part of the nuclear family organization, many of these very couples come to see that the possibility of sharing anxieties and close feelings with others in the network of the multiple couple group serves some of the purposes formerly served by the extended family.

This process may be shortened if a couple in the beginning asks for a group experience, or if they have been in some other therapy and are now interested in joining the group. The overall goal of the evaluation is to explore the current marriage situation as well as its history adequately enough so a choice can be made by both partners for commitment to the group.

Structure

In the first session basic agreements are made concerning time, absences, and termination. In my groups an accrued vacation absence of one session for each two months of therapy is the rule. Couples are asked to stay for at least two additional sessions if they make a sudden decision to leave the group. Open and direct communication is encouraged, and each member is asked to respect the confidentiality of the group members.

Bowen and Framo (4) have advocated the allocation of periods of time in each session devoted to each couple. For example, in an hour and a half group, each of three couples would be the focus of the group for 30 minutes, while the other two couples listen and quietly relate to what is occurring. In this model, group dynamics are minimized, and couples' therapy in a group is the essence. I have found this approach useful, particularly early in the group's life. Each couple has a chance to review their own history for the others, to clarify their immediate problems, and to identify their goals. In later phases I prefer the dynamic group approach, because I believe it creates the possibility of other learning experiences with more intensive cross-couple interactions. The structured approach can be introduced for short periods at any time, and does provide a way to shift group focus, and to break redundant group process.

Goals

Although many people enter individual therapy with a sense of outrage at others for having caused so much of their troubles, most still accept the idea that they must themselves do something to change if their lives are to improve. In marital therapy partners enter with an awareness of suffering, but very often their concept of the problem is that their marital partner is greatly to blame. Therefore, their attempt is to change the other partner. A major goal of couple therapy, however, is to develop awareness with the couple that no one person is responsible for the dysfunction and frustration in the system, and that each person in the system has the potential to make changes which can alter the total functioning of the family group (10, 17).

The overall goal is an improvement in total family system functioning. This is achieved by an assessment of the present functioning, and an evaluation of the realistic problems faced by the family unit, particularly related to the stage of the marriage, the constellation of the nuclear and extended families, and the economic factors. Each partner is also asked to define personal goals, and to explore individual hopes and expectations; these are compared to earlier individual and couple goals, and also compared with the goals of other couples in the group.

One group goal is to improve unclear and confusing communication through example, role-play, confrontation, and experience in more direct ways of exchanging information in the group. Nonverbal communication is emphasized, especially as it creates paradoxical messages with verbal communication that result in binds and other distortions in relationship.

My experience in the multiple couple groups reflects that of Coughlin and Wimberger (3), who wrote that a faith that improvement in one aspect of the system's functioning would raise family confidence and lead to successful change in areas which were not dealt with directly. This brings into focus the ultimate goal of the therapy, which is to encourage the development of each couple's ability to deal more directly with each other and with their total system, so that they can continue to work together in coping with the myriad real difficulties which challenge every family through the course of its life.

EVOLUTION OF THE GROUP

Early Stages

I will discuss here the development of a dynamic, open-ended group; however, many of the stages and characteristics also apply to more structured, specific goal-oriented, and time-limited groups (13, 18). Anxiety is always present as the new group begins. One woman commented in the first session that she felt so nervous that in spite of her rage at her husband, she found herself sitting beside him, and feeling very glad that she could turn to him for protection. Low self-esteem is also an important factor in the developing group. Not only may an individual feel inadequate in his own feelings of self, but in addition may feel the additional burden of shame that the marriage relationship has not been a success.

Part of the suffering of many people comes from loneliness and isolation. Just as an individual may feel different from his fellows, and may experience his own pain as unique, and somehow worse than anyone else's, so too may a couple in their isolation feel that their problems and pain are unusual and unique. The realization in group exchange that others encounter similar conflicts can help each couple develop a more realistic perspective.

During the early stage there is, then, a tension between anxiety and a desire to hide, and the opposite desire to reveal problems and seek help in resolving them. The focus may fall on the man, on the woman, or on the couple itself. One husband took the position of the objective guide through the neurotic behavior patterns of his unhappy wife. She in turn portrayed herself as a valiantly striving, but completely misunderstood woman. Both were startled when another couple reacted to them not as individuals, but as an "impossible pair." This function of other group members as cotherapist opens the way for the next stage of group work.

Middle Stages

With further experience in the group a trust level develops, and more and more risks are taken. Each individual gradually builds an understanding of himself in relation to his own past, in relation to his present family in the marriage, and in relationship to the therapy group. The group functions as a support system as well as a confronting system, and in a way plays the role of a large new family. This last function also is useful in providing couples with new types of modeling in terms of problem solving, communicating, and expressing concern.

Revelations about feelings may lead to significant information about the interaction in the partnership. A wife began to talk about her own loneliness following a tearful expression of sadness by another woman in the group. The loneliness was described as having existed since the beginning of the marriage. She felt that she had never been understood by her husband, and that she was destined to remain in this loneliness forever. The husband was astounded to hear her say this, and began to challenge her by claiming that she had on so many occasions said that she was happy, and loved being married. The more she insisted that she really felt misunderstood and alone, the more he focused his argument to prove point by point that she was wrong. Another woman in the group reacted by telling him that she would be very angry if he kept trying to talk her out of her feelings in this way. The woman who had first cried expressed sympathetic understanding for the wife. Gradually the group began to look at the way communication between the couple moved to an argumentative mode, with a competitive stance between the partners. One man in the group suggested to the husband that perhaps he felt hurt and angry to hear his wife say she had been lonely from the start of the marriage. This enabled the husband to begin to directly express some of his feelings of hurt, and the discussion in the group then moved to an exploration of the fear of open disclosure of feelings, both negative and positive.

The example shows how the flow in the group moves from one couple to interaction among all the members, and from feeling in one individual to concentration on argumentative struggle, to a refocusing on communication styles and the stance of each partner, with eventual shift to a more open and concerned exchange not only between partners, but among all members of the group sharing the experience.

Problem solving also presents another opportunity for group participation and learning. A couple talked in one group about their concern with their teenaged daughter who was becoming more and more rebellious, and who had the night before walked out of the house announcing that she would not be back until the next day. As the story unfolded and each parent added information, they began to get more and more involved in blaming each other for the way each reacted to the daughter, not only over the current crisis, but in several past instances. The husband complained of the wife's harshness to the girl, while the wife implied that the great closeness between father and daughter was making her feel excluded and incompetent as a mother. The rest of the group began to identify with the parents, and with the daughter, and information was added about similar problems in their lives. Eventually the group was able to see that the problem of teenaged girls moving toward more independence was one they all knew something about, either from their own youth or from experiences in their present families. The group discussed feelings of parents and feelings of teenagers, and then returned to the first couple. In the context of their problem's being less unique, and therefore less disastrous, this couple then looked more closely at their reactions to each other and to the daughter. The father said eventually that the only real feeling of warmth he got in the family was when he felt close to his daughter. The mother talked about her own isolation as a child, and her resentment when her daughter seemed to be getting things her own way. Both were then aware of their anxiety over the feelings of responsibility as a parent, and their own feelings of incompetence in the role of parents spilled out.

These brief sequences give examples of many group dynamics in the working middle stages of therapy. More openness and trust has been established. The group can move from being listeners to participating by empathy and support, by challenging, by confronting, by interpreting, and by personally reacting with emotions related to the immediate situation, or to experiences associated from their own lives. Identifications are made, and acknowledged. Distortions or transferences become increasingly apparent, and since not everyone in the group has the same reactions, the distortions are more easily explored with help from some of the other group members.

As the group continues it also becomes safer to talk about sensitive topics such as jealousy, sexuality, and hostility. A wife chided her husband lightly about his foolishly being jealous of her, and having once marched her out of a party by her ear. He did not take the matter lightly, and the couple had an increasingly tense exchange as he made explicit the details of her "gross flirtation" and the fact that the behavior went "beyond flirtation" to actual physical touching. Another wife pointed out the paradox that it was the husband who was concerned about his wife's flirtation, but the wife who had phobic anxiety when her husband went on trips by himself. As is common, such seeming paradox represent the flipside of the same problem of dependency and possessiveness, and the group was able to begin to explore the issue of power and control, both in the first couple's relationship and in all the marriages.

The entrapping aspects of marriage, related to the close coupling and the contract to maintain a permanent and monogamous relationship for life represent an important area of difficulty for most married people. The multiple couple group provides an unusually helpful format to investigate and counter some of the negative consequences of this parochial aspect of marriage. The narrowness of perspective which is promoted by the closed marriage system, and which is worsened by the loosening of the extended family, is in some ways encouraged when a couple works in isolation with a therapist. In the group, new possibilities are provided in the congregation of couples from other stages of marriage, from different economic and ethnic backgrounds, and with different levels of education and very different current lives. Each couple in the group is privileged to have a look inside many other relationships, and to see different lifestyles, different ways that couples have dealt with problems, and to open up new opportunities for themselves. A husband who became angry if his wife was ever away from home when he arrived from work began to rethink his attitude when he heard another couple describing the man's preparing dinner for the children when his wife had dinner appointments with clients she met in the course of her own business career. Another man developed a new understanding of his own narrowness when he learned that two other men in the group had shared much of the early childrearing chores, while he had steadfastly refused to soil his own hands in any way. This late realization and his acknowledgement of it to his wife enabled them to reevaluate their current sharing of tasks; with the participation of the others in the group, they rearranged their way of sharing work.

When one man in a group revealed the strife he and his wife had experienced when the details of an affair came to light a few months earlier, a woman in the group was able to express her own fears of attraction to other men, and the way she used fear of her husband's reaction to keep her awareness of these desires from her own consciousness. Her husband was able to talk openly about his reactions to her fantasies. Others in the group then revealed their own experiences with affairs, and their own anxieties about dealing openly or covertly with the issue.

In the middle stages, considerable support among members of the group is evidenced in a division of the participants by sex. Particularly in the last five years, women in the groups feel a strong bond with one another, and are extremely alert to sexbased discrimination. They are able to create an understanding among themselves, and also with the men, that problems derived from sexual discrimination transcend the personal nature of their relationships, and are rooted in the social and cultural attitudes transmitted and carried by boys and girls, men and women, in the continuing contexts of their lives in this society. Defining problems and attitudes in this way— that is, as rooted in socially-derived influences—has the liberating effect of relieving individuals of unwarranted personal guilt, and of helping both men and women realize that they both participate in a larger drama which assigns roles and characteristic behaviors regardless of the individual's personal experience. Because many such attitudes are reinforced in current life situations, the possibility of working in a therapy group allows the development of a different kind of relating, so that more liberated ideas and values can be reinforced.

Later Stages

As change occurs in individual attitudes, and as world views enlarge, concurrent alterations appear in the way the couples relate to one another.

Contracts are changed, often facilitated by the development of new communication skills in which there is less double-binding, and less obscurity. Couples frequently develop new sensitivity to their own reactions and feelings. They are able to emphathize with partners, and to be aware of and respond to feelings in their partners. The possibility of closeness and cooperative living is felt as a greater possibility: and, in a seeming contradiction, the capacity to disagree, to fight more directly, and to strive for one's own rights creates not less but rather more closeness, and feelings of intimacy and love.

Another consequence is that sometimes couples realize they are struggling with too many negative factors in their relationship, and with better communication are able to make a decision to separate. Of course there are also instances in which one member of a marriage develops awareness and development of self to a point beyond that of the spouse, so that a personal decision is made by the one partner to separate and end the relationship. The group in such cases can be very helpful not only to the one who feels abandoned, and frightened or furious, but also to the one who is leaving, and who may feel extremely anxious and frightened as well.

In the later stages, when changes have occurred, there may be startling reversals. A husband complained that throughout the marriage he had been disappointed in the sexual relationship with his wife. He found the frequency too low, her enthusiasm too tepid, and her lack of assertiveness rejecting. As the wife developed an awareness and appreciation of her own sexuality, brought to the surface especially by her attraction to one of the other men, and by an open discussion of details of the sexual enjoyment one of the other wives described, she began to assert her own interest in more sex with her husband, began to feel more sexual excitement, and for the first time had an orgasm in intercourse. Her husband concurrently began to experience anxiety, and for the first time felt concerned about his ability to keep an erection. His anxiety was followed by phobic feelings regarding intercourse. Within a few weeks the scenario had reversed. The wife was now interested in more sex, while he was losing his interest and making many of the same excuses she formerly gave. This kind of reversal demonstrates dramatically the fact that problems can best be understood as manifestations of systems operation, rather than just the manifestation of an intrapsychic problem. This man was able to explore his own feelings of anxiety about taking pleasure for himself in sex, and both partners became aware that each of them had difficulty in receiving from others, while both felt much more comfortable in the giving and helping role. With this insight they were able to help each other experiment with the possibility of having at least a fair share of personal satisfaction and pleasure in sex. The consequence for the other members of the group was that they too were able to gain awareness about similar difficulties in their own lives, and two of the couples dealt specifically with their own inhibitions and fears in taking pleasure. This kind of contagion is another attribute of multiple couple therapy.

Such contagion can also have a negative side. A couple who are locked in a power struggle, for example, and who compete destructively with one another may involve other members in their struggle, so that demoralization and cynicism may spread in the group. This eventuality may be countered by the reactions of some of the members of the group, but if not, the therapist must intervene to create a way of moving toward the larger group goal of a common attempt to understand and to develop new awareness.

When a couple is preparing to leave the group, there may be a return to older, less adaptive behavior, with a recurrence of old symptoms and interaction patterns. Usually this negative therapeutic reaction can be understood quickly, and related to understandings that the whole group gained during the course of its work. As one couple leaves, and a new couple joins the group there will be a return to a different trust level in the group, and the quality of the group interaction may change. However, the development of a new working atmosphere is achieved relatively quickly as the new couple learns the ground rules and group mores that have developed while the group has worked together. In this way a continuity can be maintained, and couples can leave and new couples join without the basic group functioning being seriously altered.

Role of the Therapist

Throughout the various stages the therapist has different tasks, and in this sense his role changes. But in another sense, he or she maintains the same role during the entire course of therapy. There has been much concern during the past three decades about the role of the therapist, with emphasis varying from his taking a passive, objective role, with considerable detachment, to his taking the role of teacher, with considerable direction and structuring, to his participating as an equal member and sharing in the human exchange and interaction. I see the therapist in the group as both a person with very human reactions to the others in the group, and also as a person whose specific role tasks are to lead the group and use his expertise to enhance the group experience so it will be as much as possible a human learning experience productive of change. Some role tasks are different at different stages of the group's development, while others are constant throughout. The therapist's human involvement, I believe, should be at the level of openness and willingness to participate personally in the group, and this principle holds for all stages.

A few of the role's specific tasks can be outlined briefly. In the beginning, rapport is necessary, and the therapist should be concerned with understanding where the couple stand in relation to therapy, and what they want from the experience. He has to also explore the feelings of the couple about working with him, because if a basic sense of rapport does not exist, the experience will likely not be of much help. At the start the therapist also needs to structure sessions so that each member has an opportunity to reveal personal material in an atmosphere that has safeguards and is conducive to the development of an adequate trust level.

In later stages he needs the skill to move back and leave room for members to work with each other, at the same time remaining ready to involve himself with specific therapeutic techniques which may provide special help at some moment—for example, skill in interpreting dreams, and in noticing significance in nonverbal behavior. In addition, techniques such as roleplaying, television playback, assertiveness training, and group exercises may be of significant help when introduced at opportune moments.

The other aspect of the therapist's stance, his human involvement as a person, should also be considered. The therapist's modeling influence is very great, so this is a potent force which can have immense therapeutic impact. Since human relating is at the center of consideration, the very focus of couple therapy, the way the therapist personally relates to group members, both men and women, and the way he relates to the members as couples will obviously have great importance. If the therapist is open in his own communication, is direct, and nonbinding, his example can be very helpful. If the therapist is in touch with his own feelings and reactions from moment to moment in the group, and is ready to reveal these directly and openly to the group, he will demonstrate in a most powerful way the effect of this kind of immediacy. I have also found it useful to add my own associations and experiences to the group material when it has seemed appropriate and cogent, and have found this not only personally rewarding, but also helpful to the other members in the group. Skill in therapeutics is important; but it is unrelated to other qualities of human relating, and this is a crucial differentiation. When group members become aware that the therapist too is human, and faces the same problems as all people, bringing to their solution his own experience and struggles, the group members then feel less alienated, and more ready to reveal their own struggles, in the hope of finding human companionship in the search for personal development and fulfillment.

SPECIAL TECHNIQUES

In addition to the usual therapeutic interventions which originate both in family therapy and in group therapy, other procedures may be used. Only a few will be outlined here, but the list of possibilities is very large. In addition to those I shall discuss, some others are: using the Ravich Interpersonal Game Test (15); application of gestalt methods; use of behavior modification methods, including task assignment; introduction of meditation exercise; use of guided fantasy; and utilization of nonverbal and communication exercises. I shall discuss here the introduction of family network members; division into subgroups; roleplaying techniques; use of family choreography; use of television playback; and changing the time and space structure of the group.

Family Members

Framo (4) has described a practice of having one interview with the couple and with their families of origin prior to introducing the couple in the group. This practice has the merit of identifying old family relationship and communication arrangements which may be repeated and reinforced in the new marriage. Also identified may be the repetition and reversals of role which continue to transmit certain attitudes and sequences through the generations, and which may play a significant part in mate choice. I have not routinely used this approach, but on occasion have found it very valuable, especially when the continuing negotiations and family interactions are intricately involved across generation lines.

Periodically I have had a member of the couple's family temporarily join a group, often for one or two sessions, when it seemed indicated, and of course when all those involved were willing. One woman had a very competitive relationship with a younger sister, and felt extremely inferior to her. The sister lived with them for several years after the couple had married, and later left to marry and settle in her own home. Phone conversations continued on an almost daily basis, and the wife continued to feel inferior, and also to entertain jealous fantasies about the relationship of her husband and her sister. The sister agreed to come to two group sessions in order that the three of them might clarify the conflicts, and resolve some old feelings of resentment and misunderstanding. The effect was to make the group extremely cohesive. Everyone was interested in comprehending the puzzle, and in helping in any way possible. The sister felt very welcome in the group, and the two women were able to confront one another more directly. This had the effect of releasing the husband from the triangular bind he had been in, between the wife and the sister; both women recognized the similarity between the husband's position and that of their father. In the original family, three triangles existed: the mother and father and each of the daughters; and the father and the two daughters. In the group the couple were able to make much closer contact, and to communicate more directly about fear of rejection; and others in the group were able to recognize similar patterns in their own lives, and also among members of the group itself.

Although a routine family-of-origin interview is not held at the start of therapy, I have selectively asked to have such an interview with a couple during the course of the therapy when seems that an impasse in the couple's relationship might be broken by the procedure.

Subgroups

Breaking into small groups, and then reassembling can have impressive effects in focusing resistances in the group, and in providing new possibilities for moving in different directions. At the start of one meeting there was considerable tension and a resulting silence. It seemed that everyone had something quite personal he was preoccupied with, and letting the group process go its spontaneous course was going to mean many people would feel left out. Each person was asked to pick a partner, but not the spouse, and to meet in pairs in different parts of the office for ten minutes. During that time they were to talk with each other about their most immediate concerns. After the ten minutes the group reassembled. No reporting was asked for, but the group was told to pick up at any place they wished. Two couples were able to become involved in talking to the whole group that evening, but all the members of the group commented that the opportunity of communicating with one other interested person for a few minutes had freed them to participate more in the total group.

Often the content of the group discussion reveals a man-woman split, and at such times it can be useful to ask the men and women to meet separately in two groups for any period from ten minutes to the whole session. This technique, more than any other I know, has the effect of bringing sex role differences into clear awareness. A peer group support also develops, and makes it much easier for some people to identify more forcefully their own position on many issues concerning roles of men and women. In one group the women were able to confront the men in a very different way after such a separate group meeting. The women had been able to identify the men's condescension, and to relate it to feelings of depression and low self-esteem. Labeling such reactions as part of larger social and cultural influences can be very liberating; for many of us feel such resentment and depression, but take sole personal responsibility for our feelings as being only further proof of our own inferiority.

Roleplaying

Role-play techniques can be especially valuable in bringing greater clarity to the dynamics of relationships, and in improving the effectiveness of communication. Many variations and improvisations can be used. One husband for instance, described his anger at his wife's delaying their departure for a party. He told how he had quietly resented her lateness, and how this was a frequent source of annoyance for him. The two of them were then asked to stand up and replay the incident. Part way through, they were invited to switch roles. At the finish, another woman was asked to play the wife's role, and the incident was played again. Between replays of the incident other group members gave a critique, and coached the couple on different ways they might play the scene. Originally the husband was quiet as he had reported. When the roles were switched, the wife, now playing husband, began to yell and say she was tired of all the damned waiting. When this part of the scene was played by another woman in the group, she yelled back at the husband, and was able to continue to directly express his anger. The husband reported that he knew now just how angry and frustrated he felt when he had to wait, and he was able to later report to the group that he found it much easier to make direct confrontations when he felt frustrated.

"Doubling" is another role-play technique that can be very effective. A couple is asked to replay an incident, and a double is assigned to each, to say out loud the feelings and thoughts they believe the real couple are not expressing directly. The real couple are instructed to give feedback so the doubles will know if they are correct or not in what they are saying. This method is very useful in helping each partner gain more awareness of both his own and his mate's feelings.

The doubling can also be used by the therapist, and this can be done spontaneously during the course of the group process. In this method, the therapist verbalizes some feeling he perceives to be indirectly communicated by one of the partners. For example, a husband was critical of his wife after she disagreed with him. The therapist said, "I'm also quite hurt by what you said." This made the wife sit back, and then she said, "I rarely ever think of you as being hurt. I see you really do feel that." She then reached over and took his hand, and the quality of the communication changed from attack and counterattack, to an attempt to share and understand feelings.

Family Choreography

Using members of the group, one person can arrange their postures, their facial expressions, and their movements to represent ongoing relation-

ship patterns in his current family, the family of origin, or in other designated networks. Using the space in the room as a boundary for a life space,
these sometimes unusually powerful dramatizations can be of tremendous
help in providing a visual and felt awareness of otherwise obscure transactions and contexts.

In one couple group, each member was asked to choreograph the currently important people in his life, and to show how they were dynamically
arranged in terms of their relationship to him and to each other. At the close
of each tableau, the active member took his place in the appropriate spot,
and a color Polaroid was taken. Each person then described his feelings and
reactions to the experience, and the directing member also gave his reactions and associations to the whole experience. By this method one woman
recognized how isolated she felt from both her parents, and how her brothers always intruded themselves between her and her mother. At the same
time, she saw that she had placed her in-laws between herself and her own
husband in the choreographed group, so she felt isolated in both her current
family, and in her family of origin. The group member who played the part
of her father expressed his feelings of frustration at being distant from this
daughter, and in a later report to the group she told how she had described
the episode to her real father, and how he consequently realized that he too
felt frustrated at the distance. They were closer than they ever remembered,
and she gained a sense that she could move to make relationships different.

Television Playback

If videorecording equipment is available, it can be of considerable assistance. As with the other techniques described, there are reports in the
literature detailing rationale and use (2); a brief example will be given here.
In one group the wife said, "I want to make just a short statement about
that." The husband interjected, "Really, a short statement?" Everyone
laughed, and the woman continued on to give a really protracted statement.
The session was being videotaped, and as she talked, the husband looked
up, and slowly turning his head, began to trace the pattern of electrical
conduit on the ceiling of the room. This portion was replayed on the
television screen for the group, and the husband laughed and said, "I guess
I wasn't really listening." The wife was upset, but also amazed, because she
had no awareness during the actual event that he had not been paying
attention. The encounter led them to begin a discussion of his problem in
being more assertive in interjecting and stopping her long descriptions. The
episode became known as "watching the ceiling" in the group, and at later
times when a member said to another, "Watching the ceiling, I see," the
group could in a shorthand way focus on the problem of effectively interrupting a filibuster.

Playback is also effective in reviewing the sequences which lead to impasse; in allowing each member to react to his particular behavior during some incident in the group, by replaying the scene over and over, while each person has a turn; and in revealing expressions and gestures which change the course of group interaction, but which are ordinarily outside awareness.

Time and Space

The group usually meets in the same place, the therapist's office. However, from time to time changes can be made, and these can have very useful results. In one group a couple wanted to hold a group meeting at their home, because the regular time fell on the eve of a holiday, and the group felt inclined to celebrate together. The therapist agreed, and the meeting was convened in the home. The result was unexpectedly valuable for the host couple. Their cooperation as hosts gave the group a new sense of cooperative possibilities between them which had never been apparent before. Also, the decoration of the home gave a warmth which was an additional dimension not experienced before. The total evening was so impressive that each couple decided that over time they would like a meeting to be held in their home, and this process was followed, with the therapist attending the meetings.

Another alteration of both time and space occurred when one group held a weekend meeting at the country home of one of the couples. The plan for the weekend was to have a marathon session, including preparation of meals, housekeeping as minimally necessary, and intervals of recreation. At least nine hours a day for two days were devoted to group meetings, one of which was held on the lawn beneath the trees. The whole experience provided an intense period of work which resulted in more cohesiveness in the group, more awareness of the effect of continued closeness, and the revelation of conflicts which had been hidden easily in the shorter group meetings.

The process of exploring new possibilities in the mix of relationships was enhanced with the weekend arrangement. Also, the variety of real tasks that were involved gave an experience of working and playing with each other in a new and vivid way. One husband offered to supervise the preparation of breakfast, and made arrangements to meet with the breakfast crew at 7:30 in the morning. When the time came to begin, he was out making a repair on his car. He appeared about twenty minutes later, completely unaware of having broken his contract; but his wife was very happy to see the reactions of those who had expected him on time. Events similar to this were repeated during the whole weekend, and in later meetings of the group, members would recall episodes from the weekend. Its value remained long after the occasion itself had passed.

COMMENTARY

If the therapy process is seen as a real and human experience of growth through awareness and new relationships, then the alteration of format, and the changing of time and space boundaries will not seem disruptive, but will be understood as methods compatible with wider goals. As is well known, evaluating the effectiveness of any therapy is difficult, if not impossible. Clinically, therapists feel their work is often useful, and patients continually endorse the effectiveness of methods. From a theoretical viewpoint, multiple couple therapy has much to commend it. It is an efficient use of a therapist's time, and can be undertaken at less cost by patients. Furthermore, it provides a third family for couples who have been shortchanged on earlier family life. It also opens awareness of how similar are the problems faced by all couples, which thus makes each couple feel less unusual and less disordered. It also provides a positive support system of peers, and thereby is likely to diminish undue influence by the therapist. Identifications are readily made, and the other members can help not only with insights and support, but also by participating in techniques which need several people, such as choreographing and roleplaying.

Literature on the outcome of marital therapy (5,7) acknowledges the difficulty in assessing any psychotherapeutic method, but points to a growing trend in group, as in individual, therapy to develop instruments which can measure change. This accounts in part for the move away from theory and toward a pragmatic approach to intervention, which uses an eclectic technology to resolve more sharply defined goals. My discussion here reflects this approach, since a variety of techniques are discussed; however, all techniques must be applied in context, and the importance of that value context must, I believe, be emphasized.

In multiple couple therapy the encompassing goal is the development of closer human contact through awareness and direct expression of feeling, and the development of relationships with others in a mode that encourages and promotes freedom and growth. Marriage partners who have reached the degree of personal maturity where they can respect the individuality and freedom of their mate are in a position to work with that mate in developing effective ways of living together and separately, so they can not only try to meet each other's needs, but so they can also cooperatively and effectively work together in coping with life's endless family problems and joys.

References

1. I. Alger. "Marriage and Marital Problems," in S. Arieti (ed.). *American Handbook of Psychiatry,* New York: Basic Books, 1974.
2. _____. "Audio-Visual Techniques in Family Therapy," in D. Bloch (ed.) *Techniques of Family Psychotherapy.* New York: Grune and Stratton, 1973.
3. F. Coughlin, and H. Wimberger. "Group Family Therapy," *Family Process,* 7 (1968), 37–50.
4. J. Framo. "Marriage Therapy in a Couples Group," in D. Bloch (ed.). *Techniques of Family Psychotherapy.* New York: Grune and Stratton, 1973.
5. A.S. Gurman. "Marital Therapy: Emerging Trends in Research and Practice," *Family Process,* (1973), 45–54.
6. J. Haley. "Family Therapy: A Radical Change," in J. Haley (ed.). *Changing Families—A Family Therapy Reader.* New York: Grune and Stratton, 1971.
7. D. Hardcastle, "Measuring Effectiveness in Group Marital Counselling," *Family Coordinator,* 21 (1972), 213–18.
8. P. Laqueur. "Multiple Family Therapy," in A. Ferber, M. Mendelsohn, and A. Napier (eds.). *The Book of Family Therapy.* New York: Science House, 1972.
9. M. Lebedun. "Measuring Movement in Group Marital Counselling," *Social Casework,* 51 (1970), 35–43.
10. E. Leichter. "Treatment of Married Couples Groups," *Family Coordinator,* 22 (1973), 31–41.
11. P. Low and M. Low. "Treatment of Married Couples in a Group Run by a Husband and Wife," *International Journal of Group Psychotherapy,* 25 (1975), 54–66.
12. M. Markowitz, and A. Kadis. "Short-Term Analytic Treatment of Married Couples in a Group by a Therapist Couple," in C.J. Sager, and H.S. Kaplan (eds.). *Progress in Group and Family Therapy,* New York: Brunner-Mazel, 1972.
13. T. McClellan, and D. Stieper. "A Structured Approach to Group Marriage Counselling," *Mental Hygiene,* 55 (1971), 77–84.
14. J.A. Peterson (ed.). *Marriage and Family Counselling: Perspective and Prospect.* New York: Association Press, 1968.
15. R. Ravich. "The Marriage/Divorce Paradox," in C.J. Sager, and H.S. Kaplan (eds.). *Progress in Group and Family Therapy.* New York: Brunner-Mazel, 1972.
16. C.J. Sager. "Marital Psychotherapy," in J. Masserman (ed.). *Current Psychiatric Therapies, Vol. VII.* New York: Grune and Stratton, 1967.
17. M. Roman and S. Kaplan. "Phases of Development in Family Group Therapy." Paper presented at the Annual Meeting of the New York State Psychological Association, May, 1963.

CHAPTER 22

Principles and Techniques of Multiple Family Therapy

Murray Bowen, M.D.

The method of multiple family therapy described here was developed as part of a clinical research study at Georgetown University Medical Center. The method, already successfully used by an increasing number of family therapists for a wide range of clinical problems, takes less of the therapist's time than more conventional methods, and is quite different from other methods of multiple family therapy. It was developed as an extension of my own theoretical-therapeutic system, and combines clinical observations from family research with developments in family systems theory and practice. First I shall deal with observations from the early family research which are important to the rationale for this method. Then I shall review some important changes in theory and therapy after the original research; describe my method of family psychotherapy for a single family; and finally deal with principles and techniques involved in adapting this method for use with multiple families.

BACKGROUND OBSERVATIONS

Details about the early family research have been presented in other papers (1,2), describing a five-year research project in which entire families lived on the research ward with their schizophrenic son or daughter for periods as long as thirty months. The number of families living in at any one time varied from three to five. This was determined by the size of the families and available room space. The project ran five years. The first year the focus was on mothers and patients. Each mother and each patient had individual psychotherapy. During that year the research hypothesis was modified to consider schizophrenia a process that involved the entire family.

At the beginning of the second year, fathers were required to live on the ward with the families, and "family psychotherapy" was started. All available family members attended the psychotherapy sessions. One goal in the use of the term "family psychotherapy" was to emphasize and complement the companion theoretical concept which considered "the family as the unit of illness." During the first year, with parents and patients in individual psychotherapy with separate therapists, family problems were diffuse and compartmentalized, and difficult to define for research or therapy. After that, all individual psychotherapy was discontinued and family psychotherapy became the only treatment modality.

The initial family sessions were for the families only, but there were major emotional problems in every segment of the operation. In addition there was an overall policy toward openness and moving meetings from behind closed doors into the open. Very soon the daily psychotherapy meetings included all the members of the families and all available staff members. The four therapists functioned as co-therapists, and focused on any issue whether it be between members of the same family, between one family and another, between staff members and the group of families, or between individual staff members. In the effort to achieve a completely open communication system, family members were free to read any records written about them and to attend any clinical, administrative, or research meeting. Initially there was a large family attendance, but the families did not have the time or the interest to continue the meetings, or to consistently send family delegates to the more important meetings. What was important was that the system was open and they could attend if they wished.

In retrospect, those early meetings would more accurately be called "Multiple Family-Therapeutic Milieu Network Therapy." The meetings were so important to the total operation that the project might not have survived those early months without the open communication policy and the open meetings for the entire group. The basic therapeutic method employed during that period was group therapy, although the meetings were called "Family Psychotherapy" to emphasize the primary focus on the family, and to establish a clear delineation between this and conventional group therapy. The meetings resulted in a kind of therapeutic honeymoon for the families, and enthusiasm in the staff. The conversion of the small closed system operation into an open system probably accounted for much of this. The symptoms decreased in most of the families, and there were fairly well sustained periods of enthusiasm and near exhilaration in some.

The honeymoon ended after about a year, and the Family Psychotherapy meetings became repetitive and less productive. The therapists had specific issues for focus within the families, but all too often the focus was lost in a group therapy type of feeling exchange between family members and the ward staff. The first major change in the structure of the meetings came when members of the ward staff attended the sessions as silent observers rather than participants. There were well-established administrative policies for dealing with such issues, and family members could no longer use the meetings to externalize intrafamily anxiety into conflict with the ward staff. This was the beginning of a period in which the active participants consisted of all the members of the families and four therapists. Anyone could speak at any time. This is not a place to evaluate co-therapists or multiple therapists, but in addition to the positive values, there were negative aspects. One therapist might start to define a specific point, and before he could finish, another therapist could interrupt and focus on a completely different issue. More and more time was spent on therapists trying to define issues between themselves. Most important, the families began to use this channel for externalizing intrafamily anxiety into differences between the therapists.

Eventually the therapists' roles were more clearly defined, and the structure of the meetings was changed so that a single therapist was in charge of each session. The therapist in charge could ask another therapist for an opinion, or another therapist could intervene if he had a compelling reason; but ordinarily the therapist in charge directed that session with little participation from the other therapists. This resulted in a structure in which the active participants consisted of all the members of all the families and the therapist who was designated to run the meeting for that day. Any member of any family could speak at any time. Just as the therapist was successfully working toward a definition of an issue in one family, some anxious member from another family would interrupt and change the subject to another issue in another family. It was extremely difficult to keep the issue in a single family in focus, when any member of another family could interrupt the process.

Finally, during the last year of the research project, there was the most important change in the structure of the family psychotherapy sessions. Each family session was designated for a single family, while the other families attended as silent auditors. For the first time in the entire course of the research project, it was possible to work through to clearly define intrafamily emotional issues. From the standpoint of the families, they made much more progress in this period than any other. Some families said they often obtained more benefit from auditing, when they were free to listen and to really "hear," than when they spent time preparing their next comment. The therapy-research staff members considered this year their most productive. This was the final structure of the family psychotherapy sessions when the formal research was terminated in 1959.

CHANGES IN THEORY AND THERAPY AFTER THE EARLY RESEARCH

The significant evolutionary changes in the development of this theoretical-therapeutic system have been presented in reasonable detail in other papers (3, 4, 5). One of the main efforts over the years has been to further define the systems concepts, and to replace conventional theory with new systems concepts.

A major change in practice occurred early in 1960, when the problem child for whom the parents had originally sought psychiatric help was excluded from ongoing family psychotherapy sessions with the parents. This was the result of mediocre results with some twenty-five of these children in the period between about 1957 and 1960. Though the formal research study from 1954–1959 had been devoted exclusively to families with a severely impaired schizophrenic son or daughter, there was a simultaneous clinical operation in progress for a wide range of less severe emotional problems. The children in this group varied in age from preadolescent to midteen years, and had been referred by the Juvenile Court, or by the school, for behavior problems or academic difficulty. Both of the parents and the child were routinely seen together at weekly intervals. In the sessions the parents would focus so much on details about the child's problem that it was difficult to maintain sufficient focus on the parental relationship to foster change in the parents. The average "good" result with these families was one in which they would attend the sessions about a year and then terminate at a point when the child's symptoms had decreased, the mother's "domination" had subsided, and the father's "passivity" had decreased. The family would leave with glowing praise about the success of the therapy, while I considered them to have attained little or none of the basic change of which they were capable.

Rather than continue this mediocre operation, I began to see the parents alone in the first interview to state my conviction that the basic problem lay in the relationship between the parents, and if the parents could define and modify their relationship, the children's problems would automatically disappear. A high percentage of parents readily accepted this working premise. Most of these family therapy sessions were lively and profitable instead of dull and nonproductive as they had been with the child present; most of the children became free of symptoms, so that the average "bad" result was better than the "good" results with the former approach. Since 1960 I have not seen children as part of family psychotherapy sessions, although I occasionally see the children for special reasons.

In the early 1960's I began defining my theoretical concept of "triangles," which provides a flexible and predictable way to conceptualize and modify the family emotional system. This concept has been described in detail in other papers (4, 5). The triangle is the basic building block of an emotional system. A system that includes four or more people consists of a series of interlocking triangles. The characteristics of all triangles are the same, whether in a family system, an emotional system at work, a social system, or elsewhere. A triangle is in constant motion with moves that operate automatically like emotional reflexes, and that are so predictable that one can precisely predict the next move in the system. If one can modify the functioning of a single triangle in an emotional system, and the members of that triangle stay in emotional contact with the larger system, the whole system is modified. Gross behavior in an emotional system may appear too random and strange to describe or classify; but beneath the gross behavior is the constant, predictable microfunctioning of triangles.

On a practical level, there are two major ways to modify the functioning of a triangle. One way is to put two people from a familiar emotional system into contact with a third person who knows and understands triangles, and who does not play into the emotional moves of the familiar twosome. If the third person can continue to stay in contact with the twosome without playing the familiar game of the twosome, the functioning in the twosome will automatically be modified.

Consider the father-mother-child triangle. When these three people are together, the triangle operates automatically on its already built-in circuits. Put a stranger into the system in place of the child; after a brief time he will either become programmed into the familiar patterns of the triangle, or he will withdraw—also a predictable response to triangles. Put a family thera- pist with knowledge of triangles into the triangle in the place of the child. The parents will make predictable moves designed to involve the therapist into the triangle with them. If the therapist can avoid becoming "triangled," and still remain in constant emotional contact with them over a period of time, the relationship between the parents will begin to change. This is the theoretical and practical basis for much of the family psychotherapy in this theoretical-therapeutic system, in which a family is considered to consist of the two most important people in the family, together with the therapist who constitutes a potential triangle person.

Theoretically, a family system can be changed if any triangle in the family is changed, and if that triangle can stay in meaningful emotional contact with the others. Practically, the two spouses are usually the only ones who are important enough to the rest of the family and who have the motivation and dedication for this kind of an effort.

The second way to modify a triangle is through one family member. If one member of a triangle can change, the triangle will predictably change; and if one triangle can change, an entire extended family can change. Thus, an entire family can be changed through one family member, if this moti- vated family member has sufficient dedication and life energy to work toward his goal in spite of all obstacles. The "change" mentioned here is not some superficial change in role or posture, but is deeper and more far-reaching than the change generally associated with most therapeutic systems. An entire family can be changed through the effort of one person. This "family psychotherapy with one family member" involves teaching the motivated person the predictable characteristics of triangles and emotional systems, and then coaching and supervising his efforts as he returns to his family to better observe and learn about them, and as he gains increasing ability to control his own emotional reactiveness to his family. The basic goal has to be to change and improve self, which then secondarily affects the others. This method can be used in families in which one spouse is motivated to work on a family problem and the other is antagonistic, or with young unmarried adults.

With experience, I discovered that research families did better in psychotherapy than families seen only for psychotherapy, and since then I have worked to make every family into a research family. Subtle and important things take place when the therapist functions as a "therapist" or a healer, and the family functions passively, waiting for the therapist to work his magic. Equally subtle and important factors are involved in getting a therapist out of his healing or helping position and getting the family into position to accept responsibility for its own change.

This theoretical-therapeutic system has thus evolved through several major changes and through constant minor change and modification. It began with the relatively simple theoretical notion that the problem involves the entire family; the relatively simple therpeutic method was to get the family together to talk about it. It has arrived at a much better defined and precise systems theory, composed of several interlocking theoretical concepts and at a therapeutic system in which the therapy is usually with the two most responsible family members, or the one most responsible family member.

FAMILY PSYCHOTHERAPY WITH BOTH SPOUSES

Since the principles and techniques of working with families in a multiple family setting are exactly the same as working with a single family, I will first describe the process as it applies to a single family. For therapy purposes, this theoretical approach considers a "family" to be the two most responsible family members (both spouses) with the therapist as a potential triangle person.

The technique of working with both spouses has been modified several times, especially in the early years of family practice. From about 1956 to

1960 there was strong emphasis on analyzing the intrapsychic process in each spouse in the presence of the other spouse. There was a strong focus on dreams, which provided an opportunity to analyze the process in the dreamer, and also to analyze the simultaneous emotional response in the other spouse. By 1960 the primary emphasis was on the relationship system between the spouses, with far less emphasis on the intrapsychic process in each. One goal in that period was that spouses reach the point at which each could communicate to the other anything they thought or felt about the other, or anything they thought or felt about self. The spouses were encouraged to speak directly to each other rather than to the therapist, and there was emphasis on the careful discrimination between thoughts and feelings, and the direct expression of feeling to each other. The present method started about 1962, after the triangle concept was sufficiently developed to be put into clinical operation. It developed rather rapidly until about 1964, since which time there have been fewer changes in technique and more emphasis on the differentiation of self in the therapist.

With this method of family psychotherapy, the therapist has four main functions: (1) Defining and clarifying the relationship between the spouses: (2) Keeping self detriangled from the family emotional system; (3) Teaching the functioning of emotional systems; and (4) Demonstrating differentiation by taking "I position" stands during the course of the therapy.

Defining and clarifying the relationship between the spouses. To some degree, all spouses are caught in feeling worlds, in which they react and respond to the emotional complex in the other without really *knowing* the other. This exists to a significant degree in a majority of spouses, and there is a very large group in which it exists to a paralyzing degree. Most people probably have the most open relationships in their adult lives during courtship, in common-law relationships, or in other fairly intimate relationships that are not permanent. After marriage, each quickly begins to learn the subjects that make the other anxious. To avoid the discomfort in self when the other is anxious, each avoids the subjects that make the other anxious; an increasing number of subjects thus become taboo for discussion. Most spouses attempt to resolve the communication gap by "talking it out," with less than satisfactory results. All too often the attempt to communicate only stirs up emotional reactiveness and drives them farther apart. Very early in my family psychotherapy I discouraged spouses from attempting to talk more at home; and after about 1962, I stopped suggesting that they talk directly to each other in the family therapy sessions.

In this format, I control the interchange. Each spouse talks directly to me in the calmest, low keyed, most objective possible way. In this situation, the other spouse is often able to listen and to "really hear," without reacting emotionally, for the first time in their lives together.

A typical session might go as follows. I open by asking the husband what kind of progress he has made since the last session, and ask him to give me his most objective report. If his report has reasonable content, I then turn to the wife and ask for her *thoughts* while he was talking. Early in the course of therapy, my questions are designed to elicit the intellectual process by asking for thoughts, opinions, or ideas. In other situations I ask for her response or reaction, which is a little less intellectual. Only much later in therapy, and in special situations do I ask for a reading from her subjective, inner feelings. After the wife has spoken, a question may be directed to the husband, such as, "What was going on in your thoughts while she was talking?"

There are occasional "clean" sessions, in which the therapist does nothing more than direct questions from one to the other. There are situations in which the husband's comments are too minimal for an adequate response from the wife; then I ask sufficient questions to get him to elaborate his ideas before asking the wife for her thoughts. If the wife responds with minimal comments, there are more questions to get her to elaborate before I turn to the husband again. If feelings build up and one responds emotionally and directly to the other without waiting for my questions, I increase the directness and tempo of the questions so as to return the process to me. I am always dozens of questions ahead of them. There is always a backlog of theoretical assumptions about the family about which I have questions. During sessions when there is a lull, I make notes about new areas for questions. When obvious feelings are stirred up during a session, the goal is to get them *talking about* the feeling, rather than expressing it. For instance, if the wife suddenly becomes tearful, I may ask her husband if he noticed the tears; or ask him what was going on in his thoughts when he saw the tears. An overall goal for the questions is to touch on areas known to be emotionally important for them, and to get calm, low-keyed responses.

Results of this calm, intellectual, conceptual approach with families have been much more successful than emphasizing the "therapeutic" expression of feeling. The spontaneous, free, open expression of feeling comes automatically and much faster than when therapy is directed at the feelings. One great dividend is that for the first time each spouse finally hears and knows the other. In one session, for instance, which came after about ten family sessions, the wife said she could not wait to come to the sessions because they were so wonderful. The therapist asked what was so wonderful about family problems. She answered that in the process of listening to her husband talk to the therapist, she had learned more about him than during ten years of marriage. A husband, summarizing progress after twelve monthly sessions, said the greatest value to him had been learning what went on inside his wife after having been in the dark for twenty years. Another wife, watching her husband with fixed adoration while he talked, was asked what she thought while she looked at him like that. She said she was absolutely fascinated by the way his mind worked, and that she never had any idea he thought like that.

Special attention goes to defining the system of automatic emotional responses in every marriage that operate largely out of awareness. They are so numerous that one could probably spend a lifetime and never define all of them. In general, they consist of minor emotional stimuli in one that trigger major emotional responses in the other. The response may involve any of the five senses, but most relate to visual or auditory stimuli. The stimulus may be so revulsive that the responder would do almost anything to avoid it, or so pleasurable he would work hard to elicit it. Among the negative stimuli are mannerisms, gestures, facial expressions, and tones of voice that stir jarring emotional responses in the other, or that can make the other's "flesh crawl." As one example, a husband was so attracted by, and so emotionally dependent on his wife for, a certain smile that he spent a sizable segment of his life trying to evoke it, while she was generally turned off by his efforts.

Emotional responsiveness can profoundly affect the course of a relationship. A goal in therapy is to be aware of such mechanisms, to define them in as much detail as possible, and to help the spouses become better observers in an effort to define more and more of them. Often the careful definition of the mechanism is enough to defuse it. For instance, in one conflictual marriage, the husband would slug his wife in response to a trigger stimulus. Several attempts to find the stimulus had failed. He did not hit her often, but when he did it was in the midst of noisy argument, and there appeared to be no specific stimulus. Finally, a situation without words arose when he hit her in response to "that look of hatred in her eyes." That was the last time he ever hit her. He was immensely pleased with the discovery and with his control. Thereafter when tension was high, he avoided looking at her face; she also had some control over "the look." Other stimuli that caused acting-out responsiveness have been identified as "that cold icy stare," "that sneer of contempt," and "that awful snarl in his voice." This level of emotional responsiveness in a marriage has been described as part of the emotional interdependence, and also as part of the family emotional process.

Keeping self de-triangled from the family emotional system. If the therapist is to develop the capacity to stay relatively outside the family emotional system in his clinical work, it is essential that he devote a continuing effort to differentiate his own self from the emotional system of his own family, and also from the emotional system in which he works. Said in another way, it is necessary that he learn about triangles, and that he use his knowledge successfully in the emotional systems most important to him. However, there are some rules and principles that are important in the clinical situation. It is essential that he always stay focused on process, and that he defocus the content of what is being said.

It is absolutely predictable that each spouse will use mechanisms with which each is most familiar and at which each is most adept to involve the therapist in the family emotional system. The first move is usually to cause the therapist to take sides with one or the other; but the therapist is as effectively triangled when angry as he is if charmed. To judge effective emotional distance for myself even though I may be sitting physically close, as occasionally happens in videotaped interviews, I attempt to back out emotionally to the point where I can watch the ebb and flow of the emotional process while always "thinking process," and without getting caught in the flow. Furthermore, there is usually a humorous or comical side to most serious situations. If I am too close, I can get caught in the seriousness of the situation. If I am too distant, I am not effectively in contact with them. The "right" point for me is one between seriousness and humor, when I can make either a serious or a humorous response to facilitate the process in the family.

A basic principle in this theoretical-therapeutic system is that the emotional problem between two people will resolve automatically if they remain in contact with a third person who can remain free of the emotional field between them, *while actively relating to each.* It is essential for the therapist to keep talking, especially in response to a triangling move. If he has the right degree of emotional distance—emotional contact, it is almost automatic for him to say and do the right thing. If he becomes silent and cannot think of a response, he is too emotionally involved. The spouses are continually misperceiving the therapist's involvement, or lack of it, or misperceiving him to either be for or against them. Casual comments are effective messages that he is not overinvolved. A "reversal," which is a comment that focuses on the unobvious or the opposite side of an issue, or that picks up the casual or slightly humorous aspect, is a most effective way of decompressing an overserious situation. One wife, for example, became more emotionally uptight in describing her dominating, nagging mother. I made a casual comment about her lack of appreciation for her mother's lifelong effort to make her be a good daughter; the spouses laughed, the tension was decompressed, and I had communicated awareness that there was another side to the issue.

When the therapist can remain casual about such serious situations, it is usually not long before the spouses can begin to get outside themselves to a more objective view of the situation. No one can tell a therapist what to say in such situations. If the therapist is already emotionally involved, his effort to reverse the emotional process will be heard as sarcastic and mean. Knowledge of triangles is the most effective way I know for understanding emotional systems and keeping self in meaningful emotional contact without becoming emotionally overinvolved.

Teaching the functioning of emotional systems. Some teaching or instruction is necessary with any kind of psychotherapy. With family systems theory and therapy, which explains the human phenomenon in special terms, and which utilizes intellectual concepts to guide the effort to modify emotional systems, teaching is even more necessary. There are hazards to emotional systems in talking *about* emotional systems. When family tension is moderately high, the therapist is vulnerable to being triangled into the family system if he tries to instruct or direct them away from a direction that appears unprofitable. Each spouse interprets the communication differently; then, after debating the issue at home, they return to ask the therapist for the correct interpretation. At that point the therapist's goal is to detriangle himself rather than explain, because that would involve him more deeply in the family system. Over the years I have worked out a plan which works fairly well in teaching the family about emotional systems. Communication is made in a neutral way that is not perceived as authoritative, and at a time when family anxiety is lowest. Early in therapy, when family anxiety is often high, instructional communications are put in terms of "the I position," which is explained below. Later, when anxiety is lower, teaching is done by parables, illustrated by successful clinical solutions of similar problems in other families. Still later, when there is little anxiety, the teaching can successfully be quite didactic.

Taking "I position" stands. When one member of a family can calmly state his own convictions and beliefs, and take action on his convictions without criticism of the beliefs of others and without becoming involved in emotional debate, then other family members will start the same process of becoming more sure of self and more accepting of others. The "I Position" is very useful early in therapy as an operating position in relation to the family. It is advantageous to use it whenever possible through therapy. The more the therapist can clearly define himself in relation to the families, the easier it is for family members to define themselves to each other.

A goal of this method of family psychotherapy is to provide a structure in which spouses can proceed as far toward the differentiation of self as the situation and their motivation can take them, and as rapidly as is possible for them. The therapist makes a continuing effort to challenge them to maximum effort, and to help them through the predictable episodes of anxiety that occur. They are free to stop at any point, and the therapist is free to exercise his "I Position" to define his part in the effort. A high percentage of the families have what is conventionally defined as moderate to severe neurotic problems; only a few are borderline or mildly psychotic. The average family starts with a significant degree of ego fusion or undifferentiation. This has evolved over the years to the point of acute dysfunction in a spouse (usually emotional illness, somatic illness, or social dysfunction such as drinking), to marital disharmony and conflict, or to a behavior problem or life failure problem in a child. A significant number of the families have had long exposure to other forms of psychiatric treatment. The approach for all families is to involve both spouses in this method of family psychotherapy.

The therapy proceeds through several distinct phases. One of the significant early phases is the stage through which they each come to "know" each other better. In some this is slow and gradual; in others it can be a rapid and almost exhilarating experience. Some are so pleased with the decrease in symptoms and increase in togetherness in the marriage that they are ready to terminate. There have been a number of striking early "cures" in a relatively few sessions, such as a seven-session "cure" of fairly severe frigidity in a wife.

For those motivated to proceed, the process helps each spouse to gradually begin to differentiate a self from the other spouse. Characteristically, one spouse begins to focus on self while the other pleads for togetherness. It is common for the differentiating one to yield to the togetherness pressure at least once before proceeding on a self-determined course in spite of the opposition. This results in a brief emotional reaction in the other, following which they both arrive at a new and slightly higher basic level of differentiation. This is usually followed by another fairly calm period, after which the other spouse focuses on self and takes the same steps toward differentiation while the former opposes with togetherness pressure. Thus, differentiation proceeds in small alternating steps. Each new step stirs emotional disharmony in extended families and other interlocking emotional systems, which is generally easier to handle than the disharmony between the spouses. As early as possible the therapist begins to coach spouses in differentiating a self in their families of origin. When a motivated spouse is successful at this, the total process proceeds more rapidly without the alternating pattern that occurs when there is less attention to families of origin.

This is in my experience the most successful and efficient method of family psychotherapy. The family can stop at the point of symptom relief, or they can continue toward a more satisfying, deeper resolution. If the family is well motivated, and the therapist has been relatively successful at keeping himself out of the emotional system with the family, it is usual for the family to find more and more to work on and to resolve. Abrupt termination after fairly brief therapy is often the result of the therapist's emotional involvement in the family emotional system. As the family proceeds through the nodal points of differentiation, it is common for the togetherness-oriented spouse to become negative and disenchanted with the therapy effort. The other is usually pleased and wishes to continue. It is usually fairly easy to help them through these nodal anxiety periods.

There are situations in which a fairly sudden and abrupt termination can occur at a nodal point of change. This happens when the opposing spouse demanding togetherness can stir enough momentum to overcome the more positive forces in the other. I have had experience with over twenty-five families in which a togetherness-oriented husband at such a nodal point suddenly left on a business assignment in another city or overseas, which terminated the therapy effort. An orderly termination is reached when both have achieved a reasonable level of differentiation of self from each other, and from their families of origin; when they know enough about families systems so that one or the other of them has developed the capacity to handle crises; and when they have some kind of reasonable plan and motivation to continue working toward differentiation in the years ahead.

MULTIPLE FAMILY THERAPY

The theory and technique for multiple family therapy had been developed in detail for about two years before it was actually put into operation as a clinical research experiment. Two main ideas motivated the effort. The method of family psychotherapy just described was in successful operation both in private practice and also in my various teaching and supervision programs. The clinical results were excellent with a variety of single families; in some of these families both spouses attended sessions regularly; in some large blocks of sessions were with one spouse alone; in others the total course was with a single family member.

In all areas, the family psychotherapy efforts were going well; but in going from one session to another, I found myself teaching the same principles in session after session. I began thinking of the time that could be saved, and the advantages of covering the material in more detail to many families at the same time. I heard about the striking experiences in each of the families as they worked toward the differentiation of self, but then I had to assimilate these experiences into my own experience and communicate that to others. In thinking about some kind of a structure that would bring a number of families together, yet that would avoid the social and emotional togetherness of groups, and preserve the emotional separateness between families necessary for working out the nuances of emotional interdependence and family process between the spouses, I remembered the structure my staff and I had developed for the live-in families in 1958 and 1959. Using that as a basic structure, I added the details that would be necessary for this new clinical effort.

In the following few years I made some unsuccessful efforts to start this method of multiple family therapy, starting with about three or four new families, each with neurotic level problems of about the same intensity. I spoke to a clinic about finding such families; but most of the "good" families of this type were referred for individual psychotherapy, and those referred to me were too severely impaired and fragmented and too poorly motivated for this effort. I tried to save up enough of these families to start in my private practice, but there were not enough referrals at about the same time to get started. Finally, in 1965, there was an admissions social worker who did understand what I wanted. Within a short time she had found three families applying for family therapy at about the same time that perfectly met the criteria. The families were interviewed, all agreed to participate, and we quickly worked out a relatively simple research plan for observation and the recording of sessions.

The therapy was started with families sitting in a semicircle facing the therapist, and a variety of research observers sitting in the back. The early operating rules were more strict than they have been since. The focus was to be on the emotional interdependence between the spouses in each family, with the other families as silent observers. Elaborate precautions were taken to keep the families emotionally isolated from each other, and to prevent the families from emotionally merging into one large undifferentiated family ego mass which could inundate the family process in each family. The families were all unknown to each other before the start of the project. The purpose and technique of the study was explained to each, and they agreed to avoid social contact with each other outside the sessions, and in case they might later find they had mutual friends, to not mention the other families in any of their social contacts. They had no contact with each other outside the sessions except for meeting in the hallways and elevators as they assembled or left the sessions. In the sessions, each husband and wife sat beside each other, slightly separated from the next two spouses.

The weekly sessions were planned for one and a half hours each, with no fixed rules about the amount of time with each family, and with one half-hour research summary at the end of each session. Originally I had planned a very flexible format which might allow most of the time for a single family, and little or none with the others until the following week, but very quickly we began to divide available time about equally between the families. Too often a silent family would have problems of an urgent nature with too little time. It did not work well to skip any family at any session. Too much could take place in their thinking-feeling systems in that period of time without the therapist's awareness. Originally we planned to build up the group to many more than the original three families, but this was not feasible if the therapist was to do even a brief check on each family each week. Two hours was about the maximum time that families could keep their attention on the sessions without fatigue, and four families was the optimum number for this format. Five families made the schedule too rushed and pressured.

Two major findings of this research effort had not been accurately predicted. (1) The larger group did not facilitate advantageous use of teaching time. It was even easier for the therapist to become emotionally triangled into the families' emotional systems in this setting than in dealing with individual families. (2) The surprise was the unusually rapid progress of the families. This was estimated to be about 50 per cent faster than comparable clinical problems in other families. When we asked about this, we usually got the same reason given by people starting group therapy: "It is reassuring to know that other people have the same kinds of problems." Apparently, it is easier to really see and know your own problem when you watch it in other people than when you only know about it in relation to yourself. Families learn from each other. If one family made a breakthrough in an area, within a week or two other spouses would be trying some version of that in their own families.

The rapid progress of families in the multiple family sessions led to my establishing the first multiple family group in my practice about eight months after the start of this project. This led to the establishment of more and more multiple family groups as fast as schedules could be arranged, until a major portion of my practice, in terms of number of families, is now this method of multiple family therapy. The same has been true of other research observers, and this method of multiple family therapy, which began as a pilot research study at Georgetown University Hospital, is now being widely used in the Washington area.

Another dividend of the research project was the development of a more detailed formal research study on the question of change in psychotherapy. In professional practice, the concept of change or improvement is applied to things as elusive as feeling better, or disappearance of presenting symptom. The research staff on this project has tried hard to define *change* in a way that can be measured and quantified.

This pilot research study has also affected the practice of family psychotherapy. Until this project was over two years old, it was generally accepted that families should be seen once a week in family psychotherapy. This once a week format had generally evolved over the past ten years to replace the two or three appointments per week common in the late 1950's. A year and a half after the start of this project, I began an ongoing multiple family therapy group on videotape in another medical school. My schedule allowed no more than one session every four weeks. There were many reservations about holding multiple family therapy sessions only once a month. One of the wives for the proposed venture, who had been hospitalized several times, was very anxious. She said, "With appointments that far apart, I could get into the hospital and out again between appointments." However, the outstanding success of that multiple family therapy group was responsible for my changing my practice of all kinds of family psychotherapy to monthly appointments, and families have made as much, and possibly even more, progress than equivalent families seen in other multiple family groups that have met weekly.

Considering all the ideas and the explanations offered by the families and the observers, the best explanation for the remarkable progress with the monthly sessions seems to be that families are more on their own, made to be more resourceful and less dependent on therapy to provide working solutions. This also fits with my conviction that it takes a certain amount of time on the calendar for families to change, and the length of time necessary for change is not decreased by increasing the frequency of appointments. (*Change* here refers to change as it is considered at this Center, and not to superficial manifestations of change.) The favorable experience with the monthly appointments has led me to reduce the frequency of appointments with all families, whether therapy with multiple families or single families, to once every two weeks. An increasing number are seen once a month, and a small experimental group of families are being seen once every three months.

From the perspective of this experience, my answer to the often asked, impossible question, "How long does family therapy take?" is now that some families, because of the intensity of their ingrained life patterns and their initial basic level of differentiation of self, will never be able to change significantly. Almost all people in the mental health professions, with whom most of the research has been involved, have so much deep resistance to learning about and getting to know the people in their extended families that they literally have to force themselves to work at it. Even while they are searching for data and going to see distant relatives, this resistance is working to oppose the success of their efforts. This emotional revulsion is very strong in some people, and operates to deny them meaningful contact with the past. There is some indirect evidence that the people who do best at the differentiation of a self in family psychotherapy have some of the same qualities of people who do well in searching out and getting to know people in their extended families. This example may convey some idea of the forces that permit people to do well in family psychotherapy or that prevent them from significant change. As far as upper-middle class families who are motivated to continue working until they have achieved significant change in family psychotherapy are concerned, the average family continues for about four years, whether appointments are once a month or twice a month.

One last word. As should be obvious, it is inaccurate to refer to the clinical method described here as "psychotherapy." I would like to drop the entire concept of "psychotherapy," but there is no accurate and acceptable word to replace it. As we move more and more into systems thinking, we will have to find new terms to describe what we are doing, for conventional terms simply no longer apply.

REFERENCES

1. M. Bowen. "A Family Concept of Schizophrenia," in D. Jackson (ed.), *The Etiology of Schizophrenia.* New York: Basic Books, 1960.
2. _____. "Family Psychotherapy," *American Journal of Orthopsychiatry,* 30(1961), 40–60.
3. _____. "Family Psychotherapy with Schizophrenia in the Hospital and in Private Practice," in I. Boszormenyi-Nagy and J. Framo (eds.), *Intensive Family Therapy.* New York: Harper and Row, 1965.
4. _____. "The Use of Family Theory in Clinical Practice," *Comprehensive Psych.,* 7(1966), 345–74.
5. _____. "Family and Family Group Therapy," in Kapland (ed.), *Comprehensive Group Psychotherapy.*

CHAPTER 23

Multiple Family Therapy

H. Peter Laqueur, M.D.

HISTORY OF MULTIPLE FAMILY THERAPY

Multiple Family Therapy (MFT) was born in 1950 in a New York State Hospital where the author was in charge of a 100 bed ward of mostly young schizophrenic patients under insulin coma therapy. Noticing the well-known phenomenon of patients improving steadily until their first home visit and then returning to the hospital in worse shape, we decided to have a closer look at the families. Families were invited for informative question-answer meetings. This soon made the patients suspicious that the doctor "conspired" with the families whom they generally saw as their adversaries. Joint meetings of patients together with their families were then instituted. After a few years, the sheer number of people present at these meetings made them ineffectual and we then decided to split these families up into groups of four or five families in a group.

Very soon we observed that this was not only expedient, saving time and personnel, but that the interaction of several families seemed to produce change in behavior faster than the treatment of individual families, which we also had used in some cases. It seems that certain mechanisms active in MFT, such as learning through analogy, indirect interpretation, and identification, make it easier for family members to improve communication and to try out new behavior in an atmosphere that is more permissive than when only one family is the center of attention at all times. MFT has been aptly called "a sheltered workshop in family communication."

We mentioned our work with families for the first time briefly in 1959, in a paper on our specific method of insulin coma therapy (9), but not until 1963 did we present a paper on Multiple Family Therapy (10). Since then insulin coma therapy has practically been abandoned in this country and Multiple Family Therapy has progressed from a treatment for the most severely schizophrenic patients on an insulin ward to disturbed families with identified patients of the most diverse diagnostic descriptions in settings of all kinds—hospital, community mental health clinic, correctional facility, drug rehabilitation center and psychiatrist's office (8, 11, 12, 13).

DESCRIPTION OF MFT

A description of MFT is in order at this point. Four to five identified patients, hospitalized or ambulant, together with their families (parents, siblings, spouses, children) meet with a therapist, co-therapist, and observers (therapist trainees) in weekly sessions of 1½ hours. Meetings must be held in evening hours to make participation of working family members possible. Any large, accoustically acceptable, and decently ventilated room in which 25 to 30 chairs can be placed in an ellipse is suitable. Video taping equipment is highly desirable to record the MFT session, both for immediate playback of important sections to the group as part of the therapy, as well as for the evaluation and training sessions of therapists, co-therapists, and therapists in training following the therapy session.

Groups are open-ended. A family leaving the group for whatever reason —for instance, improved identified patient and family relationships, so that the family does not feel the need for further participation; family moving away; change of season (particularly important in Vermont where families living at a distance grow weary of traveling at night over icy winter roads); or, occasionally, a family just dropping out—is replaced by a newly referred family.

After a trial-and-error period of selecting families for a common factor —for example, psychiatric diagnosis, educational level, or economic status —we found that it is best to make MFT groups as random as possible in their socioeconomic as well as their ethnic, religious, political, age, and other characteristics. Specific factor grouping carries with it the dangers of pseudointellectuality, and of superficial discussion around so-called common interests, instead of work on basic human behavior problems, such as marital relationships, or parent-child relationships.

The family's understandable request is that the treatment should produce improvement in the clinical condition of the member who has been identified as "patient." Thus, the first task of the therapist is to explain that we don't believe in "primary patient" as opposed to "healthy" family members, but that we look for disturbed interaction patterns in the entire family in order to help them all. We explain that we see the specific symptoms in the identified patient as provoked, or at least contributed to, and therefore alterable by the response of the family system. We aim to have the families in the group actively participate in the discovery of sickness-provoking mutual behavior, so that families become "co-therapists" and help each other find possibilities for change, and for coping with problems in new ways.

STRUCTURE OF DISTURBED AND HEALTHY FAMILIES

In our attempt to understand a family, we make use of perhaps somewhat oversimplified descriptions of the structure of disturbed as opposed to healthy families.

The most severely disturbed family is one in which everyone is turned off on everyone else. Each member lives in his own world and finds it difficult, if not impossible, to communicate with the others; they cannot talk about anything except perhaps the weather.

The second kind of family is split by the age-generation gap. The parents communicate with each other; the children are in touch with each other; but parents and children have little in common and cannot communicate.

The third family is split by sex. Father and sons form a subsystem, and mothers and daughters are another subsystem; there is little communication between the two.

In the fourth family, two members are intensely tied together emotionally, while other members are not connecting with the symbiotic pair or with each other.

The fifth family has one member, usually mother, in the control tower. Communications from everyone to everyone else go through her; direct communications from one family member to another are avoided. It must be understood that a control tower has also a "loving" function—it avoids collisions.

In the sixth kind of family, most members are in good communication with each other; but one is "outside," except for a weak connection with one other member, and is perhaps being scapegoated.

The seventh kind of family has a strictly hierarchical order; the person who is in the top position may not even appear with the family in the therapy session. He may be a grandparent or other significant personality who calls the shots for the whole family.

And finally, there is the "ideal" family (which we still have to meet in real life), where everyone communicates freely with everyone else on every subject, on cognitive as well as emotional levels.

These models are, of course, only what we see as the most prevalent family types among hundreds of variants and combinations.

GENERAL SYSTEMS THEORY

We have found general systems theory (2) to be a most helpful tool in analyzing and understanding individual families, as well as the whole MFT group.

Living systems have a history of coming into being; of existing for a limited period during which they grow and expand in knowledge, skill, and capability for coping with the environment; and of ceasing to exist after having fulfilled their function. This history applies equally to families and the MFT group as a whole. The individual is seen as a subsystem of a higher system, the family, and this in turn as a subsystem of the next higher systems, the community, society, and environment (suprasystem.) Likewise, the MFT group consists of subsystems: the families and the therapeutic teams each consist of subsystems made up of the individual family members and the therapist, co-therapist, and therapist trainees.

All functioning systems, no matter how intricately composed of multiple parts (subsystems), have *input;* a *central processing unit* (C.P.U.); *output;* and a *feedback loop* which informs the C.P.U. of the quality of its performance and thereby allows control and correction of output.

The family system receives matter, information, and energy (input) from its members (subsystems), and the environment (suprasystem.) It processes this input into actions (output) that ensure productive and creative growth, or, at least, the survival of the system (family) and its subsystems (family members.) The joint decision-making apparatus of the family, whatever shape this may take—family council, informal consultation of family members, and so on—may be termed the C.P.U. of the family system.

The MFT group—and for that matter, any form of psychotherapy—can be considered a system with input (human beings and relationships in need of help), a C.P.U. (the therapeutic team, often in cooperation with family members who act as co-therapists), and output (better functioning of families and their individual members.)

Malfunction of an individual, a family, or the whole MFT group can be analyzed to find the primary focus of disturbance, and to devise methods for correction. Systems malfunction occurs when: the inputs are too powerful, or too scarce, or of irrelevant and useless nature; the C.P.U. lacks data, information, organization, or perception/recognition/checking/planning apparatus to correlate incoming signals with output in a well-structured program and in satisfactory individual style; the output channels are obstructed, distorted, or poorly operating; feedback information is incomplete, wrong, or excessive, redundant, and misleading; and too much, too little, or the wrong kind of energy, matter, and information (cognitive and affective) passes through the interface from one subsystem to the other. Any of these occurrences may cause overloads, inadequate timing, improper reactions to internal and external sensors, friction between parts, faulty bypasses, or over or underreactions.

In a system, no one part can move without influencing all other parts of the system. The therapist must be aware of this and at all times keep the MFT group and also the individual families in his mind *as* systems (6). He then will be able to perform the function of a systems analyst, which consists of analyzing interface problems, feedback, perception, recognition, association, and planning for response; and proposing new and specific possibilities for the correction of malfunctions (3, 4, 5).

DIFFERENCES BETWEEN MFT AND OTHER FORMS OF PSYCHOTHERAPY

We believe that MFT is unique insofar as it alone among the different forms of psychotherapy allows the suprasystem, the outside world, society, to enter into the therapeutic relationship.

In individual therapy, for theoretical reasons, the therapist and the patient close themselves off from the rest of the world. Information from "out there" only enters through the patient's perception, and the therapist has no direct means of checking how correct this perception may be.

Peer group therapy brings the therapist together with several patients, but again information from the "outside" only reaches the therapist through the patients' perception. He cannot see the patients' interactions with the significant others in their immediate environment, let alone with society.

Conjoint family therapy and social network therapy both focus primarily on the identified patient and bring in only persons directly concerned with the identified patient's problems and fate.

It seems to us that only in MFT is society, so to say, present in the form of several families other than the identified patient's, people who are not directly concerned with the identified patient's or his family's fate. The therapist not only directly observes the patient in the context of his family system, but also the family system in its relationship with a suprasystem, the MFT group. This makes the MFT group a truly open system for information input.

RECENT ADVANCES IN MFT

We have developed several techniques or adapted known techniques to our purposes in MFT by means of which we hope to expedite change and shorten the therapeutic process. Years ago we were not overly concerned with shortening therapy, because our identified patients were for the most part severely schizophrenic individuals, longterm in-hospital patients. With the trend toward shorter hospitalization and faster reintegration of the identified patient into active life, we started looking for ways to also shorten MFT.

We devised an exercise for the very beginning of a new MFT group which seems to speed up the process of getting-acquainted considerably. The mothers of the group are asked to come to the center and tell the group what they think of themselves, and how they rate themselves as mothers and wives. Then the fathers in the group are asked to rate themselves as fathers and husbands.

The youngsters are asked to divide themselves into two subgroups, one the so-called "good" children (usually the ones who consider themselves the "healthy" children), and the other, the so-called "bad" children (usually the identified patients). They are encouraged to state briefly their problems with the family; probably not surprisingly, the "good" children also have many of these. This polarization—which of course works best with families who seek help because of behavior problems of one member—leads to a process of learning by analogy. After only two sessions, the group usually obtains a good awareness of the type of family problems in each family.

The therapist may also explain and diagram the previously described family structures for the group, and ask families to indicate which model they think comes closest to their own family.

In subsequent sessions we explore specific dyadic relationships with the help of some here-and-now exercises:

In the *yes-no exercise:*, two people with differences of opinion stand opposite each other with arms outstretched and hands on each other's shoulders. One states a wish or command and then shouts "Yes," while the other shouts "No." The shouting usually becomes louder and quickly is followed by a physical attempt to push the other away from the midline. Aggressive people try to win; passive people learn to muster more strength, and in the majority of cases both partners report that they find the emotional intensity of the exercise satisfying. Only a small number of people call this demonstration "silly" or are "ashamed to show feelings," or are "afraid of hurting or being hurt" or prefer to "only talk" about their differences. There is diagnostic significance in how long it takes each person to express genuine emotion and activity; also in whether participants follow the rules or try to tickle or otherwise get the other off balance.

Three other exercises, the *yes-if,* the *yes-but,* and the *yes-and,* can be useful to explore how two people reach a tentative or qualified agreement, or if two people have to learn to agree to disagree in a friendly tolerant fashion, rather than to disagree in angry or resigned (shrugging shoulders) ways.

Another very challenging exercise is the so-called *back-to-back.* A couple is placed back to back, locking arms, and is asked to find a some way to extricate themselves from this position. Some turn around, seeking each other out, and some walk away from each other frustrated. From who does what when, we and the group as well as the participants in the exercise learn a great deal.

Hierarchy within the family can be made manifest by letting one person climb on a chair as "boss", and decide who should stand closest and who farther away.

We have somewhat modified the family sculpting technique of Peggy Papp and her colleagues. We not only ask a person to sculpt his family as he sees it now, but to model it over time, as it was when he was five years old, ten, fifteen, twenty years of age, up to the present. This chronological family sculpture is also an excellent exercise for therapist trainees during the evaluation and training session that follows the MFT session. Similarly, we find the older psychodrama techniques of "doubling," "monologue," "sociogram," and "act out a story" more useful in our training sessions for new workers than in the MFT session.

One of the most exciting innovations is the recording of MFT sessions on video tape, with its possibility for immediate playback to the group of important scenes, allowing us to study body language and contradictions between verbal and nonverbal signals. We record with two cameras, one at each end of the elliptically arranged MFT group. A special-effects generator allows the VTR director to show in a composite picture what goes on at one end of the group simultaneously with the reactions in the rest of the group.

PROCESS

For schematic purposes, we can divide the treatment process in MFT into three phases.

Phase I: Initial Interest. Families experience an initial sense of relief and even some remission of symptoms as they see that something is being done about a painful situation. It is a kind of magical relief due to unreal expectations. But there is also the chance to observe at firsthand other families suffering (and improving), and thereby to have a spark of hope kindled.

Phase II: Resistance. The family begins to see that a change in attitude and behavior is required not only of one member (the identified patient), but in all members mutually and simultaneously. This is the time when their initial fears about exposing hurts and anxieties come to the fore, and resistance to treatment sets in. Doubt that "anyone ever changes," and fears about losing "whatever little good relations we had" are voiced when they are asked to open up and to confront the sleeping dogs in their lives.

Before genuine changes in emotional response patterns based on something more than lip service can be obtained, individuals must first gain confidence that risk-taking and reaching out to the other person can be safe, and that the other person may respond positively and not with the accustomed withdrawal, irrelevancy, or rejection. Only when fear of failure gives way to mutual acceptance, can phase II slide slowly into

Phase III: Working Through. Significant changes begin to take place. With true openness and with increased confidence, families come to realize their deeper problems and also their ability to deal with them. They become more flexible in their recognition of the alternative options open to them. Families in this phase become helpful to other families in distress, and teach them by model and analogy.

MECHANISMS OF CHANGE

A description of some of the mechanisms operating in MFT may illustrate the nature of the transactions performed (7).

Delineation of the field of interaction. Following Kurt Lewin's *Field Theory in Social Science* (14), the therapist tries to see the total field of interaction between subsystems (patient, family) and suprasystem (the total social environment), and makes the participants in the group aware of the importance for sickness and health of this changing surrounding field. The range and variety of therapeutic approaches available to the therapist in this field of interacting forces is much wider than in a two-way communication with individual patients or single families.

Breaking the intrafamilial code. Families with a seriously disturbed member seem to develop secret codes for their internal verbal and nonverbal communications. These are often used to close off discussion of a dangerous area. Families have had a lifetime to learn each other's signals, and these are not readily understood by the therapist. Often other families, because of their own experience, are able to help in breaking these codes. At such moments, the therapist may be confused and unable to understand the direction things are taking, because he is unaware of the secret meaning of messages; but he can assist in circumventing this defensive process by insisting on discovering the real meaning of the transaction taking place, often with the help of explanations by other families.

Competition. Competition between systems (families) or subsystems (individuals) produces changes in the internal power distribution of the system faster than work with a single family could do. A threat to the status of a family or an individual stimulates competition, which leads, in turn, to productive interaction of the family members at an earlier stage in treatment. Later on, cooperation may take the place of competition.

Amplification and modulation of signals. A sensitive patient can pick up a signal from the therapist and amplify it to sensitize his family. Through his family, such a signal may be further amplified and modulated to other families who, without this amplification, might not yet have responded to the therapist's signal.

Learning through trial and error. The MFT group provides its members with unique opportunities to try out new modes of behavior, reinforce them if they meet with the group's approval, or discard them if the group disapproves. The MFT group is characterized by the simultaneous presence of many authority figures—the therapist, fathers, mothers, and so forth. In this setting, the relationships between identified patient and various authority figures can be worked through rapidly by means of the comparatively nonthreatening process of understanding through analogy and identification. The therapist, in the role as parent-surrogate, may transiently diminish the parent's authoritarian status, thereby encouraging the identified patient to behave more independently, to be more "daring."

New insights may also be achieved through role-playing—for example, having the son of family A play the role of the father of family B. By acting as if he were that parent, son A may not only achieve for himself, but also transmit to the other children, a greater understanding of the role of the parent in this situation.

Learning by analogy. Members of the MFT group have many opportunities to observe analogous conflict situations and learn from these examples. The knowledge that others have been there is an important incentive to learn new ways of dealing with conflict; this situation occurs frequently in the MFT group, whose members present many different types of conflict.

Learning through identification. MFT offers many opportunities for identification. Fathers learn from other fathers; mothers from other mothers; youngsters identify with youngsters in other families. The fellowship of experience in the MFT group helps each to cope with existential and situational problems.

The use of models. The therapist in MFT uses the healthier aspects of one family as a model and a challenge as a way to motivate other families to change their behavior. The potential for this is enhanced by the fact that

MFT groups are open-ended, so that in each group families at different stages of treatment are present.

Creating a focus of excitation. In our attempt to break through the resistance to change behavior that is manifested in most families, we asked ourselves: "How do people integrate new experiences in their outlook on the world and their preparation for future behavior?" Information theory postulates that those events that have the least probability of occurring, yet do occur, have the highest information value. A new pattern or a new sequence of signals that produces an excitation focus in the nervous system has high information value. Translated into MFT terms, a new, more realistic type of behavior of one family, as distinguished from their usually observed behavior, can act as a focus of excitation for the whole group if it is used skillfully by the therapist. The use of humor, a drawing, or a video picture in this context can be very successful.

Use of families as co-therapists. The open-ended MFT group includes families in different stages of treatment and improvement. Often, the more advanced families, consciously or unconsciously, directly or indirectly, offer themselves as co-therapists; how the therapist uses these opportunities is indicative of his skill. In any of the above described mechanisms families can be used in therapeutic ways to help other families.

GOALS AND RESULTS

Therapy always aims to change a system of interaction between the primary patient and his environment, even if the stated goal is not crisis intervention, but only mediating and producing better insight. Insight, after all, in systems terms, means becoming aware of more inputs to the regulatory system that maintains and steers the activities of the self. If one perceives and recognizes more external and internal forces and vectors, one subsequently can change one's behavior because of these insights. Every psychotherapist, from whatever school derived, strives to teach the primary patient and his environment to "relate better"—that is, to be less easily offended, turned off, sulky, depressed, or unproductive; to learn self-confidence, even under stress; to stand up to formerly unconquerable obstacles and overcome them; to achieve a better understanding of inner conflicts and one's goals and purposes in life. This means that patients and families are encouraged and persuaded to gain a new perspective on life and environment, no matter how non-directive the therapeutic techniques applied are.

We consider a family improved if our therapeutic intervention has achieved the following:1. Better function and creative operation of the family, even within environments that make family life more complex and difficult emotionally, economically, politically, or morally. 2. Better mutual liking and respect of family members for one another. 3. Better acceptance of shortcomings and capitalizing on each other's strengths. 4. Better ability to enjoy day-to-day living. 5. Greater capability for compassion, mutual love, understanding, support, and cooperation among family members. 6. Better insight and improved judgment. 7. Greater openness for new information. 8. Building of lasting and satisfying relationships with each other within the family, and with friends and environment.

It remains to be said that in the approximately 1500 families treated in our MFT groups over the last twenty-five years, we may have had no more than a handful of families where we thought MFT was contraindicated. These were cases where exposure of a vital secret might lead to explosive reactions. In general, however, we fully agree with Ackerman (1): "With great frequency I have found that these intimate matters, these so-called secrets, turn out not to be real secrets at all. Far more often they are common family knowledge, surrounded by a tacit conspiracy of silence. What is involved here is not so much a true secret but rather a barrier to emotional communication, a barrier to the free sharing of certain experiences."

REFERENCES

1. N.W. Ackerman. *The Psychodynamics of Family Life*. New York: Basic Books, 1958.
2. L.von Bertalanffy. "General Systems Theory and Psychiatry," in S. Arieti (ed.), *American Handbook of Psychiatry*. New York: Basic Books, 1966.
3. H.P. Laqueur. "General Systems Theory and Multiple Family Therapy," in J.H. Masserman (ed.), *Current Psychiatric Therapies*, Vol. VIII. New York: Grune & Stratton, 1968.
4. _____. "General Systems Theory and Multiple Family Therapy," in W. Gray, F.J. Duhl, and N.D. Rizzo (eds.), *General Systems Theory and Psychiatry*. Boston: Little, Brown, 1969.
5. _____. "Multiple Family Therapy and General Systems Theory," in N.W. Ackerman (ed.), *Family Therapy in Transition*. Boston: Little, Brown, 1970.
6. _____. "Systems Therapy," in J.H. Masserman (ed.), *Current Psychiatric Therapies*, Vol. XI. New York: Grune & Stratton, 1971.
7. _____. "Mechanisms of Change in Multiple Family Therapy," in C.J. Sager, and H.S. Kaplan (eds.), *Progress in Group and Family Therapy*. New York: Brunner Mazel, 1972.
8. _____. "Multiple Family Therapy: Questions and Answers," *Seminars in Psychiatry*, 5 (1973).
9. H.P. Laqueur and H.A. LaBurt. "Coma Therapy with Multiple Insulin Doses," *J. Neuropsychiat.*, 1 (1960), 135–47.

10. H.P. Laqueur, H.A. LaBurt, and E. Morong. "Multiple Family Therapy," in J.H. Masserman (ed.), *Current Psychiatric Therapies, Vol. IV.* New York: Grune & Stratton, 1964.
11. _____. "Multiple Family Therapy: Further Developments," *Internat.J.Soc.-Psychiat.* (1964), 69–80.
12. H.P. Laqueur and S.L. Safirstein. "Comparison of Treatment in the Psychiatric Division of a General Hospital and in a State Hospital," *Excerpta Medica Internat.Congress Series No. 150.* Madrid, 1966.
13. H.P. Laqueur, C.F. Wells, and M. Agresti "Multiple Family Therapy in a State Hospital," *Hosp. Community Psychiat.,* 20 (1969), 13–19.
14. K. Lewin. *Field Theory in Social Science.* New York: Harper & Row, 1951.

CHAPTER 24

Co-Therapy in the Treatment of Families

Michael Holt, Ph.D.

and Doris Greiner, R.N., M.S.

Just as many swimmers who are uneasy about drowning will associate with a life preserver, so do many family therapists prefer company when they dive into a family.

Jay Haley (1)

During the past twenty-five years, increasing attention has been paid to the value of involving two professionals in the therapeutic setting. This procedure has been called "co therapy," "multiple therapy," "co-operative psychotherapy," and "three-cornered therapy" (2). These labels suggest differences in goals and methods which must be examined in order for procedure to be defined; however, for purposes of convenience the term *co-therapy* will be used here to mean the simultaneous involvement of two therapists in the treatment setting. Co-therapy has been employed in a variety of treatment settings with differing goals and patient populations (3,4,5,6). Unfortunately, the disorganized state of the literature obscures important elements of co-therapy and clouds the significance of various goals, therapeutic situations, and patient populations. Thus, the current status of co-therapy is paradoxical: co-therapy has been discovered and re-discovered in differing settings, and used for varying goals with different patient populations in a rather disorganized manner. An increasing number of therapists, particularly family therapists, feel that it is a successful and preferred procedure; however, despite claims of success almost no empirical research exists that investigates the process or outcome of co-therapy.

Our purpose here is to briefly review the history of co-therapy and suggest ways to organize the approach to co-therapy. Secondly, a scheme designed to clarify its nature will be proposed. Thirdly, we will define our own approach to co-therapy by showing how we apply this organizational scheme. Fourthly, the benefits assumed to attend the use of co-therapy with families will be examined; our argument in this regard is that co-therapy is more complicated than it initially appears. Fifthly, the potential of this process and means of facilitating this potential with families will be discussed. Finally, philosophical implications of co-therapy with families will be explored.

Interestingly, co-therapy arose in connection with the family setting. In 1930 Adler described discussions of a child's problems by two counselors, the child, and the parents (7). He reported that this procedure had therapeutic value for the child. Later, Reeve and Hadden (8,9) described the use of two therapists in individual and group psychotherapy for training and supervisory purposes. Therapeutic as well as training benefits were noted. Whitaker (10) was the first to report the use of co-therapy for primarily therapeutic purposes. He and his associates emphasized the efficacy of co-therapy in working through impasses in the treatment of individuals, particularly severely disturbed patients (11,12). Shortly after Whitaker described the therapeutic benefits of co-therapy, Dreikurs (13) reported the use of co-therapy for training, supervisory, and therapeutic purposes. He mentioned the following specific advantages: the establishment of a proper transference relationship; a better analysis of the patient's problems; enhanced insight for the patient; and a more effective change of the patient's attitude and behavior. Later, he and his associates discussed these values for both the therapists and the patient in more detail (14,15). More recently, Mullen and Sangiuliano (16) have developed a comprehensive list of 28 advantages of co-therapy. Reports of the success of co-therapy in the individual treatment situation have continued up to the present (17,18,19).

Reports of the use of co-therapy in the group psychotherapy situation quickly followed its initiation in the individual treatment setting (20,21,22). According to Gans, the first goal was to provide a shortcut to the training of group psychotherapists (23). Advantages described by others were that: transference was enhanced; countertransference was better controlled; the family setting was recreated; identification was facilitated, especially when male and female therapists were used; a model interpersonal relationship was provided; a more objective basis for evaluation and diagnosis was developed (24,25,26). It should be noted that these are similar to the values reported above by Dreikurs as applying to co-therapy in individual psychotherapy. There are numerous reports in the literature of successful results with co-therapy in the group situation involving psychotic, neurotic, and psychopathic patients (27,28,29).

Belmont and Jasnow, Framo, and Haley first reported the involvement of two therapists in the treatment of families (30,31,32). Initial purposes of co-therapy in the family therapy setting were that it afforded protection for the therapists against being overwhelmed and engulfed in the pathological family system. Beels and Ferber described the family therapists who were proponents of co-therapy as having a reactive and analytical orientation to family therapy (33); also, they stated (34) that this group of therapists were particularly concerned about "dangers, pitfalls, and the need for help." Family therapists (35,36,37) have reported that co-therapy prevents the therapists from becoming dependent on the family for support and acceptance, presents a clearer understanding of family dynamics, provides the family with a model relationship, and gives the family a new set of "parents." Many family therapists describe co-therapy as a preferred procedure, and some question whether effective family therapy can take place without the involvement of two therapists (38,39). When co-therapy was first reported in family therapy it was most often initiated in the treatment of families containing schizophrenic or psychotic members (40,41).

Several important themes emerge from the history of co-therapy. Co-therapy often originated in treatment situations, whether individual psychotherapy, group psychotherapy, or family therapy, that involved psychotic or schizophrenic patients. Co-therapy has been most often developed by therapists, again whether in individual psychotherapy, group psychotherapy, or family therapy, who have an analytic orientation or at least share terminology and interests within the analytic tradition.

Therapists employing co-therapy usually report it to be effective and successful (42). Criticism of co-therapy has emerged almost exclusively from the group psychotherapy situation. MacLennan, Slavson, and Johnson (43,44,45) have each questioned the value of co-therapy, and suggested that it confounds and confuses important issues, particularly involving transference and countertransference. The strongest criticism is that of Berne (46). He states that co-therapy necessitates that both therapists are professionally and administratively equal, which rarely occurs. Co-therapy is generally described as an evasion of responsibility on the part of the therapist. According to Berne, practical advantages of co-therapy have not been explained, and it obscures and complicates important issues.

The importance of the dynamics of the co-therapy relationship has been frequently mentioned in the literature, (52,53,54). Rubinstein and Weiner (55) have provided a good discussion of the dynamics of the co-therapy team in family therapy. Other family therapists have mentioned or suggested the similarities that occur between the dynamics of the co-therapy relationship and the dynamics in the family (56,57).

There is a deficit in empirical research which is difficult to account for especially considering the almost universal claims of success by those who use co-therapy. A brief review of representative empirical studies illustrates the problems of research in co-therapy. Rabin (47) surveyed therapists and found that co-therapy was a preferred method and that emphasis was placed on a "good" relationship between co-therapists. No specific definition was proposed for a "good" relationship. Rice, Fey, and Kepecs (48) investigated therapist experience and style as factors in co-therapy. They found six therapeutic styles. They also found that experienced and inexperienced therapists had different styles; that subjectively rated effectiveness correlated with the level of comfort in the co-therapy relationship; and that there was a negative correlation between amount of co-therapy and satisfaction in co-therapy. Unfortunately, their study had serious methodological problems so that their findings, at best, are tentative.

Gurman (49) found no significant differences in outcome of marital therapy when co-therapy and single therapists were compared, although again methodological problems make this finding almost meaningless. For example, data were combined which were based on vastly differing types of co-therapy with different types of patients and compared to data derived from marital therapy with single therapists without in any way insuring equivalence between the situations. This lack of empirical research in co-therapy is shared with the entire field of family therapy. It would be productive for family therapists, and specifically those engaging in co-therapy, to follow the model established in individual psychotherapy, where a significant research literature has been developed (50,51). Research would assist in the organization of both family therapy and co-therapy, and it could illustrate the importance of outcome variables involving therapeutic method, patient, and therapists' characteristics. Investigations of process variables could illustrate factors and variables influencing the interactions and interventions between therapists and families and between the two therapists. Both outcome and process research is needed in co-therapy and family therapy.

While a historical review suggests several themes that emerge from the development of co-therapy, the disorganization in the literature makes it difficult to identify important issues and variables that could result in a meaningful definition of co-therapy. We believe that clarification would result from an organizational scheme in which co-therapy was defined by its goals, treatment situation, patient population, therapists' characteristics, and theoretical orientation. Such an organizational scheme would raise questions for the therapist interested in utilizing co-therapy as well as for the researcher of co-therapy.

Co-therapy undertaken for therapeutic goals can be differentiated from co-therapy for purposes of training, supervision, or consultation. Criteria of process and outcome will vary depending on whether the co-therapy is primarily for the patients' or for the therapists' benefit. It would be helpful to investigate which type of goal is most often established and which tends to be most often achieved. A second consideration focuses on the objectives of the therapy itself. More specifically, co-therapy in short-term therapy is likely to be very different from co-therapy in intensive or long-term psycho-therapy. There are suggestions in the family therapy literature that co-therapy is more often used in intensive family therapy, although no definite conclusion can be made.

Secondly, individual psychotherapy, group psychotherapy, and family therapy treatment situations can be differentiated. There are particularly important differences between family therapy and individual and group psychotherapy. Both individual and group psychotherapy are essentially artificial situations established for the purpose of assisting or changing an individual; however, in family therapy the objective involves assisting or changing an ongoing family system of interactions, and the resulting change of individuals is of secondary interest. It would be helpful to know whether there are differences in effectiveness among these situations. Co-therapy seems to be often used in family therapy with the hope that it will reduce the more difficult therapeutic task. There is little empirical evidence that supports this hope.

Neurotic, psychotic—particularly schizophrenic—and personality dis-ordered patient populations can be differentiated. It is important to question whether there are differences in outcome among these populations. In the past, co-therapy has been most often developed in situations involving psychotic patients. Here again, co-therapy seems to have been founded on the belief that it reduces the difficulty of the more formidable therapeutic task of working with severely disturbed patients.

Fourthly, it would be beneficial to differentiate whether cotherapy is associated with particular types of therapists. For example, Beels and Fer-ber (58) dichotomize family therapists into conductors, who are powerful, active, and persuasive, and reactors, who are less directive and particularly concerned about difficulty associated with family therapy. Reactors with an analytic orientation most frequently have initiated co-therapy in the family setting. Conductors rarely utilize co-therapy. At the present, it is impossible to determine whether co-therapy is primarily practiced by reactive and analytic family therapists because it is most consistent with that orientation, or whether that orientation was coincidental to the situations in which co-therapy was first used with families. In addition, it is interesting to consider the A-B therapist variable of Whitehorn and Betz (59). They found evidence that type A therapists are more effective with schizophrenics, while there is other equivocal evidence suggesting that type B therapists are more effective with neurotics (60, 61). Since co-therapy has been often initiated with schizophrenic patients, it would be interesting to investigate whether it was developed by type B therapists to possibly compensate for their lower success rate. Other considerations about the type of therapist focus on whether peer or equal therapists' relationships are more effective than senior-junior relationships.

Fifthly, it would be helpful to differentiate theoretical orientations to determine whether co-therapy is more consistent with particular orientations. Although most therapists who developed co-therapy had an analytic orientation, it does not necessarily hold that co-therapy is inconsistent with other theoretical positions. Mullen and Sangiuliano's use of co-therapy within an existential orientation (62) illustrates a different orientation.

In summary, co-therapy can be better understood by asking the following questions: co-therapy for what goals? in what treatment situation? with what type of patient? with what type of therapists? with what theoretical orientation? The systematic application of these questions would lead to a more accurate conceptualization of co-therapy both in clinical and research areas.

The primary concern of the authors has been the use of co-therapy for therapeutic rather than training purposes, with families rather than in individual or group psychotherapy. Most often, the families with which we have worked have contained one or more psychotic members. We involve ourselves in intensive examinations of rational and emotional issues that have precluded the family's development of its own strengths. We have engaged in co-therapy in out-patient family therapy over the past 3½ years. In terms of Beels and Ferber's dichotomous classification, we are closer to the reactive group. The co-therapy we practice involves an equal relationship in which each of us assumes responsibility both to the family and to each other. We perceive the co-therapy relationship as integral to the family therapy process. More specifically, we believe that the dynamics of our relationship are important because they have impact on the families with which we work. The impact goes beyond each of us as individual therapist and behaviorally communicates values and interests which we share. Secondly, we see the dynamics of our relationship as often reflecting important dynamics within the families with which we work. When we encounter particular difficulties with families, we have found that it is productive to evaluate whether the difficulty is evident in the process of our own relationship.

ASSUMED ADVANTAGES OF CO-THERAPY WITH FAMILIES

We assume five benefits of co-therapy with families: security and protection; more objective evaluation; exposure to a good relationship; increased effectiveness of heterosexual co-therapy teams; satisfaction and pleasure deriving from co-therapy. The increased security and protection which co-therapy affords family therapist has been mentioned frequently in the literature (63,64,65). The basic assumption seems to be that involving two therapists with a family will make the therapeutic task easier or at the very least more comfortable. While personal and professional security are prerequisite for engaging in therapy, entering into a co-therapy relationship for the primary purpose of increasing this security should, at best, be done cautiously. For one thing, the risk that security becomes an end in itself is great, and the pursuit of this end is directly opposed to the therapeutic process. Additionally, Slavson and MacLennan (66,67) report that co-therapy results in increased manifestation of dependency and security needs. If these issues are not carefully examined the likely result will be confusion and a lack of therapeutic progress. Essentially, the therapeutic tasks are increased rather than decreased by the use of co-therapy.

McGee and Schuman (68) suggest that sexual needs may be central to the relationship between the therapists. Dependency, security, and sexual issues are closely related for families who present themselves for therapy. Usually, little effort has been made to identify these needs, and the way they are met. Therefore, it is incumbent on the therapists to initially and continually differentiate these needs and issues in their own relationship if the process is to be effectively pursued with the family. Again, the therapeutic tasks increase rather than decrease when co-therapy is employed.

A second assumed benefit of co-therapy is that it results in less bias, increased "objectivity," and more valid evaluative and diagnostic information (69,70). This may seem initially obvious, so that it may not be carefully questioned. If security, protection, and dependency issues have not been identified and considered it appears doubtful that two therapists could safely share conflicting or opposing impressions. Clarification and validation could simply become a means of supporting each other rather than obtaining a more accurate understanding of family and team dynamics. The maintenance of unbiased and independent perspectives is a difficult task once the two therapists become involved not only with the family, but also in their own relationship. If the assumed benefit of increased "objectivity" is naively expected, it might prevent the therapists from seeking needed independent evaluation. Thus, once again, the benefits and difficulties of co-therapy are more complicated than they superficially appear.

The first two assumed benefits of co-therapy are primarily for the therapists. From the family's point of view additional benefits are assumed in the literature (71,72), the most noteworthy being that the family has a good relationship with which to work and to use as a model. Family members may initially perceive a potential for relating between the therapists, and this perception may be a significant factor in beginning the work and in setting a focus for the therapy. Family members may feel overwhelmed at the prospect of having to deal with two therapists; or they may be relieved by thinking that the forces of destruction they experience in their family may not so easily overwhelm a team. Therapists do well to be alert to both of these possibilities. Moving beyond the initial phases of family therapy, the relationship of the therapists as a potential benefit to the family takes on increased significance. It is generally accepted that this relationship needs to be a "good one." What "good" means is difficult to specify. A basic assumption seems to be that one aspect involves the ability to tolerate and work with what Boszormenyi-Nagy (73) has summed up as the "incredible tensions, generated by what can be called the family member's unconscious manipulation of the therapists into resolving the family's covert incestuous and murderous conflicts."

It seems from the literature and from the experience of these therapists that work often begins with relatively little preplanning or examination of the relationship that the co-therapists are offering the family (74,75). The parallel between a natural or convenient selection of therapists and the similar approach that many of the parents and troubled families have taken to selecting each other is striking. This similarity suggests that there may be many aspects of the potentially good relationship unavailable to conscious examination early in the relationship. When these aspects enter awareness they may have more to do with the therapists' early family and peer relationships than the current needs of a particular family. Again, the potential develops for additional therapist work in order to realize the potential of co-therapy.

If a positively developing relationship is available to a family, family members may connect with it in a variety of ways. The co-therapy team has been mentioned in the literature (76, 77) as providing a new set of parents for the family. The degree to which this aspect of the relationship is fostered and explored varies; much depends on the theoretical basis and objectives of therapy. Whether or not they are fostered and explored, dynamics that parallel the family struggle exist. To some extent testing takes the form of a continual effort to split the co-therapy team. Whether or not this is dealt with depends partially on the recognition of this dynamic and partially on the specific goals of therapy. The relationship that absorbs such testing without splitting and without solidifying in defense may be one example of that good relationship mentioned in the literature.

Closely related to the parental model is the discussion of the value of a heterosexual team. Again, advantages have been assumed, through not universally (78,79). The benefits of a heterosexual therapy team cut across many levels of interaction and intensity. At a less intense level, socialized roles and expectations are examined in the family therapy process. A male and female by their very presence in the therapy setting may break into conventional male-female stereotypes (for instance, women are not competent outside of the home and family; men act and do not examine personal behavior and feelings openly). At a more intense level, clarifying sexuality in relationships is an aspect of the work to be done with families in therapy.

Confusion about sexual needs and expression is enmeshed in whatever presenting and continuing difficulties families bring to therapy. At some level, the sexual aspects of the relationship between the therapists is part of the family therapy process. The clearer the therapists are about the sexual implications of their ongoing relationship, the greater the possibility of being aware of the distorted expressions of sexual needs in the family. If the therapists fail to examine these issues in their own relationship the chances are that confusion in the family may be increased by the therapy team.

A fifth benefit of co-therapy is that of satisfaction and pleasure for both the therapist and the family. It is interesting to note that the value of satisfaction and pleasure for both therapists and family is not often mentioned in the literature. Mullen and Sangiuliano (80) as well as Kell and Burrow (81) report that co-therapy for individual patients results in satisfaction for the therapists that outweighs the added effort and difficulty. Several family therapists have briefly or implicitly suggested that pleasure is derived from co-therapy (82,83).

For the therapists, satisfaction is necessary for the development of their relationship. It results from the experience each therapists has with the family and from the relationship between the therapists. A crucial dilemma in therapy discussed by Boszormenyi-Nagy (84) individuates the importance of satisfaction and support for co-therapists. He states that the therapist may be rejected for wanting to help the family to change. The solo therapist may be confronted with a paradox: he may obtain the family's acceptance by supporting their resistance to change and "giving up his professional integrity"; if he confronts the family's resistance to change and therefore maintains his professional integrity, he risks losing the family's acceptance and support and probably his own satisfaction. A satisfying and accepting relationship with another therapist affords at least a partial resolution of this dilemma.

For the family, satisfaction and pleasure from co-therapy probably stem from the multiplicity of health relationships which are possible. In working intensively with two therapists, each family member can experience support and acceptance from each therapist and from the co-therapy relationship. Also, co-therapy mitigates the fears of rejection and isolation which may be involved in termination. The family does not have to experience anxiety about leaving the therapists alone if a satisfying and pleasurable relationship exists for the therapists.

FACILITATING THE POWER OF CO-THERAPY

These five assumed benefits of co-therapy make it clear that co-therapy is a more complicated and less understood procedure than it may initially seem. The complications and confusion are particularly evident when co-therapy is being employed in intensive family therapy. While the advantages which have been assumed do not always hold up under close scrutiny, it is important to identify means of maximizing the therapeutic effectiveness of co-therapy. We think that the potential of co-therapy can be achieved by the co-therapists' participation in the process of examination, clarification, and change of their interactions as well as those of the family. If the co-therapists do not participate in the process of examination, clarification, and change, they invite an element of hypocrisy into their relationship and into the therapy.

In order to maximize the power of co-therapy, the following questions may be asked: what are the goals of the family therapy and how does co-therapy relate to the goals? what are the goals of co-therapy and how are they communicated to the family? what is known about the family that suggests that co-therapy would be beneficial? what elements of personal style are important to each co-therapist, and what is available to change? in what areas can strengths and weaknesses be expected to develop in the co-therapy relationship? how do the theoretical orientations of the co-therapists compare, and how do they relate to co-therapy? Other questions assist in exploring the co-therapy relationship: to what degree is our co-therapy relationship based on needs for security and protection? how free is each of us to share or raise different or contradictory impressions or perceptions? do we professionally and personally respect and trust each other? what are the sexual implications and aspects of our relationship? do we enjoy and take pleasure in working with each other? An assessment of the issues raised by these questions may keep the therapists and family from becoming sidetracked.

Several brief examples illustrate the importance of the continuing examination of the co-therapy relationship. The first family we saw in co-therapy consisted of parents in their fifties and six children ranging from 10 to 30 years of age. There was an awesome amount of tension, dependency, and anger in the family, especially centering on the relationship between the parents. During the initial sessions we took a passive role, primarily reassuring each other. For a variety of reasons our planned meetings to discuss the family sessions did not occur. When our lack of progress became evident we did begin to meet regularly to discuss our approach. At first we identified our passivity and protectiveness as preventing the mother from having a psychotic break. Upon a closer examination we realized that we were protecting ourselves from confronting the turmoil of change. Following this realization, we were able to clarify and confront the confused authority structure in the family, and to assist the parents to become more assertive and cooperative. It is doubtful that we could have challenged the family's resistance to change had we been unwilling to examine our security needs.

Two other examples illustrate the importance of differentiating security and dependency needs from sexual issues. The authors were working with a family in which the parents were professionals and about our age. After initial sessions involving both parents and children, we were working primarily with the parents. Both had former marriages that had terminated in divorce, and they feared their current relationship was destined to have a similar fate. While it was probable that their sexual adjustment was less than desirable, sexuality was not discussed. On one occasion the wife came in dressed very provocatively, but neither of us made any comment about the unusual style of her dress. We conspired with the husband to keep sexual issues secret due to our fear of raising sexual issues in our relationship. Several months later, following the relatively unsuccessful termination of this family, we tentatively decided that it was necessary to clarify sexual issues within our relationship. We view sexuality as being involved at some level in any close relationship between a man and woman, and the co-therapy relationship is no exception. There is no way to discount or "resolve" sexuality because it is an ongoing aspect of the relationship. Therefore, we continually attempt to identify and differentiate sexual responsiveness from the covert expression of dependency, security, or anger through what seems superficially to involve sexual issues.

Our recent work with a couple illustrates the outcome of the manner in which we attempt to deal with issues involving security and sexuality. The couple consists of a somewhat hysterical woman who seemed to be developing a rather incapacitating disorder, and a man who was rather passive and compulsive. In exploring conflicts, strengths, and weaknesses of their relationship, both husband and wife identified sexual problems as an area involving particular difficulty, and an area in which they wished to work. In sharp contrast to our earlier awkward denial in the example above, we were able to reinforce the importance of their sexual relationship as an aspect of their marriage. We were able to assist each of them in differentiating sexual needs and feelings from expressions of dependency and hostility. In sum, we believe that the primary way to facilitate the power of co-therapy is for the co-therapists to share with the family and each other a commitment toward the examination, clarification, and change of their interactions in order to strengthen each system of relationships.

PHILOSOPHICAL IMPLICATIONS OF CO-THERAPY

When co-therapy is seen as a process integral to family therapy and not a "technique" of family therapy, several philosophical implications exist for both the therapists and the family. One implication for both therapists and the family is addressed by Haley (85) in his statement quoted as an epigraph above. If a therapist seeks security and protection in co-therapy, even if only in the sense of making the therapeutic tasks easier and more comfortable, then the other therapist becomes, as Haley points out, a life preserver. The other therapist personifies the hope for some rescue, some easy and comfortable means of coming to grips with the anger, anxiety, and despair with which the family and therapists must struggle if family systems are to be strengthened. If the therapists are there to rescue each other, who is there to assist the family? On the other hand, if an honest relationship with a respected and valued co-worker is integral to work with the family, then the therapists make a clear statement for themselves and for the family about the importance of relatedness and relationship. The quality of the co-therapy relationship and the ability of the co-therapists to focus that relationship on work with the family inevitably make a strong statement about the values and interests that will shape the therapeutic process.

A second implication arises from an application of Becker's discussion (86,87) of the myth of the hero. According to him, one of the most universal human problems involves the attempts of the individual to assert his narcissism and "cosmic significance," and to reject his mortality and fallibility by some heroic act. Applying Becker's idea to work with families, we may say that disturbed families are likely to contain many destructive hero myths. The single family therapist working with families is vulnerable to motives of heroism seen in his remarkable "cures" or "rescues" of families. As Whitaker points out (88), the solo therapist may use the family "like the mother who uses the child for a lapel button." A strong co-therapy relationship confronts the myth of the hero for both the therapists and the family.

A final implication of co-therapy for both the therapists and the family is that it expands the reality base of the therapy. Many family therapists have pointed out the tendency of the family to overwhelm, manipulate, or distort the abilities or the single family therapist. Two therapists working together can more adequately confront the family's manipulative and resistive behaviors. Equally important, two therapists can confront each other's manipulativeness and deception. Co-therapy makes a great demand that the therapists practice that which they espouse. Easier, it is not. It is, however, potentially more satisfying and effective for therapists and families.

REFERENCES

1. J. Haley, "Whither Family Therapy," *Family Process,* 1 (1962), 72.
2. B. Rubinstein and D. R. Weiner, "Co-Therapy Teamwork Relationships in Family Therapy," *Family Therapy and Disturbed Families.* Palo Alto: Science and Behavior Books, 1967, 206.
3. H. Mullen and I. Sangiuliano. *The Therapist's Contribution to the Treatment Process.* Springfield, Illinois: Thomas, 1964, 117–271.
4. W. H. Lundin and B. M. Arnov, "The Use of Co-Therapists in Group Psychotherapy," *Journal of Consulting Psychology,* XVI (1952), 76–80.
5. I. Boszormenyi-Nagy, "Intensive Family Therapy as Process," *Intensive Family Therapy,* New York: Harper and Row, 1965, 137–141.
6. J. A. Treppa, "Multiple Therapy: Its Growth and Importance," *American Journal of Psychotherapy,* XXV (1971), 447–57.
7. A. Adler, *The Education of Children.* New York: Greenberg, 1930.
8. G. H. Reever, "Trends in Therapy: V.A. Methods of Coordinated Treatment," *American Journal of Orthopsychiatry* IX (1939), 743–47.
9. S. B. Hadden, "The Utilization of a Therapy Group in Teaching Psychotherapy," *American Journal of Psychiatry,* 103 (1947), 644–48.
10. C. A. Whitaker, J. Warkentin, and N. L. Johnson, "A Philosophical Basis for Brief Psychotherapy," *Psychiatric Quarterly,* 23 (1949), 439.
11. _____, "The Psychotherapeutic Impasse," *American Journal of Orthopsychiatry,* 20 (1950), 641–47.
12. _____, "A Comparison of Individual and Multiple Psychotherapy," *Psychiatry,* 14 (1951), 415.
13. R. Dreikurs, "Techniques and Dynamics of Multiple Psychotherapy," *Psychiatric Quarterly,* 24 (1950), 788.
14. R. Dreikurs, B. H. Shulman, and H. Mosak, "Patient-Therapist Relationship in Multiple Psychotherapy," *Psychiatric Quarterly,* 26 (1952), 219–27.
15. _____, "Patient-Therapist Relationship in Multiple Psychotherapy II," *Psychiatric Quarterly,* 26 (1952), 590–96.
16. H. Mullen and I. Sangiuliano, "Multiple Psychotherapeutic Practice: Preliminary Report," *American Journal of Psychotherapy,* 14 (1960), 558.
17. J. A. Treppa and K. G. Nunnelly, "Interpersonal Dynamics Related to the Utilization of Multiple Therapy," *American Journal of Psychotherapy,* 28 (1974), 71–84.
18. Mullen and Sangiuliano, 1964, 117–271.
19. G. W. Piaget and M. Serber, "Multiple Impact Therapy," *Psychiatric Quarterly,* 44 (1970), 114–24.
20. Lundin and Arnov, 1952, 76–80.
21. A. Solomon, F. J. Leoffler, and G. H. Frank, "An Analysis of Co-Therapists Interaction in Group Psychotherapy," *International Journal of Group Psychotherapy,* 3 (1954), 171.
22. A. R. Slavson, *Analytic Group Psychotherapy.* New York: Columbia University Press, 1950.
23. R. W. Gans, "Group Co-Therapists and the Therapeutic Situation: A Critical Evaluation," *International Journal of Group Psychotherapy,* 12 (1962), 82–88.
24. E. W. Demarest and A. Ticher, "Transference in Group Therapy: Its Use by Co-Therapists of Opposite Sexes," *Psychiatry,* 17 (1954), 187–202.
25. Lundin and Arnov, 1952, 76–80.
26. Solomon, Loeffler, and Frank, 1954, 171.

27. Treppa, 1971, 447–57.
28. Lundin and Arnov, 1952, 76–80.
29. J. Adler and I. R. Berman, "Multiple Leadership in Group Treatment of Delinquent Adolescents," *International Journal of Group Psychotherapy*, 10 (1960), 213.
30. L. P. Belmont and A. Jasnow, "The Utilization of Co-Therapists and of Group Therapy Techniques in Family Oriented Approach to a Disturbed Child," *International Journal of Group Psychotherapy*, 11 (1961), 319.
31. J. L. Framo, "The Theory of the Technique of Family Treatment of Schizophrenia," *Family Process*, I (1962), 119–31.
32. Haley, 1962, 72.
33. C. C. Beels and A. Ferber, "Family Therapy: A View," *Family Process*, VIII (1969), 280–318. Beels and Ferber report that co-therapy was initiated by a group of family therapists they refer to as "reactors" who were concerned about the dangers and pitfalls of family therapy.
34. _____, 296.
35. Rubinstein and Weiner, 1967, 206–20.
36. Treppa, 1971, 452.
37. Boszormenyi-Nagy and G. M. Spark. *Invisible Loyalties*. New York: Harper and Row, 1973.
38. A. S. Friedman, I. Boszormenyi-Nagy, J. E. Jungreis, G. Lincoln, H. E. Mitchell, J. C. Sonne, R. V. Speck, G. Spivak. *Psychotherapy For The Whole Family*. New York: Springer, 1965.
39. B. W. MacLennan, "Co-Therapy," *International Journal of Group Psychotherapy*, 15 (1965), 154–65.
40. Friedman *et al.*, 1965.
41. Boszormenyi-Nagy, 1965.
42. D. G. Rice, W. F. Fey, and J. G. Kepecs, "Therapist Experience and Style as Factors in Co-Therapy," *Family Process*, 11 (1972), 1–12.
43. D. W. MacLennan, "Co-Therapy," *International Journal of Group Psychotherapy*, 15 (1965), 154–65.
44. A. R. Slavson. *A Textbook in Analytic Group Psychotherapy*. New York: International University Press, 1964.
45. J. A. Johnson. *Group Therapy: A Practical Approach*. New York: McGraw Hill, 1963.
46. E. Berne. *Principles of Group Treatment*. New York: Grove Press, 1966.
47. H. M. Rabin, "How Does Co-Therapy Compare With Regular Group Therapy," *American Journal of Psychotherapy*, 21 (1967), 244–55.
48. Rice, Fey, and Kepecs, 1972.
49. A. S. Gurman, "The Effects and Effectiveness of Marital Therapy: A Review of Outcome Research," *Family Process*, 12 (1973), 145–70.
50. J. Meltzoff and M. Kornreich. *Research in Psychotherapy*. Chicago: Aldine-Atherton, 1970.
51. L. Luborsky, M. Chandler, A. H. Auerbach, J. Cohen, and H. M. Bachrach, "Factors Influencing the Outcome of Psychotherapy: A Review of Quantitative Research," *Psychological Bulletin*, 75 (1971), 145–85.
52. Rubinstein and Weiner, 1967.
53. J. L. Framo, "Rationale and Techniques of Intensive Family Therapy," in *Intensive Family Therapy*. New York: Harper and Row, 1965, 198–201.
54. A. Napier and C. Whitaker, "A Conversation About Co-Therapy," in *The Book of Family Therapy*. New York: Science House, 1972, 480–506.

55. Rubinstein and Weiner, 1967.
56. J. C. Sonne and G. Lincoln, "Heterosexual Co-Therapy Relationship and Its Significance in Family Therapy," in *Psychotherapy for the Whole Family.* New York: Springer Publishing Company, 1965, 213–27.
57. Framo, "Theory."
58. Beels and Ferber, "Family Therapy."
59. J. C. Whitehorn and D. Betz, "A Study of Psychotherapeutic Relationships Between Physicians and Schizophrenic Patients," *American Journal of Psychiatry,* III (1954), 321–31.
60. A. M. Razin, "A-B Variable in Psychotherapy: A Critical Review," *Psychological Bulletin,* 75 (1971), 1–21.
61. G. M. Chartier, "A-B Therapist Variable: Real or Imagined?" *Psychological Bulletin,* 75 (1971), 22–33.
62. Mullen and Sangiuliano, 1964.
63. Haley, 1962.
64. Framo, 1965.
65. Rubinstein and Weiner, 1967.
66. Slavson, 1964.
67. MacLennan, 1965.
68. T. F. McGee and B. N. Schuman, "The Nature of the Co-Therapy Relationship," *International Journal of Group Psychotherapy,* 20 (1970), 25–47.
69. Rubinstein and Weiner, 1967.
70. Treppa, 1971.
71. Rubinstein and Weiner, 1967.
72. Framo, 1965.
73. Boszormenyi-Nagy, 1965.
74. Napier and Whitaker, 1972.
75. Rubinstein and Weiner, 1967.
76. Framo, 1965.
77. Rubinstein and Weiner, 1967.
78. Sonne and Lincoln, 1965.
79. Rubinstein and Weiner, 1967.
80. Mullen and Sangiuliano, 1964.
81. B. L. Kell and J. M. Burrow. *Developmental Counseling and Therapy.* Boston: Houghton Mifflin, 1970, 212–21.
82. Napier and Whitaker, 1972.
83. Rubinstein and Weiner, 1967.
84. Boszormenyi-Nagy, 1965.
85. Haley, 1962.
86. E. Becker. *The Birth and Death of Meaning.* New York: Free Press, 1971.
87. ———. *The Denial of Death.* New York: Free Press, 1973.
88. Napier and Whitaker, 1972.

CHAPTER 25

UNDERORGANIZATION IN THE POOR FAMILY

Harry J. Aponte, M.S.W.

To write about therapy with a poor family may imply that there is something psychologically peculiar about such families that requires explaining. To equate poverty with psychological deviance would take a lot of explaining, since the poor are the larger portion of the population. The rich are the minority, and in that sense deviant from the average; yet, one never sees an article about therapy for the rich. To suggest that to be poor is to be mentally ill leads to the conclusion that income is a determinant of mental health. Should we then require dissertations about how therapy should be conducted in relation to income? A graduated therapy, locked into personal tax returns? The idea is absurd. The relationship between mental health and poverty is not so much a matter of the emotional consequences of the lack of capital as it is the social conditions sometimes associated with being poor.

To begin with, poverty in all its various shapes can be an impediment to treatment. The people below the poverty line are a diverse group—old, disabled, unemployed, and underemployed—not only in income but also in social conditions. Therapy for these individuals who are poor poses a problem for middle-income therapists if for no other reason than that the socioeconomic difference creates a communication gap that complicates the task of mutual understanding. This obstacle may possibly be supported by both sides, and can become even more problematical if compounded by cultural and racial differences. Poverty associated with a cultural minority can present an impenetrable barrier to a middle-class therapist who is not a member of that minority. It must be made clear that the problems for the therapy created by these differences are not the result of any pathology in the minority patient—a rationalization that can protect the therapist from a sense of personal responsibility for failure in therapy. The distance between the walls of the canyon is no greater if measured from one side than if measured from the other.

There is another problem that comes with poverty, and certainly not the exclusive possession of the poor, which is related to social organization. Social organization is an aspect of social ecology. It can be weakened at every socioeconomic level, but it is particularly vulnerable to dysfunction under the social conditions linked to poverty and other forms of powerlessness. Some call the cluster of organizational problems that poor families often have *disorganization;* I prefer to call it *underorganization,* to suggest not so much an improper kind of organization, as a deficiency in the degree of constancy, differentiation, and flexibility of the structural organization of the family system. This kind of internal underorganization is accompanied by a lack of organizational continuity of the family with the structure of its societal context, that is, its ecology.

Social ecology refers to a complex of interdependent social systems organized at family, social, and community-institutional levels. People relate to one another through these social organizations. The social network is traced through the relationships people form to carry out social functions, whether these functions be a family work task, recreational efforts among friends, or large-scale political action on a formal level. Functions in their respective systems determine the nature of the relationships that people develop at any level of social organization. In a family, a man relates himself to his wife in accordance with the special requirements of each of the functions inherent to the marital relationships. His behavior and attitude toward her are quite different when he responds to her as a lover than when he deals with her as an economic partner in household management. Those function-related activities that flow out of the nature of a system are the *operations* of the system.

Every system has a cluster of operations through which the system is actuated, and each system develops its own characteristic patterns for carrying out these operations. In a family, people form patterns for loving, for recreation, for working, and so on. These patterns become part of a repertoire specific to the family system, which forms a framework for all transactions of the members in the system. For example, when it comes to handling money, a husband and wife have certain implicit or explicit rules that guide their actions in relation to one another in its management within their family. However, these rules exist within the context of the other patterns in their relationship, such as those that are principally directed to the demonstration and sharing of affection, whether these be activities of love-making or gift-giving. Patterns formed for any one activity or operation form a backdrop that colors every other activity engaged in by the members of the same social system.

The patterns formed by people for these operations need to be sufficiently elaborated and flexible to allow for the range of complexity that the activity itself may call for. The patterns must also be stable enough to be an influencing factor during the time another operation is being carried out.

This all means that a couple can engage in a heated and involved negotiation about the use of their money and still feel confident that their affection for one another will temper the discussion, and will survive the financial negotiations. Of course, these patterns are not static. They are continuously played out in time through sequential actions in a social context that itself is evolving. Consequently, the patterns develop in ways that permit alterations in their structure without necessarily endangering the essential nature of the relationships in their system.

The structural underpinnings of operational patterns in social systems are *alignment, force,* and *boundary. Alignment* refers to the joining or opposition of one member of a system to another in carrying out an operation. *Force* defines the relative influence of each member on the outcome of an activity. *Boundary* tells who is included and excluded from the activity in question. The structural underpinnings of the relationships people have in a system are the bases for the organizational patterns of the system. A partner in a marriage is described as dominant because of the frequency and degree of forcefulness of his or her influence over the other in a range of operations. The dominant partner can not be the determining factor in every activity, since there will always be situations in which the weaker partner will have his or her way. However, what gives a system its special organizational character is the degree of predictability of the structural patterns from activity to activity.

Individuals or groups who are not effectively integrated within their ecological set lack alignments with other units in their society to help them achieve their social goals. They are short on the force to exert their portion of control over the actions taken in their social context that affect them. They also find themselves outside many of the operations of their society that are meant to enrich the units within that system. These structural conditions are descriptive of the poor in our society.

The consequence of this lack of effective structural integration with their society is that the social network of the poor is not organized for their maximum benefit. These individuals and groups must arrange their lives to satisfy more powerful outside forces, often at significant sacrifice to their personal goals. At the institutional level—political representation, organized business activity, educational facilities—a social group which lacks political and economic influence is incorporated into a position of weakness in the structural organization of the larger society. This situation is more dramatic and more destructive if the society is actively exploiting the weaker sector.

The nature of ecology is such that the larger societal entity does much to shape the societal units within it. A group that develops within an ecological set that reflects its values will find that the encompassing society complements and supports, in most spheres and levels, the formal and informal social organizations the group requires for its development. This support facilitates the evolution and elaboration of the structural organization of the group, insuring not only survival, but a successful progression in development. In contrast, the isolated, weaker group may have to accommodate to the point that it loses its identity (its boundaries are diffused because it is within the boundaries of the dominant societal unit); or it may only compromise to the extent minimally necessary for survival, otherwise insulating itself from the larger society by rigidifying its boundaries and looking within itself for what support it needs. Of course, the smaller group may also rebel, attempting either to gain more power within the larger unit or to extricate itself from it, radically changing its social context.

Whatever happens to a social group within the larger political context is reflected in the formation of the families within that group, and in the development of the individuals in those families. The poor and weaker social groups in our society have not successfully meshed with the host society. The structural organization of these groups is not supported by their ecological set, and the families that belong to these groups suffer accordingly. As a result, we have the underorganization of families living in nonsupportive social conditions, such as poverty.

FAMILY ALIGNMENTS

A family that has developed successfully will have a dependable, differentiated, and flexible internal system of structural alignments. Each family member will have other members on whom he or she can count to carry out family-related operations. An individual has relationship patterns in his family that provide him with a complex of personal alignments with the family members who can best assist him in carrying out each family task at any given moment. For example, a young woman in a family knows that her mother is usually helpful in advising her about problems with people. However, when it comes to her boyfriends, she may prefer to talk with her sister who is only a year older than she. While her mother is a good confidant for most social matters, her sister, as a virtual peer, may serve as a less censoring adviser for her love life.

Such a young woman knows she has persons within the family who will help her with her personal problems; she also knows who, at any particular time in her life and in her family's development, is best suited to help her with what issue. She knows to whom to turn for money, for help in selecting clothes, for protection when walking to the store at night. As time goes on, she will shift alignments in the family, since as she and the family change, tasks within the family sphere will also change. But she has reached out to these people in the past, and has good reason to believe she can turn to them in the future. She has a family whose patterns of alignments are reliable, a family that will also have the resources and flexibility to make the appropriate changes in the structural patterns of the family alignments as she and it shift over time.

In a family that is underorganized, the pattern of family alignments is not so well elaborated or so reliable. The structure may be so organized that a young woman could seek assistance only from her mother, no matter what the social contingency, and regardless of the passage of time and development. Her mother may so centralize all activities at home around herself that her children can align themselves with hardly anyone else in most family activities. At the other end of the spectrum, the young woman may turn to any family member with little discrimination, talking about her problems to whomever sits beside her on the livingroom couch. The logical consequence is that her conversation with each person will likely end as each gets up from the couch to do something else. This young woman is not apt to conclude a discussion with any of her family except by accident. She may have persons within the family with whom she prefers to share certain interests and efforts, but she may not be able to consistently follow through her activities to conclusion with them.

At one extreme, the inflexible and limited structure of this underorganized family will overtax the relationship between mother and daughter, as the young woman asks for her mother's help in too many operations; also, if she has siblings, she will be in competition with them for their mother's attention, since the mother is their only source of support. At the other extreme, the lack of a developed pattern of alignments makes for indiscriminate communications, and a minimally crystallized image of specific sources of help in the family. Alignments in an underorganized family may be scarce and/or too rigid or too loose. In either case, they are not adequate for the range of operations that must be engaged to deal with the vicissitudes of the family's existence, and the effect is a discontinuous pattern of structural alignments.

FAMILY FORCE DISTRIBUTION

In a social system, the distribution of force among the component units is delicately balanced. An operation in a family must be able to be carried out by the individuals engaged in the activity without unduly sacrificing the family and its members, and at the same time hopefully it will further the family's interests. Family members themselves must have enough power in the family to be able to protect their personal interests in the family at all times, while keeping the wellbeing of the other members, and of the family as a whole, in mind. This can be an active power or an ascribed power, that is, one that is self-initiated, or one that is possessed because others in the family bestow it, such as the power of a loved infant in a household. The power of each family member must be such that it influences the execution of any and all operations in the family. In a family system, force is being distributed in relation to the developmental requirements of the family system and each of its members. This exercise of power in the family and among its members shifts according to the goals of the operations being exercised. On a car trip, a father who is the only driver in the family may assert more than the usual control he does at home at the dinner table.

The distribution of force forms a pattern that is functionally determined. It has a stability that can be depended upon, and a degree of elaboration and flexibility that is adaptable to a variety of contingencies. In a family where a differentiated power structure exists, an individual can expect to have special influence over the outcome of certain activities, in accordance with his/her position in the family. For example, a parent will usually assume that adult rank merits certain prerogatives. The reliability of the pattern provides a framework within which the family system and its member subsystems will develop over time. But this pattern of distribution of force within the family will change with time, as the functional requirements of the family change. For example, the mother's power vis-à-vis her son changes as the child grows. The more mature the child, the greater his power relative to his mother, and the less his mother is required to care for him.

In an underorganized family, force is not distributed in an orderly way. A single or a few family members may possess an inordinate amount of control over all operations, regardless of function. Since any single person, or even an exclusive few, can never, by the force of their talents, make every family undertaking work, this kind of overconcentrated power is inefficient. If a mother holds on to all the family controls, her young children may be very well-behaved in her presence, but very disorderly and negligent about carrying out household duties whenever she is out of the home. Such concentration of power in the family is effective only within certain narrow limits; it may be ideally suited for certain operations where the mother's extra control is structurally called for, but not at all for other operations. Furthermore, prepubescent children may adapt reasonably well to the mother-dominated structure, but may find the family way of doing things intolerable as each one reaches adolescence and requires a context in which he or she can exercise more autonomy. In such a family, we may see one youngster after another leave home prematurely while the one who does adapt his/her personality to the family power structure does so at a serious personal sacrifice to his/her personal emotional development.

At the other end of the continuum is the family in which power is distributed in a discoordinated manner. In the underorganized family where power is loosely distributed, the power of any one individual is not effectively woven through the various operations in which he or she is involved, nor is it balanced flexibly with the power exercised by other family members. In an underorganized family, a parent may not be able to take for granted his/her power and may be able to exercise it only when he/she asserts it with exceptional force. In such a household, one is likely to see a mother repeatedly yelling or striking her children to obtain some order. Some families are so loosely organized that the seat of power for the same operation changes frequently. An oldest child may have been delegated control by her mother over younger siblings for the house cleaning, but may find that her mother's support is not consistently forthcoming, so that she has no effective leadership.

A pattern of sorts exists within a family in which power is loosely or rigidly distributed in the sense that, over a period of time, one comes to know the likely outcomes of many interactions. However, even in an underorganized family where structural patterns of force distribution tend to be rigid, the ultimate configuration is discontinuous. The rigid structure cannot respond to all contingencies, and so will frequently dissolve into a minimally coordinated effort not unlike the fragmented patterns of a loosely organized family. In either case, the efforts involved in the family's operations are not consistently coordinated and so much energy is dissipated in repeatedly negotiating power, that personal energy does not become effectively channeled into operational outcomes. In a more organized family, efforts at power negotiations result in organizational structures that become the bases for action. In an underorganized family, the struggle for power burns up too much energy in an effort to assert one's presence and significance, and relatively little of the struggle bears fruit for basic family operations.

FAMILY BOUNDARIES

Every system must define itself vis-à-vis others in its context. In doing so it establishes its boundaries. In each and every operation, the system in action determines who is and who is not included in the scope of its activity, and thereby delineates its boundaries for the duration of the operation. Each system has a constellation of operations through which the system actuates itself. The boundary-making aspects of the actions and interactions of the operation form a pattern that defines the functional boundaries of a system. A furniture manufacturer is one through all the activities involved in the process of making and selling furniture. These operations form, over a period of time, a pattern that gives to his company its particular identity.

A family has its own variety of activities in which its members engage. The individuals in the family must be able to participate in these family-related actions in ways that affirm their personal identities, the identity of the family subsystems, and the family as a whole as the bases from which the operations spring. This means a stability of boundary, and a complexity and a flexibility of boundary structures that allows even for subtle shifts in defining functional entities. The structure must be able to withstand the conflict that always exists in some degree among these functional entities, and yet be able to reconcile the differences among them through an ecological balance that fosters personal individuality as well as family subgroups and family identities.

The members of a family engage in a myriad of activities with one another, and in each of these activities boundary is an essential issue. As a woman engages in a social function with her husband, how does she maintain her separate identity within the marital partnership? When the couple is involved in a peerlike activity, such as a tennis game with their teenaged children, how do they preserve in that context their generational distinction as parents in relation to their children? Some operations have complementary tasks for the participants that serve to include them within the boundaries of the activity, while reinforcing their differentness. The very nature of breast-feeding accomplishes this, even though in the earliest months the infant cannot perceive separateness from the mother. Other operations tend to diffuse the individual boundaries of participants. The effort of a set of parents to present a united front in a disciplinary action toward their children will stress the generational boundary at the expense of their personal boundaries vis-à-vis one another. In this instance, the complex of other, more differentiating parental tasks, as well as the other distinctly independent roles which each has, forms a context that helps to preserve for each their separate identities.

As an individual, a family member faces personal boundary issues from activity to activity. A man in a family has his identity as an income-producing, working person, and as such, he functions within the boundaries of his job; he is a husband, and has activities specifically related to his position within the husband-wife subsystem of his family; and he is a father, with all the activities entailed by his partnerships with the children's mother and with the children themselves. And through all these roles he must maintain some sort of basic personal identity. As he shifts from one role to another, he must maintain, at some level, all his other functions, and must somehow reconcile them.

Individuals and subgroups in a family not only must maintain distinct and yet flexible boundaries, but must also do so in ways that take into account the roles played by other family members. A man's wife can hardly engage in wifely activities without his cooperation at some level. And to engage in a husband-wife activity, such as lovemaking, the man and his wife, as a couple, must consider the others in the family system. They will plan sexual activity at a time and place that will allow them privacy from the children. While that boundary around their sexual activities as spouses will exclude the children, they must plan their sexual life so that it does not subvert their functions as parents to the children. The boundaries around all of these diverse and complementary operations of the family's members must be so organized as to enhance the efforts of the individuals engaged in them, and not detract but when possible support the activities of the other family members and the family itself.

In the underorganized family, boundaries will tend to be too rigid or too diffuse, or will vacillate from one to the other. As an example of overly-rigid boundaries, take the situation of the boyfriend who has lived for years in the home, but neither allows himself nor is allowed by the woman with whom he lives to have anything to do with her children from a previous union or even from her current relationship with him. The father who maintains all the power in his family is another example of rigid boundaries, as he refuses to allow anyone else in the family to share his executive functions.

When it comes to diffuseness of boundary, we have the incestuous father who engages in sexual activity with his children. Less dramatically, there are those parents who for periods of time will depend on a young child in the family to care and nurture them, reversing roles in certain activities with the child. In both of these instances, while the parents confuse boundaries with their children in certain operations, they still maintain clear boundaries in others. Again, in a underorganized family, shifts in boundaries can be either too difficult or too easy to make, and are certainly ineffective, since they do not serve to facilitate the various operations of the family and its members.

PATTERNS OF UNDERORGANIZATION

The structural patterns of the alignments, boundaries, and force distribution in the underorganized family are often difficult to identify. Sudden shifts in these patterns make them appear unpredictable. Yet, there are always patterns of some kind, even if relatively loose. A pattern of interaction can be built over a period of time on accrued fragments of behavior. The young woman who attempts to discuss her problem with each family member who sits on the couch forms the beginnings of an alignment with each person who takes enough interest to respond to her remarks. These responses may be partly negative or positive, but each represents a step toward drawing a member of the family into her worry; therefore, each effort represents one segment of a sequence which might lead to someone's helping her work out her problem. Even if no one even finishes the discussion with her, the repetition of this effort over a period of time with a number of different problems would represent the rudiments of an alignment pattern that show her to be connected with her family.

The incompleteness of structural organization in the underorganized family, in both overly rigid and loose patterns, impedes the effective outcome of operations that are essential to well-coordinated family development. The structural balance is often sufficiently imperfect so that it is accompanied by much frustration; somatizing or acting out is often in evidence as strenuous efforts are repeatedly, but inconclusively, made by individuals to achieve a stable and personally favorable balance in their family situation.

Communications within an underorganized family reflect the family's degree of organization, since communications are the means through which the family members structure their activities. Alignment, power, and boundary are communicated in the way the family member engages in an operation with or without another member. In an underorganized family, one is likely to hear much simultaneous talk, loud competition for attention, long periods of silent unconnectedness, and sudden shifts in mood expression among individuals. Basically, the communications do not form the richly interwoven and continuous pattern that exists within a family with a well-elaborated structure.

AN UNDERORGANIZED POOR FAMILY

Following are excerpts from an initial interview conducted by the author with a family that in a number of respects fits our description of an underorganized family. This family lives on Public Assistance. The family is black, and consists of a mother and four children: Charles, age 12; Marge, age 11; Joe, age 9; and Dennis, age 5. The family was referred by a member of the social service department of a pediatric clinic. The mother had complained to the pediatrician about her twelve year old, who she said was incorrigible. The pediatrician referred the mother to social service, where she was seen with some regularity for about two months. The caseworker finally called the author in desperation, saying that the mother was insisting on placing Charles in an institution, but that Charles was in no way delinquent and that his rebellion was no more than resistance to his mother's severe restrictions and controls. He was, in fact, a mild mannered, shy youngster. The author agreed to see the family in a consultation with the counselor present.

As the family sat for the interview all the children clustered around the mother except for Charles, who took a chair in a corner and sat with his back to his mother. The author, who will refer to himself as the therapist, began by asking Charles where he lived, and the directions to his house. The boy haltingly tried to give the directions; but his sister Marge completed them, partly wanting to join her brother but also trying to outdo him. Knowing that the mother wanted Charles institutionalized, and having observed the family's seating arrangement, the therapist's first problem was how to utilize these data as he entered the family system. He hypothesized that this youngster was coming into the interview as an isolate; he had no one overtly aligned with him, and was powerless, with his mother pushing him outside the boundaries of the family.

The therapist made his decision. His first move, asking Charles his address, was an attempt to align himself with the boy, thereby bringing him within the boundaries of the interview and placing him in a position of some power as the focus of the therapist's attention. Marge's effort to join in the discussion apparently reflected her perception, at some level, that this was happening, and showed her own wish to be included and to be at least as central as her brother in the activity.

However, the mother countered instinctively. With no explicit introduction to the subject, she volunteered, "Charles, he doesn't like his sisters and brothers." Her move was to isolate him again. The therapist then maneuvered to interpose himself as a boundary between her and the children over the next several sequences, and to exclude the mother from his explorations with the children about implicit alignments within the sibling subsystem. What follows is a verbatim account of this part of the interview. What it cannot convey is the amount of noise and confusion that ensued when the mother was cut off and the children were interacting without her supervision. They repeatedly interrupted one another, and the therapist repeatedly attempted to secure some order and relative quiet.

INTERVIEW

Mother: And Charles, he doesn't like his sisters and brothers.
Therapist: Oh, is that true?
Mo.: He's just evil around them and just as cross and fretful as he can be. *(Marge and Charles attempt to talk at the same time, even as mother is talking.)*

Th.: (To the children) Okay. Wait a minute! Charles, do you realize what she just said? Is she right, you don't like your sisters and brothers?

Charles: Yeah, I like them. I didn't say that.

Th.: You do like them?

C.: Yeah.

Dennis: He likes me.

Th.: He likes you?

D.: I don't know why he doesn't like the rest of them.

Th.: Okay. Charles, do you like Dennis?

C.: Yeah.

Th.: You do. All right. What about you, Marge? You and Charles. How do you two get along?

Marge: Terrible. I help him with his homework.

C.: You do not. You never help me with my homework.

M.: I have homework and I don't know how to do it and he won't even show me how to do it, but I show him how to do it. *(Marge and Charles start shouting at one another.)*

Th.: Wait, wait, wait!

M.: He doesn't like for me to look on his paper.

Th.: Is that true?

C.: Yeah.

Th.: Why not? *(To Dennis, who was talking over everyone else)* Wait, Dennis! You're very good but I want you to wait . . .

Mo.: (Addressing Charles in an attempt to reassert herself) Now you turn around and look at people when they're talking to you.

Th.: (To Charles) Why don't you like her (Marge)? What does she do to you?

C.: She tells lies on me all the time.

Th.: Who does she tell the lies to?

C.: Me.

Th.: Who does she tell? She tells on you? She tells your mother on you?

M.: Everything they do and I see . . . *(Joe and Dennis argue, also competing to be heard.)*

Th.: Wait, wait. . . .

Mo.: Didn't you hear him say wait? One at a time.

Th.: I want Marge to talk.

M.: Everything they do and I see that my mother don't want them to do, I tells on them.

Th.: I see. That's why you don't . . . *(To Joe, who again interrupts)* I will let you talk in a minute. *(To Charles)* That's why you don't like Marge. Because she tells on you.

C.: She tells lies on me, and every time Joe does something she blames it on me.

Th.: (Up to this point, Charles only has Dennis on his side, and is in danger of alienating Joe. So the therapist moves to that relationship.) (To Joe) What about that? Is that true what he just said?

Joe: Yes.

Th.: Really?

M.: It is not.

Th.: Wait a minute Marge, now it's Joe's turn.

J.: When she hits me, she says I hit her. She cries and then makes me get a beating.

M.: I do not.

J.: You do.

M.: Them two right there *(Charles and Joe)* they tell lies on me. Like if my mother goes somewhere—they tell lies. *(Now Marge is inadvertently pushing Joe towards Charles. Then Dennis again starts talking.)*

Th.: (To Dennis) Okay. We'll get to you.

M.: They tell lies on me, and them two they are always fighting and me and him *(Dennis)* we don't fight as much as them two. *(She tries to at least bring Dennis to her side.)*

Th.: Okay but wait a minute *(to Marge)*. But right now, Joe and Charles, the two of you say that Marge tells on you. *(They indicate agreement.)*

M.: They say I'm a tattletale.

Th.: They say you're a tattletale?

Th.: Does she tell on you, Dennis? *(Testing Dennis' loyalties)*

D.: Yeah. When she gets mad at Charles, I get mad at her.

Th.: Because Charles is your friend, right?

D.: Yeah. I like them two. *(Pointing at Charles and Joe)*

Th.: I see.

J.: I like them two.

Th.: You like which two?

J.: I like them two. *(Pointing to Charles and Dennis)*

Th.: So you three guys are all together here, and poor Marge is all by herself. *(When the boys isolated Marge, the therapist made a gesture to support her. He then explored the family reaction to her isolation by pushing it further.)*

Th.: Are you the family tattletale?

M.: No, I'm not.

D.: Marge and mom. *(Pointing to them, suggesting collusion)*

Th.: That's it? Okay, all right. Now I understand. *(To mother)* Is that the way it is?

Mo.: Well, I carry her with me a lot.

Th.: Yes . . .

Mo.: And I leave the boys a lot. *(Mother and Marge now begin pulling together)*

M.: And they get mad at me, because most of the time I go to New York and we have been up here going on five years in September, I think. Is it, mom?

Mo.: Yeah, I think so.

M.: September and . . .

Mo.: I believe it's four years.

M.: We came in 1970.

Mo.: I think it's about five years. I have it written down.

M.: And I've been going to New York ever since then. I've been to New York about ten or fifteen times and they've been only about two times.

Th.: Is that true? *(Dennis begins talking and the others jump in.)* What are you talking about? Stop! Mrs. Cass, does this happen at home?

Mo.: Well, I don't know what he's talking about. We were on one conversation. . . .

Th.: No, I'm talking about, do they all talk at the same time?

Mo.: Well, that's the way they do. I tried to beat it out of them. I can't beat it out of them to save my life. And Charles carries on so bad that he gives me a headache, and I have a headache for two or three days.

Th.: Oh, really . . .

Mo.: I think that causes me to be cross like I am. Charles is the worst one. He's the main one. And he don't like Philadelphia and wants to go down south.

Th.: Actually, all the boys, the three boys, are coming together and causing noise, and causing some trouble?

Mo.: Yeah.

The therapist ends this part of the interview by trying to lump the boys together in the mother's eyes. If she can see Charles as one of three troublemakers, he will not stand alone in her view. She will experience him as aligned with the other two, and she will not be able to assign to Charles all the blame for the disarray. She may not need to extrude him from the family. As is evident, when she is not actively controlling all the transactions among the children, there is little order in the communications. When she is controlling the transactions, the children through their silence isolate Charles; but when the therapist interrupts her control, the boys unite against Marge, linking her with mother. There is no hierarchy of function (boundaries), or authority—that is, power among the children; so, when they are left alone, they are disorderly. The problem of constantly forcing order is too much for mother, and she has chosen to scapegoat Charles and eject him as a way to relieve the strain.

Following the reported portion of the interview, the therapist tried several times to realign family members so as to get Charles re-included in his family, but could not succeed. The longest effort was one in which the therapist tried directly to draw the mother and Charles together. The mother brought this sequence to a head when she openly said, "Yeah, unwanted, that's right, unwanted. I don't want him." Charles cried; the therapist, talking with him, was able to get him to acknowledge he loved his mother. He also elicited from the mother an admission that she would feel differently about Charles if he were to stop "sassing" her. "Yeah, I would feel better towards him. You know, you can't love a sassy big one." Even here, she identifies that what makes sassing intolerable is Charles' maturity. She is less disturbed by the sassiness of the two younger boys.

With this statement of the mother, the therapist felt he had gone as far as he could in his attempts to bring mother and son together. So, he chose to try to align Marge, the mother's closest ally, to Charles. The clue to this possible opening was given by Marge at the beginning of the interview, when she complained that Charles would not help her with her school work. The therapist started the move toward his goal by spending a bit of time talking with Marge about her perception of her problems, attempting to align himself more closely with her. He had already gained Charles' confidence, and he attempts to draw Marge and Charles together.

M.: He don't like for me to be in the same room with him. My mother tells me to try to help him when we have something new in the classroom, a new subject in the classroom, and he don't know how to do it and I know how to do it. I show him how to do it. And when we get another new subject and I don't know how to do it, he don't even want to show me.

C.: When we get something new, the teacher always shows us because I stay after school. She *(Marge)* didn't never show me nothing. I know how to do my own work.

Th.: You wouldn't want to help Marge if she needed your help, Charles? If she needs your help for the school work, you wouldn't want to help her?

C.: No, she might be wrong. Cause she's not that good in arithmetic.

M.: I'm good in reading.

Th.: *(To Marge)* Okay. Wait a minute. *(To Charles)* Are you good in arithmetic?

C.: Not that good.

Th.: Are you better than she is? Or are you worse than she is?

C.: I'm better than she is.

M.: I'm smarter than he is in spelling.

Th.: Is that true? She's smarter than you in spelling?

C.: I have trouble. I can't pronounce the word out.

Th.: Oh, I see. Do you get homework every day?

M.: Every single day.

Th.: Every single day you get homework! Gee, that's a terrible thing. What's going on between you two about the homework *(to Marge)*, because you're so good in spelling and I don't know why you're not helping him, and *(to Charles)* you're so good in math and I don't know why you're not helping her.

C.: She's telling a story.

Th.: What story is she telling?

C.: She's telling a story about she's smart in spelling and I'm not smart. Only thing I can't do is *(defensively)*, I can't pronounce the word out correct.

Th.: But can she pronounce the word out better than you can?

C.: I don't know.

Th.: Can you, Marge? *(She agrees. To Charles)* Well, maybe she can do something a little better than you can, and maybe you can do something better than she, right? There's nothing wrong with that. I'm terrible in math. I mean, that's me. That's the truth. I'm absolutely a bust. I'd like to be good in it but I'm no good in it. I used to have to get others to help me with my math.

M.: When I was in the third grade and I didn't know my tables as good as he did, he would pick at me and say you old dumb thing, you don't even know tables.

Th.: You would have done the same thing to me, Charles, because I would have been an old dumb thing who didn't know his tables. *(To Marge)* What are you saying?

M.: Now I know them, I know them now. *(She is hoping to turn the therapist's alignment with her against Charles. The therapist changes focus as he pulls them together through himself.)*

Th.: Well, what worries me is what's happening with this homework. I think it's a terrible thing. You know, do you think you could come over here to the clinic to do your homework together?

C.: *(Tentatively)* Yeah . . .

Th.: Well, when do you do your homework?

C.: At night.

Th.: Uhuh!

C.: Sometimes in the day. Sometimes I stay after school and do it in school.

Th.: Well, how long does it take you to do your homework? How long does it take you, half an hour? *(Charles nods yes.)* Doesn't take too long, does it? How about if I could get the two of you to come over here right after school, and just spend half an hour and somebody here would help you to do your homework together?

. . . Well? . . . I think I have a great idea, but nobody's saying anything. What do you think about my idea? You would have someone to help you to do real good homework. Would you like that, Charles? *(Charles again nods in agreement.)* Would you like that? *(Marge, smiling, says she would.)* Because we have some tutors here, special teachers, and they can help kids with homework, and they can help you do better in your school work. They could help you to do it together.

M.: I wanted to go to tutoring. Some other girls in my classroom, they go to tutoring, and I don't know why I can't go? *(Marge, while special in mother's eyes, does not want to be excluded from her peers.)*

Th.: You can go to tutoring. You can go to tutoring here with this guy *(indicating Charles)*, right?

C.: Yeah.

Th.: Hey, mom, what do you think about that? *(Soliciting mother's blessing, thereby including her in the operation.)*

Mo.: Well, it will be all right . . .

Mother agreed, but did not let the interview terminate without again expressing reservations about Charles. The therapist assured her that he heard her concern, and that this was only the first step in the hundred steps that would need to be taken in the effort to solve her problems. The interview ended with the mother agreeing to continue with her caseworker, and to send Charles and Marge together to the tutor. The therapist never did receive a follow-up from the caseworker; but some months later, his sleeve was tugged during a visit to a library in the family's neighborhood; was Charles, who obviously was still living at home.

The first object of this interview was to prevent Charles from being pushed outside the family boundaries. Underlying the effort to align Charles with Marge was the assumption that, by becoming Marge's friend, Charles could move closer to becoming mother's friend. This effort also served to include Marge within the boundaries of the sibling subsystems of the family, obviously a position she craved. Within the sibling group, the therapist would hope to place Charles in the special post of the eldest child, with Marge a close second, sharing with him the responsibilities of older siblings among a group of children. If these two could assume these hierarchical positions, they could share the mother's task in bringing more order among the children. They would share in the mother's executive power in the household, power that would support the mother and not compete with her authority. If this were to happen, hopefully she would feel free to allow these youngsters to individuate themselves more within the family, that is, develop their boundaries around themselves as individuals and exercise more control or power over their lives. These structural changes in the family should benefit all of its members.

SUMMARY

The problems that therapists encounter in working with a family are manifestations of structural conflicts among and within the social units in the family system. Individuals and subgroups are stressed in the family around the structural issues of alignment, force, and boundary. As the social units of the family struggle for survival and fulfillment, problems arise about the need for allies in tasks, for force to influence outcomes, and for the inclusion and exclusion of others in family operations that will insure personally favorable results.

In discussing therapy with a poor family, we have added a dimension to problems of systems conflict, which we have called *underorganization.* This structural problem refers to the lack of constancy, differentiation, and flexibility in the social organization of the individuals and subgroups in the family system.

Families who are poor, and therefore often powerless, friendless, and excluded from the vital operations of society, do not have the kind of institutional and community supports necessary for their ongoing development as organizations in their own right. This factor contributes to denying the individuals in the families the optimum context within which to develop their own personalities. In the clinical example presented, we offered not only a view of such a family, but also an example of how a therapist maneuvered to become part of the structural dynamics of the family, and to use himself to affect the alignments, force distribution, and boundaries of the family system and its subsystems.

BIBLIOGRAPHY

H. Aponte. "Psychotherapy for the Poor: An Eco-Structural Approach to Treatment," *Delaware Medical Journal,* 46 (1974).

S. Minuchin, B. Montalvo, *et al. Families of the Slums: An Exploration of Their Structure and Treatment.* New York: Basic Books, 1967.

PART IV

TECHNIQUES

CHAPTER 26

Evaluation of Family System and Genogram

Philip J. Guerin, Jr., M.D. and Eileen G. Pendagast, M.A., M.Ed.

A family rarely enters therapy with a clearcut idea of exactly where its problems lie. The therapist's major job in the first interview is to elucidate and organize the facts and characteristics of the family, and dissect the emotional process in a way that pinpoints the trouble spots in the relationship system. It is to the advantage of both the therapist and the family that this process be simple, and accomplished in a relatively short period of time.

The choice of a particular method for evaluating a family depends upon the ideology of the therapist and the state of the family when it enters therapy. A family that comes to the initial session in an agitated state may need to be allowed the beginning of the session to talk about their view of the crisis. While they are doing this, the therapist can attempt to cool down the affective overload in the system before proceeding with more structured information gathering. If the family is not in crisis the therapist is able to move quickly on to the structure of his particular method.

The first contact is usually by telephone, and at that point, membership issues involving the first session will be decided. Most family therapists have their own set of guidelines for these issues, which to some degree depend on the therapist's definition of the clinical unit "family." If family is defined as the household, all members of that particular household will be brought in. Therapists who emphasize family as a conceptual base, rather than a natural group, consistently see only the spouses, or, at times, just one motivated family member. Another factor that must be considered at this point is the family's view of the problem. If they define the problem as a marital crisis, the husband and wife may wish to be seen without the children; a child-centered family will most often want the children included.

We believe therapists should maintain a flexible response so that their options will be open to serve multigenerational families or one family member, depending on the circumstances.

If one family member is seen alone as the initial contact, the issue of confidentiality should be dealt with at the beginning. The most functional position is one in which the therapist refuses to make secret pacts, and thus establishes his freedom to introduce into the larger family system information received from one family member, if clinical judgment warrants such disclosures.

Many kinds of information can be looked for in the initial session. Some therapists choose to combine observation of nonverbal behavior and kinesic communication with an elaboration of the family's view of the problem. Others always proceed using a regularly structured format. There are pros and cons to both positions. In the end it comes down to a matter of clinical judgment, and to the short and longrange goals formulated from the therapist's own particular theoretical position.

We start off by telling the family that we will ask a few background questions that are important to an overview of the situation. We then use the structure of the genogram to spell out the physical and emotional boundaries, the characteristics of the membership, the nodal events, toxic issues, emotional cutoffs, the general openness/closedness index, and the multiplicity or paucity of available relationship options. Ideally, by the end of the first session we should have a reasonably clear definition of the membership and boundaries of the system, and some beginning definition of the emotional process surrounding the presenting symptom. At the same time, we try to make what we are doing relevant to the family's view of the problem, and to assist the engagement process by saving enough time to give the family some feedback before the end of the session.

In our experience, the evaluation time can be used most efficiently if a therapist has a well-defined structure and method for gathering necessary information about the family. We will therefore elaborate our particular method for evaluating a family, starting with the overview and genogram, and going on to engage the family to define their view of the problem.

There are some general contextual questions that should be part of the overview. Cultural, ethnic, and religious affiliations of a family should be explored, as should also its cultural heritage, socioeconomic level, the way the family relates to the community, and the social network in which it lives. If a family lives in a very affluent section of Westchester County, and yet makes only $10,000 a year, the chances are good that it is in dyssynchrony with its affluent surroundings. This can lead to isolation of the family unit within that community. Also, the therapist has to wonder how much financial backing is coming from the extended family. The real problems of poverty-level families must be recognized and validated, without making them feel patronized. Income level and placement within the community affect not only personal options and expectations, but also relationships with other families in the area. What is the extent of the social network of a family? How isolated is this particular nuclear family unit? It is important to document social and familial isolation because it can create an emotional cocoon that intensifies emotional processes in the nuclear family, and significantly limits the relationships available to dissipate anxiety and emotional distress.

In moving from the general contextual issues to more specific issues of boundary, membership, and process the genogram is our most useful tool. A genogram is a structural diagram of a family's three-generational relationship system. It uses the following symbols to illustrate these relationships.

☐ = male	◯ = female	△ = child in utero
⬘ = abortion or stillbirth	horizontal line = marriage	vertical line │ = offspring
⬙ = divorce	✗ = death	

These symbols, together with other pertinent factual data, are used to show the relationships and positions for each family member. This diagram is a roadmap of the family relationship system. Once the names, the age of each person, the dates of marriages, deaths, divorces, and of births are filled in, other pertinent facts about the relationship process can be gathered, including the family's physical location, frequency and type of contact, emotional cutoffs, toxic issues, nodal events, and open/closed relationship index. Each of these facts will help the therapist to form a picture of the family's characteristics.

Physical location of the family is important for tracing the physical boundaries of the system. Mapping gives information about the degree to which physical distance is used to solve relationship problems, and how much of a support network is present for a particular nuclear family segment. Families can be classified as either explosive or cohesive, depending on how close they have stayed to their original location. For example, in the Italian-American section of New Haven, Connecticut, there are many families who live within walking distance of most of the members of their extended families, and they have never lived anywhere else. Ella Grasso, for instance, lived in such a section in her hometown. She has said that her work

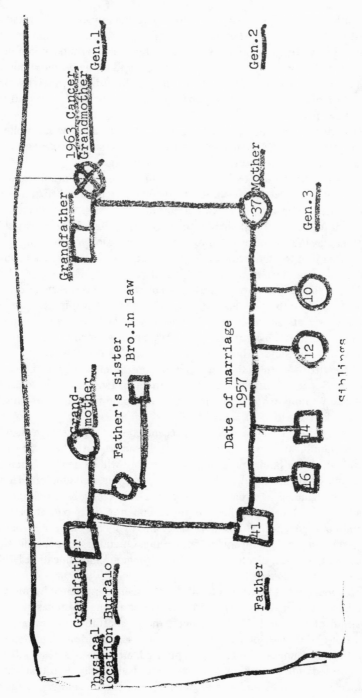

in politics and her eventual rise to the governorship of Connecticut depended on the fact that when her children were growing up she was never afraid to leave them at home, as everyone for blocks around was either a family member or a close friend. On the other hand, some people would find such cohesion a source of potential apoplexy and emotional paralysis. Often a member of an explosive family marries into a cohesive family and tries to make it his own.

Another important piece of information is who calls, visits, writes to whom, and with what frequency? Is there one person who serves as the family communications switchboard? Grandmothers and oldest siblings frequently occupy this position. It is not uncommon to find an explosive family that remained cohesive until the switchboard person died and no one moved into the vacated slot. Ritualized family visiting, territoriality, and telephone addiction are all phenomena to be recognized. Ritualized visiting accompanies the use of physical distance as a solution to emotional problems—that is, a totally predictable timetable of visits, involving an equally predictable repertoire of behavior while there.

Most frequently territoriality is shown by whose house everyone congregates at on the important holidays. Are grandparents willing to visit, eat, and stay over at their children's homes, as well as vice versa? Telephone contact also reveals a lot about the family process. Who calls whom and with what frequency? Who answers the phone? When the grandparental home is called, does the father answer and immediately hand the phone over to mother? Is it impossible to get to talk to one person alone? Who are the members of family who prime the anxiety pump or calm their own insides by an addictive use of the telephone?

As the patterns of closeness, distance, and conflict emerge from elucidating the family system boundaries and characteristics, the toxic issues around which the family process gets played out will be defined. There are some almost universal issues—money, sex, parenting, and children. How is the money handled in a marriage? who makes it, controls it, doles it out? Which side of the family has the most, and how is it passed on from generation to generation? His, hers, ours, and theirs are categories that are simultaneously toxic, amusing, and revealing. Often there are specific toxic issues—for instance, alcohol abuse, death, religion, and education level—that are worth tracking.

The open-closed index of a family system can be estimated by studying toxic issues and the relationship process around them. Examples would be the death of a central family member, the premature death of a young parent or child, onset of serious physical illness, an oldest child's leaving for college, a youngest child's getting married, an only son's being killed in war. Are individual family members able to deal openly with toxic issues in some relationships and not in others? or is there a more generalized conspiracy of silence? The presence or absence of emotional cutoffs is another indication of the open-closed ratio. Emotional cutoffs can be brought about by the use of physical distance, but can also be present in relationships with considerable proximity.

Nodal events are those crossroads times and events in the family life cycle that shape the future form and structure of the relationship process. Normative crises and catastrophic events fit into this category.

PORTIONS OF AN EVALUATION INTERVIEW: THE FLYNNS

Tom Flynn is 49 years old; his wife Mary is 41. From previous marriages they have between them a total of seven children. Mary called and asked if she and Tom could come in for consultation around the effect on the family of Tom's being out of work. In the initial phase of the evaluation interview, the genogram was employed, and the basic facts were gathered. One of the facts that surfaced early in tracking the genogram with this family was that both Tom and Mary have lost mates: Tom's first wife and Mary's first husband both died in 1964.

In this first interview, it is important to strike a balance between hearing the family members out and not getting totally distracted from the goal of obtaining an overview. The following segment illustrates the way this kind of questioning is done:

Dr. Guerin: You're how old, Tom?
Tom: Forty-nine.
Dr. Guerin: And you, Mary?
Mary: Forty-one.
Dr. Guerin: You were married when?
Mary: It will be eight years this June.
Dr. Guerin: That was in June, 1968? Is it an only marriage for both of you?
Mary: No, it's a second marriage for both of us.
Dr. Guerin: You were married to your first husband when, Mary?
Mary: 1957.
Dr. Guerin: His name?
Mary: Bill.
Dr. Guerin: He is how old?
Mary: He is no longer living.
Dr. Guerin: When did he die?
Mary: In 1964.
Dr. Guerin: Of what?
Mary: He took his own life.
Dr. Guerin: Was that a surprise? Had he been depressed? Ill? Or was it a sudden kind of thing?
Mary: No, it was a complete surprise.
Dr. Guerin: Have you spent any time trying to sort that out? Were you in any

kind of therapy? I know you spent a lot of time trying to sort it out, but did you use professional assistance to try to sort it out?

    Mary: Only the family doctor.

    Dr. Guerin: Did you have any kids with Bill?

    Mary: Yes, two.

    Dr. Guerin: And they are?

    Mary: A boy and a girl.

    Dr. Guerin: Oldest?

    Mary: She will be sixteen next Monday.

    Dr. Guerin: Her name is?

    Mary: Nancy, and there's John who is fourteen.

    Dr. Guerin: Both of them doing okay?

    Mary: Both of them are doing okay, but I worry about Nancy's moodiness.

    Dr. Guerin: Do you have any children from this marriage?

    Mary: No.

    Dr. Guerin: Your first marriage was when, Tom?

    Tom: 1951.

    Dr. Guerin: What was her name?

    Tom: Katherine Kelly—she died in 1964 also, the same year as Bill. In 1964, in childbirth.

    Dr. Guerin: In childbirth? That's kind of unusual these days.

    Tom: Yes, it is.

    Dr. Guerin: Did the baby live?

    Tom: No.

    Dr. Guerin: Hemorrhage? Or what?

    Tom: A long labor, something to do with the membranes.

    Dr. Guerin: Then no delivery until the next day?

    Tom: No delivery. We had five children, that was our sixth.

    Dr. Guerin: So you both have the symmetrical experience of losing the first spouse to death?

    Tom: It was at about the same time, too.

    Dr. Guerin: Your five kids are joined with Mary's to make seven, is that the way it has worked?

    Tom: Yes, but my one son was killed two years ago—accident during the summer. The rest of mine are all girls.

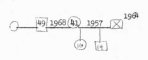

    As this segment illustrates, a routine manner of questioning about dates of deaths and marriages quickly elicits the facts about the structural characteristics, membership, nodal events, and toxic issues in a family. This line of questioning has established that there has been a symmetrical emotional experience for these two marital partners. Mary lost her husband through suicide; the therapist files away for some appropriate time a series of questions about how responsible Mary felt for her husband's suicide. If she did, then how did she deal with that? Who can she talk to most openly about it? Later on, the therapist learns that his suicide is a major secret being kept from her children. Tom's wife died in childbirth, an unusual happening in this day and age. The fact that she died giving birth to a sixth child, which today may be viewed as contributing to overpopulation, leads speculation about the degree of responsibility Tom felt for his wife's death. This family has sustained a number of losses in a very short period of time.

One of the major benefits of taking this kind of family history is that important things are learned about right away that otherwise might not come out until much later. One of the goals of each session is to locate toxic issues and open up communication around them which hopefully will detoxify them and open multiple relationship options. As the therapist proceeds, he will focus on pinning down the process and emotional reactions to some of the factual happenings.

As the genogram is filled in and the family process is spelled out the therapist organizes the information around these significant areas: the family's operating principles; its operating principles in times of stress; the function of time in these relationships; generational and personal boundaries; the conflictual issues—sex, money, in-laws, kids; triangles; personal closeness, tenderness, and honesty; and the extended family's relevance to the stated problem.

Once having done this, the therapist and family can go on to thoroughly investigate the family's view of the problem. This is important to the process of engagement between the therapist and the family, which depends on many factors. The therapist must make a personal connection with each family member present. How he does this will depend on his style. In making this connection the therapist must remain alert to the family's boundary guard. Frequently the boundary guard is the father, and successful initial contact with him will implicitly open the remainder of the system to contact with the therapist. It is also important that he communicate an understanding of each family member's position vis-à-vis the presenting problem. The evaluation session then becomes an emotionally validating experience for the family, and as such fosters the process of engagement.

The therapist turns to Mary first for her view of the problem. She states that she has been feeling better just since making the appointment to come in. The fact that her mother has been visiting for the previous week is offered as the most recent disorganizing experience. The therapist decides to be untracked for a moment, and find out just what position Mary's mother occupies in the present family structure. Mother is described as anxious, critical, and easily upset. The therapist probes the openness of that relationship by inquiring if Mary told her mother she was coming in for consultation. Mary replies that her mother couldn't handle that sort of information. The therapist, referring to his genogram, sees that Mary is an only child, and investigates the impact of that fact on the intensity of their relationship. Going further, he looks for three-generational triangulation, and asks, "Which of your kids is Grandma's favorite?" The answer is Nancy, who just happens to be the daughter Mary is most concerned about.

A number of things come together at this point. Earlier in the interview Mary has remarked on how much Nancy reminds her of her father, Mary's

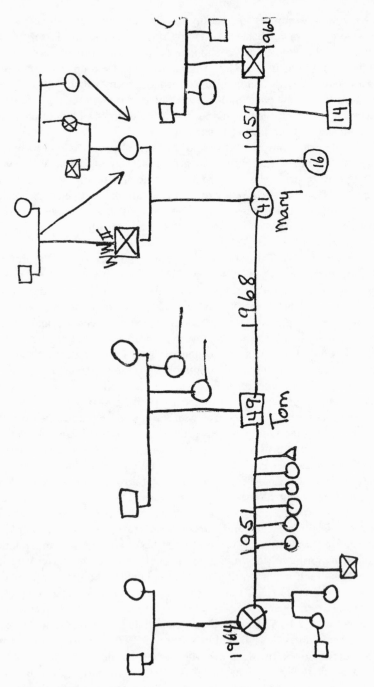

first husband, Bill. One of her worries about Nancy, Mary reveals, is that Nancy might repeat her father's suicide. This revelation, combined with the therapist's observation that while this line of questioning is going on with Mary, Tom is relieved to the point of being pleased, causes the therapist to take a series of steps. He frames his move by first recalling Mary's concern for Nancy's possible suicide; then he gradually moves to open the issue of potential suicide in the marriage.

The first target of the therapist's questioning is Mary's feeling of responsibility for her first husband's death, and to what extent that ties in to her present worry about her daughter. Next the therapist checks on Mary herself. "With all of this trouble that you have been having recently with the children, and Tom's lack of work, have you ever thought of cashing in your own chips as a solution?" Mary replies that while she frequently feels that the entire household would improve greatly if she packed a bag and left, she does not see suicide as the answer to her problems.

The therapist then moves to cover the primary target, and asks a reverse question. "You'd never find yourself worrying about Tom becoming so despondent about his own career that he would take his own life?" Mary's answer requires no period of deep thought. She says immediately, "Definitely. Quite often." This is then opened up with Tom and checked out with him. Tom does a disclaimer, stating that suicide is not his style; but he does admit being bugged at not being able to reassure Mary. Much of the presenting problem as it appears from Mary's vantage point has been spelled out. She has never come to terms with her feelings of responsibility for her first husband's death. She is determined to prevent a recurrence in her daughter. She has virtually no one that she can talk to about her deepest worries in this regard. When she does let them out into the relationship with her husband Tom, he reasons at her intense feelings. Her mother, too, lost a husband prematurely. But the intensity of that relationship can't contain Mary's emotions. In her isolation Mary is constantly taking Tom's emotional temperature, trying to deal with his children as well as her own, and feeling supported by no one.

The therapist has heard the problem from Mary's viewpoint. Tom has also been connected with about his views on the issue of suicide. Tom relates his central concern to be no job and an upset wife. The therapist asks, "Are you ever aware that Mary is sitting there worrying that you will become so depressed about your lack of a job that you might resort to suicide as a way out?" This question has a dual purpose: it allows the therapist to move toward the areas of Tom's concern, and it also sets the stage for questions about how the Mary/Tom relationship works on an operational level—that is, how aware of Mary's concern is Tom, how much is he tuned in to her and the way she thinks?

Tom appears to be a calm reasonable man who takes most things in his stride. He even appears to have the present state of affairs under control, and describes his situation with a half-smile and a gentle joking manner. The therapist observes this, and puts it together with the fact that Tom is an Irishman, and perhaps therefore has inherited some of the cultural patterns of his forefathers. How much is his calm, jocular exterior related to the Irish manner of holding in feelings of rage? Pride is often the napkin that covers everything else in the Irish picnic basket.

Here is a man who is used to making $50,000 a year in an important job. Now his wife supports the family on considerably less. How low has his pride index fallen? The therapist's questioning follows this train of thought. He asks, "What are some of the problems you personally face around your present work difficulties?" "Frustration, mostly," is Tom's reply, "I mean, I never get violent or anything." The therapist remarks, "The Irish are famous for their underground rage." Tom laughs and confides that he does experience a significant degree of rage, and that most of the time he just does not know where to put that feeling. He tries hard to control it. He does doubt himself and his abilities. "Supposing I really am not all that good. . . . then what?" He worries about this daily, and sometimes feels that this constant internal battle will result in a loss of confidence in himself, so that when he does go to an interview, his embarassment and lack of belief in himself will show, and work against the impression that he makes.

The therapist asks, "Do you have the freedom to put these kinds of thoughts and upsets into your relationship with Mary?" Tom confides that he really is holding most of this in, because he does not want to complain and burden everyone, especially Mary, with a situation that he can do nothing about. The therapist points out that talking about it to Mary might validate her thoughts and feelings, and be a relief to her. If she knew he was suffering, she would be less upset and he would have less to contend with. Also, she wouldn't have to fill the vacuum with thoughts of his suicide.

A good deal of time in this part of the interview is spent discussing the practical difficulties in job hunting, overqualification, lack of readily available jobs due to the economic crunch, and so on. The therapist questions Tom about the possibilities of relocating to another more prosperous area. Tom says that of late he has been considering it. The therapist also remarks that Tom is being interviewed by men who are less qualified to do the jobs they are doing than Tom himself is; Tom states that he has learned to write his resume to fit the description of the job for which he is applying. This tells the therapist that Tom is not sitting around the house waiting for a job to come to him, and is in fact doing everything that he can for himself.

The operating principles that each of this marital pair uses to govern his or her own individual action and reactions has been evident throughout the interview. The therapist knows, for instance, that Mary is a distancer when it comes to her mother, but a pursuer of her husband and children. She is the self-appointed protector of her charges who tries to keep them from all harm. She oversees everything from the laundry to her daughter's and her husband's depression index. Tom, on the other hand, distances from everything but his work. He used his work as a source of refuge when his first wife and baby died, and also later on, after the untimely death of his son. Here is a man whose major prop—the work in which he took pride—has been removed. In his own words, "Pride gets in my way and sometimes it colors my judgment about things. Sometimes I think that now it is my pride that I protect the most."

The problems that this couple have with their two middle daughters (one each from their former marriages), who strongly resemble their respective dead parents, point up the need to deal with the ghosts of these former spouses, so that the children do not indeed become pushed into repeating those parts of the family script. At the end of this interview Mary and Tom were asked to bring in the children for the next visit. In addition, they discussed the possible advantages of having a session that included Tom's two oldest daughters, both in their twenties and living away from home.

We usually set aside an initial period of two hours, followed by two one-hour sessions, for a family evaluation, but the many complex problems in this family made another two-hour session including the children necessary. Ideally, the next step might be a home visit with the whole family, perhaps at dinner, but this is usually not possible with most families.

In the last evaluation session, the therapist presents the things he has learned about the family and charts a general course of action to be followed in subsequent meetings. This interview often includes specific assignments for each partner, which will be checked on in the next meeting.

A great deal of information is gathered in an evaluation interview, which has to be synthesized and recorded. To facilitate this process we have developed a form, reprinted below, which we offer as a model.

PRESENTING PROBLEM

Tom has been out of work for 2½ years. He is a graduate of Fordham with a B.S. in Business Administration and an M.A. in Engineering. His salary when last employed was $50,000. He was a consultant to a major engineering firm. Mary is currently employed in administration at a Mental Health Clinic at a salary of $11,500.

The couple cites a variety of emotional adjustments they have found difficult to make as a result of the loss in income; father's being a housewife with scant business prospects; and behavior problems in Mary's daughter.

REFERRAL SOURCE: Jane Thorndike, M.S.W., Director of Rehabilitation Services at North Park Mental Health Clinic.

EXTENDED FAMILY RELATIONSHIPS

Mary's Family. Only child of Father killed in an automobile accident

E-1

EVALUATION. INTERVIEW------------------GUERIN/PENDAGAST

Name--------------------Address----------------Date----------

Phone--------------------   ----------------------Time------------

Genogram--- 3 Generations

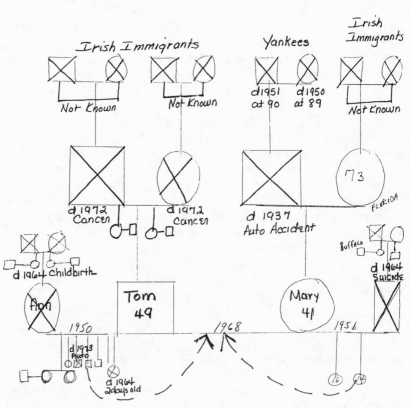

when she was three years old. Mother (73) still living in Florida. They have little contact except for yearly "duty visits," from Mother, "to see my grandchildren." Mary's distance from Mother has been in existence since adolescence. Mother objected strongly to both of Mary's marriages, and wished her to remain at home. Mary very close to first husband's sisters, sees them frequently, calls them every other week on the phone.

Tom's Family. Both parents dead within six months of one another. Rarely sees either of his sisters or their families. Has remained in contact with first wife's sisters. Had very little contact with parents after leaving for college.

N.B. Neither spouse has developed close friends in social network. Friends appear to be for good times only.

NUCLEAR FAMILY

Mary—pursuer and accumulator, easily upset. She is overinvolved with all kids, and while working still tries to monitor husband/kids/house. Feels responsible for first husband's death, just as Tom feels responsible for his first wife's death. One of her kids and one of his get caught up in this.

Tom—is a distancer, into objects and books. He is very depressed, since he is a man who distanced into his work and survived his losses through death by immersing himself in work. No support for nuclear family from the extended family.

Mary is allergic to Tom's housewifing and he to her role as provider. She worries about his depression and fears it might lead to suicide. Also worries about this in her own daughter.

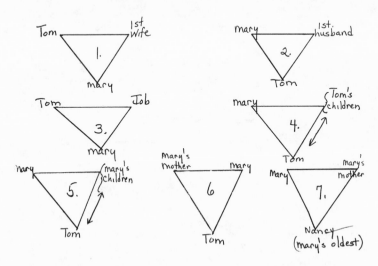

DIAGNOSIS OF PROBLEMS & PLAN FOR TREATMENT
1. Detoxify issues of death, suicide, and Father's job loss by lowering

anxiety level and opening the relationship around these issues.

2. Dissect the relationship process and dysfunctional patterns that orbit around all of the issues listed above.

3. Challenge dysfunctional patterns by offering alternative options and tasks that will reverse the direction of movement in the present process.

4. (a) Make known and then structurally alter triangles involving Tom and Mary and both of their dead spouses.

(b) Do the same with all other triangles, especially those involving the children and dead parents.

5. Attempt to open up the extended family on both sides.

PROGNOSIS

The tenderness/caring index in this particular family is quite high, which is a positive prognostic sign. But this first session demonstrates that there is a significant amount of closed communication in the family system. There are cutoffs from the extended family, and these signs tend to make the prognosis somewhat guarded. From the initial evaluation time, Tom and Mary appear (with the therapist's help) to be able to label the areas of dysfunction. However, how they take to tasks aimed at intervention in the ongoing process, and how well they sustain a focus on the thread of movement toward change, remains to be seen.

The willingness of Tom and Mary to re-enter their respective extended family fields will be an important indicator as to whether the family will settle for some form of symptomatic relief, or move into an ongoing process of longterm change.

CHAPTER 27

Family Choreography

Peggy Papp, M.S.W.

Family choreography is an outgrowth of family sculpture, which was developed by David Kantor and Fred and Bunny Duhl at the Boston Family Institute. Historically, family sculpturing began with Dr. Kantor's attempts to translate systems theory into physical form through spatial arrangements. In 1950 Dr. Kantor had begun to explore the significance of space in human relationships, and became preoccupied with the use of space as a metaphor for understanding human relationships. In 1965, when he came into contact with the systems theory, he decided that "relations," "context," and "situations," all of which described systems, could best be grasped with the use of spatial metaphors. His experiments combining these concepts gave birth to what he called *family sculpturing*.

Although widely used, this phrase is inadequate to describe the process, since it implies a static rather than a fluid state. Since emotional relationships are always in motion, sculpturing is an instrument of movement. It choreographs transactional patterns—alliances, triangles, and shifting emotional currents—and projects them outward as a silent motion picture. For this reason, I prefer to describe this process as *choreography* rather than as sculpturing, since I think it is a more accurate way to describe the technique.

It is no accident that this technique was developed within the field of family therapy, rather than within the frameworks of individual, group, or encounter therapy, for interrelatedness involving space, time, energy, and movement is inherent to the systems concept of human behavior.

Because of its malleability, family choreography can be adapted to any theoretical approach, modified to suit any style, and used to implement many goals. Dr. Kantor's use of it is influenced by his fascination with psychodrama, and rooted in his belief in experiential learning. He emphasizes the boundaries of personal space, the recreation of past experiences, and the understanding of these in a new way. The Duhls' use is based on a learning theory: "We believe that the individual can change only if he can transcend the system which is his context, and he cannot transcend it until he knows how it works." Virginia Satir, another pioneer in family sculpturing, has used it innovatively as a tool for teaching and for demonstrating family patterns before large community groups. In working with families, she uses it to characterize what she believes to be the four most common stances of family members; the accuser, the placater, the rational one, and the irrelevant one.

My own use of this technique, while also influenced by all these ideas, is based not so much on experiencing or understanding the system to which one belongs as on creating new patterns and thus changing the system. Choreography is used as a method of actively intervening in the nuclear and extended family by realigning family relationships. This realignment is done through exploring alternative transactional patterns in terms of physical movement and positioning.

In order to give the reader an idea of its vast potential, I will describe here the wide range of settings and purposes for which family choreography can be used, from the therapeutic to the educational, from the nuclear to the extended family, from long term to short term therapy, from one family to groups of families, from the inner to the outer system and back again. Regardless of specific purpose, its major value remains constant: its ability to reveal human relationships within a social, psychological, and physical system. Choreography is a technique, rather than an approach or method. It should be added to a therapist's repertoire of other techniques, and used to further an established goal.

REALIGNING THE NUCLEAR FAMILY

Perhaps the most pertinent use of family choreography is in realigning relationships in the nuclear family. Most family problems become locked into linguistic traps. Families are adept at intellectual exercises that use language to deny, rationalize, accuse, defend, and cover up secret family rules. These exercises, through repetition and predictability, congeal problems into a frozen form. This form is changed by the choreography, which transcends language. It introduces the element of the unexpected, the unknown, the unpredictable. Family members seldom surprise one another by what they say, since they have heard it all before. They are surprised by what they choreograph, because they haven't seen it before. Freed from words, the underlying emotional tracks on which the family runs emerge. Once these are made explicit, alternative pathways can be explored.

One example of the use of family choreography in a first interview as a tool for first delineating and then realigning the family system involved a couple in their middle fifties. They came with marital difficulties and conflictual relationships with their two grown children, their married son and daughter, who were 31 and 29. The family was alienated and in a high state of anxiety. The mother hadn't spoken to the son for three months, and wasn't speaking to the husband either, except through the children. There was growing hostility between son and daughter. The choreography was initiated within ten minutes after the session began as a means of cutting through their barrage of attack and counterattack.

Each person was asked to show a visual picture of the way he or she experienced the problem. In order to elicit a systemic picture, the therapist asked systemic questions always aimed at illuminating the transactional patterns. The father's picture immediately showed the rift between these two parents. He placed himself close to his son in the den watching a sports event, separated from his wife and daughter who were close together in the kitchen with the door closed. The daughter showed herself going back and forth, trying to bridge the two camps. She ended up not knowing where to place her feelings, swaying back and forth in the doorway. If she leaned too far one way she would offend her mother, if she leaned too far the other way she would offend father and brother.

The brother showed himself as caught between three different positions: remaining in the den as father's companion; sitting at the dining room table placating mother; or going out the door and staying away "because it is too painful for me to be in the center of that family." However, he could not stay outside the door as it was "dark and cold," and was constantly pulled back into the family through his need to fill up the vacuum between mother and father.

When asked to show the family as he would like it, he placed them in a circle on the floor holding hands, his sister on one side of him, his father on the other. He was suddenly dismayed at not having a third hand to reach across to mother who sat opposite him. The therapist then asked if he felt this was his responsibility, since father was sitting next to her; and he replied, after a long pause, "Yes I have, all my life."

The basic dysfunctional triangle had been given physical form, and could now be altered within that form. The therapist then focused on the marital relationship, asking father to take responsibility for doing something about mother's unhappy face. After several halfhearted attempts at moving closer and trying to establish contact, he gave up, and the son immediately jumped in to take over.

Refocusing once again on the marriage, the therapist then asked the mother to show just where she would like father to be. She placed him out the door (leaving a three-inch crack) and placed both children in front of her. She hesitated as she contemplated the distance between herself and her son, saying they used to be close. Asked to show how close by standing at the opposite sides of the room and approaching each other until they arrived at the distance that would indicate this, the mother stopped when they were approximately two feet apart; the therapist commented that this was within talking distance. The mother then stated they used to be "very very close." When asked to show this, she embraced her son, breaking into loud sobs. With the mother and son in a tight embrace, the therapist asked the crucial question. "Ask your husband to come in, please, and let's see where will he go?" The mother called her husband back into the room; then, after a long pause, she released her son with one arm and extended it to the father. He approached her slowly, and she embraced him. This left the daughter on the outside of the circle. Mother released her other arm from around the son and embraced the daughter, forming a circle which separated mother and son. The children were gradually excluded from the circle, leaving mother and father to confront the unresolved issues between them, thus releasing the children from their entanglement. The choreography had served as an instrument for physically tracing old patterns and drawing new ones.

SYMPTOMS IN CHILDREN

Family choreography is often useful in connecting a child's symptoms to family patterns. Children are often more apt to reveal the secret family rules so closely guarded by adults. Being imaginative and playful, the choreography provides them with a channel for expressing what they cannot express verbally. Their unspoken fears, fantasies, wishes, and hopes can be put into pictures more easily than into words.

A widowed mother brought her eleven-year-old daughter to the clinic because she was failing in school. She was accompanied by her fifteen-year-old son and eighty-year-old aunt, who had raised the mother and who was now living with the family, looking after the children. The daughter sat silent and withdrawn, answering questions noncommittally with "I don't know," "Maybe," "I guess so," "Sometimes." The mother launched into a tirade against her daughter, and defended herself as a mother, saying how much she cared, how hard she had tried, how difficult her life was as the only provider, and how hopeless she felt now that all her good intentions had proved to no avail. Nothing she did helped her daughter, and she could not understand why she was failing. The aunt was incommunicado, speaking almost no English, and the son remained neutral.

The therapist turned to the daughter, saying she didn't have a clear picture of what happened at home, and asked her to make a slowmotion picture of how her family lived together. The daughter became uninhibited and expressive. She placed her mother and brother with their arms around one another, looking admiringly into each other's eyes, "almost like a honeymoon picture." When mother did look at her, it was down her nose with a disdainful glance. She stood her aunt directly in front of her, and said, "I can't get to my mother because my brother and aunt are always in between." Asked to show what she would like to do, she brushed past her aunt, pushed her brother aside, and threw herself into her mother's arms, crying. The mother, who later confided she had never been able to embrace her daughter, was stunned and clung to her. Verbal communication cannot duplicate a physical enactment of a scene, nor can it change a scene. Enacting what was never allowed to happen, what one wishes would happen, what could happen creates a different reality, replete with possibility. This choreography was particularly important in breaking through the stalemate and giving mother and daughter hope.

The mother's first remark to the therapist at the following session was, "Thank you for changing my life. I can never forget that experience." Realizing how a child feels will sometimes shock a parent into temporary affectual changes; however, this therapist has learned through grievous experience that simple understanding is not enough, and that change must be structured into daily life. This was done through subsequent tasks aimed at fostering a closer mother/daughter relationship. The choreography was a significant factor in motivating the mother to follow through on the tasks. It had also provided a family map indicating what changes were needed.

In another family the choreography was used to facilitate communication between a distant father and son. Recreating excerpts from the father's childhood provided them with a common meeting ground.

This was an upper-middleclass black family trying desperately to make it in an exclusive white community. They presented themselves as the perfect family—perfect parents, perfect relationships, perfect patients. It was difficult to break through their facade of niceness. The sixteen-year-old son, suffering symptoms of withdrawal from family, friends, and school, was asked to picture himself in all three situations. He showed himself with his colleagues after a football game, when everyone was invited to a party except him. In the classroom he sat in the back of the room, feeling inadequate and isolated. Coming home with these feelings, he found his mother laughing on the telephone in one room, his sister laughing on the telephone in another room, and the father buried in his newspaper. The boy ended up in his own room, pacing and downcast. The therapeutic move was focused on the son's great need to identify with his distant father. In rerunning the scene, he was asked to see what would happen if he approached his father and told him something of what was troubling him. The father put down his newspaper and, being the perfect parent, began to give his son perfect advice a la *Reader's Digest.* The son stated that he didn't find this helpful, and the father was requested to see how long he could listen without giving advice. Within minutes his eyes became misty, and he spoke of having had similar problems in growing up. He was asked to show these by using members of the staff to play the different people from his past. The scenes were strikingly similar to those of his son involving friends, at school, and at home. His son, who until then had known very little about his father or his life, had thought that it must have been perfect, and was always comparing his "imperfect self" with his father's "perfect image." The choreography provided a pathway of communication between the father and son, shattering the perfect image and permitting them to share life experiences. While the harsh realities of both past and present could not be erased, they were easier for the son to face when he could share them within a family.

TRACKING AND INTERRUPTING A VICIOUS CYCLE

The vicious cycle syndrome is a common characteristic of intimate emotional relationships. Before it can be interrupted, one must have a clear picture of the mutual behavior which keeps it activated. This is often difficult to arrive at through verbal description because of the generalities of language and the vagueness of perception. Choreographing the cycle can provide a detailed picture of the sequences which lead to the escalation.

A husband who habitually disappears from home for several days at a time, approximately every three months, spoke of feeling trapped on those occasions. He blamed himself for being a person who simply couldn't take the domestic scene for too long, and had to blow. There was no particular event which he could single out which precipitated these feelings. He was asked to show the domestic scene, beginning with his coming home from work in the evening. How did he approach the house? He moved slowly, and with trepidation. "I know she is going to want something from me." He opened the door cautiously, greeted his wife perfunctorily, and walked into the bedroom. This incited the wife to try and make contact. She followed him from room to room in her efforts to establish communication. The pursuit was etched in detail, with the wife using every device at her command to engage, the husband using every device at his command to disengage. This escalated until the wife ended up in the bathroom crying, while the husband sat in the living room feeling trapped and looking for the exit. This evening sequence epitomized their relationship.

In order to emphasize the futility of their behavior, they were asked to repeat the sequence with each trying harder to do what they were doing. This telescoped their interaction and intensified it to the point of absurdity. The wife finally threw up her hands, "The harder I try, the faster he runs."

The system, having been projected outward, could now be played with.

Different alternatives were explored through position and movement. The wife was taken out of hearing distance of the husband, and instructed to move away immediately after greeting him and involve herself in an activity. They began the sequence over, and as she moved away, the husband stood transfixed. He folded his arms and cocked a curious eye at her. When asked why he didn't move, he replied "I'm intrigued. She seems interesting to me now." The wife was astonished. "You mean, it's as simple as that? After all these years!" They were then asked to repeat the initial sequence once again, with the husband being given a different alternative. He entered the house, swept his wife off her feet, and danced her around the room. An entrenched cycle had been interrupted by introjecting surprise and unpredictability. An old problem had been experienced differently. Enacting this change in the session under the direction of the therapist made it easier to recreate at home.

TRAINING

Family choreography is an excellent training tool, due to its ability to demonstrate visually the cybernetics of a family. It can create a graphic picture of family processes over time, including labeling, projecting, triangulating, reciprocity, and homeostasis. Those who believe that an understanding of the trainee's own family is essential to understanding treatment families can use the choreography for this purpose. It provides the trainee with the unique experience of observing himself within his family system at the same time he is experiencing it, so that he can see his position in relation to the other family members, the function he serves in maintaining the family homeostasis and his behavior patterns that emanate from the overall family design. It is difficult if not impossible to comprehend the part one plays in a system, particularly a system as intensely emotional as the family, without externalizing it in some way. Some therapists draw systems on paper or on the blackboard to make them more graphic. Choreography allows the therapist to draw the system with space, time, sight, hearing, energy, and movement.

One of the most difficult problems in monitoring a choreography is to keep the trainee from expressing himself verbally rather than through pictures and movement. We are essentially a verbal culture, highly articulate and adept at using words not only to express our feelings but to cover them up, to deny, project, intellectualize, and rationalize. The power of the choreography comes through *seeing* and *physically moving through* the situation.

The trainee begins by choosing participants from the training seminar to stand in as members of his family, including someone to play himself. This permits him initially to stand on the sidelines as an observer.

One trainee's choreography revealed family processes across three generations. The trainee, a woman, was asked to begin by having a fantasy of her parents' expectation of her before she was born. She was then asked to pictorialize these fantasies through the choreography. Her father's fantasy took place in an operating room with the trainee performing superb open heart surgery. Her mother's fantasy showed the trainee as a renowned professor lecturing in a reputable university. She was married to a "gorgeous wonderful man and had perfect children." This projected a picture of preordaining influences of the system into which she was born.

The trainee was then asked to show the relationship between her father and mother at the time of her birth. Being the first born, she had inevitably absorbed what was unresolved between the two of them. Specific questions were asked in terms of psychological stances and gestures. How were their feet planted on the ground? What were their hands doing? What was each hand saying? Where was each foot going? Where were they looking? With what kind of expression? How did they touch? It is only in the particulars that the unique quality of the relationship emerges.

The trainee placed her parents holding hands, father turned looking away from mother, one foot headed out the door toward his work. Mother was leaning toward father, hands outstretched, one hand saying "I need you," the other saying "I need more." Father responded with one of his hands holding mother's, saying "I am here for you," the other waving her away with "I can't give you any more."

After the therapist gets the exact positioning, he puts the picture in motion by asking action questions. "Who moves toward or away from whom?" "How?" "What is the other person's reaction?" "What are the cues which regulate the relationship?"

Father is the first to move, breaking away from mother when her clutch becomes too tight. He moves toward his work or toward his parents, again moving away from his mother when her clutch becomes too tight. He ends up escaping into his work to avoid the clutching hands of both wife and mother. (Whenever the grandparents play an active role in the family, they are brought into the picture). When father moves away from mother, she moves toward her own parents who have their fists raised "up and at each other." She comes bearing gifts in order to try and stop the fighting, but they hardly notice her. She returns to her husband, and the sequence begins all over again. This gives one an overview of the three generational schema into which the trainee was born.

As the trainee enters the picture as a newborn baby, she is clutched by the outstretched hand of mother to fill the empty space between her parents. She quickly begins trying to fulfill their expectations by climbing a ladder, looking back over her shoulder particularly at father to see how she is doing. Father is moving restlessly about and not noticing. She then stages a temper tantrum, hoping to get father's attention; but it is mother who notices and comes in. Mother, unable to get father's attention herself, uses the tantrum to involve him, grabbing him to calm down the daughter. Father comes in reluctantly and stops the temper tantrum. All three hold hands until it gets too close for father, and he moves away.

We now have a clear idea of the way in which the daughter has been labeled the white hope of the family, and is used by mother to involve father in family affairs.

The second child is brought into the picture—a brother. Mother remains focused on the daughter, and the brother fends for himself, fighting with sister. The mother then uses the fighting between the siblings to try and involve father. Father breaks up the fight, then moves out; the daughter starts climbing the ladder again; and the cycle renews itself with the addition of the sibling fighting as a new focus for bringing in father. The grandparents stand absorbed with her climb up the ladder, always applauding her efforts to reach the top. The mother now takes the daughter as a gift to her parents, and this time they stop their fighting.

The trainee is then asked to show how the picture changes over time. At adolescence she begins her rebellion. She swiftly pushes the ladder away, locks arms with a female friend, and truants from school, "to fight the world with compulsion, anger, and fun." Mother now uses her rebellion as one more way to try and involve father. She falls to her hands and knees, pleading and crying over her daughter's wildness; father comes running to solve the crisis.

Having directed the operations of her family from the sidelines, the trainee is now asked to enter the system experientially by playing herself. Her position as a spectator has given her a bird's-eye view of the total system and each person's position in it.

The trainee moves through the central patterns of her life, repeating the sequences over and over just as life tends to repeat itself. This gives her a sharpened sense of the way in which her emotional circuits are connected with the central family theme.

The past is then connected with the present by having her choreograph her current relationships with her family. Her mother is dead, and she enacts her role as the over-responsible caretaker, watching out for her brother, still trying to repair the relationship between her grandparents, and still trying to get father involved with both her and her brother. She stops in the middle of this to say, "I realize I am taking over the role of mother. What she didn't do, I am trying to finish. The battles she didn't fight I am trying to fight. I am even trying to bridge the distance she couldn't bridge with father. The anger she didn't speak I carried." She expressed her desire to change her relationship with her father, but didn't know how. Every time she approached him, she felt he moved away, leaving her frustrated and angry. She was asked to show just how she approached. She moved toward him in an aggressively demanding manner, hands outstretched, much the same as mother. The stand-in for father automatically backed away saying, "That scares me. I'm afraid I can't meet your demands." Asked how she felt she could approach him so that he would respond differently, he replied "Approach me slowly and just wait." As she did this, he stated, "I am not threatened now," and he took a step toward her. The stand-ins often give pertinent feedback based on physically experiencing a particular position in a family.

A month later, in a followup report, the trainee stated, "I stopped calling all my family—gave up trying to keep everybody involved and happy. A funny thing has happened. Now they are calling me—including my father."

The most important part of learning about change is to see that the past cannot be changed, but the continuation of the patterns into the present and future can be. By attempting to do this, the trainee learned something about unbalancing homeostatic tendencies in her family.

There are many different ways of entering a family system. Another way is through the use of metaphors. Metaphors are a quick way of abstracting the essence of family relationships. One trainee was asked to think of a metaphor for each family member, and place them together. His father was a locomotive going full steam ahead, his mother a threatening sky, his sister a bright field of flowers, and he himself was a bridge over which the locomotive passed. When asked what the problem for him in this gestalt was, he said there was a crack in the bridge. The crack was grown over with ivy so no one could see it, but its existence was a gnawing source of anxiety to him. If the bridge fell his father would crash, his mother would rain tears, and his sister would witness the scene of a disaster. When asked to translate these metaphors into his real life scene, he showed his mother and father in a violent fight, after which his mother, who had a heart condition, dragged herself pantingly up the stairs (he was always afraid she wouldn't make it to the top), and his father raced out of the house. The trainee ran to his sister's room for help. She dismissed him with a carefree shrug, leaving him alone and feeling that he must hold everything together. Asked to show how he did this, he ran back and forth between his sister, mother, and father to no avail, becoming more frustrated and ending up tearing his shirt apart in desperation. The crack in the bridge, representing his symbolic "inadequacy," was now seen as a reaction to trying to resolve an impossible situation rather than as a defect within him. He was left with some thoughts about his bridge playing role in his present family and the feeling of an imminent crack as a result of again trying to hold everything together.

EDUCATION

Because family choreography is a dramatic medium for demonstrating the family system, it can be used advantageously for both public and professional education in community mental health programs, workshops, and on television. One format, designed for an educational community program sponsored by the Center for Family Learning, actively engaged the audience in demonstrating common operations of a family system. This program was presented in churches, synagogues, PTA meetings, YMCA's, and neighborhood associations—wherever family education meetings were sponsored. Three scenes were designed to portray the operations of a family in everyday terms, and unrelated volunteers from the audience were used to move through familiar family situations as the therapist described them.

Who has the problem? shows a husband coming home from work and withdrawing into his newspaper; a wife trying to get his attention and taking out her frustration on her son; the son, unable to deal with his parents, hitting his sister; his sister, too small to defend herself, screaming for Daddy; and Daddy ending up fighting with Mother over the children. This graphically illustrates the circularity of interaction, showing the family members physically locked into a circle. The audience is then asked, "Who has the problem?"

The individual solution shows the dissolution of the family. Each person develops a symptom, and is individually diagnosed and sent to a different source for help. The father goes to a doctor for migraine headaches; the mother to a womens' liberation group for depression; the son to the school guidance counselor for school failure; and the daughter to a pediatrician for asthma. The individual solutions, although giving temporary relief, present a picture of a distant and scattered family.

In the last scene, *All in the family,* the members are brought back together, and the problem is handled among them by physically negotiating different positions. With the help of the therapist each person finds a position in which he feels he can comfortably relate to the others. Usually a great deal of humor and fun is shared by both participants and audience as they recognize themselves and their families in the various situations.

USE IN GROUPS

Family choreography is ideally suited to a group setting. The dramatic form of the choreography and the theatrical setting of a group are a perfect match. The group provides an audience which both actively participates in the process and looks at it from the perspective of distance and detachment.

It can be used in a couples group, in multiple family groups, or in conventional group therapy with unrelated individuals. In a couples group, choreography can be used to connect the present with the past, or simply to delineate the relationship in the here and now. In one couples group it was used successfully to define the dilemma between the couples through the use of metaphors elicited in daydreams. In a long-term couples group, the families of origin of each couple were choreographed, followed immediately by the choreography of their present relationship. This condensed the patterns and emphasized their repetitious nature. Corresponding tasks were then given around extended family and marital relationships.

For example, a wife's choreography revealed criticism to be a central issue for her across three generations—with her father, her husband, and her children. Her father was pointing an accusing finger at her in a childhood scene, her husband was doing the same in a marital scene, and she herself was pointing an accusing finger at both of her daughters. Her reaction to father's and husband's criticism was to become argumentative. Following the choreography, she was given tasks aimed at reversing her defensive position with her father and husband. The next time her father criticized her, she was to ask his advice about her problem of being too critical of her daughters. In the first personal conversation they had ever had, the father confided his own struggle with self-criticism. "I have spent my whole life tearing myself down. I guess I have been too hard on you too," and then went on to praise her for all her virtues and those of her children. In reversing her position with her husband, she was instructed to agree with his criticism rather than fight it, to denounce herself even more than he, and to wonder how he had put up with her for so long. His criticism immediately decreased, and he began to contradict her low appraisal of herself. The end result was that she became less critical of herself and her children. This example points up the necessity of the therapist's integrating the material which emerges from the choreography into an overall treatment design. The choreography serves simply as an instrument, like a pen, to draw a picture, which once made clear can be changed.

In a multiple family therapy group, the choreography can serve many purposes. Choreographing the parent's family of origin can be especially effective, as it gives the children a glimpse of what it was like for their parents to be children. Usually children think of parents in a one dimensional picture—nagging, disciplining, criticizing, worrying, distancing, unavailable, demanding. The choreography reveals each parent as a total person struggling with problems similar to those the children have, which makes them more human. Group members who stand in for original family members see the family unit with the eyes of a newcomer, and are able to give valuable feedback about the experience. Choreographing the parents' families of origin followed by choreographing the nuclear family shows the converging of family themes from both sides, and gives a historical perspective that aids in preventing problems.

USE IN CONSULTATION

When a therapist finds himself immobilized with a family it is often helpful to take advantage of the fresh eye of another therapist. The choreography is an effective device for consultation, as it provides not only a different point of view but a different form. It can stretch a system to its outer limits, contract it, magnify it, or refocus it.

A therapist sought consultation about a family who had for years lived in a never-never land of pseudo-divorce. The mother had definitely made up her mind to separate years ago, but she was immobilized by her husband's inability to accept the actual separation, even though he himself felt it was impossible to continue the relationship. The children, ages 9, 13, 14, and 16, were caught up in the turmoil of conflict and ambivalence, and had developed distressing symptoms. All four children wished their parents to separate. In the consultation interview the therapist took the entire family through a rehearsal of a trial separation, asking each member to show his greatest fear and his greatest hope. As each enacted the problem he or she might encounter, different solutions were experienced in terms of positions and movement. Rigid alliances were shifted, allowing more flexibility in moving in and out of relationships. A composite designed for the future was mapped out, encompassing the family's striving for a new way of life, and emphasizing the hope and possibility of a better future. The choreography enabled the father, a quiet inhibited man, to express through pictures many feelings and observations about the family and himself which he had been unable to express in direct conversation. All eyes were focused intently on him as he unfolded his concerns about himself and the family. His comment at the end was, "Once out there, things don't look so horrible. They look more manageable."

As the consulting family therapist observed the interview and studied the tape, it was clear to him how the plans for the separation should be carried out, which relationships were the most vulnerable, and where trouble spots were most likely to develop.

CRITERIA AND PITFALLS

Family choreography speaks with the universal language of sight and movement; therefore it is comprehensible to any family, from the most highly educated and articulate to the most impoverished and inarticulate. Being primarily nonverbal, it is an excellent technique for families who do not verbalize easily. Families with any kind of a language problem can often express themselves more freely through action than through words, particularly if they are involved in complicated community networks and outside institutions such as schools, hospitals, or welfare. Both problems and alternative solutions can be presented in terms of action, which greatly simplifies the confusion.

Used with discretion it can make explicit the double binding processes in psychotic families. Since there is a taboo against defining relationships, these processes are covert and difficult to trace sequentially. The choreography provides an artifice through which they can be revealed and examined. As with any other technique, its successful implementation depends upon the skill, judgment and sensitivity of the therapist. It should be added to a therapist's repertoire, and used whenever verbal pathways prove inadequate.

The greatest pitfall is that it may be ineffective. Families are difficult to damage or destroy. They are expert in maintaining a homeostatic system, and the greatest danger is that the therapist will not be able to upset it. Most professional therapists are knowledgeable enough to handle the fallout from any changes stirred up from the choreography. Choreography should, of course, be limited to professional use. It is not a parlor game, and demands an objective observer.

Some family therapists have experimented using choreography with their own families, and have reported illuminating experiences. Others have reported that it simply stirred up old issues without illuminating them at all. When choreography fails, it is generally because the therapist is overwhelmed by the richness of the material that emerges, and has not evolved any clear notion of what to do with it. The best way to learn family choreography is to teach oneself by watching replays of one's own videotapes, while constantly asking, "What do I wish to accomplish?"

BIBLIOGRAPHY

F. Duhl, B. Duhl, and D. Kantor. "Learning, Space and Action in Family Therapy: A Primer of Sculpture." in D. Bloch, ed., *Techniques of Family Psychotherapy.* New York: Grune and Stratton, 1973.

R. Simon. "Sculpting the Family," *Family Process,* 2 (1972), 49–57.

P. Papp, O. Silverstein, and E. Carter. "Family Sculpting in Preventive Work with 'Well Families." *Family Process,* 12 (1973).

V. Satir. *People Making.* Palo Alto: Science and Behavior Books, Inc. 1972.

Making the Invisible Visible, training tape demonstrating the use of family choreography. Available through the Nathan W. Ackerman Family Institute, 149 East 78th Street, New York City.

CHAPTER 28

The Use of the Arts in Family Therapy: I Never Sang for my Father

Philip J. Guerin, Jr., M.D.

> *Death ends a life, but it does not end a relationship which struggles on in the survivor's mind toward some resolution which it never finds. . . . Alice said I would not accept the sadness of this world. What did it matter if I never loved him, or he never loved me? . . . Perhaps she was right. But still, when I hear the word "Father" . . . it matters.*
>
> Robert Anderson, *I Never Sang for My Father*

The use of the arts in family therapy is a natural spinoff from the use of displacement material in other areas. Therapists, educators, theologians, and parents have used displacement materials for generations to help people focus on problems that they are too involved in emotionally to see clearly. Long before the arrival of family therapists, people sat in open fields and in darkened theaters and watched skilled performers acting out situations that were a part of their own everyday existence. The externalization of the process of day-to-day family life seems to facilitate a more objective view of how it works. Children's literature, for instance, is often concerned with stories that teach lessons about how to handle most of the problems of childhood, including stories about imaginary creatures, fashioned out of their own fear and uncertainty, and assorted ways to outwit parents and siblings. Child psychiatrists frequently use displacement techniques in play therapy with an individual child. The story about a baby bird who falls from the nest while his mother is out searching for food can serve to open up to verbalization and examination the child's own anxiety about being separated from his mother.

One of the reasons frequently given to explain the effectiveness of multiple family therapy is that it enables families to gain a new perspective on their own emotional process by listening to other families describe the problems that they are experiencing. In the early 1960s, Bowen began using the technique of telling families in treatment about other anonymous families that he was working with in order to prod them into new ways of thinking about their own problems. I became intrigued with this technique, which I called the use of displacement stories, and expanded it to include the use of movies, plays, and other displacement forms. I will illustrate the technique here using the film *I Never Sang For My Father* as an example —first from a historical perspective, and then from a more operational, practical perspective.

In 1970, Columbia Pictures released the film of Robert Anderson's play *I Never Sang For My Father*. It is a story about the Garrisons, an upper-middle class WASP family. Its major thematic thread is the relationship between father and son over two generations.

The father, Tom, and mother, Margaret, are in their eighties. They live in Westchester County in a house that has been theirs since their children were small. The father is a successful businessman, who was also a former mayor of the town. He has been retired for fifteen years. The mother is in poor health with a deteriorating cardiac condition. Anderson tells us nothing of the mother's extended family, and she is clearly idealized by the author; however, there is a pattern of almost continual criticism from her aimed at her husband.

The father's extended family is presented through the father's eyes. He was the oldest of three children, and his mother died when he was ten years old. She had been deserted by her husband who was an alcoholic. Tom clearly bastardized his father and idealized his mother. The process of idealization began while she was alive, and became further intensified following her premature death. Tom Garrison is portrayed as a self-made man, pompous and opinionated, invulnerable to feeling, who sees himself as devoted to his wife Margaret whom he also idealizes.

The marriage of Tom and Margaret Garrison has produced two children. The older, a daughter Alice, is married and living with her husband and children in Chicago. She has been cut off from her parents and her brother after having been "banished" by father for marrying a Jew. Gene, the younger, is an author who lives in New York City, but who travels on tours to other parts of the country. His wife has been dead for approximately a year. She died of cancer, and the couple had no children. On a recent tour to California, Gene has met and fallen in love with a woman doctor who has been married before and has children. The fate of her first marriage is not made known.

The film opens with Gene picking up his parents on their return to New York from Florida. They drive from the airport to their home. During the ride home, certain parts of the family process become clear. The brusque pompousness of the father is contrasted with the soft over-tolerant mother, whose faint twist of bitterness lies somewhere just beneath the surface. The distance between the parents becomes evident. This and later developments in the film define the father as an emotional distancer, one who moves toward objects, productivity, and material markers of accomplishment. He is somewhat addicted to ritual, and his prevalent mood varies from negative to hyped-up enthusiastic.

Mother on the other hand is a normalizer, more of an optimist, emotionally more tuned in and more relationship-oriented than her husband. She has obviously handled her husband's distance by emotionally overinvesting in her children. She has accepted his distance, and resigned herself to his negativism. The father has been relieved of the job of dealing with his wife's intensity by her overclose relationship with her children, especially with her son. Only at times has the father allowed himself to feel that he is on the outside looking in.

My wife and I saw the film a few short months after the death of my father-in-law, and it set off a lot of emotional triggers in me. After seeing the movie, I spent a lot of time thinking about how quickly time and life pass by, and how very important fathers are to the quality of one's own life. I had a lot of thoughts about my wife's relationship with her father, and also about my own relationship with him, which led me to think about my relationship with my own father and his relationship with his father and so on through the generations. I also thought a lot about my kids, and how I might make myself more knowable to them as their father without occupying too much of their life space. Although the movie was thus a very moving experience for me personally, as a family theoretician and clinician I also could not help thinking what a beautiful piece of teaching material the movie would make for family therapists and families in therapy. A few weeks later I discussed this aspect of the film with a colleague; it turned out that through a combination of circumstances and people, she was able to get the rights to use the film for study, teaching, and noncommercial showing.

The full-length film was first used for family therapy training at the 1970 Fordham-Einstein Family Symposium. The audience was made up of about 300 mental health professionals from throughout the country, and their responses were mixed. Some walked out about half way through, while others left in the middle of the confrontation scene. Some people cried, while their neighbors appeared bored and indifferent. In the discussion that followed, it was evident that the audience for the most part quickly personalized the story, especially in terms of the difficulties entailed in trying to attain a person-to-person adult relationship with one's parents. Some were angered at the father, and saw him as an impossible bastard; others were angry with the son for not confronting his father sooner. The movie clearly triggered intense affect, but the question was, how to channel this affect so that it became more than just another emotional experience. How could we use this film so that its effect could be carried over into a new way of thinking about a different relationship with one's own family?

Over the past five years I have used the film with large groups, such as the Fordham-Einstein Symposium; with Therapists-Own-Family Seminars and Community Education Programs with Families; and also at specific points in therapy with an individual family. In this last context, it is usually used when a family is having particular difficulty seeing the importance and relevance of their extended family to both their present and future emotional functioning. What has been developed is a teaching structure, the major components of which are the genogram, capsulized theoretical concepts, and a series of questions that can be proposed to the audience prior to showing the film or segments of the film. A genogram is a structural representation of the family relationship system which allows facts about the family to be organized in such a way that the process in the important relationships is easily demonstrated. The pertinent information available in the film is then pulled out and placed into the structure of the genogram.

A brief attempt is then made to teach a few basic concepts about viewing the family as a system, and the meaning of an emotional relationship system as it pertains to the family. The basic concept that no family member exists in isolation, and that each member occupies a place in the family emotional field is discussed. Each family member is seen as constantly receiving inputs from the field, and depositing his own outputs. What affects any one family member in some way has an effect on every other family member. After these basic assumptions are established, a scenario is proposed that takes the Garrison family as it appears in the film and uses the genogram that has just been drawn.

The audience is asked for example, to suppose that they are entering a time tunnel which will take them back thirty-five years to a time when the Garrison children were still young. We know from the genogram that father has an intense sensitivity to alcoholism and drunken behavior as a result of his experiences with his father. Suppose that on his way home from work, while stopped at a traffic light, the father sees a disheveled, obviously intoxicated man staggering down the street. He feels a tightness in his stomach, and begins to replay in his head a lot of painful stuff from the past. He forcibly blots it out of his consciousness, but on arrival home the toxic parts of his own behavior become prevalent. He is edgy, critical, and wants somebody to listen to a hero story about his latest business accomplishment.

This type of behavior will predictably trigger an emotional reaction in mother. On the one hand, she feels criticized and undervalued, on the other somewhat guilty and responsible for her husband's unhappiness. There is also a trace of anger in her at his self-preoccupation and his not coming home ready to move in and take over with the kids. This reaction on mother's part gets converted into behavior. She moves toward a more intense involvement with fixing dinner and helping the children with their homework. Father senses the move away. To some degree he's bugged, and the thought runs through his head that no one cares about him here anyway; all he is is the money-making machine. On the other hand he's relieved to be able to go up to his study, be alone with his miseries, and take refuge in the leftover work from the office. A short time later at dinner, daughter becomes whiney and demanding; father quiets her with a more than adequate dose of "for your own good" criticism. Mother is quiet, somewhat sulky, and subdued. Son tries to cheer everybody up, especially father, by telling his own hero story about winning the prize essay contest at school. Father responds by telling son how nice that is, but that he'd better put more effort into becoming proficient in math, because that's what will serve him well in the real world. Father then proceeds to tell another hero story of his accomplishments in business. As he proceeds, mother, daughter, and son, at varying rates, slowly sink into their mashed potatoes. At the end of his story father senses this reaction, and, becoming somewhat embarrassed, excuses himself and returns to his room to take refuge again in his work. Mother excuses daughter to do her homework. She and son clean up after dinner, and then he plays his latest piano piece for her in the livingroom.

What are the problems in that family? Is the father's isolation his problem? Is the daughter's whiney behavior and unhappiness her problem? Is mother's distance from her husband and overinvolvement with her son her problem? Are son's anxious attempts to please his problem? Or are they all symptomatic representation of what isn't working well in that family? Everyone will answer on cue. This leads to a brief consideration of the concept of triangulation, which also serves to reinforce the idea of the family as a system. At this point, I usually defer to those people in the audience who have had ten years of psychoanalysis by mentioning that this way of conceptualizing the process in a family is only one of many ways of doing it, since any theory is an abstraction of a natural process, and as such is merely one explanation. The suggestion is made that any theory should be tested by its usefulness as a guide to producing change, which usually detoxifies any ideological warfare that may be brewing and simplifies and enriches the experience for most of the participants.

In introducing the concept of the triangle, it is often useful to explain briefly what it means and then return to the previous scenario for a short elaboration. The concept of triangulation is based on the premise that in a dyadic relationship the process between the two people involved is an unstable one. Think of your best functioning personal relationship. Now imagine isolating that relationship in time and space. Having done that, imagine attempting to confine all communication to personal thoughts and feelings about your own self and the other. It won't be long before you are talking about the Mets, Aunt Suzie, or somebody or something else. The process in the relationship has moved to stabilize itself by triangulating in a third person and/or object.

In order to understand how this process operates in a system, suppose that the Garrison son develops a sysmptom of fear of darkness to the degree that he can't sleep, and neither can the rest of the family. To make it even more incredible, let's suppose his parents bring him to a family systems therapist. The therapist listens to the family, asks some questions, and decides on a plan for engaging the family and responding to the symptom. The central triangle as viewed by the therapist is one in which the distant conflictual relationship between the parents has been covered over. The mother ends up in an overclose relationship with the son, the son and father have an overly distant relationship. In his initial intervention, the therapist has the father take over responsibility for dealing with the son's fear of darkness; he also assigns the father the task of taking his son to work with him for two days in one week, and the following week take his son to the city to see a play. The result is magical. Son's symptom disappears, father and son become closer. Hey, but what about mother? How is she taking all of this? It is impossible to tamper with the father/son relationship without disturbing the mother/son relationship. Mother is now on the outside looking in. She becomes depressed. The triangle has shifted, and so has the symptomatic focus in the family. The problem is no longer a son problem, but has now redefined itself as a family system problem.

After this discussion, a brief description of how family scripts tend to pass from generation to generation is elaborated. This can be done by using the script of distant fathers, and its reoccurrence over the generations in spite of pledges to the contrary. An interesting point can be used here— namely, that the generational repeat of distant fathers involves people carrying a last name from the paternal side of the family, while emotionally being a part of the mother's side of the family. Raising this point is often an effective way to get distant daddies to see the relevance of extended family to their present relationships with their kids.

The stage is now set for offering a set of questions to the audience to serve as a structure for viewing the emotional process in the film. The questions most commonly used are:

1. What are the conflictual issues in the family?

2. What are the central triangles, and how do they appear to operate?

3. What is your idea of a personal relationship? Is it possible to have a personal relationship with the father in this film?

4. What are the nodal point or points around which, if one member of the family changed his/her predictable, behavioral pattern, a whole new

series of options might have opened up for the family?

If the entire film is being shown you are now, as they say, ready to roll. When restrictions of time make the use of ninety minutes of film, plus teaching time, impossible, however, selected segments of the film may be used. Ideally, it is best to have a group view the film in its entirety, and then rerun segments for review and study; but the use of segments, plus teaching and discussion, generally is more practical. The choice of segments from this film will vary according to purpose. Segments dealing with the process of aging and death may be chosen, but for general family process teaching, I usually use two segments. One I call the "garage scene"—it begins in the parents' garage and ends as the son pulls out of his parents' driveway to return to his own apartment. The second segment is the last thirteen minutes of the film, which I call the "confrontation scene."

In watching the garage scene segment, the audience is asked to keep in mind the first two of the four key questions.

1. What are the conflictual issues in the family?

2. What are the central triangles, and how do they appear to operate? In order for the therapist who is presenting this film to clarify the process he should review the script of the play before the showing and keep these key questions in mind.

Here is the garage scene, with a running commentary about the main points in the family process.

(GENE *can hear* FATHER *trying to start the car in the garage. He starts out the kitchen door toward his* FATHER, *and gets there as his* FATHER *starts the old Buick. Tom shows immense satisfaction that the old car starts. He guns it a few times and then shuts it off.*)

Tom: Where did you say your mother was?

Gene: In her garden.

Tom: You know, Gene, the strain has been awful.

Gene: Well, she looks well.

Tom: I know. But you can never tell when she might get another of those damned seizures.

(he looks at the ground and shakes his head at the problem of it all)

Gene: It's rough, I know.

(puts his arm around his FATHER'S *shoulder)*

Tom: Well, we'll manage. She's a good soldier. But she eats too fast. The doctor said she must slow down . . . Oh, well. . . .

(GENE *moves toward the door of the garage.*)

Tom: Gene . . . We got your letters from California.

(fishes in his inside coat pocket)

I've got them here someplace. Well, we do look forward to your letters, old man. . . . there isn't much else for us these days. . . . But this girl, this woman you mentioned several times. . . .

Gene: I'll tell you all about California at dinnertime.

(he starts to move.)

[The development of the central triangle in this family evolves from the beginning of this scene.

Father talks to son about mother, transmitting his anxiety about mother's health and his inability to deal with her in Gene's absence. Gene's letter about a possible move to California has triggered his father's anxiety, and he moves to reinforce son's position as his mother's emotional lifeline and anxiety sponge.

The configuration in the triangle is:]

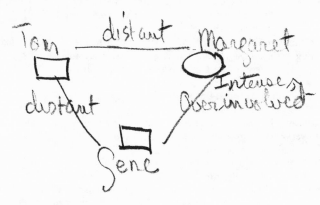

Tom: You seemed to see a lot of her.
Gene: I did.
Tom: Carol's been dead, let's see now, what is it?
Gene: Over a year.
Tom: And there's no reason why you shouldn't go out with another woman.
Gene: No.
(GENE *just waits, puzzled.*)
Tom: I was in California once many years ago. Beautiful country. I can understand your enthusiasm for it.
Gene: I liked it a lot.
Tom: But, Gene . . .
(he bites his upper lip and his voice is heavy with emotion)
If you were to go out there, I mean to live, it would kill your mother.
(He looks at his son with piercing eyes, his tears starting. This has been in the nature of a plea and an order. GENE *says nothing. He is outraged that his father would say such a thing.)*
God, you know you're her whole life.
(GENE *is further troubled by his father's expressing what he knows to be the truth.*)
Gene: Dad . . .
Tom: Yes, you are! . . . Oh, she's fond of your sister, but you . . . are her . . . life! Don't you suppose I've known that all these years?
[Father pulls out all the stops, and continues the triangulation. He makes no statement about what effect the son's leaving for California would have on him. Father reinforces son as Mother's emotional lifeline.]
Gene: Dad, I realize we've always been very close, but . . .
(MOTHER *appears in the near distance. They both notice her.*)
Tom: Just remember what I've said. Well, now let's look after the luggage.
[After getting settled in the house, Gene takes his parents out to dinner. During this restaurant scene, the distance between Tom and Margaret is demonstrated. This

is an important part of the process that ties Gene to Margaret in an overly intense way. The scene also introduces Father's oft-repeated diatribe on the horrors of his boyhood. The central parts of this are the bastardization of his father, and the idealization of his mother.]

   Tom: Have I ever shown you this ring?
   Margaret: You've shown it to him a hundred times.
[Mother's reactive intolerance to Father's ritualized story telling.]
   Tom: (ignoring her remark)
I never thought I'd wear a diamond ring, but when T. J. Parks died, I wanted something of his. Last time I had it appraised, they told me it was worth four thousand. Of course, when I go to see a doctor, I turn it around.
   (a sly smile as he turns it around)
Don't want them to think I'm rolling in money.
[Father, undaunted continues.]
   Margaret: It's his favorite occupation, getting that ring appraised . . . that and telling everyone the gruesome details of his life.
[Mother escalates her complaints.]
   Tom: Now wait a minute!
[Father tries to draw the line.]
   Margaret: I can't have anyone in. Your father won't play bridge or do anything. He just wants to watch Westerns on TV or tell the story of his life.
   Tom: People seem to be interested.
   Margaret: What?
   Tom: I said, people seem to be interested.
   Margaret: He keeps going over and over the old times. Other people have miserable childhoods, but they don't keep going over and over them. That story of your mother's funeral.
[Mother continues complaining to son, describing her social isolation, father's distance from her, and his involvement with objects (TV), along with his ritual story telling. Almost by the character of her complaint she paradoxically encourages father to add yet another of his ritualized tales.]
Gene: I don't remember that one.
[Gene, sensing his father's hurt, moves to placate him. The stage is set, and in two more steps the father will fall into his predictable pattern.]
   Margaret: Oh, don't get him started. He keeps telling everyone how he wouldn't allow his father to come to his mother's funeral.
   Tom: Are you suggesting I should have let him?
   Margaret: I'm not saying—
   Tom: —He'd run out on us when we were kids—
   Margaret: Can you imagine going around telling everyone how he shoved his father off the funeral coach.
   Tom: And I'd do it again. I was only ten and we hadn't seen him in over a year —living, the four of us, in a miserable two-room tenement, and suddenly he shows up at the funeral, weeping, and begging and drunk as usual. And I shoved him off. I never saw him again till some years later, when he was dying in Bellevue . . . of drink.
[Father's tale spells out clearly his intensely negative relationship with his own father. His intense idealization of mother is left until after Margaret's death, when in the casket room of the funeral parlor Tom weeps over a casket that reminds him of his mother's. His idealized version of his mother flows spontaneously. At this point in the play, the repetitive intergenerational triangles and the family scripts are obvious.]

(His hatred and anger are barely held in. GENE *is fascinated by the intensity and hatred after all these years.)*

    Margaret: (has been looking at menu)
What looks good to you?

    Tom: I have not finished yet. . . . I went down to see him, to ask if he wanted anything. He said he wanted an orange. I sent him in half a dozen oranges. I would have sent more, except I knew he was dying, and there was no point in just giving oranges to the nurses. . . . The next morning he died.

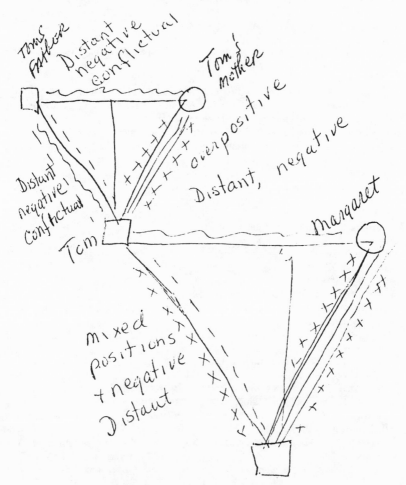

(There is silence for a moment, while GENE *and* MARGARET *look at the menu, and* TOM *grips and ungrips his hand in memory of the hatred of his father.)*

    Margaret: (gently)
Look at your menu now, Father. What are you going to eat?

    Tom: I don't feel like anything. I have no appetite.

    (he lights a cigarette)

    Margaret: This is the way it's been.

INT: MOTHER'S ROOM IN THE HOUSE—NIGHT

(This is a nice room with family photographs, a comfortable old chaise longue, which is mother's "place," sewing table nearby—comfortable old pieces of furniture. As GENE *enters the room from the upstairs hall, we can hear the blare of the television downstairs, a Western with plenty of gunfire.* MARGARET *is looking through Gene's new book of short stories.)*

Margaret: This is lovely, dear.

Gene: Thank you.

Margaret: I don't know how he can stand listening to those Westerns hour after hour.

[As the process continues in the parents' home, we see a further elaboration of the central triangle.]

Gene: I think he always wanted to be a cowboy.

Margaret: He won't listen to the things I want to hear. Down in Florida there's only one TV in the lounge, and he rode herd on it. And then he'd go to sleep in two minutes. . . . Still, he's a remarkable man.

[Mother catches herself, and shifts to excusing father's idiosyncrosies. She seems to want Gene to know that his parents' relationship wasn't always so distant and empty.]

Gene: Good old Mom.

Margaret: Well, he is. Not many boys have fathers they can be as proud of.

Gene: I know that. I'm very proud of him.

Margaret: (she catches his tone)

Everything he's done, he's done for his family.

(GENE *just looks at her smiling*)

So he didn't dance with me at parties.

(she smiles at GENE*)*

You took care of that.

Gene: You were just a great dancer, Mother.

Margaret: What a shame that children can't see their parents when they're young and courting, and in love.

Tom (O.S.): Gene . . . Gene . . . Come and watch this one. This is a real shoot-'em-up.

Gene: I'll be down in a minute, Dad.

(closes door)

Margaret: (as she moves toward her chaise longue)

Now . . . tell me about California.

Gene: (uneasy . . . but he has decided to tell her)

Well, I liked it a lot.

Margaret: It was good for you to get away for a while from the apartment and memories of Carol.

Gene: (wonders for a moment if he'll pick up that "for a while" . . . then:)

Yes.

Margaret: I didn't want to suggest it earlier, but I think you should consider moving out of that apartment. It's so bound up with Carol.

Gene: (after a moment)

Mother . . .

(There is a long pause. . . . MOTHER *has some sense and fear of what is coming.)*

Gene: I wrote you about the woman I met out there, Peggy.

Margaret: The doctor with the children.

(There is a long look between them. She now knows . . . but waits. He goes on very gently.)

[On Mother's prodding, Gene proceeds to tell her about California, his new woman, and his plan to move out there and marry her. Up to this point the configuration in the central triangle has put mother and son as overclose and father in the outside, distant position. As she senses Gene's leaving for California his mother pulls somewhat back from him and toward father, almost as if she were trying to loosen the bond between them to shield herself and allow him to go. True to form, she says little about her own reactions to Gene's leaving, denies it will kill her, and instead translates that to father. We thus have each parent talking about the other's response, and not his or her own.]

Gene: I'm thinking of marrying her.

Margaret: She sounds like a lovely person. And people would expect a man of your age to marry again.

(She apparently hasn't gotten the whole point.)

Gene: She has a practice out there, and her children have their friends and school. . . .

Margaret: (tears come to her eyes . . . she nods)

Well . . . there are still trains and planes. And Alice comes from Chicago once or twice a year with the children.

(GENE smiles gently, understanding her pain. He takes her hand.)

Margaret: Your father and I can take care of each other. He makes the beds, which is the only housework I'm not allowed to do, and I'll remember where he put his checkbook.

Gene: I'm sorry it's worked out this way.

Margaret: (holding herself in control with difficulty)

We've been fortunate to have you so near us for so long. . . . Have you told your Father?

Gene: No. But he guessed something from my letters, and told me if I went out there to live it would kill you.

Margaret: Why can't he say it would kill him? He doesn't think it would hold you or mean anything to you.

(she shakes her head)

(GENE doesn't want to go into that, and just looks down at their hands.)

Margaret: I'll talk to him. He'll make a dreadful scene, but—

(MARGARET looks down at their clasped hands. At last her emotion is beyond control, and she cries. GENE understands that this was inevitable . . . but his MOTHER does not mean it to deter him. She just can't help it. He touches her face gently.)

Gene: —No. You always have done that for Alice and me. I'll do it.

[The triangle operates in such a way as to prevent a mutual personal communication in any twosome. Mother talks to Gene about father, father talks to Gene about mother, he talks to each of them about the other, and on it goes. Momentarily we have seen the triangle shift so that Gene is on the outside; however, mother's anxiety about father's reaction to Gene's news pulls her back into offering to be his spokesman. Gene, hoping to be grown up, refuses her offer. He goes downstairs and finds his father has moved from one object of his distance, the TV, to another, sleep.]

INT: NIGHT

(As GENE enters the room where his FATHER is watching TV, he pauses. He is saddened by the picture of the old man asleep in front of a babbling TV screen.

. . . He wonders too, if he should talk to his father tonight. He turns down the volume knob on the TV.)

    Tom: (waking up at the silence)

What? What?

    (sees GENE *crouching near him)*

Where's your mother?

    Gene: She's all right. She's upstairs, going to bed.

    Tom: (sits back)

Oh . . .

    (blinks his eyes to wake up)

    Gene: (hesitantly)

Dad . . .

    Tom: (looking at TV)

Oh, this is a good one. This fella can really handle the guns.

    (he reaches past GENE *to turn up the volume)*

    Gene: Dad . . . I want to talk to you.

    Tom: Just a minute.

    (he adjusts the picture, and leans forward to watch)

    Gene: (gives up, after watching FATHER *a few moments)*

Well, I've got to go now.

[Gene makes a valiant effort to connect with his father. He stands in front of the TV, and wakens him. Father physically moves Gene out of the way, re-establishing the link between himself and the TV, with Gene on the outside. Gene's reactive triggers are fired, and all hope of connecting fades.]

    Tom: Oh, so soon? We see so little of you.

    Gene: I'm up at least once a week, Dad.

    Tom: Oh, I'm not complaining.

    (but he is)

There just doesn't seem to be any time. And when you are here, your mother's doing all the talking. Well . . . "All's lost, all's spent, when we our desires get without content. 'Tis better to be that which we destroy, than by destruction dwell with doubtful joy."

*(*GENE *is always puzzled by his father's frequent use of this quotation. It never is immediately appropriate, but it indicates such unhappiness that it is sad and touching to him.)*

    Gene: We'll get a chance to talk, Dad. Maybe you could have lunch with me in town in a couple of days. I'd like to talk to you.

    Tom: That's a wonderful idea. You set the date.

    Gene: I'll call.

(They move to the porch.)

EXT: PORCH—NIGHT

(Single light in roof of porch) . . .

[Father puts the finishing touch on by adding a ritualized quote, and by instructing his son on how to pull out of the driveway and what directions to take on his way home.]

    Tom: I can't tell you what a comfort it is knowing you are just down in the city. Don't know what we'd do without you. No hat or coat?

Gene: No.

Tom: It's still chilly. You should be careful.

(GENE *kisses* FATHER *on cheek.*)

Tom: . . . You're coming up for your Mother's birthday, aren't you?

Gene: Yes.

Tom: It'll be my party. . . . And, Gene . . . remember what I said about California.

Gene: (*pauses on the step for a moment, then turns to go*)

Good night, Dad.

Tom: (*calling*)

Drive carefully. I noticed you were inclined to push it up there a little.

(GENE *moves on.*)

Tom: Make a full stop going out of the driveway, then turn, right . . . traffic is terrible out there now . . . take your first left and second right. It's a little tricky down there.

[This segment defines the conflictual issues as the father's death, alcohol, emotional distance and closeness, physical distance, emotional cutoffs, bitterness, and business accomplishment versus artistic accomplishment. Each of these issues can be tracked through the relationships over the generations.]

EXT: DRIVEWAY—NIGHT

(GENE *has opened the car door and sat down. He now slams the door unnecessarily hard, and starts the car with a vengeance. He turns the car in the drive and leaves.* TOM *is left alone on the porch, under the one light, waving vaguely after the car.*)

This segment clearly illustrates the fact that one of the methods most commonly used by parents to keep from getting into painful issues with their adult children is to treat them exactly as they did when they were very young. Gene plays right into this by allowing it to happen; he eases his own conscience about not discussing his California trip by making an appointment to discuss it with his father at a later date. After this segment, Gene's mother has a heart attack, and is placed in an intensive care unit. Gene and his father retreat when she falls asleep, and go out for the evening to a Rotary Club meeting. During the night Margaret dies. The daughter, Alice, comes for the funeral, and she and Gene discuss what is to be done with Tom. Alice advises Gene to get out of town, remarry, and leave him to live alone with a paid housekeeper. They also talk about how sorry they are for not having found more time to spend with their mother, and Gene mentions that he became his mother's life because his father had "quit on her."

After the funeral Alice reiterates her position on what should be done with their father, and says that having him live with her and her family would be impossible. She volunteers to approach Tom on the subject of hiring a housekeeper, and tells Gene to back her up when the father turns to him. Tom predictably dismisses her from any obligations, but hastens to add, "Gene will keep an eye on me." It is Alice who finally reopens the topic of Gene's remarriage and move to California, and Gene who just as predictably backs down and tries to get Alice to drop the subject. The scene ends with Tom telling Alice that everyone has gotten along just fine without her.

Gene's next step, after Alice leaves, is to visit nursing homes; he becomes thoroughly depressed. Peggy comes from California for a meeting; she comes to see Tom, who does his best to pretend that he does not know who she is. Their meeting leads inevitably to the final confrontation scene, which follows. Before screening it, the audience is asked:

(1) What is your idea of a personal relationship?

(2) Is a personal relationship possible with this father?

(3) What are the nodal points where the son could have turned the process around?

(TOM *is in his pajamas and bathrobe kneeling by his bed, saying his prayers. Again, a touching sight.* GENE *enters when* TOM *starts to rise.)*

Gene: Ready to be tucked in?

[This scene begins with an enactment of a pseudobuddy-buddy ritual between Gene and his father. In spite of this ritual, the mutual longing for closeness comes through. Again they try. Earlier, while talking with Alice about the days following their mother's death, Gene complained that he wanted to talk with his father about his dead mother, but that his father wouldn't allow it. He is about to get his chance.]

Tom: (smiling at the phrase)

Yes . . . look at the weight I've lost.

Gene: Well, you had quite a little pot there, Dad.

Tom: But look, all through here. Through my chest.

Gene: Well, we'll put some back on.

Tom: (looking at his own chest)

You know, I never had hair on my chest. I don't understand it. You have hair on your chest. I just didn't have any. . . . Well, I'm confident if I could get some exercise. . . . Do you remember when I used to get you up in the morning, and we'd go down and do calisthenics to the radio?

Gene: (smiling)

Yes.

Tom: (stands very straight and swings his arms)

One, two, three, four. One, two, three, four . . .

(he totters a bit)

Gene: Hey, take it easy. . . . why don't you wait till morning for that?

Tom: And we used to put on the gloves and spar down on the side porch? The manly art of self-defense.

(he crouches in boxing position)

Gentleman Jim Corbett . . .

(he spars a moment with Gene . . .)

Oh, well . . . I intend to get over to the club and play some golf, sit around and swap stories with the boys. Too bad you never took up golf.

(he fishes in his top bureau drawer, which he has brought to his bed)
I was looking through my bureau drawer . . . I don't know, just going over things . . .
(takes out a packet of photographs wrapped in tissue paper)
Pictures . . . I think you've seen most of them . . . the family.
    Gene: (very tentatively)
You know, Dad, I've never seen a picture of your father.
*(*TOM *looks at him a long time. Then finally, with his hatred showing in his face, he unwraps another tissue, and hands over a small picture.)*
    Gene: (surprised)
He's just a boy.
    Tom: That was taken about the time he was married. . . . Oh, he was a fine-looking man before he started to drink. Big, square, high color. But he became my mortal enemy. . . . Did I ever show you that?
    (takes out a small piece of paper, hands it to GENE*)*
Careful . . . When I set up a home for my brother and sister, one day we were all out, and he came around and ripped up all my sister's clothes and shoes. Drunk, of course. A few days later, he came around to apologize *and* ask for some money, and I threw him out. . . . The next day he left that note. . . .
[Tom again builds a case for bastardizing his father, and openly proclaims him as his mortal enemy. In response, Gene searches for something positive that might mitigate Tom's intensely negative stance.]
(Rumpled piece of paper . . . scrawled on it: "You are welcome to your burden.")
    Tom (V.O.): You are welcome to your burden.
    Gene: And you kept it?
    Tom: Yes, I never saw him again until many years later he was dying, in Bellevue, and someone got word to me and I went down, and asked him if he wanted anything. He said he'd like some fruit. So I sent him in a few oranges. He died the next day.
    Gene: There must have been something there to love, to understand.
[Tom blocks Gene's attempt, and shifts to the positive things about his relationship with Gene. It is as if each of them has made a pledge not to let their relationship with one another be a repeat of the previous generation.]
    Tom: In my father?
(he shakes his head no . . . then he shows GENE *another card)*
Do you remember this? "To the best dad in the world on Father's Day."
    (turns it over and reads the notation)
1946. . . . Yes.
    (emotional)
I appreciate that, Gene. That's a lovely tribute. I think I have all your Father's Day cards here. . . . You know, I didn't want children, coming from the background I did . . . and we didn't have Alice for a long time. But your mother finally persuaded me. She said they would be a comfort in our old age. And you are, Gene.
    Gene: (touched, but embarrassed and uncomfortable)
Well . . .
    Tom: (fishes in the drawer and brings out a program)
A program of yours from college . . . some glee club concert . . . I've got everything but the kitchen stove in here. . . . Do you still sing?
    Gene: (smiling)
Not in years.
    Tom: That's too bad. You had a good voice. But we can't do everything.

... I remember your mother would sit at the piano, hour after hour, and I'd be up here at my desk, and I'd hear you singing.

[The theme of singing for father is clearest here. We see the process in the central triangle: Tom, alone in his room upstairs working, Gene downstairs singing to the accompaniment of his mother. Here father and son almost touch in a real way, when the process of how it really was surfaces, and father is again thrown back into the past.]

Gene: You always asked me to sing "When I Grow Too Old To Dream."

Tom: Did I? . . . I don't remember your ever singing that. . . . You always seemed to be just finishing when I came into the room.

(*looks at* GENE)

Did you used to sing that for me?

Gene: (not a joke any more)

No. . . . But you always asked me to sing it for you.

Tom: Oh.

(puts program away)

Well, I enjoyed sitting up here and listening.

(he pokes around in the drawer, and takes something out . . . in tissue paper. He unwraps a picture carefully)

And that's my mother.

Gene: (gently)

Yes, I've seen that, Dad. It's lovely.

Tom: She was twenty-five when that was taken. She died the next year . . . I carried it in my wallet for years . . . And then I felt it was wearing it out. So I put it away. . . . Just a little bit of a thing . . .

[As Tom again begins his idealized version of his mother, his vulnerability surfaces for the first time. It is hard to tell whether he is mourning his wife or his mother, or a combination of the two. The stage is set—two men, father and son, both longing for a mutual closeness. Both have experienced the loss of their mothers and their wives.]

(He starts to cry, and the deep, deep sobs finally come and his emaciated body is wracked by them. It is a terrible, almost soundless sobbing. GENE *comes to his* FATHER *and puts his arms around him and holds him. Then, after some moments . . .)*

Tom: I didn't think it would be this way . . . I always thought I'd go first.

(He sobs again, gasping for air. GENE *continues to hold him, inevitably moved and touched by this genuine suffering. Finally,* TOM *gets a stern grip on himself.)*

Tom: I'm sorry . . .

(tries to shake it off)

It just comes over me. It'll pass . . . I'll get a hold of myself.

Gene: Don't try, Dad. . . . Believe me, it's best.

Tom: (angry with himself)

No . . . It's just that . . . I'll be all right.

(he turns and blows his nose)

Gene: It's rough, Dad. . . . It's bound to be rough.

Tom: (shakes his head to snap out of it)

It'll pass. . . . It'll pass.

(starts to wrap up the picture of his mother)

Gene: Can I help you put these things away, Dad?

[Gene faces his wished-for opening. His father is vulnerable, bleeding openly. How does he respond? Does he talk about his own emotional reaction to the death of his wife or his mother? No. Instead he responds on an object level, offering to help father put his things away. All is still not lost. His over competent father allows him to do it, and the opening still exists. Gene, with magnificent timing, opens the issue of moving to California and marrying Peggy. The opening is slammed shut. The automatic reactive pattern reestablishes itself. Gene and his Father now proceed, against both of their wishes, to repeat a piece of painful process from the generation before.]

Tom: No . . . no . . . I can . . .

(he seems to be looking for something he can't find)

Well, if you would.

(GENE starts to help.)

Tom: I don't know what we'd do without you, Gene.

(And together they put the things back in the box. . . . As they do so, GENE is deeply moved with feelings of tenderness for his father. After a few moments, he starts, with great consideration.)

Gene: Dad?

Tom: Yes?

Gene: (putting it carefully and slowly)

How did you like Peggy?

Tom: Who? . . . Oh . . . Oh, yes. Very nice. Very attractive.

Gene: I'm thinking very seriously, Dad . . . of marrying Peggy . . . and going out to California . . . to live.

(TOM straightens a little.)

Gene: Now, I know this is your home, where you're used to . . . but I'd like you to come out there with me, Dad. It's lovely out there, and we could find an apartment for you near us.

(this is the most loving gesture GENE has made to his father in his life)

Tom: (thinks for a moment, then looks at GENE with a smile)

You know, I'd like to make a suggestion. . . . Why don't you all come live here?

Gene: (explaining calmly)

Peggy has a practice out there.

Tom: A what?

Gene: She's a doctor. I told you. And children with schools and friends.

Tom: We have a big house here. You always liked this house. It's wonderful for children. You used to play baseball out back, and there's that basketball thing.

Gene: Dad, I'd like to get away from this part of the country for a while. It's been rough here, ever since Carol died. It would be good for you too, getting away.

Tom: Your mother would be very happy to have the house full of children again. I won't be around long, and then it will be all yours.

Gene: That's very kind of you, Dad. But I don't think it would work. Besides her work and the children, all Peggy's family is out there.

Tom: Your family is here.

Gene: Yes, I know.

Tom: You know, Gene, I'm only saying this for your own good, but you went out there very soon after Carol's death, and you were exhausted from her long illness, and well, naturally, very susceptible. . . . I'm wondering if you've really waited long enough to know your own mind.

[As this insidious process surfaces, Tom tries to coax Gene into compliance. Gene holds onto his California anchor in desperation. Father pulls out the stops and pushes all the guilt buttons.]

Gene: I know my own mind.

Tom: I mean, taking on another man's children.

(looks at GENE *a long moment, sees it's hopeless)*

Did you mention this business of California to your mother?

Gene: (gets the accusation, but keeps calm)

Yes. She told me to go ahead, with her blessings.

[Mother's ghost appears, and the central triangle is again spelled out.]

Tom: She would say that, of course. But I warned you.

Gene: (turns away)

For God's sake.

Tom: (gives up, angry)

All right, go ahead. I can manage.

(sarcastic)

Send me a Christmas card . . . if you remember.

Gene: (enraged)

Dad!

Tom: What?

Gene: I've asked you to come with me.

Tom: And I've told you I'm not going.

Gene: I understand that, but not this "Send me a Christmas card, if you remember."

Tom: I'm very sorry if I've offended you. Your mother always said I mustn't raise my voice to you.

(suddenly hard and vicious)

Did you want me to make it easy for you the way your mother did? Well, I won't. If you want to go, go!

[Mother's ghost, plus her position in between them.]

Gene: God damn it.

Tom: (running on)

I've always known it would come to this when your mother was gone. I was tolerated around this house because I paid the bills and—

[Tom's feeling of being left out and tolerated.]

Gene: Shut up!

[The dam bursts.]

Tom: (coming at him)

Don't you—

Gene: (shouting)

Shut up! I asked you to come with me. What do you want? What the hell do you want? If I lived here the rest of my life it wouldn't be enough for you. I've tried, God damn it, I've tried to be the dutiful son . . . commanded into your presence on every conceivable occasion, Easter, Christmas, birthdays, Thanksgiving. . . . Even that Thanksgiving when Carol was dying and I was staying with her at the hospital. "We miss you so. Our day is nothing without you. Couldn't you come up for an hour or two after you leave Carol?" You had no regard for what was really going on. . . . My wife was dying!

Tom: Is it so terrible to want to see your own son?

Gene: It is terrible to want to possess him . . . entirely and completely!

Tom: (after a moment . . . coldly)

There will be some papers to sign, for your mother's estate. Be sure you leave an address with my lawyer.

[Tom attempts to dismiss his son, and bring their discussion back to object level.]

Gene: (cutting in)
Dad!
Tom: (cutting, with no self-pity)
From tonight on, you can consider me dead.
(turns on him in a rage of resentment)
I gave you everything. Since I was a snot-nosed kid, I've worked my fingers to the bone. You've had everything and I had nothing. I put a roof over your head, clothes on your back—
[Tom's answer is the same as with his own father and his daughter Alice: a complete emotional cutoff.]
Gene: —Food on the table.
Tom: —Things I never had.
Gene: I know.
Tom: You ungrateful bastard.
Gene: (as though he would hit him)
What do you want for gratitude? Nothing, nothing would be enough. You have resented everything you ever gave me. The orphan boy in you has resented everything. . . . I'm sorry as hell about your miserable childhood. When I was a kid, and you told me those stories, I used to go up to my room at night and cry. But there is nothing I can do about it . . . and it does not excuse everything . . . I *am* grateful to you. I also admire and respect you, and stand in awe of what you have done with your life. I will never be able to touch it.
(TOM looks at him with contempt.)
Gene: But it does not make me love you, and I wanted to love you. . . . You hated your father. I saw what it did to you. I did not want to hate you.
Tom: I don't care what you feel about me.
Gene: I do!

CONCLUSION

Enlightened by the successful use of *I Never Sang for My Father,* I have looked for other films which might be equally useful. *Double Solitaire,* another of Robert Anderson's works, deals with a marriage that is twenty-five years old, and is about to rupture. This marriage is seen against the backdrop of the marriage of the husband's parents, who are celebrating their fiftieth wedding anniversary. The similarities between the two marriages are very clear. The fifty-year-old relationship survives by closing things over, pretending everything is all right, and living at a fixed distance, a distance filled with games of solitaire. The younger marriage is a series of repeating patterns in the marital fusion. This is elucidated very clearly in a sequence in which the husband and wife spend a weekend together in a remote beach house, and the husband tries vainly to reach his wife and change her mind about leaving him.

Another film that is an excellent study of marital fusion, especially reciprocity, is Ingmar Bergman's *Scenes from a Marriage.* This film shows how the relationship between Marianna and Johann shifts over the course of his affair, their separation, and the subsequent process of their divorce and reconnecting after they have both married other people.

John Cassavetes' film *Woman Under the Influence* lends itself very nicely to a study of the invalidation process in families as it ties into acute psychotic reactions.

The study of human relationships and the way they determine how much of the potential of any individual is realized never ceases to fascinate. It has been estimated that most people use something like one-fifth of their actual abilities in a lifetime. How much more of their inherent talents and intelligence might people use if they were masters of their own relationship space. It has always been easier to see what's gone wrong with the family across the street, or how other wives and husbands might improve their lot. And life would be easier if your spouse would change, so that you wouldn't have to. Displacement material offers the student of humanity an exercise in planning how to change others, while offering a chance to learn enough also to change himself.*

*All quotations from *I Never Sang For My Father* copyright © 1966, 1968 by Robert Anderson, Rep. Random House, Inc. Reprinted by permission. The author gratefully acknowledges the assistance of Richard and Eloise Julius, Leslie and Elizabeth Ogden, and Seymour and Muriel Epstein, whose benevolence and network connections were responsible for my being able to acquire a copy of the film for my research and teaching.

CHAPTER 29

Breaking the Homeostatic Cycle

Lynn Hoffman, C.S.W.

A virtue of family therapy is that it allows one to identify the sequences associated with irrational behavior in small social fields. Many family therapists have created personal vocabularies to describe the dynamics or the structure of these sequences. Bowen talks of a network of linked triangles in which twosomes are always changing partners (1). Minuchin speaks of a child and his parents caught in "rigid triads," which may take a variety of forms (2). Haley, who was one of the first to call attention to cross-generation coalitions as a sign of dysfunction in a family, is now telling clinicians to look for a triangle consisting of an overinvolved parent-child dyad and a more peripheral parent (3).

The diversity of these descriptions conveys the dilemma of the art. How is one to know which pattern to look for, let alone identify, when one is in the presence of a strange family, peering into the gloom of its manifold transactions? Surely there is a formulation which would operationalize triadic concepts so that one could say to oneself during a family interview, "There it is! That one there!"

Haley spoke to this issue many years ago, when he made a plea for a descriptive language for interaction that was not purely dyadic. For illustration, he chose a repetitive sequence in a family with a disruptive child (4).

The child would misbehave in some way, for example, by leaning down and looking under the table. The father would speak to the child and tell him to straighten up. Mother would then speak to father and tell him that he should not have chastised the child at that time or in that way. Father would say he was merely reprimanding the boy because it seemed necessary, and mother would look exasperated with him.

Haley has suggested that such a sequence may occur at a time when the family, or a particular relationship in a family, is threatened with change.

The sequence, not just the misbehavior, served some kind of change-resist-ant, or homeostatic, function. Moreover, this kind of sequence did not represent causality in the usual sense, it was a cycle. Each person's behavior was influenced by the behavior of the other persons, and influenced their behaviors in turn. Getting one element to change would only cause the other elements to readjust so that the outcome was the same.

Haley used this example as a take-off point for a model of the family as a cybernetic system, rather than staying with the program he described. What a pity. Even though this little piece of interaction seems nondescript, lacking the grandeur of a truly pathogenic display, it deserves attention. Haley had caught a sequence which child-oriented family therapists see or hear reported over and over again in their offices. It is a common example of a group of homeostatic cycles relating to the symptom of a child. When experienced family therapists find this cycle, they direct an intervention toward it with the precision of a laser beam.

If one could isolate and describe a few instances of cycles of this type, even if one could not exactly explain their dynamics, it would be a step toward achieving greater accuracy in making assessments and formulating interventions. In this paper I will not examine interaction cycles of every kind (couple cycles, for instance), but will concentrate on only this one. Illustrations will be from family interviews with two-parent families where a child is the problem, and will be limited to those occasions when a knowlegeable family therapist recognized this cycle and carefully inter-rupted it. First, however, it might be useful to place this type of cycle within a larger class of behaviors which are not specific to our species, but occur in many other creature groups.

A recent book by E.O. Wilson, *Sociobiology,* offers a novel explanation for selfless behavior among animals (5). His thesis is that populations with a capacity for cooperation, generosity, and self-sacrifice have a better chance to survive than more selfish groups. Examples from the animal and insect kingdoms are numerous: dolphins who carry a stricken comrade on their backs; soldier ants who give their lives to defend the queen and her eggs; the bird who trails a wing to lead a predator from the nest. Wilson surmises that such behaviors came about through the process of natural selection, since by the sacrifice of individuals the group was enabled to survive; and that a predisposition toward these behaviors was eventually imprinted in the DNA of the fortunate species.

Like most animal ethologists, Wilson cannot resist making a connection between animal and human groups. The idea of a gene for altruism is the result. A suggestion is offered that disinterested benevolence, charity, self-sacrifice, even martyrdom, may be inbuilt predispositions useful for the survival of the society, rather than difficult spiritual attainments.

Extrapolating from animal behavior in this way can lead to somewhat untenable claims. However, observation of irrational behaviors in families supports the idea that there are indeed programs for altruism which occur over and over again in human groups. These are not, sad to say, always the kind which involve personal courage or choice. In fact, they often appear involuntary; it is of the essence that they do appear involuntary. I am talking here about a certain class of psychiatric symptoms, previously thought of as maladaptive behaviors or illnesses, but now beginning to be described as functional for at least one of the contexts in which they occur. Writers in the sociology of deviance have frequently commented on the role of the deviant in ensuring group cohesion. Goffman goes so far as to describe the "career" of the mental patient, as if his product were part of the normal division of labor in the community: the village "needs" its idiot, just as the town "needs" its drunk.

Family therapy has contributed to this group of ideas. Laing, one of the earliest students of the connection between the family and mental illness, has gone so far as to elevate the status of the schizophrenic to that of saint. Pioneer family therapists like Ackerman spoke of the disturbed child as the "family healer"; and Bell and Vogel, in a similar vein, describe him as the "family scapegoat." One of family therapy's most venerable beliefs has been that the child develops symptoms in order to save his parents' marriage. As Satir (6) puts it in her classic work, *Conjoint Family Therapy,* the child's symptoms are "an SOS about his parents' pain and the resulting family imbalance."

The difficulty with such formulations is that they suggest an involuntary self-sacrifice. Like Wilson's implied gene for altruism, this is almost a self-contradiction: martyrdom and altruism are by definition voluntary offerings, not coerced or programmed. Nevertheless, we must be grateful to the family therapy movement, because it has called attention to the fact that, however you define them, symptomatic behaviors occur in a matrix of other behaviors, that they are linked to and supported by these behaviors, and that the totality constitutes some sort of formal program which has to do with the survival of a larger unit, usually the family.

THE ANATOMY OF A CYCLE

Let us move to an example of such a program, a recurrent sequence between father and son reported in the family interview "No Man's Land" in Haley and Hoffman's *Techniques of Family Therapy* (7). The triangle consists of an ineffectively domineering father, a mildly rebellious adolescent son, and a mother who sides with son. Father keeps getting into an argument with son over smoking, which both mother and father say they disapprove of. However, mother will break into these escalating arguments to agree with son, after which father will back down. Eventually father does not even wait for her to come in; he backs down anyway. This sequence occurs several times, with variations, during the interview. To give some idea of the flavor, here is one of the shorter versions; the mother has just said she is not in favor of taking away the boy's allowance:

Mr. K: (to Mike) Would it please you, I presume it would, it would please you if I said that it was all right with me for you to smoke: Would that make you feel better?

Mike: Yes, I guess it would.

Mr. K: Well, for your sake, Mike, I wish I could, but I honestly and truly can't. I still don't think it is the right thing to do.

(Pause)

I really don't.

Mike: Well, by taking my allowance away, you're, you're both, not being, I'm not able to buy cigarettes, or I'm not being, I'm not able to do anything. I can't go to the show, I can't . . .

Mr. K: Now, Mike, whenever you have come to me in the last two or three weeks and asked me for money for some specific thing, I have given it to you.

Mike: Those things I had to do.

(Pause)

Mr. K.: You're right. You're right.

This cycle is an example of a homeostatic mechanism which redirects tension away from some other area of the family. Here, this other area involves a parental conflict. If the parents began to struggle with each other more directly, their own relationship might be imperiled. One can see that the stakes are high in favor of some arrangement which will allow the parents to express their disagreement, but which will limit the disagreement to the topic of the boy's behavior. Since this arrangement usually means that one parent will take a positive or neutral and the other a negative attitude toward the behavior, we will use Stanton and Schwartz's term for this type of polarization: the "mirror-image disagreement" (8).

In their book *The Mental Hospital,* these authors found that when two authorities on a ward were in an unacknowleged struggle with one another, they would often begin to disagree over the management of a case. One authority, a psychiatrist perhaps, might take a protective interest in a particular patient, while the other, possibly a nurse, would become strict and even punitive. The patient would get progressively more agitated as the polarization of attitudes between the two staff members intensified. However, if they could be brought to settle their differences face to face, the patient's agitation would usually subside.

In a family, the mirror-image disagreement may be hidden beneath the parents' concern for the symptomatic child, or it may appear as antagonism toward him, but a persistent effort to get each parent to express his attitude toward the symptom will usually cause the disagreement to appear. Most family therapy with a child includes an attempt to uncover this disagreement, if it is not obvious, and to refocus it as an issue between the parents. But any move to block or shift elements in the cycle in which the symptom is embedded will often bring the polarization between the parents to the fore.

A question now arises. If one speaks of a homeostatic cycle, one also should be able to define the factors which are being monitored by this cycle. It is too general to say "tension between the parents" and let it go at that. Presumably, there are essential variables which the parents—or whatever executive dyad is operating—must maintain within certain limits if they are to function together successfully. What might such variables be? Let us make a few guesses.

A prerequisite for couples where there is trouble in the child is often an unusually tight bond. Whether the source of this be a fear of abandonment or isolation in the spouses, or some other reason, neither spouse ever goes as far as to actually separate no matter how intensely they may feel they want to. Given this basic fact, there have to be some ways, some devices, for creating distance in an otherwise suffocating closeness. One is reminded of studies of cats in their natural surroundings. Cats seem to need well-defined spatial territories, and if they have conflicts over a space, will solve them by allotting different time spans for occupying a particular spot. Cat A will sit by the hearth in the morning, while Cat B will enjoy it in the evening. Cats approaching each other at an intersection of two habitual cat-paths will sit some distance from the intersection and wait, apparently not looking at or noticing each other. At a certain point, one of the cats will casually walk through, and then the other cat will follow suit. Cats invading the territory of another will be greeted by a ritualized aggression display by the home cat, which seems to monitor the boundary between them.

Although humans and cats have different closeness-distance requirements, the behavior of cats does furnish a valuable way to think about the predicament of an overclose couple. Clinicians are familiar with the array of mechanisms for distancing that couples use. One device is to maintain separate physical spaces; different bedrooms, sometimes even different houses. Spouses still close to their own families of origin often use their childhood homes as places to escape to. Another device is temporal distancing, as when a couple manages to arrange a work schedule so that one spouse works nights and the other days; or a working spouse comes home late, and then is exhausted or unavailable. The term "emotional distancing" may be used to describe the kind of behavior that people use in crowded elevators: their bodies are physically pressed together, but they avoid eye contact or other communication. Spouses who are practised in this type of avoidance find it hard to look at each other while talking during a family session. Another form of distancing, which might better be called a modulator of both distancing and closeness, is the periodic bicker. This type of conflict is closer to the boundary-marking aggression displays one finds in animal groups than anything resembling an argument that resolves a real issue. A key to whether these behaviors are true conflicts or merely part of a closeness-distance cycle is whether there is a "cut-off point"—a sudden cessation of hostilities triggered by some minimal cue. A bout of bickering seems to occur after a couple has experienced a period of withdrawal. Thus, despite its negative aspect, it must still be construed as a kind of contact, preliminary to a renewal of distancing.

However, open conflict is such a threat to the pair bond that overclose couples are often fearful of any show of differences. A relationship style commonly associated with conflict-avoidant families is one in which one spouse is apparently dominant and the other submissive, subject to an occasional flipflop. Ravich, (9) who has tested many couples with a train game which differentiates between symmetrical and dominant-submissive patterns (among others), comments on the tendency of dominant-submissive pairs to stay together, no matter how miserable they may be. They will resist any attempt to change this pattern, and if the therapist does introduce a change, they will often drop out of treatment.

The mechanism which makes the dominant-submissive pattern so ideal for masking conflict has been suggested by Wild et. al. (10) in a study comparing the communication styles of families of hospitalized schizophrenic males with a control group of hospitalized character disorders. The authors found, among other things, that the behavior of an unusual number of fathers with schizophrenic sons could be described as "overcontrolling," while the communications of the mothers were classified as "amorphous." This combination allows one spouse, the father, to seem dominant, but a close reading of conversations shows that mothers, by the use of non-sequiturs, scattered thinking, topic changes, and the like, were able to nullify any decisions the fathers might try to make. The authors point out that these behaviors have a mutual causal effect: "Mothers' vagueness increases the likelihood that fathers will take over and control situations, and fathers' arbitrary and often irrational style of control increases mothers' vagueness." One can see how these linked behaviors would minimize any appearance of disagreement between the parents, while still fostering an intense struggle, and might also account for some of the confused thinking displayed by sons.

Ravich (11) comments on a striking characteristic of dominant-submissive couples; they seem to have more than their share of seriously disturbed children. A predominantly symmetrical relationship will be more likely to come into therapy for a marital problem than a child problem, unless that problem is the outcome of a separation crisis or divorce proceedings. If the child or young adult has a severe symptom, like a life-threatening psychosomatic disorder or some form of psychotic behavior, it is uncanny how often the parental axis is markedly unequal. The classic work on this subject is Lidz and Fleck's study depicting "marital schism" and "marital skew" in families of hospitalized schizophrenics. Although the first group displayed overt marital struggle and the second did not, couples in both groups were descibed as being wife-dominant or husband-dominant, although these were not the terms that were used.

An interesting speculation arises as to the function of a dominant-submissive relationship in the case of an overclose pair. Two points could be made. One, explored by Bateson, (13) has to do with the way complementary (unequal) and symmetrical (equal) forms serve as control mechanisms for each other in human relationship systems. For instance, a couple where one spouse is extremely dependent on the other will find it hard to separate. The function of a symptom in such a couple seems to be to create a deeper dependency when a split threatens. It is as though the parties are only in danger of disengaging from each other if they are in a symmetrical position. At the same time, a move toward symmetry often counteracts the strains generated by a dominance-submission cycle. Many couples oscillate between these basic forms. But a dominant-submissive couple has a special problem with symmetry, with all that this state implies for splitting or divorce.

The second point has to do with the closeness-distance axis. Let us go back to studies done on cats. When a number of cats is placed in a small cage, so that spatial or temporal distancers are not available, a rigid pecking order will rapidly evolve. There will be a top cat and the others will deploy themselves down the status ladder until one gets to the bottom cat, a miserable, cringing creature who gets picked on by all the rest. This observation suggests that a strongly complementary (in Bateson's sense) arrangement might act as a distancing device in a situation where degree of closeness is a vital issue. If a married couple were to adopt such an arrangement, this would allow maximum closeness, while at the same time the status differential would create enough of a barrier to give the parties breathing space. If this status differential were to surpass its given limits in either direction, the marriage tie or the well-being of one of the partners would probably be threatened. As we have said, a move toward more equality might end in a separation, where a move toward greater inequality might provoke in one partner severe symptomatic response.

But neither of these horrid possibilities need happen if a third party, usually a child, can be brought in to monitor both the overcloseness and the status difference which is so often associated with it. Couples who must paradoxically seek distance because they are so tightly stuck together are inordinately vulnerable to coalitions with others. A spouse who can use a friend, relative, or child as a major source of support will have the edge over one who cannot. Thus the life-or-death nature of loyalty issues in such

families. However, a family is not a war, and coalitions tend to be constricted by rules operating in the interests of the larger unit. It is here that
the type of cycle we have been describing comes in.

THE CHILD AS A THIRD PARTY MONITOR

In the light of the above discussion, how can we understand the cycle
featured in the "No Man's Land" interview? For one thing, the marital
dyad seems to be mildly dominant-submissive, with the husband trying to
take an authoritarian stance toward his not-too-compliant wife. We find out
that he maintains considerable emotional distance from her, a situation she
reinforces by investing herself in other relationships, like a girlfriend of
whom the husband is jealous, and, of course, the son. The wife's weaker
position in the marital subsystem is counterbalanced by her strong position
in the parental subsystem, where she has the son as an ally. The son's
involvement is able to affect both the power difference in the marriage and
the closeness-distance axis, so that neither variable is driven too far from
its usual limit.

What has apparently happened to upset the family balance is the advent
of a major transition point: the adolescence of the son. He is entering a
period where he can realistically challenge his father. On the other hand,
the normal pulls of growing up tend to detach him from his mother and
female ways. It is logical that the behavior that brought the family to
therapy was his breaking into a tobacco store and stealing cigarettes and
some change. The action also relates to the major issue between the father
and son: smoking.

In the repetitive argument over smoking, the problem the boy faces is
the mirror-image disagreement between his parents. If he does not smoke
(is not rebellious), he supports his father against his mother; if he does
smoke (is rebellious), he supports his mother against his father. If this kind
of interaction had been allowed to continue, the boy would probably have
taken flight into another piece of behavior which would force his parents
to unite to deal with him.

The therapist, Charles Fulweiler, seemed to know that this sequence was
important to move in on. The methods he used were mostly blocking
maneuvers, supported by interpretations. However, a part of his style is to
enter and leave the room without warning. He took advantage of his en-
trances to inhibit the cycle we have described at strategic points, and turn
it step by step into a different direction. He used his first entrance to cue
the mother to be more explicit in her defense of the son; the second entrance
to pick out the disagreement between mother and father; the third entrance

to back up the father's authority in the face of the mother-son combine; and the next two or three to stop the father from taking the role of victim, while at the same time clarifying the mother's part in rendering the father ineffective. The interview ended with nobody to blame, because all these events had their roots in the past.

So much for the immediate intervention. Over the longer haul, which may mean anywhere from ten sessions to two years, depending on therapist and family, it is best to prepare for the consequences of breaking this cycle. A disruptive child offers his behavior like sticky bait to the overinvolved parent (in this case the father), and the resultant conflict triggers the less-involved parent (the mother) to step in. Here the mother is able to make a coalition with the boy quite openly; if she had been more covert about it, one might have expected a more serious symptom. The overinvolved parent is usually the outsider in the triangle, and much of his inappropriate anger, and, in this instance, sense of helplessness and backing down, may come from this fact. In the closeness-distance area, the wife maintains the upper hand by having an affair to go to, so to speak. In this way she can reverse the imbalance in their relationship. And her husband, by exaggerating, even inviting, his own helplessness, uses the magic power of complementarity to stick them back together.

Obviously, if a therapist breaks this cycle, he has to help the couple both with the closeness-distance problem and the one-up/one-down problem, so that they no longer need a third party monitor. Fulweiler made a beginning attempt in the first interview to alter both dimensions and apparently was successful. The boy stopped being perceived as a problem very soon, and the couple went on in therapy without him.

A PARSIMONIOUS TECHNIQUE

If a clinician is successful in identifying the cycle of which the symptom is a vital part, a very small change can presumably be pinpointed accurately enough to have a wide-reaching effect. Watzlawick, Weakland, and Fisch, the authors of a recent book called *Change* (14), represent an extremely parsimonious school of family therapy in this respect. This writer was present at a demonstration of their techniques by Dr. Richard Fisch, who interviewed a couple at the Center for Family Learning in New Rochelle. The problem the family reported on was embedded in much the same type of cycle we have been talking about. But the therapist's method for intervening in this cycle was completely different from the approach previously described.

The family in this instance consisted of the father and mother, both in their thirties, a girl of nine, and a boy of six. The children were not present. Dr. Fisch asked what the problem was, and the parents stated that they were having difficulty controlling the girl, who was willful, self-centered, obstinate, and disobedient. She was so unpleasant that she had only one friend, and even that friend she treated badly. Mother would get into daily battles with this child over issues like drinking her orange juice at breakfast. Mother might win, but these were Pyrrhic victories, as mother's nerves would then be shattered. When the father was home in the evening, the struggle would get to such a pitch that the father would come out of his study and browbeat the girl into obedience. The parents described their own relationship as close and loving, and stated that they knew the fault could not be in their parenting, since their little boy was as delightful as his sister was difficult. Dr. Fisch made the declaration of pessimism characteristic of the work of his group, but offered one small suggestion. He observed that one reason the parents were unable to combat the child's behavior might be because they had become too predictable. If they were to confuse her by doing something odd and unexpected, they might have more success. He then told the father that the next time he came out of his study to chastise his daughter, he simply give her a penny. If she asked him why, he was to say, "Because I felt like it," and go back to his room.

This intervention might seem clever but inconsequential, unless one examines the nature of the cycle it is designed to interrupt. The pattern described by Haley is again apparent: one parent who is overinvolved with the symptom of the child, and the other parent concerned but less involved. Usually, if one studies the family carefully, the more peripheral parent turns out to be in some kind of covert coalition with the child, even though he overtly disapproves of him. In the Fulweiler example, the less-involved parent could acknowledge the coalition. But here, perhaps because of the need to keep up the appearance of a united front, despite a hint of covert disagreements, the father never challenged his wife in favor of his daughter. He could only go so far as to say that he did not have as negative a view of her as his wife, since she and he both liked music and he enjoyed taking her to the opera. Thus the task given to the father altered the cycle in an important way: it undermined the myth of the child-monster which was working to keep the spouses tightly joined.

At the same time, the therapist anticipated some of the consequences of altering this cycle. There would be some side-effects, he warned them, if their daughter, despite the hopelessness of the case, did improve. First, the "good" child might begin to seem less than perfect once the "bad" child no longer offered such a total contrast. The father agreed that the boy was indeed somewhat childish and immature, signalling another matter on which he differed with his wife. Second, the therapist said, the mother might miss the intensity of her feelings for her daughter, which were a product of her mother's concern and a proof that she really did love her. The mother accepted both the positive relabeling of her hostility and the idea that she might find the change a hard one. Third, the therapist warned, the mother might at some point have to restrain her rather mild and rational husband from losing his temper and going too far. If one thinks about it, these consequences alter or reverse the affect of nearly every relationship reported on in that family.

But the most interesting event of the session was that after the therapist agreed with the mother that the most that could be hoped for was that the mother react less strongly to her impossible daughter, the father stated that he was not about to give up hope that easily. He, for one, had higher expectations of her. The mirror-image disagreement, up to now out of sight, came to the fore.

The outcome of this interview is not known, but this is not crucial to an examination of the homeostatic cycle involved in this example, and the methods used by the therapist to break it up. The Palo Alto group specializes in small changes, by their own say-so, and even in their tasks they stick to "small change." The contrast between the limited nature of the intervention and the many points of interaction which it touched, make this a good illustration of therapeutic economy.

BREAKING THE CYCLE IN THE ROOM

Minuchin, unlike the Palo Alto group, attempts consciously to revise relationships while the family is sitting in the room. Inexperienced therapists watching Minuchin shift and restructure relationship patterns within two or three minutes of meeting a family for the first time are surprised. Minuchin will say that there is no need for surprise; he has seen this particular family constellation so many times that he needs only minimal cues to recognize it.

It is also possible that what Minuchin is talking about has to do with the cycles we have been trying to describe. He does not particularly emphasize cycles in his writing, but an examination of his therapy reveals that he is sensitively attuned to them. Let us take, for an illustration, the first few minutes of an interview with a family of a little girl of four, described by the parents as "uncontrollable." The session included the parents; Karen, the patient; her two-year-old sister, Laurie; the family's therapist, Dr. F.; and Dr. Minuchin, who came in as a consultant. The father, who was a policeman, was in the habit of wearing his gun to the session.

Karen: Hi.
Dr. M: Hello. How are you?

Karen: Fine. Can we play with toys?

Dr. F: We're going to get some toys.

Dr. M: *(To Karen, smiling)* You said that your name is Karen?

Mr. K.: Yeah.

Dr. M.: Karen, what's the name of your sister?

Karen: Laurie.

Dr. M.: Laurie? Hello, Laurie.

Karen: Don't pick her up. Don't pick her up. Don't pick her up . . . do you know why?

Dr. M.: Why?

Karen: Cause she has a sore arm.

Dr. M.: She has a what?

Karen: She has a sore arm because she fell out of her crib.

Dr. M.: Which arm . . . this one, or this one?

Karen: Which one, Mommy?

Mrs. K.: The left one. Which one is that?

Karen: This one, right?

Mrs. K.: Uh hm.

Karen: She cracked her, ah . . .

Mrs. K.: Collarbone.

Karen: Collarbone.

Dr. M.: Oh my goodness!

Karen: It went ka-bam! And Aunt Dorothy . . . do you know why she fell out of the cri—she put, she fell out of her portacrib again.

Dr. M.: *(To parents)* Let's share that; so we need to sit together.

Mr. K.: Okay.

Dr. F.: I asked Dr. Minuchin to join us because—four eyes are better than two. Dr. Minuchin is director of the clinic here.

Karen: Is that mine?

Dr. M.: No, that's mine. *(She gives it back, goes and sits on a table)*

Mrs. K.: Don't sit on the table, Karen. What is that?

Karen: That's the table.

Mrs. K.: Okay. Don't sit on the table, okay? You sit on chairs. Okay, honey?

Karen: Doc . . . doc . . . doc . . . doc . . . *(continues to repeat this as she she runs around the edge of the room, touching the backs of the chairs.)*

Mrs. K.: She seemed pretty wound up lately. I don't know whether it is Christmas or maybe . . . No, Laurie, no sweetie.

Karen: Are there any toys?

Dr. F.: Here are some toys.

Karen: I want to play with . . . here, Laurie, you play with the dragon.

Mr. K.: *(Chuckling)* Dragon.

Karen: Do you have any paper?

Mrs. K.: Not today, sweetheart. No, put that back, we don't have any paper to draw on. Put them back, Karen. Karen, do what you were told. Put them back. *(To Dr. M.)* Her belligerence is so . . .

Dr. M.: Is that how you run your life? Is that how Karen and you spend your time together?

Mrs. K.: Yes . . . yes.

Dr. M.: It takes just a minute and a half to see it.

Mrs. K.: Yeah. Like, it's a continuous battle.

Dr. M.: Um hm.

Mrs. K.: You know . . . at least for me.

Dr. M.: Um hm. Who wins?

Mrs. K.: It varies. If I'm *(sighs)* up to fighting with her, at that point, sometimes I do. You know, I leave her win sometimes too. You know . . . but we do try and get her to do what we say even if it is a fight. *(To Mr. K.)* Don't we?

Mr. K.: I make her.

Mrs. K.: Yeah, right.

Dr. M.: *(To Mr. K.)* What was your answer?

Mr. K.: I make her do it.

Mrs. K.: Right.

Mr. K.: I always win.

Karen: (In background) Doc . . . doc . . . doc . . . doc . . .

Dr. M.: I feel there is a little difference.

Mrs. K.: Yeah, there is.

Dr. M.: *(To Mr. K.)* You make her do it . . .

Mr. K.: Yeah, I make her do it.

Dr. M.: . . . but she *(indicating Mrs. K.)* doesn't.

Mrs. K.: No, not all the time . . . no.

Dr. M.: Do you find this present arrangement a difficult one? For example, the two girls going around while we talk? How do you respond to that?

Mrs. K.: How do I respond to it? I get tense.

Dr. M.: You get tense?

Mrs. K.: Yeah, I do get tense.

Dr. M.: So, you would prefer that she stay in one place?

Mrs. K.: No, I can see them walking around when there are toys for them to play with.

Dr. M.: What would you like?

Mrs. K.: Right now?

Dr. M.: Yes. What would make it more comfortable for you?

Mrs. K.: For them to sit over there and play with the puppets.

Dr. M.: Okay. Do that. Make her do that.

Mrs. K.: Karen, go over there and play with the puppets, okay? Go ahead. No, not here. No.

Karen: Why?

Mrs. K.: Go over and play with the puppets.

Karen: I don't love you.

Mrs. K.: I love you. Go ahead, go play with your puppets.

Karen: I don't want to play.

Mrs. K.: Karen . . .

Mrs. K.: Laurie's playing with them.

Mr. K.: Karen, will you sit down?

Dr. M.: Let mother do it. You know, she's the one who does it when you are not there.

Mr. K.: Yeah, yeah.

Dr. M.: So, let her do it.

The presenting problem in this family, like the others dealt with in this paper, is a disruptive behavior. The scenario which includes this behavior is, in the case of a young child, easily provoked into happening in the room. In fact, it usually occurs without prompting. Within a few minutes of the beginning of this interview, the mother is asking to child not to sit on the table, but instead of following up the order with action, asks her the name of the thing she is sitting on and again tells her to get off it because "you sit on chairs." The child does get off, but she does not sit on chairs, she begins to circle the room very noisily. Mother tries to make her behave, then turns to Minuchin, indicating how helpless she is.

Minuchin then ascertains that this is the way the child behaves at home, and also that father is the only one who can make her obey. He suggests to the mother that she could ask her little girl to stop running around the room if she does not like it. Mother tries again, and when she does not succeed, father comes in as usual to establish law and order. Minuchin blocks his helpful maneuver, telling him that since his wife has to contend with this behavior at home, she is the one who must control it. Thus the scenario which generally happens does not happen. The therapist has interrupted a cycle.

What follows this intervention is a suggestion to the mother which helps her to succeed in quieting the little girl down. Minuchin has her get down on the floor and play hand puppets with her. This is a positive rather than a negative reinforcement for behaving well, and is an action rather than words. The mother plays for a bit, but soon her tendency to criticize takes over. Minuchin then invites the father to sit on the floor, and soon he and the other therapist and Minuchin are all playing with the little girl. The therapist ends this sequence by commenting on the father's gentle way of playing with his daughter. By now, of course, she is behaving like an angel.

Toward the end of the session, Minuchin excuses the children and speaks alone with the parents. He finds out that the mother is afraid that when her husband intervenes to control the little girl, he may lose his temper and hurt her. Minuchin expresses surprise and asks why she thinks that this father, who has just been playing affectionately with his little girl, could be capable of such a thing. The mother says that once, ten years ago, her husband got angry and had a violent outburst. He did not hurt anybody, but it was a memorable occasion and the mother has never forgotten it. The therapist questions whether this is still a possibility, since in ten years the father has never had a similar outburst. He suggests that perhaps the mother has been fabricating a personality for her husband that is not correct. The mother leaves the session with some doubts in her mind, and the father is obviously delighted to be relieved of the stigma of being the "monster."

Therapy went very well with this family. The father stopped bringing his gun to the sessions. In fact, whether this event was related or not, he eventually left the police force.

This cycle is a little different from the other two we have looked at in at least one respect. The helpless wife and the authoritarian husband carries a flavor of a dominant-submissive arrangement. The child, as was true in the other situations, is overinvolved with one parent (mother), who becomes so unable to control her that she has to bring in her husband. Since both father and daughter are billed as "monsters" who are able to terrorize mother, one can assume that mother feels in some way like an outsider to these two, and also that she feels neglected by her husband. Her struggle with the little girl has the flavor of hitting out at a preferred rival. However, when the husband does come in to control the child, the mother turns on him and sides with the child. It is a neat switch, since by one move she not only separates father and daughter, but becomes daughter's protector against father. Now it is father who is the outsider. But the child has been the weight who changes the balance of the two sides of the scale.

WHEN THE CYCLE INCLUDES LARGER SYSTEMS

Haley redefines the problem of working with hospitalized adolescent schizophrenics as one of helping them leave home. The process which takes these young adults from home to hospital and back again is merely another version of a homeostatic cycle which monitors the parents' relationship. However, to break a cycle which includes not only the family but other social systems is an unusually complex operation which requires a series of maneuvers inserted sequentially over time.

Haley documents this process in a training tape he supervised in collaboration with Sam Scott, a therapist at the Philadelphia Child Guidance Clinic. The tape is entitled "Leaving Home," and involves a twenty-four-year-old deaf man who had shuttled between home and hospital for eight years. The sequence was predictable: after he came back home, he would become threatening and abusive; he would then be moved out to an apartment; after that, he would get on drugs, and go out and cause trouble in the community. The police would find him, the parents would hospitalize him, and the whole cycle would start again.

Haley conceptualizes the therapeutic task as one of breaking up this cycle. If one part is blocked, the whole will have to change. The therapist who was working on this case could use sign language, and therefore could communicate both with the boy and his parents, who did not use sign language. The first intervention he made was to change the type of institution the boy would go to the next time he was picked up by the police. He had the parents sign a paper, in the presence of the boy, saying that the next time the boy got into trouble, they would have the police put him in jail. This not only changed the consequences for the boy, but also for the parents. They could still maintain some control over him if he were in a hospital. For instance, they could visit him frequently. In jail, this would no longer be possible. In addition, the boy's actions were reframed from behavior that could not be controlled to behavior he was held accountable for.

Another change was to interrupt the cycle at the point when the tension between the parents usually increased. This would happen if the boy maintained good behavior for a while. Irritation between the parents would begin to surface, and the boy would start to get into fights with his mother. She and he were in a kind of sticky bond: she would protect him from his father, who would beat him up if he misbehaved; on the other hand, she would push him away from her, insisting that he go out of the house and not make so many demands on her. In a sense, the mother could ignite an outburst from her son just by this way of treating him.

The therapist, during a period when the boy was home, prolonged the period of good behavior beyond its usual limits by betting him a sum of money that he would not get into trouble with the police during the next two weeks. The boy stayed out of trouble and won the bet. As a result of this period of calm, the father went on a trip he had long been planning. During his absence, the mother angered the boy by trying to make him spend time out of the house. He became violent, threatening her with a knife and his sister with a bat. At the next family therapy session, the therapist showed up with a knife and a bat and laid them on the floor. Although the boy acted as if he was not responsible for what he had done to his mother and sister, the therapist pushed him so hard that he grabbed the bat and threatened the therapist. The father took the bat from him. The therapist then insisted, and had the parents insist, that the boy was not allowed to use violent threats and weapons to intimidate people. He could argue or criticize, but he could not use knives or bats. This move blocked the patient's part in the cycle, labeling it as intolerable behavior and making the other parties in the cycle join to resist it.

The next shift was to have the boy move into an apartment and continue to live there. In the past, he had usually moved away when he and his parents were angry at each other. In addition, they treated him as a handicapped person who could not be expected to live by himself. The therapist laid some groundwork by insisting that the boy do his own laundry while he was still at home, and contribute housekeeping money from his welfare check. He was also expected to repay debts. Thus the self-fulfilling prophecy that labeled him incompetent was cut into in an active way. After the scene with the bat, the boy moved out once more. He got into trouble with the police again and was briefly hospitalized, but this time his parents stayed out and he handled the situation on his own. According to the therapist, this was the last time he got into trouble, and, more importantly, the last time he was hospitalized.

A question that comes to mind is why, if the parents' marital tensions were being deflected by the boy's troublesome behavior, did the therapist not treat their problems directly? The answer may be that it is not necessary to shift all aspects of a cycle, only enough of them to cause a major symptom to disappear. If the parents' relationship did not start to fall apart, or if one of them did not come up with a serious symptom, one could assume that the couple system had achieved a new equilibrium that would allow them to stick together without the need for a symptomatic child.

Family therapy includes many more maneuvers than breaking the chain of behaviors in a homeostatic loop. But therapists who address themselves to relieving specific complaints do seem to be looking for that cycle. If the problem behavior is a disruptive one, it usually stands out clearly and the cycle it is embedded in is not hard to find. This makes the question of how to intervene and where much easier than in cases where the problem behavior is a chronically pervasive condition, like many psychosomatic illnesses or communicational disorders associated with psychosis. Here the clinician may have to work to find the cycle, and usually it appears most readily if he focuses on *management* of the condition rather than the condition itself. This will usually cause the mirror-image disagreement between the parents to emerge, and the problem can be redefined as one of helping them to get together so that they can make the child behave responsibly in spite of his "illness."

A big question always arises when methods that circumscribe the therapeutic goal are presented: will the symptom disappear, only to come back later? or will some other complaint take its place? And what about all the other obvious problems that are floating around in the family which ought to be fixed? The answer is not easy, unless one is a purist about change. There are some purists who say that growth and a better life for each person in the family is the goal of therapy. There are opposite purists who say that they have no interest in changing the structure of the family and that they only wish to relieve people of the particular pain they complained of when they came in. Actually, since therapy is as complex a construct as families are, few of these purists do what they say they believe in doing. Experienced small-change purists go after a shift which will make interconnecting shifts take place elsewhere in the family. Experienced growth purists are extremely concerned about the presenting complaint, and use all kinds of maneuvers to remove it.

However, the merit of training therapists to think in a more circumscribed way is that it brings therapy a little closer to the ideal of a precision instrument. There is an analogy here to the advances in medicine which allow specific cures to be devised for particular ailments. Until very recently, doctors used generalized practices like leeching, cupping, purging, and bleeding, which not only did no good, but actually did harm, since all these methods dehydrated people. Psychotherapy, including family therapy, is just emerging from a similar dark age in which one global technique after another has been applied indiscriminately across the board. Family therapy has pushed cathartic approaches, in which getting out anger or grief or longheld secrets would supposedly cure all symptoms; better communication approaches, which would supposedly help any relationship in trouble; paradoxical approaches which work best with families caught in rigid homeostatic constraints but have been presented as if they applied to all families; and if all else failed, the ideal of self-actualization could be held up for family members to aspire to, so that even if they continued to experience their symptoms, they would at least be more autonomous human beings.

However, the concept of a more parsimonious psychotherapy is a coming idea in mental health, not just for economic reasons, but because it is beginning to seem possible. The advantage of focusing on the homeostatic cycle which supports a symptom is that it speaks to this issue of parsimony. The therapist can ascertain the variable that is being maintained, isolate the part played in it by the symptom, and then seek out the most effective way to block the cycle, using the fewest possible moves consonant with effective family functioning. This, at the very least, is what a client should receive when he comes to a healer to get rid of his pain.

REFERENCES

1) M. Bowen. "The Use of Family Theory in Clinical Practice," *Comprehensive Psychiatry,* 7 (1966), 345–74.
2) S. Minuchin. *Families and Family Therapy.* Cambridge, Mass.: Harvard University Press, 1974.
3) J. Haley. "Strategic Therapy When A Child Is Presented As The Problem," *The Journal of the American Academy of Child Psychiatry,* 12 (1973), 641–59.
4) _____. *Strategies of Psychotherapy.* New York: Grune and Stratton, 1963, 158.
5) Edward O. Wilson. *Sociobiology: The New Synthesis.* Cambridge, Mass: Belknap Press of Harvard University, 1975.
6) V. Satir. *Conjoint Family Therapy.* Palo Alto, Calif.: Science and Behavior Books, 1964, 2.
7) J. Haley, and L. Hoffman. *Techniques of Family Therapy.* New York: Basic Books, 1967.
8) A.H. Stanton, and M.S. Schwartz. *The Mental Hospital.* New York: Basic Books, 1954.
9) R. Ravich. *Predictable Pairing.* New York: Peter H. Wyden, 1974.
10) C. Wild, *et. al.* "Transactional Communication Disturbances in Families of Male Schizophrenics," *Family Process,* 14 (1975), 131–60.
11) Ravich, *op. cit.,* 68.
12) T. Lidz, *et. al.* "The Intrafamilial Environment of Schizophrenic Patients:

Marital Schism and Marital Skew," *American Journal of Psychiatry,* 28 (1958), 764–76.

13) G. Bateson. *Naven.* Stanford Calif: Stanford University Press, 1967.

14) P. Watzlawick, J. Weakland, R. Fisch. *Change: Principles of Problem Forme tion and Problem Resolution.* New York: W.W. Norton, 1974.

CHAPTER 30

Cross-Confrontation

Norman L. Paul, M.D.

Cross-confrontation techniques evolved due to my gnawing impatience with the halting pace of the traditional therapeutic process. It seemed to me that all too often words obscured a client's ability to become aware of his own unpleasant feelings. The more articulate the individual or the couple, the more inaccessible these feelings seemed to be.

Beginning in 1964, I began to use audio tapes containing unpleasant, emotionally-charged material derived from one set of client-families as stressor stimuli for another set of client families. The tapes were used with the written permission of the families originally recorded, and contained no identifying data. These original tapes depicted feeling states regarded as universal; for example, delayed grief reactions, intense sibling rivalry, and separation anxiety between mother and child.

Gradually since then I have added to my library of stressor stimuli poems, letters, pieces of literature, and video tapes. In various ways these all provide sanctions for clients to allow themselves to consider that unpleasant feeling-states are normal features of living, and can be shared. The experiences selected for use are designed to encourage clients to empathize with other human beings, and then with themselves. Most recently, sexually provocative films have been used (1).

The rationale underlying these procedures is the need to assist people to perceive and understand that all feeling states are normal, and that there are no abnormal fantasies. Furthermore, any assignment of deviance is to be made exclusively on the basis of behavior. My purpose is to broaden the range of both ego-alien fantasies and affects which can be shared when appropriate. All materials are regarded as empathogenic, and clients are encouraged to empathize with the emotions in which they are bathed. Subjects are encouraged to remember and then to verbalize similar experiences in their lives.

The sexual films include scenes of heterosexual and homosexual behavior; sadistic sexual behavior is excluded. These films have been used to lessen, and hopefully eradicate oscillating and disabling fears of sexual fantasies. The homosexual films are used to help promote comfort with such fantasies as a way of increasing empathy for the spouse's gender.

The individual, couple, or family is confronted by the audio tape, poem, or letter, which is referred to as stimulus stressor. The reactions subsequently recorded on audio or video tape are later played back to the subject in a type of self-confrontation. To date the sample includes at least eight hundred different families. The reactions range from frank derogation, to resistance, to shock. Sensitive, empathic support for clients' reactions is vital for effective use of these techniques.

The following stressor tape is one example of how stimuli are used in the cross-confrontation procedure. It is taken from the early part of the fourth session with the Lewis couple. The Lewises, at the time of the excerpt, were both thirty-nine years old, married for twenty years, with six children. The presenting crisis was that Mr. Lewis was planning to divorce his wife in order to marry Charlotte, a twenty-one-year-old woman living in a large, distant city. The level of acrimony between the spouses was very reminiscent of the dialogue in *Who's Afraid of Virginia Woolf.* One crucial factor in their premarital history was that Mr. Lewis had been conceived and born out of wedlock, and had successfully persuaded his father to marry his mother when he was about twelve years old. Another important fact is that both Mrs. Lewis's parents committed suicide—her mother when she was sixteen, and her father when she was thirty-two.

At the beginning of this fourth meeting, Mr. Lewis announced that this was to be our last meeting insofar as he had made a final commitment to marry Charlotte, and had consulted with his attorney the previous evening to initiate a legal separation. At the point at which this excerpt begins, Mr. Lewis was discussing his feeling that he and his father had been trapped into marriage.

During this excerpt, he exposed previously unrecognized and hidden intense feelings of grief, of which his wife had also been ignorant. Four months after this interview took place, Mr. Lewis abandoned his plans to marry Charlotte and returned to live with his wife.

EXCERPT FROM LEWIS COUPLE INTERVIEW—FOURTH MEETING

Dr. Paul: How often did you ask your father to marry your mother?
Mr. Lewis: Oh, quite often.
Dr. Paul: Beginning at what age?
Mr. Lewis: Oh, probably when I was about nine.
Dr. Paul: And how would he greet you?

Mr. Lewis: He would be very indulgent. He would be, we, we, my father and I, when we get along very well, we can have very friendly pleasant relationships, I mean, at times.

Dr. Paul: Again, I draw the parallel between you and your wife; you get along, you have pleasant relationships. Go ahead.

Mr. Lewis: But, I mean, for example, I'd say, I've usually, in fact I think this has been one of the reasons I was successful in my own work is that I've always had to persuade, I mean, I was a kid, my parents were older. They were, they were foreigners in this country. They couldn't speak English. I was sort of the educator, the critic, and the persuader.

Dr. Paul: You were assuming leadership in some ways in the home?

Mr. Lewis: Oh . . .

Mrs. Lewis: Oh, yes.

Mr. Lewis: I led that family from the time I was probably five years old, and uh, in many, many ways, in many ways. I really marshalled the family's direction in many ways. And they appreciated it. They were very proud of me for this. I mean they . . . But I would say to my father sometimes when we were alone, I would say, Pop, you know it would be very nice if you married Mom. After all, she is a woman, and she, she'd feel better if she were married. Incidentally, my mother would sometimes mention this to me.

Dr. Paul: That she'd like to be married.

Mr. Lewis: Yes. I mean she would mention it. See, I don't know how I ever got the impression that I was illegitimate because no one ever said it to me. It's a funny thing. Now, speaking of hearings things. No one ever told me that.

Dr. Paul: Did you ever see any documents?

Mr. Lewis: No. There's a funny thing. It's a funny thing. I just knew. I don't know.

Dr. Paul: Do you believe in the supernatural?

Mr. Lewis: No. But something must have told me.

Dr. Paul: The vapor in the air, sort of . . .

Mr. Lewis: No, no, but I think maybe my mother must have said, I remember, I know what, I was with my mother and aunt and one of the things I think has influenced me a lot, my aunt Mary was a most wonderful person. Oh, she was . . .

Dr. Paul: Her sister?

Mr. Lewis: Yeah, my mother's sister.

Dr. Paul: Older?

Mr. Lewis: Younger, and we were, we would go on vacation, not vacation but we'd go to visit my aunt Mary in North Carolina, and I would be in bed with the two women as a boy.

Mrs. Lewis: Yes, you told me that you used to overhear the women talking.

Mr. Lewis: And they were talking. They wouldn't see each other for a year and they talked for all night.

Dr. Paul: You'd sleep what, on the end or between . . .

Mr. Lewis: I'd sleep on the end, and they'd be in the other . . .

Dr. Paul: What age?

Mr. Lewis: Oh, I must have been eight, seven. And they would talk all night about men, and all night they'd be, the sisters, having a real personal and intimate relationship and, . . .

Dr. Paul: What?

Mr. Lewis: A personal and intimate relationship, discussing men and discussing life with men and the problems of men and every so often, I'd just get, just wake up and hear . . . men are so and so, men are so and so.

Dr. Paul: Did that make you feel sort of positive about growing up to be a man?

Mr. Lewis: Make me feel positive? Well, I don't know about that.

Dr. Paul: What do you think?

Mr. Lewis: I don't know. My mother would always criticize my father. You know, she'd, she'd always be very critical at some times. Then she'd be nice at other times. My aunt Mary was wonderful, though. There was a remarkable woman. She was a remarkable person.

Dr. Paul: When did she die?

Mr. Lewis: She was thirty-five.

Dr. Paul: And you were how old?

Mr. Lewis: I was about, oh, ten or eleven. She was a remarkable, nice person.

Dr. Paul: And how did you feel when she died?

Mr. Lewis: Oh, I felt sadder about my aunt's death than anybody.

Dr. Paul: How's that?

Mr. Lewis: Miserable, miserable.

Dr. Paul: How miserable?

Mr. Lewis: Terrible.

Dr. Paul: What do you remember, huh?

Mr. Lewis: (Weeping) I feel terrible.

Dr. Paul: Do you feel that you still miss her?

Mr. Lewis: Oh, yes, I do. She was so nice *(weeping)*. She was so nice.

Mrs. Lewis: She had, she did all the things, you know, for him, you know, when he was a little boy that little kids need that he didn't get at home. You know, she had animals around the house and things, you know, his parents never understood things like that.

Mr. Lewis: She's really the woman I've been looking for, really. She was so nice. She was a beautiful woman. She was so kind.

Dr. Paul: She was single?

Mr. Lewis: No, she was married. She had a family. She had her children, and, uh, but she was always understanding.

Dr. Paul: Do you ever see her family?

Mr. Lewis: No. Never had any really close relationship with her family.

Dr. Paul: Since she died.

Mr. Lewis: Since she died. She was a remarkable, kind person.

Dr. Paul: Do you know where she's buried?

Mr. Lewis: Yeah, Charlotte, North Carolina. I've never been to her grave.

Dr. Paul: Never?

Mr. Lewis: No. You see, I don't know why I've never been to her grave, but I haven't been to anybody's grave. She's the only person I ever, the only close person that's ever died in our family, you know.

Dr. Paul: Do you feel that, uh, she's the only one that you really loved that way? *(Mr. Lewis weeping, then silence)*

Mr. Lewis: I've always loved her. She was very kind to me.

Dr. Paul: She loved you?

Mr. Lewis: Yes, she did *(sobbing)*. I don't know what I'm crying about.

Dr. Paul: You don't know what you're crying about.

Mr. Lewis: I don't know.

Dr. Paul: You don't? You still miss her.

Mr. Lewis: She was so nice. It wasn't anything she did, especially, it was just . . . she was always so nice *(sobbing)*. She always, she was always so sweet and so kind, and there was never a mean or a bad word *(sobbing loudly)* coming from her lips. She always liked me. There was never anything phony, she was always accepting me as I am. Being with her was like peace, just peace, just absolute peace.

    Dr. Paul: So, in many ways you have been looking for her over the years.

    Mr. Lewis: Yeah, I think I've found her. I think I have.

A REACTION TO CROSS-CONFRONTATION STIMULUS

This excerpt from a session with the Lewises was played to the wife of a couple, Mr. and Mrs. Dunn, during her second session. There had been one prior meeting with Mrs. Dunn and her husband, during which I saw each alone for fifteen minutes and then both together for about half an hour. Mr. Dunn, a history professor, was thirty-eight years old, his wife, a lawyer, was thirty-five. She had had a hysterectomy for cancer fourteen months before they consulted me. They had one child, a daughter, ten years old. They had been married eleven years. The presenting problem was that Mrs. Dunn, unable to tolerate her husband, had served him with divorce papers two weeks prior to their first visit with me. She expressed her determination to get out of the marriage.

Mrs. Dunn's parents had both died of tuberculosis in a sanitorium, her mother when she was four and her father when she was five years old. She and two younger brothers were cared for in the sanitorium until she was eight years old. She claims never to have had active tuberculosis. At eight, she was placed in a foster home which lacked a father. She remained there until she was twelve, at which time she was sent to a convent. When she was sixteen, she was deemed too worldly by the convent administrators. After leaving the convent, she went on to a series of different jobs and different living situations until she met her husband-to-be. Their courtship lasted for three years; she became pregnant and had an abortion before their marriage.

The marriage was characterized by sexual incompatibility and biting sarcastic interplay. On a couple of occasions Mrs. Dunn acted out her threats to abandon their child by taking extended trips to Europe, with her husband's ambivalent approval. Unknown to her husband, she decided to marry a lawyer after their divorce was final.

Her first affair occurred when her daughter was five years old. She went to Europe then, and again two years later in January, the month in which her father had died. She learned about this coincidence later in treatment when she consulted her parents' hospital records. She had served divorce papers on her husband on January 5, the thirtieth anniversary of her father's death.

The hypothesis dictating my use of a delayed grief reaction stressor stimulus via cross-confrontation was that she was unconsciously jealous of her daughter's having a father, and that she needed to have her aborted mourning process reactivated and empathize with herself as an orphan before she could decide which life course was appropriate for her. Her conditions for consulting with me initially included that she see me alone; that her husband also consult me alone; and that her husband move out of the house. At this point, momentum toward divorce ceased and they agreed to a temporary informal separation.

Often therapeutic progress can be more easily achieved by having a couple live apart in different residences, and by focusing on the self, particularly the emotional history antedating courtship. I regard marital friction as a reciprocating defense against remembering traumatic childhood experiences, especially traumas related to loss.

At the beginning of the playing of the stressor tape, Mrs. Dunn sat attentively with her hands folded. Shortly afterward she appeared saddened, and asked for pen and paper, which I regarded as an attempt to hold back her tears. Upon the conclusion of the stressor tape, her initial remarks were about her father-in-law—how he had once asked her husband if she were a bastard, and how he had humiliated her husband by telling him that he was terribly ugly. The following is verbatim:

Excerpt from Interview with Mrs. Dunn—First Meeting

Mrs. Dunn: Now, in this last scene where the man is crying, uh, I was a bit shaken.

Dr. Paul: In what sense?

Mrs. Dunn: Well, I, I, uh, I think without much ado, without much control I could have started crying myself. But more important I think was when you asked him, I was writing before you asked him if he knew what he was crying about, and he said, yes, that she, uh, she understood him, she accepted him. Now, uh, before he said that, I felt as if he really didn't know what he was crying about, uh, that what, what he is talking about is not really the reason that he is crying, but that he is rather, uh, he is rather crying about himself actually and not about this aunt, that the fact that he was crying about this aunt was secondary to the fact that he was crying about himself for some reason.

Dr. Paul: And you say you were sort of shaken?

Mrs. Dunn: I was, I was disturbed by the fact that he was crying. I've seen men cry before. Uh, perhaps, I really don't know what, I was upset that he was crying.

Dr. Paul: Upset in what sense? It's not too clear to me what you mean by upset.

Mrs. Dunn: Emotionally I was upset *(tearful).*

Dr. Paul: When you say emotionally upset, what did you feel?

Mrs. Dunn: I could have cried.

Dr. Paul: About what?

Mrs. Dunn: About the fact that he was crying. But yet, I, I was, there was a feeling that, uh, that this man didn't really, wasn't really crying about this aunt, that he was crying about, about himself, or for himself.

Dr. Paul: In a sense that's to me . . .

Mrs. Dunn: . . . that he was seeing himself in, in relation to this aunt, and that he was crying about this individual that he saw rather than about the aunt, that the fact that she had passed away and that she had been so kind to him.

Dr. Paul: Well, I . . .

Mrs. Dunn: And this happens to me very often, uh, perhaps this will give you some, some insight. I haven't cried very much in this last year, in these last few years. I've been feeling quite positive. I find that when I start to think about myself and am depressed or moody and given to crying, it's, uh, it's not over a . . . the situation that provokes it, let's say the cross word or the way that somebody looked at me. It isn't actually *that* that's making me cry. It's rather, uh, I, I see this—this little me appears *(cries quietly)*.

Dr. Paul: Which little you?

Mrs. Dunn: (Crying) Excuse me.

Dr. Paul: That's okay. *(Pause)* Which little you?

Mrs. Dunn: (Still crying) It's this . . . I, I can only think of one way to describe it. It's this, it's this puny little kid who's running around sickly all the time *(pause)*.

Dr. Paul: Alone . . . inside?

Mrs. Dunn: Yes, and feeling sorry for herself and very often it's . . . I don't allow myself to think this way very often, and I haven't been, as I said, it isn't until coming back to you that this scene has been coming back to my mind lately.

Dr. Paul: Of this puny little girl? Is this the way you looked, you felt about yourself, growing up?

Mrs. Dunn: Oh yes, as a matter of fact, I was, I was a very ugly little girl, and always had been feeling terribly unsure of myself.

Dr. Paul: Whom nobody loved?

Mrs. Dunn: Uh, I really don't know. I, I called it pity, I think, rather than love.

Dr. Paul: You called it what?

Mrs. Dunn: Pity.

Dr. Paul: What do you mean, pity?

Mrs. Dunn: That these people weren't doing it because they loved me or perhaps I didn't understand love, that if they showed me any interest or concern it was more because they pitied me, that I was an orphan, uh, that she has no home, no parents, and that I was being given this consideration because of this. And I did not consider this love, I considered it pity. And I . . .

Dr. Paul: It wasn't love, was it?

Mrs. Dunn: I'm sure it wasn't. Uh, and I ran from this, as a matter of fact I resented it and became quite, quite hostile and began to feel that . . . and began to react in a, in a fashion that, that I'll show them that I'm, I really can do very well without their assistance, without their help.

Dr. Paul: Screw them?

Mrs. Dunn: No, it wasn't, it wasn't that. Well, interestingly enough, I used that term just the other day in talking to John. I can't recall now what the incident was, I don't remember that. But it seems that whenever I did try to fly alone, as it were, completely on my own, that, uh, the conflict within me or the inability to see the situation true would very often perhaps bring about or would be terminated by— I'm again talking about this effort to fly alone—would be terminated by a situation where I became, uh, it was a recurrence of this *(unclear)*. I guess that's what it was called, or a trip to the hospital and any kind of, uh, as I said, attempt to be on my own would culminate or terminate in something like this, so that I was again made to feel that I was reliant, or had to rely . . .

Dr. Paul: But basically feeling inside a puny little girl.

Mrs. Dunn: This I feel is what I see myself as when I am indulging myself or engaging in any kind of self-pity. And I don't like to accept this role. I would much rather feel that I'm self-sufficient and, and able to cope quite adequately.

Dr. Paul: Well, when you get into the self-pitying situation, do you sort of feel an inner sense of loneliness that you touch base with that otherwise you don't, or aloneness?

Mrs. Dunn: Uh, yes, I would, I'd say I do, uh, at these moments. And very often, uh, John has never been, has not often been aware of them because I tend to go off by myself or am quiet, or if I do cry, it's generally by myself. There are some times when I cry in his presence . . . .

Dr. Paul: But you wouldn't let him know what it was about, probably.

Mrs. Dunn: I just, I just couldn't feel that I could communicate this to him.

Dr. Paul: Do you feel that if you were, if you ever let anybody know, he might take advantage of you?

Mrs. Dunn: I don't think it would be a situation where they would take advantage of me, no.

Dr. Paul: That you were then in a vulnerable position.

Mrs. Dunn: Yes, as a matter of fact, I've often used that term in regard to myself, that I feel quite vulnerable *(tearful)*.

Dr. Paul: So, in some ways, the picture that I get of you going through life is someone who in her own way is trying to be a brave little soldier and be positive.

The process of Mrs. Dunn's empathy for that puny little girl had now begun. Over the next thirteen months, she and her husband were seen in different components: separately, together, and with their daughter. The family was included in a multiple family therapy group during the last six months of the treatment program. After four months, she gave up her prospective second husband; she and her husband began to have an active sexual life.

Mrs. Dunn's belated grief for her parents and herself as a youngster and an orphan was gradually resolved as she visited with her husband her parents' unmarked graves, the places she lived as a child, and the convent. Two year follow-up disclosed that the couple are happy with their daughter and with their lives. They regularly review the historical account of this process by listening to audio tapes of their meetings during the fourteen months they were seen.

Various forms of cross-confrontation can be regarded as dynamic Rorschach test procedures. Instead of using symbols in the form of inkblots to elicit projections of unconscious personality determinants, excerpts of emotional states and fantasies regarded as universal are used. Self-confrontation of the clients' reactions to such taped or filmed material focuses sharply on a person's ability to bear both the original stimuli and his means of coping with them.

These techniques afford individuals the opportunity to become responsible and responsive to themselves and others. It is apparent that the inner self-image represents the internalization of varying attitudes and affects perceived by the self about the self over the sweep of life. As an oversimplification, it includes some elements of which one is conscious, and some which are hidden by suppression and repression. To survive and function, most individuals have to forget painful experiences of grief, rage, helplessness, and especially guilt. But in forgetting, they also fail to integrate these experiences into a perspective on their lives.

Flexibility in the use of the stressor stimuli is important. A husband, for instance, may not react empathically with his wife present, because he may feel that to shed tears in front of her is a display of his weakness. On the other hand, he may do so readily when seen alone by a male therapist. Occasionally a given stressor stimulus may have to be used on three separate occasions before a positive empathic reaction is elicited.

The therapist must be able to empathize with the listener's positive resonance or his resistance to feelings aroused by stressors. He must also de-emphasize the exposure of such pain as evidence of sickness or pathology, and focus on it rather as evidence of a hitherto concealed hurt in the listener. The therapist's role, other than that of an empathic benevolent parent-type, is somewhat akin to that of a playwright, who draws out the experience as it was lived, including the setting, the time, and the transactions between the relevant persons present.

Man's search for new worlds to discover and conquer, including the dramatic voyage to the moon, must be matched by an equal thrust to discover who and what he is, the process of his being. He must eventually make empathic contact with himself and those about him, if he is to survive. His eagerness to bridge the gap in his external environment between the known and the unknown can also be used to achieve a new knowledge of the self, but only if he has the courage to do so.

REFERENCES

1. N. L. Paul and B. B. Paul. *A Marital Puzzle.* New York: W.W. Norton, 1975, 102–04; 233; 236.
   See also:
Milton M. Berger, ed. *Videotape Techniques in Psychiatric Training and Treatment.* New York: Brunner/Mazel, Inc. 1970.
Walter Haas, David Mendell, Celia Mitchell, Hugh Mullan, and Norman Paul. *Exploring Therapeutic Encounter.* A professional discussion with LP recording of a therapy session. Audio Press, 1970, Briarwood Lane, Pleasantville, New York 10570.
Bertram D. Lewin. *The Image and the Past.* New York: International Universities Press, 1968.

Samuel Novey. *The Second Look: The Reconstruction of Personal History in Psychiatry and Psychoanalysis.* Baltimore, Md.: The John Hopkins Press, 1968.

Norman Paul. "Parental Empathy," in E. James Anthony and Therese Benedek (eds.), *Parenthood, Its Psychology and Psychopathology.* Boston: Little, Brown, 1970.

_____. "Effects of Playback on Family Members of Their Own Previously Recorded Conjoint Therapy Material," *Psychiatric Research Report 20, American Psychiatric Association,* February, 1966.

CHAPTER 31

Integrating Immediate Videoplayback in Family Therapy

Ian Alger, M.D.

INTRODUCTION

The quarterback steps back into the pocket, takes time as his defense blocks well, then, aiming carefully, spirals the ball to his wide receiver near the eight-yard line. The receiver, racing toward the side, makes a tremendous leap, and pulls the ball from the air, first by his fingertips, then with his whole hand. The tackler crashes into him, and the referee wildly signals the receiver out of bounds. The magnificent pass went for nothing, and the crowd roars its rage. In the television broadcast booth the announcer says, "Let's watch the replay in slow motion." And there is the action again, slowing down at the crucial moment as we see the ball caught, and the receiver's foot coming down . . . well within the line! It was a fair catch! The referee was wrong. He couldn't see it clearly when it happened. But his ruling is upheld. Indeed, the use of instant replay by the officials has been rejected as being too time-consuming. An instant here is just too long.

At times, apparently it is more important that life be dealt with as people want to see it; and at other times it is important to see it as it is. In therapy immediate videoplayback has provided an opportunity to capture behavioral data, and to examine and re-examine it on the spot. This potential has been available for over fifteen years, and a considerable literature has accumulated, including a constant updating of technical improvements. Little will be said about the history and technology of videotape recording in this chapter. Rather, the emphasis will be on the clinical use of immediate videoplayback in family therapy (1,6).

Video became available at a time when communication theory, field theory, and general systems theory were providing alternate explanations for human behavior. The idea of understanding a person's behavior from exploring internal motives was being expanded by the idea that if we understand larger group behavior—systems behavior—we can gain a better comprehension of the meaning of one individual's behavior in that larger context. The search was no longer for the truth about an intrapsychic process, but rather for a view of the behavioral sequences and signalling complexities in a systems unit. Family therapy quite naturally came of age during this period, and it is especially appropriate that videorecording has found particular use in the study of family behavior.

Therapy focuses on change; the relevant question, immediately posed, is therefore, how can video be useful in promoting therapeutic change? The study of recorded data provides insight, but it is the immediate playback during a session that provides the new possibility. With this feedback information the actual course of the session can be changed. This corrective maneuver is a cybernetic intervention. The second consequence of the playback is that the role relationship of therapist and family members is changed. During the replay both family and therapist step to a different position. All of them now are data researchers, and all of them are equally engaged in the task of reviewing and reacting to the recorded material. This shift not only alters the therapist-patient relationship, but also interferes with the usual hierarchical relationships between family members. This alternating shifting of role relationships provides an additional impetus for change.

TECHNICAL ASPECTS

There are numerous references about equipment and technical operation; these can be consulted (9,11). The setting will determine the elaborateness of the operation. In teaching clinics, technical personnel will be available to operate cameras, and a coordinated effort can be directed by a therapist-director who may not even be present in the therapy room. In many small clinics and in private practice, however, simple equipment and the least elaborate operation have been the most successful. I have found that a simple one-camera system, with a half-inch reel-to-reel recorder and a single TV monitor, is very adequate. The camera can be put on wide-angle so that the whole group, including therapist, is recorded; or the camera, equipped with a zoom lens, can be placed beside the therapist on a low tripod, and operated by the therapist himself during the session. The recorder is placed conveniently by the other side of the therapist, and can be stopped, reversed, and put into freeze-frame or slow motion with great ease.

The TV monitor is placed so everyone can see it, and the therapist operating the camera can use it for a view-finder during the recording.

When co-therapists are working with a family, one can operate the camera, but still retain the role of co-therapist. In consultation between sessions the co-therapists may develop an understanding of certain dynamics and interactions which then can be easily captured on tape during subsequent sessions, with an immediate replay highlighting the particular sequence (8). Family members also may learn to use the camera, and the focus they choose provides additional useful clinical material. The tapes can be saved, or particular sections can be edited, so that a library of relevant segments is accumulated for each family. The review of this material on a periodic basis can also have important therapeutic impact, but I will not explore that point further here.

CLINICAL USE

The equipment may be used the first time the family is seen, or may be introduced at a later session. In either case the attitude of the therapist toward the camera and recorder, and his ease with them will be important in determining the family's comfort and willingness to participate in the videorecording. In my practice the equipment is not concealed, and fits into the regular decor of the office. When I meet the family, after initial introductions, I make a statement similar to the following: "You see this camera and videorecorder, and television set. I find it useful to make videorecordings of our sessions, so from time to time we can look together at what we are doing. It gives us a chance to look at things again, and to better understand our reactions with each other. I'll be operating the camera now, and if at any time one of you would like to replay something, just speak out and we can do it immediately. Have any of you seen yourselves on TV before?"

From answers to this question I learn whether anyone has seen his image on TV, and I ask further about that experience. If no one has, I ask how they feel about the prospect. I then go on to say, "It's important to realize that what you see on the TV screen is your television image. It is only in two dimensions, it is in black and white here, and the picture is affected by the lighting, and by distortions of the camera angles, and the particular lens. The recordings will show us how we interact together, and also will provide a television image. But I am saying that the image is not exactly the way you look in life. Also, it will seem different to you from your image in a mirror for two reasons. First, the image in a mirror is reversed, while on TV you see, for example, your right side as your right side. This makes the image seem somewhat unfamiliar. The second difference from looking in a mirror is that the image on TV will move in a way unrelated to your immediate actions, since you will be watching a recording of earlier behavior." These explanations are given because the television image varies greatly with different technical conditions, and knowledge of this gives each person some protection from an immediate harsh view of his actual appearance.

I also add that the recordings will be used only for review by the family, and will not be shown to others without the written permission of the family. If treatment is carried on in a hospital or clinic with training groups, it is important to obtain releases from the patients, and if any material is used for other teaching purposes, it is also important to obtain adequate releases from all the family members. Sample release forms are printed in *Videotape in Psychiatric Training and Treatment,* edited by M. Berger (4).

At the first session the family is also told that the recording is a method which may be helpful in the work we plan together, but that it will not be used continually, and possibly not in every session.

Once the first recording session has begun, some family members may be quite eager to look at the playback. As a rule it is wise to wait until one is sure there is an established rapport with each family member. If the family has been seen for one or more sessions prior to this initial video session, rapport will not be an issue; but if this is actually the beginning of the relationship, showing playback too soon may make it extremely difficult to discuss reactions, and to assess the impact on the viewers.

If the first playback reveals some information about the structure of the family, or about a transaction involving several members, it will likely reinforce the importance of learning and how people in the system react with one another. On the other hand, focusing first on one person's appearance may create support for the belief that video is a way to probe deeply into one individual's psyche.

Experience has also demonstrated the effectiveness of making only two or three playback interventions in the course of one hour. More than this tends to disrupt the flow of the session, and hinders rather than promotes integration of new awareness. Of course, for any one sequence there may be numerous replays of the same material as different members of the family react to their own perceptions and memories of the sequence.

Basic Principles

When a wide-angle camera is used, all the behavior is captured. With closer shots using a zoom lens, decisions must be made at the time of the action as to which aspect to capture on tape. In either case, knowledge of the significance of nonverbal behavior is essential if one is to follow the transactions and develop awareness of the crucial behavioral signalling which is going on. In *Body Language and Social Order* (10), Scheflen presents an extremely useful guide to the classification and comprehension of nonverbal behavior. He makes the point that nonverbal behavior is much more than a revelation of inner states of being; it is additionally a traditional code maintaining and regulating human relationships without reference to language and conscious mental process. This approach provides a basic framework which one can use to classify nonverbal communication and thereby become more conscious of it in a family.

In therapy the setting is a face-to-face grouping, and movements may be related to bonding an affiliation, including courting and quasi-courting behavior, and also to dominance-submission behavior. Facial gestures, raised brows, sidelong glances, and preening and flushing may be noted in the quasi-courting mode, which may of course not proceed to physical contact, but may be used to signal a desire for the development of a friendly exchange.

The dominance-submission reciprocals may be seen in the thrust of the jaw, the position of arms, and the posture in standing or sitting. In addition, people involved in face-to-face groupings also frame their transactions by the way they place their bodies when they sit or stand.

A further series of signals and gestures give order to the transactions, creating initial definition, determining the speaking and listening arrangements, and commenting on the quality of the relationships. This category of behavior often involves metacommunication; that is, communication *about* some other communication. Metacommunication thus modifies another communication and gives information as to the way the first communication is to be received.

Another set of behaviors are transcontextuals. This means that the behaviors seem out of place, or not in context, and therefore their significance is obscure, puzzling, or anxiety provoking. Such behaviors are frequently seen in families seeking help. Finally, verbal communication itself, which usually in our culture is experienced as a means of conveying information, can be used in a metacommunicative mode. Also, the messages delivered verbally can be quite discrepant with those delivered through the nonverbal channels. This kind of contradictory message, particularly in groups where intense bonding has occurred so the members cannot easily separate from one another, is the basis of the double-binding behavior described by Bateson *et al.* (3) in their work on disturbed families.

In the actual interview, then, one can see the importance of capturing facial expressions and gestures, of being alert to the seating arrangements, and changes in the seating, as well as the posture taken and any changes in that posture. Monitoring behavior may occur through covering the face with a hand, or drawing the finger beneath the nose. Alliances may be indicated by shifts in body position, by crossing of the legs so as to exclude someone, or pointing an elbow so as to wall off a certain territory. Alliances may also be apparent through synchronous movements, behaviors where one family member picks up rhythmically the body movement of another. The videorecording captures the flow of verbal exchange, with its informational and metacommunicative aspects, along with the kinesics of the interactions, and displays and reproduces all this information immediately and as many times as required. Once the material is recorded, the next task is to determine the moments when replay would be therapeutically useful, and then to integrate what is learned in the replay into the ongoing session.

I will now present several clinical examples of this kind of integration, taken from different cases in family therapy. Following each clinical description, I will briefly discuss my criteria for selecting and recording the particular nonverbal communications; explain my reasons for selecting a replay segment; and illustrate the integration of the video replay as a therapeutic intervention. However, no guide can indicate exactly when the replay is most appropriate in a particular family meeting. This clinical skill comes from a combination of experience and overall therapeutic capacity which is best learned through actual application of the method.

Alliances and Distance

In a family, the alliance between two people may also function to exclude another family member. In the following case, each parent felt a special closeness to one of the children, while the mother and father were distant and indirect with one another. The primary therapeutic goal was to shift alliances, and thereby shift the focus from the identified patient.

The family initially presented their problem as centering around the 14-year-old daughter who was failing in school and who was behaving in a very sulky and rebellious way at home. Her 11-year-old sister was quiet, and the only anxiety expressed by the parents over her was a concern that she was not involved with any friends, and stayed at home a great deal. The mother, in her forties, looked drawn and anxious, while the father, who was a few years older, dressed stylishly, and appeared very confident but somewhat aloof.

The family readily accepted the idea of recording the sessions, whereupon the father took the lead in presenting the background of the family, and the problems the family was having with the older daughter. As he talked I noted that the mother turned in her chair, which was beside his, and put her head in her hand while looking down and away. This was the focus of the replay occurring in the first session with the family. I asked the family to watch the sequence, and then raised a question about their reactions. The children were at first quiet, but the mother said that she got embarrassed when her husband went on and on. She reported that his behavior bothered her particularly when they were at social affairs. The father said he hadn't noticed her turning away, but even after the first replay he showed no particular concern about her behavior. When questioned about this he said he wasn't going to be controlled by her behavior. The wife then reacted by saying that she felt hopeless about trying to change him, and she guessed this was why she just turned away, because nothing would do any good anyway.

In two subsequent sessions the same reactions were recorded, and shown back to the family. After the third instance, the wife became more direct with him, and on several occasions during the next few sessions she took more aggressive steps to interrupt him when she felt embarrassed. Apparently in response to this, he became more aware of his reactions, and was seen on later replays to be glancing frequently toward her as he started to speak. When he began to do this, it was also observed that her head was being held higher, and that her gaze often met his, instead of being turned to the side.

While the above reactions were being considered, other material was also recorded. It was noted that the older daughter and the father often sat in a similar position, and once the camera caught both of them moving their feet in perfect rhythm. This was replayed, and both daughter and father said they felt very close to one another. At the time he was supporting her about shopping for some things she wanted, while the mother was expressing great question about the wisdom of her purchases.

In another sequence, the mother and youngest daughter were seen to hold the same position for several minutes, with their heads turned in the same direction, and with their arms and hands in the same posture. On replay they were able to confirm an alliance, both feeling very close to each other, and both experiencing a kind of sad disenchantment with their lives, the mother in her work, and the younger girl at school. This was the first expression directly by the younger daughter of her own unhappiness, and following this session she was able to include direct comments more frequently in the family sessions.

The videotape highlighted alliances in the family, as well as the distance in the relationship of mother and father. The replay also seemed to enable the mother to confront the father more directly about her discomfort with his style of communication. The general focus moved away from the central attention on the older girl, and toward the total family dynamic.

Nonverbal Modifiers

Some nonverbal behavior has the effect of signalling another person to change or modify his behavior. In the following case the husband engaged in a display of behaviors indicating his distraction, sending the message to his wife that she should discontinue her line of communication. Such nonverbal communication is very often carried on below the level of conscious awareness of both persons involved in the interaction.

In the first session with this particular family, consisting of mother, father, a daughter aged eight, and two sons, ten and fourteen, the mother talked of her concern and anxiety. She continued to speak of her feeling that her husband was not interested in the problems she saw, and described her sense that he was usually distracted, and unavailable to her.

While she was saying these things, the husband was turning his head, and gazing at pictures on the wall, and up at the ceiling. He was asked to watch the replay, and was utterly amazed to see that he was so blatantly distracted, and apparently not interested in what was being said. Following this, he was able to directly engage in more open exchange with his wife, and later reported that the visual image of himself looking at the ceiling remained with him, and was brought to his mind often when he sensed a feeling of boredom. Using that signal he said that he now was often able to respond, and become involved in the exchange. He went on to investigate what he found boring, and the couple became more open in confronting each other, with less fear that they would injure one another.

Transcontextual Behavior

This category of behavior causes disruption and confusion in the flow of ordinary communication. It can be expressed through either verbal or nonverbal channels, and is called *transcontextual* because it cuts across the ongoing context. It is difficult to comprehend because the content is irrelevant, but once one grasps the fact that its significance is not in its content, but rather in its effect on relationships, its meaning can be understood from this new perspective. The following case demonstrates a brief example of this form expressed in both verbal and nonverbal modes.

A family with three boys, 14, 16 and 20, and mother and father, sought help because of concern about the 16-year-old who was erratic in school performance. He was having great difficulty with peers, often becoming the butt of jokes because of his interests in esoteric subjects, and because of an impulsiveness which at times seemed inappropriate.

In the eighth session the focus had shifted to some degree from the middle boy to the youngest. The mother complained about his disinterest in the house, and his unwillingness to do work. The middle son began to play with an ashtray, dropped a pencil on the floor, and interrupted with apparently unrelated pieces of information about problems he encountered the day before (transcontextual).

After several such sequences, the family watched a videoreplay and a pattern was identified. Each time the mother began to criticize the younger boy, the next older started some distracting behavior. The effect was to shift attention from the younger. The middle son was then able to tell the mother how much her criticism always bugged him. He was identifying with his younger brother, and this realization was important, because ordinarily he also bugged the younger one, and denied that he had any real interest in him.

This sequence led the three boys to a more unified alliance and the parents began to talk at greater length about their disappointments with each other, shifting the focus of therapy markedly.

Denial of Depression

Turmoil around the behavior of one member of a family can serve to obscure the deep feelings of depression which may be felt by other members, and yet go unacknowledged. In the next case the depression in the family was masked by the anxiety and struggle around the daughter.

The parents initially said that the problem was with the 16-year-old daughter who was staying out late at night, and was extremely defiant. Her brother, 22, and at college, also came to the session, along with the mother and father. The mother expressed great anxiety and concern about the daughter, while the father tended to side with the girl, and to take her part against the mother. The son was fairly quiet, and did not seem to want to get involved. The family seated themselves at the start of the session with the mother on one end, the son on the other, and the daughter and father in between. At first the father was somewhat belligerent and challenging with me. The first videoreplay was shown early in the session to allow the members to express an initial reaction to their own images. The father made the first remark, and criticized my use of the zoom lens, saying that his son was partly left out of the picture.

As he made this comment to me his jaw was protruding in an aggressive gesture, and I realized he was taking the position of gatekeeper for the family. If I wanted to establish rapport with the family I realized I would have to meet him in the challenge, and gain his acceptance. I thought otherwise we could easily become engaged in a futile power struggle. I knew he worked as a stock broker, and felt he could be reached man-to-man on the level of his competence in his profession. I told him I could see that in the session he was using the same skills and perceptiveness that he obviously used in his job as a stock broker, and that this would be of assistance and value to me in the therapy. Instead of creating a further challenge, my reaction recognized his need to become a cohelper in this process so he would not lose completely his role of father, and leader in the family. His belligerence, and the resistance of the rest of the family vanished as I made this alliance with him.

Since I could also see that the father and daughter were closely connected, and were sitting beside one another, I decided to create some separation by asking the father to switch seats with the son. This put the two children in the middle, and a parent at each end. In the course of the session I asked the son and daughter to talk with each other, and while they did, the father put his hands over his face, and lowered his head. At the same moment, but a fraction of a second later, the mother brought her left hand up over her own mouth.

When this sequence was replayed on video, the mother was astonished to see her husband in this depressed position. He also looked at himself, and then said how depressed he felt. The mother exclaimed, "I had no idea he was so depressed." I then asked the two children to move down one seat, and the mother sat beside the father. They touched each other, and both began to express their feelings of concern and depression over their health, and also over their difficult financial condition.

What was particularly startling was the marked change in mood of the whole family group from one of belligerence and anger, to one of depression and quiet concern, with the focus having shifted from the daughter to the plight of the whole family, and the worry of the parents.

Intellectualized Versus Gut Communication

Family therapy is a conceptual approach as well as a technique. The number of people in a family attending any one session is not the crucial issue. Instead, looking at total family behavior as a systems manifestation is much the more central factor. The family in this next example consisted of husband and wife, and two children; however, in the session described only the husband and wife were present.

In the course of the exchange the academic and intellectualized quality of exchange became apparent through the use of replay, and the technique of role-scripting was utilized, along with further replay to encourage a shift to a more directly emotional engagement.

Both partners were obviously very guarded with one another. Speech was carefully chosen, voice level was well-modulated, and spacing between the two was carefully delineated. At one point in the session the couple were discussing power issues, and the wife was commenting that she felt that it was difficult to criticize her husband under some conditions. He asked if she were going to start her depressive number again, and she continued in a manner which seemed to make him angry; but at the same time he appeared subdued, and ready to continue at the same conversational level.

The episode was replayed to that point, and then I asked if the husband would try to follow a different script. He agreed, and I told him to respond to his wife's depressive complaints by saying, "Tough shit, baby!" He agreed, and the episode was acted out by the two of them again. But when it came time for his new line, he gave a completely different, and much more bland version. I stopped the action, and told him he must have misunderstood. The husband appeared puzzled, and inquired what he had been told to say. It was repeated to him, and this time he was able to follow through. The wife was now involved in the role-play, and responded with, "Fuck you!" He also, now well into the mood, responded in kind, by saying, "Don't put your shit on me." Suddenly the wife began to withdraw, and to show tears.

I then suggested that maybe *she* could use a temporary script writer, and since I had given lines to the husband, it only seemed fair to give her some as well. She agreed, and I told her to reply to her husband's last injunction of "Don't put your shit on me" by responding, "On you, under you, beside you, everywhere I want to!" She seemed amused at the idea, and her tears stopped forthwith. In the new role-play she actually did me one better, adding, "On you, under you, on top of your head, all over you. I'll put it where I want to!"

The husband began to respond, looked abashed, smiled in a somewhat startled way, put his arms out with palms turned up, and finally appeared completely helpless, yet still somewhat amused. He finally said with a laugh, "Well, that *is* a different response!" The whole sequence was then replayed on video and the couple reacted by recognizing the futility of their careful way of interacting with each other, which usually ended with the wife finally retreating into a tearful withdrawal, and the husband reacting with an angry silence. The assertive encounter in the exchange remained vivid for both of them as they watched the extraordinary difference in the two sequences.

By directing this couple to engage in abusive exchange with one another in a style so utterly in contrast with their usual intellectualized and proper approach—that is, in the academic style of the therapists they actually were in their professional lives—I paradoxically was able to help them confront themselves with the feelings they had toward each other. These feelings, of course, had been hidden to them previously because of the repetition of their nonproductive communication patterns.

Nonverbal Synchrony

Alliances are revealed through synchronous behavior. These are movements of the body in rhythmical synchronization with the body movements of another person. Although they occur beneath the level of awareness, they indicate a close sympathetic (resonating) response.

A couple were involved in discussing the wife's depressed feelings about her disappointment at not having as fulfilling an occupation as her husband, who was a therapist. He was telling her that he was very ready for her to undertake a new direction for herself in pursuing her interest in art. She appeared quite sad, and was sitting with one leg crossed over the other, while her eyes were averted downwards. He was leaning towards her, but neither was touching the other. She responded to his assurance of his interest in her by saying, "I don't really feel that you understand, and I feel quite alone." As she said this she simultaneously began to gently stroke the soft cuff of her trouser. About three seconds later the husband began to rub the side of his own foot, which was also crossed over his other leg in a way identical to that of his wife.

This sequence was replayed on video, and still-framed as the wife began to stroke her cuff. I asked her how she was feeling at that moment, and she said, "Sad, and lonely." She then confirmed that the stroking gave her a feeling of warmth and comfort. I then continued the playback and a moment later the image of the husband stroking his foot came on the screen. The two of them were amazed to watch the absolute synchrony of the postures and the stroking. The wife was suddenly convinced of her husband's concern, and caring as she watched its nonverbal expression. They both began to talk in a more direct way, and the impasse of distance and depression was broken.

OTHER CLINICAL APPLICATIONS

Several therapeutic techniques which are useful in family therapy gain an extra dimension when augmented by the use of videorecording and immediate playback. Transactional analysts have found videorecording and replay especially useful, particularly in the identification of different ego states. Gestalt therapists have also found the technology of help. One method I have described (2) is a confrontation of self using the video image instead of the empty chair technique. This can be used in family sessions; one member of the family can engage in a dialogue with his own image, and then other family members can join in the discussion, and address themselves either to the real person, or to the TV image.

Special applications can also be created because of the unique characteristics of the video equipment. The camera's capacity to zoom, for example, is one that the human eye does not have, and it offers a new perspective which can produce sudden awareness of something which previously was obscure. For example, a large closeup of the face may reveal sadness or anxiety that ordinarily is not seen.

Techniques of interpersonal process recall developed by Kagan have been widely used. A couple is videotaped during a session. In subsequent sessions, with separate interviewers, each partner is assisted in recalling emotional and ideational material while watching a replay of the original session. In order to reduce the stress level of the recall sessions, the interviewers are not the original therapists. Following the recall sessions, the couple is re-interviewed together while once more watching the original videoreplay, in order to facilitate an integration of the new understandings they gained in their individual recall experiences.

Other effects can be obtained by varying the speed of the replay. Slow motion and still-framing can accurately pinpoint the beginning of a sequence, even though the actions of two people in a sequence may be separated by no more than a fraction of a second. The action can also be speeded up by adjusting the videorecorder, and this too can bring awareness of the differences in activity between members of a family. One person may be exhibiting agitated behavior, but at a regular time rate the difference is not readily noticed.

Other methods of utilizing the videoplayback method are:

Confrontation in Assertiveness Training

Family therapy cannot be defined by the number of family members present in any one session. The following example illustrates family therapy with only one member of the family.

Joan, in her late thirties, and mother of five children, complained in the session that she and her husband had had a disagreement, and that she felt bitterly disappointed and hurt at his callousness toward her and the children. Her husband was going on a trip, and she and two of the children drove him to the airport. He found there were no insurance machines available, and said that he was not going to get *any* insurance, because the machines would have cost only a dollar-and-a-half, but buying insurance at a counter meant a minimum of seven and a half dollars. Joan was incensed that he would not spend the additional money for his family's protection, but he was adamant. She had remained subdued, hurt, depressed, and angry since that moment.

I invited her to try an experiment to see if there was another way she could cope with the situation. She agreed and her image, full-face, was shown by closed circuit TV on the screen which she was directly facing. At the same time, a videorecording was made of the self-confrontation. She then was requested to play the scene as if it were happening again, and that her husband was telling her he was not going to buy the insurance. She looked at her face, began to cry, and said she couldn't do it. She complained it was artificial. I agreed that the role-playing was a simulation, but since it was such an important issue I urged her to try and see if she could react to the directions, to tell her husband directly to buy the insurance.

With this encouragement, she started; while watching her own image, she began to talk. "I want you to buy the insurance!" She was encouraged to repeat the sequence over and over again. At first her dialogue and manner was tearful and pleading, and at the same time blaming. With each new try her affect in the portrayal changed. Soon, even though she was still crying, her direct anger was evident as she became more animated, and as the level of her voice rose. Eventually she stopped crying. She was urged to diminish the pleading quality, and to state more directly what she wanted. "Martin, I want you to buy the insurance!" She then said, half-musingly, and looking up, "He might have *heard* that!"

Following this entire sequence, the videotape was replayed, and Joan reacted to her own developing assertiveness, agreeing that the last version was more direct, more powerful, and might have been effective.

The following week she appeared quite calm, and sure of herself. She reported that she had received a letter from her husband in which he wrote that he had seen her through plane window, and had noticed that she was blowing her nose a great deal. She told the group that she had written back to him, saying that indeed he had seen her blow her nose because she was crying and felt very badly. She wrote further that she was worried when he was away, and that she felt even more worried at the prospect that some accident might befall him. She added that she wanted him to buy the insurance for his trip home because it was important to her.

Joan reported later that this visual experience stayed with her, and in other situations she had been able to carry over the learning in finding a more direct way of looking after herself. She recalled that her own mother had not demanded enough of her father, and she realized that both her father and her husband needed direct demands if they were to respond to the needs of others. She went on to reveal that she would really like to be taken care of without having to ask, but now realized that she was not likely to get that response from her husband, and would have to take the responsibility for giving more care to herself.

Splitscreen Replay

In order to use this technique an additional piece of equipment, called a "special effects generator," is required. A second camera is also needed. With this additional equipment several innovations can be tried. One is called "corner insert." While the entire family constellation is shown on the television screen, a closeup of one member can be inserted in one corner of the screen. In this way the details of facial expression and gesture can be clearly seen, while the total context with all nonverbal interaction among members is shown simultaneously.

Another technical possibility with this equipment is the splitscreen: the image from one camera can be shown on the left side of the screen, and the image from another camera shown at the same time on the right side. This method is especially useful with couples, as a side-by-side replay.

A couple in their late fifties argued mostly over financial issues, and their exchange usually escalated into an impasse in which the husband finally became silent and fuming, and the wife began to cry. In one session when he raised the issue of excessive spending again, I suggested trying a new approach. The couple was seated with their backs to one another, and a camera at each end of the room televised the image of each. These images were fed into the special equipment so that on the television screen they would appear side-by-side in later playback.

During the encounter neither partner could see the screen. They were asked to continue their discussion of the financial problem. This they did, with the usual impasse developing in spite of the fact that they were not facing one another. Both were then asked to sit beside each other, and to watch the replay. The tape was stopped when either of them asked for it in order to make comments. Both were utterly amazed to see the expressions on their faces. One fact soon became apparent, namely, that neither seemed to be listening while the other was talking. The facial expressions appeared to be connected to their own inner processes. This was confirmed by both, and they began to exchange their fantasies and feelings. This realization was crucial in their making a new attempt to stay connected with each other, and to stop the other if each was unable to continue listening.

The total effect of the experience was not only to identify the communication blockage, but to help each of them know what the other was really feeling. This marked the beginning of a long series of similar attempts by both of them to really listen to the other and thereby deepen the level of their intimacy.

Family Roleplay

The following version of roleplay technique has been found especially valuable in helping families identify issues which arise at home, but which seem very difficult to report in the sessions.

The family is instructed to caucus among themselves at the start of a session, and to decided on an episode which has been important for them during the past week. The family is then asked to roleplay the episode by taking their own parts and to reproduce it the way it actually happened. The entire play is videotaped, and then shown back. During the replay any member of the family can stop the machine and give a critique, either of his own part, or that of any other family member. Discrepancies in the way members recall the real event come to light.

The family is then asked to repeat the episode, including what they have learned from their own critique. This revision is then replayed in entirety without stop. Finally, the family is asked to play out the episode again, spontaneously as they feel it at the moment. In this last version resolutions to old difficulties are frequently found by the family, even though there has been no organized consultation about the exact changes that could be made. Usually the family enjoys this exercise, and sometimes the fun of the project is an important addition to the therapy.

Home Visit

A portable television recorder makes this type of experiment possible. The equipment is light and reliable, and the camera is such that even in ordinary room light, excellent pictures can be taken. With an adaptor the tape can be replayed on the television set in any home, so playback is also immediately available.

A visit was made to a family with three girls, five, eight and twelve. The original complaint had been the impulsive and hyperactive behavior of the eight-year-old. At the beginning, it must be said that the value of this technique is primarily derived from the home visit itself (5), but the addition of the television recording capacity adds an extra dimension.

The family had prepared the livingroom, and there were snacks on the dining room table. I set the camera on a tripod and adjusted it to take in the whole livingroom. We began our session. Throughout, the eight-year-old was much quieter than in my office, and actually took on a hostess role. The mother seemed to sit back, and was apparently unsure of what to do next, while the father remained polite and cordial, but somewhat stiff. On replay it was noted by the twelve-year-old that the parents seemed uncomfortable, and the therapist mentioned how at ease all three girls seemed.

A tour was later made of the apartment, and video playback was then shown of each room. It was apparent to the mother and the father that the apartment was in a state of considerable disarray, and that many of the ordinary, comfortable, homey touches were missing. This deprivation emerged starkly through the screen, and led to associations by the parents of the feelings of emotional deprivation in their own lives. The visit marked a shift in therapy from the concentration on the middle child, to the quality of life in the whole family, centering around feelings of deprivation in the parents.

COMMENTARY

I have described only a few of the many possibilities of videorecording and playback in therapy. The variety and the invention is limited only by the experimentation and the innovation of the therapist. Technology has now advanced to the point where the equipment is reliable, and simple to operate. The cost of owning the equipment is within reason, and the usefulness of this tool as an adjunct in therapy seems beyond question.

Future research will be done on measuring effects of self-confrontation, on designing studies to determine the most effective means of fostering learning, and on assessing the overall value of becoming aware of behavior in context through the observation of television recordings. At the moment, clinical experience indicates that videoreplay can be significantly effective as an adjunct in family therapy.

The complication of equipment may be a drawback to some, but I believe most therapists can easily manage a simple system, such as I have described. It is important not to let the equipment overshadow the therapy, but to keep it in its role as an additional technical aid. Some people have a negative reaction to their own image, and this consequence must be dealt with sensitively. Usually very depressed people need extra help in identifying the factors which may increase their unhappiness in watching themselves, and the therapist should carefully monitor the playback experience with such patients. Those who have paranoid feelings usually are pleased by the recording, feeling reassured by the presence of more accurate data about what really happens.

Children have for the most part been quite delighted with the videotaping, and this probably reflects the fact that we they are used to living in an electronic age with television a daily friend. Almost no patients have refused to be recorded, and a surprisingly large number have been agreeable to the use of the recorded material for teaching purposes.

Two especially significant values merit emphasis. One is that the possibility of obtaining objective behavioral data, and having it immediately available for integration into an ongoing transaction marks a truly significant advance in the development of the therapeutic art into a combination of art and science. Secondly, the shift of role position which occurs when therapist and family step back from the usual hierarchical positions to that of cooperative researchers in a common task marks another significant move in making therapy a more truly human and mutual adventure.

REFERENCES

1. I. Alger. "Audio-Visual Techniques in Family Therapy," in D. Bloch (ed.), *Techniques of Family Therapy.* New York: Grune and Stratton, 1973.
2. _____, "Television Image Confrontation in Group Therapy," in C. J. Sager and H.S. Kaplan (eds.). *Progress in Group and Family Therapy.* New York: Brunner-Mazel, 1972.
3. G. Bateson, D.D. Jackson, J. Haley and J.H. Weakland. "A Note on The Double-bind, 1962," *Family Process,* 2 (1963), 154–62.
4. M. Berger (ed.). *Videotape Techniques in Psychiatric Training and Treatment,* New York: Brunner-Mazel, 1970.
5. D. Bloch. "The Clinical Home Visit," in D. Bloch (ed.). *Techniques of Family Psychotherapy.* New York: Grune and Stratton, 1973.
6. A. Bodin. "The Use of Video tapes," in A. Ferber, M. Mendelsohn, and A. Napier (eds.). *The Book of Family Therapy.* New York: Science House, 1972.
7. N. Kagan, *et al. Studies in Human Interaction.* Educational Publication Services, Michigan State University, 1967.
8. J. Metcoff. "A Problem-Oriented Approach to Structuring Videotape Playbacks in Family Therapy," Institute for Juvenile Research, Chicago, 1975. Unpublished.
9. M. Murray. *The Videotape Book.* New York: Bantam, 1975.
10. A.E. Scheflen and A. Scheflen. *Body Language and Social Order.* Englewood Cliffs, N.J.: Prentice-Hall, 1972.
11. Videofreex. *The Spaghetti City Video Manual.* New York: Praeger, 1973.

INDEX